Donald Trump

The Man Who Would Be King

Twelve Years and Forty Titles of Award-Winning Entertainment
About How America Interprets
Its Actors, Its Spinmeisters, and Its Celebrity Politicians

www.BloodMoonProductions.com

Donald Trump

The Man
Who Would Be King

Darwin Porter & Danforth Prince

Donald Trump
The Man Who Would Be King

Darwin Porter and Danforth Prince

Copyright 2016, Blood Moon Productions, Ltd.
All Rights Reserved

www.BloodMoonProductions.com

Manufactured in the United States of America

ISBN 978-1-936003-51-8

Cover Designs by Danforth Prince

To Anyone Who Is Watching,
and to Whom It May Concern,

A message from this book's publisher and co-author, Danforth Prince

This is an unprecedented, original book about an unprecedented, original candidate for U.S. President. We crafted it as a reflection of the bizarre, pop-driven *Zeitgeist* of America and its passions during the postmodern, post-recession election campaign of 2016.

Consistent with our previous publishing agendas, it focuses on the American concept of fame as it affects media, entertainment, and—as it specifically relates to Donald Trump—politics.

Please do not assume that our powers of criticism are exclusively reserved for "THE DONALD," or exclusively aimed at Republicans. The illustration on the ne t page indicates that we have already lacerated some illusions about the Clinton campaign, too.

Therefore, as "equal opportunity muckrakers," we respectfully suggest that both of these books would be helpful for a concerned voter's understanding of the double jeopardy he or she faces during this election season.

Many thanks for interpreting this as a patriotic overview of the ironies of this, the Greatest Nation on Earth. With reverence, we salute the American concepts of Democracy, Free Speech, Prosperity, and Justice for All.

As both candidates said at the end of their acceptance speeches after their nomination for President by their respective parties:

GOD BLESS YOU ALL, &
GOD BLESS AMERICA!

Steve McQueen, King of Cool, Tales of a Lurid Life

Paul Newman, The Man Behind the Baby Blues

Merv Griffin, A Life in the Closet

Brando Unzipped

Katharine the Great, Hepburn, Secrets of a Lifetime Revealed

Jacko, His Rise and Fall, The Social and Sexual History of Michael Jackson

Damn You, Scarlett O'Hara, The Private Lives of Vivien Leigh and Laurence Olivier (co-authored with Roy Moseley)

FILM CRITICISM
Blood Moon's 2005 Guide to the Glitter Awards
Blood Moon's 2006 Guide to Film
Blood Moon's 2007 Guide to Film, and
50 Years of Queer Cinema, 500 of the Best GLBTQ Films Ever Made

NON-FICTION
Hollywood Babylon, It's Back! and Hollywood Babylon Strikes Again!

NOVELS
Blood Moon,
Hollywood's Silent Closet,
Rhinestone Country,
Razzle Dazzle
Midnight in Savannah

OTHER PUBLICATIONS BY DARWIN PORTER
NOT DIRECTLY ASSOCIATED WITH BLOOD MOON

NOVELS

The Delinquent Heart
The Taste of Steak Tartare
Butterflies in Heat
Marika (*a roman à clef based on the life of Marlene Dietrich*)
Venus (*a roman à clef based on the life of Anaïs Nin*)
Bitter Orange
Sister Rose

TRAVEL GUIDES

Many Editions and Many Variations of *The Frommer Guides,*
The American Express Guides, and/or TWA Guides, et alia to:

Andalusia, Andorra, Anguilla, Aruba, Atlanta, Austria, the Azores, The Bahamas, Barbados, the Bavarian Alps, Berlin, Bermuda, Bonaire and Curaçao, Boston, the British Virgin Islands, Budapest, Bulgaria, California, the Canary Islands, the Caribbean and its "Ports of Call," the Cayman Islands, Ceuta, the Channel Islands (UK), Charleston (SC), Corsica, Costa del Sol (Spain), Denmark, Dominica, the Dominican Republic, Edinburgh, England, Estonia, Europe, "Europe by Rail," the Faroe Islands, Finland, Florence, France, Frankfurt, the French Riviera, Geneva, Georgia (USA), Germany, Gibraltar, Glasgow, Granada (Spain), Great Britain, Greenland, Grenada (West Indies), Haiti, Hungary, Iceland, Ireland, Isle of Man, Italy, Jamaica, Key West & the Florida Keys, Las Vegas, Liechtenstein, Lisbon, London, Los Angeles, Madrid, Maine, Malta, Martinique & Guadeloupe, Massachusetts, Melilla, Morocco, Munich, New England, New Orleans, North Carolina, Norway, Paris, Poland, Portugal, Provence, Puerto Rico, Romania, Rome, Salzburg, San Diego, San Francisco, San Marino, Sardinia, Savannah, Scandinavia, Scotland, Seville, the Shetland Islands, Sicily, St. Martin & Sint Maarten, St. Vincent & the Grenadines, South Carolina, Spain, St. Kitts & Nevis, Sweden, Switzerland, the Turks & Caicos, the U.S.A., the U.S. Virgin Islands, Venice, Vienna and the Danube, Wales, and Zurich.

BIOGRAPHIES

From Diaghilev to Balanchine, The Saga of Ballerina Tamara Geva

Lucille Lortel, The Queen of Off-Broadway

Greta Keller, Germany's Other Lili Marlene

Sophie Tucker, The Last of the Red Hot Mamas

Anne Bancroft, Where Have You Gone, Mrs. Robinson?
(co-authored with Stanley Mills Haggart)

Veronica Lake, The Peek-a-Boo Girl

Running Wild in Babylon, Confessions of a Hollywood Press Agent

HISTORIES

Thurlow Weed, Whig Kingpin

Chester A. Arthur, Gilded Age Coxcomb in the White House

Discover Old America, What's Left of It

CUISINE

Food For Love, Hussar Recipes from the Austro-Hungarian Empire,
with collaboration from the cabaret chanteuse, Greta Keller

AND COMING SOON, FROM BLOOD MOON

Lana Turner, Hearts and Diamonds Take All
Rock Hudson, Erotic Fire
Rita Hayworth, Love Goddess of the World
Hefner, Guccione, and Flynt: Empires of Skin

With Pride, We Dedicate This Book

to anyone who has been enraged or embarrassed by political developments in America during its 2016 electoral campaigns.

God Bless America!

I support Hillary Clinton as the first female to run for President, but not the last. Yet I do not rail against Trump supporters. You have to find the sources of it and not overreact to the craziness in it. The woes of the declining middle class are real. Conversation has to address the feeling of uselessness and despair and marginalization on the part of people who were never rich, but had a job they could rely on. Now they can't, for several generations now. There's meth and opioids. There's real despair. That's part of inclusivity as well.

—Meryl Streep

Contents

PART ONE
Origins and Emergence of The Donald and His Empire

White House Like Jacqueline Kennedy." **Eric:** "Perfect Except for His Slaughter of Wild Animals in Zimbabwe." **Tiffany**: "Pursuing the Pleasures of the One Percent."

PART TWO

THE SUMMER OF TRUMP

AMERICA'S GREATEST DEAL MAKER MAKES A BID FOR
THE WHITE HOUSE
HOW DID IT HAPPEN?

PART THREE

THE AUTUMN OF TRUMP

"I'M TOO RICH TO BE BOUGHT" DONALD PROCLAIMS

INSULT BY INSULT, HE CLIMBS IN THE POLLS

PART FOUR

THE WINTER OF TRUMP

THE POPE VS. THE BILLIONAIRE

IN A MEDIA-SAVVY HOLY WAR OF WORDS

DONALD IS FORCED TO DEFEND THE SIZE OF HIS PENIS

PART FIVE

THE SPRING OF TRUMP

DONALD SWEEPS TO VICTORY IN THE NORTHEAST AND KNOCKS HIS REMAINING RIVAL (CRUZ) OUT OF THE RACE

MUCH OF EUROPE VIEWS DONALD AS "THE WORLD'S MOST DANGEROUS MAN"

Blood Moon Productions, in case you don't know, is a small publishing house on Staten Island that cranks out Hollywood gossip books, about two or three a year, usually of five-, six-, or 700-page length, chocked with stories and pictures about people who used to consume the imaginations of the American public, back when we actually had a public imagination. That is, when people were really interested in each other, rather than in Apple 'devices.' In other words, back when we had vices, not devices."

—The Huffington Post

PART ONE

Origins and Emergence of The Donald and His Empire

Chapter One

 *

TRUMP DYNASTY FOUNDED ON HARD LIQUOR & PROSTITUTION

From the Tenements of New York to the Klondike Gold Rush Trail, a Young German Barber Sets Out to Conquer the New World

DECAYING HORSEMEAT STEAK & OVER-THE-HILL WHORES
Lure Gold Miners into Trump's Alaskan Restaurant

Donald Trump prevailed in a court battle to have his own Scottish coat-of-arms, four years after falling foul of ancient heraldic laws.

Who were the ancestors of Donald John Trump? They were not what he claimed in his bestseller, *The Art of the Deal.*

He falsely cited Sweden as his ancestral home. Not so. His family was solidly German on his father's side, and on his mother's, Scottish.

Over the course of five centuries, the Trump named evolved, at least according to the church register in Kallstadt, Germany through mutations that included Drumb, Tromb, Trum, Trumpff, Drumpf, Dromb, and finally, Trump.

For thousands of years, throughout as many traumatic centuries of recorded history as central Europe had witnessed, cold winds from the Haardt Mountains had blown down upon the Palatinate region of southwestern Germany. Set some forty miles west of the Rhine (a.k.a., the "Highway of Europe"), Kallstadt was a little village thriving on agriculture, the breeding of livestock, especially pigs, and viticulture.

In regional dialect, the wine-making locals of Kallstadt are known as *Brulljesmacher,* a word which translates from the German as "braggart." The townspeople were said to almost chronically exaggerate their accomplishments and their achievements, a charge that would be leveled in 2016 against their most famous son.

Two famous American dynasties had originated in Kallstadt: Johann Heinrich Heinz was the father of the American food mogul, Henry J. Heinz, "King of Catsup;" and Friedrich Drumpf (he changed his name in 1892 to

Kallstadt was famous as the home to the founder of Heinz catsup, and home turf of *Saumagen* (stuffed sow's stomach, as depicted in this ad, whose wording translates as *Saumagen Paradise-Always a Pleasure*). To an increasing degree, it's famous throughout Germany as the site from which the Trump family patriarch emigrated in economic despair in the late 1800s.

Frederick Trump) was the grandfather of Donald Trump, the real estate and entertainment magnate, who had entered the 2016 race to become President of the United States.

Ironically, despite his origins, many German newspapers had already referred to Donald as "the reincarnation of Adolf Hitler." One particularly outspoken editor in Stuttgart went so far as to predict that if he were ever elected president, the stars in the American flag would be replaced by Nazi Swastikas.

In the modest Hansel-and-Gretel house occupied by Donald Trump's forebears, Christian Johannes Trump (born in 1829) and his wife, Katherina Kober Trump, would sit by the fire in the pre-radio and television age and relate details to their son, Friedrich (born March 14, 1869), about the town's tragic past.

Over the centuries, waves of invading armies—Austrian, Prussian, Russian, French, and Spanish—had marched through Kallstadt, draining its wooden kegs of wine and often raping its young girls and women. In many instances, after their brutalities, the invaders had burned the villagers' homes to the ground.

Since the early decades of the

Friedrich Trump, family patriarch, above the banner for the Rhenish district of The Palatinate.

In contrast to Trump family lore, as distributed for years based on anti-German sentiment during World War I, the family's dynastic origins are firmly rooted in *Deutschland*, not in Sweden, as was often claimed.

18th century, many of the Pfalzers (as inhabitants of the Palatinate were called), had maintained a sometimes obsessive dream about emigrating to America. German-speaking communities soon sprung up across the New World. The Amish and Mennonites established German-speaking communities in the early 1700s, and the Moravians had founded communities in Pennsylvania in the 1740s that later expanded into North Carolina. [The

"Pennsylvania Dutch" dialect spoken by the Amish of Pennsylvania derived primarily from the German dialect as spoken in the Palatinate.]

Frederick's mother cooked him a hearty diet. Kallstadt was known for its most celebrated dish, *Saumagen*, literally "sow's stomach." In the Trump Tower in Manhattan, Donald, even today, still orders his chefs to make this dish. It consists of a thick, crispy fried casing of a pig stomach stuffed with a mixture of minced pork, potatoes, and seasonings. Blood pudding sausage (*grieweworscht*) is another favorite dish, as well as *bratwurst* (a white sausage) served for breakfast when Palatinate liverwurst wasn't otherwise available.

Lewwerknedel (liver dumplings) was another favorite dish. Brown gravy seemed to accompany all the dishes. "My ancestors were definitely carnivores," Donald once said.

Frederick's grandfather, Johannes, was frail and suffered from emphysema. During the last decade of his life, constantly coughing, he devolved into a virtual invalid. As a young boy, he had painted vine leaves with copper sulfate to keep the pests away. That and the noxious fumes from fertilizer used at the time may have contributed to his lung condition.

In 1877, at the age of forty-eight, Johannes died, leaving his wife with six hungry mouths to feed and no money, except for what she could earn

Katherina Kober Trump, Donald Trump's great-grandmother, was a stern, God-fearing Teutonic woman.

At the age of forty-one, the death of her husband left her with six mouths to feed, a pile of debts, and very few ways of earning a living, except baking bread for her neighbors.

When Friedrich Trump (above, left) spotted the five-year-old, Elizabeth Christ, daughter of a tinker man, he decided that one day after he became rich in the New World, he would return to Germany and take her as his bride.

He eventually carried out his original vow.

4

from rising at 4AM every morning and baking fresh bread for the local families.

Frederick emerged from all this with a steely determination to gain wealth. He was eight years old when his father died, and like him, frail. He would endure hardships in his youth, however, that might have killed a stronger man.

In 1883, when he turned fourteen, his mother, no longer able to provide for him, sent him to the small town of Frankenthal. There he became an apprentice to the local barber, Friedrich Lang, who taught the teenager how to cut hair with a straightedge razor. It was a profession that the lad would eventually export with him to New York. In Frankenthal, his duties involved running frequently across the street to the Bierstube to fetch mugs of brew for the burghers waiting to get a haircut.

In 1885, he returned to Kallstadt as the autumn leaves on the Haardt Mountains were turning red and golden. He moved back in with his family, finding them still underfed and struggling. He was also rudely awakened to the reality that since the men of Kallstadt expected their wives to cut their hair, there was no need there for a barber.

Complicating matters, he soon received notification that, at the age of sixteen, he would soon be drafted into the Army. Refusal to serve meant a jail term.

Frederick noticed that other young men were packing their meager possessions into battered suitcases, dodging the draft, and heading for the New World for access to its seemingly endless possibilities.

He'd managed to put away a small stash of money, enough to pay for his passage to New York. Instead of sharing his purse with his mother, Katherina, he opted to buy a one-way ticket in steerage class to America. Not wanting to face his mother, he arose one morning at 3AM and scribbled a note for her, leaving it on the kitchen table.

Despite his weak constitu-

Immigration processing at Ellis Island in the 1890s. Anonymous, depersonalized, and, ultimately, terrifying.

tion, his determination had risen to a fever pitch.

The day before his departure, as he'd headed into his house, he noticed a little girl playing in her yard, along Frankenheim Strasse. Only five years old, she waved at him and called out, "Would you come and play with me?"

He would later claim that he was overcome with this strange premonition. He'd later tell her that he decided right there and then that one day he'd return to Kallstadt and propose marriage to her. It wasn't her beauty as a child, but a certain free spirit about her that attracted him.

His older sister, Katherine, was already living in New York. She had migrated there with her new husband, Fred Schuster, who was also from Kallstadt. He had found work in New York as a shipping clerk, and she was a maid at a local hotel.

On the 350-mile rail trip to the teeming port of Bremen, Frederick had taken three bottles of Riesling and a dozen apples. There, he found that hundreds of other emigrants were leaving for a hoped for better life in the New World.

He had booked passage aboard the SS *Eider*, which had originally been built in the grimy port of Glasgow. As it sailed out of Bremen, he told a fellow passenger, "Germany has just too many damn barbers and doesn't need me."

Day after day, he stood on the ship's deck, wanting to be the first to see the coastline of America. Although his heart was still in Germany, his hope for the future lay in the United States, a brash and innovative country which in the upcoming 20th Century would change the world.

***

In 1892, Ellis Island in New York Harbor had opened its doors as the processing center for millions of immigrants. It was a bustling, foul-smelling place, as many of its newcomers had not had an opportunity to bathe in weeks. Some of them had lice and carried pests. Rigorously segregated into separate sections, men and women had to strip down and be fumigated before being sent to the baths.

Frederick's processing, during which he asserted that he was qualified to earn his living as a barber, took about five hours. Although his health had passed inspection, he witnessed dozens of men turned away for reasons based on illnesses, sent back to their point of origins after long transatlantic voyages, from what came to be called "Heartbreak Island."

Released into the United States, Frederick was met by his older sister and brother-in-law, Katherine and Fred Schuster at "The Kissing Post," a wooden column where new arrivals were greeted with tears, hugs, and kisses, and went off to live with them.

He wandered like a dazzled pilgrim into this strange new world of more than a million people from many parts of the world, mostly Europe. Late 19th-century New York was a vast cauldron: Bustling, filled with noise and filth, with piles of decaying garbage everywhere. Animal excrement from feral pigs, cows, and horses littered the filthy, muddy streets. Stagecoaches carried residents about.

He traveled uptown with his sister and brother-in-law to Forsythe Street, a block from Grand Street on the Lower East Side of Manhattan, and was assigned a room in their dark, small apartment. When he heard the locals conversing in German dialects, he felt as if he were back in Germany. Even a bakery next door turned out breads like his mother baked in Kallstadt.

His sister had secured him a job with a German barber, which was open on the Sunday morning when he reported for work. Many workers had only Sunday to get their hair cut. A wooden Indian stood outside on the sidewalk. The owner, who hailed from Frankfurt, taught Frederick some of the finer lessons of what was fashionable in the New World at the time, including such tonsorial

Slums of tenement New York. Bad, in an international, melting-pot way. Here is a scene Frederick encountered upon his arrival.

Communal outhouses in back of a NYC tenement building, late 1800s, and water source for the residents inside. Despite the bad conditions, they were still better than what many immigrants to the city had left behind.

This buxom late 19th Century young prostitute, with plunging *décollétage,* was typical of the women Frederick "auditioned" before hiring to cater to the male clients of his restaurant.

He built cubicles over his restaurant in which the prostitutes plied their trade, in the Tenderloin District of Seattle.

Frederick called his working girls "soiled doves." Some women working the late night shift were grossly overweight, since many men preferred women "with meat on their bones."

When women began to lose their allure, they were shipped to the frigid Klondike, where men were not so particular.

techniques as creating a "Van Dyke" beard.

Most nights, during his walk back to his sister's apartment on Forsythe Street, he was accosted by prostitutes. When he'd saved seventy-five cents, he hired one, a big, buxom, blonde-haired woman from Munich. She took him back to her dingy apartment where he lost his virginity.

Sometimes, he ducked out of sight to avoid street gangs, these thugs armed with pistols and knives. On his rare day off, he set out to explore Manhattan, sometimes passing foul-smelling slaughterhouses and tanneries.

In the late spring of 1887, Frederick, along with his sister and brother-in-law, moved uptown to 2012 Second Avenue near East 104th Street. The crowded tenement held eight families, and the halls were filled with the smell of boiling cabbage and the sound of babies crying. To get to work in Lower Manhattan, Frederick and his brother-in-law rode an elevated train south.

After ten months, Frederick decided he'd had it with New York. He wasn't getting rich—in fact, he managed to make just enough money to stay alive.

He decided to heed a popular slogan of the day, a call for immigrants to "Go West, Young Man!"

At this point in his life, he'd spent five years in New York and had acquired a handlebar mustache. He stood five feet, nine inches, and had put on thirty-five pounds since coming to America.

As New York heaved and vibrated under the gray clouds of November, 1891, Frederick headed for Seattle in the great, untamed Northwest to make his fortune in the emerging U.S. territory of Washington.

***

In 1891, Frederick traveled west on the Northern Pacific Rail Line. For a one-way ticket priced at $37.50, he was assigned a seat in the emigrant car along with representatives from a medley of ethnic groups. He rented bedding, but had to pick up provisions along the way. He later claimed that he thrived mostly on apples, stale bread, and moldy cheese.

He arriving in the bustling city of Seattle, a settlement that at the time was reinventing itself during an era of previously unimaginable change. Founded on the log industry, Seattle was recovering from the Great Fire of June 6, 1889, which had burned away the (log-built) heart of the town. What Frederick discovered here was a raw and wide-open frontier town where gambling, liquor, prostitution, and all kinds of graft and extortion flourished.

The town's first brothel had opened in 1861 and, after that, other whorehouses seemed to erupt like mushrooms from the mixtures of mud and manure that lined the streets. Within a population that was mostly male and

Young women were shipped from Seattle to the gold-mining town of Monte Cristo. At dinner, these women donned white aprons to serve food and drink to the miners. Later in the evening, miners retreated to one of the upstairs cubicles with the waitress of his choice. By now, Frederick had learned that a consistently profitable enterprise during the Gold Rush was a restaurant-cum-bordello.

without any permanent roots, negotiable sex had become one of Seattle's most flourishing enterprises.

Frederick was eager to reap profits from this new "industry," whose red lights sprawled out from the "Lava Beds," and whose brothels included "peg houses," whose clients preferred to sodomize young boys. It was here that Frederick looked for a location for his business, adopting the motto, "The miners mined for gold, and Seattle mined the miners."

He began patronizing one of the bordellos, usually on Mondays, when the whores offered discounts, based on slow trade that day, after the bustling trade of Saturday night.

He settled on a location at 208 Washington Street, immediately adjacent to an opium den run by Chinese, for the opening of the "Pet Poodle Restaurant," which he later renamed The Dairy Restaurant. This was the first Trump enterprise in America, the beginning of a business empire which would ultimately include skyscrapers in Manhattan.

With his meager staff, he served sour beer, Sauerkraut, steaks, salt pork, and locally harvested fish twenty-four hours a day.

Upstairs, he rented cubicles staffed by eight prostitutes, who had migrated north from San Francisco. He'd sampled each girl before hiring them. Throughout his stay in the Pacific Northwest and Alaska, he would turn to his own in-house whores when he desired sex for himself. As he later boasted to his brother-in-law, Fred Schuster, after his return to New York, "I never paid for it ever again."

In 1888, Washington State joined the Union, and on October 27, 1892, Frederick became a naturalized U.S. citizen. As part of the process, he had to renounce his fidelity to the Emperor Wilhelm II of Germany.

From within his restaurant/bordello, he welcomed ruddy-cheeked lumberjacks and the blackened miners who emerged from the nearby coal mines. Whenever sailors arrived in port, business boomed, with Frederick taking three-quarters of his girls' earnings.

He had spent a year in Seattle, and had made and saved some money, but he was far from being as rich as he wanted to be. He'd heard stories of the riches to be made in a settlement in north-central Washington State, Monte Cristo, the largest mining boomtown in North America. He was told that there was gold and silver in "them thar hills."

In 1894, word spread that the richest man in the world, John D. Rockefeller, was bankrolling a mining operation in Monte Cristo. It was time to sell out in Seattle and move on to richer fields.

"MINING" THE MINERS
OF MONTE CRISTO

Monte Cristo in the Cascade Mountains is a ghost town today, and hazardous materials, including arsenic, still remain from its mining heyday. Between 1889 and 1907, Monte Cristo produced some 310,000 tons of zinc, gold, silver, and copper, which destructively exposed miners and their health to such poisons as lead, mercury, and arsenic.

In all, more than two-hundred claims were filed, including a false one by Frederick. According to the laws of the day (most of them never enforced), if a person discovered gold on a plot of land, it became his, providing he mined it.

Frederick had not struck gold—in fact, he did no mining at all.

"Let the miners dig for gold," he said. "I plan to dig the nuggets from their pockets."

In Monte Cristo, as a means of accomplishing that, he erected a shabby hotel, a restaurant that served the same German-style food he'd "perfected" in Seattle, and some cubicles for his prostitutes, whom he'd imported from Seattle.

"Booze, plenty to eat, and ladies who are not ladies," he proclaimed to his motley, satisfied customers.

Frederick had turned twenty-four when he faced his first major setback. Word soon reached him that although Rockefeller still publicly touted the wealth to be unearthed in Monte Cristo, he was actually selling his assets

John D. Rockefeller had sent out propaganda that there was gold to be dug up in Monte Cristo. Soon, it was peopled with prospectors who lived in smoky shacks and tents.

Frederick Trump was among them. He arrived here in 1893, not to dig for gold, but to offer miners badly cooked food, drafty lodgings, liquor, and over-the-hill prostitutes.

11

there and arranging a fast exit. In the summer of 1897, when business was still thriving, Frederick hastily sold everything and headed back to Seattle.

Once again, he decided to pursue his own gold in the way to which he'd become accustomed. He knew that hundreds of miners had to be "fed, housed, and fucked," as he bluntly phrased it.

FREDERICK TRUMP & HIS "DEPRAVED LADIES"
Head North for the Klondike Gold Rush

On August 16, 1896, gold was discovered by miners in the Yukon Territory in Northwestern Canada. News of it set off a stampede that attracted more than 100,000 prospectors from 1896 to 1899. A few got rich, but thousands did not, after enduring almost inhuman hardships. Reaching the gold fields would be as hazardous as what Leonardo DiCaprio faced in his 2015 movie, *The Revenant*.

Loaded down with supplies, Frederick shouted "North!" and set out on his perilous journey.

Items he did not take were picks and shovels, as he had no intention of ever prospecting for gold. For this perilous journey, some of which would be on foot across dangerous and snow-blocked mountain passes, he took

Understaffed and overwhelmed by the tsunami of Gold-Rush would-be prospectors heading for the Klondike, the Northwest Territory Mounted Police cracked down before allowing the migrants to cross into the Yukon. They insisted they carry a certain amount of provisions before letting them go forward, knowing that if they did not, they might starve to death.

When gold was discovered in the Yukon Territory, the Gold Rush was on, luring thousands upon thousands of get-rich-quick Americans. Prospectors arrived in San Francisco, heading north to Seattle, before embarking on a trip to the Klondike.

Most would-be prospectors landed in the overcrowded and bustling port of Skagway, Alaska, at the head of the Lynn Canal. Boats arrived daily from the south, laden with passengers. From here, they would have to make the perilous journey north, many never to return.

Northern Bound: View of the Chilkoot Pass at the U.S/Canadian border. Misery, hunger, frostbite, wretchedness, and endemic price-gouging.

along restaurant supplies, as he planned to open trail-side eateries.

Old paddle wheelers, fishing boats, barges, and filthy coal ships were pressed into service to haul would-be prospectors to the Klondike. Many of the overloaded vessels sank, as every passenger carried staggering amounts of equipment and supplies, all of them desperately necessary for survival in the wilderness.

Sluicing and panning in the Yukon Territories. These hearty, rugged prospectors dreamed of untold riches they'd find when they came upon a mother lode of gold.

From Seattle, aboard an overcrowded boat carrying eighty passengers, Frederick landed at Skagway on the jagged southeastern "panhandle" of Alaska, directly south of the Yukon Territory of Canada. From there, with his load of supplies, he had to travel overland, passing through Canadian customs in British Columbia before reaching landlocked, jagged, and frequently frozen expanses of The Yukon Territory

Frozen white death: Humans as beasts of burden, crossing the White Pass en route to the gold fields near Dawson.

As the gateway to the Klondike Gold Rush, Skagway—home base of the Chilkoot and Chilkat tribes— was bustling and breaking loose at its seams. Almost daily, a steam-wheeler filed with gold-seekers arrived from Portland, Seattle, or San Francisco.

Skagway was a cold, smoky, smog-laden hellhole of human and animal excrement and muddy streets lined with hastily rigged tents and weather beaten shacks easily permeated by the constant winds.

New arrivals were often robbed in this lawless frontier town, and Frederick had to take extreme caution. He soon became accustomed to his designation as a "cheechako," a derisive term used by the native Inuit tribe to designate a stranger.

As a means of achieving his daunting setup, Frederick took the White Pass, a narrow canyon-like route that stretched for almost forty-five steeply inclined miles. Pack animals moved along this route laden with supplies. These poor creatures were literally worked to death and often died beside the trail, their carcasses abandoned or sold.

Hungry trekkers often cut flesh from these dead animals as "steaks" to be cooked over open fires. The route soon became known as "Dead Horse Trail." Rock walls, rising at one point to 1,600 feet, lined both sides of the canyon.

Canada's North West Mounted Police vigorously checked each visitor's equipment and supplies. They strictly enforced a Canadian law that demanded that each traveler, for his own survival, be accompanied with a ton of provisions before they were allowed to cross the Canadian border into the Yukon. Men attempting the transit often divided their supplies into as many as forty separate loads, carrying their provisions in backpacks, the contents of which were deposited on the shore of Lake Bennett, on the distant side of the often-frozen White Pass. Those who could afford it hired local laborers to haul their goods for them, if they could find someone to trust. Those who arrived early on the scene were notorious for

These Klondike prostitutes, perhaps associated with Frederick, bore no resemblance to contestants in his grandson's Miss Universe pageants. Although some of them doubled as "actresses," who in some cases could demand payment in gold nuggets, others barely managed to eke out a miserable living amid the rigors of the northern frontier.

At the settlement of Dyea, at the height of the Gold Rush, prospectors camped out in horrid conditions waiting for boat transportation.

exploiting the new arrivals.

As a means of conserving his fast-dwindling supply of cash, Frederick opted to make a series of separate trips over the mountain pass, dividing his supplies into fifty-pound lots. It took him three months to haul them overland along the treacherous terrain, where there was always the danger of his goods being looted.

He endured bitter temperatures that sometimes froze the fingers and toes of ill-equipped trekkers, many of whom died along the way. He'd later describe the feeling of the harsh winds: "It was like a knife cutting into your chest. I thought the monstrous pass would never end." He had to shave with a frozen razor; otherwise, his beard and handlebar mustache would freeze into a mask of ice.

Even before he reached the end of the trail, Frederick came up with the idea of making money along the route. In the spring of 1898, he opened his first "tent canteen," where he could feed as many as eight men under very crowded, smoke-filed conditions. For his meats, he had a constant supply of horses which had dropped dead from overwork on the trail.

From his cache of supplies, he managed to make sourdough biscuits, like his mother had taught him. He always had a supply of dried beans which he'd boil with slabs of salt pork. For dessert, he'd serve dried fruits he'd brought with him.

Unwilling to remain in one place too long, he packed up and moved along the length of the trail, opening another canteen. Before he reached his final destination, he had established, and disassembled, four separate and self-sustained canteens, each generating cash from the sale of "vittles" to desperately hungry would-be prospectors.

At the end of the trail lay the bustling little town of Bennett, on the edge of icy-cold Lake Bennett, a glacially carved finger lake that challenged the survival instincts of any adventurer who tried to cross it.

Mostly consisting of makeshift tents, Bennett received new arrivals every day. Most of them needed boats for transit across a series of waterways that eventually flowed downstream to the set-

Actresses, actually prostitutes, crossing the Dyea River, *en route* to provide entertainment to bored, lonely, and horny prospectors.

tlement of Dawson.

Many of the "Gold Rushers" managed to assemble enough wood to nail together, or lash together, enough planks and/or logs for a makeshift watercraft (often a raft made from logs) to float their supplies to Dawson. Hastily erected sawmills soon denuded the local forests, and soon, nearly every tree that was reasonably accessible had been felled, and the area ran out of timber.

For an entire year, beginning in the summer of 1897, it is estimated that some 20,000 people, including 650 women, migrated from the settlement at Bennett aboard some kind of water craft, seaworthy or not, floating down the Yukon River to the gold fields at Dawson.

Many of these hastily assembled craft—later nicknamed "coffins"—were not seaworthy and many would-be prospectors drowned.

For a while, Frederick operated a tent restaurant at Bennett, eventually constructing a watercraft of his own to haul his supplies.

He named his two-story frame eatery The New Arctic Restaurant. Foraging from whatever managed to live on the surrounding tundra, he specialized in crude preparations of grouse, ptarmigan, swan, caribou, rabbit, squirrel, duck, and moose meat.

Upstairs, he rented "boxes" where five

Frederick's Arctic Restaurant, with hotel rooms and cubicles, thrived in the settlement at Whitehorse, next to its two larger competitors, the Whitehorse Hotel and the Hotel Grand (it really wasn't). At this 1899 establishment, Frederick prospered, making a fortune that become the foundation of a powerful empire in New York City.

He placed an ad in the local paper, promoting his hotel and restaurant. In the ad, he shortened his name to Fred. He falsely promised that "We have come to stay." Actually, he skipped out of town.

prostitutes were kept busy day and night with the miner trade. He made more money on hard liquor and sex than he did on the cuisine. He kept a scale for weighing gold nuggets, which the miners gave him as payment for the food, liquor, and sex. A little local paper that had sprung up defined his "ladies" as "depraved."

Before he moved on from his makeshift premises in Bennett, he estimated, "I made a small fortune."

Just two years after Frederick's arrival in the frozen north, access to the Yukon changed abruptly, for the better, thanks to the opening—at an appalling cost of human life—of a narrow gauge rail line known as the "White Pass and Yukon Route." It would link the Alaskan port of Skagway with the Canadian settlement of Whitehorse, a treacherous distance of 100 frozen miles north from the settlement at Bennett. Within a few weeks of its completion in 1900, it became the primary route of access to the interior of the Yukon, supplanting the dangerous and narrow pedestrian passes that, until the rail line's construction, had been the only route of access.

Shortly after the rail line's completion, sensing that there was money to be make in the region's subsequent boom, Frederick opted to move his business interests to Whitehorse, a jerrymandered, makeshift settlement that sprang up virtually overnight in 1898. He arranged for a wood-framed building to be pre-assembled and then loaded aboard a scow. A crew then attempted to float it down the river to Whitehorse. In its assembled form, it did not survive the rapids, collapsing into pieces when the scow hit some rocks. But Frederick was able, with hired help, to salvage the timbers and rebuild it beside the muddy expanse of Front Street in Whitehorse, very close to the recently inaugurated railway terminus known as the Yukon Depot. He named it the New Arctic. Just before it opened, a load of prostitutes arrived to service clients within the "boxes" he'd built over his eatery.

As Frederick's restaurant, hotel, and brothel boomed, there was incentive for him to expand his premises with another set of boxes. He did this by adding a log-sided annex onto the main structure of his hotel. To staff them, he sent for another twenty "ladies" from Seattle. It was rumored that he tried out each of them before hiring them, learning about their respective "specialties" as a means of advising his clients and customers.

But the fickle fortunes of the gold trade soon turned, and trouble loomed for the town as well as his enterprise. Miners were quickly becoming aware that the Yukon did not have acres of gold deposits that had been rumored. In fact, it was getting harder and harder for prospectors to find gold. Then, news reached Whitehorse that elusive gold deposits had been discovered in the even more remote region around Nome, on the far-distant west coast of Alaska, about 2,000 miles across spectacularly hostile terrain.

More trouble was on the way when Whitehorse's new mayor took over, promising to rid the town of prostitutes—a campaign commitment that would directly threaten Frederick's sex trade.

Making matters even more complicated, based on claims from other settlers challenging his ownership of the building site he'd commandeered on Front Street, Frederick found himself on the verge of losing his restaurant and bordello.

By now he'd grown tired of life in the frozen north, and although he'd become rich based on his marketing of liquor and prostitutes, he harbored a preference for life as a burgher in Germany. Quick-witted and imaginative, and perhaps perceiving that a future in the harsh conditions of the rapidly gentrifying Yukon might no longer be as profitable as it had been during the early days of its Gold Rush, he wanted to settle down, marry a German girl, and raise a family.

Based on his personal experience, most of the women he'd met in the New World had been prostitutes. In his search for a decent marriage partner, he opted to return to Kallstadt. Nostalgically, he retained the memory of that bright-eyed five-year-old he'd spotted the day before he'd emigrated from Bremen. She must be grown up by now.

Turning his back forever on the rowdy, raucous, life-threatening frontier, he headed for New York with the intention of boarding a ship to Germany.

In many ways, Frederick might be said to have invented the tired cliché, "New York is a great place to visit, but I wouldn't want to live there." In his way, he had already achieved his version of the American Dream—that is, to strike it rich in the New World before returning to "civilization."

America's Northwest, Alaska, and western Canada, were still raging, untamed frontiers, not the kind of places a decent, respectable man would select as a home for his God-fearing wife and family.

During his ocean transit back to Bremen, a secret he'd hold close to his chest involved the fact that his newly acquired wealth was based for the most part on prostitution.

He was still an American citizen, and could return to the New World any time he wanted to.

But a nagging question lurked in the back of his brain: Would he—perhaps based on a bribe or two—be allowed to reclaim his German citizenship, considering the circumstances of his hasty departure years before?

***

Frederick Trump had left Kallstadt as a poverty-riddled sixteen-year-old. Now, at the age of thirty-two, he walked once again along the familiar streets of his native town, except now—based on the standards of his era, he was moderately wealthy, worth at least $400,000 in U.S. dollars of 2016.

After a reunion with his family, he walked across Frankenheim Strasse and knocked on the door of the Christ family. To his surprise, the door was opened by that same little girl he'd seen years ago, except now she was Elizabeth Christ, a twenty-one year old.

Based on the standards of that era, she had emerged as a beauty, a Teutonic ideal with blonde hair and blue eyes and what later became known in America as a Mae West "hour-glass figure."

The Christ family was looked down upon in the town because of their extreme poverty. Its patriarch, Philip Christ, supported his family by selling pots and pans, and was known as "The Tinker Man."

Much to the disapproval of Frederick's mother, Katherina—who had, years before, been virtually abandoned by her son—he began courting the young woman.

Frederick eventually placed an engagement ring on Elizabeth's finger, with a promise to return for her after he closed out his affairs in America. The date of their wedding was set for August 26, 1902. Before he left, he issued a stern warning that she avoid other men during his absence. He also gave her the equivalent of $1,000 U.S. dollars, instructing her to buy a better wardrobe, the most important component of which would be a wedding dress.

Elizabeth quickly fell in love with Frederick. He later claimed that "she made herself available to me," but he chose not to immediately pursue it, wanting her "pure" on her wedding night, when he

Virginal and unsoiled, a "Kallstadt Lily," Elizabeth Christ represented an idealized form of Teutonic womanhood for the jaded and deeply cynical Frederick upon his return to Germany from the rigors and fleshpots of the New World's Western frontier.

Since his departure from Kallstadt as a teenager, he had amassed a large fortune (for its time). She had not married in the interim, and he asked her to be his bride.

planned, as her husband, to take her virginity.

As promised, after concluding some business matters in America, Frederick returned to Kallstadt, and the wedding took place on the pre-arranged date, with representatives from both families present. Although he was satisfied that Elizabeth was, indeed, a virgin during their lovemaking after the wedding, she reportedly cried until morning, as she had no idea that sex involved a penetration that she interpreted as brutal. She had never seen the sex organ of a male, and apparently refused to perform "certain acts."

Frederick, in contrast, who had been trained by prostitutes in America, was said to have been a skilled seducer and a demanding lover.

Soon after their wedding, they left Germany for a life together in the United States. After their arrival at the Port of New York, Frederick took his bride to the fast-growing borough to the north of Manhattan known as the Bronx, where they would live, as he had in years past, with his sister, Katherine, and her husband, Fred Schuster.

Elizabeth found the New World bewildering, disapproving of much of what she saw. In those days, there was a gin mill for every eight residents. Gambling halls proliferated, and streetwalkers were clearly in evidence plying their trade. Startling new "discoveries" included electricity and a home with indoor plumbing (she would no longer use an outhouse).

In 1898, the Bronx was incorporated into the newly consolidated City of New York as one of five distinct boroughs.

Frederick moved with his bride to the South Bronx, a neighborhood with a high percentage of German-speaking people that was known at the time as Morrissania, hoping that his wife would assimilate and be happy. On Westchester Avenue, she lived in an apartment building whose other units were occupied for the most part by other German-speaking people. But public phones and trolleys terrified her. She'd never known of such modern advances.

After a year in the Bronx, she was desperately homesick for Kallstadt, and she begged her husband to return to Germany. She did not like America or its customs, and she did not want to be-

Elizabeth Christ Trump, after her marriage.

It was said that she never really felt comfortable in the bold, brassy New World carved out by her forceful, fiercely entrepreneurial husband, whom she barely knew at the time of her wedding. .

come an American citizen like her husband.

On April 30, 1904, she gave birth to a child, also named Elizabeth.

So once again, at the beginning of summer of that year, Frederick returned to Kallstadt with both mother Elizabeth and daughter Elizabeth.

Defining himself as a solid and loyal German who had returned to his ancestral home, he attempted to renounce his American citizenship and become, once again,

Smelly, loud, cacophonous, and dirty, this is the kind of Manhattan street scene Elizabeth Christ confronted upon her arrival in the New World. She hated it. Never really fitting in, she yearned for the rolling green fields of the Palatinate and the perceived grace of Old Germany.

a citizen of his native Fatherland. But to his rage and astonishment, local authorities refused his application. A stricter and more militaristic Germany had emerged under Kaiser Wilhelm II, who would eventually, with tragic consequences, lead his country into World War I.

Humiliated, Frederick was defined as a draft dodger. Authorities in Speyer noted that he had scorned his military obligations, dodged the draft, and insulted the Fatherland. Consequently, they seriously considered expelling him from Germany forever.

"The news hit Elizabeth and me like lightning," he wrote to sister Katherine in the Bronx. "A dark cloud had been cast over us. We will have to leave Germany, perhaps forever."

With endless appeals exhausted, Elizabeth, Frederick, and their daughter said goodbye to Germany on June 30, 1905. Sailing back to America with a raft of mixed feelings, Elizabeth Trump was five months pregnant.

In the Bronx, amid everything she disliked about the New World, another child would be born, Frederick ("Fred") Christ Trump. Emerging later in life as a millionaire real estate developer, he would do much to change the skylines of some of New York City's Outer Boroughs.

He would also father a child who would grow up to run for President of the United States.

Chapter Two

CHANGING THE SKYLINES
OF BROOKLYN & QUEENS

*Fred Trump Emerges from the Depression and a World
War as "The Henry Ford of the Building Industry"*

RE-DEFINING THE GOLD RUSH

How a Bonnie Lassie from
SCOTLAND
*Melted Fred's Cold, Cold Heart, and How a Workaholic
Building Mogul Carved Time Out for*
LOVE

Frederick Christ Trump—later known as Fred—was developing within his mother's womb during his family's transit on the *SS Pennsylvania* from the German port of Bremen to New York Harbor. There, as a U.S. citizen, he would be born on October 11, 1905.

He was the first son of Frederick Trump and his wife, Elizabeth, who had turned twenty-five just before Fred's birth. She had not wanted to return to a life in New York, but she had been more or less deported by German bureaucrats who had rejected her husband's attempt to reclaim his citizenship.

By this point in their marriage, Elizabeth had noted that her roguish, free-wheeling husband was beginning to drink rather heavily, not only at night but during the daytime, too.

As a newborn birthed within the premises of an American hospital, the infant Fred was carried to his family's very modest apartment—a cold water flat with a shared bathroom in a hall—at 539 East 177th Street in the Bronx.

Upon his return to America, baby Fred's father, Frederick, resumed his career as a barber. Eventually, in league with his brother-in-law, Fred Schuster, he opened a large and profitable barber shop of his own at 60 Wall Street in Lower Manhattan. It became the preferred early-morning venue for

Left photo: Two views of NYC from around the time of Fred Trump's arrival. (left photo shows Financial District (Maiden Lane, near Frederick Trump's Barbershop at 60 Wall Street, in the Financial District) in 1905.

stockbrokers, who came by for a professional shave before reporting to work.

The increased income allowed Frederick to move his family into an apartment building in the Woodstock section of the Bronx.

Because he didn't want to continue shaving beards and cutting hair for the rest of his life, he was constantly on the lookout for other fields to conquer. His family had grown. His third child, John George, had been born on August 26, 1907. Unlike Fred, who did not go to college, John would become the scientific genius of the Trump clan, earning his Ph.D from M.I.T. and becoming a professor of physics.

For business opportunities, Frederick looked south to the relatively undeveloped borough of Queens. Occupying, with Brooklyn, the western tip of Long Island, it would explode based on factors that included the opening of the Queensboro Bridge in 1909. The construction of railway tunnels under the East River would follow. By 1915, much of the borough would be linked to Manhattan and the rest of the city via the subway system. [Eventually, Queens, although technically classified as a borough of New York City and

More genteel than the Klondike, and less frenetic than Manhattan with its fast-emerging slums, Queens was ready, willing, and able to appreciate the rough-and-tumble entrepreneurial, "frontier pizzazz with the German accent" of Frederick Trump.

Frederick Trump had trained as a barber in his native Germany. He brought his tonsorial skills to New York, and with his brother-in-law, Fred Schuster, opened a thriving barbershop at 60 Wall Street in Lower Manhattan.

Before stockbrokers reported to work during the loosely regulated "robber-baron" financial markets of that era, he gave some of them an early morning shave.

not, technically a city in its own right, would become the fourth most densely populated community in the United States, surpassed only by Los Angeles, Chicago, and its neighboring borough of Brooklyn.]

At the time, Queens was known as "the cornfield borough," peppered as it was with farms growing produce for the residents of Manhattan and Brooklyn. Fred became specifically interested in the Woodlawn district, a community flanking the borough's western edge.

Those farms would soon be bought up and transformed into housing developments. Over the ensuing decades, real estate prices would soar as the borough's population increased by 40 percent. Whereas at the turn of the 20th Century, the population here had been one-quarter German, during the ensuing decades, it would emerge as one of the most ethnically diverse areas on the globe.

In 1905, the Trumps abandoned the Bronx, moving to Queens into a house on Jamaica Avenue in Woodhaven. By now, Frederick viewed real estate as an investment, and with money he'd saved, he purchased a second two-story house nearby. Historians might one day conclude that that house was the first stone laid in what would, during the administrations of Frederick's son and grandson, become a vast real estate empire.

He abandoned his vocation as a barber and took a position as the manager of the Medallion Hotel in Manhattan. That meant that he was rarely at home, returning to Queens mostly to sleep before departing once again early the next morning.

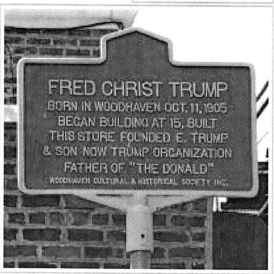

Fred Trump became a legend within his community even before the rise of his son, Donald, to the presidential race. This memorial plaque honors his memory today to passersby in Woodhaven, Queens.

Perhaps because his father was mostly absent, and perhaps because of the overweening supervision of his mother, Fred became labeled as a "mama's boy," frequently encountering bullies within his neighborhood.

Although the United States remained neutral during the early years of World War I, life within the Trump household changed after 1914. Most Americans sided with the British, and anti-German sentiment grew. To an increasing degree, Germans were despised. To offset the animosity building against them, the Trumps' reinvented their Teutonic heritage, redefining it as Swedish, based on a fictitious claim that they had emigrated from Stockholm

Public opinion in the U.S. against "the Hun" intensified in May of 1915, after a German submarine torpedoed and sank the *Lusitania*, a British liner flying an American flag. The fallout from that act of aggression strongly influenced America's decision to declare war against Germany in 1917, two years later. The Trumps reacted with bitterness, shame, and horror as Sauerkraut was redefined as "Liberty Cabbage," and hamburger reappeared on American menus as "Salisbury steak." Outside the Trump home, Boy Scouts assembled bonfires for the burning of German-language newspapers.

Even though World War I ended in 1918, more tragedy loomed for the Trumps as "Spanish influenza" morphed into a worldwide pandemic, eventually claiming 21 million lives, more than had been killed from armed hostilities during the war. Among its victims were Frederick, the family's adventurous and roguish patriarch, and his brother-in-law, Fred Schuster.

Subsequently, young Fred became "the man of the family." As a preteen eleven-year-old, he helped to put food on the table, procuring it however he could. Although the family had been left with a nest egg that would be worth about $350,000 in 2016 terms, the Trumps saw much of that largesse disappearing during the post-war economic downturn, as inflation spiraled out of control.

For a while, young Fred worked as a shoeshine boy, and his widowed mother took in sewing. On January 10, 1923, as a thin, blonde-haired, and ambitious young man, he was graduated from the then-largest high school in Queens, Richmond Hill High School, founded in 1898. Although he had little time for them, he was already attracting the attention of many girls at his school.

Those years at Richmond Hill would be the extent of his formal education. After that, he educated himself in the rough and tumble world of New York real estate, a milieu overflowing with labor disputes, crooked politicians, and mob bosses. Even as a teenager, he saw the unlimited possibilities of developing housing for a rapidly expanding population. As such, most of the family's livelihood derived from their construction and subsequent sale of small, single-family houses. The family would, in essence, finance their sale to (supposedly) qualified buyers, and hold the mortgage in-house, collecting the monthly payments as a means of providing income. All three of Frederick Trump's children, as spearheaded by Fred, joined in the enterprise.

In Woodhaven, Fred earned extra money as a golf course caddie, a paper boy, and a grocery delivery boy. Many boys at that time wanted to grow up to be firemen or police officers, but Fred wanted to carry through on his father's dream and become a builder, or, as he put it, "the best real estate developer in New York City—that is, New York City except Manhattan. That's poison."

Enrolling in night courses at the local YMCA, he learned the technical intricacies of the building trades, including wiring and masonry. In later years, even as a multi-millionaire, whenever he spotted a workman executing a task incorrectly, he'd take over and demonstrate how he wanted it done.

Fred's entry into the building trades occurred at the industry's lowest end. Whereas in summer, he'd enlist the aid of a horse and cart for delivery of supplies to building sites, in winter, when the roads were blocked, "I became the goddamned mule hauling heavy loads myself," he said.

In 1922, the Trumps received news that the grand matriarch of their family, Katherina Kober, had died in faraway Kallstadt. After a lifetime of struggle amid changing political and economic fortunes, she had expired at the age of eighty-six.

Her death marked the beginning of the schism wherein the Trumps of the New World lost touch with the Trumps of the Old World. With her passing, the Trumps of the New Order would become thoroughly Americanized and increasingly distant from their Teutonic roots. To an increasing degree, especially in his dealings with Jewish clients and colleagues, Fred asserted that his family's ancestral roots derived from Sweden.

Since he was legally underaged, Fred, during the two years that followed his high school graduation, relied on his mother, Elizabeth, to function as the figurehead for the newly formed E. Trump & Son. Her signature "E. Trump" became a means of concealing, to the degree she could, her gender in an era noted for his barriers against the advancement of women.

Since banks at the time were unwilling to lend him or his company any money, Fred would build a house, sell it, and use the proceeds to construct another. Before the age of 21, he had erected nearly two dozen homes in the neighborhood of Queens known as "Hollis."

Fred wasn't part of the flapper contingent that to some degree defined

"The Roaring Twenties," and he didn't spend his nights like some of his former classmates dancing the Charleston with lookalike Joan Crawfords in the speakeasies of that time. Instead, he spent his energies at construction sites throughout Queens. The Trumps became a family of gypsies moving into one new house after another, sometimes before its interior was complete, locating elsewhere whenever they managed to sell it, usually for a profit.

Fred Trump operated his fledgling enterprise during relatively undocumented times, so records on his political and business activities remain sketchy. An exception to this was provided on June 1, 1927, by *The New York Times*, which reported that Fred Trump, then living at 175-24 Devonshire Road in Queen, was arrested and later discharged after an incident involving members of the Ku Klux Klan. A political protest had led to a brawl, and Queens police were called to the scene. In all, according to the news story, there were more than a thousand Klansmen involved, drawing some 100 police officers to the *melée*. Seven men were arrested, including Fred, who later maintained that he'd been a casual, otherwise uninvolved bystander.

David Julius Lehrenkraus, as depicted on the frontpage of *The Brooklyn Eagle*, January 24, 1934, operated a Ponzi-like scheme. When it was exposed, Fred Trump stepped in to pick up the pieces.

Fred's sister, Elizabeth, was the first among her siblings to marry. The wedding occurred in June of 1929. Her groom was William Walter, a bank clerk of German origin.

Working seven days a week, and keeping long hours, Fred took over undeveloped lots in Jamaica Estates, a neighborhood in east-central Queens, near the borough's eastern edge. His houses became more elaborate, often designed in Queen Anne, English Tudor, or Georgian colonial. Houses with five bedrooms sold for as much as $35,000, a luxurious and upscale price tag in those days.

Fred proclaimed at a family gathering, "Thank God we left Germany, which is facing horrendous troubles. America is the land of dreams. Every-

29

thing good and glorious is coming true for us."

In spite of that rosy outlook, disasters lay ahead, not only for the Trumps, but for the United States in general.

Among them was the Wall Street crash of 1929. In its aftermath, the real estate market collapsed, too, as few people could purchase new homes. In a departure from his usual mode of operations, Fred opened a retail outlet for groceries. Formatted as a serve-yourself supermarket, it was a novel idea at the time. He modeled it on King Kullen, a fast- emerging retail food chain that would eventually buy his supermarket, reconfiguring it into one of their branch outlets after the economy improved.

During the darkest years of the Great Depression, unemployment rose to twenty-five percent. The outgoing U.S. President, Herbert Hoover, was widely perceived as having done virtually nothing to help, and Fred placed his hopes in the newly elected President, Franklin D. Roosevelt, whose first presidential term began in 1933.

When FDR took over, real estate values had dropped twenty percent, and foreclosures stretched from sea to sea across America. Homes were seized for nonpayment of mortgages, and thousands upon thousands were left homeless.

In the malaise sweeping the country, and perhaps inspired by a cliché favored by his mother [*"If you're given lemons, make lemonade"*], Fred saw a chance to grab up foreclosed real estate from banks who wanted to unload

"When Johnny Came Marching Home from War," the FHA was there to help him buy a house.

A huge postwar demand for housing, coupled with ferocious resolve, an ironbound work ethic, and the easy availability of vast amounts of government money, all conspired to make Fred Trump rich.

the properties they'd seized "at firesale prices," as Fred defined them.

By the mid-1930s, he saw an opening where he could profit from the downfall of others. The Brooklyn-based J. Lehrenkrauss Corporation, mortgage-servicing lender, had become insolvent. The papers proclaimed that the firm had failed to pay dividends to holders of mortgage certificates, and that on January 25, 1935, Julius Lehrenkrauss, the company's CEO, a native of Stuttgart, Germany had been convicted of mail fraud during the marketing and sale of $1,600,000 worth of preferred stock. Government prosecutors alleged that the firm had been insolvent at the time it had sold the worthless stock, and that investors who bought them had been defrauded.

Young entrepreneur Fred Trump, rebuilding the face of housing in Queens.

His good looks were compared to those of a silent screen *matinée* idol.

Lehrenkrauss had been operating a Ponzi-like scheme, fraudulently disguising the weakness of his operation by shifting cash from one account to another. Many of his problems derived from his loss, during the stock market crash of 1929, of the equivalent of $8.5 million in 2016 dollars.

After a trial, Julius was sentenced to a term of five to ten years at Sing-Sing. Handcuffed to a petty thief from Brooklyn, Julius, sobbing and crying, was led away from the courtroom still wearing his pince-nez and striped pants.

Fred showed up in court the next day as what remained of the Lehrenkrauss holdings were being allocated and auctioned to buyers. Its mortgage servicing department, once valued at $28 million, had shrunk to $6 million, and was eroding every day. Fred had to move quickly to salvage what remained.

After a series of intricate maneuvers, the underfinanced Fred, in league with another developer from Queens, William Demm, was awarded the remains of the Lehrenkrauss holdings.

"I can now stop selling catsup and hawking carrots, cabbage, and onions," he said, in reference to his food emporium. "I'm back in the real estate business."

Fred needed money. He found it in the fine print of FDR's New Deal. As a stimulus to the moribund housing industry, the Federal Housing Administration (FHA) came into existence. The sudden availability of Federally guaranteed funds for construction of residential buildings represented a new "Gold Rush" for Fred. Reacting to the availability of vast amounts of capital, he embarked on a program to accessorize the Outer Boroughs of New York City with urban housing. Under his guidance, farmlands were soon transformed into real estate developments in a borough whose population was rapidly expanding.

"You can have Manhattan," he said. "I'll concentrate on Brooklyn and Queens."

That policy of avoiding Manhattan, of course, would not be endorsed by his son, Donald, who was years from being born.

With steely determination, and courage bolstered by the new fiscal policies of the FHA, Fred took over the mortgages of families plunged into default. This was with the understanding that any loss incurred through making a bad loan to a prospective buyer of one of his units, even to a risky client, would be reimbursed, in the event of default, by the FHA.

For generations, the Flatbush section of Brooklyn had been devoted to growing produce such as cabbage, cauliflower, and lettuce for the food markets of Manhattan. During the social and economic upheavals of the early 20th century, Fred saw opportunities for business. As trolley and subway service expanded out into Flatbush from Manhattan's core, homes sprang up to house the workers making daily commutes. Taking advantage of the Depression-era subsidies offered by the U.S. government, Fred emerged as a multi-millionaire.

Based on the desires of its administrators to avoid get-rich-quick schemers and the influence of the mob, the bureaucratic FHA was girded and fenced with regulations described by a local farmer as "bull high and pig tight."

From 1935 until the entry of the United States into World War II in 1941, Fred, using FHA-backed financing, built 2,350 private homes, each well-constructed and adhering to government standards of sanitation, safety, and design.

It was during this period that the till-then-unprecedented twenty-year mortgage emerged as a financial vehicle, enabling ownership of a home to millions of Americans.

Within six years, Fred emerged as one of the Outer Boroughs' major homebuilders. By 1950, his building projects had expanded into one of Brooklyn's final expanses of scrub and wetlands, the Farragut Woods (a region roughly synonymous with what had formerly been called the Paerdegat Basin), a six-acre habitat for raccoons, muskrats, and otters, where

Canarsie Indians had once hunted for pheasant and deer.

As a means of accomplishing his goals, Fred was sometimes forced into contact with mob bosses who had infiltrated local politics and the construction industry. They had the power to sabotage a construction project unless the builder paid them. In later life, Fred painfuly recalled, "The Mafia made building a home within the limits of New York City the most hazardous and the costliest of any other large city in the United States."

Even though America suffered yet another economic downturn in 1937, *The Brooklyn Eagle* hailed Fred Trump as "The Henry Ford of the building industry." Sales of his new-built homes were brisk. In an article in *The New York Evening Post,* a reporter claimed that "mobs of hysterical buyers at Fred Trump's Brooklyn real estate office forced him to call in the police."

During the late 1930s, Fred employed a work force of some 400 men, most of them from Europe. Each of them had a specialty. He learned that the best plasterers came from Italy, the best wood workers from Sweden. At one of his work sites, a reporter said the combinations of languages spoken at the site evoked the Tower of Babel, as one home after another went up in rapid succession. They were priced at from $3,500 for a no-frills version to as much as $7,500 for a larger and more luxurious version with three bedrooms and two bathrooms.

Many of the homes he built were attached or semi-attached, edge to edge, with common walls. Stretching for blocks, they evoked a sea of dark sienna-colored bricks whose practical, no-nonsense style became a trademark of "Trump homes." Most contained a garage, something that until then had been a luxury reserved only for the rich. At the time, many of the buyers didn't own a car or know how to drive one, but all of that changed over time.

A great hunk of Fred Trump's consumers consisted of

Mary McLeod—a recently emigrated lass from one of the most remote, barren and isolated islands in Scotland—became Mary Trump in January of 1936 and thereafter became a part of the American legend of her unexpectedly famous middle son, Donald.

young professionals—doctors, lawyers, and government workers—many of whom were recently married and starting families.

Based on the hardships of his teen years, and the intensity of his work ethic, most of Fred's life had been devoted to work, not pleasure. But at the age of 30, he had reached the point in his life when he wanted to settle down and rear a family.

One night at a party, from across a crowded room, he eyed a lovely young woman. Her name was Mary Anne MacLeod, and she'd emigrated to New York after a tough, no-nonsense childhood on Stornoway, a northern, wind-whipped island outpost of Scotland in the remote Outer Hebrides.

No doubt some Viking blood flowed through her veins. She was still learning English when she arrived on Ellis Island, having grown up in an age, and in a region of the British Isles, where Gaelic was the language of choice.

She was assigned a small bedroom in the apartment of her sister, who had inaugurated a new life for herself in Astoria, Queens. Her sister had invited Mary Anne to this party, and it was there that she first met Fred. She was very shy around him, but he seemed to like that quality in a young woman.

Within days, they began to date. Subsequently, she wrote back to her relatives in Scotland, "Fred Trump, a German, looks like he will make a good provider. He is very successful in building public housing. He seems to like my raven hair and fresh-faced, freckled look. We've gone out ten times. I expect a proposal of marriage tonight. No need to worry about me in America anymore."

In January of 1936, when he was 31, Fred married her. Based on business commitments, he allowed himself only one night for a honeymoon escape to Atlantic City, a resort which, in time, would become a gambling mecca forever associated with one of their sons.

During the months to come, Mary gave birth to their first child,

Keep the home fires burning

MORE PRODUCTION!

This is typical of the motivational and instructional posters issued by FDR's Wartime Office of Production Management.

In the frenzy catalyzed by the Nazi offensive, building supplies during the war were mostly snapped up for the war effort, making Fred Trump's life as a building contractor nearly impossible.....Until the government hired him to erect military housing in Norfolk.

Maryanne, who would evolve into a successful lawyer and later, a Federal judge.

Fred Jr. came along in 1938, Elizabeth in 1942. Two other sons, Donald and Robert, would wait until after World War II before emerging as postwar "Baby Boomers."

In 1940, Fred had completed the construction of 350 residences, with annual sales of one million dollars. In Brighton Beach, a Brooklyn neighborhood adjacent to the Atlantic, he began erecting newer, better, and more upscale homes, the sales of which he promoted with an ongoing series of $100 prizes. A "Trump Baby" was a designation for any infant born during the residency of his or her parent(s) in one of the houses he had built.

To an increasing degree, his name was becoming famous throughout New York City. There was even talk about propelling him into public office as the Borough President of Queens.

By now, war was looming from across the Atlantic. In 1941, a battered Britain stood almost alone against the overpowering military forces of Nazi Germany, whose Luftwaffe was firebombing London almost every night. Adding to the horror was the increasing aggression of the Empire of Japan. Based on these and other factors, Fred understood that a U.S. entry as an armed combatant in the war effort was virtually inevitable, and that a war would directly affect the housing market.

As U.S. President, during his unprecedented third term, FDR established the Office of Production Management (OPM) to prepare America for war. Construction materials were impounded for almost exclusive use by the war effort. Subsequently, the building of private homes ground to a standstill.

With adroit foresight, Fred managed to escape most of the OPM restrictions by retooling his organization into something synchronized with the war effort. Some of his efforts focused on the construction of housing for workers associated with the burgeoning Brooklyn Naval Yard. Defense workers were flocking to New York from towns across the Eastern Seaboard. To

The Trump family homestead on Wareham Street in Jamaica Estates. This is where "The Donald" grew up, in the "Tara of Queens."

house them, Fred built, in rapid succession, 750 new houses on a 55-acre tract of land in Bensonhurst.

Then an opportunity arose to construct emergency housing for defense plant employees at the Norfolk Naval Base and Air Station in Virginia. After finalizing the necessary contracts from the government, he roared into production of fast-built, standardized housing within what, until then, had been a red-light district catering to horny sailors.

This occurred during an era when Norfolk became such a boomtown that it was even hard to get a seat at a movie theater. *[Part of the Trump family lore associated with that period of Fred's life relates that once, during a Norfolk screening of the then-most-popular movie in town, Fred had to call in a political favor to procure seating at a screening of* Somewhere I'll Find You, *co-starring Clark Gable and Lana Turner.]*

During the war years, commutes between New York City and Norfolk were so restrictive, and so likely to be diverted or delayed based on the needs of the military, that Fred opted to transfer his wife and three children to Norfolk. Day after day, Fred, self-identifying as "a Swede," heard sailors and soldiers, in their loathing of all things German, attacking "The Krauts." In response, he sometimes asserted, "But Japs are an even bigger menace." He also began to contribute to Jewish charities. Many people who met him assumed he was a Jew.

In 1944, as the tides of war turned in favor of the Allies, Fred had completed the construction of approximately 1,500 desperately needed wartime housing units.

As it became more obvious that the United States was winning the war in both Europe and the Pacific, construction for wartime workers in coastal Virginia was no longer a government priority. By June of 1944, Fred told his family, now based in Norfolk, "FDR has pulled the plug on us. We're selling out and moving back to New York."

Consequently, Fred, with his family, moved back to Queens, to a two-story faux Tudor structure on an inconveniently small lot on Wareham Street in Jamaica Estates. In time, it would prove too cramped for their needs. Fred would erect and move them into a much larger home.

For income, he focused on residential housing in neighborhoods that included Bensonhurst and Brighton Beach in Brooklyn, erecting shelter for veterans returning from the war. Construction materials, however, were expensive and scarce, creating dramatic shortages, skyrocketing prices, speculation, competitive bidding, and in some cases, graft and kickbacks.

Some six million soldiers were flooding into New York after wartime stints in Europe and/or the Pacific, and the housing shortage was at crisis levels. Some ex-soldiers were assigned to live in dormitory-style accommodations gerrymandered from railway boxcars. In many cities, including Chicago, vets were homeless.

Harry S Truman, anxious to solve the problem, created the Veterans Emergency Housing Program (VEHP), which—in an attempt to encourage home construction and discourage speculation and graft—imposed price controls on building supplies. Much to the chagrin of Fred and other builders, the program failed.

Despite the many problems he faced, Fred came up with a daring plan then-novel in postwar America. It involved the creation of residential housing with a shopping center and the "feel" of a custom-designed and relatively self-contained "country village."

Ambitious and innovative, and incorporating thirty-two six-story apartment towers, it was launched on a fourteen-acre site at the edge of the bay in the Brooklyn neighborhood of Shore Haven. Its 7,000 units would eventually house many veterans and their baby-booming families within a development named "Trump City." Its configuration as rental units represented a departure from Fred's earlier preference for the construction of private homes.

Trump City was followed by Beach Haven, near Brighton Beach, a complex containing nearly 2,000 apartments within two dozen buildings.

Hovering in the background, exploiting what they could, were the crime families. The Genovese and Gambino families, and Lucky Luciano, would soon become household names.

By now, Fred Trump himself was known throughout New York because of the reams of newspaper publicity he'd generated. There was talk that he might one day run for Mayor. His tailor-made suits filled more than one closet, and by 1950, he

Fred Trump's son, Donald, would later become one of the best dressed men in town, even manufacturing (in China) expensive suits and ties.

Donald learned his penchant for dressing from his father, who, in 1950, competed with General Dwight D. Eisenhower for status as one of the ten best dressed men in the United States.

Within two years, the well-dressed Dwight, depicted on election night in November of 1952 with his wife, Mamie, was elected President.

In 2015, Fred Trump's son, Donald, announced his own bid for the White House.

joined General Dwight D. Eisenhower on a list of the ten best-dressed men in America.

He was also rich. When he wanted to stage a benefit concert for some charity, perhaps for the emerging state of Israel, he'd bark a command at one of his assistants: "Get me Benny Goodman. Perhaps throw in Roberta Peters."

***

On June 14, 1946, an infant was born who would alter the direction of the Trump family forever, redesign the skylines of Manhattan, and perhaps change the course of world history.

He was Donald John Trump. His birth was celebrated as a blessed event in the Trump family, although latter-day critics would equate it with the birth of "Rosemary's Baby."

Chapter Three

AMID CULTURAL UPHEAVALS
*A "Rebellious Bumpkin with Big Teeth"
Becomes a Baby Boomer Pit Bull*

FORCIBLY ENROLLED AT A MILITARY ACADEMY AS A DETERRENT TO JUVENILE DELINQUENCY,
"Jocko" Trump Bullies and Terrorizes the Nerds

AS THE HOUSING MARKET BOOMS,
*Fred Trump is Scandalously Associated with
Accusations of Government Theft*

SHOWTIME!
Donald's Broadway Dream

DADDY TRUMP GETS SLAMMED
*An Activist Songwriter Accuses Him of Racial Hatred in
the Housing Markets*

Late in the summer of 1945, with vast parts of Germany in ruins, World War II came to an inglorious end. As ordered by then-President Harry S Truman, the United States dropped atomic bombs on Hiroshima and Nagasaki. Within minutes, the Empire of Japan and its imperial ambitions came to an abrupt, ghastly, and horrifying end.

A B-29 flies over Osaka, Japan, days before atomic bombs are unleashed on Hiroshima and Nagasaki, devastating Japan and thereby ending WWII.

In distinct contrast, New York would soon experience unparalleled prosperity and a Golden Age, fast morphing into the cultural center of the world. In the words of the British author, J.B. Priestley, "It was a truly American city before it became a glittering cosmopolis that belonged to the world."

Despite optimism that permeated the urban landscape, 1946 was nonetheless fraught with

Long-suffering G.I.s returned from the front in urgent need of R&R, some partying, and HOUSING.

problems. Millions of soldiers were returning from the war, and all of them wanted jobs and affordable housing.

According to Daddy Fred, "After their return from Europe and the Pacific, those horny soldiers and sailors were fucking day and night. Babies were dropping out of wombs faster than they could be housed. Babies were booming, and the housing markets roared."

North Carolina women in Greensboro line up to welcome their warriors home, circa 1945.

"Little Boy" mushrooms atomic annihilation on Nagasaki, propelling the United States into the role of of the world's premier military and economic superpower.

Soldiers returning from the wars in Europe and the Pacific, and the baby-booming families they spawned, needed housing, and FAST.

Human values and pastimes across America changed as the country shifted away from a wartime economy. In department stores, shoppers unaccustomed to the sudden availability of luxury goods, rioted when nylons became available after the deprivations of war.

Government issued promotional ad advocating the virtues of family-making after the depopulation of WWII.

Confronted with the urgent need for new housing, Fred faced a shortage of building materials, sometimes having to procure them at inflated prices on the black market. When they became available, accommodations were snapped up by eager consumers. New houses sold for an average price of $5,600 to workers making an average annual wage of $2,500. Most of them drove to work in a car dating from the 1930s. They paid an average of 15¢

a gallon for gasoline, usually with the expectation of replacing their beat-up antiques with newer vehicles from assembly-line Detroit.

As residents of New York, the Trumps were well positioned to benefit from the country's radical demographic changes. The city had become the world's largest manufacturing center, home to some 40,000 factories employing a staggering one million workers. The Port of New York handled some forty percent of the country's waterborne freight. Manhattan was the headquarters of such industrial giants as Standard Oil and U.S. Steel. The United Nations was also located in the city, making New York, at least symbolically, the capital of the world. The city's reputation as a center of relatively tolerant liberals was reinforced. Many American men, introduced to homosexuality during the war, and in lieu of returning to conservative communities back in the grain belt, opted to permanently relocate.

Tupperware parties became the rage across America as consumers changed their shopping, cooking, and dining rituals. Standards of morality changed almost overnight, too. In the summer of 1946, although it was later banned from U.S. beaches, the micro-bikini was introduced to the French Riviera. Political presuppositions were redefined as governments collapsed and subsequently reconfigured. The British Empire was fading into history; Japan was in ruins; some thirty million Chinese were on the verge of dying of starvation; and the Cold War was about to burst into a terrifying *fleur du mal*. At Fulton, Missouri, in one of his most famous speeches, Sir Winston Churchill sounded an alarm that an "Iron Curtain" had fallen like a shroud over Eastern Europe.

Even the English language changed, based on the introduction of new words with global implications: The G.I. Bill, closed shop, right-to-work laws, union shops, feather bedding, a 'Do Nothing Congress, the Fair Deal, dynamic conservatism, the Federal Highway Act.

News organizations aimed their lenses on a charismatic roster

Peacetime economies focused on home, hearth, and postwar prosperity. Depicted above is a Tupperware party, circa 1950.

of newcomers, each of whom exploded into the public consciousness as key players in power games and pop culture. Examples included Richard Nixon, Marilyn Monroe, and Martin Luther King, Jr.

As the fear and mistrust of the Soviets intensified, the "commie-hating" Senator Joseph McCarthy asserted that Reds were taking over both Hollywood and the State Department. Careers were ruined and standards of censorship and free speech became battle zones as creative people were blacklisted.

Homophobia ruled: The concept that America was the land of the free did not extend to homosexuals. Their manifestation of love was illegal, and all of them risked being arrested. They were not even allowed to congregate in a public place. If and when they defied the law, as in a bar, for example, that establishment could be raided by the police and subsequently shut down.

Despite the glaring shortcomings of the postwar boom, seventy years

As a young boy facing a financially privileged but uncertain future, Donald's face reflected a certain arrogant independence:

Would he grow up to be the man who made America great again, or would he tear the country apart in partisan bickering?

later, a member of the Trump family, seeking the presidency, would express his vision for the future as a return to the days when America was "great."

Baby Boomers, including Donald, grew up within a culturally schizophrenic context of bomb shelters and the Cold War. Simultaneously, in an ironic contrast to the era's fear and pessimism, entertainers like Elvis Presley flourished, young people danced to the sounds of rock 'n roll, and families sat together in front of their new television sets watching Lucille Ball [who had registered as a communist in the 1930s] and Desi Arnaz in their hit sitcom, *I Love Lucy*.

During this era of cultural upheaval and change, on August 26, 1948, Robert, the last of Fred and Mary Anne Trump's children was born. He would grow into a man as different from his brother, Donald, as John Wayne was from John Derek. When they were growing up, Donald bullied Robert and commandeered his toys. But as they matured, he came to love his little brother. As an adult, on the phone or face-to-face, he often referred to him as "honey," confusing and confounding whomever happened to be listening.

The Trumps lived together in one of the more opulent houses Fred Trump had built, a red-brick colonial residence with twenty-three rooms and nine bathrooms. He positioned it in Jamaica Estates, Queens. Its façade boasted four 210-foot Greek columns, a feature demanded by his Scottish wife, Mary, who had an affinity for the trappings of British royalty. The year it was built, the family attended a screening of Cary Grant starring in *Mr. Blandings Builds His Dream House* (1948). Although Daddy Trump was a lot less naïve about homebuilding than the protagonist (Cary Grant) of that film, in some ways, it evoked some aspects of their real-life experience.

Donald grew up heavily influenced by his mother's sense of decoration and style. Decades later, in the décor of the most splendid residence (his own) in Trump Tower, he made lavish use of gilt, a decorative style his critics described as "Louis XIV on steroids."

Even though by now the Trumps were rich—winter vacations in Florida, summer camps in the Catskills—Fred hammered each of his children with the work ethic, insisting that each of them earn his or her own money. Donald was assigned responsibility for a paper route. In winter, he was perhaps the only schoolboy in Queens who serviced his subscribers from the back seat of a chauffeur-driven limousine.

Fred Trump,

Years after World War II ended, memories of its traumas remained deeply entrenched.

Depicted above is a U.S. Army photo of soldiers embarking onto a beach in Normandy on D-Day, the first step in the Allies' armed invasion of Europe in June of 1944.

the first of his lineage born on American soil, had achieved the American dream. The family was rich, with a domestic staff that included a white maid (Emma) and a black chauffeur (George), habitually clad in a moss-green or charcoal-gray uniform.

Fred was mostly absent from frequent or prolonged contact with his children, always working, always at some construction site, barking orders to his crew and "putting out brush fires," as he called them.

"I never felt like some pampered rich kid growing up," Donald claimed. "My father worked day and night, and my mother cooked, cleaned, darned socks and helped out at the local charity hospital. I was not a model son, I admit, and as I grew older, I stood my ground against my father. He was a real tough son-of-a-gun, but he respected me for asserting my individuality. Unlike Fred Jr. and Robert, I was the tough son."

His older sister, Maryanne, referred to Donald as "a rebellious youth." He was a terror among his classmates, throwing water balloons and launching spitball missiles. He liked to spray sodas on the girls in his class. If invited to a birthday party, he cut off pieces of the cake and threw it at the other boys. He liked football and baseball, and followed Fred around to muddy construction sites.

One teacher said he made "Dennis the Menace" look like a choirboy. He often talked back to his teachers and in the second grade, he punched his music teacher in the face, giving him a black eye. He told his father, "The guy deserved it. He didn't know a damn thing about music."

By the time Donald had turned four, America was at war again, this time in Korea.

According to Daddy Fred, "America will come out of this and go on to fight other wars, but I don't want any of my sons to go into the army to die on the battlefield of some god forsaken country

Britain, and probably most of her former colonies as well, celebrated the 1953 coronation of Elizabeth II with a ferver that went way beyond a mere acknowledgement of celebration of a dynastic change. It had been eight years since the war had ended, prosperity was underway, and it was time to celebrate, and to the degree it was possible, emulate.

Donald's mother, a native Scotswoman who had emigrated in her early 20s, followed key events in the life of the British Royals with a virtually obsessive interest.

of rice-eating savages."

"Of all my children, you are the one destined to be great," he told Donald. "Remember my advice: Be a killer! You are a king."

Fred later amended that: "Of course, I meant a future king. Right now, you're a prince-in-waiting to ascend my throne. Now, I'll teach you how to read a blueprint. Remember my motto in building: Get the best work done for the lowest price!"

Fred was extremely frugal, ordering Donald to go around a construction site picking up unused nails for some future project. At home, Mary was no retiring wallflower. She had a sense of the dramatic, often manifesting a genuine showmanship. Donald claimed, "She really wanted to go on the stage, but marriage derailed her career. At Queen Elizabeth's coronation, mother sat glued to the television set, watching the pomp, the circumstance, the glamor."

From the first to the seventh grade, Donald attended the Kew-Forest School, an independently run, coed, preparatory institution. Opened in 1918, it was a school for children of elite families on the north shore of Queen's County. Daddy Fred—who sat on the school board and had donated materials for the construction of the school's new wing—demanded that his son be given preferential treatment.

Donald would later admit, "I was a very bad boy. I wasn't violent or anything like that. But I wasn't well-behaved. You might call me a brat. No one said I was perfect."

"I learned to fight back," he said. "If someone attacked me, he'd end up with a bloody nose. In that sense, I carried that trait over into adulthood. The rebellious tough-fisted boy grew into a Pit Bull young man."

***

In 1954, Donald observed firsthand the fighting savvy of his father during his confrontations with "political hacks and mob bosses" at his building sites. Donald learned even more when, during the hot, humid summer of that year, Fred engaged in battle with government bureaucrats at the Federal Housing Authority (FHA). Legislated into existence in 1934 as part of the National Housing Act, the FHA defined and enforced building standards and the underwriting mortgage loans issued by banks and insured by the U.S. government. Fred, who had applied for and received FHA money to finance his housing projects, had been denounced by some regulators and critics as "a real estate pirate reaping large windfalls from government money." Even worse, he'd been reported by *The New York Times* and *The Brooklyn Eagle* for allegedly pocketing some four million dollars in FHA loans earmarked for use in public housing.

During testimony Fred delivered in Washington, his most visible adversary was the chairman of the Senate Banking Committee, Earl Capehart, an Indiana Republican. *Fortune* magazine had defined Capehart as "one of the highest-power, highest pressure salesman America has ever produced." Before becoming a senator, he was known as "The King of the Jukeboxes," various models of which had been installed across America. Capehart, whose interrogation techniques conveyed aspects of a politically motivated show trial, held Fred in total disdain, referring to his skimming of FHA money as "the profiteering scandal of the century."

Fred's interrogations were conducted against a backdrop of U.S. President Eisenhower's attempts to operate a government "as clean as a hound's tooth." When Eisenhower, a Republican, learned that some FHA officials were profiteering fraudulently from the government's largesse, he issued an order: "Fire the sons-of-bitches," and insisted that private real estate developers accused of wrongdoing (i.e., Daddy Trump) be hauled before the Senate for questioning.

Making matters worse, at least for Trump, Capehart, as a far-right conservative, vehemently objected to government-funded public housing, defining everything associated with it as socialism. Just before a vote on public housing, during a battle with Senate majority leader Lyndon B. Johnson, Capehart threatened the future American President, "I'm going to rub your Texas nose in shit."

In response, Johnson growled, "And I'm going to jam a twelve-foot firecracker up your Hoosier asshole and light a match."

Johnson won, and the vote passed in favor of government-funded housing.

At Daddy Trump's Senate hearing, under tough questioning, Fred faced Capehart and his other accusers. He denied any misuse of funds, and cited how successful he'd been, providing homes for veterans and their fast-growing families. "I operate under the free enterprise system in this country, a system that our brave men in World War II fought to preserve. It's what makes America great!"

Despite his patriotic rhetoric, under intense questioning from Capehart, Fred had to admit that up to four million dollars on deposit in one of his bank accounts had, on occasion, been issued as loans for use by one or another of his business interests. But despite those admission, he nonetheless claimed that "The accusations against me are very wrong. They hurt me. The only thing I am happy about is that they are not true."

"Tenants are using the charge against me by refusing to pay their rents, which is greatly harming my business. I am suffering. Not only that, but I have received untold damage to my standing in the community. My reputation as an honest builder is being destroyed."

Ultimately, although he was grilled, repeatedly and mercilessly by Capehart during the Senate hearings, it was decided that Fred had not broken any law or committed any criminal acts.

His reputation, however, had been seriously damaged, and in years to come, he would face torrents of skepticism, opposition, and more intense scrutiny during his launch of future projects.

Even after his return to New York, his troubles continued when he was accused of racial bias in his selection of tenants. The most visible charge derived from Woody Guthrie, the liberal and activist singer and songwriter. [He was nicknamed the Dust Bowl Troubadour for his articulate defense of the working man. His best known tune, still used as background for political rallies, is "This Land Is Your Land."]

Guthrie defined Fred Trump as a racist and a fascist. He also accused him of membership within the Ku Klux Klan. Ironically, Guthrie's own father, Charles Guthrie, had been involved in the 1911 KKK lynching of Laura and Lawrence Nelson, an African-American couple.

The folk icon, since 1950, had been a disgruntled tenant in one of Fred's apartment complexes in Brooklyn. He chronicled his contempt for his landlord in lyrics of one of his songs, accusing Fred of "stirring up racial hatred in the bloodpot of human hearts."

***

As one author phrased it, "Donald Trump grew into a jealous, rebellious, blonde bumpkin with big white teeth and a passion for baseball, football, and muddy shoes on trips to his father's construction sites."

Frequently preoccupied, and the victim of long, overextended workdays, Fred did not always supervise his son. Relatively unrestricted and on his own, Donald began to hang out

The dustbowl troubadour, Woody Guthrie, accused Fred Trump of being "a racist and a fascist," and attacked him as "a member of the Ku Klux Klan."

with a gang of other boys almost as unruly as he was. He soon became the leader of a band of high-octane boy hoodlums.

In 1961, West Side Story depicted switchblade-carrying street gangs roaming through downtrodden neighborhoods of New York City. The "Jets" and the "Sharks" were depicted (with beautiful choreography by Jerome Robbins) on screen, to some degree, as underappreciated folk heroes.

Long before the release of that movie, Donald rode the subway to Manhattan to purchase switchblades, one of them eleven inches long and marketed as "the heart plunger." At a novelty store, he also bought smoke bombs, stink bombs, and gross-looking novelties such as plastic vomit.

In a search of his son's bedroom one afternoon, and alert to his thirteen-year-old son's penchant for mischief, Fred discovered his stash of knives. Fearing his boy would become involved in some sort of violent confrontation, perhaps with the police, he made a decision to send him off to the sanctions of boarding school. The setting he selected was the New York Military Academy (NYMA), informally known as "Neema."

On the Hudson River, eight miles from West Point and sixty miles north of New York City, it had been founded in 1889 by Charles Jefferson, a Civil War veteran. Positioned on an "apron" of the Palisades, it resembled a fortress, with turreted rooftops. Marketing its ability to impose stern discipline on hyperactive males and an intense discipline inspired by the U.S. military, it was dismissed by its critics as "a junior grade West Point for gun-toting boy soldiers straight from the comic opera."

Over the years, its graduates had included the movie star, Troy Donahue, and John Gotti, son of the Mafia don. Cadets who attended the academy but moved to other schools before graduating included the filmmaker Francis Ford Coppola, and the brilliant composer/songwriter Stephen Sondheim.

Donald was thrown into a mixture of young but strong-willed boys who in-

Sent to a military academy for disciplinary reasons, Donald was awakened every morning to the sound of the beating of pots and pans before sunrise.

He had to endure hard training exercises—push-ups, sit-ups, and laps. There were rewards for the cleanest shoes and the best-looking uniforms.

cluded everybody from the sons of Wall Street bankers to the spoiled brats of South American dictators. Displaying a mixture of tough love and benign neglect, Fred promised—probably with the best of intentions—that he and Mary would come for visits every weekend, or, at least, every other weekend. He then returned to his pressing business interests, leaving thirteen-year-old Donald, basically, to fend for himself.

He entered a brutal world whose tenets and rules, written and unspoken, were completely foreign to him. The academy allowed (some say "encouraged") hazing, a series of raucous, controversial, and deliberately degrading "breaking-in" ceremonies designed and implemented by both the supervisors and the older cadets.

Unaccustomed to obeying commands, Donald found himself being ordered to belch or fart on cue, or perhaps to describe the vaginal functions of a cow and what a bull does to her. He also had to recite silly rhyming formulas for conveying what time it was.

Another device adopted by the hazers involved stripping a newcomer and forcing him into the communal showers with all the shower heads pouring forth hot water.

During one session, a freshman cadet was stripped naked by upper-classmen, who collectively urinated on him after chugging a lot of beer.

"Those guys at the academy used to beat the shit out of us," Donald claimed. "They were a pack of rough bastards. They'd deliberately pick a fight with you. If guys in today's colleges did stuff like that to students, they'd be jailed for twenty-five years. A guy could plant his fist right in your kisser. POW! All you could do was wipe up the blood and say, 'Yes Sir! May I shine your shoes, sir?'"

Freshmen had to take care of an older cadet's laundry and were given leftovers for dinner. "There

Donald, in this yearbook picture, is second from the left.

In running for President, Donald was ridiculed by veterans when he compared his military school life as something "more rigorous" than actual training in the U.S.' armed forces. His Academy was once mocked for its "gun-toting soldiers straight from a comic opera."

was a lot of hollering in your face," Donald said. "Names were thrown at you like 'punk, jerk, or faggot.'"

By the time of Donald's evolution into an upperclassman, he'd become one of the most aggressive hazers at the Academy.

Behind his back, his classmates called him "Jocko," a name perhaps taken from Calder Willingham's popular novel at the time, *End as a Man*, detailing the brutal context of a military academy and its gratuitous terrorizing of its cadets by bullies.

Donald was especially brutal to his roommate, Ted Levine, "a 120-pound weakling," the smallest kid at the academy. When Levine could take it no more and was on the verge of a nervous breakdown, he appealed to his best friend, the school's football captain, Stanley Holuba. He approached Donald and attempted to beat him up, but he was hit over the head and temporarily dazed. Donald used that opportunity to toss him out the window, but at the last minute, two other classmates entered the room and prevented Holuba from falling to his possible death.

In theory, at least, there were limits, which weren't always enforced, associated with how far hazing could go. When the Academy learned that some of the older cadets were forcing freshmen to perform fellatio on them, these cadets were either expelled or severely lectured about conduct interpreted as "immoral." [The administration did not want to use the term, or define the act, as "homosexual." Girls were forbidden on campus. The more effeminate boys were cast in drag as girls in school plays.]

One night, after a particularly sadistic episode of hazing, a cadet was severely beaten with chains, but then managed to escape, seriously injured, to a nearby hospital.

Fred Trump, Sr., Mary Trump, and Donald.

Donald, years later, told CNN, "I wasn't the most well-behaved person in the world, and my parents had no idea what to do with me. They heard about this school that was a tough place. They sent me there so I would learn some discipline."

After examining him, and probably with a sense of outrage and horror, one of the doctors reported his injuries to the police. That led to a probe, a public outcry, and the resignation of three of the academy's top administrators.

During the investigation, Donald himself was cited for "overhazing" and was subsequently demoted to a lesser position within the chain of student command. Despite the "dishonor" this implied, he nonetheless defined his demotion as a promotion.

During his time at the Academy, Donald made friends with "the meanest man on campus," Ted Tobias, a rough-and-tumble former Marine drill sergeant, who was coach of the baseball team. He designated Donald as its captain.

During their time together, Tobias fascinated Donald with his tales of Italy during the war and the U.S. military's march north to Rome, battling Nazis all the way. "It was a tale of foxholes, blood, and screaming," Donald said. "Ted was a fucking prick, but I loved him."

"Donald was a real pain in the ass," Tobias said, "but I came to admire the kid. He had guts. He'd do anything to win… and I mean anything."

Donald looked forward to weekend visits from Fred and Mary. "It was my only chance to get a decent meal. The food at the Academy was poisonous."

He'd entered as a bratty eighth grader, with lingering signs of baby fat. He later graduated as a 6'1", 180-pound "hunk of beefcake, a babe magnet that excelled at baseball," in his estimation. Photos show him standing, chin out, with a steel spine and eyes forward.

He'd been a success at the Academy, becoming the captain of both the football and baseball teams. In his senior year, he attained the highest cadet rank: First Captain.

Hot date, 1964: "I was not only the star athlete, but the best-looking guy at the Academy," Donald boasted. "All the girls were after me. I won trophies in intramural softball, basketball, bowling, and freshman football. I was also the Academy's babe magnet."

"Upon graduation, I had become the best baseball player in New York State," he said.

Baseball talent scouts showed up on campus, trying to entice him to become a professional. He turned them down. "Baseball doesn't pay enough."

Upon graduation, he was not voted "Most Likely to Succeed." Instead, he was given the title of "Ladies' Man."

"I was not thrilled to be sent to the Academy," he recalled. "But it turned out to be the right decision for me. I learned to channel my aggression into achievement."

"I was never particularly interested in schoolwork," he said. "It bored me. What counts for a young man is what he does after college."

[In 2015, during the Academy's drive to stave off bankruptcy, Donald was asked to donate $7 million to his Alma Mater. He rejected the request, claiming, "It is not a good investment."

In March of that year, confronted with a serious falloff in enrollment, the Academy filed for Chapter Eleven Bankruptcy protection. Around the time Donald was announcing his bid for the presidency, his old Academy shut its doors forever. At an auction, it was sold to a group of Chinese investors.]

***

In September of 1964, Donald began a two-year stint at Fordham University, a Roman Catholic institution in the Bronx mostly staffed by Jesuits. Fordham was admittedly an odd choice, since he was not Catholic. But since it did not require that he live on campus, it allowed him to commute to classes from home. Later, his older sister, Maryanne, was asked, "Why Fordham for Donald?"

"Because that's where he got in," she replied, bluntly.

A fellow student at Fordham, also named Donald (Winston), said, "Trump sometimes shared his hopes and dreams with us. He talked a lot about himself, actually only about himself. Back then, his dreams sounded preposterously ambitious. He told us he was going to change the skyline of Manhattan—bullshit like that."

At Fordham, Donald was the richest kid in his class, showing up for classes in a flashy red sports car and a tailor-made suit and hand-crafted leather shoes. In contrast to the bulk of the (mostly Catholic) student body, he self-identified as a Presbyterian. Most of his fellow students drank and smoked. Donald did neither.

No longer restricted by the militaristic regimes at "Neema," he could stay out late and date a string of girls. He sometimes bragged to his fellow males that, "I got lucky last night." And in a change from his pre-college pursuits of baseball and football, he took up squash and golf, a pastime that he'd avidly pursue later in life.

In reference to his observations about Donald, a classmate who didn't want to release his name because "Who knows: I might apply to him for a job one day, and I don't want to piss him off," said, "Unlike me, who was a bit of a nerd, it seemed that Donald got lucky every night, at least to hear him tell it."

At one point during the two years he studied at Fordham, Donald accompanied his father to the opening of the Verrazano Narrows Bridge linking Staten Island to Brooklyn. The "last hurrah" of Robert Moses, Csar of New York City construction, it was the longest suspension bridge in the United States.

Donald always remembered the occasion, as he watched 85-year-old Othmar Hermann Amman, a Swiss-born immigrant, standing all alone and neglected during the festivities as others took credit for the bridge he had designed.

"I learned a lesson that day," Donald said. "I planned to put my name on all the future buildings I would erect. No one was going to play me for a sucker in my future. I did not plan to be ignored."

During his time at Fordham, Donald had witnessed firsthand the hazards associated with the building trades, watching what Fred was enduring during the creation of "Trump Village" at Coney Island in Brooklyn, the first housing project to bear the Trump name.

Fred would later refer to that housing project as "my greatest achievement and my biggest fucking headache." It had begun in 1964, when he'd set out to build 3,800 apartments on a site that became available after the city-sanctioned condemnation of several smaller, side-by-side properties. Each building within it would eventually rise twenty-three floors. Donald and Fred discussed what a challenge it was. The project was ultimately completed through government assistance and low-cost financing. "Delicious tax breaks," as Fred described it, "were part of the deal."

During its conceptualization and completion, Donald enjoyed an up-close-and-personal overview of the financial and political manipulations required to succeed at such a project. On weekends, or during spring breaks, Donald worked "hand in glove," as Fred claimed, helping him launch Trump Village, sometimes with the cooperation of "friendly judges."

"I learned more from my father than I ever did at Fordham," he said.

After many trials, tribulations, lawsuits, and setbacks, Trump Village opened. Ironically, the housing project that bore Fred's name wasn't actually built by him. However, he collected $3.8 million of the builder's grant of $4.8 million.

That lesson was not lost on young Donald.

Trump Village had no doorman, no concierge, no gym, and not a lot of architectural razzmatazz, either, sheathed as it was with a "skin" of dull brown brick. Its modest apartments, mostly occupied by professionals, accountants, and teachers, rented for about $250 a month.

Donald later said, "Gucci is a hot store of one of my buildings in Manhattan. My father settled for Waldbaum's, and he even had to go collect the rent himself on occasion."

***

For the final two years of his four-year college education, Donald enrolled at the Wharton School of Finance and Commerce, a subdivision of the Ivy League University of Pennsylvania. It had been established in 1881 as the first business school in the United States.

At Wharton, he studied real estate, which was a minor pursuit at Wharton, with just one professor and a total of six male students. He also studied high finance, account, banking, and, most definitely, mortgages.

In his autobiography, *The Art of the Deal*, he wrote, "It didn't take me long to realize that there was nothing particularly awesome or exceptional about my classmates. I competed just fine."

"The other important thing I got from Wharton was a degree. That degree doesn't prove very much, but a lot of people I do business with take it very seriously, and it's considered very prestigious. So all things considered, I'm glad I went to Wharton."

He had previously considered the Harvard Business School, but rejected the idea of applying. "If you want to become a CEO, then go to Harvard," he said. "If you want to become a multi-millionaire entrepreneur, enroll at Wharton, if you can get in."

[In 2015 and 2016, since Donald had invoked Wharton as a reference during his race for the presidency, reporters checked to see if he'd been a heavy contributor. They learned that he had contributed nothing, post-graduation, to his Alma Mater.

In ironic contrast, Jon Huntsman—the plastics magnate, former governor of Utah, and 2012 presidential candidate—had donated an astonishing $40 million contribution to Wharton in 1998. One of the most impressive buildings on the Wharton campus is named after him today.

In reference to his course studies at Wharton, Donald had claimed, "I was really good at this stuff." In response, during a Republican debate, Florida senator Marco Rubio mocked Donald's business prowess. During a televised Republican debate, in front of millions of viewers, Rubio outlined Donald's business failures and quadruple bankruptcies.

Incidentally, three of Donald's children—Donald Jr., Ivanka, and Tiffany—attended Wharton. Ivanka graduated with the highest honors.

Yet in spite of the Trump family's ongoing links with Wharton, during Donald's bid for the Republican nomination, Wharton's administrators remained rather hush-hush about the business school's link to, and its opinion of, its most celebrated graduate.]

***

With Wharton behind him, it seemed inevitable that Donald would follow in his father's footsteps as a real estate developer.

But for a few weeks, he considered the pursuit of a career as an entertainment mogul in Hollywood. As such, he wanted to enroll in the film school at the University of Southern California, hoping to follow in the footsteps of Darryl F. Zanuck, Harry P. Cohn, and Louis B. ("a great showman!") Mayer.

One afternoon, he walked into the office of Broadway producer David Black. It was positioned above the Palace Theater in Manhattan.

Donald clearly articulated his proposal: If Black would give him equal billing on the posters and in *Playbill*, he would pay half the production costs of his next play.

Paris Is Out! was a domestic comedy starring Milly Picon, the biggest star of the Yiddish Theater in New York.

"Most of the guys who put up money wanted to do so just to meet girls," Black said. "Not Trump. He was a serious backer who wanted to know the intricacies of bringing a play to Broadway. Donald put up $70,000 for a show capitalized at

Producer David Black, Donald's Broadway mentor:

"Had our joint production of *Paris Is Out!* succeeded, Donald might have gone on to become Broadway's next David Merrick instead of the real estate mogul he became. Many rich guys put up money for Broadway shows, mostly musicals with lots of gals, but Donald was serious about becoming a producer."

56

$140,000.

Donald would arrive at the theater in a white convertible, often with a young woman in the front seat with him.

The show, which opened in 1970, was a flop, closing after 112 performances. Clive Barnes of The New York Times wrote, "I pitied it more than I disliked it."

Its script was by Richard Seff, who had been working in the theater since he made his acting debut in support of Claude Rains in the prize-winning *Darkness at Noon*. He later toured as a supporting player to Edward G. Robinson. Later, as an agent, Seff developed such young talents as Chita Rivera and John Kander, before returning to his first love, which was acting and writing for the theater.

Donald helped produce his 1970 comedy on Broadway, *Paris Is Out!*.

Even though it was a flop and received some scathing reviews, many critics liked it. Hobe Morrison of Variety called it "as rich and delicious and filling as a large helping of apple strudel."

Donald's interest in Broadway continued long after that inaugural failure. Years later, he almost became the centerpiece of a Broadway show based on producer Pierre Cossette's musical interpretation of his life. "He's a bigger-than-life person. It might have been great, but the show went nowhere."

In 2005, Donald considered adapting his hit TV show, *The Apprentice*, into a Broadway musical. Another time, he actually discussed appearing on Broadway as an actor, interpreting the role of Billy Flynn in the hit musical, *Chicago*.

In 2007, Donald talked about producing The Trump Follies, a revue featuring the music of Irving Berlin. That

Brooks Atkinson Theatre

PLAYBILL

the national magazine for theatregoers

PARIS IS OUT !

Molly Picon was the most popular Jewish star of her day, and Richard Seff's script might have succeeded, as it had its moments.

In the plot, Hortense (Picon) must decide how she feels about the man with whom she has shared a life for forty years. They embark together on a trip "across the pond." But her husband, Daniel, has certain demands: "No Paris!" (hence the title). "No Venice; no shopping, no sightseeing, no speaking French."

show, too, never found its legs.]

Now in his 80s, Black recalled, "Donald had a flair for show business, and he liked putting his name on something that was not real estate. A potential David Merrick. *If Paris Is Out!* had been a hit, who knows what might have happened to his career?"

In 1970, Donald met with Black in a coffee shop, where they agreed to, and discussed the details associated with, closing down the show.

According to Black, "He looked disappointed and asked me, 'David, what should I do now?'"

"Try real estate!" Black answered.

"I'm one jump ahead of you," Donald said. "I've joined the Trump Management Company. Let my Dad take Queens, Brooklyn, and Staten Island. I'll take Manhattan."

47 — EMPIRE STATE BUILDING AND SKYLINE AT NIGHT, NEW YORK CITY

NEW YORK the WONDER CITY

Chapter Four

Left to right, siblings Donald, Fred Jr., Elizabeth, Maryanne, and Robert Trump

"THE DONALD" AND HIS SIBLINGS
Triumphs & Tragedies, Successes & Failures, & Court Disputes Over Money

A MOGUL IN TRAINING
In Ohio as "The Cincinnati Kid" Donald Pressures Uncooperative Tenants to "Pay Up or Get Out!"

"My Family Put the Fun in 'Dysfunctional.'"
—Fred Trump III

In Trump Tower, during his announcement of his bid for the U.S. presidency, in June of 2015, Donald shared a memory from when he was eight years old: "I remember sitting at my father's feet playing with building blocks and listening to him negotiate with subcontractors."

As columnist Caitlin Flanagan wrote: "If you've never heard the heartlifting sound of a Queens guy negotiating with subcontractors, circa 1952, or never seen a mid-century mob movie, the emotional romance of this family scene may be lost on you."

Business associates of Fred, Sr. always referred to him as a hard-nosed contractor. Years later, they evaluated Donald as "like father, like son."

As an adult, Donald recalled, "My father's scene was a little rough for my tastes—and by that, I mean physically rough." As a teenager, Donald accompanied a bill collector to an uncooperative tenant's apartment in Queens. The older associate taught the boy a valuable lesson, warning him to stand to the side, and then to lean over, extending his hand to pound on the door. "If you stand to the side, a bullet fired at the door might blow off you hand, but at least it won't hit you in the chest."

As a landlord, Donald found himself in the unwelcome position of having to demand that some of his tenants not throw their garbage out the window, but to carry it to the incinerator chute.

Later in life, he concluded that he found it preferable to rent to tenants such as Michael Jackson and Steven Spielberg.

Early on, Donald confessed "I had far loftier dreams and visions than my father."

Sometimes, when criticism from his father "lashed at my soul," he

On screen in 1965, Steve McQueen (above) played *The Cincinnati Kid*, but in real life, Donald was "The Cincinnati Kid" in a rundown housing development that he and Fred Trump took over. Half-empty, it was the largest and most dangerous apartment complex in the city.

Donald learned the rules of survival in this crime-filled building which housed tenants who might shoot you instead of giving you the rent.

turned to his mother, Mary, for comfort. "Perhaps I got my sense of splendor and magnificence from her, not my father, who was a very down-to-earth man who got excited only by competence and efficiency."

As a 25-year-old, Donald cooperated with Fred Sr., in the takeover of Swifton Village, a 1,200-unit apartment complex in Cincinnati, Ohio. Originally built in 1953 for a cost of between $10 and $12 million, and "plagued from the beginning" by bad luck and low occupancy rates, it had fallen, unwanted, and unwelcomed, into the orbit of the FHA, which defined it as a ruined failure of a once-promising housing development. Two-thirds of its units (i.e., 800 of them) were vacant. Although credit for the concept is usually attributed to Fred Sr., the actual transformation of this slum tenement represented Donald's first big real estate deal.

During the course of its renovation, Donald began referring to himself as "The Cincinnati Kid," perhaps taking the name from the steely, poker-playing, poker-faced character portrayed by Steve McQueen in the 1965 movie with the same name.

Like vultures feeding on a corpse that very few other construction outfits would touch—a fact that made the Trump family's bankers extremely nervous—Fred and Donald took over the project at a sheriff's sale of foreclosed property for $5.7 million, putting up almost no cash as part of the sale, with the understanding that they would improve and upgrade the property.

En route to this goal, they had to confront some difficult tenants.

In *The Art of the Deal*, Donald cited examples of some of the renters living within Swifton Village at the time of their takeover. They included families who had fled from the hills of Kentucky, a married couple with seven or eight children, crammed into a one-bedroom apartment. "The kids in the building went wild, wreaking havoc on the property," Donald claimed.

Gradually, they managed to get "poverty row" tenants they interpreted as undesirable, and rent to more desirable tenants. From the point of view of future investors, that meant occupants who paid and/or were employed.

After their upgrade of the complex, and a net cash outlay of what was reported at $500,000, the Trumps sold Swifton Village for $12 million, having increased its occupancy rate to nearly 100%. Fleeing Ohio, they returned to New York.

"It was my baptism of fire," Donald said. "I was now ready to compete in the dog-eat-possum world of New York real estate."

The first father-and-son photograph of Fred and Donald to appear in *The New York Times* was in 1973, when Donald was twenty-seven. Author Timothy L. O'Brien claimed that Donald still looked like a kid, with light blonde hair spilling over his forehead. In contrast, "Fred looks utterly and inexhaustibly formidable. Staring out coolly from beneath a fedora, jaw set, and so in possession of himself that he comfortably sports an outrageous polka-dot tie."

"My father did not show off his wealth," Donald said. "But he had one indulgence: He always wanted to be seen driving a new Cadillac, navy blue, never black, with a license that contained his initials, 'FCT.'"

Unlike his son, Fred worked out of a surprisingly modest office. It occupied what had been converted from a dentist's office in the Beach Haven housing complex near Brooklyn's Coney Island.

Richard Levy, a senior vice president of Tishman Real Estate, remembers calling on Fred Sr., with a sense of foreboding: "I felt like Custer."

[George Armstrong Custer (1839-1876) was a U.S. cavalry commander whose massacre, along with all of his soldiers, by a coalition of Native American tribesmen in Montana in 1876 overshadowed all of his earlier achievements.]

"There were all these huge wooden Indians all over the place," Levy continued. "One wall was covered with awards from various organizations he aided; another had pictures of him with U.S. presidents and celebrities. He was a giant of a man, well over six feet tall."

Robert Trump, the family's youngest son, said, "My dad lent Donald support when he aspired to be a developer in Manhattan. But what he lent him was mostly know-how, but not a lot of money. Donald really did it on his own, along with whatever boost he got from being Fred Trump's son."

Even though Fred Sr., became a multi-millionaire, he liked to be surrounded by familiar things and people. He was married to his Scottish bride for sixty-one years, and they never moved from the red-brick colonial house they'd constructed in 1951 on a half-acre in the middle class suburb of Jamaica Estates in Queens.

The neighborhood deteriorated over the years, and Donald frequently urged them to move away from "the combat zone." Newspapers wrote of what had happened to the district which, in time, became filled with underpaid working class or unemployed African Americans. Hispanic immigrants, legal or otherwise, formed one of New York's most ethnically diverse neighborhoods, many of the inhabitants homeless.

Yet throughout Fred Sr.'s regime, if an employee proved loyal and efficient, Fred liked to keep him or her for years. Such was the case with his secretary, Amy Luersson, who held onto her job for almost six decades.

"Fred was so different from his son," said New York Mayor Ed Koch. "Fred was a meat-and-potatoes man, Donald a caviar-and-smoked salmon guy. Fred was a thick-skinned survivor whose word was his bond. He had a dry sense of humor and did not suffer fools lightly. He was all work, day and night, all business. He had an appetite for a fire-sale bargain, and he always made off with the best deal in any business negotiation."

In 1973, Fred became embroiled in a rather tawdry lawsuit when the U.S. Justice Department's Civil Rights Division filed a suit against the Trump Organization, charging that it consistently refused to rent to African American families.

Secretly, the Urban League had tested this discrimination, sending both white and black "tester applicants" searching to rent apartments. The prospective white tenants were granted leases, the African Americans were not.

In an exposé in *The Village Voice*, a former rental agent asserted that Fred had personally and specifically instructed him not to rent to black tenants, and to encourage/coerce African Americans already in residence within his building complexes to move out.

After a prolonged and embarrassing investigation, the government forced Fred to advertise his vacancies in minority newspapers and to list his rentals with the Urban League.

Fred, however, did not always comply with those mandates. The Justice Department began receiving more complaints about racial discriminations from real estate agents. Finally, the Justice Department was

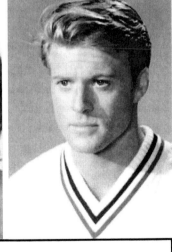

As a young man, Donald on his visits to Hollywood was urged to try his luck as a movie star, auditioning for parts.

Many in the business compared his looks favorably to those of Robert Redford.

Years later, Robert Redford was told that Donald Trump, had he gone into the movies, might have been a major challenger to him.

"Actually, Trump might have fitted into my role in *The Candidate* (1972). The part I played issued one shocking statement after another."

forced to issue a warning that "such frequent discrimination has created a substantial impediment to the full enjoyment of equal opportunity for all tenants."

***

As Donald moved up in the world, also becoming a familiar face in California, Fred seemed flattered that much of the Hollywood press compared his appearance to that of Robert Redford.

"My son Donald is the smartest man I know," he boasted. "I gave him free rein to make major business decisions when he was only twelve years old. That's how smart he was even back then. He had a great vision even as a boy. Today, everything he touches turns to gold. He definitely has the Midas Touch."

In spite of that compliment, and in spite of his long and enduring love for his wife, Fred Sr., could also grow disenchanted with any assertion his children or their wives made about their respective independence. To an associate, he delivered a shocking statement: The occasion was when Donald and Mary flew to Czechoslovakia to attend the funeral of Milos Zelnicekova, the father of Donald's wife, Ivana. Ivana and her children had flown to Europe the day before.

Fred told Amy Luersson, "I hope their plane crashes. Then all my problems will be solved."

Surely he could not have meant that. Perhaps he was only momentarily disenchanted with both Mary and Donald because, as he often complained, both of them were independent and sometimes caused him grief when they didn't carry out his orders. Except for that one rash statement, on other occasions, he showed great love and compassion for both Donald and Mary.

Around 1993, although he still retained his title as Chairman of the Board of Trump Management, a position he would never relinquish, Fred was stricken with Alzheimer's disease.

Young Mary, future U.S. immigrant, a model U.S. citizen, but definitely NOT a natural-born American.

Until he could no longer work, he maintained a hands-on management style, even mixing his own floor cleaners for use in his housing projects.

Then he developed pneumonia. At the age of ninety-three, he died during his hospitalization at the Long Island Jewish Medical Center in New Hyde Park, New York.

***

Throughout their lives, although controversy would frequently envelop her husband and her son, Donald, Mary Anne MacLeod, like Caesar's wife, lived a life above reproach.

Born in 1912 in Scotland, two years before the outbreak of World War I, she emigrated to the United States when she was eighteen. There she met Fred, her future husband, whom she married in 1936. They would have five children: Maryanne (1937), Fred Jr. (1938), Elizabeth (1942), Donald (1946), and Robert (1948).

Mary had grown up in Tong, a remote, storm-tossed hamlet on the Isle of Lewis, in the Scottish Hebrides. [*Identified in Gaelic as Tunga, it's located about four miles northeast of the larger village of Stornoway. In 2001, the population of Tong was 527 hardy souls.*] Mary's father, Malcolm MacLeod, was a fisherman who had married his wife, (*née* Mary Smith), in 1891. Both of them spoke Gaelic.

Until she mastered English, their daughter, Mary, also spoke Gaelic as a first language. Even in America, long after she'd abandoned the fishing and shepherding ways of her native village, she sometimes sang her babies to sleep with Gaelic lullabies.

She attended school in her closely knit Hebridean community with the hearty sons and daughters of fishermen and crofters, most of whom followed in

This was intended for display in a prominent position within Donald's Scottish golf hotel, in honor of his Scottish mother, Mary McLeod, who grew up in a simple croft, having been born into a family of extremely modest means.

Still trying to learn English (her original language was Gaelic), she landed in Manhattan at the age of twenty.

the same professions as their ancestors.

They lived in a stone-sided "black house," with thick, low walls and a rustic-looking roof of thatch whose topside sported birds' nests and patches of moss, and whose underside had been seasoned with generations of soot.

At the age of six, Mary gathered peat from the moorland to keep the home fires burning. She later told tales to her children about the hard lives of the locals, growing up amid boggy landscapes almost completely devoid of trees. Throughout the long, stormy winters, she had longed for the late spring, when the bogs and tundra blossomed with heather.

As a teenager, she had dreamed of going to America to escape from the harsh realities of life in Tong. On many a winter night, her mother had to dilute her soups and stews with water as a means of feeding everyone at her table. "We put almost anything edible into that black pot," Mary recalled. "I longed for a better life in America. But never in my wildest dreams did I know I'd marry a multi-millionaire and that together we would have a multi-billionaire for a son. Riches I never imagined."

As a mother in Jamaica Estates, she had evolved into a strict household authority, claiming, "I run a tight ship." When her daughter, Maryanne, came home from school wearing lipstick, Mary took a napkin and forcibly wiped her lips clean. No curse words were ever to be uttered in her presence. When Donald didn't obey her, she took her big wooden spoon and spanked him with it, hard.

At dinner, she demanded that each of her offspring eat everything on his or her plate, reminding them that children were starving in China. She was also good at recycling leftovers.

Even though married to a rich man, she went around the house turning off lights. She also ordered her boys to collect empty bottles from Fred's building sites so their deposits could be reclaimed as their spending money.

"Even though I left the U.K. and emigrated to America, I maintained my loyalty to Queen Elizabeth," she said. "Once I wrote a letter to Buckingham Palace, to the Queen, telling her that I was ready to pay her a lot of money for her old Rolls-Royce before she traded it in for a new one. She never answered."

When Mary didn't get Elizabeth's used Rolls, Fred bought her a new one. Despite her status as a wealthy woman, she nonetheless retained her Scottish frugality, driving the Rolls herself during her rounds she made collecting coins from the laundromats in the basements of her husband's housing projects.

After the passage of many years, she had to abandon that pursuit. At the age of seventy-seven, she developed a severe case of osteoporosis, a condition that made climbing a short flight of steps a slow and painful task for her.

After her children matured, Mary found that she had more time to devote to fundraising for charities and for volunteer work at the Women's Auxiliary of Jamaica Hospital.

In vivid contrast to the fourth (Donald) of her five children, Mary tended to avoid publicity. She made headlines, however, on October 31, 1991 when a sixteen-year-old boy in a Queens shopping center attacked the seventy-nine year-old, rather frail woman and stole her purse. During the course of the incident, she was knocked to the ground, breaking her hip and three ribs.

A bystander, Lawrence Herbert, a 44-year-old African American, grabbed her assailant and sat on him until the police arrived.

The teenager was released on $25,000 bail, a judgment that angered Donald. "The thug almost killed my mother. Now he's free to go about as he pleases while Mary lies in the hospital, fighting for her life."

Later, Donald invited Herbert for dinner at the Plaza Hotel in Manhattan as a gesture of thanks for holding down the assailant.

Mary recovered, although her health would never be the same again. Gradually, she resumed her authority in the household.

Selena Scott was voted "the sexiest broadcaster in Britain" but when Donald viewed one of her broadcasts about him as unflattering, he publicly reviled her as "sleazy and unattractive."

She shot back at him, accusing him of being "the comb-over creep who hates women."

Selina was a friend of Princess Diana, upon whom Donald had a fixation. "Eat your heart out, Donald," Scott said. "Billionaires can't have everything they want."

Selina Scott, one of England's best known journalists, and also voted "the sexiest broadcaster in Britain," visited New York in 1995 and interviewed Mary.

Later, when Selina returned to London, she appeared in documentary broadcast that was most unflattering to Donald, referring to him as "a mama's boy. He was given everything he wanted and gave back little in return. Mary, growing up on a remote Scottish island and enduring great hardship, didn't want Donald to suffer, so she indulged him. His mother is a saint, but Donald reminds me of one of those bullies in the schoolyard."

When the program aired on the BBC, it provoked Donald's anger. He accused Scott of being "very sleazy," "unattractive," "obnoxious," and "boring."

He fired off a missile to her, accusing her of "having little talent and even fewer viewers. You are no longer 'hot.' Perhaps that is the curse of dishonesty. You would obviously go to any length to try to restore your fading image, but guess what? The public is aware and apparently much brighter than you. They aren't tuning in. I hope you're able to solve your problems before it is too late."

In January of 2016, when Donald was running for the White House, Scott, in London, wrote a scathing article about him for *The Mail on Sunday*. She called him "the comb-over creep who hates women," claiming that he once tried to seduce her and, when he failed, spent twenty years stalking her.

Aboard his private plane en route to Florida, and at 30,000 feet in the air, he invited her to share his white leather double bed, presumably for an airborne fuck. According to Scott, that incident occurred in 1995. She cited Donald, as a candidate, for appealing "to the dark heart of the American psyche."

"Trump is a shark," she wrote. "A

Proud and fiercely independent, Scotland is a historically and culturally unique semi-autonomous nation within the United Kingdom, aggressively opposing impositions from England and from outside developers such as Donald Trump.

Depicted above are some of the famous longhorn Highland cattle for which Scotland's landscapes are famous.

shark has no yesterday and no tomorrow. Just the next meal, the next victim to be destroyed and consumed. And a shark must keep moving or die."

She discovered that he was filled with "bluff, bombast, and braggadocio," as he falsely claimed that he owned one-hundred percent of the Empire State Building. He made this boast during a helicopter ride with her over Manhattan.

At one point, Scott was introduced to Marla Maples. The journalist found her "blonde and beautiful but also vacuous, with little conversation. She was submissive and silent around Trump."

As for Mary, Scott viewed her as "the perfect wealthy American matron, all traces of the humble Scottish lass airbrushed away. A trophy mother."

At some point, Scott chatted with Princess Diana in London. She had learned that Donald viewed her as his "dream lady."

Scott asked the former Lady Diana Spencer what she thought of Donald.

"He gives me the creeps," answered Her Royal Highness.

***

Mary, perfectly groomed and far removed from her origins as the shy daughter of an impoverished fisherman from an island outpost in the North Atlantic, was in a wheelchair when she attended Fred's funeral in June of 1990. There, she was surrounded by celebrities, each of them on hand to pay their respects. Visitors included comedian Joan Rivers and New York Senator Alphonse D'Amato. Mayor Rudy Giuliani kissed her hand. Donald showed up with a shapely model, Marla Maples, who by then had become his second wife.

Mary would die soon after her husband's funeral, in 2000, at the age of eighty-eight.

"At least she made it to the 21st Century," Donald said. "She remained a very traditional wife, very religious, a devoted wife and a devoted mother. After my father died, she, too, seemed to fade. She told her children, 'It is time I go to join Fred in Heaven.'"

***

Her own mother called Maryanne Trump [aka Maryanne Trump Barry] "the smartest of my children." She won the endorsement of such different Presidents as Ronald Reagan and Bill Clinton.

Failed presidential candidate, Ted Cruz, defined her as a "radical abortion extremist."

In 2007, as Donald was formulating major-league plans for development in Scotland, he, along with his sister, Maryanne, made a sentimental visit to the village of Tong, his mother's ancestral home, in the remote Hebrides.

His assistants had arranged for him to rent a Porsche for the day from the only millionaire on the island. A local journalist accompanied him, noting that he spent ninety-seven minutes in his mother's former home. There, he met many of his relatives. Most of them were bilingual, speaking Gaelic as well as English with a Scottish brogue.

He told them about the high ratings of his television series, *The Apprentice*. "If you get high ratings, you're the king of television. I am a king. If you don't get high ratings, you're thrown out on your ass."

When Donald announced his run for the presidency in 2015, a journalist speculated, "I can't help but wonder what Mary McLeod Trump would say about her son's goal to make it harder for immigrants to start their new lives in the United States, as she did herself."

***

Donald's older sister, Maryanne Trump, named for her mother, entered the world on April 5, 1937, more than two years before the outbreak of World War II. The first born of Fred and Mary, she grew up in New York where, even as a girl, she was called "competent and self-possessed."

"We always knew our daughter would make good," Mary said. "We didn't know in which way. Don't quote me, but by the early 1950s, I thought she was the smartest of all my children."

In describing her early years, Maryanne noted that she was the first of her family to attend college. She received her B.A. from Mount Holyoke College in 1958 and her M.A. from Columbia University in 1962. Twelve years later, she received her law degree from the Hofstra University School of Law. Before becoming a judge, she was an assistant U.S. attorney for the District of New York.

"When I first went away, I was desperately homesick," Maryanne said. "I was scared. I didn't do very well during my first year. But I stuck to it and got my degree. I had a long interlude being a wife and mother before returning to law school. I was the first woman in New Jersey to do criminal work before appearing before male judges. I was scared every day of my life."

In 1960, she married David Desmond, a lieutenant in the U.S. Air force.

A son was born that year. She divorced her husband in 1980, and, two years later, she married John J. Barry, a New Jersey lawyer who would later represent Donald in litigation associated with his investments in the casinos of Atlantic City. Barry died in 2000.

Maryanne had no desire to join her brothers in real estate development. She loved her brother, Donald, but later admitted, "He was a real brat when he was a boy."

Her first major appointment came on September 14, 1983, when President Ronald Reagan appointed her to the U.S. District Court of New Jersey. She was unanimously confirmed by the U.S. Senate.

Despite her allegiance to the Republicans, Bill Clinton nominated her as a judge on the U.S. Court of Appeals for the Third District in June of 1999.

After the U.S. Senate once again approved her nomination, she said, "I'm glad that politics was not the priority."

She soon built a reputation as a tough judge in total command of her courtroom, and she tackled many high profile cases. One of them involved the conviction of Louis Manna, the Genovese crime family boss accused of plotting to assassinate John Gotti.

Maryanne's most widely publicized infamy derived from her testimony in support of the 2006 nomination by George W. Bush to the Supreme Court of Samuel Alito. *[Abhorrent to liberals, and the darling of far-right conservatives, Alito, along with Clarence Thomas, became two of the most reviled judges on the U.S. Supreme Court.]*

Maryanne suffered the glare of unwanted publicity more than any of her siblings during Donald's bid for the presidency in 2016. Despite her testimony in favor of the ultra-conservative Samuel Alito, Texas Senator Ted Cruz defined her as "a radical abortion extremist."

In retaliation against the opponent he had by now nicknamed "Lyin' Ted," Donald (perhaps jokingly, but perhaps not, and perhaps

P.T. Barnum with his sideshow midget, "General Tom Thumb."

Donald Trump was compared to the fabled circus huckster.

merely to irritate him) said, "When I become President, I'll name her to fill a vacancy on the Supreme Court."

Cruz's slanderous charge against Maryanne was based on an opinion she wrote in 2000 when a three-judge panel struck down a New Jersey law banning "partial birth abortions." She interpreted the law as "so broad and vague that it could be read to ban almost any abortion at any stage."

Attorney Matthew Stiegler, who writes a blog [The CA3blog] on events transpiring within the New Jersey and Federal courts, defended her ruling. "Her opinion was competent, professional, and utterly mainstream. If this opinion makes Judge Barry a radical extremist, then so is ninety-eight percent of the Federal judiciary."

Maryanne appears to be almost the polar opposite of her brother, Donald, preferring a very private life. When she does give a speech, her words are well chosen, without a hint of braggadocio. In 2016, she told the press that the media coverage of her brother's run for president "is just great. The media covers him with a lot of affection. Given all the things he does, I think he gets fabulous publicity. He is P.T. Barnum."

[Phineas Taylor Barnum was the godfather of "hot press" and self-promotion. Contrary to legend, he never said, "There's a sucker born every minute." He did say, however, "The people like to be humbugged."

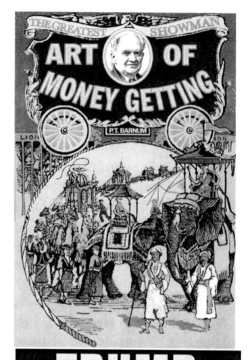

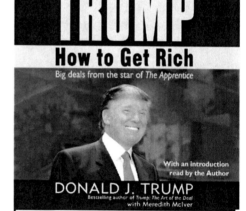

Two showmen-cum-moguls, each with powerful appeals to their eras, each with best-selling advice about lifestyles and money-getting.

An ad for his book read: "First he made five billion dollars. Then he made *The Apprentice*. Now The Donald shows you how to make a fortune, Trump style."

In his shows and circuses, Barnum presented sideshows that would be denounced as inhumane and dehumanizing today. They included "The Bearded Lady," the 161-year-old woman, Siamese twins Eng and Chang Bunker, and the "Fejee Mermaid," a mummified monkey's head attached to the body of a dead mackerel.

Reporters have drawn many parallels between Donald's life and career, including his sponsorships of a national beauty pageant, to that of P.T. Barnum. Along the publishing spectrum, Barnum's The Art of Money Getting (1880), is sometimes defined as a precursor to Donald's How to Get Rich (2004).]

Like her younger brother, Maryanne sometimes comes down hard on political correctness.

> *"I stand second to none when it comes to condemning sexual harassment of women," she said in 1992. "But what is happening is that every sexy joke of long ago, every flirtation, recalled by some women and re-evaluated, is viewed as sexual harassment. Many of these accusations are frivolous and do much, if not eliminate, communication between men and women of any kind of playfulness or banter. Where has laughter gone?"*

"I'm no different from any other brothers who love their sisters," Donald said. "My sister got the Federal appointment on her merit."

In a modest, and appealingly self-deprecating denial of that, Judge Maryanne Barry gave some of the credit to him. "He helped me get on the bench. I was good, but not that good."

***

The second child of Fred and Mary Trump, the couple's first son, Fred Christ Trump, Jr., was born in 1938. His father had been hoping for a male heir who might one day take over his fast-expanding real estate empire.

Biographer Gwenda Blaire wrote:

> *"Skinny, blonde, and nervous, the boy was a live wire, always active, always moving, always doing something. Even when sitting down, he*

Three young heirs to the legacy of Frederick Trump (left to right), Donald, Fred Jr., and Robert Trump.)

One of them would become spectacularly famous; one would die relatively young; and one would opt for a life of quasi-obscurity.

73

would invariably be tapping his toe or jiggling the chair. He had a sense of humor. He was a wise guy who specialized in raised eyebrows and double entendres, always ready to poke fun at anyone, including himself."

Instead of going to Kew-Forest, the private co-ed prep school that Donald attended, he enrolled at St. Paul's, an Episcopalian boy's prep school on Long Island. Unlike Donald, he did not care for baseball or football, and, unlike his very smart older sister, Maryanne, he was not a bookworm.

"Dad wanted a killer, but got me instead," Fred Jr. (known as Freddy) said. "I grew up imitating W.C. Fields rather than having any interest in real estate."

A classmate in high school claimed that Freddy informed him that his father was worried "that I'd grow up to be a fairy. My dad said I didn't seem interested in doing what other boys of my age do. He told me that if they ever remade *Gone With the Wind*, I could play Ashley Wilkes."

As a boy, Freddy was caught between the 'bookends" of his father, a perfectionist and intensely demanding patriarch; and Donald, an aggressive, intensely competitive younger brother.

Despite some friction, as they matured, Donald retained an abiding affection for Freddy. But Donald could also lecture, scold, and humiliate him. At table together, at a family dinner one night in Queens, Donald turned to his older brother and said: "Grow up! Get serious and make something of yourself in the family business!"

Although he didn't want to, Freddy applied for admission at Wharton School of Business, but was not accepted. Subsequently, he attended Lehigh University, an institution with strong links to Bethlehem Steel and renowned at the time for its prowess in science and engineering, in Bethlehem, Pennsylvania. There, he enrolled in ROTC and pursued his real interest—aviation. As a member of Lehigh's flying club, he was a daring (some say reckless) pilot, sometimes maneuvering his plane perilously beneath electrical wires and racing his aircraft dangerously close to lightning storms.

Ironically, Freddy, the son of a German immigrants, opted to join a Jewish fraternity. Within their midst, his brothers found comic relief in his middle name ("Christ.")

One fraternity brother remembered Freddy as a rich kid who drove a Corvette, wore the latest Brooks Brothers fashion, and owned a Century speedboat.

Once, after Freddy invited a classmate to join him aboard a fishing expedition off the coast of Long Island, he warned him, "I hope you don't mind if I take along my younger brother. I've got to warn you: He's a pain in the ass."

During one of his return visits to Jamaica Estates, Freddy informed his father that he wanted to be an airplane pilot. Fred Sr. was horrified, admonishing his son, "Do you realize that that is on the same professional level as a bus driver?"

When classmates from Lehigh visited Freddy in New York, he invited them to such chic night clubs as the Copacabana. "Having Fred Trump for a father means we'll be guaranteed a ringside seat."

Unlike his father, who remained firmly resistant, Donald came to accept Freddy's aviation goals. "He belongs in the clouds and not amid bricks and mortar."

In the years that followed his stint at Lehigh, Freddy, acquiescing to his father's pressure, made a valiant attempt to join him in the real estate business, but he seemed painfully doomed for failure. Frequently, sometimes within full view of his extended family, Fred cracked down on his oldest son, often blasting him for decisions he'd made. One such reprimand was associated with the installation of new windows within a building where the old ones were still serviceable. "Freddy was always behind the eight ball," Donald recalled. "He could not stand up to Dad. I could."

Freddy was as handsome as could be, and he loved parties and had a great, warm personality and a real zest for life," Donald wrote. "He didn't have an enemy in the world."

Self-destructive, willful, and idealistic, Freddy eventually left the real estate business and the immediate tutelage of his demanding father. He relocated to Florida, where he became a pilot for Trans World Airlines.

In 1962, at the age of twenty-three, he married Linda Clapp, a beautiful airline stewardess. Eventually, they would produce two children, Mary and Fred III. Fred Jr., insisted that he had named them after his parents.

Ultimately, life for Freddy didn't work out happily. In the end, he divorced Linda and abandoned piloting based on the dangers associated with his uncontrolled alcoholism. After an unsuccessful stint as a commercial fisherman in Florida, he moved back to his parents' home in Jamaica Estates, working for the family business as a low level member of one of its maintenance teams. To an increasing degree, he self-destructed. More and more, as Donald observed, he descended into alcoholism.

"As Donald moved ahead, Freddy went on a downward spiral," said Maryanne. "Freddy was sweet and generous, not competitive like Donald."

In 1977, Donald asked Freddy to be his best man at his marriage to the Czech model, Ivana Winklmayr. He showed up drunk. Emaciated and in ill health, in four years he would be dead.

At the age of forty-two in September of 1981, he suffered a massive heart attack. His drinking had become so severe that his few remaining friends attributed it to "suicide by Scotch."

Donald was severely shaken by his older brother's death. "Freddy, just wasn't a killer. I saw people take advantage of him. The lesson I learned was always to keep your guard up one hundred percent. If I had any guilt about his death, it was that I benefitted from my brother's mistakes. He was the first son and heir apparent, but that role fell onto me."

Tragically, the pain associated with Freddy's life, failures, and early death spilled over—in ways reminiscent of the words of the Old Testament patriarchs— to the Trump family's next generation.

In 1999, when Fred Sr. died after a long illness and a prolonged bout with Alzheimer's disease, his adult grandchild, Fred III—himself the victim of his father's alcohol-related failures—spoke at the patriarch's funeral.

That very night, Fred III's wife, Lisa, went into labor, giving birth to William Trump at Mount Sinai Medical Center. Their infant son was born with a rare neurological disorder that would lead brain damage, violent seizures, soaring medical bills, and carloads of parental pain. At one point, Fred III owed the hospital $300,000 for procedures associated with brain scans, spinal taps, and blood tests.

To his alarm, when the contents of Fred Sr.'s will was read, Fred III and Lisa were horrified: He had bequeathed all his assets to his children and their offspring, "with the exception of the off-spring of my son, Fred C. Trump, Jr."

That meant that Fred III and his sister, Mary, had been disinherited, cut off from the family largesse that otherwise extended to each of the patriarch's other grandchildren. Desperate to pay for his infant son's medical bills, Fred III, in league with his sister Mary, sued, charging in court that Fred Sr., based on his Alzheimer-induced dementia, had been mentally unfit when he signed his (revised) will.

In retaliation, Donald, exercising his authority as executor of his father's estate, withdrew the medical benefits—previously provided by the Trump business interests—for his nephew's infant son.

Although Fred III's rage continued for years after the litigation was somehow settled

Fred Trump III faced disinheritance and mounting medical bills for his children.

out of court, he later wryly commented, saying, "Our family puts the 'fun' in dysfunctional."

He eventually went into real estate himself, "but not for Donald's people."

In reference to the affair, perhaps in self-justification, Donald was later quoted as saying, "My dead brother's children live like kings and queens. This is not the story of two people left out in the gutter."

***

The quietest and least known of the Fred Sr. and Maryanne Trump's five children is their third (i.e., "middle") child, Elizabeth. Shy and retiring, she was born in 1942, during the darkest year of America's involvement in World War II.

Donald's sister, Elizabeth Trump Grau, administrative assistant at Chase Bank, marries James Grau.

Elizabeth was named after her paternal grandmother and was born shortly after her parents had moved to Norfolk, Virginia to construct wartime housing.

"She lived life under the radar screen," Freddy, her older brother, said.

As a pre-teen and teenager, she attended the Kew-Forest School and later, Southern Seminary College in Buena Vista, Virginia. After graduation, she became an administrative assistant at the Chase Manhattan Bank in New York.

In March of 1989, she married James Grau, the president of Charisma Productions, known for documentaries and sports movies. A graduate of Northwestern University, he had been married before. Elizabeth's siblings, Maryanne and Donald, were prominent at their wedding, having been designated as the matron of honor and as one of their ushers, respectively.

Today, Elizabeth is retired, and rarely seen in public. She made an appearance at her father's funeral in 1999, along with 650 other guests, where she was seen talking to New York Mayor Rudy Giuliani. In front of the assembled mourners, she read a poem, "Don't Quit," claiming it was her father's favorite.

Donald has had little to say about Elizabeth. "She is kind and bright, but less ambitious than Maryanne."

***

Fred Sr., had once expressed an interest in producing a big family with perhaps as many as eight or ten kids. Although with Mary, he produced five, that dream was curtailed after the delivery of their final child, Robert, who was born in 1948, two years after the birth of Donald. In the immediate aftermath of the birth of her fifth and final child, Mary started to hemorrhage. Fred agreed with her doctors that they needed to perform an emergency hysterectomy.

That was only the beginning of her physical woes. She later developed peritonitis, which is a horrible and very serious abdominal infection. To save her life, she had to undergo four more operations within a period of two weeks.

Summoning his children for a family conference, Fred informed them that their mother might die at any moment. But the following day, instead of standing "guard" beside her at the hospital, they were ordered to attend school.

In time, Mary recovered, but she never regained her former strength.

Unlike his siblings, the youngest of the Trump children, Robert, was not named after one of the Trump family forebears. In time, he'd become the sibling Donald referred to as "my Honey."

Neighbors in Jamaica Estates recalled Maryanne, Donald, and Robert as "three tow-headed children, all fair skinned, roaming around or playing. One housewife, who lived next door, remembered the Trump kids coming over for visits which often included getting something to eat between meals. [Snacks were strictly forbidden in the Trump household.] Another neighbor recalled the three siblings as looking "buttery."

"Donald decided what games we were to play together," Robert said. "He was the boss."

Set apart to some degree as a family "subdivision" of their own, as the family's youngest siblings, Donald and Robert competed for access to certain toys. According to Trump family legend, in an act that might have been a forecast for his later occupation, Donald once forcibly commandeered Robert's building blocks for his own make-believe construction project.

As boys, the two youngest brothers sometimes accompanied Fred Sr. to his building projects. "We would go with him as he checked on his buildings. We'd take the elevator to the top floor and then walk down, floor by floor, with father barking orders to his crew. We rented to tenants on weekends."

Eventually, Robert attended Boston University. After graduation, he did not immediately enter his father's real estate business, but became an investment banker instead.

For a period of his life, he lived in an apartment formerly occupied by Donald's on Manhattan's East 65th Street. Fred Sr. "accessorized" him with a decades-old Oldsmobile Cutlass for transportation.

Perhaps to escape from his father's authoritarian shadow, Robert went to work on Wall Street, having accepted a position in finance at Kidder Peabody, Later, he migrated to Eastdil Realty and then detoured off to Shearson Loeb Rhodes. Finally, he returned to the family fold, joining the Trump Organization.

There, he partnered with Donald, who referred to Robert as "my lookalike, only handsomer. I knew I could rely on the kid. But I warned him he'd have to clank balls on occasion. At first, he let me be the tough guy. If he had a fault, it was that he was just too god damn nice."

In 1981, Donald brought Robert in as a partner in a deal to erect a thirty-nine story luxury cooperative on Third Avenue at 61st Street in Manhattan. It became known as Trump Plaza.

Robert got his biggest and most complicated assignment when he was given the job of overseeing the completion of the plagued Taj Mahal Casino in Atlantic City.

***

For twenty-five years, Robert was married to Blaine Trump, a figure who, over the years, had become prominent on the Manhattan's society circuit. Their marriage collapsed after Robert fell in love with his secretary, Ann Marie Pallan, and bought a $3.7 million home for her in Garden City,

Blaine Trump, post divorce from Robert, emerged relatively unscathed, appearing on the cover of the February, 2015 edition of *Avenue* magazine in a story entitled "Act II."

New York.

When she learned of their affair, Blaine was said to have overdosed on sleeping pills, later recovering within a hospital room at the city's Mount Sinai Hospital.

Today, Robert is (in his words) "gainfully retired." He has told the press that he can't wait to see Donald sitting in the Oval Office. "Donald has a great message for the American people, and I support him one-thousand percent."

***

Donald Trump and his siblings have shared a turbulent past. Their relationships—like those of millions of other families—have survived more or less intact after multiple changes, rages, feuds, and upheavals. In the aftermath of decades of interchanges, some of them happy, some of them traumatic, it's certain that if he and his candidacy survive until and triumph on Inauguration Day in January of 2017, Maryanne, Elizabeth, and Robert will be standing on that platform watching their brother sworn in as President of the United States.

Chapter Five

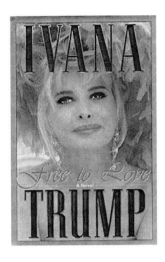

CZECH MATE
Across a Crowded Singles Bar, Donald Spots Ivana

TORN BETWEEN TWO LOVERS
Guess Which of Them Held the Trump Card?

ROY COHN
*Donald's Uneasy Alliance with the Most Notorious
Lawyer in New York. Crooked Deals, Ongoing Feuds, and
Murky Prenups with Ivana*

IVANA'S BESTSELLING ROMANCE
*Pulpy, Purple, and Romantic, Is It Fact or Is It Fiction?
Its Heroine "Can't Wait to Get Naked in His Arms"*

In 1971, Donald Trump left Queens, moved to Manhattan, and rented his first apartment, a bachelor pad studio on the 17th floor of a glazed white brick building on East 75th Street, near Third Avenue.

Dark, dingy, and positioned four floors beneath the building's summit, it encompassed a grimy closeup view of a water tank. Despite its drawbacks, he nonetheless began referring to it as his "penthouse."

A visitor described it as mostly outfitted with, "mirrors, furry furniture, and pictures of Manhattan real estate. Donald was obviously thinking of future building projects."

For transportation, he drove around the city in a new white Cadillac with red upholsteries. From his bachelor apartment in Manhattan, he'd commute every workday to the Trump family's office at 600 Avenue Z in Brooklyn. "Trumps don't take subways," he boasted.

Debonaire and single, he was handsome, young, and rich by the standards of the day. He had a net worth of about $200,000, most of it tied up in real estate with a lack of ready cash.

"I've become a Manhattan dude," he boasted, "No longer 'The Kid from Queens,'" On his days off, he spent time prowling through Manhattan on foot, forever on the lookout for a large tract of bargain basement real estate that could be mega-developed. In search of it, he sometimes drove his Cadillac along the West Side Highway into the northern stretches of Manhattan.

One day, Fred Sr. announced that he was naming himself Chairman of the Board of the Trump Organization, a move that would call for Donald to reconfigure himself as the organization's president. From the vantage of his new office, Donald began articulating his dreams about "changing the skyline of Manhattan," and dreaming on a scale bigger than anything his father had previously attempted.

He lobbied for admission to the exclusive Le Club, a swanky restaurant and nightclub on east 54th Street. It had been founded in 1960 by Igor Cassini (aka "Cholly Knickerbocker"), author of one of the city's most celebrity-obsessed

Rich, single and swinging, young Donald as he appeared during his bachelor days at Le Club and at Maxwell's Plum.

gossip columns. Igor's brother, fashion designer Oleg Cassini, provided financial backing. It had become known for a wealthy clientele, socially prominent membership that included many older industrialists accompanied by one, and often more than one, strikingly beautiful and much younger women. Lady Astor, the doyenne of New York society, dropped in on occasion, along with other members of the Social Registry. Some of them appraised him as an *arriviste* and a nouveau riche. As a member of the old guard told her friends, "He's a diamond, but a diamond in the rough. He's too brash, too loud, too commercial, and he really isn't one of us... I doubt that he'll ever make it in New York society."

But despite the sniffs, snubs, and dismissals of the Old Guard, Donald soon learned he didn't have to pursue the young and beautiful daughters of the upper tiers: gold-digging debutantes looking for a rich bachelor to marry flocked to him in droves. He also rubbed shoulders, and perhaps other body parts, with the daughters of fading aristocrats from long-gone European kingdoms; models who stepped out of the pages of *Vogue*; olive-skinned progeny of Latin American dictators; and the rich, spoiled offspring of Mafia dons whose diamonds and haute couture were financed by drugs and prostitution. He became especially popular with young, ambitious women who whispered to each other about how skilled Donald was in bed.

At the age of twenty-five, the thing he wasn't looking for was a wife. He often told associates, "I'll never marry. I want to achieve so very much in such a short time and have as much fun as I can because I don't think I'll live to turn forty." He never explained why he believed he wouldn't enjoy a long life.

Based on dalliances with a female *smörgåsbord* populated with fashion models and flight attendants, he quickly reinforced his image as a "ladies' man," a moniker first associated with him in military school. "The women at Le Club were vain, some were crazy, some were wild, and many of them were phonies," he said. According to an assistant manager at Le Club, "Donald didn't smoke or drink. Sex was his only indulgence."

Throughout it all, he was pursuing more than just "something on the hoof," as he put it. He was also developing valuable business contacts among the stockbrokers and bankers who patronized Le Club during their free-spending off-hours. He was often seen in the company of famous men, such as George Steinbrenner, the owner of The New York Yankees.

In a latter-day evaluation of his years as a free-wheeling and eligible bachelor on the make, Donald asserted, "At Le Club, I learned the art of deal-making. I would later become the world's authority on the subject."

The high-stakes attorney, Roy Cohn, a larcenous regular at Le Club, had an enormous impact on Donald Trump during this period of his life. As a kid, Donald had watched him on television at the Senate hearings led by the "red-baiting" Senator Joseph McCarthy, focal point of the communist "witch hunt" of the mid- to late 1950s. Young Roy Cohn was McCarthy's chief counsel. The two men, each a malevolent closeted homosexual, became famous for always being caught up in a conspiratorial private conference, whispering to each other as news cameras clicked.

Loathed by millions, especially in Washington and in Hollywood, Cohn was notorious as the most brilliant and the most crooked attorney in America, always under investigation by the IRS for unreported income. He became increasingly known for his demand that his wealthy clients pay in "hard, cold cash."

"Roy was not a pretty face," Donald admitted. "Instead of Scarface, I called him 'Scarnose,'—behind his back, of course." His nose had been scarred by a "quack doctor" during childhood surgery.

Cohn was short, balding, and combative, his eyes so heavily lidded that he looked half asleep. His menacing stare sometimes terrified his opponents. He constantly faced charges of bribery and bank fraud.

"Right from the first, I knew that Roy was no Boy Scout," Donald said. "He admitted that he'd spent two-thirds of his adult life under indictment for some charge or another. But he had one redeeming quality. If he became your friend, he'd be incredibly loyal to you. You could call him at two o'clock in the morning, and say 'I just murdered someone.' Roy would invariably say, 'Don't worry about it: I'll get you off.'"

Cohn was known for making dubiously legal, behind-closed-doors deals. His motto was, "Don't tell me what the law is. Just let me know who the fuck-

Early fine-tuning of the combativeness that made him a terror: Roy Cohn as counsel for the Senate Investigating Committee in the 1950s and chief aide to Joseph McCarthy.

ing judge is."

Cohn's illustrious clients included Ronald and Nancy Reagan; North Carolina Senator Jesse Helms ("America's leading homophobe"); Chrysler chairman Lee Iacocca; media tycoons Si Newhouse and Rupert Murdoch, and eventually, Donald Trump.

Cohn's best pals tended to be other closeted homosexuals: They included the FBI Director J. Edgar Hoover and the gay literary agent, Jay Garon. At night, Cohn often prowled the gay clubs of Manhattan with Garon, picking up young men, preferably "midnight cowboys" who had just arrived, ambitious, desperate, and broke, at the Port Authority Bus Station.

His best female friend was Barbara Walters; his worst enemy was Robert Kennedy. When not with media barons, he was seen with Mafia bosses or with glittering members of society cliques.

Biographer Nicholas von Hoffman wrote: "Roy Cohn was a cunning mentality. He loved to use people, get favors, give favors, build up patronage the way a ward politician would. I don't know what a shrink would say."

Even the former mayor of New York City, John Lindsay, had definite opinions about Roy Cohn: "If it were against the law, or if a case needed power brokering, call Roy Cohn, the most notorious attorney in New York City."

"All of Roy's friends knew he was gay," Donald wrote. "If you saw him socially, he was invariably with some very good-looking young man. But Roy never talked about it. He just didn't like the image. He felt that to the average person, being gay was almost synonymous with being a wimp. Roy was always the first one to speak out against gay rights."

Cohn shared that piece of hypocrisy with other closeted, and frequently malevolent, gay, J. Edgar Hoover.

One night, Cohn confessed to Jay Garon, "I have the hots for Donald Trump. I'm dying to find out how he's hung. I'd like a taste, but I have to cool it around him. He doesn't swing in that direction—he's a real pussy boy. If he drank, I might get him drunk one night, and I could take advantage, but he doesn't touch booze."

"In that case, drug his coke and devour him when he passes out," Garon advised. "When he wakes up the next morning, he won't know what you did to him. Have a ball...or two."

Almost immediately after hooking up with Cohn, Donald sought his legal advice, telling him that the U.S. Justice Department was after his father. Based on his systematic refusal to rent to African Americans, Fred Sr.

had been accused of violating the Fair Housing Act of 1973.

After studying the case, Cohn told Donald, "It's only a spit in the ocean. I'll get your dad off."

Cohn was right: Fred practically gloated in triumph when the Justice Department released a decision that onlookers defined as "a slap on the wrist." Although he was forced to advertise his rentals in the Harlem-based *Amsterdam News*, he privately he told his associates, "Advertising to these jungle bunnies is one thing. Actually renting to one of them is another. Also, I've made it clear I don't rent to welfare tenants, regardless of the color of their skin."

Soon, Donald began negotiating on his own. In the beginning stages, his father often showed up. One of Donald's chief honchos, Jeffrey Walker, remembered Fred Sr. as "having bright blue eyes and bushy eyebrows like the Catalán artist, Salvador Dalí. A high energy guy, he arrived on the launching pad like a rocket, taking two steps up the stairs at a time. Younger men had a hard time keeping up with him." A longtime realtor, Benjamin Lambert, said, "Donald Trump is full of shit, at least the line he feeds the gullible. In spite of all the publicity, he still hasn't put two bricks together, unlike his father, a real builder."

***

Based on Cohn's advice, Donald was advised to start "buying off" politicians of either party. He would follow such a practice as late as the 2012 elections, in which he contributed to both GOP and Democratic candidates.

He took great interest when Congressman Hugh Carey announced he was going to run for governor of New York. An Irish Catholic Democrat, he was the father of twelve children. He had begun his professional life in his family's fuel oil business, but soon switched to politics.

To help finance Carey's campaign for the governorship in Albany, Donald issued a direct contribution for $50,000 and co-signed a loan for $300,000.

"Hugh Carey is perfect," one of Donald's aides said. "He'll do anything for money." Trump companies became the second largest donor during the Carey campaign.

Based to some degree on Trump's financial support, Carey hosted his victory party in Manhattan at the Commodore Hotel next to Grand Central Terminal, a decaying relic that Donald would later acquire.

Assured, to some degree, of the backing of these, and other, political contacts, Donald realized "I'm the most aggressive of the Baby Boomers to take Manhattan. The skyline's the limit."

In his fervid search for new horizons to develop and conquer, his greedy eyes fell on the ill-fated Penn Central Transportation Company.

[Headquartered in Philadelphia, The Penn Central Transportation Company (Penn Central) existed only between 1968 until its dissolution into bankruptcy in 1976. It had been created by the 1968 merger of three previously independent railways — The New York Central, the Pennsylvania, and the New York, New Haven, & Hartford Railways. Each had been deeply injured by the rise of government-funded Interstate Highway System and the subsequent growth of the trucking industry. At the time of Donald Trump's involvement, it was fighting for its life and (frantically) divesting itself of its vast holdings.]

In real estate alone, it held 1,300 properties, maybe more. One of them was the decaying Commodore Hotel at Grand Central Station in the heart of Manhattan. Another lay beside the West Side Highway between 49th and 75th Streets, opening onto the Hudson River. Donald was aware that it was the largest undeveloped land mass in Manhattan, entirely owned by Penn Central.

Penn Central was not the only entity in fiscal trouble: Another was the City of New York. "The time to strike is now," Donald said. "Mired in twenty billion dollars worth of debt, New York is a sinking ship, praying for some bail-out rescue from the Federal government."

[By 1973, the NYC real estate market was deteriorating rapidly, and city officials turned to Washington. They did not get a friendly reception. At the White House, President Gerald Ford, a former male model, compared NYC to "a wayward daughter hooked on heroin."

In retaliation, The New York Daily News ran an infamous headline FORD TO CITY—DROP DEAD.]

Despite the deeply depressed market, Donald was optimistic, seeing a golden opportunity. He set about his plan, proposing to build a convention center at 34th Street, which he wanted to name in honor of his father, the Fred C. Trump Convention Center. He also had a grandiose plan to purchase Madison Square Garden.

He repeatedly surveyed the Penn Central properties alongside the West Side Highway, even venturing inland and walking block after block to check out the neighborhoods. He remembered seeing welfare hotels on almost every block.

The streets nearby were peopled with young men hawking illegal drugs. Many of them assumed that a well-dressed white man like Donald was in their decaying neighborhood seeking either a prostitute or heroin, maybe both. As he strolled about, he constantly resisted solicitations for sex and drugs.

Confronted with this fermenting cauldron of decay, Donald turned to Fred Sr. to exploit his political connections, especially his longtime friendship with Abe Beame, the mayor of New York. Fred had contributed heavily to Beame's re-election campaign. "To get you what you want, you're going to need changes in zoning," Fred warned his ambitious son.

Donald was granted a meeting with attorney Ned Eichler, who had been hired by Penn Central to help divest itself of its unnecessary real estate. "I found Donald Trump a young man of epic character, straight out of a Stendhal novel," Eichler said.

To impress him, Donald took him to see Mayor Beame, a diminutive former Brooklyn accountant now installed at Gracie Mansion. Fred Sr. joined the meeting. Eichler was astonished when the NYC mayor embraced the two six-footers, Fred and Donald. "Whatever my boys want, give it to them," Beame told Eichler.

Finally, after many tough negotiations, Donald bought options to develop both the Penn Central property beside the West Side Highway and the Commodore Hotel, too.

But trouble, more than he ever bargained for, lay ahead.

"There was a roadblock around every corner," he said. "I found myself in a crocodile-infested swamp. Other developers joined in the fray, pressing their agendas. It was hell getting everyone to agree on a site for the convention center. Some jerks wanted to build it at the lower tip of Manhattan in the Battery. 'Real convenient to midtown,' they said. Like hell it was."

Donald finally won, nicknaming his triumph "The Miracle on 34th Street," a reference to the popular 1947 movie of the same name, starring Maureen O'Hara and John Payne.

As it happened, Donald lost in the race to develop the Penn Central properties beside the West Side Highway, and he wasn't des-

Then NYC Mayor Abe Beame holding the famously headlined edition of *The Daily News'* reaction to the "message" of then-president Gerald Ford.

ignated as the builder of the sprawling new Convention Center. He was, however, offered a buyout of his option. During negotiations to determine its value, he claimed that he was owed $4.4 million. But a careful reading of his contract by opposing lawyers netted him only $500,000.

Throughout the entire tormented process, however, he retained his option on the Commodore Hotel.

"The city regretted it didn't name me as the builder of the convention center," Donald said. "The project was fucked up. Finally, the Jacob Javits Center opened four years late and $250 million over budget.

Depicted above is an engraving of the late 19th century's equivalent of Donald Trump, railway mogul Cornelius ("The Commodore") Vanderbilt, namesake of the Commodore Hotel, and chairman of the New York Central Railroad Company as depicted on a stock certificate for 100 shares of Common Stock in his railway enterprise.

His vast fortune of $100 million was almost unimaginable by the standards of his day.

"As a young wheeler-dealer setting out to take Manhattan, I expected setbacks," Donald said. "I learned a lot, even if the deal fell through. In my next move, I promised my father I would emerge triumphant...and I did!"

***

Immediately east of Grand Central Terminal in midtown Manhattan, The Commodore Hotel had opened on January 28, 1919, in the immediate aftermath of World War I. It was destined to become the first big property that Donald acquired in Manhattan. It had been named for "Commodore" (he really wasn't) Cornelius Vanderbilt, then one of the richest men in America and the founder of the New York Central Railway system.

Vanderbilt had risen from ferryboat operator to robber baron and ultimately to the railroad czar of America.

At its opening, the hotel boasted "the most beautiful lobby in the world," along with 2,000 bedrooms, some of them the size of closets. A waterfall in the lobby was designed by John B. Smeraldi.

Right from the beginning, The Commodore welcomed visitors from around the globe.

At its opening, P.T. Barnum staged a circus—complete with elephants—in the Grand Ballroom. The Century Room, a night club, boasted its own orchestra, and was patronized by *tout* Manhattan. "Those were the days," Donald said.

But by the 1970s, the hotel was deep in its twilight, on the brink of closure. High-paying guests no longer checked in, preferring The Plaza or the Waldorf-Astoria instead. When Donald took over, The Commodore was losing $1.5 million a year.

He brazened his way into control of The Commodore at the lowest point in its history. "By renovating this hotel, other developers will also move into the area," he predicted. "It will be the beginning of a long-overdue Renaissance for New York City."

His son's takeover of The Commodore did not inspire Fred Sr.'s approval: "It's like fighting to get a berth on the *Titanic*."

The neighborhood around Grand Central had deteriorated, and many nearby storefronts were boarded up, with many homeless men and women sleeping in the doorways. Garbage seemed to chronically litter the streets, which were lined with massage parlors. Prostitution and heroin abuse were rampant.

Not only that, but as a sign of the times, the Chrysler Building across the street was in receivership.

When Donald first walked into the lobby of the once glorious Commodore, he said, "I thought I was in a welfare hotel. I was in the lobby for only ten minutes when two different prostitutes had propositioned me."

These women were free lancers, when not otherwise engaged within the on-site massage parlor where young women gave out-of-towners blowjobs for only ten dollars.

One floor was almost totally a bordello, with clients, many of them in transit from arrivals and departures from Grand Central Station, next door, often occupying a bedroom for less than an hour. Management sometimes didn't even change the sheets unless they found blood or feces or semen.

Prostitutes weren't the only unwelcome guests. Donald explored the hotel's boiler room, finding homeless people living there, some of them cooking meals over open fires. They inhabited the dank underbelly of the building with colonies of "the biggest red-eyed rats since their ancestors brought the Bubonic Plague to Britain."

He hired out-of-work men to capture feral cats roaming through the streets of New York, and to release them into the bowels of the hotel. As it happened, the rats were so big, they sometimes ate the cats.

Some reporters labeled Donald's next move "the big lie." He announced to *The New York Times* that he had paid $250,000 for an option to buy The Commodore Hotel for $10 million. It was a bluff, since it was later discerned that he was only worth about $200,000 at the time—and very little of that was available as ready cash.

To pull off his brash and daring plan, he desperately needed a tax abatement from the city, approval for which lay with Mayor Beame and a handful of other officials. Even though he was relatively inexperienced, and still very young, Donald managed to organize one of the best deals of his life, something unprecedented in New York City's history: A forty-year tax abatement worth approximately $175 million.

Beame later said, "New York taxpayers became the key to making Donald Trump a rich man."

Critics defined the tax abatement as "a sweetheart deal hatched by political cronies on the take." Its ramifications especially enraged Donald's rivals, hoteliers and property managers Harry and Leona Helmsley.

After that spectacular success, Donald decided it was time for him to move up in the world. He turned over his cramped bachelor pad to his brother, Robert, and rented a "genuine" penthouse on the top floor of the Phoenix Hotel at 160 East 65th Street.

A while later, he upgraded his living space again, migrating to the top floor of the Olympic Tower, a new high-rise in "a bull's eye target" location at Fifth Avenue at 51st Street, across from St. Patrick's Cathedral.

Despite his success at wangling the tax abatement, crucial as a vehicle for raising the financing for The Commodore's radical restoration, he

With bluff and bluster, a young and inexperienced Donald acquired the landmark Commodore Hotel next to New York City's Grand Central Terminal.

He pulled off one of the great :sweetheart deals in the history of New York, but had to chase out the prostitutes and giant red-eyed rats.

needed a guarantee from a top hotel chain to define itself as his co-partner and the eventual administrator of the massive entity that would emerge from the debris of The Commodore. The road eventually led to Jay Pritzker, the CEO of the prestigious Hyatt chain.

After a long courtship and lengthy negotiations, Donald got Pritzker's name on the contract. Two nights later, as he told his attorney, Roy Cohn, "Fuck Hyatt. I have them signed. Now I can do what I damn please."

Cohn later said, "It was vital that Donald show that he was a genius in his own right, and not just Fred Trump's son."

The time had come for him to release his development plan for the Commodore to the New York press. He needed a young and aspiring architect who would work for low fees but who was "also brilliant and perhaps a genius on the rise in architecture." He settled on Der Scutt, who came up with a stunning new design for The Commodore.

Donald wanted to cover the crumpling brick façade with a "skin of glass." He told his architect, "I want you to take an old relic and turn it into a Tiffany diamond."

The once famous lobby was restyled with brown Paradiso marble, along with Grecian columns and shiny brass railings. The 2,000 bedrooms were reduced to 1,400 accommodations, making all the chambers larger. Donald also ordered the lower floors to be stripped down to their steel skeletons. He wanted to retain the layout of the once fabulous public rooms, but demanded that they be restyled, except for the neoclassical columns and the plasterwork in the Grand Ballroom.

When presented with problems, Donald told his crew, "Don't tell me how it can't be done. Tell me how it can be done."

In addition to the rooms, a lavish presidential suite, priced at $2,000 a night, was made available for rent. Donald said, "If Ronald Reagan wins the presidency, I hope he'll stay with us, even bring Nancy along, if she insists."

As The Commodore was transformed, Steven Spinola, head of the Real Estate Board of New York, praised Donald for launching a revival of the grimy Grand Central district.

In September of 1977, Beame suffered a crushing defeat in the Democratic mayoral primary. New York's five-time congressman from Manhattan, Edward Irving Koch, a closeted gay, swept into power, becoming the city's 105th mayor. Among his platforms, he opposed "sweetheart deals" with realtors, perhaps a reference to Donald and his father.

Koch claimed that "for a man still under thirty, restoring The Commodore was an outrageous feat of chutzpah."

He also claimed, "I never knew what role Donald Trump was playing on any given day. Howard Hughes one day, James Bond the next, perhaps Errol Flynn in the boudoir. Soon, New Yorkers were saying, 'That's so Trump of you,' to describe anything that was real ritzy."

After many sleepless nights and many negotiations, Donald arranged multi-million dollar financing through the joint efforts of the Bowery Savings Bank and the Equitable Insurance Company. After closing that, Donald proclaimed, "One day, I'm going to write a bestseller, entitling it *The Art of the Deal*."

At the time he closed the final deal on The Commodore, amazing bargains were available throughout Manhattan. The notorious Reverend Sun Myung Moon bought the 2,000-room landmark New Yorker Hotel on 34th Street for just $8 million, one of the city's alltime real estate "steals."

In 1980, the Grand Hyatt opened with fanfare and during its first year of operation, it made a $30 million profit.

[In 1998, when Donald was ready to move on from his Grand Hyatt venture, he sold his interest in the hotel to the Hyatt chain for $200 million.

In 2011, The New York Times headlined a story—MAKEOVER AT GRAND HYATT SHEDS THE TRUMP GLITTER. That year, Hyatt launched a $130 million renovation with the goal of erasing the old Trump image. "Everything gold and shiny is going," said Carol Bentel, a Long Island architect, referring to the Trump era's reflective surfaces, such as mirrored ceilings and the highly polished metal columns of the casino-like lobby. The goal was to adapt the hotel's style and décor to a level that was consistent with that of the Hyatt brand, something by then familiar to the chain's clients around the globe.

Of course, even after the hotel's 2011 makeover, the masonry of the old Commodore remained hidden behind the mirrored glass façade installed by Donald way back when.]

The ultimate NYC politician, with a style that might have, to some degree, influenced that of Donald Trump, the frequently kvetching NYC mayor, Ed Koch, was sometimes complimentary, sometimes raucous, and always a booster for his native city.

***

When time allowed during his almost hysterically busy schedule, Donald patronized the chic eateries of Manhattan, including "21," where he encountered Joan Crawford. With her provocative, flirtatious manner, she made herself available. But he allegedly told an associate, "I'm not into grannies this year. Crawford is much-used goods."

He was also seen at Elaine's, at P.J. Clarke's, and at Le Club, his other favorite stopovers.

At all of these watering holes, he had his pick of the sexiest women in New York, if he wanted them. Some evoked Rita Hayworth in 1944; blondes like Marilyn Monroe in 1952; and brunettes like Hedy Lamarr in 1940.

He told Roy Cohn, "Most of these gals don't have their heads screwed on right."

Shortly after Maxwell's Plum opened in 1966 at 1181 First Avenue at 64th Street in Manhattan, it became the most swinging singles bar in New York City. Into its outlandish Art Nouveau décor might walk, on any given night, Warren Beatty escorting Barbra Streisand, or perhaps Audrey Hepburn on the arm of Cary Grant.

Under kaleidoscopic glass ceilings hung Tiffany lamps illuminating a menu whose trademark staples included a "triangular" hamburger and Iranian caviar. Donald sometimes showed up with Roy Cohn, despite the marked difference in their respective gender preferences.

Nightly, a bevy of the most glamorous of the fashion models of New York could be seen at Maxwell's mammoth bar, perhaps talking with men who evoked Tab Hunter or Robert Wagner.

Donald frequented the place as often as three or four times a week, becoming acquainted with its owner, Warner LeRoy, son of the fabled Hollywood producer of such movie hits as *The Wizard of Oz* (1939) and *Mister Roberts* (1955). The 230-pounder always bounded up to greet Donald, often wearing a "screaming" paisley-patterned suit.

LeRoy recalled an episode from his past when his father was di-

The Grand Hyatt, post The Donald's upgrade with its façade of a "glass skin."

recting Judy Garland in *The Wizard of Oz*. "After Judy had danced down the yellow brick road in those ruby-red slippers, I, as a four-year-old, waited until the sound stage emptied. Then I tried it myself, running along. But I slipped and fell down, bashing my head against a wall. I decided then and there not to follow in the footsteps of Miss Garland."

It was a hot and oppressive August night when Donald arrived alone, escaping from the grimy heat into the restaurant's air-conditioned interior. He looked rather dashing that night, wearing a tailored burgundy-colored suit, burgundy tie, Robin's egg blue shirt, burgundy socks, and hand-crafted burgundy-colored leather shoes. He cut a dashing figure, an object of sexual desire among nearly all the women in the bar as well as among the coven of gay men, a few of whom got off on "seducing straight guys."

Of all the blondes at Maxwell's including "bottled ones," one young woman stood out. She was standing in a long waiting line with three other women, all of whom looked like models.

Donald made eye contact with the model of his choice. Somehow, she became aware that she was being evaluated. The shapely, hazel-eyed blonde flashed a smile at him.

Donald summoned LeRoy and said, "See those young women over there, probably models. I want you to give them one of those tables you hold in reserve. Whatever they want, give it to them and put it on my tab."

He walked toward them, and came up behind his pick of the blondes. He tapped her on the shoulder. "If you're looking for a table, I can help you," he said.

She turned to stare into the blue eyes of a good-looking, tall, blonde-haired man.

"I'm Donald Trump."

She thanked him and he went away briefly to huddle with LeRoy. She turned to her girlfriends. "The good news is, we're going to get a table real fast. The bad news is, this guy is going to be sitting with us."

That didn't happen. After signing a blank tab with LeRoy, Donald disappeared.

Maxwell's Plum, psychedelic "singles scene" playground of the swinging 60s and 70s.

However, when the models left Maxwell's, he was waiting for them outside in the driver's seat of his limousine. There was no driver. He motioned for all of them to get inside. His favorite model joined him in the front seat.

"He drove us to the Hotel Roosevelt, and I gave him my phone number," she said. "After that, we started to date."

***

Just who was this mysterious woman Donald Trump spotted across the crowded room of horny singles at Maxwell's Plum? The world may never really know, since Ivana Marie Zelnickova has deliberately obscured her own controversial background. She was born in the town of Zlin (now Gottwaldov) in Soviet-controlled Moravia, a region within what used to be known as Czechoslovakia.

In spite of other years stated in published reports, her actual birth date was February 20, 1949. She was the daughter of Milos Zelnicek, an electrical engineer, and Marie Francova.

[Ivana's full name (Zelnickova) is different from that of her father (Zelnicek) because in her native Czech language, a feminine "-ova" is added to the masculine form of the name, and an "e" is dropped.]

She was born prematurely, and had to spend the first six months of her life in a hospital, since she was too small at birth. As she grew up, based on her perky appeal, she was called "the Bohemian Shirley Temple."

Her father, a former swimming champion, had great ambitions for her. He taught her not only how to swim, but how to ski. At the age of six, she was recklessly gliding down the slopes on midget skis. Six years later, she was enrolled in a regimented and draconian Communist Bloc training camp for child athletes.

Labeled a daredevil, she was at this point a specialist in downhill ski-

Born in postwar communist Czechoslovakia, Ivana became one of the most famous capitalist women in America. It all had to do with her marriage to the man she forever labeled "The Donald."

The facts of her early life are rather elusive—many contradictions.

ing and the giant slalom. "I broke my bones many times," she lamented. On five separate occasions, she did break one or another of her legs.

As she matured, she wanted to go to college and was enrolled in the prestigious Charles University, named after Charles IV, the Emperor of the Holy Roman Empire. Located in Prague, it dated from 1348.

She had another reason for wanting to move to Prague. She'd fallen in love with George Syrovatka, and had begun an intense affair with this handsome young man, who was one of the best skiers in Czechoslovakia. He didn't see any need for marriage: He detested life behind the Iron Curtain and planned to defect.

His chance came in 1971, when he competed in a ski race in Austria. Spiriting himself away from his "handlers," he abandoned Europe and settled in Montréal, all the while staying in contact with Ivana.

Through a series of covert and clandestine manipulations, George later helped her escape from Prague. When Ivana traveled to Austria for a ski competition, he arranged for a fellow skier friend of his, Alfred Winklmayr, an Austrian, to marry her in 1971. He was twenty-five and she was twenty-two. It was a "Cold War marriage."

With her new Austrian passport, Ivana flew to Montréal to settle in with George, who was running a ski boutique there and selling sporting goods. George and Ivana often spent weekends skiing together in the Laurentian Mountains of Québec.

Her divorce from Winklmayr would eventually be granted in 1973 in the Los Angeles Superior Court.

It was in Montréal that Ivana began her life-long passion for decorating. George's kid brother, Michael Syrovatka, said "She didn't really have a taste of her own. She had no background in interior decoration. She would just see something in the latest magazine and set out to duplicate it. I found her to be a spoiled brat, not good enough for my brother."

To earn money of her own, using George's contacts, Ivana decided to become a model. Her natural brown hair had been dyed blonde, and she had developed a shapely model's figure, that was accepted as suitable for most fashion styles with the exception of haute couture, which required taller and thinner models.

A meeting was arranged with Audrey Morris, an agent representing a clientele of top models. "She was poised, immaculately groomed, with never a hair out of place," Morris said. "The more she modeled, the more skilled she became. Perhaps with too much makeup, she strutted down the runways, as regal as a princess. I felt she was going places. But where? The career of a model has the life of a sickly butterfly."

Although Ivana spoke several languages, English wasn't one of them. To remedy that, she enrolled in night courses at McGill University. In time, she became one of the top three models of Montréal, earning $50,000 a year. Millions lay in her future.

She became so popular that she was interviewed by magazines, claiming that George was "my husband." Actually, that was not true. When he was asked later if he'd ever married Ivana, he said, "Well, not exactly."

In August of 1976, Ivana was asked to join two other models for a trip to New York for the promotion of Canadian furs and to hype the upcoming Olympic Summer Games in Montréal.

***

The next morning, shortly after Ivana woke up at her hotel, she was greeted by the sight of two dozen of the most beautiful roses she had ever seen.

She decided to stick around the hotel until late afternoon, expecting that this mystery man would call her, but he never did. When she got back after a modeling session, she checked for messages. There were none.

Later, after her return to Montréal and the arms of George Skrovatka, she seemed to forget about this brash New Yorker in the burgundy suit.

Two weeks later, she was modeling furs for an upmarket audience that included some rich Canadian industrialists. From the runway, she thought she recognized Donald sitting in front, but wasn't sure.

After the show, she wandered out to meet the buyers and spotted Donald. She approached him and said, "Thanks for the roses."

"My pleasure," he said, extending his hand.

"Welcome to Montréal."

"I must go now," he said. "You were terrific modeling those furs."

She was obviously mistaken in thinking he had flown to Montréal just to track her down.

Two days later, Donald called Audrey Morris at the modeling agency and secured Ivana's phone number. During the next two weeks, he phoned her two or three times a day.

At one point, she confessed that she was living with a longtime friend whom she identified only as George. That didn't seem to concern him greatly, and he told her he was sending her a round-trip ticket to New York, where he'd reserved a suite for her at the Plaza Hotel.

She accepted his invitation and flew to New York, where he had arranged for a limousine to take her to a flower-filled suite at the Plaza. In her wildest dreams, she could not imagine that in a few years, she'd be the president of this luxury landmark.

He phoned her shortly after her arrival and invited her to have dinner with him at Le Club, promising to pick her up at eight o'clock. As a token of his affection, he presented her with a "get-acquainted gift"—a diamond bracelet from Tiffany's.

At Le Club, he introduced her to New York society, falsely claiming that she was an Olympic swimming champion, and boasting that she was fluent in Czech, French, and Russian.

When she went to powder her nose, Donald told his male friends, "Khrushchev, that fucked-up fat slob commie dictator, wanted her for his mistress, but she turned him down."

That story wasn't true, but Ivana was learning fast that Donald was very impressed with hype. She never knew what utterance would emerge from him, minute by minute.

She wasn't particularly offended by this characteristic. She'd been told long ago that some famous person—she didn't remember who—had once said that truth is like poetry, and that a lot of people didn't like poetry.

Ivana's affair with Donald reportedly began during that Donald-sponsored trip to New York. Details are missing, but one can surmise based on what she wrote in a romantic novel she later penned, a *New York Times* bestseller, entitled *For Love Alone*. In this sizzling and quasi-autobiographical page-turner, Ivana clearly emerges as the heroine, Katrinka, whose love interest is Adam Graham.

Her written description of Katrinka's seduction by Adam is as follows:

> *"He began to kiss her again, his mouth moving up from her throat to her ear, her cheek, her eyes, down her nose, to her mouth. His tongue slipped inside and met hers, and she thought she heard him groan. Or was it herself? If he took his arms away, she would fall, she thought, she felt so weak with desire. His left hand stroked her throat, her shoulder, moved down and cupped her breast. His right hand moved from her hair to her back, found the zipper of her dress. Oh, yes, she thought, this is what making love should be like. She had almost forgotten. She could not wait to be naked in his arms. She could not wait to feel him inside her. Reaching for his tie, she began to undo it."*

Audrey Morris was the first to realize that a serious relationship was fast-developing in New York. Ivana was away every weekend, warning Morris not to book her for any assignments early in any week.

Apparently, she told George that she had made a connection with a modeling agency in New York and was getting assignments down there.

That explained her vastly upgraded wardrobe from some of the most prominent and upscale emporiums along Fifth Avenue. She never showed him the diamond bracelet.

When Donald learned that Ivana was flying to Aspen, Colorado, with a group of her girlfriends for an annual Christmas holiday, he arrived at the resort two weeks before she did.

There was a problem, however, and he set about to remedy it: He did not know how to ski. Consequently, he hired the resort's most renowned ski instructor, approaching the sport with the same dedication he applied to a building site. After two weeks of intense instruction, he knew how to ski, winning praise from his coach who added, "Of course, his is not of Olympic caliber."

In Aspen, he had a reunion with Ivana. After a night of lovemaking, they hit the ski slopes the following morning. Of course, with her skill on the slopes, she zoomed right by him, leaving a mass of snow flurries in her wake. He knew he would never be able to ski like she could, but she was impressed that he tried so hard. "At least I learned how to ski down a slope without breaking my neck."

On the second night, they sat before a fireplace enjoying the après-ski ritual. Within this intimate setting, he confessed to her that she was the type of woman he'd searched for a very long time. "Both of us aren't spring chickens any more. We're two mature adults who should know what they want. Both of us are fiercely competitive. I've sensed that in you. With you at my side, I could climb the highest rungs on the ladders of New York. As my wife, we could raise a family. I want at least five kids, hoping that one of them will turn out to be like me, just like I was like my father in our family of three boys."

That impressed her as she, too, wanted to have children, and her love, George, did not. She was still the daughter of a mother who, back in Czechoslovakia, often spoke yearningly about Ivana's arrival with grandchildren in tow.

In all of Ivana's years with George, he had never proposed marriage. Both men were good looking, and each could have been called a desirable catch. But only Donald wanted marriage and kids. Not only that, but George probably would never rise above the level of a skier who sold sporting goods. For Donald, the world seemed not beyond his reach. Manhattan, of course, would be his first conquest.

During her time in New York, Ivana read newspaper clippings about Donald and his takeover of the Commodore Hotel, then under reconstruction. As a man about town, he was already tabloid fodder and was frequently mentioned in gossip columns.

He told her that he didn't aspire to be a millionaire. "I plan to be a billionaire. One day, as my wife, you'll preside over a household with a million-dollar-a-month budget for living expenses."

"Donald has a great future in real estate," Ivana told Morris. "But with George, what will happen if the snow one winter is only a bit of powder? Donald is already a rich man and a celebrity in New York. As his wife, I, too, will become a celebrity. Maybe one day the *grande dame* of New York. I could even become famous in America, perhaps getting movie offers."

Years later, Roy Cohn revealed that Donald had shared his future ambitions with him, including what he needed in a wife. "He wanted to become not only a real estate mogul in Manhattan, but one day hoped to erect buildings in other parts of America, even around the world. To have a vast empire. But even that would not be enough for him. He told me as early as 1976 that he might one day run for President of the United States."

"I've got to be careful in the wife I select," Donald said. "Of course, I could have any shapely Ford model I want. Beauty is not enough. The woman I marry has got to be intelligent. After all, she might be presiding over State Dinners at The White House one day. No doubt I will have to escort her to Buckingham Palace. I can't show up on Queen Elizabeth's doorstep and introduce her to a cheap floozie."

"Ivana was torn between two lovers," Morris said. "George and Donald. But only one of them held the Trump card. Forgive the pun."

One weekend in New York, Donald and Ivana arrived by chauffeur-driven limousine at the Jamaica Estates home of Fred and Mary Trump. There, Ivana was introduced to his family. Their dinner went very well—the family found her charming.

The next day, Fred called his son. "I approve," he said. "This is the first gal you've dated you can even consider becoming your wife. The other whores you took out were just cheap gold-diggers, empty-headed trollops."

Ivana was delighted to hear that the family approved of her. Back in Montréal, she told Morris, "I can go from being a top model and champion skier to becoming a fairytale Cinderella."

By January of 1977, Ivana finally made up her mind to marry Donald, despite some misgivings about George. Flying to New York, she accepted his proposal of marriage. The next day, he presented her with an engagement ring, a five-carat oval diamond from Tiffany's.

She had to tell George, and she wasn't looking forward to their confrontation. She'd fallen in love with him a decade ago, way back in Czechoslovakia. Together, they'd survived upheavals that included their respective defections to the West. But the time had come for her to move on with her life.

She later confided to Morris, "I told George that he'd been the sweetheart of my girlhood, and that I would always have a kind chamber of my heart reserved for him. But I had to tell him he still was not mature enough for marriage, in spite of his age."

"It was time for me to get married and have a family. I assured George that he was a wonderful man and a great lover, and I was certain that one day, he'd find the right girl to marry and could settle down and raise a family of his own."

Five days later, Morris met with Donald and Ivana in Montréal. "They made a wonderful looking couple. They were definitely two people in love. He was so kind, so loving, so considerate of her. I determined that he was the type of man who put women on a pedestal."

Michael Syrovatka, George's kid brother, took a more cynical view. "George took Ivana's departure very, very hard. He had always counted on her to be there for him. She broke his heart. Once, I rode into the mountains with him, and I was in the passenger seat. He was speeding and driving recklessly on a slippery road. In his fury, I felt he wanted to kill himself. But I didn't want to go there with him. As for Ivana, she made her choice. She went for the gold."

***

Before the wedding, Donald's lawyer, Roy Cohn, drew up a prenuptial agreement for Ivana to sign. He told Donald, "When love's lust fades, and it invariably does, you don't want her to take half of everything you've worked so hard for."

When the document was presented to Ivana, she asked, "What is a prenuptial? We don't have such things in my country."

When Cohn explained it to her, she said, "To me, it seems like you're giving up on the marriage before it even begins. Marriage should be forever."

On March 18, 1977, Ivana and her lawyer, Lawrence Lavner, who had worked hand-in-glove with Cohn on other deals, met with Donald. The enraged outcome of that meeting almost let to the dissolution of their engagement.

Cohn had inserted into the prenup that in case of a divorce, Ivana would have to give back any gifts, including jewelry, that Donald had presented to her. She was furious at the suggestion. "A gift is a gift," she shouted at

102

Cohn.

She also demanded a "rainy day clause," wherein Donald would set aside, in her name, in escrow, the sum of $150,000. When Donald refused, she rose to her feet and stormed out of the restaurant. He went after her. For about fifteen minutes, they stood outside on the sidewalk, arguing and attracting attention. Finally, she relented and agreed to continue their negotiations.

Finally, Ivana lowered the amount of the "rain check" to $100,000. At this time in his career, Donald did not have a lot of ready cash, and even that (relatively) small amount would have been difficult to raise. *[At the time, he was reporting a taxable income of only $2,200 a week. (Annualized, that would work out to $114,400 a year.)]*

Cohn finally conceded that she could keep her jewelry in the event of a divorce. According to the final contract, if the marriage collapsed, Donald volunteered that he would pay her $20,000 a year in alimony.

***

On April 9, 1977, Donald and Ivana were married at the Marble Collegiate Church on Fifth Avenue. The minister who presided, Norman Vincent Peale, was also a famous author. Some two-hundred invited guests showed up along with a few family retainers. The most distinguished guest was New York's mayor Abe Beame. Ed Koch, soon to replace him in that office, also attended.

Milos, Ivana's father, also flew in, not being able to afford the cost of a ticket for Ivana's mother.

Ivana made a stunning appearance in her wedding dress, an off-the-shoulder creation with a chiffon full skirt of mid-calf length. She wore a veil but no train. Since it was the Easter season, the church was filled with white lilies, a magnificent array.

Donald's sisters, Maryanne and Elizabeth, were bridesmaids, leading a procession of flower girls in pink

Entrance to the Marble Collegiate Church, where Ivana married "The Donald" in 1977.

"Mr. Trump is not an active member."

dresses. Fred Jr. was best man, with Robert serving as an usher.

That morning before the wedding, Ivana had been a "nervous wreck," perhaps having second thoughts. At one point, she didn't think she could go through with it, but friends calmed her down. "I don't know anybody here," she lamented, "except my father. I'm afraid."

The wedding reception was held at Donald's favorite "bistro," the "21 Club." Joey Adams, the husband of Cindy Adams, the gossip columnist, was the toastmaster. The party lasted until well past midnight.

On her wedding night, Ivana was hardly a virgin, and she was by now accustomed to Donald's lovemaking, so she had no surprises.

She did confide to friends, "I still miss George. I can't get over him so easily, even though I am now in the arms of another man, even one I'm married to for a change."

The next day, Mr. and Mrs. Donald J. Trump were on a plane bound for Acapulco, following in the footsteps of John F. Kennedy and his bride, Jacqueline, who had also selected that resort for their honeymoon, decades before.

On the second night of their honeymoon, he restated his ambition for their future, but phrased in a new way: "It's not just about making money—I also want to be famous, a household name like McDonald's or Roy Rogers."

"Who is this Roy Rogers?" she asked.

There were still some surprises in store for Donald from his bride: On the plane back to New York, she startled him by announcing, "I'm not going to be some stay-at-home housewife baking cookies and having babies on demand. Come Monday morning, I'll put on a hardhat and be at that construction site where you're transforming The Commodore. I'll be on the lookout for waste, inefficiency, and corruption. When I find it, I'll shout, 'You're fired!'"

Did Ivana, the new Mrs. Donald Trump, invent her husband's famous punch line for his future hit TV show, *The Apprentice?*"

Chapter Six

FAME AND FORTUNE
Donald & Ivana Launch a Real Estate Empire

THE SUPERNOVA OF FIFTH AVENUE
Despite Massive Outrage & Resistance, Donald Erects Trump Tower

CELEBRITY TENANTS
Liberace, Michael Jackson, "that Nasty Bastard," Johnny Carson, and a Coven of "Eurotrash"

After his return from his honeymoon in Mexico, Donald Trump was swept up in a whirlwind of activities, with grandiose plans for his next big real estate development.

He moved his new bride, Ivana, into his bachelor apartment within Olympic Towers at 641 Fifth Avenue, promising her other, more elaborate living quarters as soon as they could be arranged.

The Olympic Tower was a 52-story modern luxury building covered with bronze-tinted glass. It was financially linked to Aristotle Onassis, the Greek shipping magnate who was married at the time to Jacqueline Kennedy. Ivana called it "a huge box."

In the fast-paced months to come, she started referring to her husband as "The Donald," and the name caught on in the tabloid press.

She had hoped to continue her modeling career, but that dream faded fast. Her new life was packed with actions and reactions, and in short order, she became pregnant. As she lamented, "What could I model? Maternity dresses?"

"If it's a boy, I plan to name it Donald Trump, Jr.," Donald announced, without consulting her.

Despite her pregnancy, Ivana did not curtail her frantic lifestyle—in fact, the night before she gave birth to Junior, she was seen out dancing.

When confronted by the press, she refused to provide details of her background, or even information about how she had met Donald. She said, "Whatever The Donald wants, The Donald gets."

She was a good cook and specialized in French-style sauces. But she soon learned that she had married a "meat-and-potatoes" kind of guy, as he informed her.

In addition to their Manhattan address, the Trumps also purchased a ski retreat in Aspen and a summer house in Wainscott on Long Island.

While Donald busied himself with his real estate, Ivana shopped for a larger and more luxurious apartment, finding one at 800 Fifth Avenue, on top of an old Manhattan mansion. She hired Barbara Greene, of G.K.R Associates, to help her decorate it. The location was off Central Park with panoramic views

A visitor to the apartment recalled that it was adorned with sofas in beige-colored velvet, and with an ample display of Steuben glass animals, a virtual glass menagerie in the front hall. The shelves were lit by tiny white lights, evoking Christmas year-round. The dining room was dominated by a bone-and-goatskin table.

When Donald saw the final result, he praised Ivana for her "imagination and flair, always in good taste."

Writing in *Vanity Fair*, Marie Brenner described Donald at this point in his life: "He was like an overgrown kid, all rough edges and inflated ego. He had brought the broad style of Brooklyn and Queens to Manhattan, flouting what he considered effete conventions, such as landmark preservation. His suits were badly cut, with wide cuffs on the trousers. He was just a shade away from cigars. 'I don't put on airs,' he said. He tooled around New York in a silver Cadillac with the initials 'DJT' on the license plates. It had tinted windows and was driven by a former city cop."

In the construction of Trump Tower, Donald wanted to use large sheets of glass instead of brick, claiming, "Glass is as cute as hell itself." In spite of criticism, including from his father, Donald moved ahead to erect a monument to himself, and his future home.

Opening in April of 1983, it became one of the most visited landmarks on Fifth Avenue, drawing some 2.5 million visitors annually. As sheathing for the stunning six-story atrium, he boasted, "We had to buy a whole damn mountain of pink marble in Italy."

After the success with The Commodore (aka the Grand Hyatt) at Grand Central, his next "towering" achievement, one for which he would be forever known, became the Trump Tower. A bold statement of imagination and glamour, its construction would be consummated only after the most subtle, skilled, and far-reaching real estate negotiations.

Almost every day, he walked past the eleven-story Bonwit Teller building (Fifth Avenue at 57th Street). At the time, he defined it as, "The greatest single piece of real estate in the city…a Tiffany of a location," a reference to the upmarket jewelry store next door. [*The celebrity cachet of this deeply en-*

trenched icon received a mega-boost after the release, in 1961, of Breakfast at Tiffany's, *a film starring Audrey Hepburn that was based on the novella by Truman Capote.]*

During the planning stages for the Trump Tower, Donald became painfully aware of the many hurdles he'd have to face. One of the most crucial would involve a change in the zoning laws of the neighborhood that surrounded it.

The Bonwit Teller building stood on leased land with twenty-five years remaining on its contract. He learned that the land the building sat on was actually owned by his partner, Equitable, with whom he had collaborated on previous (and profitable) deals. The most obvious of these involved the rebuilding of what had previously been known as The Commodore Hotel.

To erect the building he envisioned, he'd need to purchase the air rights over Tiffany's, but before he proceeded, he called his favorite architect, Der Scutt, who had devised the designs for the rebuilt Grand Hyatt.

The wheeling and dealing needed would almost require a book in itself. Donald wrote about it extensively in *The Art of the Deal.*

With disappointments, heartbreaks, controversies, lawsuits, financial manipulations, and easements from the city, he moved ahead, step by step, until he got what he wanted.

Two views of the once famous Manhattan landmark, the old Bonwit Teller building, with its famous decorative iron grille and its celebrated friezes, which were demolished by underpaid Polish workers (i.e., "cheap immigrant labor").

Architectural critics such as Roberta Brandes Gratz attacked the proposal to demolish the landmark, claiming that it would destroy the architectural harmony of old Fifth Avenue.

Donald's response? "What a ball-buster she is!"

"My tower would be located at a bull's eye address that only a kind of wealthy person could afford," he said. "It would be the hottest ticket in Manhattan. I would sell fantasy."

Scutt developed several different designs until he devised "my dream skyscraper." It meant demolishing the old Bonwit Teller flagship at 725 Fifth Avenue (between East 56th and 57th Street in midtown) and replacing it with a soaring, glittering, mixed-use tower.

He wanted it to become the headquarters of the Trump Organization, and he planned to move his growing family to its penthouse.

As part of an amazing deal, he bought the Bonwit Teller lease for $25 million and acquired the air rights over the Tiffany Building for only $5 million, which was considered "a steal" in real estate circles. To secure the land beneath Bonwit, he once again entered a partnership with Equitable, offering them a fifty percent stake in the gargantuan undertaking, for which the insurance giant launched the construction process with a cash infusion of $100 million.

There were immediate objections to the construction of such a towering monument. It was ascertained that it would cast a giant shadow over Fifth Avenue. "If you want sunlight, move to Kansas," Scutt told critics of his design.

Bonwit Teller, an upscale department store and fashion emporium, had opened at this location in 1929 at a ceremony attended by Eleanor Roosevelt. It was a terrible time to launch a store for the luxury trade. The stock market crashed two weeks after its inaugural ceremony.

Preservation-minded New Yorkers insisted that the limestone Art Deco bas-reliefs of half-nude goddesses adorning the store's façade should be preserved. Donald mollified their objections by promising to donate them to the Metropolitan Museum of Art, along with an ornate 15-foot by 25-foot iron grille that had been positioned above the store's main entrance.

But after ascertaining that the removal, intact, of the mammoth friezes would cost at least half a million dollars, and delay construction for almost two weeks, he ordered his workers to jackhammer them into chunks and fragments. As for the decorative grille, it disappeared into a large moving van and was never seen again. These demolitions were executed in defiance of the strident objections of the tower's architect, Der Scutt, who desperately wanted, and had publicly committed, to preserve them.

In response to the subsequent outcry, Donald asked a reporter, "Who cares? Those friezes are junk. If I'd presented them to the Met, they would have stored them in their basement. I'll never please the effete tastemakers of New York. The jerks would love to see me fail. In fact, they'd be thrilled.

I don't give a damn about earning their goodwill...something I'll never have anyway."

The New York Times, in a rueful analysis of the brouhaha, wrote: "Obviously, big buildings do not make big human beings, nor do big deals make art experts."

As part of a negotiation separate from the preservation of the Bonwit Teller frieze, after some bitter fighting with Mayor Ed Koch, Donald got his tax abatement. Later, in reference to Koch, one of his honchos proclaimed, "We fucked that faggot."

The press called the sweetheart deal and the subsequent skyscraper, "a supernova that descended on Fifth Avenue."

Architecturally, Scutt had devised a daring and innovative plan, envisioning a skyscraper that rose in a zigzag effect, a design that positioned the tower's sides with twenty-eight different planes, in effect allowing panoramic vistas from multiple glass-sided "corners" within the interiors. The resulting mass, accented with ornamental trees in terraced gardens, was neither chunky nor boxy.

What emerged was a sawtooth profile, where chunks of the tower were arranged like the teeth of a saw, allowing a network of terraces looking down upon Fifth Avenue. Each apartment

At first, Donald wanted to call it Tiffany Tower, because of the brand name recognition of the nearby jewelry store. But then one night he asked himself, "What the hell? Let's call it Trump Tower!"

Architect Der Scutt's stunning "sawtooth" profile allowed for a network of terraces looking down on Fifth Avenue with distant vistas of Central Park.

The tower became one of the wonders of Fifth Avenue.

within this "architectural wonder of Fifth Avenue" would have a "to-die-for" panoramic view in two different directions, many of them with vistas over Central Park.

Adding to the furor associated with the public outcry, it was revealed that Donald had hired undocumented Polish immigrant laborers at $4 an hour to demolish the old Bonwit Teller building and its controversial friezes. Sometimes, as a supplement to their low, off-the-book wages, his foreman gave these heavy drinkers bottles of Polish vodka. Many of them slept at the construction site.

Working without hardhats, some of the Poles labored eighteen hours a day during the demolition process, trying to meet their almost impossible deadlines.

[Filed in 1983, a class-action lawsuit against Donald over unpaid labor union pension and medical obligations dragged on through several appeals and non-jury trials. It was ultimately settled in 1999, with all records sealed.

Years later, during his 2016 presidential race, Donald was attacked for hiring low-paid Polish workers to restore Mar-a-Lago, his lavish estate in Palm Beach. His practice of doing that became a political football that was repeatedly hurled in his face for months after its first disclosure.]

When it came time to pour massive amounts of concrete at the tower's building site, Donald had to interact with John Cody, the mob boss who ruled over the city's concrete truckers. If a building contractor didn't meet his demands, he could shut down a site, running up outrageous costs. He held great power over any new building that used concrete, and the tower required tons of it.

Donald later revealed how he dealt with Cody's threats. "I told him to go fuck himself. He was one psychotic shithead, a real scumbag, definitely a mental case."

Cody was called a "buddy" of Roy Cohn, and it appeared that Cohn kept the peace with the union boss, which meant that Donald's construction site was not shut down in 1982 when other concrete truckers went on strike. It was suggested that as a means of accomplishing this, Cohn acquired and subsequently threatened to expose serious blackmail evidence that implicated Cody.

Eventually, the disgraced union boss served a prison term for racketeering and died in 2001.

Barbara Corcoran, the empress of real estate brokers, was quoted as saying that to erect Trump Tower, "Donald was a real bullshitter. But his bullshitting paid off handsomely."

***

As unpaid labor herself, Ivana was called in to decorate the Trump Tower's six-story atrium, one of the most dramatic high-ceilinged interiors in New York. As sheathing, she was instrumental in the selection of a variety

111

of pinkish-peach Italian marble named Breccia Pernice—250 tons of it. "It was so beautiful, it took my breath away," she said.

Donald later proclaimed, "We used so much marble, we actually took off the top of a mountain in Italy." In reference to the atrium, a visitor exclaimed, "Its eighty-foot waterfall made me feel I was in Wonderland."

Ivana wanted lots of mirrors and brass, not aluminum. That brass had to be polished every two weeks.

For the doormen, Ivana designed red military overcoats, embellishing them with gold braid and high black boots. The effect evoked the British "redcoats" who lost the American Revolutionary War. Capping it all, and inspired by the guards at Buckingham Palace, she insisted that they wear black bearskin hats ("busbies").

When asked, "Why so British?" she suggested that it would make the recently married Prince Charles and Diana feel at home when they moved in. A rumor spread that the Prince and his sometimes estranged Princess were considering renting a deluxe apartment within the Trump Tower, a "hideaway" during extended stays in America.

The rumor, unfounded or not, spurred a boost in sales of the units inside. So pleased was Donald with Ivana's contribution that he named her Executive Vice President in charge of Interior Design for the Trump Organization.

Later, Donald admitted, perhaps with a sigh of relief, that he didn't really believe that Prince Charles would ever become one of his tenants. "When Charles last came to New York for a visit, the IRA came out in full force to protest. As he walked into Lincoln Center for a concert, hundreds of protesters stood outside, hissing, screaming, and throwing bottles at him. It must have been a frightening experience for him, and I couldn't imagine he had any desire to take an apartment at Trump Tower. Also, I didn't want protesters gathering in the atrium."

Despite the non-presence of the Windsors, some of the most exclusive retailers in the world (Asprey, Charles Jourdan, Cartier, Buccellati, and Harry Winston) opted to open branches in the tower, boutiques interspersed among chic cafés. Gucci established its flagship inside, with signage out on Fifth Avenue. A pedestrian bridge spanned part of the atrium, within sightlines of the waterfall.

When it was completed, the tower rose 58 stories, despite some initial speculation that it would, or might, rise even higher.

When the final costs were ascertained, financial experts concluded that whereas some $200 million had been spent to erect the tower, the sale of its residential units generated revenues of about $250 million. Based on the profits thereby generated, Donald bought out his partner, Equitable, in 1986.

During the administration of Ronald Reagan (1981-1989), with all its kitsch and glitz, Trump Tower stood among the world's most dazzling architectural achievements. The word TRUMP, laid out in two-foot gold letters, accented its façade. Public approval soared: TV talk show host Regis Philbin claimed that Donald had not only launched the restoration of the Grand Central Terminal area, but also brought a Renaissance to Fifth Avenue, which had begun to decline.

According to Donald, "I decided to name the building Trump—after all, that's the winning card!"

The Tower opened in the spring of 1983 and almost overnight became one of New York's most recognizable landmarks. By the turn of the 21st Century, it would be drawing more than two and a half million visitors, coming from all parts of the world, annually.

It became one of the most recognizable great skyscrapers of the world. At its inauguration, it was the tallest glass building in Manhattan, even though it sat on less than an acre of land. It was visually stunning, with its glass curtain wall and sawtooth faceting. Structural engineers cited the solidity of the building as based, to some extent, on a concrete "hat-truss" system that linked together the building's exterior columns. It later became the setting of the hit NBC TV series, *The Apprentice*, site of the celebrated boardroom where Donald fired at least one person as the dramatic conclusion at the end of every show.

He reserved the best of the condos inside for himself. He eventually combined adjoining triplex penthouses into a single unit, a move which gave him a dramatic eighty-foot living room with a spectacular view of Manhattan. Their interiors were adorned with onyx. Even the bathtubs were made of lilac onyx with gold faucets. Gold leaf dominated, evoking the aesthetics of Louis XIV at the Palace of Versailles.

Prince Mutaib bin Abdulaziz Saud was only too willing to turn over bundles of petrol dollars to become one of Donald's first tenants in Trump Tower.

As one of Donald's sales agents later recalled, "At that point, he welcomed Muslims, providing they were rich. There was no talk of banning them as long as they were rich. Don't quote me, or, if you do, don't name me."

The living room sprawled out under a frescoed ceiling whose artwork Donald claimed surpassed that of Michelangelo's Sistine Chapel.

One of its focal points was a twelve-foot waterfall that cascaded against a backdrop of translucent onyx. The ceiling's elaborate trim and moldings were plated with 23-carat gold. "I was thinking of how the rich popes decorated the Vatican," he said.

To top it off was perhaps the grandest rooftop garden in Manhattan.

As someone later quipped, "How can the Donald ever settle for a dreary bedroom in the White House after living it up on top of the Trump Tower, where he could be King of the World?"

It seemed that some of the most celebrated people on earth, even the most notorious, wanted Donald Trump as their landlord.

Some of his clients he preferred not to publicize. One of them was "Baby Doc" Duvalier, the deposed ruler of Haiti, son of the most brutal and murderous dictators in the history of the Caribbean, François Duvalier ("Papa Doc").

Show business clients bought apartments. They included David Merrick and Frank Lloyd Weber. Actors such as Bruce Willis and Sophia Loren became tenants, too.

Oil-rich sheiks also signed on. One of them was Prince Mutaib bin Abdulaziz Saud.

Two of Donald's most famous tenants were Michael Jackson and Liberace. On television, Donald later said, "I knew what was going on in my tower, and I didn't see Michael bringing in any young boys to molest."

During his inspection of the unit he'd eventually move into, Liberace showed up wearing a rhinestone-studded jacket with white "Nancy Sinatra" boots." He was accompanied by two startlingly handsome young men in skin-tight

Johnny Carson...Enraged because of a missing vicuña coat.

The Gloved One...Did he or did he not slip in young boys?

Liberace: "Compared to my other lavish homes, my apartment at Trump Tower might be called a 'crash pad.'"

114

white pants, shiny black boots, and gold-braided uniforms evocative of the Hungarian Hussars. "I want only the best, and that's why I'm here," Liberace claimed.

Donald's least favorite tenant was TV's most popular talk show host, Johnny Carson. At first, they got along, especially when Carson claimed that "Donald Trump made it cool to be a New Yorker again after the city went into a slump."

One highly embarrassing day, Carson phoned Donald at his office, claiming that two members of his staff had stolen a most valuable vicuña coat from his apartment. Although each of the men maintained his innocence, Carson demanded that each of them be fired. Donald, or members of his staff, complied.

Two months later, Carson found the vicuña coat at the back of his large closet and informed Donald of that. However, neither of the two men were rehired.

Afterward, Donald said, "That Carson was one nasty man. To judge by the women coming and going from his apartment at all hours, he must have been a sex fiend, although I heard he was no good in bed."

***

Over the years, even more buildings would be emblazoned in big, bold letters with the TRUMP name.

With his architectural triumph (Trump Tower) operating smoothly, he turned his attention to other projects. At a cost of $125 million, he erected, in 1984, another mixed-use skyscraper, the Trump Plaza on Third Avenue and 61st Street near Bloomingdales, on Manhattan's Upper East Side. Many South Americans, including millionaires from Argentina with dubious backgrounds, rented some of the 175 apartments, as did many rich Asians and Arabs.

***

Trump Parc, a sleek, elegant condominium tower at 106 Central Park South, was originally incarnated in 1930 as the Barbizon Plaza Hotel. In January of 1988, when it re-opened with 347 units after a radical renovation, each of its residential units had already been sold. Its views of Manhattan—advertised as "from river to river"—are among the most panoramic in the city, and usually include vistas over Central Park.

Trump Palace Condominiums, a tall skyscraper at 20 East 69th Street in Manhattan, was completed in 1991 with 54 floors. Its majestic façade commands an entire block of Third Avenue on the island's tony Upper East Side. It is distinguished by an illuminated spire that is now a Manhattan landmark.

***

Trump International Hotel & Tower, located at One Central Park West, is the 52-story, 583-foot- tall focal point of the southwestern corner of Central Park. Inside are 176 magnificent guest rooms and suites, each with a fully equipped kitchen and floor-to-ceiling windows designed for clear-sighted views. It also contains a five-star and five-diamond restaurant that's spearheaded by Jean-George Vongerichten, sometimes hailed as the best chef in the United States.

It was originally built in 1969 as the ill-fated Gulf+Western building, as designed by Thomas E. Stanley. Cursed with structural problems, it swayed in the wind, reminding some of the occupants on its upper floors of California during an earthquake. With a design inspired by an airplane wing, its outer curtain walls were sheathed at the time with cheap aluminum and glass, elements of which flew off during strong winds. Making matters worse, the building at the time was laden with asbestos.

Beginning in 1995, as part of a $30 million renovation/rebuilding that was completed in 1997, the building was stripped to its skeletal frame, reinforced, re-sheathed with a new façade designed by Philip Johnson and Costas Kondylis, and elegantly redecorated inside and throughout. Owned today by the General Electric Pension Fund, it was used as the setting of the 2011 comedy/crime drama, *Tower Heist*.

***

In 1929, J.E.R. Carpenter, the leading architect for luxury apartments of his generation, designed the 450-room Mayfair Regent Hotel at 610 Park Avenue. It became one of the most prestigious addresses in Manhattan, and enjoyed its greatest fame when Le Cirque—then one of the most ballyhooed restaurants on the East Coast—opened here in 1974.

By 1997, its glory days had ended, and the Mayfair was purchased at a bankruptcy auction for only $15 million by Colony Capital, Inc., a real-estate development group based in Los Angeles.

The new owners became partners with the Trump Organization and poured $55 million into it, converting its interior into 70 luxurious condos. The reconfigured, radically upgraded monument became the venue for the four-star restaurant Daniel, one of the best in Manhattan.

***

When the Trump World Tower was built in 1999, a kind of panic arose, based on the fact that it would dwarf the world headquarters of the United Nations, just across the street. Walter Cronkite opposed its construction because of its daunting height and its lack of distinguishing features. Rising like a glassy, bronze-tinted, rectangular box soaring 72 floors above the sidewalk, it was designed by the Greek architect Costas Kondylis.

For a brief time, it was the tallest all-residential tower in the world. That was before the 2003 completion of the 21st-Century Tower in Dubai.

Built at a cost of $300 million, the Trump World Tower offers 376 units, selling for anywhere from $650,000 to $28 million. In 2003, the International Real Estate Federation designated it as the Best Residential Building in the World. The building and some of its interiors have been used as film sets in NBC's *The Apprentice*.

***

In 2002, Donald purchased the old Delmonico Hotel for $115 million and converted it into condo apartments. Once again, he relied on architect Costas Kondylis. The 32-story building at the northwest corner of Park Avenue at 59th Street contains 120 luxury condos and eight penthouses.

It first opened in 1929, the same year as the Wall Street crash. Over the years, in addition to its designation as the Delmonico, it was also known as the Viceroy Hotel and the Cromwell Arms.

THE GM BUILDING
A Heavenly Match" that Went to Hell

In 1999, the mating of Donald Trump and Stephen Hilbert, the executive who chaired the Conseco Insurance Company of Indiana, teamed up to buy the General Motors Building on Manhattan's Fifth Avenue. A vast and modernist fifty-story landmark, it carried a price tag of $878 million.

Hilbert and Donald got along, each executive admiring the other's style. Donald was amused to learn that his new partner had met the woman who became his sixth wife when she jumped out of a cake at a party he'd hosted for his son's 21st birthday.

Built between 1964 and '68, the GM Building lies between 58th and 59th Streets, one of the few skyscrapers in Manhattan to occupy a full city block. Its façade is an unbroken verticality of glistening white Georgian marble and sheets of glass.

In 1998, Donald and Conseco viewed the acquisition of this building as a potential gold mine.

Donald and Conseco bought it when the real estate market was at its peak. Donald got the better part of the deal, putting only $11 million into the pot. In contrast, Conseco, with little experience in the New York real estate market, shelled out $211 million in return for a preferred return and a fifty percent ownership. Additional financing was arranged through Lehman Brothers.

Donald immediately set about improving the lobby, sheathing it with Vermont Verdi marble and brass trim, and redesigning the sunken and not-very-practical outdoor plaza. As a final touch (or insult, according to some accounts), he installed his name on the building in four-foot gold letters.

At the time of this writing, positioned at the base of the building is a 32-foot glass cube, the entranceway to Apple, Inc.'s flagship store. Architectural critics have compared its dimensions and angularities to the Louvre pyramid in Paris.

The happy partnership soon

The General Motors (GM) Building, shown here with the Sherry-Netherland Hotel in the foreground, was built in 1964. Occupying a full city block midtown, it became one of the most contested properties in New York City.

Donald later admitted, "the wheeling and dealing, the revolving door ownership, the betrayals, and the lawsuits would make a great battle-of-the-moguls movie, perhaps starring Michael Douglas."

came crashing to an end. In 2000, Hilbert was tossed out of Conseco, as the company nearly collapsed under a mountain of debt. Conseco negotiated for more than a year to dump its stake in the building onto Donald for $295 million, but that deal fell through.

Donald and Conseco battled each other with ugly recriminations and lawsuits. At one point, Conseco threatened to rip Trump's name from the façade of the building and auction off its oversized letters on eBay.

Finally, in 2003, Donald and Conseco managed to sell the building for $1.4 billion, which at that time was the highest price ever paid for an office building in North America.

The proceeds of the sale went to pay off a $700 million mortgage. Conseco got $211 million, with Donald getting $15.6 million. Conseco got most of any remaining proceedings.

Donald expressed satisfaction with the transaction.

The Macklowe Organization took it over until February of 2008, when they put it back on the market. They faced a credit crisis among lenders. In May of that year, they sold it for $2.8 billion to a joint venture among Boston Properties, Goldman Sachs Real Estate Opportunities Fund, and Meraas Capital, a Dubai-based real estate private equity fund. The sale was the largest single transaction of 2008.

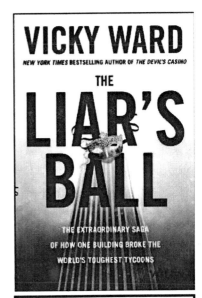

The turbulent proceedings associated with the GM Building were later outlined in a book entitled *The Liar's Ball: The Extraordinary Saga of How One Building Broke the World's Toughest Tycoons* by Vicky Ward. It detailed the random horrors associated with major-league real estate "deals among thieves" in New York.

Donald was furious at what he read about himself in the book, and trashed Ward on Twitter. He charged that the book "was poorly written and boring—she did a lousy job. I made a tremendous amount of money on the deal. The book doesn't capture the essence, the glamor, or the excitement of what went on."

Donald was furious at how he was portrayed in Vicky Ward's book, *The Liar's Ball*. It detailed the feuds and fights of "how one building (the GM building) broke the world's toughest tycoons, including Donald himself.

***

Trump knew that the City of New York, after many expensive delays, had spent several years trying to renovate and/or rebuild the Wellman Ice Skating Rink in Central Park. "Trumpeting" the city's inefficiency and his ability to get things done, along came Donald, and within four months, in November of 1986, the rink was finally opened in time for the winter season.

As one rival realtor noted, "Suddenly, all of New York knew the name of Donald Trump. Soon, he would become a household name throughout America. That left only the world to conquer. When he showed up at a bank and wanted to borrow a cool $60 million, a banker turned him down, offering $125 million instead.

***

With all this publicity and acclaim, the press began to write with an increasing frenzy about Donald and Ivana, both as a couple and as strong-willed individuals. Many reporters commented on her charming accent, which made excessive use of Vs and Zs. One writer compared her speech patterns to "the shoe-obsessed Imelda Marcos," First Lady of the Philippines, and Leona Helmsley, the hotel czarina nicknamed "the Queen of Mean."

In time, some staffers would designate Ivana "the most famous woman in the world," although that was an exaggeration. She seemed, however, to always be in the headlines.

Donald soon learned the downside of his growing fame, based on the tendency of the press to first build up a celebrity, and then to delight in bringing him or her down. Within months of his designation as a Boy Wonder bringing an architectural renaissance to a decaying city's core, he was labeled as an "anti-tenant," "landlord from hell," "exploiter of immigrant workers," "a promise breaker," "an art vandal," "a sorehead," "a conniver," "an anti-black racist," and "a god damn lying son of a bitch."

During the months and years to come, he would be called much, much worse.

Chapter Seven

HOW DONALD BECAME
A GAMBLING CZAR
Saber Rattling with the Heir to the Hilton Legacy

"Welcome Suckers, to Atlantic City—I've Never Gambled in My Life."
—*Donald Trump*

MIKE TYSON
Donald's Hookup with "The Baddest Man on the Planet"

IVANA REJECTS HIS OFFER OF AN
OPEN MARRIAGE, BUT COMPLAINS
"Donald Has Trouble Rising to the Occasion."

EXPENSIVE PLAYTHINGS AND TOYS
The Trump Princess, The Trump Shuttle, &

Mar-a-Lago

By 1870, accessorized with its newly built Boardwalk and bolstered by the publicity associated with the opening of a railway line and a major hotel, Atlantic City had become a resort. That hotel, The United States, was immediately heralded as the largest in the country, with 600 rooms and grounds that sprawled across fourteen acres.

The city didn't enter its Golden Age until the 1920s, when it flourished during Prohibition. Liquor and gambling (both illegal) flowed and flourished in the back rooms of hotels and speakeasies.

For a while, Atlantic City blossomed as "The World's Playground." But with the coming of new kinds of travel options in the jet age, vacationers opted instead for Miami Beach or The Bahamas, and Atlantic City entered a long, tormented decline, plagued with poverty, crime, and corruption. Proud hotels that had once flourished were converted into cheap rentals or nursing homes.

Donald Trump only became interested in Atlantic City when the voters of New Jersey passed a referendum in 1976 that legalized gambling. In 1978, Resorts International opened the first legal casino in the East.

To investigate the possibilities of opening his own casino hotel, Donald made the 120-mile transit from New York City to the Jersey shore, where he was presented with a sad and decrepit sight of

Atlantic City around 1910. Genteel resort escapism from the heat and oppression of the pre-air conditioned age for overheated New Yorkers.

Donald gambled on real estate, not at the gaming tables. He regarded those who did a "suckers," but he gleefully accepted their money when they lost, as most of them invariably did.

boarded-up stores, burned-out buildings, and rot. He likened it to a ghost town filled with people mired in poverty and despair.

But with news that gambling had suddenly been legalized, real estate prices—fueled by speculators—were soaring. As Donald wrote, "Houses that couldn't even fetch $5,000 were selling for $300,000, even $500,000, maybe even a million, depending on location.

He decided to proceed with caution, even though he knew that by delaying, he might end up paying more. But first, he wanted a gambling license. Barron Hilton later made a mistake by building a Hilton, only to find that he'd been denied the license that was essential to make it profitable.

What Donald wanted was "location, location, location. "Actually, he sought the best site at the resort, and he decided that it was a 2 ½ acre plot next to the Depression-era Convention Hall, which he compared architecturally to "a giant cement Quonset hut." His plan involved the construction of a hotel that would be interconnected to the Convention Center by an elevated "skywalk."

The center's main reason for existing seemed to revolve around its role as home port for the annual Miss America Beauty Pageant.

John P. O'Donnell, former president of the Trump Plaza Hotel & Casino, wrote: "Donald Trump came to Atlantic City in the middle of the early boom years. Like the rest, he was seeking new worlds to conquer. He was lured by the same excitement that worked its magic on us all. Primarily, he saw that the income from his New York hotels, even the most luxurious and successful, pales in comparison with the fast and easy cash of a gambling hall."

Some of Donald's jealous rivals said, "He thinks he's some White Knight rescuing Atlantic City, a damsel in distress."

Bypassing the first rush of land speculation, Donald waited until 1980 to move ahead with the acquisition of a building site opening onto the Boardwalk. He noted that both Hugh Hefner of *Playboy* and Bob Guccione of *Penthouse* had failed in their respective attempts to launch casinos there.

By careful maneuvering, and by buying at a time when the casino bubble had temporarily deflated, he set out to assemble a desirable tract of real estate from a medley of different owners, many of whom, it seemed, were suing each other. One by one, Donald negotiated with them, buying one small lot after another and paying the highest price per square foot of any properties previously sold in Atlantic City.

One particularly difficult transaction derived from Vera Coking, a tough landlady who owned the Sea Shell Guest House, perched smack in the center of the location Donald wanted for his casino. Her building might have been valued at around $35,000, but she reportedly wanted $2 million. She had already resisted a takeover attempt by Guccione. Donald's legendary salesmanship was utterly wasted. She called him "a cockroach, a maggot, and a crumb."

She took him to court, and emerged victorious, thwarting his plan to carve out a parking lot for limousines.

Donald was informed that Hefner lost his bid for a gambling license because at a crucial hearing, he had showed up "dressed like a dandy, all in silk, two blonde bimbos on each arm."

For Donald's appearance before the New Jersey Casino Control Commission, he had partnered with his very respectable-looking brother, Robert ("the good Trump"), who had managed to maintain a pristine, long-term business record.

Their hearing before the casino commission lasted two hours, with Donald testifying for only fifteen minutes. According to a later evaluation, he may have "shaded" the truth a bit. But he was granted the gambling license in record time. Other casino operators languished for months waiting for a decision.

In May of 1982, ground was broken on Trump Plaza, envisioned as a hotel/casino complex with an estimated building cost of $220 million. At the time, Donald had only $5,000 in his savings account and about $385,000 in his checking account.

He had approached five New York banks, each of whom had rejected him, each of them cautious of any investment in New Jersey gambling casinos.

A breakthrough came from Manufacturers Hanover Trust: "Manny Hanny came through for me, but I had to personally guarantee the loan."

national park service/jack boucher

Coking House, the home of the very stubborn Vera Coking, became the most disputed real estate in Atlantic City, and the focus of a controversial eminent domain case which was used against Donald by Marco Rubio in their race for the presidency in 2016.

Coking purchased the property at 127 Columbia Place for $20,000 in 1961. In the 1970s, *Penthouse* publisher Bob Guccione offered her $1 million but she turned him down. In 1993, she also refused to sell to Donald Trump, which led to a series of lawsuits.

[The loan was for $170 million. Ironically, a rival hotelier sat on the board of the bank, Barron Hilton, the hotel heir. "There was another condition that the bank imposed," Donald said. "That Barron and I be in love."]

With his gambling license approved, and with financing arranged, Donald moved ahead with his ambitious building plan. It called for thirty-seven floors with 614 bedrooms and a 60,000 square-foot casino.

All of those processes were inaugurated with the understanding that whatever got built would urgently need an entity to operate it after its construction. His problem was solved when a call came in from Michael Rose, chairman of Holiday Inn Hotels and Resorts. He wanted to meet Donald in Atlantic City.

Donald usually towered over most men, but when he met Rose, who measured six feet seven inches, the inverse was the case.

Vera Coking holds up her hands in a victory salute after a court ruling in her favor.

But after greedily holding out for $5 million, the property lost its value during the city's financial crisis of 2007-2008.

Eventually, it was sold at auction in 2014 for $583,000 and demolished.

Together, they hammered out a fifty-fifty partnership wherein Holiday Inn would advance $50 million toward construction, plus a reimbursement to Donald of $22 million in expenses that he had already incurred.

The resort's new name would be Harrah's at Trump Plaza *[at the time, Harrah's was in partnership with Holiday Inns]*, and its opening would be scheduled for May, 1984. The complex would feature seven restaurants, a health club, and a 750-seat showroom.

"Get Frank Sinatra," Donald ordered.

Donald brought Ivana in to decorate the public rooms, which displeased the Holiday Inn executives. One VP attacked "the ponderous chrome fixtures and wall treatment done in a cacophony of bright reds, oranges, yellows, and purples" that she installed.

Donald pronounced it "the most magnificent building in the world." In vivid contrast, a Holiday Inn executive asserted privately, "It looks like a Las Vegas whorehouse, and I should know. I've patronized all of those Nevada bordellos."

Donald's only instruction to Ivana had been "to dazzle the suckers." Subsequently, she created a cocktail lounge called Trump's, and named one of the resort's most upscale restaurants Ivana's. [Specializing in French nouvelle cuisine, it was renamed Ivanka's after the couple's divorce.]

There were other troubles, too, some the result of bad planning. Stairways led to nowhere, and the escalators didn't work. There were huge pillars in the lobby that ruined the vista. Even the slot machines weren't working the first year, and the first alarm system went off "ten million times," an irate executive told *The Wall Street Journal*.

After its opening, Trump Plaza did not generate rave reviews, one critic comparing its stocky silhouette to "two mammoth Edsel radiator grilles set end to end."

A worthless trinket, a nostalgic souvenir of one of many casino hotels that failed in the seas of red ink that engulfed Atlantic City, including some of the casino hotels owned by The Donald.

Donald didn't like his personal guarantee of the loan, and he later got out of it by persuading Bear, Stearns & Company, a prominent Wall Street investment firm, to float a privately placed bond issue. This resulted in Donald getting a $353 million mortgage bond issue. Not only did he get one-hundred percent financing and a release from his personal guarantee of the original loan, but a $5 million personal fee, too.

Holiday Inn soon expressed displeasure with the revenue generated by their new resort, evaluating it as the second-lowest of any hotel in Atlantic City.

Rose was later quoted as saying, "My goal was to make money for Holiday Inn shareholders, whereas Donald wanted to bag millions for himself. Perhaps a clash was inevitable."

At the time of his dealings with Holiday Inn executives, Donald was said to be taking a controlled substance. Tenuate Dospan, something "pharmacologically similar to amphetamines." The drug had been prescribed to him by an endocrinologist, Dr. Joseph Greenberg, as a means of controlling his weight.

Within five months, the Harrah's name was removed, and the resort became known as Trump Plaza. "The original name was associated with too many low-rolling gamblers, and we wanted a better class," Donald said.

In 1989, the East Tower opened, thereby raising the room count to 906.

The honeymoon with Holiday Inn was short and not sweet. The two different managements conflicted on an almost daily basis. Donald claimed that he brought the construction of the building in on time and under budget, but Holiday counter-charged that he ran "tens of millions of dollar over the agreed-upon price." Almost violent arguments ensued on every detail of the operation.

After all these disagreements, Donald finally bought out Holiday Inn's interest in the resort. It was now his to do with as he wished.

[By 2014, Donald retained only ten percent owners of Trump Entertainment Resorts, which owned the Trump Taj Mahal and Trump Plaza. He filed a lawsuit to get his name removed from the Plaza, since he was no longer its sole owner. In 2014, Trump Entertainment Resorts entered Chapter 11 bankruptcy and closed Trump Plaza indefinitely, laying off some 1,000 employees.]

***

With all the work she was doing for Donald's enterprises, Ivana demanded that another pre-nuptial agreement be drawn up. Once again, in the presence of Roy Cohn, on May 25, 1984, a revised version of the pre-nup was signed by both parties. It would grant her $2.5 million in the event of a divorce, plus their country estate in Greenwich.

In appreciation for drawing up the revised deal, Donald presented Cohn with a diamond-studded Tiffany watch. Later, this luxurious gift was reportedly stolen one night by a male hustler.

Cohn later confided to agent Jay Garon, his cruising buddy, that Donald's passion for Ivana had cooled after she gave birth to their last child, Eric. "Donald is sexually indifferent to her and mocks her behind her back," Cohn claimed. "He told me he'd proposed an 'open marriage' to her and that she had refused. He would allow her to take on all the studs she wanted, whereas he could have any of the beautiful young women who pursued him relentlessly. She said no to all his deals. I expect a divorce lies in their future. I'll be his lawyer."

Roy Cohn, the most larcenous and terror-inducing lawyer New York ever produced.

FOOTBALLING WITH DONALD

Trump Buys the New Jersey Generals and Sues the NFL

Donald's winning streak came to an end in September of 1983. He summoned the New York press to the atrium of Trump Tower to hype his latest purchase, the New Jersey Generals, a relatively untested franchise of the United States Football League (USFL) which had begun playing that year. Some members of the press had mocked USFL, claiming its initials stood for "Unusually Stupid Football League."

In marked contrast to the teams of the more deeply entrenched NFL (National Football League), whose autumn games were televised before millions of TV viewers, the Generals played in the spring.

Donald, who wanted the USFL to stage its football games in the autumn, too, received a lot of press coverage when he announced that he was suing the NFL. He claimed, "My team could beat hell out of some of those loser NFL teams. Many of their players should play touch football against the Kennedys, but they'd probably lose."

Although he would be dead before the case was tried, Roy Cohn filed the lawsuit on October 17, 1984. Charging the NFL with monopolistic practices, he asked for damages of $1.32 billion.

To beef up his team, Donald hired Herschel Walker, a former Heisman Trophy winner, as his chief player. Donald also signed Lawrence Taylor, the linebacker for the New York Giants, offering him a $3.2 million contract.

For the players' uniforms, Donald turned to Ivana who came up with the team colors of white, scarlet, royal blue, and sunflower gold. The logo of the team became a gold wreath inspired by something that might be awarded to a military commander. Her most controversial rule was to forbid the players from dating the cheerleaders. That command made her very unpopular with the footballers.

By the end of the team's first full season, in June of 1984, Donald came to realize that he'd made a bad investment.

He lost $5 million, an amount that contributed to an overall deficit of $14 million since he had first acquired the team. He referred to his purchase of the Generals as "hemorrhaging."

Even though he'd lost money since purchasing the team, his exposure to millions of sports fans had made him more famous than ever.

But instead of admitting that the Generals were a losing proposition, he announced that his team was worth $60 million.

Cohn, who had been suffering from complications associated with AIDS for the previous two years, was in denial, trying to convince such friends as Barbara Walters that he had liver cancer. Almost until the end of his life, he carried on with both his sexual and legal affairs.

On March 1, 1986, Ivana and Donald threw a spectacular party in his honor at Mar-a-Lago in Palm Beach. When he showed up, it was immediately obvious to the other guests that Cohn was desperately ill. Nonetheless, he brought his male companion, Jay Taylor, who had grown up on a farm in New Zealand. Taylor was introduced to such luminaries as Lee Iacocca, the

Herschel Walker, a newly minted player for the NJ Generals, is officially welcomed to the new football league by Donald.

In 1984 and 1985, a manufacturer of sports memorabilia and trading cards (Topps.com) produced what are now collectors' items, souvenirs of Donald Trump's short-lived United States Football League.

Whereas Jim Kelly, Steve Young, Reggie White and Herschel Walker would achieve superstardom with the NFL, the souvenirs that commemorate their links to the USFL are marketed today as collectible objects of nostalgic value.

Souvenirs like those displayed above are all that remains from Donald's financially disastrous dabbling in the world of professional football.

chairman of Chrysler.

By the time Donald's complaint against the NFL went to court, Cohn was dead. Donald's replacement lawyer faced a bevy of high-paid, major-league attorneys from the NFL. They painted a picture of him as a "vicious, greedy, Machiavellian billionaire, intent only on serving his selfish ends at the expense of everyone else."

The case had gone to trial in May of 1986, with a verdict rendered on July 9. The jury found the NFL guilty of willfully acquiring or maintaining a monopoly on football games. However, to Donald's dismay, the league was fined only one dollar. He immediately announced that he would appeal the court's decision.

From 1983 to 1986, Donald lost $22 million because of his investment in the Generals. As he put it, "It was time to get out of Dodge."

The USFL suspended its operations in August of 1986, and the Generals never played another game.

"The sports business is a lousy business," Donald told *Playboy*.

THE ART OF THE DEAL:
How to Beat a Rival? Buy Him Out

In 1984, a rival hotelier, Barron Hilton, set out to establish a "beachhead" in what was by now known as "the economic war zone" of Atlantic City. His name was famous around the world as the socialite heir to Conrad Hilton. His brother, Nicky Hilton, had married a young Elizabeth Taylor, and his father had been famously wed to Zsa Zsa Gabor, the blonde bombshell from Budapest.

One of Barron's grandchildren, Paris Hilton, is better known today than her grandfather.

Barron had already waded into the gambling casino quagmire in 1972, when he purchased two Nevada casinos (the Flamingo Hilton and the Las Vegas Hilton) for $12 million. By 1985, these two moneymakers accounted for forty-five percent of all Hilton hotel revenue. The eyes of this Dallas-born Texan turned eastward, focusing on Atlantic City, where he would become a Johnny-come-lately in the casino sweepstakes.

Many of his competitors had already established glittering citadels there, attracting high rollers, including the Sands, Harrah's, Bally's, Caesars, and the Golden Nugget. Once he decided to become a player in Atlantic

City, Barron moved swiftly, too swiftly.

In distinct contrast to the placement of Donald's 2 ½-acre building site on the Boardwalk, Hilton acquired a fourteen-acre site near Atlantic City's marina. His Atlantic City Hilton would be the largest undertaking in the history of the Hilton Empire.

His hotel rose twenty-six stories, with 703 guest rooms. It included a thirty-foot high atrium and a nine-story parking garage for 3,000 vehicles. Its gaming hall sprawled a mammoth 60,000 square feet.

Even before it opened, Barron envisioned an even grander plan that would eventually include an additional 2,000 accommodations.

But in his rush to join his rivals, Hilton made a costly mistake: Assuring his shareholders that procuring a gambling license from the Casino Board of New Jersey would be merely a formality after submission of the extensive paperwork, he launched construction before he had a gambling license in hand. In marked contrast, Donald delayed construction until he had a gambling license in hand.

Barron Hilton was the heir to a great hotel chain named after his illustrious father, Conrad Hilton.

In a surprise move in Atlantic City, Barron was denied a gaming license because of his alleged links to organized crime. Everyone was shocked   except Donald, who "moved in for the kill."

It was assumed that Barron and Donald were avowed business enemies, but, if that were so, why did Donald name his son with Melania Barron?

Like Donald, Barron had also morphed into a prominent figure in the sports world. He'd been a founding partner in the American Football League, and the original owner of the San Diego Chargers.

It came as a heart-wrenching shock to Barron when the New Jersey casino commissioners refused to grant him a gambling license. Their decision, they reported, was based on Hilton's link to Sidney Korshak, an attorney rumored to have established links to the mob. Throughout the previous decade, Barron had paid Korshak $50,000 annually to help resolve labor disputes.

When it had become increasingly clear that a gambling license for the new Hilton resort would not be approved, Barron fired Korshak, but it was too late. As one of the commissioners told the press, "Hilton didn't get religion until he was already pounding on the Pearly Gates."

Barron—enraged, embittered, and berated by his shareholders—was in a horrible position. He'd been so certain that he'd be granted a license that he had announced the gala opening of his resort in three months, and had already hired 4,000 employees. Not only that, but he had ruinously invested $320 million Hilton dollars in the resort's construction and development.

Hoping to benefit from Barron's failure, Donald called him in San Francisco. After some polite small talk, Donald came to the point: "If you want to throw in the towel, you can toss it to me. I might buy you out if the price is right."

Barron didn't rush to accept the offer, because he was hoping that he would be able to reverse the commission's decision and nab a gambling license after all. He told Donald, "Thanks for the offer. I'll get back to you...maybe."

In Manhattan, Donald met Barron for the first time at the townhouse of Ben Lambert, who sat on the Hilton board of directors. Donald discussed a possible purchase of the Atlantic City Hilton with Barron, who seemed cautious, not anxious to enter into a deal.

"I played it low-key," Donald claimed.

Suddenly, Steve Wynn, a kingpin in the casino and hotel industry, entered the picture in a threatening sort of way. He

Zsa Zsa Gabor, the 'Bombshell from Budapest," was once married to Conrad Hilton, the hotel chain's founder. During her ill-fated marriage, she spent more time in bed with her son-in-law, Nicky Hilton, than she did with her husband. This occurred during Nicky's marriage to Elizabeth Taylor.

Zsa Zsa's love affairs ranged from Prince Aly Khan to John F., Kennedy, and she had eight husbands. She confided to her mother, Jolie, that she planned to make Donald Trump her upcoming husband, but somehow her plan went astray.

Donald told an aide, "I was born in 1946. A woman born in 1917, or even earlier, is more a great-grandmother than a wife."

was known for both his Las Vegas and Atlantic City casinos, one of which was the Golden Nugget. *Forbes* magazine listed the art collector as one of the richest Americans.

Wynn was threatening a takeover of Hilton stock, which made Barron much more eager to listen to Donald's proposition. Wynn cut an impressive figure in his $3,000 suits and silk shirts, and could easily have made the best-dressed list along with the richest.

With at least part of his childhood spent in upstate New York, Wynn had grown up in and around his father's string of bingo parlors. According to legend, perhaps unfounded, Wynn had learned to play poker when he was five.

Capitalizing on Barron's fear of a Wynn takeover, Donald offered $250 million for the Atlantic City Hilton, eventually raising that bid to $320 million. That was the exact amount Barron had invested. Whereas he would not make a profit if he sold to Donald, he would at least recover his bad investment.

Amazingly, when Donald made that offer, he had never set foot inside the Hilton property, then in its final stages of construction. "Before buying a property, my father inspected every nook and cranny," Donald said. "If I'd told him I'd offered $320 million for a hotel without going inside to inspect it, he would have thought I was out of my mind."

For his final "art of dealmaking," Donald assessed his biggest advantage. "Barron wanted to get the hell out of Atlantic City and leave the nightmare behind him."

After many tense negotiations, with the Hilton lawyers sometimes walking out of their shared meetings, Donald closed the deal. At last, and for the first time, and as its new owner, he walked into the unfinished building, and was impressed with its solid construction. [He later uncovered some problems that had to be corrected.]

He renamed it the Trump Palace, a name it retained until Caesars Palace threatened to sue. He then renamed it Trump Castle. He had received the funds for its purchase from Manufacturers Hanover's board of directors, a loan that

Steve Wynn threatened both Donald and Barron Hilton when he tried to take over the entire Hilton Hotel chain just as Donald was trying to buy Barron's Atlantic City property.

Donald feared that Wynn might dominate Atlantic City with a gaming complex big enough to devour the lion's share of the profits.

was backed by his personal guarantee, but he wanted to get himself off that hook as soon as possible. [The Castle had to meet a debt service of $40 million annually.]

In pursuit of that goal, in that era of easy credit and go-go financing (an era which abruptly, and disastrously ended with the beginning of the Great Recession in 2008), he was able to make a deal with Bear, Stearns on Wall Street to float a bond issue that would replace his own bank financing from "Manny Hanny."

"Bear Stearns did a fabulous job. I got a good deal. So did the bondholders."

With financing settled, Donald made what seemed a rash decision to some Atlantic City operators. He appointed Ivana as manager of the hotel and its casino, even though she had no experience at running such a vast operation.

***

Arriving in Atlantic City by helicopter after the dust from the acquisition had settled, Ivana immediately established her authority. "She was a slave driver, inspecting every corner," said an employee. "She lashed out if she found anything wrong. A pile of garbage in the hall, a waitress who looked sloppy—it seemed that every sentence that came out of her mouth used the word 'fucking.' I'm sure she learned that from Donald."

She viewed herself differently. "I'm a lady and I run the hotel with dignity. My managers aren't afraid of me. That hideous rumor is unfounded."

From the first day and night of its operation, during which it took in

"Ivanarama!" was sweeping the land, as evoked by this cover shot of a gummy Ivana on the cover of *Spy* magazine.

When Donald put her in charge of his big resort and casino there, she set out to become "The Queen of Atlantic City." The hotel she managed had actually been built by the Hilton hotel chain, and picked up by Donald after the refusal of the gaming commission to grant Hilton a license.

By the time she reached Atlantic City, her "fiery presence and explosive temper were already a legend."

around $750,000, Trump Castle was a roaring success. Before end of 1985, six months later, Donald had grossed $130 million. Under Ivana's management, the casino, in 1986 (the first full year of its operation), brought Donald gross revenues of $225 million.

"I never abuse my authority," Ivana maintained. "My job is to inspire and motivate an employee to do his or her best. In dealing with the maids, I found that a gift of languages was necessary. So few of them spoke English."

"I have a lot of energy, and I love to work," she said. "There's not a lazy bone in my body. Of course, I had no experience in running a casino hotel. People under me often resented that. But I was doing a great job, and I think that after a few months, had won their respect. My feeling is this: If you're thrown into the ocean, you swim or you drown. Donald gave me the chance. He knew I would emerge as a champion swimmer."

"I felt like the mayor of a small town," Ivana continued, "governing 4,000 employees and welcoming 10,000 guests a day, with a weekly payroll of $1.2 million. From the laundry room to the dressing room of the showgirls, I ran a tight ship. Nothing escaped my eagle eye. No one was going to call me a pussycat, or, God forbid, a blonde Playboy bimbo."

"She cracked down on the waitresses," one of the headwaiters said. "She designed their uniforms. She would not hire any gal with a nose ring. She demanded that the gals sweep their hair up off their foreheads in a modified 'Ivana cut' like her own."

A reporter once asked Ivana, "Are you a gambler?"

"Perhaps on life itself," she answered. "But not at the gambling table. I'd rather buy a pair of stylish shoes."

On her TV show, *20/20*, Barbara Walters asked Ivana what her salary was.

"One dollar a year," she an-

Donald Trump's lawyer, Roy Cohn, was best friends with Barbara Walters, who was already a TV legend when Donald was introduced to her.

During a Christmas vacation, Donald was invited to Walters' home in Aspen to celebrate New Year's Eve. He was overheard telling her his wish for the coming year. "I wish I had another Merv Griffin to bat around."

swered, "and all the dresses I can buy."

When that interview was broadcast, a cry arose from feminists across the country about inequality in pay between men and women.

But Donald later defended himself: "When I got her dress bill for the year, I realized she was paid a vast amount, at least as much as the annual budget of Nepal."

During the first three months of 1987, Trump Castle, based on its gross operating profits, emerged as number one in Atlantic City. But during the seasons that followed, as monthly revenues fell by between 2.9% and 9.4%, Donald didn't like the bottom line.

"It's time for Ivana to go," he said. "But she's going to a better position, so it's not like I'm kicking her out on her highly perfumed ass. I'm going to make her the president of the Plaza Hotel in Manhattan."

Although many employees had interpreted her style as dictatorial, others lined up to say goodbye and wish her well on the day of her departure. Many had tears in their eyes. Ivana made a graceful exit, as her eyes misted. Donald trailed dutifully behind.

To fill her post, Donald named Stephen Hyde, who was also the president of Trump Plaza on the Boardwalk. He was so very different from Ivana. A tough Westerner and outdoorsman from the wilds of Utah, he was a recognized expert at running casino hotels.

When Ivana was asked for her opinion of her replacement, she reportedly said, "He's nothing but a big fat piece of shit."

Freed of Atlantic City, Ivana enjoyed a lifestyle that prompted some to define her as "an empress."

She began one well-scruti-

On July 6, 2016, almost 30 years after the inauguration of the Trump Plaza, while memories of its collapse and failure were still raw, Hillary Clinton delivered a campaign speech from a symbolically devastating postion in front of the remains of Donald Trump's ruined dream.

Her widely televised denunciation highlighted what she called Trump's "fraudulent business history."

nized and widely chronicled day with her hairdresser, manicurist, and pedi-curist, before taking friends to Paris aboard Donald's private plane.

There, as *Women's Wear Daily* reported, she was spotted at the *haute cou-ture* houses of Paris, perhaps being fitted for a $20,000 Chanel suit. That might be followed by dinner with the Rothschilds at Lassere.

A day later, she flew back to Palm Beach to receive weekend guests at Mar-a-Lago. Then it was back to the Plaza Hotel in Manhattan to supervise its restoration.

[The future of Trump Castle would not move gracefully toward a golden age. It was taken over by Trump Entertainment Resorts, and by 1997, it was renamed Trump Marina. When Trump Entertainment entered bankruptcy, Landry's, Inc. (a conglomerate comprising more than 500 restaurants and hotels) purchased the property for only $38 million, wresting control of it in May, 2011, and renaming it the Golden Nugget Atlantic City.

A staggering $150 million was needed to repair it. Renovations were finished by the spring of 2012. New restaurants were configured within, as well as a health club and an outdoor pool.

The glory years of the reign of Ivana and Donald—previously known as the Empress and White Knight of Atlantic City, respectively—became a distant mem-ory.]

DONALD IN THE RING
The Troubled, Tragic Story of Mike Tyson

As unbelievable as it sounds, Donald Trump for several months became a sort of "mentor" to the deeply troubled and conflicted Mike Tyson, the undisputed world heavyweight boxing champion. For twenty years, the fighter known as "Iron Mike," "Kid Dynamite," and "The Baddest Man on the Planet," held the record as the youngest boxer to win the WBC, WBA, and IBF titles.

On October 16, 1987, Donald entered the murky world of boxing. He launched his involvement in Atlantic City, where he hosted the heavy-weight championship fight that pitted Tyson, then a rising star, against Tyrell Biggs.

Biggs, a 6'5" giant, had won a gold medal at the 1984 Olympic Games in the super heavyweight division. After that, he became a pro, scoring a six-round unanimous decision over Mike Evans on November 15, 1984 at

Manhattan's Madison Square Garden in his first bout.

As arranged by Donald at the Atlantic City Convention Center, Biggs' biggest pro fight would be against Tyson for the latter's heavyweight title. Days before the event, Tyson and Biggs had made their distaste for each other known to sports writers. Biggs was loud and, according some, venomous, in his pre-fight mockery of Tyson. Donald's publicist billed the fight as "The Clash for the Crown."

Just before the fight, Donald descended into the lobby of the Trump Plaza, immediately next door to the Convention Center with its boxing ring, to greet and be photographed with such visiting celebrities as Robert De Niro, Sugar Ray Leonard, James Caan, and Dustin Hoffman.

Other than real estate or women, Donald's consuming passion had become boxing. Ivana viewed the sport as "barbaric." It seemed that he had come to view it as a metaphor for his own career, where he symbolically met his ri-

Givens and Tyson—for a while, until it all blew up—were the most-watched, most-discussed couple in the world.

The cover of Sports Illustrated asked "Will Love and Marriage (and His Mother-in-Law) K.O. Mike Tyson?"

vals in a ring for battles over control of his ever-growing real estate empire.

Of course, even as a young athlete, he'd never had any interest in entering a ring himself. As he told Stephen Hyde, manager of the Trump Plaza, "Who but an idiot would want to be punched in the face by some iron fist? I wouldn't want to put on a boxer's jersey trunks for one fucking minute!"

After the opening bell, using fancy footwork and his "jab," Biggs tried to outbox Tyson. But Tyson seemed to be winning right from the beginning, landing big punch after big punch, gradually wearing Biggs down. The referee halted the match in the seventh round, declaring Tyson the winner. Tyson later claimed he deliberately extended the fight to wear down a battered Biggs and to inflict as much physical damage as possible to avenge his pre-match lambasts.

When it was over, Donald was delighted when the boxing fans swarmed into his next door casino, where his nightly gross shot up by thirty percent.

After that, Donald became acutely aware of how much money could be made from Tyson, although other greedy eyes were also moving in on the boxer. Tyson's "temper and tantrums" had already been widely publicized, his condition later diagnosed as "bipolar."

Trump went on to plan a series of even bigger bouts for Tyson. On the evening of June 27, 1988, he staged a match between the champ and Michael Spinks, an African American from St. Louis, a former Olympic gold medalist and world champion in both the light heavyweight and heavyweight divisions.

In the immediate aftermath of his Olympic victory, Spinks had returned to his job at a chemical factory in Missouri, "scrubbing floors and cleaning toilets." But by 1977, he decided to turn pro. With amazing speed, he went from one victory to another.

Don King, the boxing promoter with the "Electric Shock Coif," was flamboyant and combative.

John R. O'Donnell, former President of Trump Plaza Hotel & Casino, claimed that King "was a brash and overt bigot, hammering away at Tyson with one compelling message: 'Don't trust the white Man!'"

But on that June night in Atlantic City, his winning streak came to an embarrassing end. Some 21,000 fans packed themselves into the city's Convention Hall, where ringside seats cost $1,500. Millions of sports fans watched on TV.

For sponsorship rights to this historic bout, Donald had entered a bidding war with gambling kingpin Steve Wynn. "Get the god damn fight," Donald had ordered his subordinates. "Don't fuck around. Do anything to beat Wynn's ass."

Donald won, but had to shell out $11 million, the most expensive price tag for a boxing match in the history of the sport. To the press, he announced that the Tyson/Spinks fight "will be a bellweather day in the history of Atlantic City."

But then, to his intense disappointment, he watched in amazement as Tyson scored a knockout in just ninety-one seconds. According to Donald, "The damn fight ended before it had even begun. Some people were just taking their seats. In homes around America, guys were just opening their first can of Bud, sitting down for some gladiator combat worthy of a Roman emperor."

With a speed and single-mindedness that boxing fans recall years later as memorable, Tyson, with his "fist of steel," had moved menacingly toward Spinks, "giving him a left hook that could be heard in Alaska" and sending him sprawling backward. He fell against the ropes before he dropped dazed and defeated to the floor. Angry fans loudly denounced the fight as a "bomb."

After a record thirty-one wins, Spinks had lost. He retired from boxing the following night, an inglorious end to an otherwise fabulous career. In the history of boxing, he remains the only

One of the greatest punchers of all time, Michael Spinks—as arranged by Donald Trump—got into the ring with Mike Tyson.

Some fans had looked forward to it as "The Fight of the Century." But in just 91 seconds, Tyson delivered the killer KO, much to the disappointment of fans who were screaming for a gladiatorial combat that would have delighted the bloodthirsty Caligula.

reigning light heavyweight to win the heavyweight title, and *Ring* magazine listed him among the 100 greatest punchers of all time.

In spite of the quick KO, Donald was delighted when fans flocked to his next door casino, shelling out $18 million in losses before midnight. Even Donald's competitors benefitted from the fight's overflow crowds. That night, Atlantic City recorded the highest grosses in the city's history.

As regards profits from the fight, Donald "cleaned up" as he phrased it, having sold pay-for-view TV rights and making other subsidiary deals. As a sum-total, that evening's one-minute fight brought in $470 million for him, the highest-grossing event in the history of boxing.

Ivana presided over a victory party for Tyson in her hotel's Imperial Ballroom. When it wound down, she was seen leaving in a limousine headed back to her lavish suite at Trump Castle.

Long after midnight, Donald, too, was seen leaving in a limousine—but not with Ivana. He was making his first public appearance with Marla Maples, a stunning blonde model. Apparently, her escort that evening, Tom Fitzsimmons, was now her ex-boyfriend.

Earlier that evening, at the fight, "the Georgia Peach" had been seen with Fitzsimmons, who'd been rumored to be her lover.

Two weeks after Tyson's victory over Spinks, Donald held a press conference at Trump Plaza, announcing the formation of Tyson Enterprises, of which he would be a board member. Other members of the board would include Tyson's attorney, Michael Winston, and the boxer's dynamic mother-in-law, Ruth Roper.

In 1988, the boxer had entered into an ill-fated marriage to an African American beauty, Robin Givens, a New Yorker who starred in the role of Darlene Merriman in ABC's hit sitcom, *Head of the Class*. The series would have a five-year run. Her short marriage (they divorced the following year) would be marred by violence, lawsuits, countercharges, and massive publicity. Tyson would leave the marriage considerably poorer.

Donald told the press, "I am a friend of Mike's, and I want to see that he has a substantial future, and that he's not taken advantage of."

Givens and her mother were not the only ones profiting from Tyson's knockouts in the ring. Donald met another Donald, Don King, Tyson's boxing promoter.

King, an African American whose hair stood up on his head as if it had received an electric shock, was spectacularly flamboyant, perhaps the most controversial boxing promoter in the history of the sport. He would leave an indelible mark on the history of boxing when he staged some of the sport's most historic matches.

Tyson wasn't the only boxer promoted by King: His other champions included Muhammad Ali, Joe Frazier, Larry Holmes, George Foreman, and Evander Holyfield, among others. Almost all of them would sue King on charges that he defrauded them. Avoiding litigation in the courts, King settled, out of court, lawsuit after lawsuit, sometimes with eight-digit payoffs, to avoid conviction for felony fraud or time in prison.

In the beginning, when the boxing champ still trusted him, King had said to Tyson, "Never trust a white man, and I mean Donald Trump, who is lilywhite."

Bill Clayton, Tyson's former manager, told Donald, "Mike is suffering from the Patty Hearst syndrome. He's fallen in love with his captor," a reference, of course, to Don King.

King wanted to curtail the possibility of money grabs from Givens and her mother, whom he collectively described as "a greedy pair of tarantulas out to grab Mike's money." He went from bank to bank with Tyson, cutting off their access to his accounts. [He managed, in the nick of time, to stop a payment to "Robin Givens Productions" for $600,000, issued as a "reimbursement of expenses."

[In time, Tyson, too, would turn on King, denouncing him as "a wretched, slimy, reptilian motherfucker. He is supposed to be my black brother, right? He's just a bad man, a real bad man. He would kill his own mother for a dollar. He's ruthless, he's deplorable, he's greedy, and he doesn't know how to love anybody."

Eventually, Tyson would sue King for $100 million, alleging that the promoter cheated him out of millions for more than a decade. The case was settled out of court for $14 million.]

***

At first, Donald tried to pacify King and get along with him. When King called Stephen Hyde, the manager at The Plaza, and requested thirty (free) rooms for use over the course of a weekend for members of his entourage, Hyde phoned his boss for authorization. Donald responded, "Give the fucker the rooms," and Hyde reluctantly acquiesced.

Then King called again. "My boys have increased. I now need forty rooms."

Although he deeply resented the promoter's greed, Hyde was once again forced to go along. From all reports, King and Hyde never got along. At one point, King accused him of "treating me niggardly," making the words sound like a racial slur.

Unknown to Donald, King had hired a private detective to gather reports on any clandestine intimacies between Donald and Tyson's wife, Robin Givens.

Disgruntled members of Donald's hotel staff had reported that Givens and Donald were often seen together after Tyson had retired, exhausted from his training, for the night. "The Donald is playing with fire," one of them asserted.

As rumors spread, Donald denied any sexual involvement with Givens. He told his aides, "Get serious. I'd be crazy to have something going on with the wife of the world's heavyweight champion. That's a good way to get killed, and Mike's the guy to do it."

In his biography of Donald Trump, *The Lost Tycoon*, author Harry Hurt III confronted rumors about the Trump/Givens affair:

> *"According to Montieth Illingworth, associates of Don King told Tyson that they had overheard Donald complaining that Givens was 'inept at oral sex.'*
>
> *'She's got the sharpest teeth in the world,' Donald was alleged to have said. It was also claimed that Donald advised Givens to change her address to California so that she would be entitled to that state's Community Property Law when, as it appeared, divorce was inevitable."*

According to an unconfirmed report, the detective hired by King revealed that he had gathered evidence that Donald and Givens had spent a night aboard his yacht, *Trump Princess*.

One night during the most troubled period of his marriage, Tyson phoned Donald. Donald wrote that Tyson was "completely coming apart at the seams. I told him he had to get a grip on himself."

"Mr. Trump," Tyson said. "You've got to understand something. I just love that fucking bitch."

As Donald had predicted, the Givens/Tyson union eventually collapsed. Appearing on Barbara Walters *20/20* TV talk show, the actress claimed that life with Tyson was "torture, pure hell, worse than anything one could possibly imagine." She went on to define him as a manic depressive.

Their divorce was finalized on Valentine's Day, February 14, 1989.

***

It was around this time that Donald moved from boxing promoter to producer, based on his formation of Trump Sports and Entertainment as a branch of his Trump Organization. He named Mark Grossinger Etess as president, asking him to develop big projects, such as engaging superstars like the Rolling Stones for concerts in Atlantic City. He was also instructed to stage big wrestling events there, too.

Aides claimed that Etess and Donald were quite close, and that Donald treated him almost like a surrogate son. His family owned Grossinger's, a fabulous resort in the Catskills, that often attracted big name stars. In the past, they had included Eddie Fisher and Elizabeth Taylor while he was still married to Debbie Reynolds.

On July 21, 1989, Donald announced his sponsorship of another Tyson boxing match at the Atlantic City Convention Center, which he rented for $2.1 million for the night.

The champ would face off against Carl ("The Truth") Williams. The Florida-born boxer was the USBA United States Heavyweight Boxing Champion. He had had already fought in several notable matches earlier in the decade.

Mark Grossinger Etess, the scion of a fabled resort in the Catskills, became one of Donald's most trusted aides.

Although he was called "a born showman with tremendous energy and ambition," he would die tragically in a helicopter crash.

As one sports writer recorded about the Tyson/Williams match: "Williams fought and lost to Tyson in a battle for the heavyweight championship. The first round knockout loss to Tyson was a devastating defeat for him. Midway through the round, Tyson slipped a jab from Williams and loaded up with one of the most devastating counter punches of his career, smashing Williams and sending him down for an eight count."

"The referee waved off the fight, and Williams immediately launched a protest to the official ringside judges, but to no avail. He demanded a rematch, which never occurred."

Carl "The Truth" Williams, one of the most underrated heavyweights of our time.

144

Spectators were angered and disappointed. Since the fight had lasted only two seconds longer than the Tyson/Spinks bout, some of them demanded (unsuccessfully) for a refund of their tickets.

Years later, in Manhattan on September 11, 2001, Williams was working as a security guard at the World Trade Center when two highjacked airplanes crashed into the sides of the Twin Towers, bringing them down in a crash that would change the world forever. Williams survived, but died in 2013 of esophageal cancer. He never recovered from the pain of "my unfair loss to the Tyson monster."

***

Based on setbacks associated with the Williams/Tyson fight, Donald suffered a loss of $1.2 million, and his preoccupation with Tyson faded. He watched as he went on to defend his championship with victories over Larry Holmes, a fighter known as "the Easton Assassin," after his home town of Easton, Pennsylvana. His left jab had been evaluated as among the best in boxing history.

Tyson's luck ran out in 1990 when he lost his titles to underdog James ("Buster") Douglas, through a knockout in Round Ten.

From afar, Donald watched Tyson descend into a living hell. In 1992, he was convicted of raping Desirée Washington, a contestant in the Miss Black America contest. Tyson was sentenced to six years in prison, but released after serving a term of three years.

He attempted multiple comebacks fights, the most notorious in 1997, when he faced boxer Evander Holyfield, known as both "The Real Deal" and "The Warrior."

"The Bite Fight" as it came to be known, took place on June 28, 1997.

During its third round, Tyson bit Holyfield's ear. Although two points were deducted from his

Donald looked on from afar, and with a certain sense of horror, as he watched his ear-biting friend, Mike Tyson, descend into a kind of hell.

To make matters really horrific, Desirée Washington, a contestant in the Miss Black America Pageant , accused him of rape, for which the boxing champ would serve three years in prison.

score, the fight continued. Then Tyson bit Holyfield on the other ear, his sharp teeth ripping off a section of the ear known as the helix. Then, in front of the televised view of millions, he spat the bit of bloody flesh out onto the canvas. He was disqualified, and a *melée* ensued.

Tyson retired from boxing in 2006, having declared bankruptcy three years before. During his career, he'd made some $300 million, all of which had been scooped up by others. He was $25 million in debt and admitted that "I'm living from paycheck to paycheck." Then, as part of a religious conversion, he self-defined as a Muslim, saying, "I need Allah!"

Despite his setbacks, and based on his skill, he was inducted into the International Boxing Hall of Fame.

In 2015, when Donald announced his bid for the presidency, Tyson said, "I'm for this guy. I want to see him in the White House. He'll put this country back on the fast track. I bet in his first month in office, he'll score a KO."

TRUMP AND HIS PRINCESS

A Bargain Basement Price for a World-Class Yacht
from an International Arms Dealer &
the Sultan of Brunei

As befits his new status as a multi-millionaire, Donald acquired something associated only with the upper one-half of one percent of the world's population. He bought a yacht. And not just any yacht. It was a 281-foot super yacht originally commissioned in 1980 by Adnan Khashoggi for a staggering cost of $100 million. For its interior décor, a decorating enterprise adorned it lavishly, "sparing no expense."

Khashoggi named it *Nabila* in honor of his daughter. It was later featured in the James Bond thriller, *Never Say Never Again*. In the film, it was cast as *Flying Saucer*, the oceangoing headquarters of the film's implacable villain.

Eight years later, after Khashoggi experienced some financial setbacks, he sold it to the Sultan of Brunei. Shortly after its acquisition, the Sultan opted to get rid of it as soon as possible.

Donald had always defined Khashoggi as "one of the world's great brokers. No one is better at bullshit than this guy, who knows how to party and how to schmooze. He uses wine, women, and wild times to amass billions of dollars' worth of deals."

Born in Mecca, Saudi Arabia, in 1935, to a family of Turkish and Syrian ancestry, Khashoggi was worth up to $10 billion at the peak of his power and wealth during the early 1980s.

He became infamous as an arms dealer, brokering deals between U.S. firms and the Saudi government. Beginning in 1970, and lasting for five years, Lockheed shelled out $106 million to him in commissions. During the Reagan administration, he was implicated in the Iran-Contra affair as a key middleman in the arms-for-hostages exchange.

Before purchasing the yacht, Donald inspected every nut and bolt of the five-deck "pleasure palace," finding a disco, a cinema, a helipad, a swimming pool, and eleven of the most opulent suites of any ship afloat. It even had an emergency operating theater. "I reserved that for my most serious operations," Donald said: "Like breast reductions, as I hate plastic tits." [*Of course, he was joking.*]

Donald went on to discover that during his hasty departure, Khashoggi had left behind precious items crafted from gold, silver, and porcelain.

Rechristened as the *Trump Princess*, the yacht traveled at a top speed of twenty knots, and required a crew of forty-eight to sail it. It held enough fuel to cruise across the Atlantic twice and the Pacific once.

During his tour of the vessel, Donald learned some of the sexual secrets of Khashoggi. In addition to the huge kitchens and wine cellars, there were concealed one-way mirrors for

There's been plenty of Trump commerce with Muslims, including (top left) the Sultan of Brunei, and (top right) Saudi arms dealer Adnan Khashoggi.

Acquired through these power brokers, the *Trump Princess* came into Donald's posession, along with its concealed one-way mirrors for voyeurs and secret doors for off-the-record seductions.

147

voyeurs and secret doors that allowed someone to slip into and out of a stateroom for off-the-record seductions that presumably might go unnoticed by other guests or members of the crew.

A member of the crew directed Donald to the master bedroom, whose giant bed comfortably slept six. "I've seen as many as six gorgeous women and one man in action on that bed," the aide said. The bedroom sprawled beneath an elegant tortoiseshell ceiling.

Donald called the Princess "the ultimate party boat. Eat your heart out, Ari Onassis."

When Ivana came aboard, Donald thought she would prefer the spectacular Diamond Suite. Its décor included starbursts of patterned onyx on the floors and walls. Its features included an elaborate "grooming station," and a bathroom whose shape was inspired by an oversized scallop with lavish sheathings of black onyx.

Instead, she preferred the smaller Sapphire Suite, whose mammoth bathtub—fed by two waterfalls—had been carved from white onyx. She went on to redecorate and refurbish the entire yacht, filling it with snow-white carpeting with the understanding that henceforth, colored liquor and liqueurs would be banished from the bars based on the fear that some guests might spill their drinks on the (theoretically) pristine carpet and on the 3,500 yards of upholsteries crafted from chamois leather.

On May 25, 1988, Ivana took time out to join 141 other petitioners in Federal Court in Manhattan, where she became a naturalized citizen of the United States. Outside the building, Donald announced to the press, "A great woman has become a citizen of the world's greatest country."

For Donald's maiden voyage aboard his yacht, he flew to the Azores (owned by Portugal) for a sailing scheduled to arrive in New York Harbor on July 4th.

His aide, John R. O'Donnell, claimed that Donald became "so terrified when the crew weighed anchor—the movement convinced him that it was sinking—that he never slept on the yacht after that maiden voyage."

In contrast, Ivana and her three children often sailed it during excursions along the Eastern Seaboard, with frequent stops at Martha's Vineyard and Palm Beach. And whereas Donald never used the yacht for cruising, he employed it as a promotional venue, and for the entertainment of celebrities who included Merv Griffin, Don Johnson, Melanie Griffith, Liza Minnelli, Michael Douglas, and—before their feud—Malcolm Forbes.

In Atlantic City, he invited high rollers at his casinos to spend a night aboard, within one of its suites. He also used it as a glitzy setting for receptions honoring dignitaries; and orchestrated it as the venue for the announcement of upcoming real estate developments.

Ivana, with or without the yacht, seemed to have her own publicity machine, oiled and ready to spring into action at a moment's notice. No columnist did more to fan her self-created myths than Liz Smith, then a columnist for the *New York Daily News*.

In the summer of 1988, she gave Ivana "kudos" for her refurbishment of the yacht, asserting that the redecoration was not garish but "almost understated."

In her columns, she positioned Donald and Ivana into that rare celestial world of "royal tabloid couples," such as Ari and Jacqueline Onassis, or Elizabeth Taylor and Richard Burton.

Reciprocally, Ivana was effusive in her applause for Smith, referring to her (ridiculously) as "a great writer."

In December of 1989, Ivana flew to Tahiti without Donald to link up with the *Trump Princess* for a tour of the neighboring islands. During one of her sailing trips, she lost one of the large diamonds of her wedding band. She viewed the loss as an omen that her marriage to Donald would eventually fail.

Ironically, owning this mammoth yacht wasn't enough for Donald. He wanted an even larger and more lavish *Trump Princess II*. After discussions with a shipbuilder in the Netherlands, it was decided that it would be 420 feet long and that its construction would cost an estimated $200 million.

His dream, like many dreams, never materialized. It was 1991, and his financial empire seemed on the verge of crumbling. His *Princess*, among a lot of other possessions, had to go. He announced that he'd sell it for $150 million, but in the end, he let it go for $10 million to Saudi Prince Al-Waleed bin Talah [Forbes estimated his net worth in 2015 at $26.1 billion] with the understanding that he'd assume its $42 million mortgage.

Bin Talah immediately renamed the yacht based on a combination of his lucky number (5) and the initials (K and R) of the names of his children. Today, yacht aficionados who spot the vessel within a marina (usually, in France) or on the high seas recognize the *Kingdom 5KR* as the oceangoing

Ivana acolyte and sycophantic Trumpette: Liz Smith, New York's aging gossip maven.

former status symbol of the man who would be king, or at least, President.

THE TRUMP SHUTTLE
How it Crashed

In his 1990 memoir, *Surviving at the Top*, Donald wrote: "At five o'clock on May 24, 1989, a loud cheer went up in my suite of offices. Thanks to a court ruling in my favor, the Eastern Shuttle would at last become the Trump Shuttle and take to the skies."

His acquisition of the shuttle would turn out to be one of the worst financial mistakes of his career.

The Eastern Shuttle had pioneered short commuter flights between New York and the cities of Boston and Washington, D.C.

On October 12, 1988, Donald strode into the ballroom of the Plaza Hotel in Manhattan to announce to the press that, "I have acquired another trophy property." Filled with gargantuan confidence, Donald at that moment in his life was a brash 42-year-old Manhattan real estate tycoon. "It's a diamond, an absolute diamond," he crowed to the packed ballroom.

Henry Harteveldt, a former TWA executive who'd been designated as marketing director of the Trump Shuttle, stated privately, "When he started with that 'diamonds in the sky' line, I knew we'd have to settle for cubic zirconia."

"What we'd bought was more than nearly two dozen of the country's oldest 727's. Our job was to clean them up and plaster the Trump name in bold letters on them. Donald wanted us to make the planes his flying billboard for Trump projects. Back then, jet fuel was relatively cheap. That situation was about to change for the worse."

Donald's bigger dream involved the creation of a national airline ten times the size of the shuttle, maybe with as many as seventy aircraft in the air at all times.

The Boeing 727s flew from LaGuardia in New York City to Logan in Boston and to the Washington National Airport (now known as the Ronald Reagan Airport) in Washington, D.C. Donald also inaugurated flights from LaGuardia to Orlando.

An Eastern executive who refused to be named, said, "We were looking for a sucker on whom we could dump these aging carriers. By 1989, our financial picture was heading south on a rocket."

Donald had to make a deal with a syndicate of twenty-two banks to raise the $380 million needed to purchase the shuttle.

His new airline began regular flights on June 23, 1990. He had ordered that his planes be newly painted in white. Airplane interiors were redecorated with lavish use of maple wood veneers and gold-colored lavatory fixtures.

Almost immediately, Trump Shuttle ran into financial setbacks. In August, two months after the new airline's inaugural flight, Iraq invaded Kuwait, causing jet-fuel prices to double. And despite the eventual shutdown of Eastern Airlines, in lieu of shifting to the Trump Shuttle, passengers in droves opted to defect to the Pan Am shuttle instead.

John R. O'Donnell, former president of Trump Plaza in Atlantic City, in a memoir entitled *Trumped!* painted a dismal picture of the takeover.

Wall St. To LaGuardia In Six Minutes.

Donald was played for a sucker when he purchased a fleet of aging jet planes from Eastern Airlines. He rechristened it the Trump Shuttle, and hoped to make millions from it.

However, it cost him $85 million in its first year of operation

"Those people at Eastern must have laughed all the way to the bank. We got a vintage, fuel-guzzling fleet and paid an outrageous fortune, but the shuttle was worth only $80 million. Within six months, its value fell to $30 million. In addition to an outlandish purchase, he had to spend millions to repair and refurbish the tired old jets."

"Donald was acting more and more impulsively, giving less and less thought to the consequences of everything he did. His affair with Marla Maples was moving into the open."

The year he acquired the shuttle, his empire was bleeding at the rate of $100 million annually. In 1990, it was reported that Donald had lost $85 million since acquiring the airline. At the Friars Club, that fraternity of skeptics, bets were placed on the date Donald would file for bankruptcy.

"Donald and his brother, Robert, just assumed that the shuttle would be a cash cow," an executive at Eastern said. "They knew nothing of the airline industry, and should have investigated more."

By September of 1990, Donald's airline business collapsed under a heavy debt load. The loans were in default, and ownership passed to its creditor banks, spearheaded by Citicorp. Three hectic years later, on November 19, 1997, U.S. Airways purchased the shuttle and began operating it under their name.

In the aftermath of the debacle, Bruce Nobles, the shuttle's former president, told *The Daily Beast*, "I cringed every time Donald Trump opened his mouth."

In *Surviving at the Top* (1990) Donald delivered his (spectacularly inaccurate) opinion of his airline: "The Shuttle is now profitable. I'm glad I saved it. I'm proud of the way it's been improved. It's now the best!"

He wrote that opinion and published the book in the same year the airline had collapsed.

THE DONALD VS. THE QUEEN OF MEAN
"He's an egomaniac."
—*Leona Helmsley*

Donald Trump and Leona Helmsley, wife of Harry Helmsley, both of grand hotel fame, had long detested each other. Leona, dubbed "The Queen of Mean" by the tabloid press, took delight in the failure of the Trump Shuttle. Part of her venomous hatred derived from his attacks on her, as published months before, in *Playboy*.

It was time to get even.

She gave her own interview to *Playboy*, outing his affair with Marla Maples. Leona was cited by Playboy as saying, "Marla Meeple, Marble Maple, or Marlo Mipple, whatever her name is. Trump is no Harry. Can you imagine guaranteeing $500 million personally for a bank loan? He's an egomaniac. Just plain stupid. He's great at playing OPM (Other People's Money). Why not? It's not his. Then the maniac has the nerve to think that putting his name on something makes it better. You watch: He's going to fall on his can and it couldn't happen to a nicer person."

Leona learned that when you attack The Donald, he bites back. "She is a vicious, horrible woman who systematically destroyed the Helmsley name. Also, Leona in not a great businesswoman. A very bad one, in fact. She's set the women's movement back fifty years. She is a living nightmare, and to be married to her must be like living in hell. She's out of her mind, a truly evil human being. She's dangerous."

Reciprocating, she shot back, "I wouldn't believe Donald Trump if his tongue were notarized! I also wouldn't have done what Ivana has done: Leave a young, good-looking, very rich husband alone to work in Atlantic City four days a week? Gorgeous girls go after a cripple if they hear he's got billions."

[Although Leona continued to take delight in Donald's bankruptcies, it was Donald who closely followed, and eventually celebrated, her fall from grace. She was investigated and convicted, in 1989, of Federal income tax evasion and other crimes.

Initially, she was sentenced to sixteen years in prison, but served only nineteen months in jail and two months under house arrest.

Leona's former housekeeper reported having overheard Leona say, "We don't pay taxes. Only the little people pay taxes." This notorious aphorism followed her throughout the rest of her life, which ended on August 20, 2007.]

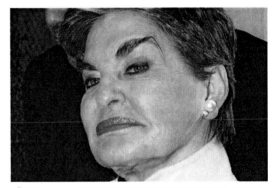

Her life was a tale of ironies: In 1920, she'd been born to Polish Jewish immigrants struggling to make a living, but ended up with an $8 billion dollar fortune—far greater than Donald's net worth. Her assets included the Empire State Building.

In her will, she left a $12 million trust fund to her beloved "but nasty-tempered" dog (a Maltese) who was aptly named Trouble. Throughout the

Rebecca of Sunnybrook Farm Leona Helmsley was not.

rest of his life, Trouble received death threats, in the wake of which the annual costs associated with his security rose to $100,000. Hailed as the richest dog in the history of the world, he died at the age of twelve in 2010.

A 1990 TV movie, *Leona Helmsley: The Queen of Mean*, starred Suzanne Pleshette.

Donald avidly tuned in the night of its premiere. Later, he asked Ivana: "What actor is talented and good-looking enough to play me in a movie? Based on his looks alone, Robert Redford, but he's too old."]

MAR-A-LAGO
Donald & Ivana vs. Palm Beach

Would Its Snobbish and WASPY Socialites Accept a Glitzy Nouveau Riche Couple like the Trumps?

During the time Donald had owned the *Trump Princess*, one of the world's greatest yachts, his greedy eye turned southward to Palm Beach, where he focused on the Mar-a-Lago estate, one of the world's most spectacular residences.

It had been constructed during the Roaring Twenties by the "Post Toasties Queen," Marjorie Merriweather Smith (also known as Marjorie Merriweather Post).

Donald had long been familiar with her fabulous estate, set on twenty manicured acres of coral reef between the Atlantic Ocean and Lake Worth.

The legends associated with the American socialite vastly intrigued him. Born in 1887, Marjorie became the richest woman in the United States, with a fortune worth $250 million. It was such a staggering sum back then that it could almost have bought a small country.

She was the daughter of C.W. Post, who had died when she was twenty-seven. Subsequent to his death, she became the owner of the Postum Cereal Company and later, the founder of General Foods.

In time, she'd marry four husbands. It was during the course of her second marriage (to financier Edward Francis Hutton) that she launched Mar-a-Lago, a vast project whose construction lasted four years. Marjorie and Edward were the parents of the elegant actress, Dina Merrill, who for a time (1966-1989) was married to movie star Cliff Robertson. [In 1959, Dina was proclaimed, "Hollywood's new Grace Kelly."]

Marjorie's third marriage was to Washington attorney Joseph E. Davis, whose appointment by Franklin D. Roosevelt as the American Ambassador to the Soviet Union led to her residency in the Soviet Union during some of the chilliest years of the Cold War.

At that time, as a means of raising hard currency, Josef Stalin, the brutal dictator, was selling the art treasures of the Royal Romanovs. Consequently, as reported by the press of that era, she acquired many of these rare treasures at "bargain basement" prices.

Mar-a-Lago had been built during Palm Beach's heyday, when it reigned during the winter months as WASP society's most stylish rendezvous. It had been designed by Joseph Urban, whom Marjorie had met during his tenure as a set designer for Flo Ziegfeld and his famous Ziegfeld Follies. He claimed he had designed buildings for Emperor Franz Joseph of Austria, but there is no documentation of that.

Urban designed the mansion in an "Arabian Nights" mélange of styles that incorporated Venetian, Moorish, and Spanish motifs. Its most visible feature was a ninety-foot tower opening onto panoramic views.

Marjorie Merriweather Post was said to be the richest woman in the world. She was also known as the "Post Toasties Queen," when that brand was America's most popular breakfast cereal.

Her husband, E.F. Hutton, quadrupled her money through shrewd investments, including the building of Americ'a most lavish home, Mar-a-Lago in Palm Beach, where Madame Post reigned as the Queen. The question is, what would this doyenne of high society have thought of *Divana* (i.e., Donald and Ivana)?

Marjorie wanted 118 lavishly furnished bedrooms for her guests. Most of the building materials were imported from abroad. Three large ships loaded with Dorian stone quarried in Italy deposited their loads near the building site. Some 36,000 tiles were imported from Spain, each of them salvaged from buildings dating back to the 15th century.

To decorate and furnish the interior, Marjorie purchased Persian carpets, Ming vases, precious antiques (many from England), Grecian sculptures, and enough silverware to serve 200 dinner guests. Some of her exquisite crystal goblets cost $1,800 each.

Her great prize was a massive two-toned marble dinner table crafted from peach-colored Italian marble and inlaid with red stone from the Pyrénées, red jasper from Sicily, lapis lazuli from Iran, and alabaster from Egypt.

When Marjorie died in 1973, much of her glitz and glamor died with her. Mar-a-Lago had become a white elephant. Rumor had it that it cost one million dollars a year to maintain. She had bequeathed it to the U.S. government as a retreat for presidents and/or visiting dignitaries.

The Secret Service, however, determined that the estate would not be safe for a president, since it lay directly beneath the flight path of Palm Beach International Airport. There was fear that a terrorist might hijack a plane and either bomb or crash-land into the property.

In 1980, seemingly unimpressed with the artistic and historic important of her bequest, the U.S. government returned Mar-a-Lago to the Marjorie Merriweather Foundation. They immediately put it up for sale, asking only $25 million.

In 1982, Donald inspected the property, calling it "the Hope Diamond of real estate." He bid $15 million, which the foundation rejected. Three years later, after offers from other buyers had each fallen through, and the building continued to languish, unrepaired, it was more receptive to Donald's bid.

Except that by now, he had lowered his offer to the ridiculous figure of $5 million, plus another $3 million for its museum-quality furnishings and *objets d'art*. Amazingly, the foundation accepted his offer, thereby actualizing one of the most spectacular real estate bargains in the history of America.

What was even more shocking was that he forked over only $2,811 out of pocket, the rest of the money provided by the Chase Manhattan Bank, as part of a deal arranged by one of its senior managers, Donald's friend Conrad Stephenson.

As the new owner, Donald ordered the installation on its grounds of a 9-hole, par 3 golf course and an Olympic swimming pool. He immediately hired Buffy Donlon, a local interior designer, to refurbish it. Her assignment: "bring back Mar-a-Lago's beauty."

After surveying the rich furnishings and accessories of the estate he had just purchased, Donald claimed, "This may be as close to paradise as I will ever come. I feel like Jay Gatsby, that character in the F. Scott Fitzgerald novel, *The Great Gatsby*."

After surveying the renovation, he told Ivana, "One thing is missing. A mammoth oil painting of me in the reception area. I want visitors to know immediately that I'm the king of his castle."

***

The narcissist in Donald got a boost to his ego when *Playgirl*, in its August 4, 1986 issue, [which included a full color centerfold of a male nude], named him "one of the ten sexiest men in America." Although he'd long been a reader of *Playboy*, he'd never read a copy of *Playgirl* until he was so honored.

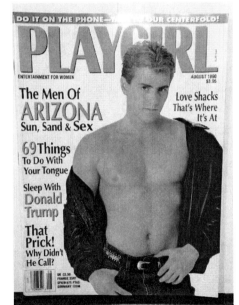

He was later informed, however, that *Playgirl* had almost as many homosexual male readers as heterosexual females. Friends on the golf course chided him with "So now you're the pinup boy darling of America's gays?"

It soon became apparent that Ivana had social aspirations about breaking into Palm Beach society. But Donald did not, claiming, "If you want to be the doyenne of the social scene, count me out. Get another husband."

"I have nothing but disdain for the social scene," he said. "It's full of unattractive people who often have done nothing smarter than inherit somebody else's money. I call them the Lucky Sperm Club. I prefer to sit in my bed and watch some movie on TV, or else a sports event."

Ivana began inviting guests to

SLEEP WITH DONALD TRUMP? *Playgirl* with its male nudes and its large homosexual readership raised that as a possibility. However, editors discreetly chose not to put a replica of Donald on the cover, preferring this male pinup instead.

her lavish house parties, including the likes of Barbara Walters, opera diva Beverly Sills, even George Steinbrenner of the *New York Giants*.

Social embarrassments inevitably followed: At one large dinner party they hosted, she stood up and toasted her husband: "I am married to the most wonderful man. He is so generous, so very smart. I love the way we live."

He looked very clearly bored with her pandering and left the table as soon as the baked Alaska was served, not saying good night to any of the guests, even Ivana.

"He is so very cruel to me," she claimed. "But I am very much in love with him."

He always liked to retire early to his private quarters. "Let the other guests hang out and get drunk on my dime. I have to make money, check closing market prices, make deals over the phone, see what the asking price is for the rundown Beverly Hills Hotel. It must be a pile of shit now. Howard Hughes long ago checked out. Some jerk should have made a sex tape of John F. Kennedy fucking some bimbo. That film clip would be worth a fortune today."

Mar-a-Lago stood next door to the prestigious WASP enclave, the Bath & Tennis Club, nicknamed "B&T." One member was quoted as saying, "Donald Trump will have to break down our door with a bazooka. That's the only way he'll get into our club."

"I don't want to join their club, because they don't accept Jews or blacks," Donald said.

After overcoming massive zoning issues, Donald turned Mar-a-Lago into a private club. Membership fees, which he boastfully contrasted to "the paltry $30,000 that B&T charges," had been cited at different times over a period of several months at $150,000, $250,000, even $350,000.

"Those phonies at B&T flock to Mar-a-Lago where they eat and drink," Donald said. "Then the following night at some cocktail party, you can hear them refer to me as 'gauche' or as 'that horrible man.' But fuck 'em! They drive me nuts. My message to them: Kiss my ass!"

At one point during his presidential campaign in 2015, Donald announced: "I'm going to make Mar-a-Lago the Winter White House."

Chapter Eight

RESORTS INTERNATIONAL
Wheeling and Dealmaking with Merv

A DREAM GONE SOUR
Television City, the World's Tallest Building
Donald Calls New York's Mayor a "Moron"

THE PLAZA HOTEL
Restoring Its Ritzy Heyday

BANKRUPTCIES!
Opening Night at the Taj

LEONA HELMSLEY
Donald Vs. The Queen of Mean

NOMENCLATURE GAMES
The Trump Building, Better Known as 40 Wall Street

In the mid-1980s, still flush from his success in the late 1970s transfiguration of The Commodore Hotel, Donald Trump announced his most daring redevelopment plan for Manhattan. Audacious and stunning, it called for construction of the world's tallest building, a 150-story new headquarters for NBC on the 75-acre that began at the western extremity of 59th Street and stretched north to 72nd Street. Decrepit, rusted, abandoned, and grimy, the acreage had functioned as the Penn Central Rail yards

Television City, as it was dubbed, would soar more than 1,670 feet, forty stories taller than the Sears Building in Chicago, then the highest building in the world.

Included within would be 7,500 apartment units, a 6,100-car garage, a two-million-square-foot shopping mall, and what Donald asserted would be "the largest and most spectacular TV studio complex in the world."

[Donald's plan had to some degree been catalyzed by NBC's recent threats to abandon their cramped quarters at Rockefeller Center, and a possible re-location to New Jersey.]

Almost immediately, Donald's plan met with fierce opposition from nearby residents and Manhattan politicos, none more vocal than New York City's Mayor, Ed Koch.

[Ever since they'd squabbled over tax abatements associated with his Grand Hyatt project, Koch and Donald had had an uneasy relationship.]

Donald met with Koch, seeking a twenty-year tax abatement from the city, something that Koch vigorously opposed, saying "The greedy, greedy, greedy Mr. Piggy wants me to empty the city's cash reserves."

In response, Donald publicly referred to Koch as a "moron." In private, he began referring to him as a "cocksucker."

"His administration is a disaster," Donald told the press. "I call upon him to resign for the sake of the

Donald Trump's grandest dream, the creation of "Television City," was to include the world's tallest building at 1,670 feet.

Fighting back against his critics, he said, "I don't want it to be contextual, blending into everything else. It shouldn't be like getting a haircut and telling the barber, 'I don't want anyone to know I've gotten one.'"

city."

"I must be doing something right," Koch shot back at reporters. "To have him attack me like that."

Representing the "fighting mad" residents of Manhattan's West Side, most of whom seemed to oppose the development plan. Rep. Jerrold Nadler (D-NY) denounced Donald's architectural plan as "grotesque."

During the widely publicized campaigns that followed, Donald used fear, based on the possible flight of NBC to New Jersey, to win public support for his plan. Aggravating his conflict with Koch were frequent press speculations, which he denied, that he wanted to run for mayor himself.

Ultimately, Koch thwarted Donald's plans for TV City, vetoing many of its key provisions and cutting off the possibility of public financing. In the aftermath, Donald appraised the mayor's decision as "ludicrous and disgraceful. Not only is the mayor an idiot, but his top advisers are jerks."

After floods of negative publicity, NBC decided to stay in Manhattan. Their decision was at least partly based on the lucrative tax breaks the city awarded as an incentive for them to stay.

"I handed Trump a bigtime defeat," Koch said, before making an inaccurate prediction. "I marked the end of a decade of splashy successes. Expect no more from him."

Jerrold Nadler, D-NY, Donald Trump's nightmare.

Long before Donald claimed he'd build a wall separating Mexico from the United States, he was attacked for the "wall" that would cast a large dark shadow across Manhattan's West Side, blocking out the sunshine and destroying the harmony of that neighborhood.

Fourteen blocks long, the sprawling complex promoted as "Television City" would have separated the bulk of the Upper West Side from easy access to the Hudson River.

[FAST FORWARD to December of 1992, when New York's City Council approved a vastly watered-down project, identifying it as Trump City, a name that later changed to the Trump Place Apartments, and which is sometimes known as Riverside South. It granted permission for him to construct sixteen free-standing apartment buildings collectively containing 5,700 units, some of which included affordable housing.

As a gesture of good will, he created a twenty-five acre park when the agreement called for only twenty-one acres. Today, that development, hugely influential in the geography and sociology of Manhattan's Upper West Side, was made possible because of Donald's collaboration with six separate bureaucracies.]

As for the ill-fated Television (or TV) City, a reporter, Daniel Bush, claimed, "Trump's failure to finance the project, coupled with local concerns over its density, scale, and environmental impact, ultimately cost him the deal. Soon after, as his professional and personal lives were imploding under the pressures of highly public bankruptcy and divorce proceedings, it looked as if his run as a big-time developer was over."

Based to some degree on issues associated with his divorce and financial troubles, Donald, in the mid-1990s, sold off much of his stake in the development to investors from Hong Kong. But it wasn't until 1997 that the first building permit was issued. In 2005, the Extell and Carlyle Group purchased the property for $1.76 billion.

***

The Plaza Hotel, one of Manhattan's most revered historic landmarks, at the corner of Fifth Avenue and 59th Street, is a twenty-story citadel of comfort, luxury, and elegance. It has provided the venue for some of the most publicized social events of the 20th century. One of the most talked-about was Truman Capote's Black-and-White Ball (1966), where the glitterati, clawing one another for one of the coveted invitations, turned out to honor Katharine Graham, publisher of *The Washington Post*.

Movie stars, diplomats, high-class courtesans, financiers, Saudi princes, dethroned European kings, U.S. presidents, and international socialites have signed the register here.

Donald had long been intrigued by the social and cultural history of the Plaza writing that "the Vanderbilts, Wanamakers, and Whitneys have stayed in the luxurious suites and sipped champagne with visiting royalty in the Grand Ballroom."

The titans of Manhattan real estate ridiculed the outrageous price Donald paid for the landmark Plaza Hotel.

It was determined that the Plaza would never be able to pay the interest on its bank loans from its cash flow. For that to have happened, Donald would have had to rent out each of its 814 rooms every night of the year at a price of $500 per accommodation.

The New York Times once wrote: "The Plaza has been the spot where gray-haired dowagers demurely sipped tea in the Palm Court, and giggling debutantes twirled through the Grand Ballroom until dawn."

Some of the biggest entertainers of the 20th Century have performed in its Persian Room: Marlene Dietrich, Lena Horne, Eartha Kitt, Peggy Lee, Ethel Merman, and Josephine Baker.

During February of 1964, hundreds of hysterical fans gathered in front of the hotel for a glimpse of the Beatles, who stayed here during their first visit to the United States.

Countless movie scenes or TV dramas have been filmed at the hotel. One of the best known of these was edited into the final, tear-jerking scenes of *The Way We Were* (1973), starring Barbra Streisand and Robert Redford.

At least part of the Plaza's fame derived from its choice as the setting by Kay Thompson, author of a series of children's books that became spectacularly popular in the 1950s. Eloise was a savvy and somewhat eccentric pre-teen whose (absentee) parents had stashed her, with limited supervision by a maid or governess, at the Plaza, where her "incorrigible" behavior seemed to satirize most of the assumptions of capitalism. Terrorizing the staff, but endearing herself to readers, Eloise became known for pouring water down mail chutes and for calling room service to place an order for "one roast beef bone, one raisin, seven spoons—and 'charge it, please.'"

Designed by Henry Janeway Hardenberg, and built in the French Renaissance château style, the Plaza opened on October

Includes scrapbook with photos and drawings by Hilary Knight!

Like any hardworking show-biz pro, actor/dancer/singer Kay Thompson maneuvered her best-selling children's series into other media ventures.

In the lower photo, she's seen with Evelynn Rudie, as Eloise, presumably at the Plaza, in the Playhouse 90 television production, *Eloise*. It aired in November, 1956.

1, 1907, when it charged $2.07 per night, per room.

Over the decades, it fell under different owners. Its most famous owner was Conrad Hilton, who, in 1943, paid $7.4 million for it (the equivalent of $100 million in 2016 currency). He spent the equivalent of $85 million in today's dollars to renovate it to its original glory.

The changing roster of owners continued until it was acquired by the Westin chain, which immediately configured it as their flagship. When that chain came up for sale, Donald bid $1 billion for it, although admitting it was "an unrealistically low figure." Other bidders included the oil-rich Kuwaiti government.

The winning bid of $1.53 billion was placed by Bob Bass, the Texas oil magnate, and John Aoki, the head of a mammoth Tokyo-based construction firm. Shortly thereafter, Donald heard that Bass, disenchanted, might want to unload it.

Donald had successfully concluded business with Bass before, paying $50 million for Alexander's retail chain. [At the time, Donald was more interested in their land holdings than he was in hawking their merchandise or in running a department store chain.]

Donald and the lawyers for "the opposing team" spent weeks playing nuanced and high-stakes cat-and-mouse games together before a deal was struck.

Based on previous experience, Donald knew that despite months of preliminaries, a real estate deal could easily collapse when two teams of attorneys met for the closing. He'd had a particularly horrible experience with Leona Helmsley and her husband, Harry, when he'd acquired their hotel, the St. Moritz, on Central Park South at Sixth Avenue. "That bitch, Leona, went about counting every towel and teacup in the hotel."

In 1988, as part of his acquisition of the Plaza, Donald paid the previous owners $407.5 million, an amount equivalent to $814 million in 2016 dollars. The money was borrowed from banks.

He announced his acquisition in *The New York Times*. "I haven't purchased a building. I've purchased a masterpiece—the Mona Lisa. For the first time in my life, I have knowingly made a deal that was not economic—for I can never justify the price I paid, no matter how successful the Plaza becomes."

He later said that when he took over the Plaza, "It had lost its luster. The carpets, in service for at least a quarter of a century, had grown shabby. The once-fabled Persian Room had been rented to a nondescript dress shop for a ridiculously low rent—and I could go on and on, outlining problems I would have to face."

He had already eased out his wife, Ivana, as President of Trump Castle in Atlantic City. Now, he decided to promote her and make her the President of the Plaza, overseeing both its management and its restoration. [Gossips had it that he wanted her out of Atlantic City so that he could more openly carry on his affair with the beautiful blonde model, Marla Maples. He'd installed her in a suite at the resort's Trump Plaza.]

Reprising within the Plaza the style she had previously developed as the overseer of Trump Castle, Ivana became an "absolute tyrant," in the words of her critics. She claimed, "The staff used to crawl. After I took over, I taught them how to walk. Pretty soon, I will have them running."

She concerned herself with the smallest details. In reference to the closets of the accommodations, she mandated, "No more wire hangers. Only satin-covered wooden ones." One reporter claimed that she evoked Joan Crawford, as depicted in Christina Crawford's notorious memoir of her movie star mother, *Mommie Dearest*.

Day by day, week by week, Ivana set about restoring the Plaza to its original luster. After years of silence and darkness, she ordered the restoration and reopening of the "Champagne Porch." Positioned on a balcony-style mezzanine overlooking the bustling lobby, it had previously been a watering hole for, among others, the novelist, F. Scott Fitzgerald, and his occasionally unstable wife, Zelda.

Reportedly, Ivana lavishly renovated the hotel, spending enormous money and energy restoring the public areas, installing gourmet restaurants, and spending $150,000 for the renovation of each individual suite.

"I wasn't satisfied until all the gold leaf glittered again, each inch of marble sparkled, and each bronze handrail shone."

Then, in addition to the Plaza, Ivana—after Donald complained that she was beginning to look "old and haggard"—rejuvenated herself as well. After major work by "beauty butchers," she emerged from plastic surgery looking ten years younger.

Despite all that, Donald told her that he was no longer attracted to her body. "You're flat chested!" he lamented.

She responded with surgical implants. Even so, she still couldn't lure him back to her boudoir. "I can't stand imitation breasts!" he reportedly told her. "I want the real thing!"

***

On April 9, 1991, *The New York Times* announced that Donald planned to convert many of the Plaza's accommodations into condominiums priced at $1,600 per square foot. That was more than triple what he charged clients at Trump Tower.

The banking world was filled with rumors that Citibank was about to foreclose on the Plaza for failure to maintain its mortgage payments. All those rumors turned out to be true, forcing Donald to relinquish forty-nine percent of his ownership of the Plaza.

In 1992, the Plaza filed for bankruptcy. Under a ruling by a Federal court, Citibank and three other banks were allowed to restructure Donald's first mortgage loan and to release him from his personal guarantee (structured as a second mortgage) for $125 million.

[After his divorce from Ivana, Donald sold the hotel for $325 million (the equivalent of $505 million in 2016 dollars.)

After that, the Plaza underwent a series of takeovers by, in addition to several others, Sahara India Pariwar, a business group from India.

"The heyday of the glitz and glamour of the Plaza is over," Donald was quoted as saying. "Foreigners have moved in to take over an American landmark. That's proof of how this once great country has put out the 'FOR SALE sign.'"

IT WASN'T A HOLIDAY
Resorts International

"I've always thought that Resorts International was the strangest deal I've ever done."
—Donald Trump

It's been suggested that Donald Trump's unlucky association with the gaming industry began when he realized that one of his competitors, James M. Crosby, would emerge with a fast-buck fortune if and when gambling was legalized in New Jersey.

Even before gambling was green-lighted there, Crosby "jumped the gun" (Donald's words) "buying up property in Atlantic City like a crazy man. No vacant lot was overlooked."

Donald had long been familiar with Crosby's career. His family had purchased the former Mary Carter Paint Company in 1958 and installed him as its chairman. From that unlikely beginning, he moved into casino gambling, and virtually created Paradise Island (formerly "Hog Island"), a low-lying strip of sand and coral off the coast of Nassau, capital of The Bahamas.

In 1967, after making bigtime payoffs under the table to The Bahamas' Prime Minister, he opened Paradise Island Casino and Paradise Beach Hotel, at which time he changed the name of his company to Resorts International, and got rid of Mary Carter and all those unsold cans of paint. By 1978, he'd migrated and expanded to Grand Bahama Island, opening a casino in Freeport, its capital.

In the mid-1970s, when it seemed likely that New Jersey, through its Casino Board, would approve gambling in Atlantic City, Crosby moved quickly, buying and assembling fifty-six acres of oceanfront land into the biggest parcel in town. Included within it was the famous Steel Pier (billed after its construction decades before as the longest amusement pier in the United States). He also bought Chalk's International Airline as a vehicle for the transport of gamblers to his casinos in The Bahamas.

Then, despite his ill health and advanced age, Crosby almost immediately launched his greatest project of all, defining it publicly as "my dream of dreams"—the Taj Mahal in Atlantic City. Inspired by the fabled monument in India, its construction costs were estimated at something close to a billion dollars.

Crosby's death in April of 1986 interrupted the realization of that dream. Gravel-voiced and stoop-shouldered, he had been a lifelong bachelor (there were rumors), survived only by his mother, two sisters, and two brothers. Without children willing to pick up its reins, his company and its interests in the as-yet-incomplete Taj Mahal went up for grabs. Into the arena stepped Donald Trump. "In the beginning [of the renaissance of Atlantic City], Crosby was the only game in town," Donald said.

Crosby's dream would become his nightmare.

Donald began to eye a takeover of Resorts International. Work had already begun on what the company had been billing as "the largest casino in the world."

[In Atlantic City, simultaneous with his focus on the Taj Mahal, Donald also became mired in issues associated with Haddon Hall.

In 1977, when gambling was legalized in Atlantic City, the first hotel catering to the casino trade was Haddon Hall, (aka The Resorts Casino Hotel). Its brick-sided premises, along with its 1,000 accommodations, some of them within a neighboring structure, the Chalfonte Hotel, had been built in the early in the 20th century on the sites of two older (demolished) wood-sided guest houses from the 1860s. During World War II, it had been requisitioned as a military hospital and for housing by the U.S. Army.

During the early days of Atlantic City as a gambling mecca, Resorts, under the direction of Crosby, had commandeered the faded hotel and launched a much-

needed upgrade. They reduced its room count to 566 bedrooms, opened a casino, shops, restaurants, and a showroom that booked such nightclub talent as Julio Iglesias, Rodney Dangerfield, and Don Rickles. Despite the efforts of its owners, Donald, perhaps based on his strenuous promotion of the as-yet-unfinished Taj Mahal, referred to Haddon Hall as "a faded lady in her 1920s finery." And as larger, splashier casino hotels opened in and around Atlantic City, Haddon Hall, whose names changed during the course of its troubled existence, eventually became obsolete.]

Financial difficulties had prevented Resorts from completing its Taj Mahal project, and in 1987, it became a takeover target for Donald based on his purchase of a controlling block of Resorts stock.

To his dismay, Donald soon realized that the Taj Mahal was an entity with more problems than he had realized. And although $500 million had already been spent on its construction and development, it was doubtful if it would ever open. "The only thing I liked about it was its name, Taj Mahal, which evoked glamor and mystery in three wonderfully soft syllables," he said.

In his book, *Surviving at the Top* (published in 1990), Donald wrote:

> *"The Taj had become an embarrassment. Its construction had been delayed, and convention bookings had been accepted and canceled so many times that people in the travel business snickered each time another 'grand opening' was announced. Some of the contractors hired by Resorts still rattled around inside the huge skeleton of a structure, doing a little electrical work here or putting in sheetrock there. But mostly, the Taj just sat on the Boardwalk, a monument to world-*

In 1984, an article in *Time* profiled Donald, placing a picture of his cardplaying as a metaphor for his business-related (and perhaps political) games of chance.

"At 6 ft. 2 in., real estate tycoon Donald J. (for John) Trump does not really loom colossus-high above the horizon of New York and New Jersey. He has created no great work of art or ideas, and even as a maker or possessor of money he does not rank among the top ten, or even 50."

"Yet at 42, he has seized a large fistful of that contemporary coin known as celebrity. There has been artfully hyped talk about his having political ambitions, worrying about nuclear proliferation, even someday running for President. No matter how farfetched that may be, something about his combination of blue-eyed swagger and success has caught the public fancy and made him in many ways a symbol of an acquisitive and mercenary age."

168

class mismanagement — and to the difficulty of making a truly great dream come true."

Its financial setup was unusual in that its stock had been issued with an A-B structuring—that is, Class A stock traded publicly but had little voting muscle. In contrast, Class B stock represented less than ten percent of Resorts' equity, but had the upper hand in voting, making it superior to the A stock by one hundred to one. Because the Crosby family had retained ownership of most of the B stock, they remained more or less in charge of the company.

Donald wanted to run the company, so he bought 750,000 shares of the Class B stock (some ninety percent of what was available), from the Crosby family, paying $135 a share. The cost to the Trump Organization was around $105 million. A condition of the sale involved positioning Donald—with the understanding that he'd remain fully responsible to the board of directors—as CEO. Another condition of the sale involved the Crosby estate's grant to Donald of seventy-three percent of their voting power.

Even after these adjustments, Donald still faced a rather shaky company. At the time of Crosby's death, Resorts had $300 million in cash and no debt. After Donald's takeover, he found it owed around $750 million in debt "with enough cash to buy a ride on the Staten Island ferry."

"My job was awesome," Donald admitted. "I had to transform a train wreck into a multi-million dollar-grossing winner in the Atlantic City sweepstakes."

He claimed that Resorts was so shaky it could not get a bank loan. Nevertheless, he managed to leverage "the power of my name" to wangle an immediate $125 million loan. He also won approval of a management contract for himself, an arrangement that granted him three percent of the Taj's construc-

TRUMP HOTELS & CASINO RESORTS, INC.
INCORPORATED UNDER THE LAWS OF THE STATE OF DELAWARE

The original version of this stock certificate once validated ownership of shares in Donald Trump's version of the Taj.

Today, the certificates, once prized and highly speculative, are nostalgic but otherwise worthless souvenirs.

Donald detractors noted that his hair, as represented on the certificates, had never looked better.

tion costs and 1.75 percent of its gross revenues, with the understanding that he wouldn't demand payment until the Taj opened and started making money.

Donald immediately began addressing his challenges. He ordered that the resort change its name to Trump's Taj Mahal, and he appointed Mark Etess—who had previously managed his family's famous resort, Grossinger's, in the Catskills—as its president.

Then he threw himself into the construction of the Taj. "I'd constructed great buildings before, and I'd kept some of the original plans, discarding the stupid or tacky one. I greenlighted construction of a complex that would be only a bit smaller than the Pentagon."

Disaster struck in October ("Black Monday") of 1987 when bank financing dried up in the aftermath of that year's stock market crash and its subsequent recession.

Acting quickly, Donald boldly decided to take advantage of the falling market and buy up all those A shares through a tender offer whose result would redefine Resorts, once again, as a private company.

He decided to be generous. Resorts' A shares had traded publicly for $11.50 a share, but he offered $15 a share. The board of directors dismissed his offer as too little, so he raised his offer to $22 a share. "That was double the market value, and I expected immediate approval," he said.

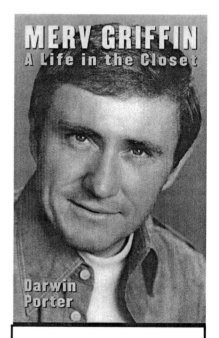

Twenty millions viewers a day and almost as many secrets... *HEERE'S MERV.*

His first and only tell-all biography, *Merv Griffin, A Life in the Closet,* from the same team who brought you this biography of Donald Trump, documented the public and private lives of TV's richest and most powerful mogul.

Included in this saga are insights into Merv's disastrous, to some degree ego-driven, entanglements with "The Donald."

***

As soon as he filed his tender offer, all sorts of rumbling was heard, including some to-be-expected shareholder lawsuits. "A lot of the static was coming from Merv Griffin. As a business man, not an entertainer, he had just pocketed $250 million from Coca-Cola for the rights to such game shows as *Wheel of Fortune* and *Jeopardy!*"

Over the Dow Jones wire, Donald learned that Griffin had placed a rival bid of $35 a share, substantially more than Donald's offer of $22. "I never understood why he made such a stupid move," Donald said.

Griffin sued Donald and Donald, being Donald, countersued.

The former "big band" singer with Freddy Martin's band, and later a TV talk show host, was now in gladia-torial combat with a powerful New York mogul, who knew how to play rough. As one Wall Street lawyer (ho-mophobically) characterized the on-coming duel, "The faggot cocksucker takes on the bully womanizer."

After Griffin sued him, Donald asked, "Is Merv Griffin fucking crazy? In fact, his offer is so crazy that I don't think I should ask for more. Normally, I might make it $40 a share and 'it's yours, sweetheart.' Not in this case. Talk about *Jeopardy!* He'll learn what *Jeopardy!* is when he gets deep into the dung heap of the gaming business."

During Donald's dispute with Grif-fin, Al Glasgow, a consultant for Trump casinos, made disparaging remarks about Griffin's sexual preference. But despite his widely documented niche as a (closeted) gay, he'd often been seen in public with Eva Gabor (his "arm candy"), one of the glamorous Gabor sisters from Budapest

Glasgow claimed, "I think Griffin has a better chance of getting Eva pregnant than he does in making money from his casino resorts. As for Donald with his Taj Mahal, he can't miss. It'll be as easy for him as spitting on the floor."

After flying to New York in his pri-vate jet, Griffin arranged for a show-

Merv was said to have the Midas Touch, developing two of Holly-wood's most popular and profitable game shows, *Jeopardy!* and *Wheel of Fortune.*

Bystanders said that the former boy singer didn't known what Jeopardy was until he tangled with Donald Trump.

down with "The Donald" at his offices at Trump Tower. He came alone, without benefit of his high-priced attorneys.

Their introductory meeting lasted an hour, beginning with Donald's rather nasty comment, "Merv, it looks like a lot of pasta has gone into your mouth, only some of which escaped from the other end. I say, boy, you must have put on fifty pounds since I last saw you on TV. You know, Merv, skin only stretches so far."

After that awkward beginning, Donald gave him an autographed copy of his best-selling *The Art of the Deal*. Griffin read a quote, positioned on one of its covers, from *CBS News* correspondent, Mike Wallace: "This reads like Trump unvarnished—vainglorious, combative, ambitious, and unafraid to let us know about it."

After that, Trump guided him by the hand *["How romantic!" Griffin had quipped]* to a picture window to show off his latest acquisition, the Plaza Hotel. "It's the crown jewel of Manhattan," Donald boasted. "Some 800 rooms."

Griffin shot back, "Gee, Donald, that's how many rooms you'll need to house all the lawyers it will take to fight me."

Merv's relationship with "those glamorous Gabors" was long, amusing, complicated, and usually mutually beneficial. Here he is interviewing Zsa Zsa on his show.

But despite the humor and formidable charms of Zsa Zsa, it was her younger sister, Eva, who became the unofficial "official escort" of the closeted billionaire.

Above, she's depicted as Lisa, a city girl transplanted to the country, next to her husband, Eddie Albert, in the long-running TV sitcom, *Green Acres*.

Once seated, Griffin told Donald, "I guess I've thrown this gigantic wrench into your plans for Resorts."

Hoping to dispel Griffin's interest in the Taj—that is, when he began to believe that Griffin seriously wanted to acquire it—Donald said, "Are you aware that it's going to take at least another $600 million to complete the Taj? This is no god damn *Wheel of Fortune* set. What in hell do you know about how to deal with union contractors? They'll cut off your balls and eat them raw."

Amazingly, as the two greedy capitalists talked, each came to realize that all that Donald really wanted was the Taj. As later recollected by Merv, "It was big and glitzy, a gigantic risk, a specially crafted dildo I was willing to offer Donald. He'd know where to stick it."

"Listen, I know you were a crooner, and I could give you something to croon about," Donald said. "Let's make a deal. You're a hotelier. I'm a developer. You've got that much-ballyhooed $250 million I haven't counted yet."

"Are you saber-rattling?" Griffin asked. "What if I'm willing to surrender the Taj? What else?"

"The Steel Pier. Ok?"

"Is that all?" Griffin asked.

"That's all!"

"Incidentally, what are you doing these days when not ordering your lawyers to sue me?" Donald asked. "Designing the puzzles that Vanna White flips during *Wheel of Fortune*? Perhaps taking Nancy Reagan to her astrologist? Hanging out with Liberace in Vegas?"

"All in all, it's not a bad life for a Depression baby," Griffin said. "Incidentally, when you're next on the West Coast, I'll give you a ten percent discount on a suite at my Beverly Hilton."

After making a deal that day (May 11, 1987) to divide Resorts' assets, their agreement fell apart as both sides grandly postured and preened. But about two weeks later, on May 27, the fearsome twosome signed a final con-

Those Glamorous

Bombshells from Budapest

Great Courtesans of the 20th Century

DARWIN PORTER

In 2013, Blood Moon Productions released the only full-length biography ever published of the legendary Gabor sisters, three unlikely but ferociously glamorous siblings who obsessively "boot-strapped" themselves into television-age celebrities.

Zsa Zsa, Eva, and Magda, *Those Glamorous Gabors,* is a triple-play saga detailing how these great courtesans conquered the New World, one millionaire at a time.

Their entanglements included "quality time" with Merv, with insights into how he handled his fast-deteriorating Wheels of Fortune with THE DONALD.

tract to divvy up the assets. Donald made off with the Taj for $230 million ($320 less than the company's cost on the project).

Griffin would buy Donald's B share at $135 a share and his class A shares at $35 each. Based on Donald's management contract, he won another $63 million.

After he had purchased his controlling interest in Resorts in 1987, Donald was charged with using his stake in the company "to extract cash from it" while he, in the words of one reporter, "indulged in a scorched earth policy with Resorts' other shareholders."

He was also accused of charging Resorts $5 million for the operation of his yacht, The *Trump Princess.*

Merv interviews his very close friend and *confidante,* Nancy Reagan.

In private, he was the first person she confided in, telling him that the President of the United States was suffering from dementia.

Griffin got the other Atlantic City properties (including Haddon Hall) and almost everything associated with the Paradise Island Resorts. An Atlantic City insider told author Gwenda Blair that "Haddon Hall used to be our shithouse along the Boardwalk. After the building was renovated, we called it our shithouse with carpeting."

Griffin had been able to pull off the deal by transferring ownership of $325 million of Michael Milken's junk bonds. They, in effect, were used as the currency he used to purchase Resorts.

After the deal was signed, Donald shook Griffin's hand and said, "Enjoy your Resorts, which is falling apart. Enjoy Paradise Island, which is the worst dump you've ever seen. Have a lot of fun."

"I kicked his ass!" Donald told his friends. "It was a great deal for me. I got the Taj Mahal—he got shit!"

Most Wall Street financiers agreed that Griffin got a bad deal. As Michael Craig put it, "Griffin was right to be so reluctant to complete the transaction. The deal was a horrible loser right from the start. For more than $700 million—the cost of buying out Trump and other shareholders and assuming all the debt, minus Trump's payment for the Taj Mahal—all Griffin got was decrepit Resorts, not especially well run, and in dire need of restoration."

Griffin's own lawyer, Tom Gallegher, called it "the deal from hell." But

Griffin seemed unflappable. Gallegher said "There was a good twin and a bad twin. In many ways, Trump is a Jekyll-and-Hyde character. He can be enormously charming, and you get the feeling he's nice, decent, and warm. That's when the bad twin emerges."

In the press and privately, Donald and Griffin chided and maneuvered each other, each eager to articulate which of them had "won."

"Merv was indiscreet about bragging to the press that he had 'out-Trumped Trump,'" Donald said. "He hadn't at all. I practically stole Resorts International right from under his nose."

One reporter privately asserted, "Merv got fucked in the ass by Trump. In some circumstances, from what I hear, he might have enjoyed that. But I'm speaking sexually, not in monetary terms."

As journalist from *Business Week* stated it more accurately, his story running under a banner headline: DONALD TEACHES MERV THE ART OF THE DEAL.

Mike Wallace persuaded the men to appear together on his TV show, *60 Minutes*, during which he highlighted their conflicts.

Wallace compared Griffin and Donald's coming together as a "slap-happy boxing match in the ring. Both of them looked like the Cheshire cat who had swallowed the little yellow bird."

On TV, Wallace pointed out that Griffin was saddling himself with a long-term debt of $925 million. That meant he would need to make $110,000 daily in his Atlantic City casinos to break even—and that was just to meet his debt service tab, not his operating costs.

Griffin mocked Donald for plastering his name so prominently over his properties, but then he went and did the same, billing his new company as Merv Griffin Resorts.

Griffin went so far as to call Donald's account of their negotiation, as printed within the pages of his memoir, *Surviving at the Top*, "a novel."

He later charged that Donald had completely misled him, claiming that he could "fix up the Atlantic City resort for 15 million dollars," when Griffin knew it would take that much money just to renovate the lobby.

After he took over his new investment, Griffin found himself saddled "with interest payments that equaled the treasury of many small countries." His company president, David Hanlon, told the press that "museum-piece elevators and a leaky roof have kept Merv from trading on his cachet to book celebrities."

Just paying the interest on the loans was more than Griffin's money advisors could cope with. The cash just wasn't there. Soon, strenuous attempts were underway to restructure the debt.

As clever as Griffin had been in his negotiations, often outwitting "The Donald" and his lawyers, he did not foresee the oncoming recession, with the hardships that lay ahead. Most of its debt, $600 million, had been assumed when he'd purchased Resorts International. To retain his twenty percent equity, he had to plow another $30 million of his own money into the company. Working behind the scenes, he was able to reorganize Resorts under Chapter 11 of the Federal bankruptcy laws.

He also began frantically publicizing his resorts, pulling out all the stops of his talent as a showman. He invited stars from the entertainment industry for high-visibility visits, many of them friends from yesterday, including Burt Lancaster and Dinah Shore. He even brought in one of the nation's best-selling novelists, Sidney Sheldon, for a book signing.

For entertainment he booked such stars as the operatic great, Roberta Peters, or "my old buddy," Tony Bennett, who on one drunken night in California, had been mistakenly introduced to the audience by Griffin as Tony Martin.

Griffin admitted that during his campaign to publicize Resorts International, "I tried every trick in the book to gain business and publicity, at one point giving away $150,000 in thousand dollar bags to fifteen people every hour."

Even so, he was forced to restructure the organization's debt again in 1994. Donald mockingly referred to it as "Griffin's Chapter 22."

Two years later, in 1996, it became obvious that Griffin's frenzied promotional ploys had worked. Whereas his New Jersey hotel, Resorts Atlantic City, had taken in only $16 million of revenue when he took over its management in 1988, it had brought in revenue of $64 million eight years later. Based partly on factors like that, in 1996, he was able to terminate his tumultuous venture into gaming, selling out at $20 a share to Sol Kerzner, the South African real estate developer.

All in all, it is estimated that Griffin had personally lost $50 million in his flirtation with the gaming industry.

He took the money from Kerzner and invested it in Player's International, an outfit that launched and maintained riverboat casinos in Louisiana, Missouri, and Illinois. In 2000, four years after its acquisition, he sold his investment to Harrah's at a profit.

Griffin spent $90 million making much-needed improvements to the tired Resorts Atlantic City. He was also forced to sell the Paradise Island property to Sun International Hotels, He later dumped the rest of what by then was Griffin Gaming and Entertainment in 1998, also to Sun International for the tidy sum of $350 million.

As part of a final kiss-off to "The Don-ald," Griffin called him in the 90s, when he was first considering a run for President in the Republican primaries. "Donald, I'm going to contribute one hundred dollars to your campaign. I've thought it over and that's all I can afford."

"As always, generous to a fault," Don-ald said. "I can't accept the money because I plan to drop out of the race. There are too many hands to shake. Germs, you know. In Atlantic City, I was in the men's room and this guy comes out of a booth after taking this big crap and wants to shake my hand."

Their enmity continued: During the re-cession of the early 90s, Griffin had been secretly delighted when Donald's most prized investments, including the Taj Mahal in Atlantic City and the Plaza Hotel in Manhattan, racked up a total of more than $1 billion in debt. In an interview with host Jim Palmer on WBAL Radio, Griffin was promoting his second autobi-ography. "You wrote about Donald Trump in your book…Chapter 7 isn't it?" Palmer asked.

"Actually," Griffin said with a grin and a wink, "he's in Chapter 11 now."

> "I don't want to be President. I'm 100 percent sure," Donald Trump told *Playboy* magazine in an inter-view published in its March 1990 issue.
>
> "I'd change my mind only if I saw this country continue to go down the tubes."

***

On October 10, 1989, from within his office at Trump Tower, Donald was among the first to receive news of a tragedy. Five passengers, including a trio of his top executives in the administration of his casino empire in At-lantic City, had died when their helicopter crashed in a pinewood forest off the Garden State Parkway near Forked River, New Jersey.

Before the craft took its fatal plunge, its main overhead four-blade rotor and its tail rotor had broken off. Only eight minutes before the crash, the pilot had been in radio contact with the control tower at McGuire Air Force Base in nearby Wrightstown. No problems, or any distress, were reported.

Killed were Stephen F. Hyde, 43, chief executive of Trump Casinos; Mark Grossinger Etess, 38, president and chief operating officer of the Taj Mahal, and Jonathan Benanav, 33, executive vice president of Trump Plaza.

Donald told the press, "These were fabulous young men in the prime of their lives. No better human beings ever existed. We are deeply saddened by this devastating tragedy, and our hearts go out to their families."

Also dead were the pilot and co-pilot, Robert Kent and Lawrence Diener. Paramount Aviation, an air service operating out of Lincoln Park, New Jersey, owned the craft. It was reported that the helicopter was airborne thirty-five miles north of Atlantic City when it crashed.

Federal investigators reported that the probable reason for the crash involved "fatigue failure of the main rotor blade spar, which originated as a manufacturing-induced scratch, the result of inadequate quality control."

Ironically, Donald himself immediately asserted that he'd been scheduled for transit aboard that fatal flight, but that he had canceled at the

Finally, a vodka worthy of the Trump name.

Trump, The World's Finest Super Premium Vodka
Quintuple-distilled in Holland by renowned Dutch master distiller Jacques de Lat, Trump Super Premium Vodka is the epitome of vodka that will demand the same respect and inspire the same awe as the international legacy and brand of Donald Trump himself.

TRUMP VODKA BOTTLES SEIZED IN PASSOVER SCAM

In addition to an abortive stab at the casino trades, Donald also got involved in a (failed) attempt to market cool drinks to hot guys in the U.S. But will sexy women be impressed with Trumpkins who stock this image-enhancer in their boudoirs?

In addition to the ballyhoo associated with Hillary's attack on Donald's business failures, Trump Vodka, and Donald's image, took yet another hit in April of 2016.

In the wake of a report in *The Jerusalem Post*, hundreds of bottles of Trump Vodka were seized by Israeli police from a warehouse in Haifa for sporting forged and phony "Kosher for Passover" labels. Although Trump Vodka has been out of business in most parts of the world for years, it became fashionable and popular in Israel as a (rigorously Kosher) accessory to the Passover ritual.

But according to the *Jerusalem Post*, Rabbi David Silverstone of the OK Kosher Certification Organization said, "We discovered that instead of one of the ingredients that was supposed to be kosher for Passover, they used a different one."

Although the conflict was eventually settled out of court, Trump sued the Israeli company that produced Trump Vodka in 2011 in a licensing dispute.

last minute because he was too busy at the time to leave Manhattan.

[Three of Donald's biographers have maintained that his claim of almost being aboard that flight was a fabrication. He was quoted privately as saying, "I can get some publicity out of this crash."

Indeed, he did. His near death "escape" appeared on the front pages of the tabloid press.

The Lost Tycoon, probably the most compelling of the three biographies, cites "a half dozen bona fide sources close to Donald who said that his claim was "a barefaced lie."

Bernard Dillion, vice president of Trump Sports and Entertainment, later told the Associated Press: "Trump definitely never planned to be on that fateful flight."]

***

In Atlantic City, Donald wandered into the "alligator-infested swamp" of the Taj Mahal's long-delayed construction. Faced with an ocean of difficulties, he put up a brave front, claiming he was erecting "the Eighth Wonder of the World." He told the *New York Daily News* that he had cash reserves of $200 million as a safeguard buffer. He did not.

To finance the construction of the Taj, Donald negotiated with Merrill Lynch to sell $675 million worth of junk bonds, the full amount repayable at harsh terms with high interest rates.

Many business reporters for *The Wall Street Journal* warned him that his shuttle and his gambling casinos were shaky business enterprises that might not survive a downturn in the economy.

"Don't worry," he assured the doubters. "The Taj will be a great monster success." He announced that it was set for "the grandest of openings on April 2, 1990."

During the pre-dawn hours of that day, laborers were slaving to meet the deadline. Many of the suites hadn't received their final coats of paint and others lacked carpeting. Electricians were still wiring lamps. Tensions became so severe that fistfights broke out between workers and their foremen.

On the day of its opening, the Taj was already $65 million over budget.

At least insofar as publicity was concerned, Donald made as much of a hoopla as he could, following Mae West's advice: "When you arrive in town, don't keep it a secret."

He loudly promoted the Taj's status as the tallest building at the resort, and he had positioned his name in large red neon letters near its summit.

Evoking a fantasy from the Arabian Nights, it sported candy-striped onion domes, gilded minarets, and glass effigies of elephants flanking the entrances to the casinos.

***

When the Taj opened, America was experiencing an economic downturn. After a successful period in the mid- to late 1980s, Atlantic City was said to have "tiptoed" into the early 1990s, when all the casino hotels reported a drastic drop in revenue. Nearly all of them were plagued with mammoth debt. "Where have all the high rollers gone?" asked one quietly desperate hotel manager.

After the Stock Market crash of 1987, Donald witnessed a $75 million loss on the value of his casino stock.

At 10AM that morning of April 2, hundreds of "gawkers or gamblers" poured into the resort. The day was a disaster, and the night didn't get any better.

Author Harry Hurt III wrote about opening night: "Behind its flashy, candy-colored face, the Taj looks like a shipwrecked ocean liner. The roof leaks in several places. Many of the room keys didn't fit their assigned locks. There isn't enough water pressure to reach the top floor suites. Room service is swamped, as are the waiters in the first-and second-floor restaurants."

The Taj opened to the sound of firing lasers and blaring trumpets, but inside its gaming room, it was less of a blast. Donald needed to gross a million dollars a day in winnings to pay off his debt load and keep the ice buckets filled. Now, in 1990, he was said to have only $1.6 million in his personal bank accounts, as opposed to his estimated worth of $1.5 billion during the late 1980s.

The opening night mob eagerly awaited the arrival of the movie stars that Donald had promised. Tom Cruise had been invited as the major lure, and his fans gathered outside. But he was a no-show. So was the next big name: Jack Nicholson. Fans also awaited the arrival of Liza Minnelli, Brooke Shields, Don Johnson, and Melanie Griffith.

That waited and waited, but each of those stars opted not to appear. Neither did Ivana. Even Donald's mistress, Marla Maples, was not there.

Ironically, the biggest celebrity in sight was Merv Griffin, who claimed, "I have come out of curiosity. I'm glad it's not my opening."

At the opening ceremony, James Usry, the mayor of Atlantic City, was introduced. But he was booed for the span of an entire minute, based on his recent indictment on a corruption charge.

There were 167 table games open and available for wagers, but clients had to use play money because the computer-driven change machines crashed. One irate gambler stood before a cash machine and said, "You either got no money at all, or else the goddamn thing spits out money like you've won Lotto."

The money crunch still wasn't resolved the next day. "It was a fiasco," claimed John R. O'Donnell, company president. "Donald went crazy, looking for scapegoats."

"I'm going to fire every asshole in this joint," he threatened.

Guests dined in the lavish Scheherazade Restaurant. Its pinkish glow made even unattractive people better looking.

The high rollers booked the penthouse suites named after such historical personages as Cleopatra. For $10,000 a night, a gambler could become a conquering hero in the suites honoring Alexander the Great or Napoléon.

Donald turned on his faithful brother Robert. A meeting of the chief executives was announced for 8AM on April 6. In front of his associates, Donald denounced Robert. "I though you could handle the job that I so generously gave you. But you fucked up. I must have been out of my mind to put you in charge. I'm fucking sick of all of you losers."

That morning, Robert resigned as CEO of the Taj and was seen boarding a helicopter for a return to Manhattan.

In the next few weeks, the Taj recovered, reporting gross revenues hovering around $35 million, which set a record for Atlantic City.

Members of the press joined the chorus of disappointment: In a scathing article in The *New York Daily*

When Donald ran for President in 2016, the question was often asked, "How can a person who has filed for bankruptcy four times expect to be elected President of the United States? How is Donald Trump able to file for bankruptcy so many times?"

The answer is, "He didn't." Donald himself has never filed for bankruptcy. His corporations have filed for Chapter 11 bankruptcy four times. All of these bankruptcies were connected to over-leveraged casino and hotel properties in Atlantic City.

News, reporters disputed many of Donald's claims about the casino. They said that the Taj rose only forty-one stories, not fifty-one, as Donald had asserted. Additionally, the square footage of the casino, at 120,000 square feet, was not the largest in the world. In Las Vegas, the Riviera boasted 125,000 square feet.

BANKRUPTCIES

"I don't like the 'B' word."

—*Donald Trump*

It was revealed that the Taj needed to gross $1.3 million a day to meet its expenses and debt services. Later, an even more devastating report revealed that the Taj was "cannibalizing" earnings generated by his other, older Atlantic City hotels.

Donald's oft-demonstrated skill at procuring major-league entertainers like Elton John or the Rolling Stones seemed threatened by his financial woes.

"Trump's pockets aren't deep enough to pay for such entertainers as Paul McCartney or Madonna," said a talent broker. "Who could he afford? Perhaps Mamie Van Doren doing a strip act, I haven't heard of her since the 1950s. Is she still around?"

When The Taj filed for Chapter 11 bankruptcy in 1991, Donald was forced to surrender half of his personal stake in the operation. He was also forced to sell his luxury yacht and his ill-fated shuttle.

The following year, as the outlook for Atlantic City as a casino venue continued its downward spiral, Trump Plaza also filed for bankruptcy, prompting Donald's forfeiture to his lenders of a forty-nine percent stake in the Plaza Hotel.

The Taj was eventually forced to confront a payoff of the staggering costs of its construction ($822 million). Donald had been forced to abandon his ownership of his trio of casinos. He was also put on an allowance. Up to that point, he had been spending $1 million a month, but that was reduced to $450,000 a month. His yearly salary was not to exceed $200,000.

Financial guru and journalist Allan Sloan delivered the most damaging critique: "Donald Trump is on his way down. The question isn't whether his real estate-casino-airline empire will be drastically shrunk. The question is whether Trump will be left with anything at all."

Trump Entertainment Resorts, Inc.—an entity previously in charge of booking such mega-expensive venues as the Mike Tyson fights—would file for bankruptcy four times, beginning in 1991 after the construction of the Taj.

During the 21st century, there were three additional bankruptcies: 2004, 2009, and 2014.

As a business entity, it still exists. In an appearance on MSNBC, Donald was interviewed by Michael Isikoff. Donald said, "I don't like the 'B' word."

Isikoff wanted to know what exactly he was paid for if he had "had nothing to do with running the company any more."

"Excuse me?" Donald said. "I'm paid because of my genius, okay?"

[During the years that followed, Donald consolidated his trio of Atlantic City resorts under a publicly traded company, Trump Hotels and Casino Resorts. In 2004, that organization filed for bankruptcy when confronted with a $1.8 billion debt it could not service. That forced the sale of Trump Marina, which became the Golden Nugget. Trump Plaza closed for good in 2014, and the Trump Taj Mahal is now owned by billionaire Carl Icahn.]

***

The Trump Organization has known good times and bad times, though prospering greatly during Donald's run for the presidency in 2016.

But in 1992, when it was mired in that Atlantic City mess, it owed $2.2 billion. He also personally owed $115 million. But before the banks went after him, he got a three-year extension on his loans.

As he wrote in *The Art of the Comeback*, "I hated having to go to the bankers with my hat in my hand. And, yes, my lifestyle was a little bit cramped for a while. I guess that's important. But getting a deal on the table—without filing for bankruptcy—was the most important thing of all."

Because of his troubles, he had to give up some of his biggest dreams, such as constructing the world's tallest building on the old West Side Rail Yards of the Penn Central.

The 1990s were heartbreaking for Donald, as bankers continued to "dismantle my empire like a pack of sons of bitches."

He managed to hold onto Mar-a-Lago through a series of clever maneuvers, but was forced to surrender "my jewel," the Plaza. Citibank took it over and sold it for $325 million in 1995.

Donald's biographer, Timothy O'Brien, wrote: "By 1993, with his casinos in hock, most of his real estate holdings were either forfeit or stagnant, and his father was slipping into the fog of Alzheimer's disease. Donald, at the age of forty-seven, had run out of money. It was a humiliating experience."

He had to turn to his siblings, including Maryanne, for a bailout. He needed some $10 million from their trust funds to keep operating his office and to pay for his personal living expenses. Each of them wanted a guarantee that they would be repaid, but he had no collateral. Donald got the loan, but when he later come back and asked for $20 million more, the siblings balked. He finally got another loan from them, but only after much persuasion.

At his lowest point, when it appeared that Donald might have to shut down, he told his associates, "In that case, I could always run for President of the United States."

In 1990, when his prospects of maintaining his empire were growing dim, *Playboy* had fallen for his hype. The magazine said Donald "has amassed a fortune that his father never dreamed possible, including a stash of $900 million and a geyser of $50 million a week from his Atlantic City casinos."

He put up a brave front for his staff during the bad years from 1992 to 1995. "Survive until 1995, you mother fuckers, Survive until then." He preached that a lot.

Dozens of bankers later wrote off several hundred million dollars in loans they'd made to Donald, or to entities he had strenuously sponsored. One banker, who preferred not to be named, said, "We just lent Trump money based on his name. I, among others, fell for his self-proclaimed myth about how much money he had, but also bought his delusion about how much money he was going to make. Guess what? We tossed some money into a bottomless pit."

WIN SOME, LOSE SOME
The Art of the Comeback

Make-Believe Money: If you don't have millions to play with, perhaps you can fake-pretend with Donald's money game. The game isn't over until somebody gets fired.

A recently widowed Elizabeth Christ Trump, Donald's grandmother, could not have imaged that the little company she had created with her son Fred (Donald's father) back in 1923 would one day morph into the Trump Organization.

Donald was given the company in 1971. He renamed it Trump Enterprises, LLC. Not satisfied with that, by November, he had changed its label to the Trump Organization LLC.

In 2016, this privately owned multi-national conglomerate operates out of Trump Tower in midtown Manhattan, and is owned and managed by Donald himself and three of his children—Donald Jr., Ivanka, and Eric. Together, they preside over this vast holding company for their father's wide-ranging business ventures and investments.

It would take an entire book to survey the vast range of their real estate developments alone, including all the towering structures that carry the Trump name. They include the Trump World Tower at 845 United Nations Plaza, a super-luxury, high-rise tower directly across from the United Nations secretariat. It is one of the tallest residential buildings in the country.

The Trump Organization is hardly confined to real estate development. It owns, operates, invests in, or develops properties such as hotels, resorts, residential towers, and golf courses in different countries, including Scotland. In his more than five hundred subsidiaries, entities with 264 of them bearing Donald's name and another fifty or so showcasing his initials.

It branches out to include entertainment, publishing, management, financial services, food and beverages, online travel, even a reality TV program, *The Apprentice*.

It has also been linked to beauty pageants, such as *Miss Universe, Miss USA,* and *Miss Teen USA.*

It also tiptoes into fashion, home furnishings, jewelry, books, chocolate bars, lighting fixtures, and even bottled spring water.

In 2015, Donald earned $71 million from condo sales alone, while collecting rents of $41.9 million.

Although the Trump name may have been damaged during his run for the presidency in 2016, before that, many developers paid him to market their properties and to be its public face. For that reason, Donald does not own most of the buildings that display his name.

Forbes magazine said that this section of his empire is actually run by Ivanka and her two brothers and is the most valuable part

Elizabeth Christ's signature, in her capacity as beneficiary, is on this certificate of transfer of the estate of Fred Trump into her name. Signed Oct 23, 1918, it attests to her payment of $268.71 in"transfer taxes."

At the time, no one could have imagined its long-term implications.

of his portfolio, earning at least $575 million annually.

Although Donald has campaigned to bring jobs back to the U.S. of A., he deals with an international coterie of financiers, with interests in Istanbul, Seoul, Toronto, Dubai, Panama, the Dominican Republic, Manila, Vancouver, and Israel, among other countries.

A great deal of Donald's wealth is concentrated in financial and commodities markets. He owns stock in such companies as General Electric, Coca-Cola, Bank of America, Nike, Google, Apple, Inc., Philip Morris, Citigroup, Morgan Stanley, Johnson & Johnson, and Facebook, among dozens of other corporations. One of his biggest holdings, maybe a stake as high as $50 million, is in Black Rock's Obsidian Fund. And yes, let us not forget…He also invests in U.S. Treasury Bonds.

He sometimes ventures beyond his traditional venues to lend his name to men's clothing, to energy drinks marketed within the Israeli and Palestinian markets, and even to a fragrance, SUCCESS, associated with his name.

As his rivals for the Republican presidential nomination, including "little Marco Rubio," have pointed out, not all of these ventures have been successful.

Trump Steaks was launched in 2007, but has been discontinued. Donald claimed "When it comes to great steaks, I've just raised the *stakes!* The world's greatest steaks. One bite and you'll know what I'm talking about. Steak is my favorite food."

Trump Vodka, announced as a super premium liquor in 2006, faded by 2011. "It failed to meet our threshold requirements," Donald was quoted as saying.

When it was announced, Donald said, "I fully expect Trump Vodka will be the most asked-for cocktail in America.

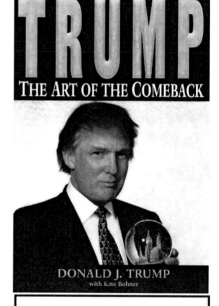

DONALD J. TRUMP
with Kate Bohner

But is it Presidential?

In this 1997 book by Donald, he delivered this as one of his top ten comeback tips:

GET EVEN.

"During the bad times, I learned who was loyal and who wasn't. I believe in an eye for an eye. A couple of people who betrayed me need my help now, and I'm screwing them against the wall! I am doing a number…and I'm having such fun."

Call it T&T or Trump and Tonic."

Many of his other enterprises went belly up, including Trump Mortgage, announced in 2006, shutting down in 2007. Donald Jr. had predicted it would be the No. 1 home lender in the United States, but the crash of the housing market ended that.

In summing up, Donald said, "In the end, you're measured not by how much you undertake, but by what you finally accomplish."

KING KONG
Donald Scales the Empire State Building

In *The Art of the Comeback,* published in 1997, Donald Trump ran a picture of Manhattan's Empire State Building, by night and fully illuminated. Once the tallest building in the world. It is a landmark known around the world, like the Leaning Tower of Pisa.

Under a picture of the soaring skyscraper, he wrote, "I own this one, too."

That was not accurate. Here's the scoop:

Among other fragrances, SUCCESS by Trump includes an alcohol-free deodorant guaranteed to mask body odors generated by long, repetitive stints of self-promotion.

Trump Magazine...a self-promotional branding device. SURPRISE! Ivanka gets to be a cover girl.

Construction started on its 102 floors in 1930 in the aftermath of the Wall Street crash. Opened in 1931, it was built for $41 million. Governor Franklin D. Roosevelt spoke at its inauguration. The entire world became aware of it in 1933 when King Kong ascended it during the film's dramatic finale in this popular box office success.

On July 28, 1945, as World War II was coming to an end, a B-25 on a routine flight to Newark crashed into the north side of the fog-shrouded skyscraper, leaving a gash between the 78th and 80th floors and killing fourteen people.

In a year that saw Nazi Germany surrender, the U.S. dropping two atomic bombs on Japan, and the end of the Japanese Empire, this crash was voted as one of the most important news events of that year.

In 1961, hotelier Harry B. Helmsley, Lawrence A Wien, and Peter Malkin bought control of the skyscraper in a $65 million syndication deal.

That same year, Harry sold the building's title to the Prudential Insurance for $29 million. Thirty years later, Prudential unloaded the title for $42 million to Oliver Grace, Jr., Actually, he was just a front man working on behalf of Hideki Yokoi, a Japanese hotelier serving a prison sentence in connection with a deadly fire at one of his hotels that killed thirty-three people.

On the death of Yokoi, his daughter, Kiiko Nakahara, teamed up with Donald to gain some control over the skyscraper.

Not pleased with a "passive investment because of that damn Helmsley lease," Donald suggested that he and Kiiko sue Helmsley, which they did. The case would drag on for seven years, Donald claiming that the Helmsleys had turned the

It was said that Donald often pictured himself as *King Kong* (see upper photo, from one of the movie versions), scaling the heights of the Empire State Building, one of the world's most recognizable landmarks.

He often told out-of-towners that he owned the building..."one hundred percent." He did not.

188

landmark town into a "high-rise slum." In court, he charged that Leona and Harry had broken their contract in a hundred different ways.

Harry's wife, Leona, hated Donald, and was horrified that he had any connection to the building. "He'll have bragging rights—and that's it. Actually, my beloved Harry and I own the building."

Donald detested the deal the Helmsleys had made for the controlling stock in the building. He referred to the lease as "onerous," because it gave Harry and his partners the right to rent out the entire building in exchange for the "measly" sum of $1.9 million annually. The tenants paid $80 million in rent, the Helmsleys, through their Helmsley-Spear Management group, benefitted from "the deal of a lifetime. The lease would remain in effect until 2075.

During his tenure, Donald tried to restore some of the fading luster of the Empire State Building, investing $70 million in a capital improvement program using Japanese money.

The litigation was still ongoing in 1997 when Harry died. Throughout its duration, Leona was imprisoned from 1992 to 1994 for Federal income tax evasion.

With legal bills mounting year after year, Donald convinced Kiiko to abandon the lawsuit. She and her associates had been unable to break the Helmsley lease, so in 2002, they sold their interest in the building for $57.5 million. Donald acted as their agent for the sale.

He did not own the Empire State Building, as he'd claimed. His settlement with Kiiko was never made public, but it is believed that he profited by more than $6 million based on his management of her interests.

"THE WOLF OF 40 WALL STREET"

Donald Buys a Chunk of NYC's Financial District for a Measly One Million Dollars. Analysts Define It as "The Real Estate Deal of a Lifetime"

The building widely recognized as 40 Wall Street, with 70 stories, between Nassau Street and William Street, had briefly, and with oceans of controversy, reigned for a few months after its completion in 1930 as the tallest building in the world. Soon after, during the depths of the Great Depression, its height was surpassed by a spire affixed, midtown, to the top of the Chrysler Building in midtown. The debate ("Does a spire constitute a bona-fide floor and does it therefore contribute to the 'tallest building' designation?) became a moot point when the even taller Empire State Building opened, a year later.

During the course of its long and much-traded life, it bore names which included The Bank of Manhattan Trust Building, and the Manhattan Company Building before settling into its present moniker, 40 Wall Street.

It experienced an eerie parallel to the better-known crash of a small plane into the side of its competitor, The Empire State Building.

On the night of May 20, 1946, during a heavy fog, a Beechcraft C-45F expediter under the auspices of the U.S. Army Air Force crashed into the building's 58th floor as it was heading toward New Jersey's Newark Airport.

"I won't settle for skimpy towels. Why should you?" — Leona M. Helmsley, President

HARLEY of New York. A great hotel doesn't have to be expensive.

Leona Helmsley in an example of "I AM THE QUEEN" ads, which increased business by infusing overnight guests with a sense of high-octane entitlement.

Inset is the cover of *People* magazine adding to Leona's devastating humiliations. No one gloated more than Donald.

In 1982, Ferdinand Marcos, the controversial and crooked president of the Philippines, secretly purchased the building through proxies. When he was removed from power in the wake of corruption charges, his assets in the United States were seized. One of the gems of the collection was Forty Wall Street. It languished in litigation and limbo until 1995.

That's when it caught the eye of Donald Trump, who, in spite of his other financial troubles, still had his eye out "for the real estate deal of a lifetime."

"After the building was pointed out to me, I couldn't resist."

He had long cherished a dream about owning a skyscraper on Wall Street, the pre-eminent symbol of wealth in America. "I needed a symbol of my ever-growing power," he claimed.

As part of his plan to acquire it, he toured all seventy-two of its floors, including its fabled tower. "In my opinion, 40 Wall Street, which I renamed

The Trump Building, is the most beautiful building in New York, and its green copper spire is in a class by itself."

He found that its tenants consisted mainly of banks and the offices of Wall Street attorneys. When Marcos lost control of the Philippines, the building was up for grabs. Early flirtations with potential investors didn't pan out.

In the mid-1990s, despite the terrible real estate market, coupled with Donald's own financial woes, he decided to make a move toward buying it. Complicating matters was the keen interest from the Kinson Company, a group of investors from Hong Kong, who also wanted it.

The Kinson people immediately confronted a daunting obstacle in the form of the Hinnebergs, a rich German family who owned the land on which the building sat. Only the lease, which still had sixty-three years before its expired, was available for sale. Many of the lease's antiquated provisions dated from the 1930s, and were subject to a wide variety of legal interpretations. Banks were consequently leery of any involvement in the purchase.

Yet despite its many problems, the Kinson group poured millions into the building, usually for issues associated with the infrastructures. *[These included, among others, an upgrading of the building's air conditioning facilities.]*

Donald learned that building contractors were having a field day billing millions of dollars of shoddy (or non-existent) "improvements" to the Kinson Group. They were also facing an avalanche of lawsuits from tenants, and the "discovery" of many "expensive to resolve" liens on the building.

In desperation, the Hong Kong investors turned to Donald. Specializing in the manufacture of sneakers back in Hong Kong, they had no experience with the nightmares associated with New York City real estate.

Meeting with the group, Donald found them eager to "get the hell out of New York." He made an offer that he thought would be greeted with derision and laughter. "A cool million dollars. They accepted my deal with-

During its brief reign, 40 Wall Street was the tallest building in the world.

Before Donald took it over, its most notorious owner was Ferdinand Marcos, the deposed dictator of the Philippines.

191

out a complaint." Donald was shocked.

He understood their eagerness to leave. "As I learned on my father's knee, New York is a minefield, and if you don't know what you're doing, you're screwed."

Immediately, Donald dealt with Walter Hinneberg, the head of the German family who owned the land. "It was a love fest," he claimed. With him, Donald worked out a deal, extending the lease on the building for two-hundred years.

His next move was to get rid of the liens and lawsuits, which he proceeded to do. "After all, I'm the master of the deal."

Donald closed the agreement on November 30, 1995. "Another landmark skyscraper was 'my baby,' with my name on it."

Once he was in control, he learned that he was entitled to tax refunds amounting to $10 million. He also signed leases entitling him to collect $20 million a year in rents.

Donald tried to sell the Trump Building in 2003, but no offer materialized.

In 2005, during the ninth episode of the fourth season of *The Apprentice*, he claimed that he paid only $1 million for a skyscraper worth $400 million.

Two years later, in 2007, on CNBC's *The Billionaire Inside*, he once again stated that he'd paid only $1 million for the building whose value he had by then redefined at $600 million.

***

Aside from his business ventures, Donald faced problems on a personal level.

He had a big decision to make: Which woman should he dump? His wife, Ivana? Or perhaps his blonde-haired mistress, Marla Maples?

Chapter Nine

FLASH AND CASH,
"The Imperial Couple"

DYSFUNCTIONAL, GREEDY, BRASH, & BRAZEN
They're Larger than Dynasty

GOING FOR THE GOLD
Donald Dumps His "Mitteleuropa Blonde."
Ivana Fights Back

HOTLY PURSUED BY ITALIAN STALLIONS
Ivana Inflates Her Chest and Her Bank Account

For an athletic girl of modest means, born in communist-controlled Czechoslovakia, Ivana Zelnicekova rose to become what some reporters called "the most famous woman in the world." She would also become one of the richest.

Of course, to reach such a lofty position, it helped that she married the man she nicknamed "The Donald." He introduced her to a world of sex, glamor, power, and money beyond her wildest dreams. Had she stayed married to The Donald, she might one day have become First Lady, returning beauty, elegance, and grandeur to the White House, in the view of some Republicans.

Ivana's unauthorized biographer, Norma King, listed some of the words used to describe Ivana in the press: "Statuesque, dynamic, outgoing, beautiful, fearless, brash, intelligent, energetic, competitive, self-sufficient, fashion-wise, and dominating."

Her critics called her "tasteless, tawdry, tacky, blowzy, overblown, kitschy, snide, picky, nasty, and bitchy." Her diction was called "a bouillabaisse of words sounding like a James Bond villainess and delivered with a machine-gun rattle."

She couldn't have been more different from Donald's second wife, model Marla Maples. In contrast, Ivana liked to work instead of spending the day making herself look more beautiful.

"I work hard because I have a lot of energy," Ivana said. "After work, I love to dine out and dance, and I adore entertainment. I'm also devoted to my children."

Life was beautiful then: Pictured here at the apogee of her fame and glory, Ivana Trump, according to a poll, was "the most envied woman on the face of earth." She even had "The Donald."

Donald was attacked when he put her in charge of his Trump Castle at Atlantic City and later made her president of the Plaza Hotel in Manhattan, but she proved capable in both capacities, overseeing the mass of details associated with both their restorations and their day-to-day operations.

As an example, at the Plaza, she hired craftspeople from Paris to reproduce the 18th Century tapestries similar to those hanging in the Louvre. She used these tapestries to adorn the Plaza's lobby, restored to its original glory, and to decorate the Oak Room and the Grand Ballroom. She also made the Plaza once again a venue for high fashion shows.

She and Donald often faced heavy criticism for their lavish lifestyle, as evoked by their yacht, the *Trump Princess*, and the dazzling Mar-a-Lago mansion in Palm Beach.

On the cover of the May, 1992 issue of *Vanity Fair*, Ivana satirized herself as a world-class star. Bob Colacello wrote of her "literary debut" with her first novel, *For Love Alone*.

In it, her heroine, Katrinka, "for one brief moment had it all."

"Donald and I have been called *nouveau riche*," she said. "Half a century ago, the Vanderbilts, the Astors, and the Rockefellers flaunted their wealth even when America was going through a devastating depression, with breadlines and soup kitchens."

"Unlike all this vast inherited wealth, Donald earned his money the old-fashioned way: He worked hard for it."

FLINGS OR FRIENDSHIPS?

Donald's Associations with Carolyne Roehm, Allison Maher, Peggy Fleming, Katarina Witt, Carol Alt, Catherine Oxenberg, & Georgette Mosbacher

Although Donald denied the particular liaisons referred to in the press, in *The Art of the Comeback*, he made a confession: "If I told the real stories of my experiences, often with seemingly very happily married and important women, this book would be a guaranteed best-seller. I'd love to tell all, using names and places, but I just don't think it's right."

In that book, without naming names, he did give some tantalizing insights into how some prominent women came on to him. Many of his New Yorker friends figured out who he was writing about, even though he didn't name names.

He related an experience at a dinner party hosted by one of the most admired men in the world. Donald was seated between him and his wife, "a lady of great social pedigree and wealth." He claimed that during dinner, she reached under the table and felt him up.

Also in that book, on another occasion, he encountered a well-known socialite a week before her wedding, to which he had been invited. He offered to give her a ride back home in his limousine. He claimed, "She jumped on top of me, wanting to get screwed."

"Women have one of the great acts of all time," he wrote. "The smart ones act very feminine and needy, but inside, they are real killers. The person who came up with the expression, 'the weaker sex" was either very naïve or had to be kidding."

***

As time went by, Donald continued to employ Ivana's business savvy and management style, but he drifted from her elegant boudoir.

He was rather frank with reporter John Taylor from *New York* magazine.

"Trump talked about girls all the time. He said, 'I can't believe I'm married. This is the prime time of my life.'"

In 1989, Ivana heard rumors that her husband was sleeping around. She was told that at social gatherings or in restaurants, "Some of New York's most gorgeous women were liter-

Taste setter Carolyne Roehm denied rumors that she was involved with Donald. She was already married to one of America's richest men.

ally making themselves available to him."

Names of women were cited in the press. It has never been determined if some of these rather prominent women were lovers, part of short-term flings, or friends. Many of these alleged girlfriends were rich, famous, or married, perhaps a combination of all three. Month after month, the tabloids and gossips cited Donald's alleged adultery, suggesting that he seduced more women than Julio Iglesias.

***

Gossip swirled that Donald was involved with the formidable Carolyne Roehm, one of the taste-makers of America, known for her classical designs, formal gardens, and sparkling dinner parties. She wrote lush, inspiring books for women and was also listed in the International Best-Dressed Hall of Fame.

She denied these reports, telling *The Washington Post*, "They are ridiculous. I'm married to the greatest man in the world."

She was referring to corporate raider Henry Kravis, the co-founder of Kohlberg, Kravis, Roberts, & Co., a private equity firm worth $95 billion. Forbes ranked Kravis as the 108th-richest man in the United States.

***

Rightly or wrongly, Donald was also linked to Allison Maher, a former model and TV producer who married billionaire Leonard Stern in 1987. This businessman, investor, and philanthropist is the chairman and CEO of the privately owned Hartz Group, which by 1984 controlled 75% to 90% of the U.S. market of pet supply goods.

***

In 1986, Donald met Peggy Fleming at the unveiling in Manhattan of the Wollman Rink in Cen-

The famous figure skater, Peggy Fleming, depicted here in all her graceful action. Did she skate into Donald's heart or just circle around him?

197

tral Park. Her manager, Karen Conrad, denied rumors of an affair. "Their paths do cross when she's in New York doing work for ABC Sports. But she's a happily married person to Dr. Greg Jenkins, a dermatologist who was once an amateur pair figure skater."

Peggy began skating at the age of nine and went on to be a 1968 Olympic Champion in Ladies Singles and a three time World Champion from 1966 to 1968.

***

Fleming wasn't the only skater who became linked to Donald. There was a flare-up with Katarina Witt, the Olympic figure-skating champion.

Born in East Germany in 1965, Witt is one of the most successful figure skaters of all time. After the reunification of Germany, Stasi files revealed that the secret police worked hard to keep her from defecting, giving her cars and gifts, deluxe accommodations, and free travel.

Years later, in 1998, she posed naked for *Playboy* under headlines that promoted her as "one of East Germany's most willing accomplices."

Donald had seen her on a few occasions, including her opening night performance at Madison Square Garden.

In the wake of that, he noted that every article about her linked his

Coming in from the cold: East German ice champion Katarina Witt on cover of *Playboy*.

Carol Alt, winner of the coveted slot on the front cover of *Sports Illustrated's* Swimsuit edition, wearing (rare for *S.I.*) a one-piece bathing suit in a landscape usually devoted to bikinis.

name to hers, including allegations that she has spurned his sexual overtures.

When *People* magazine made the claim, he fired off a letter: "Each and every time a story is written about Katarina Witt, my name is mentioned as a spurned suitor. The truth is that I hardly knew her except that on two occasions, she came to my office, the first time with Brian Boitano, another ski champion, and the second time with her agent in order to have lunch and to discuss 'endorsements.' After that, I was deluged with calls from Katarina asking me to go out with her (I have an abundance of witnesses), but I had no interest. She then invited me to a skating show at Madison Square Garden and to a party after the performance at which, because of my disinterest, she was very rude. Everyone is spurned at some time, but in this case, it was Katarina, not Donald."

Cosmetics Queen, promotions guru, and hard-driving entrepreneur, Georgette Mosbacher.

***

Donald was also linked to supermodel Carol Alt, who appeared as a contestant on his *Celebrity Apprentice* TV show. Her manager, Steve Gutstein, denied rumors of an affair, saying, "Donald Trump is a fortunate man, but he's not that fortunate."

From 1983 to 1996, Alt was married to Ron Greschnaer, a New York Rangers player. After her divorce, she had a long-term involvement with Alexei Yahsin, a former professional ice hockey player.

Born in Flushing, Queens, Alt received maximum publicity when she was featured on the 1982 cover of the *Sports Illustrated* Swimwear edition. She also appeared in December, 2008, in a nude pictorial in *Playboy*.

Over the course of her career, Alt has graced the covers of more than 500 magazines and is ranked as one of the Top Models of all time, right up there with Cindy Crawford and the super- rich Gisele Bündchen.

***

Ironically, Donald's name was linked in the press with Prairie cosmetics queen Georgette Mosbacher, one of Ivana's "ladies who lunch" friends.

A leader in Republican circles, Georgette was the national co-chairman of John McCain's run for the presidency in 2000.

In addition to being a cosmetics impresario, she's the *grande dame* of GOP fund-raising. She was married to Robert Mosbacher, the former U.S. Secretary of Commerce.

"Rumors about Donald and me are absurd," the thrice-married Georgette told a reporter. Her husband, Robert, was credited with launching her into a world of wealth, soirées, and presidential politics.

COSMOPOLITAN
June 1985 • 80p

Why Catherine O took Joan Collins' man

How to stay single though married

See Fascinating Aida at our cabaret

Never tinker with a fairy

Rare men Bob Geldof Ken Livingstone

Two 2CVs to win

Fiction Tom Wolfe's shattering forecast

Catherine Oxenberg

Catherine Oxenberg once starred as Princess Diana in a made-for-TV movie. As the daughter of Princess Elizabeth of Yugoslavia, she is in line to inherit the throne of the United Kingdom, but 1,374 royal heirs will have to die before that happens.

***

The lovely Catherine Oxenberg is an elegant New Yorker best known for her performance as Amanda Carrington on that 1980s soap opera, *Dynasty*.

Those rumors about Donald and me are a complete joke," Oxenberg told *People* magazine. "I hardly know the man."

A friend of hers told *People*, "Occasionally, Catherine and Donald do stuff, but they're not sleeping together. Trump is not a shabby escort."

Oxenberg is the daughter of Princess Elizabeth of Yugoslavia, and was once famously married to producer Robert Evans, although the union was annulled a few months after the marriage ceremony.

She made her acting debut in the 1982 made-for-TV film, *The Royal Romance of Charles and Diana*, in which she starred as the Princess of Wales.

Oxenberg is the 1,375th in the line of succession to the throne of the United Kingdom and the British Commonwealth.

DONALD AS A CENTERPIECE
(NOT Centerfold) **FOR PLAYBOY**

Hugh Hefner, publisher of *Playboy*, seemingly has had a long-enduring fascination with the lifestyle and seductions of Donald Trump. Some sources falsely claimed that the satirical magazine Hefner once launched (it was entitled *Trump*) was actually named after Donald.

It was not. This glossy magazine of satire and humor published only two editions in 1957, when Donald was about eleven years old, before Hefner had even heard of him. The magazine's mascot was a trumpeter herald inspired by the illustrations by John Tenniel in *Alice in Wonderland*.

Hefner's dream involved configuring Trump as competition for *Mad* magazine. Initially, sales were good for a magazine that sold at the time, retail, for 50 cents. It featured glossy and costly production standards, and it had the misfortune of making its debut at the time a financial crunch forced Hefner to scale back on his non-*Playboy* interests. That signaled twilight for *Trump* magazine, even before it got off the ground.

Hefner had always been noted for the cover art of his magazines. He had launched *Playboy's* first issue (December, 1953) with a cover that featured a nude photo of Marilyn Monroe, something that was very daring at the time. As Hefner became more and more fascinated by Donald Trump, he decided to feature him on the cover of an issue (March, 1990) of his world-famous magazine.

When he announced his decision, his staff asked in as-

"Mr. Playboy," Hugh Hefner himself, once said that he and Donald Trump shared at least one thing in common: "The pursuit of beautiful babes. I featured him in *Playboy*, since we shared somewhat the same reputation of being part Bill Gates, part Casanova."

Ever since *Playboy* came onto the stands in 1953 with Marilyn Monroe on the cover, Donald had been its avid reader, not realizing that one day he, too, would land on the cover of the morally unconventional magazine, often read by some men while "sitting on their thrones."

tonishment, "Has Trump agreed to pose for a nude centerfold? Maybe we should change the name to *Playgirl* and try to appeal to women and gays."

"Fuck that!" Hefner said. "No, he's not going to pose for a centerfold, but I want an interview with him."

To orchestrate it, he sent reporter Glenn Plaskin to interview Donald, but he never got the kind of tantalizing revelations that Hefner really wanted.

During his interview, Plaskin bluntly asked Donald, "Are you monogamous?"

"I don't have to answer that," Donald said, meaning, of course, that he was not. "I never speak of my wife, which is one of the advantages of not being a politician. My marriage is and should be a personal thing.

The cover of Hugh Hefner's first edition (January 1957) of *Trump.*

The reporter pressed on: "But you do enjoy flirtations?"

"I think any man enjoys flirtations, and if he said he didn't, he'd be lying, or he'd be a politician trying to get the extra four votes."

"How is your marriage," Plaskin asked.

"Ivana is a very kind and good woman, and she has the instincts and drive of a good manager. She's focused and she's a perfectionist."

"And as a wife, not a manager?" the reporter asked.

"I never comment on romance," Donald said. "She is a great mother, a good woman who does a good job."

At the time that he made that claim, Donald was involved in a torrid romance with Marla Maples.

MADONNA MIA!
The King of Hype Berates the Queen of Hype

In the late 1980s and early 90s, Donald was a bit of a gossip, leaking stories of celebrity indiscretions to the New York City tabloids. Journalist Tom Robbins claimed, "He almost single-handedly revived the fortunes of *The New York Post* and *Daily News*. More often than not, Trump's tips turned out to be true."

Tabloid writer George Rush said, "Trump was buddies with many of the gossip reporters, even calling them up on weekends just to say hello. He would phone us at home, sometimes on Saturdays, and ask, 'What do you think of this girl or that girl? What number would you give her?'"

He evaluated women on a scale of one to ten, claiming that he never dated any woman below a ten.

In 2016, a journalist wrote, "Hard to believe, but in the early 1990s, Donald Trump was as popular with supermodels as he is today with white supremacists."

Donald claimed that women—some of them very famous—made attempts to link themselves with him in a sexual sense. He also claimed that women sometimes falsely claimed that they "spurned Trump's sexual advances." He shot back that at times it was he who rejected the aggressive come-ons.

"Even Madonna, a master of hype, got in on the act," he wrote.

He had encountered the future Queen of Pop back in the heyday of Studio 54 in Manhattan. Steve Rubell, one of the founders of '54, had introduced her to him when she was relatively unknown. He also had chatted briefly with her when she was shooting a Versace photo layout at Mar-a-Lago in Palm Beach.

The Madonna/Trump publicity had begun after she became world famous. Some of it derived from their encounter at a dinner honoring fashion maven Diana Vreeland. He spotted Madonna and her entourage arriving at the door, recalling that she was beautifully dressed except for combat boots.

Over the course of that dinner, one of her male dancers approached Donald and told him that Madonna would like to chat with him, and could he please come over to her table.

Before the evening ended, Donald, indeed, came over to greet her, and witnesses said that the two of them had a friendly chat that lasted for about fifteen minutes before he left.

The next day when he read *The New York Post*, he was shocked to see a story that he had come on sexually to Madonna and that

Madonna was the Queen of Hype, and Donald was its King. They certainly knew each other, and no doubt circled each other, but reports of an illicit romance between them provided tabloid fodder...but little else. *Or not?*

she had rejected him.

"Madonna has an almost unequaled natural ability to promote herself—even at my expense," he wrote. "She knows how to be shocking. The story about my propositioning her is simply not true. She made it up. At least it was hot copy for the tabloids."

Donald often made the rounds of TV talk shows, dishing the dirt on other celebrities. When he appeared on ABC's *Nitecap* on October 21, 1992, he decided to strike back at Madonna for spreading stories about how she had rejected him.

He chatted with Robin Leach in front of the cameras, attacking Madonna's book, *Sex*, a tome filled with erotic photographs, some of which depicted her in the nude.,

He claimed that the nudity did not offend his morals. What offended him were views of Madonna's naked body. "Not great!" he claimed. "If she were in a room with young, good-looking women, she'd be the least attractive there. I went to two of her concerts, but walked out after the first fifteen minutes. They were terrible. She can't sing."

DONALD'S WATERLOO
The Future First Lady of France

Long before he married her, Donald and his girlfriend, Marla Maples, with whom he was having an adulterous affair, had many fights followed by "Splitsville." The June 26, 1991 edition of the *New York Post* had run a story headlined—MOVE OVER, MARLA. It was reported that Donald had booted her from her East Side condo.

The next day, *Newsday* ran a front page story headlined TRUMP'S NEW PAL which featured a sexy picture of Carla Bruni, and *The New York Post* claimed that "Donald's new Italian girlfriend was about to break big, leaving Marla Maples up the creek without a paddle."

Marla was said to have been devastated, as she hoped that he would soon call to make up. She wanted to know, "Who is this Carla Bruni creature?"

She got a clue when she read the gossip column of "Suzy" (aka Aileen Mehle). "Donald dumped Marla for Carla, who is the exact opposite. Instead of being blonde, bosomy, and bouncy, like Marla, Carla is flat-chested, mahogany-haired, and as sleekly smooth as a Ferrari race car."

Born in Turin, Italy, in 1967, Carla Gilberta Bruni-Tedeschi was an Italian-French model and singer-songwriter. In 2008, she told *Vanity Fair* that her biological father was Maurizio Remmert, an Italian-born grocery magnate who had sustained an affair with her mother, the Italian concert pianist, Marisa Borini.

In time, Carla became one of the world's highest-paid models, earning $7.5 million at her peak. She later abandoned modeling to become a songwriter, releasing her first album in 2002.

At a dinner party in 2007, she met the recently divorced Nicholas Sarkozy, the President of France. She married him at the Élysée Palace in February of the following year. It made her, of course, the First Lady of France.

Before that, she'd had a few dates herself, including an affair with Mick Jagger during the period he was still involved with model Jerry Hall. Other lovers included Kevin Costner, Rod Stewart, and Eric Clapton. Reportedly, she'd told Clapton, "There are only so many great men in the world, and I want to be with all of them. My parents don't consider Donald Trump one of the great men of the world."

She was also romantically linked in the press to Louis Bertignac, Léos Carax, Charles Berling, Arno Klarsfeld, Vincent Pérex, and Laurent Fabius, the former Prime

Supermodel Carla Bruni escaped from the clutches of Donald Trump and Mick Jagger to marry Nicholas Sarkozy and become First Lady of France.

For Carla, there was life after Donald.

Here she is with Michelle Obama in the Élysée Palace, where the First Lady of the United States put on a better leg show than the wife of the president of the *République française*.

Minister (1984-1986) of France.

Apparently, Donald didn't win rave reviews from Carla. His other supermodel girlfriends claimed that he had no ability for small talk and was not very social. One model reported that he was "completely paranoid about venereal disease and AIDS."

At a celebration in Atlantic City, marking the first year of business for the Taj Mahal, Donald spoke to a reporter from *Newsday*. "I have begun asking a woman I want to go out with to visit my doctor's office for an HIV test. It's one of the worst times in history to be screwing around."

Carla was said to be outraged at the suggestion of having to submit to an AIDS test.

At the time, he said, "I'm searching for the right woman, and haven't found her yet."

Sue Carswell, a former writer for *People* magazine, wanted to get the scoop on Donald's relationship with Carla. She knew that Donald had been pursuing her since her arrival in New York when she checked into the Mayfair Regent Hotel.

The next day, her room was filled with flowers, and Donald was calling to invite her out.

Carla later played a trick on him, telling him that her "sister" was coming to town. Donald generously offered this "sister" a suite at the Hotel Plaza.

Actually, it wasn't Carla's sister, but an unrelated woman friend of hers who arrived from Paris with her boyfriend. A member of the hotel staff later remembered, "Those two Parisians spent a lot of time ordering everything expensive on the room service menu."

Reportedly, Carla was said to have told her friend, "Donald is the King of Tacky."

Carswell had long pursued Donald for an interview. She sent him gifts that included Hermès ties, long before he launched his own collection. She wanted to know about his alleged affair with Carla.

At Trump Tower, she didn't get Donald on the phone, but was put through to a "John Miller," who identified himself as a spokesman for his boss. Carswell decided to record the conversation, because she suspected that this John Miller was actually Donald himself.

"Miller" openly admitted that women were pursuing Donald, not just Carla and Marla, but others as well. He cited actress Kim Basinger as an example. "Kim came to Mr. Trump to discuss a real estate deal. But she really wanted to go out with him. But the competition is rough for women after Donald. Tough on Marla Maples. Tough on Carla Bruni."

A former editor in Paris of French *Elle* claimed. "Donald Trump was no more than a passing fancy for Carla, if that. She might have liked his money and power, but she never would have put up with Trump once she really got to know him."

When he later became linked with the Slovenian model, Melania Knauss, many reporters noted that his new girlfriend was a dead ringer for Carla.

The quote may be apocryphal, but Donald was alleged to have said, "If Carla had gone with me instead of with Nicolas Sarkozy, she might have become First Lady of the United States instead of First Lady of France."

IVANA RE-SCULPTED
No Longer a "Pumpkin-Faced Moravian Matron"

Ivana had been married to Donald since 1977, and time was marching on. As biographer Harry Hurt III described her in 1989, "She seemed to be turning into a flat-chested, pumpkin-faced Moravian matron with deeply creased jowls, crow's feet around her hazel eyes, and lips so thin they resembled a bathtub ring."

Before she submitted to plastic surgery, Ivana told gossip columnist Liz Smith, "I never want to look a day over twenty-eight, and it's going to cost Donald a lot of money."

Perhaps as a means of holding onto Donald, she flew to Beverly Hills for a "makeover" at the hands of plastic surgeon Dr. Steven Hoefflin. He had worked to restore Michael Jackson's looks after he'd burned himself during an accident on the set of a Pepsi-Cola commercial.

Her instruction to the doctor was direct: "I want to emerge the Czech version of Brigitte Bardot."

When she recovered from surgery, she was no longer flat-chested. She also had re-sculpted cheekbones and fuller lips.

Allegedly, Ivana Trump told her plastic surgeon that she wanted to be re-sculpted to look like the former French sex kitten, Brigitte Bardot, who's depicted above as she appeared in 1959.

Even after the surgery, however, Ivana did not look like Bardot. Friends thought she looked like another version of Catherine Oxenberg, whose name –although it had been denied by both parties—had been linked romantically to Donald's.

A friend of Ivana's in Palm Beach said, "She did not look comfortable with her new face. It didn't work out. The nerve endings didn't seem to connect in her face, and it was something awful, like a woman wearing a mask. If you quote my name, I'll sue."

Writing in *People* magazine, Mary H.J. Farrell wrote: "Ivana pushes on. Once somewhat pudgy, overly made-up, and overly blonde, she is not the very model of 'Social X-Ray'—the transparently thin Manhattan socialite Tom Wolfe immortalized in *Bonfire of the Vanities*. Though she has never fessed up to a touch-up, a slimmer Ivana has softened her hair color and the hairdo."

As she said, "If people can improve themselves, they should."

Back in New York, and even with her makeover, Donald continued to avoid close encounters in the boudoir. He wanted some work done on himself, notably around his expanding waistline, and he also sought to conceal the bald spot at the crown of his head.

Sex without consent is

RAPE

LOST TYCOON

THE MANY LIVES OF
Donald J. Trump

HARRY HURT III

The Lost Tycoon, the Many Lives of Donald J. Trump, by Harry Hurt III, was published in 1993 and was the most controversial book ever written about Donald at that time.

Hurt claimed that Donald's private life "has become as scandalous as a prime-time soap opera."

Dr. Hoefflin had flown in from California and was working on some VIP patients in New York. Ivana recommended him, and Donald agreed to see him.

Dr. Hoefflin welcomed Donald into his office and accepted him as a patient.

Two days later, he was performing liposuction on both Donald's chin and his waistline, sucking out fatty deposits.

The operation on his scalp, in slang, was sometimes described as "head shrinking," a term more often applied to psychiatry.

The doctor removed the skin over Donald's bald spot and then sewed together the adjoining patches of hair-growing skin. After the procedure, Donald was transported in a limousine, to his sprawling estate in Greenwich, where—in theory at least—he could recover in peace.

But he had no peace, and spent most of the time in excessive pain, suffering "mind-blowing headaches." The doctor had used a tattoo machine to dye Donald's scalp, but he later complained that the skin color didn't match his original skin.

Allegedly, he phoned the doctor and threatened him telling him he wasn't going to pay his bill.

Still enraged, he returned to his penthouse at the Trump Tower in Manhattan and barged into Ivana's bedroom, He flung accusations at her and blamed her "for sending me to that "fucking doctor. I'm ruined!"

According to an account given in Harry Hurt's biography of Donald, *The Lost Tycoon*, "He pins back her arms and grabs her by the hair. He starts ripping out her hair by the handful."

She was said to have "kicked, screamed, and cried, as he ripped off her clothing and unzipped his trousers." He then, according to the account, proceeded to rape her. He hadn't had sex with her in sixteen months. His assault on her would be his last sexual involvement with her.

***

In a deposition during their divorce proceedings, Ivana alleged that, "Donald raped me." Hurt's publisher had already printed his book in 1993, and was about to ship it out to bookstores, when Donald's lawyers called him and demanded a showdown meeting. The attorneys wanted the rape passages removed from the book, but the publisher stood his ground. However, a compromise was reached in which his staff would paste in a "Notice to the Reader," dated April 6, 1993, on the opening pages of the book.

That "Notice to the Reader," (Ivana's declaration) read as follows:

> "During a deposition given by me in connection with my matrimonial case, I stated that my husband had raped me."

> "I wish to say that on one occasion during 1989, Mr. Trump and I had marital relations in which he behaved very differently toward me than he had during our marriage. As a woman, I felt violated, as the love and tenderness, which he normally exhibited toward me, was absent. I referred to this as a 'rape,' but I do not want my words to be interpreted in a literal or

criminal sense."

"Any contrary conclusion would be an incorrect and most unfortunate interpretation of my statement which I do not want to be interpreted in a speculative fashion, and I do not want the press or media to misconstrue any of the facts set forth above. All I wish is for this matter to be put to rest."

"This statement can only be released and used in its entirety."

"LISTEN, BITCH, STAY AWAY FROM MY HUSBAND!"

—*Ivana Trump to Marla Maples on the Ski Slopes of Aspen*

In the summer of 1989, Donald and Ivana had drifted apart, and he was spending his nights with Marla. She would make the tabloids as "The Other Woman."

Columnist Cindy Adams was to write: "Ivana still wants to be Donald's wife. But the bottom line is she won't give up her self-respect to do it. He offered her a chance to continue to be wed to him, but in an open marriage. She turned him down."

In December of 1989, the discord in their marriage created a tabloid frenzy as the money-crazed 1980s came to an end.

During the final daylight hours of 1989, on December 31, Marla Maples, Donald's new mistress, confronted the formidable Ivana Trump. That confrontation marked the beginning of what Donald labeled "an international soap opera." Ivana and their three children, were already installed at Aspen, Colorado, for the Christmas and New Year's holidays, having arrived in advance of her husband.

Donald flew in later, accompanied by Marla. A limousine was waiting for them at the airport to haul them into town. Its driver deposited Marla at a two-bedroom condo, which Donald had arranged for her, then delivered Donald,

Early modeling shot of Marla Maples, "the other woman" in Donald's secret life.

alone, to "Little Nell's," a newly opened deluxe hotel and restaurant owned by billionaire Marvin Davis.

There, Donald had a reunion with Ivana.

A woman friend of hers, who was from Palm Beach, was also in Aspen for the holidays. Privately, she gossiped that "Ivana—she's such a dear—is looking her age, in spite of plastic surgery, but Donald prefers a fresh-faced nineteen-year-old with an amble bosom. I hear he's shacked up with some new mistress. Perhaps some bimbo, not smart like Ivana. Maybe a gold-digger."

Presumably, Ivana may have seen Marla on a few occasions, but Donald had usually arranged for her to be escorted by a "beard"—that is, another man configured to appear as her boyfriend.

Once, Ivana had eavesdropped on a phone conversation, and had caught Donald talking to Marla. She confronted him with the damaging evidence, but he assured her, "It's just some gal who stalks me. It happens all the time to us good-looking rich guys."

Ivana had also become aware of her name, which sounded like "Moo-la."

She set about to find out who this Moo-la creature was, eventually defining her as a model trying to steal her husband.

An explosive confrontation between the two women ensued the following day. Donald and Ivana were putting on their skis outside Bonnie's restaurant. Set adjacent to the ski slopes, it was a venue where many skiers gathered for lunch.

E. Graydon Carter, co-editor of *Spy* Magazine, a publication that often indulged in Donald bashing, emerged as witness to the conflict between Marla and Ivana.

Suddenly, the two blondes—wearing identical ski suits, each a gift from Donald—confronted one another.

Marla's very provocative first words to Ivana were, "Are you in love with your husband? I cer-

Beautiful, high-altitude, high-drama Aspen... a hard-partying, infamously permissive resort that's well-rehearsed in lifestyle issues of the rich and famous, including those associated with the love triangle of The Donald, Ivana, and Marla.

tainly am!" [Donald was said to be horrified at Marla's reckless approach to his wife.]

Ivana shot back, "You must be this Moo-la I've been hearing so much about."

"I love him," Marla said. "If you don't, why don't you let him go?"

"YOU STAY AWAY FROM HIM, YOU FUCKING WHORE," Ivana shouted at Marla. "IF YOU DON'T YOU'LL REGRET IT FOR THE REST OF YOUR LIFE!"

At this point, according to the witness, "A torrent of curse words flowed from Ivana's lips, perhaps learned from Donald.

He just looked at Ivana, ignoring Marla, and then accused his wife of "being too god damn dramatic and losing your cool." After buckling on his skis, he headed down the mountain.

Turning her back on Marla, Ivana went after him. An Olympic champion, she headed downhill, screaming at him: "You cheating son of a bitch!" Then she maneuvered herself in front of him and skied backward down the slopes, wagging her finger at him and denouncing him.

That night, during an après ski session, he was overheard telling a friend, "I'm not going to let some jealous wife ruin my life. I'll do what I please. That means fucking whatever woman I want."

***

For a gala New Year's Eve Party, the oil-rich tycoon, David Koch, invited Don-

Divana Divided, a battle over babes and bucks.

The photo shows how one publication covered "the divorce of the year. "

Ironically, the same publication would splash a revised version of *Trump vs. Trump* (in this case, Donald vs. Marla) across a roughly equivalent issue a few years later.

ald and Ivana to a party of the super wealthy. He showed up, but Ivana was not on his arm. Instead, he introduced Koch to Marla Maples, who looked stunning.

It seemed that a divorce was inevitable now that Donald was making a semi-public appearance with his mistress.

A divorce could not have come at a worse time for Donald, as he was facing the financial crisis of his life, tottering on the brink of bankruptcy. In spite of her pre-nup agreement, Ivana wanted half of his net worth.

Months before, she was made aware that Donald was sleeping with other women, but, as she told her gossipy friends, "It's just a passing fancy. I know he'll always come home to me."

However, when he escorted Marla to the Koch party, in front of some of the wealthiest people in America, she knew his philandering had entered the mainstream.

Tabloid revelations were on the way.

In February of 1990, Donald informed Ivana that he was moving out of their apartment after he returned from Tokyo where he was flying to attend the prize fight between Mike Tyson and Buster Douglas. Donald's money was on Tyson.

He called the fight one of the greatest upsets in the history of professional boxing as "Iron Mike went down at the fists of a virtual unknown (Douglas)."

While he was in Japan, Ivana phoned her friend Liz Smith and gave her the front page scoop of the upcoming breakup of her marriage. Smith boasted to her editor that she was delivering to him "the scoop of the decade."

In the wake of that revelation, "Second Coming" headlines (SPLITSVILLE!) were plastered across frontpages everywhere. Donald and Ivana became tabloid fodder. Not since the first divorce of Elizabeth Taylor and Richard Burton had there been such hoopla in the press.

Since Donald and Ivana had been labeled "The Love Couple" of the extravagant 1980s, the story went international with speculation about the scope and depth of their private dynamics.

At the time, there were almost daily predictions that Donald was going under. Facing a Mount Everest of debt, he was referred to as "The Brazil of Manhattan," a reference to the staggering debts of that country.

Public opinion seemed to weigh in heavily with Ivana. Wherever she went in Manhattan, she was greeted with cheers: "Take the bastard for all he's worth!"

"Hold out for a billion, baby!"

Donald defended his empire against her. "I built it myself. Nobody did it for me, certainly not Ivana. Nobody! Just because somebody built something on their own doesn't mean they should have to give a huge chunk of it away to turn a deposed spouse into the Queen of Sheba."

Reporter Marie Brenner wrote: "By now, Donald and Ivana have become less like man and wife and more like two ambassadors from different countries, each with a separate agenda."

For the most part, Donald got nothing but a bad press, whereas—according to Liz Smith—Ivana "became a media darling on par with the likes of Princess Di, Madonna, and Elizabeth Taylor."

In the midst of her legal troubles with Donald, *People* magazine listed her on its worst dressed list, a distinction she shared with La Toya Jackson and Roseanne Arnold. Image consultant Susan Bixler publicly accused Ivana of "not understanding understatement."

During happier times, Donald had praised Ivana's skill both as a manager and as a decorator. Now he derided her accomplishments.

"What did she do for the Plaza?" he asked in an interview. "She selected some wallpaper that was so tacky I had to call in a real decorator and have it repapered!"

Donald's radical disenchantment with Ivana was revealed when he grumbled during an interview on WWOR-TV, "Ivana has gotten too arrogant. I'm afraid I have created another Leona Helmsley."

To reporter James Revson of *Newsday*, he said, "You could measure in an eyedropper all the sympathy that Donald Trump has in New York."

As news of her separation from Donald was fanned, a sort of "Ivanamania" swept across the land. She emerged as a kind of heroine of the foffaraw, a champion of women's rights, including equal pay. "I was getting more mail than Santa Claus," she claimed. On Valentine's Day, she received thirty-five proposals of marriage.

Not everyone was as enchanted: Ivana's first husband, Alfred Winklmayr, now working as a businessman in Sydney, Australia, sold the story of his marriage to Ivana to *The National Enquirer*. In the article, he accused his former wife of being a "gold-digger. She's finally get-

In the absence of Roy Cohn, Donald's newest lawyer was Jay Goldberg, a gilt-edged, Park Avenue lawyer with a daunting (some said terrifying) resumé.

ting what's coming to her."

On April 23, 1990, Donald and Ivana signed a two-page contract that in effect was a sixty-day pact allowing them to play the field. It gave each of them the permission to date during their legal separation. The agreement was supposed to be confidential, but Donald leaked the news to the *New York Post.*

The reputation of Donald's newest lawyer was as baroque as that of Roy Cohn, but Jay Goldberg was viewed as one of the most combative in New York. In a call to Cindy Adams, who was generally sympathetic to Donald, Goldberg admitted, "I'm a killer. I can rip the skin off. I know how to cause physical pain."

New York magazine once claimed that Goldberg was "among the ten most powerful, talented, and fearsome attorneys in New York." *[Previous celebrity clients had included Andy Capasso, the contractor boyfriend of Bess Myerson, a former Miss America and a close associate of NYC Mayor Ed Koch.]*

Goldberg announced to the press the terms of Ivana's agreement with "The Donald."

Goldberg said, "Adultery or sex, according to the terms, cannot be grounds for a divorce. Technically, Mr. and Mrs. Trump can have sex with partners and no one party can be guilty of adultery."

Later, Ivana wanted to void the agreement, claiming it was causing her social embarrassment. But Goldberg insisted that the contract was "iron clad."

During the course of their marriage (1977-91), Ivana had negotiated and signed four different marital property agreements. However, that was not enough for her. She demanded half of Donald's estate, claiming that she had been partially responsible for his success in the 1980s.

Donald said, "When a man leaves a woman, especially when it is perceived that he has left her for a piece of ass—and a good one at that—fifty-percent of the population, maybe a hell of a lot more, will

Everyone was surprised when Ivana hired a famously liberal (some said "leftist") lawyer, Michael J. Kennedy, depicted here outside the Alameda County Courthouse in California with a client, the Black Panther leader Huey P. Newton, in 1978.

Ultimately, he got Ivana a huge settlement.

side with the deserted woman."

Ivana's attorney was Michael Kennedy, widely viewed as an ultra-liberal defense attorney. He had previously represented murderer Jean Harris, who had killed her lover, Herman Tarnower, a cardiologist and author of the best-selling book *The Complete Scarsdale Medical Diet.*

Donald knew who Kennedy was. As he recalled, "He was someone who defended the Mitchell brothers, the porno movie kings who produced *Behind the Green Door."* It had starred Marilyn Chambers, the rival of Linda Lovelace.

On December 11, 1990, Ivana's limousine pulled up at Manhattan Superior Court. Her dress was as gray as the day. For the hearing in front of Judge Gangel-Jacob, Donald did not show up.

After statements from both lawyers, the judge granted Ivana a divorce on the grounds "of cruel and inhuman punishment and a particular flaunting of his relationship with Miss Marla Maples."

The division of cash would have to be settled later.

On March 24, 1991, Donald and Ivana came together in Goldberg's Park Avenue offices.

"Ivana's meeting with us was testy for a while," Goldberg said. "That's the way most divorce negotiations go before a cooling-off period sets in. That comes when there is an agreement about money."

Ivana ended up with a $14 million cash settlement and also demanded ownership of the family's 1989 Mercedes. "She'd been nickel and diming me over that damn car," Donald complained.

She left Goldberg's office with a $10 million cashier's check, with a promise of another $4 million before a year had passed.

She was, however, ordered to vacate their luxurious, Versailles-like triplex in the Trump Tower.

Additional terms called for her to be given the 45-room mansion in Greenwich; an

In January, 1992, just before Ivana's impromptu drop-in at the Little Rock residence of the then-governor of Arkansas, Bill Clinton was still something of a mystery to residents of far-away NYC.

Ivana, newly single and famous for her intuitive sense of who was rich, perhaps available, and A-list, might have evaluated Bill as a "person of interest."

apartment within Trump Plaza on Third Avenue, and— since she had been granted custody of Ivanka, Donald Jr., and Eric—$300,000 in annual child support. In addition, she was also allowed the use of Mar-a-Lago in Palm Beach for one month out of every year.

After all the bitter feelings and disputes, both of them seemed relieved to see their feud over money come to an end. "Now I can get on with my life and my other troubles," Donald said.

In 1992, Ivana flew to Little Rock, Arkansas, to attend a benefit of the Arkansas Multiple Sclerosis Society. Perhaps inspired by her elevated stature in the media, but without an appointment, she called on President-elect Bill Clinton. He was still living in the state-owned governor's mansion in Little Rock, since he had not yet resigned as governor of Arkansas.

She was rudely turned away by men of the Secret Service.

Years later, a writer speculated, "Had things gone differently, Ivana Trump might have become Monica Lewinsky."

IVANA POST-DONALD
Love Italian Style, Again...and Again

In the wake of Ivana's divorce, she was back on the market again, looking for romance, perhaps love, even a third marriage. After years with Donald, a byproduct of German/Scottish forebears, she turned to sunny Italy.

Donald's favorite columnist, Cindy Adams, broke news of Ivana's latest fling, headlining it TRUMP'S SURVIVING IVANA—SAYS SHE AND HER PLAYBOY ARE LIVING IN $IN.

Adams' report was based on Ivana's affair with Riccardo Mazzucchelli, a 48-year-old construction tycoon from Rome. One writer described Riccardo as "having an aquiline nose and ice-blue Siberian wolf dog eyes."

He led the life of a glamorous jet-setter and was the father of a son, 25, from a previous marriage. He owned an apartment in Prague in Ivana's native land; a condo in the Swiss Alp; two flats in London; and a powder-blue Rolls-Royce. He'd completed more than $3 billion in construction projects in the Middle East and Africa.

During Ascot Week in the summer of 1991, Riccardo had met Ivana at a dinner party at the swanky Claridges Hotel in London. The next day, he filled her suite with an array of red roses. After that, they began to date, which led to a summer fling on the French Riviera.

That autumn, they appeared together at the chic Venetian Ball with the paparazzi hot on their trail. As autumn winds blew down upon New York, the lovers were seen strolling together, hand in hand, down Fifth Avenue.

Around Christmas, Riccardo presented Ivana with a 10-carat yellow diamond. He told the press, "Trump can't stand that there is a new man in Ivana's life. He's also furious that her novel, *For Love Alone*, is a *New York Times* bestseller."

[Released by Pocket Books in 1992, it was described by Amazon.com like this: "Katrinka Graham is driven to risk everything—love, freedom, success, and wealth—because of a secret from her past, in a story of love, ambition, and determination set against the glamorous backdrop of the very rich. A first novel. 250,000 first printing."]

Donald had read her novel and called it "a thinly veiled account of our marriage and breakup. I was enraged that Ivana had broken our confidential agreement."

He obtained affidavits that Ivana and Riccardo had traveled together to Rome, Paris, St. Moritz, Venice, Houston, Los Angeles, and San Francisco, and also spent three weeks in a "love nest" at Mar-a-Lago.

"I learned that they also set up housekeeping in my mansion in Greenwich," Donald claimed. "I mean, this guy is living in homes I paid for, eating in kitchens I paid for, and sleeping in beds I paid for."

If he could prove "cohabitation" in court, he could stop paying her $700,000 annually in spousal and child support, as well as household maintenance.

Ivana told friends that she was postponing marriage to Riccardo "so I can make that bastard pay me for support for another year or two."

In 1992, Donald sued Ivana for $25 million, charging that she had violated the gag clause of their pre-nup agreement

Ivana's second marriage to an Italian, Riccardo Mazzucchelli, also ended in failure. Known for his "wolf-dog eyes," he later sued both Donald and Ivana for libel, denying accusations that he was a "gold-digging gigolo."

Actually, he was a rich man long before he met Ivana.

by revealing their marital secrets—and, as such, had committed fraud. He cited in his affidavit that he was clearly Adam Graham, that "vital sexual man with a huge personal fortune," as depicted in her [supposedly autobiographical] novel. The case was later dropped.

When Riccardo proposed marriage to Ivana in 1995, he gave her a large Burmese sapphire.

Their splashy wedding was held at Manhattan's Mayfair Hotel in November of 1995.

After only three months, Ivana announced to the press that she and Riccardo had separated. It was said that he found it difficult to live in the shadow of a famous woman and in the shadow of Donald Trump.

In her novel, Ivana described her heroine being "dropped without preparation into the middle of Adam's (read that Donald's) cluttered world, to deal with his driver, secretary, housekeeper, his mother and father, the family and friends he referred to in a bewildering avalanche of names. Her old life, in comparison, had been very frugal and solitary."

In this bizarre picture, Ivana poses with her second Italian stallion, Rossano Rubicondi, at a Halloween costume party at the home of Michelle and Frank Della in New York in 2004. Rubicondi came disguised as his impression of Donald Trump, with Ivanka appearing as Little Bo Peep...or whatever.

Ivana eventually married Rubicondi in 2008 at Mar-a-Lago. He was much younger than his bride.

In July of 1997, Riccardo sued Donald and Ivana for libel in a London court, maintaining that both of them had defamed him in slanderous statements published both in *People* magazine and the *National Enquirer*. He said that he was depicted as a "gold-digger" and a "gigolo" who had lied to Ivana to induce her to marry him.

She filed a $15 million countersuit against Riccardo, claiming that he had violated the confidentiality clause of their prenup agreement. The cast was settled out of court.

***

After Ivana dumped Riccardo, she decided to take a chance on another Italian stallion. Rossano Rubicondi was twenty-three years her junior. Ivana's "ladies who lunch" told her the obvious: younger men produce more reliable erections than men of a certain age.

For many reasons, Ivana delayed marrying Rossano for many years. At the time of their eventual marriage, she was 59 and he was 35.

He listed his profession as a "model-actor." The super-expensive wedding took place in April of 2008 at Mar-a-Lago in front of four hundred guests. Donald's sister, Judge Maryanne Trump Barry, performed the ceremony, which was attended by Donald himself. Sons Donald Jr. and Eric gave the bride away, and Ivanka was her mother's maid-of-honor.

"I'm in awe of her," Rossana told the press. "She's beautiful, smart, sexy, powerful, successful, and young in spirit. We have fun together. Otherwise, I wouldn't be marrying her."

They made a handsome couple

At another Halloween party hosted in Manhattan the following October (2005), Ivana came alone to the home of Donna and Dick Soloway, dressed in a Tijuana-inspired "South of the Border" style a few years before Donald announced his infamous plan for a wall between the U.S. and Mexico.

dancing to a 24-piece orchestra that Donald had flown in from Paris.

Her happiness did not last long, having the short life of a plucked wildflower. Her divorce from her second Italian was finalized in 2009.

Chapter Ten

MARLA MAPLES
The Donald Plucks a Shapely, Beautiful, Busty, and
Blonde Georgia Peach from the Tree of Life

THE MOST WIDELY TRUMPETED SEX SCANDAL OF THE LATE 20TH CENTURY
Marla Learns to Say "Charge It to Donald"

"(Donald is) the Best Sex I've Ever Had"
—Marla Maples

In Manhattan in 1987, while promoting his book, *The Art of the Deal*, Donald was walking by himself along Fifth Avenue. He was alone, something that would be dangerous for him to do in 2016.

He was heading for his office in Trump Tower when he spotted Marla Maples standing in front of the Pierre Hotel. Perhaps the first thing that might have flashed through his mind was the question, "Is this stunning beauty a high-class hooker, perhaps waiting for a rich john near the portal of this deluxe hotel?"

She stepped forward and reintroduced herself, reminding him that she had met him the year before when she was introduced to him by Jerry Argovitz, President of the New Jersey Generals, at a USFL gathering in Atlantic City.

After a pleasant chat, he moved on. But back at his office, he made an inquiry of his aides. "Who is this Marla Maples broad?"

Based on today's currencies, if the Marilyn Monroe movie, *How to Marry a Millionaire*, were remade, it would have to be retitled *How to Marry a Billionaire*.

As gold-diggers know, "millionaires are now a dime a dozen." Perhaps the reprised version might star an actress inspired by this Georgia peach, Marla Maples, who, according to *People* magazine, "found true love and true loot."

In just a short time, he was delivered a profile of her young life.

She was a bit actress and model. Born in the bowels of Cohutta, Georgia, in 1963, Marla as a girl dreamed of becoming the reincarnation of her idol, Marilyn Monroe, and decided to launch herself in beauty pageants. "I know I can be Miss America," she said. "Even Miss USA and possibly Miss Universe."

After dropping out of the University of Georgia, Marla, for a brief period, became a flight attendant for Delta. To break into show business, she entered a number of beauty contests, hoping to be spotted by a talent scout.

She stuffed a wild bikini for a contest in Daytona, Florida, but lost to another contestant.

Along the way, she entered the *Miss Georgia USA* contest, but lost that, too.

In Manhattan, she worked as a Ford model, hawking the glories of Delta, her former employer, and promoting a "Miracle Ceramic Tile Adhesive."

After migrating to Manhattan, she realized she needed acting lessons, and enrolled in HB Studios, where Barbra Streisand and Anne Bancroft had learned their craft.

Movie roles, small ones, were forthcoming. She appeared in Stephen King's *Maximum Overdrive* (1986), a horror film in which she was crushed to death by a load of watermelons. Film critic Leonard Matlin defined it as "a junk movie."

She also had a role as a tennis player in *The Secret of My Success* (1987), starring Michael J. Fox. It was rumored—never confirmed—that she made a play for the handsome young star.

The spring of 1987 found Marla involved with Tom Fitzsimmons, a former cop turned male model. He and his brother, a twin, stood 6'2" and were handsome and brown-eyed. Tom's desire was to break into the movies, and he'd written a feature length script, *Blue Gemini*. He and Marla became lovers, and for a time, they lived in Manhattan in a two-bedroom apartment in a high rise at 91st Street and Third Avenue.

Tom already knew Donald when both of them had dreams of going to Hollywood, Donald as a producer, Tom as an actor. He had been hoping that Donald would finance *Blue Gemini*.

Muscled and good looking,

At the beginning of their romance, nearly everything Marla and Donald did generated tabloid headlines, as when he presented her with a diamond engagement ring.

Usually, the tabloids tended to defend Ivana, depicting Marla as a homewrecking adventuress, "the other woman."

Tom made a trailer for *Blue Gemini*, a tale about twins, "men in blue," both of them employees of New York City's Police Department. The eight-minute trailer was made as a sales tool for potential backers, including Donald. There was a role in it for Marla.

Tom contacted publicist Chuck Jones, bringing him aboard to help him pitch the script. As a result, Jones was introduced to Marla, and would become notoriously linked to her, both in and out of court.

Jones' clients, one of whom was Jack Lemmon, impressed Marla, and in time, she hired him as her press agent, assigned to the advancement of her career. Soon, Jones succeeded at placing items about *Blue Gemini* in the tabloids, suggesting that shooting had begun, which it had not.

Blue Gemini never got off the ground, but those who read the script found it most viable as a movie.

In 1987, Tom escorted Marla to the book party that launched Donald's *The Art of the Deal*.

It was a gala affair, and she approached him as he chatted with the movie star, Michael Douglas. After she and Tom passed on, Donald turned to Douglas, "I saw her first."

Before the party was over, he managed discreetly to get her phone number and promised to phone her.

Even after Marla's affair with Tom ended, and she moved on to other conquests, they remained friends.

Donald's executive assistant at the time was Norma Foerderer. A forbidding gatekeeper and guardian, she had a strong impact on whomever had access to Donald, determining who could get in to see her boss—and who couldn't.

In December of 1987, she called Marla, inviting her to join Donald for lunch at the swanky St. Regis Hotel.

This was the first time the two future lovers, who had been "circling" each other, came together for a man-on-woman talk. That conversation lasted five hours, during which time they agreed to date secretly.

Marla later told her publicist, Chuck Jones, "I have reservations about dating a married man, especially a persona as famous as Donald."

Then, as if predicting their future, she said, "We might end up on the front page of the

Norma Foederer was the long term assistant and no-nonsense "gatekeeper" to matters associated with Donald Trump.

tabloids."

Jones later revealed an entry in Marla's datebook at the time. "I don't want to be something that keeps boredom away from Donald."

After that lunch at the St. Regis, Donald began to date Marla in secret. Sometimes he'd call her, and the two of them would talk until two in the morning.

The soon-to-be notorious Donald Trump/Marla Maples affair was launched around the time his book, *The Art of the Deal*, became a best-seller.

As a beauty queen, Marla had a curvaceous figure (37"-25"-37"). After she started dating Donald, she changed her hairdo, going for what was called "a Farrah Fawcett shag" to a straight-to-the shoulders cut. One author wrote, "There was not much she could do with her pouty overshot jaw and facial features so perfectly plain vanilla they appeared to be plaster of Paris."

L'affaire Marla began as a diverting interlude for Donald wanting to escape his vexing problems as he faced a fast-fading empire plagued by long-overdue bank loans and too many junk bonds. It was estimated that in 1991, he faced $1 billion in debt.

Marla remained loyal, later telling the *New York Daily News* that when they were walking together along Fifth Avenue, they spotted a wretched-looking homeless man.

Donald pointed to him and told her, "that ugly guy is worth $900 million more than me."

"I wanted to see if she'd move her ass down the street away from me, but she didn't. She's a great friend."

When Donald first decided to make Marla his mistress, while he was still wed to Ivana, he moved her into a luxury suite at the St. Moritz Hotel. He'd purchased the hotel from Harry and Leona Helmsley. Ivana was gone at least four nights a week, away in Atlantic City, managing Trump Castle, an absence that allowed Donald plenty of time to "date" Marla.

Accompanied by a bodyguard, Donald became a familiar figure to the staff at the St. Moritz. The bodyguard would be stationed outside suite No. 414 while Donald visited his mistress inside.

On the nights Ivana was away in Atlantic

When Donald was presented with a copy of this notorious front page from the tabloid, the *New York Post*, he said, "That's embarrassing, so personal, but in a way, I should be flattered."

City, Donald could arrange "sleepovers." A room service waiter remembered serving him breakfast on mornings while Marla was still getting her beauty sleep. "He wore this red silk Japanese robe that concealed his nudity, at least on most occasions. I got a brief glimpse once or twice. During the presidential campaign in 2016, Marco Rubio was wrong in suggesting the implication of Donald's small hands. Take it from an eyewitness. Small hands do not necessarily mean small anything else."

[When Donald sold the St. Moritz in February of 1988, he moved Marla temporarily into the Waldorf Astoria on Park Avenue. Later, he stashed her at the Trump Plaza in Atlantic City.]

Chuck Jones escorted Marla to the reopening of the famous Rainbow Room at Rockefeller Center in Manhattan, which even during the Great Depression was a rendezvous for the super wealthy—those fortunate few who didn't jump out of skyscrapers after the Wall Street crash of 1929.

Brooke Astor, the doyenne of New York Society, was introduced to Marla, who also met the hotel queen, Leona Helmsley.

The Rainbow Room had opened in 1934, the first restaurant and night club to be located within a high-rise building. For decades, it was the highest elevated dining venue in the United States.

Soon, Marla was seen frequently at Donald's casino hotels in Atlantic City, where she was stashed away in lavish suites, compliments of the house. Jones or Tom Fitzsimmons sometimes escorted her to public events, in which Donald stayed on one side of the room, Marla with her escort du jour on the other. When he wanted to leave a message for her at the hotel desk, Donald would sign it "The Baron."

Donald told his aide, Stephen Hyde, "Marla is a real beauty, a great little piece of ass. Perhaps I shouldn't brag, but she's also fourteen years younger than Ivana. The gal is mad about her Daddy-O."

Autographed by Marla and for sale as a collector's item, this is a promotional glossy of her during her gig advertising for Miracle, a ceramic tile adhesive.

The first mention of a romance between Marla and Donald appeared in a 1988 edition of the *New York Post.* It said that a model, Marla Maples, the "Georgia Peach, was involved with one of New York's biggest tycoons—and a married man."

The Post led all other newspapers in the scoop sweepstakes, running a picture of "the gorgeous Marla Maples" before any of its competitors.

Amid the turmoil, claiming that she was humiliated, Marla fled to Guatemala, where she stayed with a friend of hers, a member of the Peace Corps.

Reporters cornered Donald, asking him how he was holding up with all the scandal swirling around him. "It's great for business!" he shot back.

During the scandal, Marla delivered her most famous quote. The press jokingly said that in terms of the fame it would generate, it would rival General Douglas MacArthur's, "I shall return," an utterance he made when fleeing from the Japanese invasion of the Philippines.

In a "Second Coming" headline, the *Post* proclaimed, "MARLA BOASTS TO PALS ABOUT DONALD: 'BEST SEX I'VE EVER HAD.'"

In response, Donald told a reporter that he probably should have been flattered by Marla's appraisal of his sexual prowess, "But I thought it was a cheap shot aimed at hurting everyone I cared about, especially Ivana. It was a low blow."

As Hugh Hefner noted, Marla's statement suggested that she was no longer a virgin and that it implied that she'd built up a record of seduction that allowed her to evaluate Donald when stacked up against other lovers. Then, *Playboy* mag-

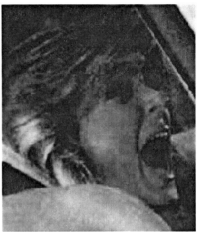

Marla's film debut as a girl in redneck hell:

In the upper photo, Marla gets crushed by watermelons during a pileup of demented 18-wheel trailer trucks in Stephen King's *Maximum Overdrive*

azine, through her agent, Chuck Jones, offered $2 million if Marla would pose nude for a centerfold.

The previously unknown Marla Maples was quickly becoming a household word. Offers poured in, allowing her to pick and choose.

Whereas she refused to lend her name to a line of lingerie that would have been branded "The Other Woman," she agreed, however, to endorse "No Excuses," a brand of jeans for "bad girls" such as Donna Rice and Paula Jones.

Unknown to Marla, Ivana, in spite of her age, had also been approached to pose for No Excuses Jeans, which she turned down as "undignified."

On May 23, 1990, a reporter asked Marla at a press conference if she were a bad girl.

"Not at all," she claimed. "I am a good girl. As proof of that, I'm donating $25,000 of my fee to the Better World Society," She was referring to an environmental organization. "Pollution really worries me. I love the ocean."

The press conference was marred when a process server showed up to hand Marla a subpoena to give a deposition in the case of *Trump vs. Trump*.

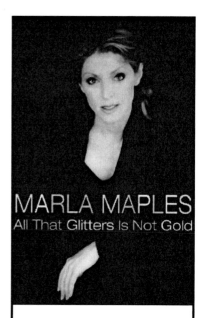

MARLA MAPLES
All That Glitters Is Not Gold

Marla's had an emotional and very public decompression after the letdown of a marriage that—although it failed—brought her fame beyond her wildest hopes.

All That Glitters Is Not Gold was announced as the name of her memoir, with the promise that it would detail her tumultuous marriage to Donald.

But it was abruptly withdrawn from the market and never published.

Other than Donald himself, Marla's agent, Chuck Jones, did more to promote her than any other person. "She is the Marilyn Monroe of the 1990s," he claimed in the *New York Daily News*. "When I walk down the street with Marla, people literally walk right into me. She's that beautiful."

He also boasted that Marla "outstripped" Ivana in celebrity status. "Mrs. Trump arrived at La Grenouille for a luncheon. It turned into a mob scene. But if I called a press conference for Marla, they would have to shut down Manhattan."

For the most part, as Ivana received glowing press coverage as the wronged woman, reporters cracked down on "the blonde vixen," Marla Maples. In 1991, in *Mirabella*, Elizabeth Kaye wrote: "Like Donna Rice or Allison Stern, or any of the flawless women who became the obsession of privileged men, Marla is the perfect coda for thirty years of the women's movement. Here is the triumph of a retro woman with retro wiles, evidence that the more things change, the more they remain the same."

In 1990, the first rumors appeared in both the *New York Post* and the *New York Daily News*, claiming that Donald and Ivana were separating. Marla was judgmentally cast as "THE OTHER WOMAN."

Tabloid writers seemed obsessed with the ups and downs of Donald's affairs. It was said that the story of his being trapped between the two demanding women (Ivana and Marla) "reached Peyton Place histrionics."

Donald told associates, "I don't really give a fuck what they write about me as long as I've got a young and beautiful piece of ass."

His love life and his ongoing divorce from Ivana had become such a hot topic that even President George H.W. Bush referred to it. He was in New York for a campaign rally. "I am here where one of the great contests of 1990 will take place. But I'm not here to talk about the Trumps."

On the Trump family's home front, Eric, Ivanka, and Donald Jr. (known as "Donny") were said to be "emotional wrecks" based on the devastation wrought by Donald's divorce of their mother. During a particularly painful father-son confrontation, Donny shouted at his dad, "You just love your money. You don't love us."

The statement was not true. Throughout it all, and despite his turbulent love life, Donald always loved his children and amply demonstrated his devotion to them.

Although Donald's local reputation as a real estate developer had long made him famous in New York, his private life made him one of the most recognizable names in America. At the age of forty-four, his nationwide legend soon began to soar.

In spite of his "dance with bankruptcy," he predicted an amazing comeback. "I might one day be President of the United States," he said. "I place no goal in the future as being beyond my power. I'm sure if I ran for President, I would win. Not only that, but I would become the greatest U.S. President of the 20th Century."

"Greater than FDR?" a reporter asked.

"Perhaps if I presided over World War III."

SO MANY LUSCIOUS MODELS
So Little Time

Their Romantic Road was rough on both Donald and Marla, as they would fight, make up, then erupt into another alienation.

During one of their separations, Donald didn't immediately seek a reconciliation with Marla. Instead, he diverted his attention to a "well-stacked" model, Rowanne Brewer.

A 26-year-old swimsuit model and former *Star Search* contestant, she was said to have sustained a brief fling with Donald who at the time was an "embattled 'billionaire-downgraded-to-millionaire' developer," according to the *New York Post*. A former (1988) *Miss Maryland USA*, Brewer would eventually appear on *Entertainment Tonight* dissing her "new honey."

She had met Donald at a pool party at Mar-a-Lago in 1990. Some fifty models turned up at the party, each a stunning beauty, but there were fewer than three dozen men.

As Brewer relayed to *The New York Times:* "For some reason, Donald seemed a little smitten with me. He just started talking to me and nobody else. He suddenly took me by the hand, and he started to show me around the mansion. He asked me if I had a swimsuit with me. I said no. I hadn't intended to swim. He took me into a room and opened drawers and asked me to put on a swimsuit."

She followed his instructions. When she came out, he said, "Wow!" He then introduced her to the rest of the party, presenting her as "a stunning Trump Girl."

Brewer and Donald began to date for a few months in 1990 and early 1991. Guests remembered them showing up at a Christmas party for the Elite Modeling Agency in Manhattan.

According to Sid Sussmann, president of American Pageants, which owns the *Miss Maryland USA* contest, "My first impression of Rowanne was that she reminded

Trump security guard to Rowanna Brewer (aka Rowanna Brewer Lane, depicted above at the centerpiece of a nationwide debate about how Trump treated women): "Call your mama and tell her you're gonna be famous."

me of a bimbo, but she's hardly that. She can speak and she's bright. She just has this outrageous body."

[Donald was not alone in his pursuit of Rowanne Brewer. An earlier beau had been "Vanilla Ice," a rapper, actor, and TV host also known as Robert Matthew Van Winkle, who had famously dated Madonna for eight months in 1990. Van Winkle and Brewer were seen together—and captured on tape—in the back seat of a limousine squirting honey onto each other's faces.]

Once again, Marla and Donald had a reconciliation, although other stormy breakups would flare again, followed by a reconciliation. Apparently, many of their fights were over her charges of "lying to me."

On September 17, 1991, Marla and Donald were seen dining with right-wing evangelist, Billy Graham. He had flown into Manhattan to deliver a sermon in Central Park, even though he was quoted privately as saying that "New York City is a land of heathens."

Why he chose an unmarried couple like Donald and Marla to dine with was a question for reporters. One journalist speculated that Donald must have given his ministry a huge donation.

Less than five days after dining with Graham, a headline appeared in the *New York Daily News*: HERE WE GO AGAIN—TRUMP DUMPS MARLA.

Donald had a special friendship with Richard Johnson, editor of the gossipy Page Six in *The New York Post*. "I want to remain good friends with Marla," Donald confided. "But it's time for me to move on. Other worlds to conquer."

Perhaps he meant other models instead of other worlds.

Donald met Kim Alley, age 21, and nick-named "Alley Cat." She was a beautiful model for the Wilhelmina Agency, hailing from Virginia.

Alley was a top-rated model, appearing in such fashion magazines as *Vogue* (both the French and Italian versions) and in the American *Elle*.

The occasion was an exclusive party at the East Side penthouse of Jerry Brandt, the nightclub impresario.

Brandt, a friend of Donald's, had launched such clubs as the Electric Circus, known between 1967 and 1971 as one of the

Kim Alley, after the brouhaha of her association with Donald had subsided, maintained that her link with him was harmful, rather than helpful, to her career and "Fame quotient."

hottest discos in New York, a mixed media pleasure dome with hallucino-genic light baths. The Velvet Underground played there, as did such bands as The Grateful Dead.

When Donald faced Alley Cat, she wore a cap with "ALLEY CAT" written atop it. He later claimed that he chatted briefly with her. After leaving the gathering, he went to the China Club on Manhattan's West Side. He noticed that Alley Cat came in later with her entourage.

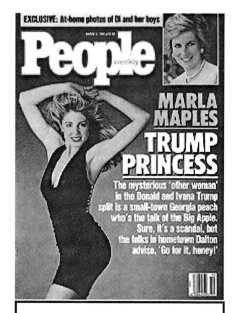

"I paid no attention to her," he wrote in *The Art of the Comeback*.

The next day he was shocked to read frontpage stories in both *The New York Post* and *New York Daily News* that she had held a news conference announcing that she was Donald's new girlfriend. "We are very much in love," she told the press.

Donald later wrote, "What the press didn't know was that the story was not true. I was incensed."

Alley Cat didn't want to keep her involvement with Donald a secret. Her version didn't match his version. "He's a lot sexier in person than he is in all those pictures," she told the tabloids. "He asked me what I thought of Marla Maples. He also kept saying to me, 'You're a beautiful woman.' I just blushed when he said that. I told him he must have quite an ego to be living in a building named after himself. He just laughed. 'Yes, sometimes I do think a lot of myself,' he said."

She confessed that he escorted her to her Park Avenue apartment in his limousine, as

People magazine, among others, helped spread the fame (read that "notoriety") of Marla Maples, but she never came close to being as widely publicized as Ivana.

An early shot of the nascent and budding relationship of Donald and Marla, taken in 1984 "when love was young."

the sound of Guns N' Roses blasted away on the limo's tape deck. "He left me, but he kissed me good night on the lips. He's a good kisser. Very, very sexy. He was polite, gentle, and didn't try any fancy stuff."

Harry Hurt III discounted Donald's version of his interchanges with Alley Cat. In his biography, *The Lost Tycoon*. Hurt alleged that Donald invited Alley Cat into his limousine for a ride to China Club, which was nearby, and, after that wound down, they got back into the limo to appear later that evening at The Roxy.

Donald was said to have told his realtor friend, Larry Russo, "Marla would slash her wrists if she really found out all the beautiful women hot on my trail...or is that tail?"

Soon, both Brewer and Alley Cat exited from Donald's life.

Re-enter Marla.

***

In June of 1991, Marla conducted another reconciliation with him rather publicly.

She appeared on the TV talk show of Kathie Lee Gifford, who was hosting the show with her husband, Frank Gifford, the former football star. Kathie Lee, too, had married an older man. Of course, her own redneck, evangelical, Southern background was different from Marla's. Kathie Lee came from a family of snake handlers, and had studied theater at the right-wing Oral Roberts University.

Donald at one point phoned Kathie Lee's studio for a live, on-the-air conversation, wherein it was confirmed that Marla had accepted his proposal of marriage. The call was broadcast on *Live with Regis and Kathie Lee* to millions of TV viewers.

Later, Marla told *People* magazine, "I think Donald deployed Carla Bruni, Madonna, and Kim Basinger to push me farther away from him. He was testing my love for him like a little boy often does with his mother, doing something really bad, knowing she'll forgive him if she really loves him. We're back together.

When Marla was temporarily separated from Donald, she fell into the arms of the handsome singer and songwriter, Michael Bolton.

She'd heard many of his recordings, and, for a while, at least, seemed mesmerized by him.

He's holding out the prospect of a big diamond ring—and, lest we forget, marriage. Perhaps."

But ten weeks later, the New York Daily News was proclaiming—HERE WE GO AGAIN…TRUMP DUMPS MARLA.

Donald told columnist Cindy Adams, "Whatever happens to Marla, my dating her has made her famous."

When Marla read that, she called *The Post*. "I don't need his help any more. I can make it on my own."

While separated from Donald, Marla was linked in the press to another beau, Michael Bolton, the American singer and songwriter. He became known for his series of pop-rock ballads in the 1980s when he sold more than 75 million records. He released eight top ten albums and two No. 1 singles on the *Billboard* charts. She appeared with him when he gave a concert at the Central Washington State Fair, arousing Donald's jealousy.

With all this publicity she was generating, Marla was offered an appearance on *Designing Women*, a CBS-TV sitcom centering on the lives of four women and one man working as interior designers at a firm in Atlanta. Occasionally, the women dealt with topical issues such as homophobia, racism, AIDS, and spousal abuse.

The backers of the show wanted to take advantage of the Marla/Donald soap opera.

On the show, Marla appeared as herself, thereby infuriating Donald. She spoke of her much publicized break with him. "That's what happens when you go out with someone who has a big ego. You wind up getting the short end of

Marla's appearance on a TV sitcom (*Designing Women*) infuriated Donald.

He objected to her suggestive reference to her "getting the short end of the stick," since it carried the veiled implication that he had a small penis.

234

the stick."

There was a brief pause before the actress who played her fictional soul-mate on the show gave a risqué interpretation to her line.

"So THAT was the problem?" she asked, a reference to Donald having a small penis.

At the time, Marla had a roommate, Kim Knapp, a freckle-face straw-berry blonde whom Marla had made friends with while attending the University of Georgia. Knapp reported that there had been a break-in at their apartment and a packet of nude photographs that Donald had taken of Marla were stolen. There was a fear that these pictures could be used for blackmail. Rumors were rampant, some of them suggesting that nude pictures of Donald had also been stolen.

After *Designing Women*, Donald—within four days—forgave Marla and flew with her to Dalton, Georgia, where she was crowned the Whitfield High School homecoming queen. TV cameras recorded his appearance there as her escort.

Donald had become a media event, his every utterance making news. When attacked, he fought back. Don Imus, on his popular radio talk show, referred to Donald's "fat, grandmotherly arms."

Donald told the press, "I'll never advertise on his show again."

Imus had the final word: "We want only advertisers who can pay their bills," a reference, of course, to Donald's bankruptcy woes.

MARLA ON BROADWAY
In Hot Pants She Shakes Her Ass Across a Stage

Marla made her Broadway debut in August of 1992, starring as Ziegfeld's mistress in the Tony-winning production of *The Will Rogers Follies* at the Palace Theater on Broadway.

She made a spectacular entrance, rising slowly from the orchestra pit like Venus floating to the surface on a hydraulic lift.

She shimmered in gold hot pants, gold cowboy boots, a gold cowboy hat, and gold hair. She sang and twirled a mammoth branding iron, and strutted and skipped across the stage, wiggling her shapely and nearly nude ass.

Jan Stuart in *Newsday* said that she was "a curvaceous prop who slinks on stage with next to nothing on to provide a butt for Rogers' off-the-cuff innuendo. In short, a cheesecake with a wink. She looks too much like an overripe Georgia cheerleader type to convey the joke. On the other hand, she doesn't embarrass."

After the show, Donald staged a big party in her honor at the Grand Ballroom of the Plaza. Only 500 "intimate" friends were invited. One reporter for *The New York Times* claimed that the entrance of Marla and Donald into the ballroom evoked William Randolph Hearst presiding at the debut of his young *protégée*, Marion Davies, who became his longtime mistress.

La Toya Jackson showed up at the party with her boa constrictor, wanting to pose with Marla, but she declined. When the diva learned that Marla was "bad mouthing me all over town," she placed an angry call to denounce her.

"You must think I'm just some god damn black bitch," La Toya shouted at her. "You're nothing but a racist who stole a husband. Kiss my ass!" Then she slammed down the phone.

Ironically, Chuck Jones, in addition to representing Marla as a client, also represented La Toya.

As the weeks passed, the wedding date for Marla and Donald was announced and then canceled. As late as October of 1992, the *New York Daily News* ran a headline: SPLITSVILLE—NEW YORK'S FUN COUPLE CALLS IT QUITS...AGAIN!

IT'S NOT A WEDDING!
But Marla & Donald & Baby Make Three!

Marla came into Donald's life when he was awash on a stormy financial sea. He was also battling Ivana in the divorce courts as she tried to get half of his assets.

Stephen Hyde, one of his chief aides, told associates that Donald at times, in his anger, blamed Marla for all his troubles, even for the gloomy skies that hovered over the Taj Mahal in Atlantic City. "He was taking it out on her, and at one point, she walked out on him."

"I'm not coming back," she shouted at him.

Months before his marriage to Marla, Donald enjoyed a heavily booked dating calendar. Columnists had a hard time keeping up with all the names of the women he was seen with: Anna Nicole, Angelica Bollinger, Frederique Van de Wall, Eva Herzigova, and such beauty title holders as

Michelle McLean (Miss Universe) and Shannon Marketic (Miss USA).

A problem soon arose. Marla was pregnant with Donald's baby.

Movie stars used to slip away and deliver their babies out of wedlock. But Marla didn't hide her "belly under a bushel," as she said. "Instead, she modeled a new line of fashionable maternity clothes for the married or unwed mother to be.

A daughter, Tiffany, was born on October 13, 1993, but Donald wasn't ready to get married until December 20, 1993. Once again, as with Ivana, he demanded that Marla sign a prenup agreement.

In his 1997 book, *The Art of the Comeback*, he devoted an entire section to prenuptial agreements. "Anyone in a complicated business should be institutionalized if he or she marries without a prenup. I know firsthand that you can't come back if you're spending all your time fighting for your financial life with a spouse."

At first, Marla refused to sign it, claiming that she felt it was "setting up the marriage for a failure. If a woman signs a prenup, it's a virtual forecast that the marriage won't work out."

After much persuasion, and perhaps a threat or two, she signed the document.

Finally, on December 20, 1993, after all those breakups, and three months after the birth of their daughter, they were married. Ivana,

Donald's marriage #2 occurred during the biggest distraction of his decade, the launch of the Taj Mahal and its associated financial horrors.

Few other brides can claim the honor of a wedding portrait attached to a casino chip.

Like the casino, the marriage failed, too.

It was a very modern wedding, accompanied with an *avant-garde* media campaign depicting a bride in white and a groom with their newborn daughter.

meanwhile, was reported to be "keeping her cool" on the ski slopes of Aspen.

For "something old," Harry Winston lent Marla a $2 million diamond tiara. Donald had already given her a $250,000 engagement ring.

The wedding was held at the Plaza, with Marla making a stunning entrance in a snow-white dress, one of Carolina Herrera's finer creations.

Donald gave his own view of his wedding to his biographer, Timothy O'Brien. "I was bored when I saw Marla walking down the aisle. I kept thinking, 'What in hell am I doing here getting married?'"

By many accounts, Marla has fine parenting skills. Baby Tiffany, depicted with her mother, wears a hat in which Marla performed in *The Will Rogers Follies*.

He would also complain to Nancy Collins, a reporter for *ABC-TV*. "I've really given a lot of breaks to women. Unfortunately, after I've made them a star, the fun is over for me. It's like a creative project, almost like creating one of my spectacular towers. After it's completed, the thrill is gone."

The guest list was impressive, and augmented with seventeen TV crews, a flood of gossip mavens, and nearly a hundred paparazzi, including the notorious photographer Ron Galella, who used to stalk Jacqueline Kennedy.

Among those appearing were Mayor David N. Dinkins, Senator Alfonse M. D'Amato, Congressman Charles Rangel, soap opera queen Susan Lucci, and such performers as Jerry Orbach, Liza Minnelli, Rosie O'Donnell, and Tommy Tune.

From the sports world came O.J. Simpson (before the murder), Evander Holyfield, Don King, and Joe Frazier. The financial sector was represented by Alan C. Greenberg, Chairman of the Executive Committee of Bear, Sterns, & Company.

Robin Leach of *Lifestyles of the Rich & Famous* likened the wedding blitz to "Charles and Diana all over again. You know what happened with that."

Also attending was Adnan Khashoggi, the Saudi arms dealer from whom Donald had purchased his yacht.

The wedding was followed by a reception where guests feasted on such delights as champagne and $60,000 worth of Beluga caviar.

For their honeymoon, Donald and Marla escaped to a secret hideaway in Telluride, Colorado.

DIVORCE
— Tycoon Style

At the wedding, shock jock Howard Stern said, "I give this marriage four months, if that."

Many of Donald's friends, perhaps his children with Ivana, didn't think it would last either.

The marriage lasted much longer than Stern had predicted. Marla and Donald separated in May of 1997, and after six rocky years of matrimony, their divorce became final in 1999.

As *The New York Times* proclaimed, in reference to their marriage, "Great sex does not guarantee an enduring love."

When news of marital discord emerged, headlines began screaming, "TRUMP MARRIAGE ON THE ROCKS."

"Marla and I just drifted apart," Donald claimed. "Our lifestyles became less and less compatible. She was content just staying at home and being with Tiffany and me. But I had a million outside interests to attend to. We were pulled in different directions."

When Marla moved ahead to divorce Donald, she, too, challenged the prenup she'd signed. As such, she followed in the footsteps of Ivana, but

At age 52, Marla made a trimphant comeback in some well-received and physically exhausting appearances on *Dancing with the Stars*, leaving memories of her marriage to Donald behind and dedicating some of her performances to Tiffany.

She danced with her partner, Tony Dovolani, and was later praised for her "natural grace."

Despite the high ratings she generated, she was eventually elimated,

not as fiercely and not with such high-powered lawyers. Marla had signed a contract stating that in the event of divorce, she'd receive a flat $2 million, plus ongoing support.

In court, she testified that Donald had promised more money, but she had no document to back up that claim.

Legal infighting between the opposing divorce lawyers lasted for eighteen months. Finally, she accepted the terms of their original agreement.

During all these proceedings, a new man had entered her life. He was Michael Mailer, the son of the famous and controversial novelist, Norman Mailer.

At one point, word reached Donald that Marla had threatened to "tell all" to a British tabloid. She was said to be revealing "what Donald is really like." But those revelations were squelched when Donald threatened to withhold $1.5 million of her divorce settlement.

***

After his divorce from Marla, Donald was inundated with proposals, both legitimate requests to become his next wife—others of a more indecent sort. One was from a (male) former matinee idol whose career was fading. "Donald," he wrote, "Why not try a man for a change? I'm very, very good."

It is not known whether Donald was shown the letter from that man, but the actor never heard from him. He was last seen disappearing into the wilds of eastern Oregon.

With Marla at last "disposed of," Donald announced that he needed to take a break from romance. At that time, he claimed that only one beautiful young woman could get him to walk down the aisle again and that was the former Lady Diana Spencer who had entered into an ill-fated marriage with Prince Charles.

As Donald wrote in *The Art of the Comeback*, "I regret I never had the opportunity to court her. I couldn't help but notice how she moved people. She lit up the room with her charm, her presence. She was a genuine princess—a dream lady."

Publicist Chuck Jones had been hired by Marla to help launch her into show business. For many months he was her chief aide, often escorting her to functions. But in time, they drifted apart.

However, in the mid-1990s, he was arrested for breaking into her apartment and making off with at least thirty pairs of her footwear, mainly high heels. He would later admit in court that he had "a sexual relationship" with that footwear. When they were eventually retrieved, some of the high heels were reported as "soiled."

He was also charged with stealing pieces of her lingerie. When his apartment was searched, police discovered an unlicensed firearm, for which he was also charged.

Since his break with Marla, he had also been accused of sending her ominous e-mails. In one of them he wrote: "I hope your Easter basket catches fire and burns your house to the ground. Now shove an egg into your slimy mouth and choke."

In another missile, he called her "a piece of shit, a homewrecker, and an all-around dumbass." In yet another attack, he labeled her "The Queen of all Scumbags."

Donald's security staff feared that Jones had also made off with nude photographs of Marla and Donald, but a thorough search of his apartment did not turn up any of these candid shots.

However, such photographs were said to have been taken in a playful moment. A "tipster" informed Richard Johnson at Page Six at the *New York Post* that "Donald Trump is shaped like a bowling pin with a cottage cheese butt."

Jones was charged with sixteen counts of harassment and with possession of an illegal weapon. But his conviction was later overturned on a technicality. Consequently, instead of serving a term of nearly five years, he was in prison for only a few months. But even after his release, he was tried once again on burglary charges. "He just seemed obsessed with Marla," said one of her attorneys. "He couldn't leave her alone and continued to harass her."

He was eventually re-sentenced to one and a half years to four years in prison. After his release, he filed a series of lawsuits against Marla, but the cases eventually drifted into a kind of limbo.

He was arrested for a second time for sending out photos that allegedly depicted Donald and Marla in positions of sexual intimacy. He was charged this time with "aggravated harassment."

In 1999, he was brought into court again on the original burglary charges, representing himself as his defense attorney. He was sentenced to three months in jail.

Amazingly, his obsession with Marla manifested itself again after his release. In 2012, he was back in court, charged once again with sending Marla harassing E-mails. This time, a plea deal got him off with only six months on probation.

***

[In 2002, it was announced that Marla was writing a tell-all about her life, with a special emphasis on her tumultuous marriage to Donald. The announcement was made even though Marla had signed an iron-clad confidentiality agreement with Donald.

ReganBooks announced that it would publish it as All That Glitters Is Not Gold. *Chuck Jones claimed that the "book will be the story behind the headlines, and it will be remarkably candid about Donald Trump. It will also deal with the pain of loving a man whose greatest passion is the empire he built."*

A few weeks later, ReganBooks announced that by mutual consent, the book would not be published. Gossip guzzlers speculated that "Donald must have moved in with threats."]

marla naples/instagram

Gorgeous mother, lovely daughter (who is more hip?), demonstrating the close reationship they share, at the observation deck of the rebuilt World Trade Center, early in 2016.

Chapter Eleven

APPRENTICES FOUR
In their birth order:
Donald Jr., Ivanka, Eric, & Tiffany
DOES FATHER KNOW BEST?

"I'm the son of Donald Trump, and here I am, a god damn boat attendant scrounging for tips."
—Donald Jr.

"So Tiffany was born out of wedlock—so what? For god's sake, this is 1993, not 1903!"
"Tiffany has the legs of her mother (Marla Maples), but the score is still out on her breasts."
—Donald, in reference to his newborn daughter

Donald and Ivana Trump never wrote any book about how to rear rich kids, but they saw around them many examples of what not to do, as they watched their fellow wealthy friends rear "spoiled brats."

There is no doubt about it: Ivana was a better mother than Donald was a father, as least during the early years where his three children were growing up.

He would take a far greater interest in his post-college kids, especially when he brought them in as executives to help him run the rapidly expanding Trump Organization with business interests around the globe.

One of his ideas about parenting involved making available a 24-hour limousine to take them to and from school, or drive them to the doctor or to the birthday party of one of their school friends.

Fortunately, he had a skilled aide, Norma Foerderer, who made him aware of all of his children's birthdays. She would, in Donald's name, purchase wonderful presents for them. She would also see that her boss actually made it to the birthday parties of each of his children.

She went beyond the call of duty and even helped Donald define and organize "talking points" when he went home to a family dinner.

"Donny (Don Jr.) had a game today," she told him. "Here's what you can ask him about it."

"Ivanka got all 'A's' on her report card," Norma continued. "You must congratulate her. In fact, I've bought a bottle of wonderful French perfume for you to give to her tonight."

"Eric has a bad cold, and Ivana has already called in a doctor," she said. "Please call on him but skip the good night kiss. You don't want to catch anything. Tomorrow, you meet with those vultures from the bank."

"Don't forget to compliment your wife on her looks tonight," Norma advised. "She's spent most of the afternoon in the beauty parlor, trying to make herself look more glamorous for you. She's complaining to her girlfriends at Le Cirque that you're not paying her much attention these days."

***

Ivana never won any "Mother of the Year" awards, but she more or less fitted her children into her hysterically busy schedule, although she was gone most of the time. She'd given birth to two sons, Donald Jr. and Eric, with a girl in between. Sometimes, her daughter's name of "Ivanka" was confused with her own name of "Ivana."

"The Donald and I don't plan to raise spoiled rich kids," Ivana once told an interviewer. "We want to give each of them a real sense of how to handle money. We don't overly indulge them, as do many parents who are friends of ours. Too often, children of rich parents grow into disasters."

"The Donald puts them on a strict weekly allowance: Five dollars for Donny; three for Ivanka; and only one for Baby Eric. At age two, he doesn't run up many night club bills."

"The trick is to keep them occupied," she said. "Busy, busy, busy—too busy to get into trouble. There is school, there is homework. Sports and plenty of exercise are also important, as is a healthy diet. I also encourage after school activities so they'll learn to mingle with kids their own age. I find out what their interests are. Take Donny for example. We found he liked sailing, so we gave him lessons from an instructor before we bought him his own sailing boat. Perhaps we'll be preparing him to be the captain of his own luxurious yacht one day."

"The Donald and I try to spend as much time as possible with our little ones," Ivana said. "We try to have breakfast as a family. They're gone all day, but whenever we can, we like to gather for a family dinner. On weekends, we try to fit them into our activities. Their father takes them to baseball games, Radio City, Broadway matinees."

"Mostly, we try to give them self-confidence. They fly with us to Palm Beach. Usually, I'm in the back of the plane with them, helping them with their homework."

To one reporter, she gave a preview of her day. "I run the Plaza Hotel, a full-time job. I wake them up at seven and get them ready for school. After a hard day's work, I come home to listen to their problems and help them with their homework before dinner. We refuse to take phone calls at that time. Later, when we send them off to bed, The Donald and I will go out to a party, at least three times a week. The stories that we stay out until dawn are not true."

DONALD TRUMP, JR.
"He Could Be Dangerous"

The first son of Donald and Ivana was born as hordes gathered in Times Square to bring in the New Year of 1978. So far as it is known, he was Donald's first child.

As he was growing up, his father did not have a lot of time to spend with him. Consequently, he turned to his maternal grandfather, Milos Zelnicek, who lived in the Trump Tower with his wife. Milos became a kind of father substitute for the growing boy.

In summer, Don Jr. flew with him to his native Czechoslovakia, where they went fishing, boating, and hunting. He even taught Don Jr. to speak Czech fluently.

It was painful for the boy when his father became estranged from his mother and became shacked up with the beautiful blonde-haired model from Georgia, Marla Maples. One teacher told Donald, "Your father is behaving like a horny teenager."

"It was a tough time for me," Don Jr. later recollected. "I was twelve years old. You're not quite a man then, but you think you are. You know everything. On the way to school, I would have the chauffeur stop so that I could pick up a tabloid to read about Marla Maples and my dad. Often, they were frontpage news, Marla proclaiming that Dad gave her the best sex she'd ever had. The boys at school ribbed me constantly."

"When they separated, I lived with my mother," he said. "You can be manipulated. Getting a one-sided perspective. I didn't speak to dad for a year."

"We reconciled and he set out to teach me the value of a dollar," Don Jr. said. "At the age of thirteen, he put me to work as a dock attendant at the marina at Trump Castle in Atlantic City. I made the minimum wage— slave pay—plus tips for tying up the boats."

He attended Hill School, a preparatory boarding school for girls and boys, in Pottstown, Pennsylvania, and later enrolled at this father's alma mater, the University of Pennsylvania, where he studied business at the Wharton School.

He admitted that he entered a rebellious part of his life, often drinking and getting into fights. "There was a lot of hard partying. For a while, I lived in 'boozy' Aspen. But one day I woke up with a hangover and decided that my brain was staring to atrophy with all that heavy drinking. I returned to New York to make something of myself."

Today, he claims, "I am my own person. I do not live under my father's shadow. But who knows what will happen if he becomes President?"

Whereas it took his father a long time and three wives to sire five children, fast-acting Don Jr. became a daddy five times between 2007 and 2012.

He hardly keeps his wife, Vanessa, "barefoot and pregnant," but he certainly keeps her pregnant.

There are those who have suggested, perhaps facetiously, that Donald should name his son as his vice presidential nominee.

Today, he is an executive vice president of the Trump Organization. He works in the Trump Tower, just a few doors away from his father. "Dad is a workaholic. Even in his free time, he's always working. It is his hobby and also his job. The man's a genius. Sometimes, I've seen him negotiate for five minutes and save a million dollars. He trusts me. However, if I write a check for more than $100,000, I have to get his approval."

"He didn't order me to watch *The Apprentice* all the time, but I always faced a tough quiz about the show the following morning, so I studied it faithfully.

"I'm glad that TV audiences got to see that Dad's a great guy—fun loving and humorous. He's not just some stiff who sits there bellowing 'YOU'RE FIRED!'"

"Before *The Apprentice* went on the air, there was this kind of corporate impression of my Dad, a kind of Napoleonic evilness," Don Jr. said. "Now people saw him interacting with normal—barely normal—individuals. It was like, 'Wait a second! He's a regular guy!'"

For *New York* magazine, Jonathan Van Meter went to interview Don Jr.: "He is tall and tan and has a thick mane of brown hair that's slicked straight back. It's not so much that he looks like his father, but that he seems like his father—big and masculine and slightly intimidating, but somehow affable. He has the charm of a professional ball player who has signed a multi-million-dollar contract. There are pinstripes and flashy cuff links and a perfectly knotted tie. If Don Jr. were to lose about twenty-five pounds, he'd be dangerous."

Don Jr. became engaged to a model, Vanessa Haydon. "Like father, like son," a reporter wrote.

He showed his father an engagement ring he wanted to buy for $65,000. "That's too cheap," Donald said.

Consequently, his son decided to make a deal: He arranged with Bailey Banks & Biddle in the Short Hills (New Jersey) Mall for a $100,000 ring to give Vanessa when he proposed to her. "It was a trade-off for turning a private event into a publicity machine for the store," Don Jr. said.

Later, however, he was denounced in the press for being "tacky," and his engagement gesture was defined as "taste deprived" for turning one of his future wife's private moments into a media circus for reporters and photographers.

Vanessa and Don Jr., were married on November 12, 2005 at Mar-a-Lago. Officiating was his aunt, Judge Maryanne Trump Barry.

Today, the couple have five children: Daughters Kai Madison (born 2007) and Chloë Sophia (born 2014). They also have three sons: Donald John III (born 2009); Tristan Milos (born 2011); and Spencer Frederick (born 2012).

IVANKA
"I'll Redecorate the White House Like Jacqueline Kennedy"
—Ivanka Trump

"The beauty with the brains," Ivanka Marie Trump, entered the world as a "mixed breed" (German, Scottish, Czech) Manhattan baby on October 30, 1981. At the age of ten, she had to experience "divided loyalties" when her parents separated.

Stylish, ambitious, and intelligent, Ivanka has the poise and self-confidence of her mother. Like her mother, she preferred life as a blonde, and she attributed a lot of her business sense to both parents.

"I grew up traipsing behind my mother as she met with executives at the Plaza Hotel, which we then owned. My father taught me the value of the often forgotten detail. He can walk through a hotel or a building and see a crown molding that's just slightly off."

She was fifteen when she enrolled at Chapin, an exclusive, all-girls school on Manhattan's Upper East Side. She later graduated from Choate's Rosemary Hall in Wallingford, Connecticut.

She later said, "If Chapin and Choate had been airline seats, they would have been first class all the way. The dorms at Choate were the first building I lived in that didn't say Trump somewhere on the façade."

Donald's older daughter, Ivanka, has been called "the brains of the family," at least in regards to her siblings.

She'd grown up in a triplex atop the Trump Tower. "I had a Madonna clock next to my white canopy bed. My walls were painted with lilac and checkered with 90210 stickers and Melrose Place trading cards. Luke Perry was my absolute favorite. Plus the usual assortment

Loving both her father and her mother, she became traumatized when her parents broke up. Sometimes, vicious classmates brought tabloid stories about her parents' breakup to school to taunt her and make her cry.

of Bon Jovi, Mötley Crüe, and Paula Abdul posters hung around the room. I was a sucker for all those big-hair artists of the late 1980s and early 1990s."

She spent two years at Georgetown University, transferring to the Wharton School at the University of Pennsylvania, following in her father's footsteps. She graduated cum laude in 2004 with a B.S. in Economics.

After college, she did not rush immediately into family enterprises. She signed with the Dynamic Diamond Corporation, a diamond trading company, where she designed and introduced a line of jewelry at the brand's first flagship store, a venue named Ivanka Trump on Madison Avenue.

She also had a detour into modeling, appearing on the cover of a 1997 issue of *Seventeen*. She also appeared on fashion runways for the likes of Versace and other designers, and modeled for ads for Sassoon Jeans and Tommy Hilfiger. She was also a cover girl for such magazines as *Golf, Forbes, Avenue, Elle Mexico,* and *Harper's Bazaar.*

In 1997, she also hosted the *Miss Teen USA* Pageant, partially owned by her father.

He watched her host the pageant, then told the press, "She did a wonderful job. The ratings for CBS were sky high. A chip off the old block."

She was later featured in a 2003 movie documentary, *Born Rich,* co-starring with other rich kids such as Georgina Bloomberg, Cody Franchetti, Si Newhouse IV, and Luke Well. "My daughter is brilliant. No one could call her spoiled, like some of those kids," Donald proclaimed.

She not only followed her father in her selection of a university, but also became an author, publishing *Trump Card*, a *New York Times* bestseller, in 2009. In it, she offered insights into the business world.

Like Ivana, Ivanka takes a hands-on approach,

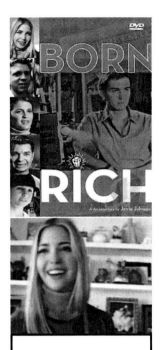

Born Rich, which premiered in 2003 at the Sundance Film Festival and was later broadcast on HBO, is a documentary in which pharmaceutical heir Jamie Johnson persuaded fellow heirs to the Trump, Bloomberg, and Vanderbilt fortunes to speak frankly about money, family pressure, and their own extravagant lifestyles.

In the movie, Ivanka cheerfully shows off her bedroom on the 68th floor of Trump Tower, with a descriptive narrative about the artifacts of her life as a "starstruck teen."

as when she helped overhaul the Trump National Doral Miami, an 800-acre resort with five golf courses that the Trump Organization purchased for $150 million and then spent more than $250 million in renovations.

Set to open late in 2016 is the Trump International Hotel in Washington, D.C., only two blocks from the White House.

"This is the place our family will host the inaugural ball if our dad becomes president," Ivanka said. "It is likely that I might like to redecorate the White House like Jacqueline Kennedy. Perhaps. Of course, Melania will get involved, too, I'm certain of that. She's got amazing style, so I imagine she would also have a big hand in it."

Today, Ivanka is the Executive Vice President of Development & Acquisitions for the Trump Organization. She also runs Ivanka Trump Fine Jewelry, and oversees the Trump Lifestyle Collection that includes fragrances, footwear, handbags, outerwear, and eyewear collections.

She is proud of her brothers, Eric and Don Jr. "There is some sibling rivalry. Dad bred us to be competitive. None of us is a drug addict like so many rich kids we know. My brothers are not chasing after women or snorting coke."

"Mother is a globe-trotter," Ivanka said. "She lives half the year in New York or Florida. She owns a home in Palm Beach and a condo in Miami. She also has a home in London and three homes in the Czech Republic. There's a vacation home in St. Tropez on the Côte d'Azur. She also has a yacht floating somewhere."

Ironically, Ivanka is also a friend of Chelsea Clinton, Hillary's daughter. In 2007, Ivanka donated $1,000 to the presidential campaign of Hillary. Later, in 2012, she endorsed Mitt Romney for President.

In a somewhat enigmatic statement, Chelsea was quoted as saying, "There is nothing skin-deep about Ivanka. I think that's a real tribute to her because certainly, anyone as gorgeous as she could probably have gone quite far being skin-deep."

Perhaps Chelsea was saying that Ivanka has beauty but also brains to go with her good looks.

Ivanka was not a party girl in college, but

Her father isn't the only one in the family who can stage beauty pageants. While still a teenager, Ivanka (right) hugs the winner of Miss Texas Teen USA, who would go on to compete in the finals for Miss Teen USA.

formed a long-term relationship with a fellow student, Greg Hirsch. From 2001 to 2005, she was the girlfriend of James ("Bingo") Gubelmann.

But in 2007, she started dating Jared Kushner, a real estate developer, the son of Charles Kushner, CEO of Kushner Properties. Jared is the owner of *The New York Observer*.

In July of 2009, Ivanka studied Judaism with Rabbi Elie Weinstock before her Orthodox conversion, when she took the name of "Yael."

On October 25, 2009, she married Jared in a Jewish ceremony at the National Golf Course in Bedminster, New Jersey, and today they live a few blocks from Trump tower. They are the parents of three children: Arabella Rose (born 2011); Joseph Frederick (born 2013), and Theodore James (born 2016).

"Our family keeps a kosher diet, and we observe the Jewish Sabbath," Ivanka said. "It creates an amazing blueprint for a family connection. From Friday to Saturday, we don't do anything but hang out with one another. We don't make phone calls then."

First Lady Jacqueline Kennedy posed for the cover of *Life* magazine in September of 1961. As her husband at the time said, "Rest assured: The White House is in classy hands."

Ivanka has spoken that as First Daughter, she, along with her stepmother, Melania, would like to bring a similar style and grace to the White House.

In 2015, as a loyal, devoted daughter, Ivanka endorsed her father's presidential bid and actively campaigned for him, taking only a few days off to have her third child.

"As a citizen, I love what he is doing, considering him the man to make us great again. As a daughter concerned for him, it's obviously more complicated."

In August of 2016, Donald stated that his daughter is his leading advisor on "women's health and women in general, and it is she who shapes my views on women's issues."

Ivanka claimed that Donald empowers women and often gives them top managerial posts within the Trump Organization.

NEW CROPS OF BABY TRUMPS:
WILL THEY INFLUENCE THE CAMPAIGN?
"My Grand Daddy Is Running for President"

What do Hillary and "The Donald" have in common? In 2016, during some of their most intense moments in their respective presidential campaigns, they both reinforced their respective roles as grandparents. That year, Chelsea Clinton and Marc Mezvinsky had their second child, and Ivanka Trump had her third baby with Jared Kushner.

[Grandparenting was not new for Donald: His oldest son, Don Jr., had already sired five children, born between 2007 and 2012, with his wife, Vanessa.]

Both Donald and Hillary were accused of using the pregnancies of their respective daughters to make themselves appear as normal, everyday people.

Jay Newton-Small, of *Time*, said, "Being a grandmother makes Hillary seem approachable."

Even before 2016, Hillary had frequently mentioned her status as a grandmother to Charlotte, Chelsea's first daughter (born 2014) as a reinforcement for some of her political platforms.

Newton-Small also pointed out the downside to being a grandmother: "A grandma-in-chief commanding the Armed Forces? You think of grannies as little old biddies—you don't think of them as U.S. Presidents."

Donald brought up the fact of Hillary's age: "Is she capable of doing the job? Is she too old? Because she's a grandmother!"

"Does she have the stamina or strength to handle the daily grind of the presidency?" he asked on Fox News.

Newton-Small called the remark "incredibly sexist and very much of a double standard. For Donald, it's especially a double standard because he is a year older than Hillary.

Newton-Small felt that being grandparents could have a softening effect on both Donald and Hillary. "It's super endearing for presidential contenders. There's nothing sort of more touching than the cycle of life, and the passing of the torch from generation to generation. Voters loved it and there's every reason in the world for their campaigns to play that up."

ERIC TRUMP
"He Seems Too Perfect for Words"

Before her marriage withered, Ivana gave birth to a third child, their second son.

Eric Frederick Trump was born in Manhattan on January 6, 1984 as America was recovering from its New Year's hangover.

He attended Trinity School and was only seven years old when his father and Ivana were divorced. Reportedly, he took the divorce rather hard and suffered as his family was torn apart because he had great love for both parents.

As a young boy at the time of his parents' divorce, he seemed trapped between his mother and father. He was midway through a vacation with Donald and his siblings when he heard his father talking on the phone with Jay Goldberg, his lawyer who handled his divorce.

Donald registered strong objections to Ivana when she published her romantic novel, *For Love Alone* in 1992. He considered it a thinly veiled account of their (pre-marital) affair, which, in his view, violated their confidentiality agreement.

Eric heard his father pressing Goldberg to sue his mother, claiming he might legally be able to cut off $350,000 in his annual alimony payments, based on her breaking of their agreement. He discussed the possibility that he might get back the millions he'd paid out to her in his divorce settlement. He even pressed the case that he should sue for custody of their three children.

The case never went forward in the courts.

Eric calls Donald Trump "my best friend," and they see each other daily whenever both of them are in New York.

He followed in his father's footsteps and is now one of the key players in running the Trump Organization.

***

Although Eric grew up in the shadow of his older brother and tycoon father, he developed into his own man.

"Girls dreamed of him when he came into the public eye," said Carolyn Skait, a model who met him once. "I made off with an eight-by-ten of him. I consider him really hot. He appears in these $3,000 suits, always immaculately groomed, standing tall and handsome. I can only dream of what he's hauling around in his Calvin Kleins. What happened to his picture? My gay brother, also named Erik (but with a different spelling), stole it and hung it up in his bathroom."

As he matured, Eric graduated from Hill School in 2002, and later graduated with honors from Georgetown University with a degree in finance and management. That served him well when he became an executive vice president charged with development and acquisitions for the Trump Organization.

He was also a boardroom judge on NBC's *The Apprentice*.

With his father, he saw the expansion of Trump Golf properties in such places as North Carolina, California, Puerto Rico, New Jersey, Pennsylvania, and New York.

Along with his siblings, he oversees Trump properties in the Trump Hotel Collections, located in, among other places, Las Vegas, Chicago, Toronto, Panama, Punta del Este, Vancouver, the Philippines, Rio de Janeiro, and Waikiki.

He also worked to acquire Kluge Winery and Vineyard in Charlottesville, Virginia, later reorganizing it as Trump Winery.

By 2012, he was named by *Forbes* as among their top "30 under 30" in real estate. *The New York Observer* named him among the "20 Most Important Young Philanthropists." In 2006, he founded the Eric Trump Foundation dedicated to raising money for terminally ill children at St. Jude's Children's Research Hospital.

Although his record seemed almost perfect, he has been hit on occasion with a brickbat. In 2010, *People for the Ethical Treatment of Animals* criticized both Eric and Don Jr. for a hunting trip they took to the Zimbabwe Parks. They went on a safari and were condemned for posing for photographs with slain animals.

Both brothers defended their safari via Twitter, affirming their actions as hunters and longtime advocates of the outdoors, calling allegations of illegality against them "baseless and false." Their father announced that he fully supported his sons.

However, the *Huffington Post* labeled it "a killing spree."

Eric seems to adore his father. "There is no more all-American guy than him," he claims. "He's a super genius and very practical. I'd compare him with Sir Winston Churchill, Andrew Carnegie, and even John D. Rockefeller."

On July 7, 2014, Eric became engaged to his longtime girlfriend, Lara Yunaska, an associate producer on the CBS TV news program, *Inside Edition*.

At Mar-a-Lago on November 6, 2014, the couple, according to a press report, had "a half-Jewish ceremony under a crystal-embellished *chuppah*" [i.e., a canopy under which the Jewish marriage ceremony is performed].

She certainly did not marry a "*po' boy*," as her husband has a net worth of $150 million, with untold millions coming his way in the future.

A reporter, Jerry Drummond, said, "I have no doubt that somewhere by mid-century, Eric F. Trump might become the President of the United States."

TIFFANY TRUMP
Pursuing the Pleasures of the One Percent

Tiffany Ariana Trump was born on October 13, 1993, a child out of wedlock. Her parents were Marla Maples and Donald Trump. "So she was born out of wedlock," her father said. "So what? This is Manhattan in 1993, not Cohutta, Georgia, in 1903." He was referring to Marla's "redneck home town."

Giving birth to her daughter involved an agonizing ten hours in labor for Marla. To soothe her nerves, she ordered the staff to have the room scented with herbs and heated aromatic oils. She also ordered that "New Age Music" be played.

Visiting his second daughter in the hospital, Donald said, "She has her mother's beautiful legs. As for the breasts, we will have to wait to see what 'busts' out."

His comments were captured on tape and later played on TV news when he ran for President in 2016. His pronouncement about his daughter's body parts was denounced as "tasteless and vulgar."

As Tiffany grew into girlhood, she was often compared to her half-sister, Ivanka, who had long before established a formidable reputation for brains and flair.

Tiffany attended Donald's *alma mater*, the University of Pennsylvania, where she majored in sociology (with a concentration in law) and urban studies.

After the university, she landed an internship at *Vogue* and worked with fashion maven Anna Wintour.

Since she hardly needs to work for a living, she can follow any path she chooses, even being a playgirl if she wants that. On *The Oprah Winfrey Show*, she expressed an interest in music. "It is my big passion. It's more of a hobby right now. We'll see what happens in a couple of years if I want to pursue it."

She also has shown some talent as a painter. In his book *Think Like a Billionaire* (2004), Donald claimed that his favorite artwork was a finger painting executed by Tiffany depicting a house.

Since Marla left New York and moved to California after her divorce from Donald, Tiffany grew up there and attended an exclusive private school.

"My mom and I have always been very close. My friends and everyone I knew told me, 'Wow! You guys really have a good relationship.' Many of my friends hated and resented their mothers. Not me. I love Marla. My mother spent a lot of time with me when I was growing up. Many of my more alienated friends found that shocking."

Although Tiffany enjoyed a rich lifestyle in California, she was awed when she visited her three half-siblings in Manhattan. Don Jr., Ivanka, and Eric were living in Versailles-like splendor at the summit of Trump Tower.

Tiffany soon became known to the security guard who controlled access to the Trump's private elevator.

Reportedly shopping in the exclusive stores in the building's lobby was a thrill to her. "When it

The fourth of Donald's (five) children, Tiffany was "cradled and cuddled" by her mother, Marla Maples, when growing up in California. On rare occasions, she got to see her famous father, as in, for some reason, the upper picture, she wanted to look at the world with only one eye.

Her parents divorced in 2000, and she didn't have as close a contact with Donald as her three older half-siblings.

comes to charging clothes, it's good to have Donald Trump as both your father and the Lord & Master of Trump Tower."

"My father was a joy," she recalled. "My mother wanted me to eat healthy, but he indulged me in my favorite food: Almond Joy bars. I don't know if that's good or bad, but I really enjoyed it. If I was craving a chocolate treat, I told Marla, "I'm going to see Dad.'"

In her late teens, Tiffany was pursued by some of the most eligible and richest millennial boyfriends in Manhattan and the Hamptons, and also by some of the young studs whose parents owned lavish estates in Palm Beach.

"But none of them lived in an estate as elegant as Mar-a-Lago," Donald claimed. "Be careful who you date. They may be a gold-digger. Many men today are gold-diggers, not just women."

Andrew Warren was one of Tiffany's most high-profile dates. He's called "the rich kid of Instagram" based on the flood of pictures documenting his lavish, over-the-top, and apparently hedonistic lifestyle on Instagram.

"It's not fair that I get so much flack for this," he said.

He told Tiffany, "I don't think I should be judged for posting a photo like eating caviar at Claridge's in London. I post photos of my girlfriends, even Tiffany. They're fabulous girls. Some guys post pictures of girls who look like unclassy hookers."

Andrew is the grandson of fashion tycoon David Warren. Tiffany's beau unveiled his new collection, "Just Drew," at Style Fashion Week at the Gotham Ball in New York on Valentine's Day, February 14, 2016.

He enlisted some of his famous friends, including Tiffany, to walk down the runway. Other millennials who participated included Kyrea Kennedy, the daughter of Robert F. Kennedy, and Elisa Johnson, the daughter of basketball great

No one gave out any "parents of the year" awards to Donald Trump and his wife, Marla, parents of Tiffany, who was born out of wedlock.

Marla was twenty years old when she met Donald, who was married at the time to Ivana.

They were famously wed for six years, and Tiffany was their only child.

Magic Johnson. They modeled outfits with plunging necklines based on a palette of black and radiant blues.

In the Hamptons in 2016, Warren and Tiffany showed up at the annual Memorial Day party sponsored by Jason Binn, the CEO of *DuJour Magazine*. *DuJour* is a new print/digital hybrid from Binn, who is the publisher of society yearbooks. Criteria for his targeted market of readers include an average net worth of at least $5 million. Journalist Eric Wilson wrote, "The magazine looks as if it belongs in Donald Trump's bathroom."

Tiffany was seen looking at the magazine, which advertises a bicycle costing $37,000 along with 100 pages of ads hawking products from such companies as Hermès.

Binn built up his reputation by publishing glossy photo-

Tiffany's cohorts, Instagram celebrities Peter Brant, Jr (left) and his brother Harry. They are the sons of billionaire paper magnate Peter Brant, Sr. and supermodel Stephanie Seymour.

When not with Tiffany, the brothers have been known to hang out with fellow heiress Kyra Kennedy, the granddaughter of Robert F. Kennedy and his wife, Ethel.

When a drunken Peter was arrested in New York trying to board a flight to West Palm Beach, his own lawyer said of the incident, "He's an idiot. Airports are really not where you want to make a big, drunken, belligerent scene these days."

graphs of the rich and famous, often concentrating on the new generation of rich millennials, which, of course, includes Tiffany's sometimes boyfriend, Warren.

In March of 2016, Binn posted a photo on Instagram featuring Ivana with her newest grandson, but the grandmother requested that it be removed.

***

Earvin (known as "EJ") Johnson III might have been an unusual choice for a date with Tiffany. His father, the former basketball champion with the Los Angeles Lakers, Magic Johnson, opened up to Anderson Cooper on CNN and said "My son's sexual orientation doesn't change my support or his for Christian religious beliefs."

Tiffany has also been spotted in Manhattan hot spots with the celebrated brothers, Harry and Peter Brandt, Jr. They were born to supermodel Stephanie Seymour and a mogul dad, Peter Brandt, Sr. the publisher, newsprint mogul, and art collector.

Vanity Fair called the Brandt brothers "the dandy teenage boulevardiers of New York society." The Brandts are "fodder" for the tabloids.

The brothers like to make an entrance. "What about arriving in a gold-plated Rolls-Royce and emerging with a baby panther wearing a diamond necklace? Or is that too ostentatious?" Harry asked.

Both Harry and Peter have also expressed their admiration for Suri Cruise (daughter of Tom Cruise and Katie Holmes). They "admire her hair, sassy frog slippers, and the wearing of Jammies in a restaurant, as well as her ladybug boots."

When Tiffany dated the brothers, she had to do so with style, knowing that they would turn up attired in finery "to make Little Lord Fauntleroy blush.

Peter's favorite color, like Oscar Wilde's, is mauve. One journalist said

From all reports, Donald's children are said to get along with the spouses their siblings married, as reflected by this harmonious gathering.

Standing left to right at a political campaign for their father (or father-in-law) are: Jared Kushner, Eric Trump, Ivanka Trump, Tiffany Trump, and Eric's wife, Lara Yunaska.

he showed up at an art gallery opening "looking like Sal Mineo playing the Great Gatsby."

Harry told Tiffany he struggles with insomnia. "Sometimes at 3AM, I read books on haute couture while texting back and forth with Courtney Love. She's always awake at that hour."

Perhaps as an attempt to fortify her for her future as a (very wealthy) public figure, Peter gave Tiffany a copy of his favorite book, *The Theory of the Leisure Class* (1899), by Thorstein Veblen.

"My greatest desire in life is to speak like Oscar Wilde," Harry told her.

Peter, or so it was alleged, "came out" to Tiffany, saying, "I might be gay. I'm both, kind of...a little bit. I do both. I like beautiful girls. Beautiful guys. If a guy spends $300 on you for dinner, afterward, you have to do whatever he wants. It used to be $500 until the recession."

Peter recalled some of his mother's previous boyfriends, such as Warren Beatty and Charlie Sheen. "She also had this thing with Axl Rose of Guns N' Roses."

Tiffany told her girlfriends, "Going out with Harry and Peter is just insane, totally crazy, but a wild ride, an adventure. The boys call it 'pursuing the pleasures of the one percent.'"

It was a family affair as the Trumps, looking fashionable, attended a gala, the Fashion Group International's "Night of Stars" at the chic Cipriani Restaurant in New York on October 27, 2005.

Pictured left to right are Vanessa Haydon (Donald Jr.'s wife), Don Jr. himself, "The Donald," his wife Melania, and daughter Ivanka.

Chapter Twelve

MELANIA
How to Marry a "Bloviating Billionaire"
and Emerge as a Potential First Lady

THE DONALD AND THE PRINCESS
Donald & Diana: The Fantasy Romance
That Never Happened

BARRON TRUMP
Cinderella's Billionaire Baby:
At the Age of Three, He Learns to Shout, "You're Fired!"

Long before he met her, Donald hoped to cash in on the publicity whirling around the royal heads of Princess Di and Charles.

When he was selling apartments at Trump Tower, Donald was allegedly the source of a rumor that Prince Charles and his Princess had purchased one of the high-end apartments, a 24-room, $5 million condo.

"They don't need bank financing," he told his associates.

In London, Buckingham Palace was asked to comment on the possible purchase, but they refused.

When cornered by reporters to confirm the rumor, Donald told them, "Only the best people in the world are buying my apartments. Charles and Princess Di are among the best people in the world. But that's all I'm saying for now."

Later, Donald would be introduced to Princess Di on at least five formal occasions in London, but it was his estranged wife, Ivana, who first got to shake her royal palm.

In July of 1990, Ivana boarded the Concorde and flew to London. Within the previous two months, she'd made three trips to Europe, treating it al-

A real estate coup that never was:

The Prince and Princess of Wales, "in residence"—that is, if anyone believed Donald's hype during sales of condos in the Trump Tower.

Donald tried to convince buyers that Charles and Diana would be part-time residents.

most like flying from New York to Palm Beach. British tabloid readers were well aware of her marital woes with Donald.

She lodged with her friend, Eva O'Neill, on Eaton Square. Who was she?

Gossip columnist Nigel Dempster, writing for the *Daily Mail*, called her "a blonde woman of an uncertain age who lives in the right part of town but is not promi-

In distinct contrast to how Diana snubbed Donald's (romantic) overtures, she related well to Hillary. Their meeting in the Map Room of the White House in 1997 is depicted in this U.S. government photo.

nent in any way. Her friends have names like Von Panz and Hohenlohe."

Wearing Parisian haute couture and plumed hats, they were seen having tea at The Ritz, dinner at The Savoy, at the tennis matches at Wimbledon, and at the horse races at Ascot attended by the Queen.

At a fashionable luncheon attended by Diana, Ivana managed to pass, along with the other guests, in front of a formal receiving line to shake hands with the tastefully dressed and charming princess herself.

Di smiled demurely at the rather overdressed and overly made up wife of Donald Trump. When she passed on down the line, Diana was caught casting a disdainful look at Ivana.

By July 8, she was on her way back to New York to meet with attorneys to give depositions in her lawsuit against Donald, seeking half of his estate for all the work she'd done for his companies, both in Atlantic City and in Manhattan.

At a time when Diana's unhappy marriage to Charles was being widely reported, although she had not filed for divorce yet, Donald, along with millions of others, learned of her marital woes. It seemed that he wanted to be among the first in her lineup of new suitors.

He began to send her bouquets of flowers and love notes. It was reported that he sent her a rare piece of jewelry that had once belonged to Marie Antoinette, although that does not appear to be the case.

Besieged by his cascade of letters, flowers, and (unwanted) attention, Diana placed a call to her friend, Selina Scott, one of Britain's most recognized TV journalists. Scott had been a key player in a documentary about Donald for the BBC. It was so unflattering that he attacked her for years after its release. During her time in America, Scott had found that, "I was especially put off by Trump's behavior toward women."

"ultimate trophy wife"

According to Selina Scott, Donald regarded the divorced Princess Diana as "the ultimate trophy wife. Of all the women in the world, she is the most desired and sought after now that Charles is out of the picture. Donald and Diana...I like the sound of that."

"What should I do with all the flowers and solicitations?" Diana asked.

"My suggestion," Scott said, "is just bin the lot" [i.e., "toss them in the dustbin."]

Apparently, the Princess told Scott just how repulsive she found Donald to be, and that there would be no romance.

Donald did not give up so easily.

Selina Scott on the BBC describing her feud with Donald Trump. She was more impressed by his Scottish mother.

He told his friends that the young Princes, William and Harry, "needed a strong macho image to be their father. I would take care of the boys while Charles was off pursuing the ugliest woman in Britain …what's her face?"

"And if Diana agreed to marry me, I would not insist on a prenup."

He had read that Diana once said, "When I was born, I was unwanted. When I married Charles, I was unwanted. When I joined the royal family, I was unwanted. I want to be wanted."

"When I heard that," Donald said, "I wrote her a very short note: 'I want you.'"

He became very miffed when Diana rejected his advances and turned to a different lover, Dodi Al Fayed.

In the late 1990s, shortly before Di's death, Alex Yemendijian, the CEO of MGM, reported that once in the Trump Tower, Donald was enraged that the Princess had been the focus of frontpage headlines and that he had been assigned "to the also-ran page three."

"Donald, surely you know that a pretty girl always wins out," the chairman said.

"This is crazy. It's not fair somehow. She's no longer in line for the throne, and is actually shacked up with this Arab. He's only an ugly Arab! Had she played her cards right, she could have had me! Women…I'll never understand them."

Weeks later, he said, "I don't think I'll ever get over the news." He was referring to August 31, 1997. "I couldn't believe she was gone. The news hit me like a shock wave."

He avidly followed world reaction in the wake of Diana's death, and was particularly interested in how Charles and the Queen were handling it. He immediately wrote sympathy notes to both William and Harry.

He learned that after hearing of Diana's car crash, the first person Charles called was not his mother, nor either of his sons, but his mistress, Camilla Parker-Bowles.

Around the same time, after her friends heard of Diana's death, some of them called Camilla to congratulate her. "My dear!" one of the ladies said. "You are going to wear the crown of the Queen of England!"

"It's ghastly," Donald told his friends, "how the royal family treated Diana. She should have been mine. I would have taken care of her. In fact, if she had married me, she'd still be alive and living in regal splendor on the top of Trump Tower."

Just eight weeks after Diana's violent death, Donald admitted on national TV that one of his biggest regrets was that he never got to date Diana. His in-

Reportedly, Donald envisioned the marketing lure of Princess Diana. "She could make millions in endorsements," he claimed. "Also, I'd invite her to the inauguration of all my properties around the world. I think we could become the power couple of the 21st Century."

terviewer, Stone Phillips, asked him, "Do you think she would have agreed to go out with you?"

"I think so," Donald said. "Yeah, I think she would. I would have had a shot. I don't recall ever being turned down by a woman."

Donald was very sympathetic to Mohamed Al Fayed, Dodi's father, who was chairman of Harrods in London. "Mohamed has gone through a rough time over the last several years. It was his son Dodi who was dating Princess Di. To many of us, it looked like they would be getting married at some point in the not too distant future, until their lives ended in that tragic car crash in Paris. Mohamed is an extremely loyal father who has fought so hard for his son and the memory of him. I wish people understood him better. He is truly a good man."

"What a couple Di and I would have made," he said. "Just imagine if I decided to run for President of the United States? With her charm and grace, she would have propelled me into the White House. There's no way we could lose."

"Di would be the greatest First Lady America has ever seen," he said. "Forget Jacqueline Kennedy and her so-called style. Di would have made Jackie look like a salesclerk in a department store."

"President Donald Trump and First Lady Diana Windsor Trump would have entered the history books, you know, along with such historical figures as Cleopatra and Marc Antony, Napoléon and Josephine, Franklin and Eleanor."

***

Since his romance with the Windsor lineage was not to be, Donald soon recovered from the shock of Di's death and turned elsewhere. "I was looking for love, and I soon found it."

When he set out on his search, he had two requirements: His new love had to be as lovely as Princess Di, or almost so, and she had to be regal enough to be a suitable First Lady if, in the future, he decided to (and was able to) move from the Trump Tower to 1600 Pennsylvania Avenue.

Fast forward from 1997 to 2004:

MELANIA'S BEAUTY:
Apprentice Contestants Invade Trump Tower.
When They Meet Her, They're Awed

Once, on *The Apprentice*, Donald extended an invitation to the winning team to dine with him and his girlfriend, model Melania Knauss, at their lavish penthouse apartment atop Trump Tower. He called it "a filet mignon dinner at twilight."

Arriving promptly at 7PM, the contestants were awed by the beauty of their hostess and the stunning décor of Donald's private quarters, even though it has been parodied on *Saturday Night Live* as "having the same interior decorator as Saddam Hussein."

In the soft lighting, Melania appeared as an incandescent beauty, with lustrous skin a dusty bronze. Photographers spoke of her "aqua eyes" that sometimes appeared a bit squinchy but in person were much wider. When she entered a room, it was like Princess Diana herself had entered. Melania was lithe and limber, with the waist of a high-fashion model, moving her 5'11" frame across the lushly carpeted room like a model on a Versace runway.

Donald delayed his entrance for thirty minutes, but Melania shook each of the contestant's hands before showing them around. For the occasion, she wore a pink cap-sleeved Antonio Berardi sheath dress with matching Louboutin high heels.

The focal point of the penthouse, and its dramatic highlight, was a Hall of Mirrors, evocative of the one at the Palace of Versailles, through which Louis XV paraded with *la comtesse du Barry*. The wide-eyed contestants took in the white marble fountain and the hand-painted ceilings with fat cherubs.

Her voice was soft and seductive, and fluent in English, Slovenian, French, German, or Serbian.

After a tour of the gold leaf décor, Melania directed the contestants toward the panoramic view of the city and Central Park at night.

The butler arrived with champagne. One of the contestants held up her glass to praise Melania. "You're very lucky."

Raising her own glass, Melania shot back, "And he's not lucky?"

At this point attention focused on Donald, descending the stairs in a suit, red tie, and shoes far more expensive than the monthly wage of some of the contestants. He walked

Falling in love with Ljubljana

Ad slogan from the Slovenian Tourist Office. Locals define Melania as the greatest incentive to tourism her country has ever seen.

over to Melania, giving her a gentle kiss on her succulent lips. "Welcome to my humble abode," he told his guests. "The beef you're about to eat tonight is the most expensive cuts in the world."

The contestants, like any readers of the New York tabloids, knew a lot about Donald Trump and his two previous wives, Ivana and Marla. But who was this "trophy girlfriend" who was not some vapid model but an intelligent, sophisticated woman of immense charm? As one contestant said of the evening, "Melania is as regal a princess as Grace Kelly or Princess Di ever was."

At the time, little was known of her background, and most of the American public outside of New York had never heard of her.

THE MODEL AND THE MOGUL
Melania and Donald

AVENUE

MARCH 2010

MELANIA HITS THE AIR ON QVC

AN INTERVIEW WITH U.N. SPECIAL DELEGATE LAURA ROSS

Melania Trump, jewelry designer

Born on April 26, 1970, in the northern tier of what was then known as Yugoslavia, within a region now known as the independent nation of Slovenia, Melanjia Knavs would eventually change her name to the more Germanized Melania Knauss.

In Manhattan and in Palm Beach, although she would preside over two of the grandest residences in the U.S, she grew up modestly.

She lived in one of the anonymous concrete apartment complexes built during Josip Tito's socialist administration of what was then known as Yugoslavia. At the time, over-the-top capitalism, and full-blown Trumpism, did not exist for her.

She came of age in Slovenia's Sevnica district in the Lower Sava Val-

In the spring of 2010, Melania posed for this sexy photograph for the cover of *Avenue* magazine, revealing an ample bosom and "Betty Grable" legs, which in World War II were voted "the world's loveliest gams."

Obviously, at this point in her career, Melania never knew that in a few short years she would be considered a possible candidate for First Lady.

ley. Her father, Viktor Knavs, owned a car dealership, and her mother, Amalija, was a seamstress who sometimes designed clothing. Melania also had an older sister, Ines.

Melania had brains as well as beauty, and she studied design and architecture at the University of Ljubljana in Slovenia.

It seemed inevitable that she would attract the attention of a photographer. Now in his early 80s, he was Stane Jerko, who discovered her and asked her to pose for him. "She was striking even with baby-fat cheeks and a Madonna-style pony tail. It could be said that I discovered her. My pictures set her down the road to fame and fortune."

Jerko's pictures were seen by a talent scout for a modeling agency in Milan. Within months, Melania had launched her career as a mannequin, appearing on high-fashion runways not only in Milan but in Paris.

"It seemed that I came across a sleeping chrysalis that transformed herself into a glamorous butterfly," Jerko said.

She dreamed of coming to New York to advance her career, and migrated there in 1996. "I was no illegal immigrant that Donald would deport. I did it the long and hard way, but the legal way."

She was in America on a visa. When it was close to expiring, she returned to Europe but re-entered again. This went on until she became a permanent resident of the United States in

Melania represents "photogenic razzmatazz," as one photographer phrased it, a glamorous figure well suited for the promotion of her beauty products.

Among her other achievements, she knew how to turn crushed fish eggs into an expensive beauty aide.

As this magazine cover demonstrates, Donald knew how to turn a hot fashion model into a symbol of domestic decorum.

In this article, she extols his virtues as a husband and as a father. She went on to say, "He would make one of America's greatest Presidents."

2001 and was granted a green card, becoming a full-fledged U.S. citizen in 2006.

"As a girl growing up in Slovenia, I was told that America was a place where dreams come true. But never in my pink-clouded fantasies did I think I would climb so far as to become a possible First Lady of my newly adopted country. I'm not there yet, of course, but one can dream. If I make it, I will use Nancy Reagan and Jacqueline Kennedy as my role models, although I will pioneer my own wardrobe."

Photographers in New York were immediately attracted to Melania's exotic beauty, and soon she was posing for Helmut Newton, Mario Testino, Patrick Demarchelier, Arthur Elgort, Ellen Von Unwerth, and Antoine Verglas.

She was the cover girl supreme, gracing the covers of such magazines as *Vogue, Harper's Bazaar, Style, Ocean Drive, Avenue, New York* magazine, *Self, Glamor*, and inevitably, *Vanity Fair.*

Her most revealing photo appeared in 2000 for the annual edition of *Sports Illustrated*'s swimwear edition in a bikini.

She was represented by several modeling agencies, including Donald Trump Model management, even though she had yet to meet the mogul.

She was also featured in a number of TV commercials, including one for Aflac, an insurance company that's associated with America's top duck icon. She would later co-host *The View* with Barbara Walters. "Behind all that beauty was one smart cookie," Walters said. "She is no mannequin, and has a passion for the arts, architecture, design, and fashion."

A person can thrive and grow in the cultural diversity of New York," Melania said. "It is, in fact, the cultural capital of the world."

One night during Fashion Week in 1998, Paolo Zampoli threw a chic party for the ID Modeling Agency. Separate and unconnected at the time, his guest list included the names of both Donald

Since her involvement with Donald, Melania has become a legend in Slavic Europe, an adventurous personification of the postmodern American Dream.

Here, striding into a bold New World, she's depicted on the front cover of the Bulgarian edition of *Harper's Bazaar.*

Trump and Melania Knauss.

Donald arrived with an "arm candy model," beautiful but vapid, and was soon surrounded by a bevy of beauties. He seemed disenchanted with his date for the evening. With his eagle eye for female pulchritude, he focused on this "stunning looker."

At the time, he had split from his second wife, Marla Maples, and was looking for another conquest.

When Donald's date went to the ladies' room, he turned to Zampoli: "That girl over there is incredible. I want you to introduce us." He was surprised to find that she had a link to his own modeling agency. Once introduced, he chatted briefly with her and asked for her phone number.

"Since he was with a date, I refused to give him my number," Melania said. "I won't give you my number, but you can give me yours," she told him. "I'll call you."

"Frankly, I wanted to see what kind of number he would give me," she said. "Perhaps it would ring through to a secretary or some aide. I was wrong. He gave me several private numbers, not only his private office number, but his penthouse number, even an unlisted number in Palm Beach."

"I had this shoot in California when I phoned him," Melania said. "He was in New York. I was struck by his energy when we spoke. He has this amazing vitality."

Back in New York, on their first date, Donald picked her up in a black stretch limousine, and, along with Zampoli and the magician, David Copperfield, he instructed his driver to take them to the deluxe Cipriani Restaurant.

When she left the table to powder her nose, Zampoli told Donald, "When you get to know Melania, you will love her. It doesn't take long for people to fall in love with her, especially men, but she's very hard to get. She's not on the party circuit."

On the following night, he took her to dinner at Mooma, which in the late 1990s was the *ne plus ultra* of celebrity-studded hot spots. "It was a great place," she said. "It was a great date. A night to remember."

Within weeks, Donald and Melania became a power couple around Manhattan, and were seen at all the lavish galas and chic restaurants, including Le Cirque. He took her there only for dinner, because his previous wife, Ivana, often lunched there with her gossipy women friends.

Very quietly and discreetly, Melania moved into his lavish quarters at the Trump Tower, sharing all those rooms with her new boyfriend. In spite of the difference in their ages (he was born in 1946, she in 1970), they clicked as a couple.

Her life with limos, helicopters, deluxe restaurants, diamonds, penthouses, lavish estates, and a fabulous "to-die-for" wardrobe had begun.

It wasn't long before the tabloids started writing about "The Mogul and the Model." The *New York Daily News* reported that "Donald Trump's latest model friend has been selected to advertise BMW cars. Did she get the job through a powerful connection?"

The couple made an appearance at the gala honoring the restoration of the Grand Central Terminal.

To the delight of photographers, Donald and Melania dazzled when they came into the lavish Costume Ball at the Metropolitan Museum of Art, where much of *tout* New York feasted their eyes on her for the first time.

"Nobody seemed to take notice of me," Donald said. "All eyes were on Melania. Perhaps that was because I didn't wear a costume myself. Hey, wasn't that Anna Wintour approaching us?"

During her courtship with Donald, Melania could sometimes create a tabloid frenzy. Such was the case when she showed up, plunging *décolletage* and all, at the funeral of Fred Trump, who died in 1999 at age 93. The funeral was at the Marble Collegiate Church in Manhattan. In spite of all the distinguished guests from both the business and political worlds, the paparazzi focused on

One thing is certain: She ain't Bess Truman, and she ain't Mamie Eisenhower...But is she anything akin to Jackie Kennedy?

Ivana probably had a lot to say when *Bella* magazine defined Melania as "The First Lady of NYC," with low-cut costumes inspired by summer in the *über*-rich Hamptons.

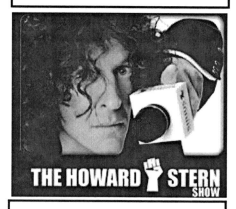

The ultimate vulgarian shock jock, Howard Stern wants to know, "What underwear are you guys wearing?"

sexy Melania, although she faced criticism for dressing so provocatively at a funeral.

In Europe, Melania had frequented some of the most glamorous spots, including St. Tropez on the French Riviera, or a palace on Lake Como. But Donald claimed that she found Mar-a-Lago the most beautiful place on earth.

At the former estate of Marjorie Merriweather Post, Donald and Melania "moved through the rooms of the estate with her acting like a princess and him some turn-of-the 19th-century grandee," a reporter wrote. "They were warm and attentive, and she looked like she stepped off the cover of *Vogue.*"

The relationship between Donald and Melania came to the attention of millions of Americans during a 1999 radio interview on *The Howard Stern Show.*

At one point, the shock jock asked Melania what she was wearing. "Not much!" she shot back. It was predictable that Stern would turn to the topic of sex. Donald admitted that he and Melania had watched the notorious sex tape of Paris Hilton. "I saw it in spite of the fact that I have known Paris since she was twelve years old, and I've been close friends of her family for years."

He told Stern that "Melania looks best—really hot—when she wears only a very small thong."

She confided, "We have sex at least once a day, maybe more. It's incredible sex. Donald is the greatest lover."

"Melania is great," Donald told Stern. "I've never heard her fart or make doodie." He also told Stern that he could trust her to take birth control every day. "She has great boobs, which is no trivia matter to me."

Stern wanted to know what Donald would do if she got into a horrible car accident, perhaps lost the use of an arm, or was disfigured in some way.

"How would the breasts look," Donald asked.

"The breasts would be okay," Stern

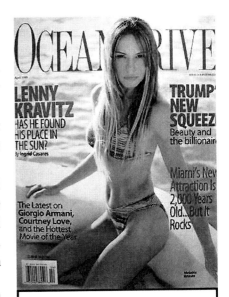

If Donald is elected President, will the Secret Service allow photo-ops of a scantily clad Melania beside the pool at the White House?

And if they do, what will she wear?

answered.

"Then yeah, of course," Donald said. "Our relationship would continue if the breasts were okay."

A friend who did not want to be named claimed that "Melania is perfect for The Donald—as if a divine plastic surgeon had sculpted her out of his rib."

"I WASN'T NAKED. I WORE A DIAMOND CHOKER"

—Donald's nude girlfriend, in reference to a photo-shoot aboard his private plane

Melania's sexy celebrity appeal received its greatest exposure through her appearance on the January 2000 cover of the British *GQ* magazine. The picture of her posing nude would later become a campaign issue in 2016, erupting into a bitter fight between Ted Cruz and Donald.

The photographer was Antoine Verglas. He had shot such models as Cindy Crawford and Claudia Schiffer. His assignment for *GQ* had been defined as a sexy photo essay about jet-

Melania and the "Naked Supermodel Special"

(Sex at 30,000 Feet)

Widely berated, and with a lot of exposed flesh, this feature in GQ from 2000 was controversial even before Donald became a presidential candidate. Ted Cruz, in advance of the Utah primaries in March of 2016, aimed dire warnings at conservative Mormon voters, taking out ads screaming "Meet Melania Trump, your next First Lady."

In response, Donald, through Twitter, released unflattering photos of Cruz's wife, Heidi "looking like a gargoyle," according to a writer from *Maxim*.

His message to Cruz? "My wife is hotter than yours."

setters, with a focus on "the sexiest model around," who was also the girlfriend of a mogul who traveled in his own private jet.

Wearing a sparkly diamond necklace—and "not a stitch of clothing"—Melania had never looked more seductive, with her icy, blue-green eyes, and her plump, pouty lips, along with her shapely butt. However, she refused to pose for certain more revealing photos that Verglas wanted.

He was also a makeup artist and hair stylist, and he spent part of that day inside Donald's custom-built jet while it was stationary and sheltered within a hangar at New York's La-Guardia airport.

"It was for the cover of a men's magazine, so I was going for the sexy image," he said. "Melania is easy to shoot because her body, unlike so many models I've photographed before, has no flaws."

On that same day, he photographed her on a fur blanket handcuffed to a leather briefcase.

Another shot depicted her standing on the wing of the plane. Pointing a pistol, evoking a James Bond girl, she wore a red bra and thong, very dark sunglasses, knee-high leather boots.

The magazine's headline was "SEX AT 30,000 FEET. MELANIA KNAUSS EARNS HER AIR MILES."

That same year, Verglas also photographed Carla Bruni, who had previously dated Donald be-

Rumors abound that Melania, like Liza Doolittle in *My Fair Lady*, is being coached for situations she's likely to face during the campaign and later, perhaps, in the White House.

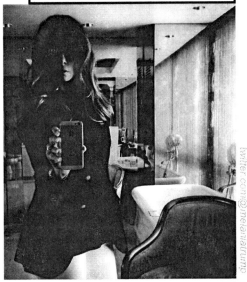

Here, as a fashion-savvy techie, Melania clicks and distributes, via Twitter, a selfie showing her outfit of the day.

Distributed on May 29, 2015, it advised, with a lack of discretion the Secret Service later curtailed, "Bye. I'm off to my summer residence."

fore marrying the French president Nicholas Sarkozy. "They both were gorgeous models, really gorgeous, with perfect figures," Verglas said. "But they were very different personalities. Before Donald, who was lusting for Princess Di at the time, Bruni had dated a lot of famous men like Mick Jagger and Eric Clapton. In contrast, Melania lived in a modest apartment and had no history of boyfriends—and that was most unusual for a model."

Verglas later photographed Melania at Palm Beach. "The girl from Slovenia was now mistress of Mar-a-Lago! It was WOW! Like Cinderella!"

"Melania was America's Carla Bruni," said image consultant Christina Logothetis.

In the years to come, Melania would develop thousands of followers on Twitter, posting selfies of her beauty rituals, private jet rides, and her bikini-clad body. However, by July of 2015, as Donald was in the first days of his campaign, the window into her private life was shut down, the curtains drawn.

"LOVE IS BETTER THE THIRD TIME AROUND"
—Donald Trump

The relationship of Donald and Melania received a lot of publicity after the launch in 2006 of *The Apprentice* when he spoke of their long courtship. "We literally have never had an argument. Forget about the word 'fight.' We are very compatible. We get along."

After surviving painful and expensive divorces from his first two wives, Donald drifted for years before he contemplated marriage again. "I didn't want to get married until I was older and wiser," he said.

"Before I married Melania, it was a big decision for me. We had a comfort zone with each other. I believe strongly in the concept of 'the woman behind the man,' or vice versa. I was with Melania for five years of my life, during which I enjoyed great success. For example, *The Apprentice* became number one on TV, and my show got nominated for five Emmys. So if figured I'd better marry the woman who stood behind me (and in front of me) during this amazing and crazy period—and fast!"

In 2000, when Donald was contemplating a run for President of the United States on the Reform Ticket, a publicist came up with "a crazy idea" for a shot.

"I was out of my mind," Donald said, "but I agreed to it."

Provocatively draped in an American flag, and lounging across his desk,

Melania was photographed gazing lovingly at her boyfriend.

When Donald saw the final print, "No way in hell!" he said. "The damn picture is over the top, even for me."

"I chose to be married because I didn't want to be single any longer," he said. "I have had a bad track record of being married, it is true, but I would rather live a married life than be single. That is because I have met the right woman. I have learned something from my previous mistakes. I am determined to do much better in my eventual marriage to Melania."

He didn't need a special occasion, such as a wedding, to present jewelry to his girlfriend. He'd been known to pop into Asprey's flagship store, conveniently positioned within Trump Tower, to purchase a "trinket" for her.

"Asprey's has been around since the 18th Century, and its jewelry makes the most beautiful women even more beautiful," he said. "But if you're in the market for diamonds, go to Harry Winston or Graff. They sell the best diamonds in the world."

Weeks before his marriage, Melania was asked to sign a prenup agreement. He'd gone through that before with both Ivanka and Marla, and ultimately, neither of them had wanted to honor their original contract with him.

He told Melania, "I love you so much, and we're going to have the greatest marriage ever. It's going to be unbelievable. Listen, just in case it doesn't work out, sign on the dotted line."

In marked contrast to both Marla and Ivana, she willingly signed her name without any fuss. He later said "It was not the most romantic thing to do, but I really, really needed her to do that."

Melania's $200,000 wedding dress was designed by the controversial John Galliano of the House of Dior. An embroidered couture creation, it took 1,000 hours of hard labor to craft.

When the cover of *Vogue*, featuring Donald's beautiful bride #3, was released, viewers had trouble seeing or recognizing Melania through the faux-virginal *froufrou*, the frills, the lettering of the cover design, the accessories, and the *whoopla*.

After many years of co-habitation, Donald Trump married Melania Knauss, his third wife. The date on the social calendar for many luminaries was January 22, 2005 in Palm Beach at the Episcopal Church of Bethesda-by-the-Sea.

Notables attending the wedding included Katie Couric, Matt Lauer, Rudy Giuliani, Heidi Klum, Star Jones, P. Diddy, Shaquille O'Neal, Barbara Walters, Conrad Black, Regis Philbin, Simon Cowell, Oprah Winfrey, and Kelly Ripa.

The veiled bride would appear as the focal point of a stunning cover of Vogue.

For her hair, Melania flew in a top stylist. Donald quipped, "I did my own hair…unfortunately for the world."

After the wedding, a lavish reception was staged at Mar-a-Lago. To entertain, Billy Joel serenaded the crowd with "Just the Way You Are," and

In the aftermath of the Trump-Knauss wedding, his enemies released this photograph of Donald at his wedding with Melania. A friendly and charming Bill and Hillary Clinton were sandwiched between them.

Widely distributed by both campaigns, it emerged as controversial and, for Donald, embarrassing. Its implications and bragging rights, and (perhaps false) professions of respect and friendship would become a furiously contested campaign issue.

Hillary later said, "I thought attending the wedding would be fun—and it was!"

Responding to his critics, Donald said, "I am a businessman. It was important to me to be friendly with people in both political camps."

supplied new lyrics about Donald to the tune of "The Lady Is a Tramp." The wedding cake was a fifty-pounder, a spectacular orange Grand Marnier chocolate truffle cake with a Grand Marnier butter-cream filling. It was covered with 3,000 dewy fresh red roses.

Tina Brown, the former editor of *Vanity Fair*, wrote in a column for *The New York Post*: "Bill and Hillary Clinton were there to do what they always like to do best for R&R: Raise money."

In 2015, early in his campaign for president, Donald was criticized for having invited the Clintons. "She had no choice but attend when I asked her to," he said. "After all, I had contributed generously to her foundation."

To explain what she was doing there, she said, "I happened to be in Florida and I thought it would be fun to go to his wedding because it was certain to be entertaining."

Brad Johns, a celebrity colorist who added "caramel highlights" to Melania's hair, said, "She's incapable of being mean. She's not gossipy at all, not bitchy and just really nice, though I know that's not exciting to hear."

Tina Brown wrote of Melania: "Underneath all the fabulousness and gloss, Melania Knauss's staying power in Donald's life is based on a shrewd understanding of her quasi-commercial role. One feels she will not make Ivana's mistake of competing with the Trump brand. But she also knows, as second wife Marla Maples did not, the difference between being mere arm candy and high-definition product enhancement. As one of her friends puts it, 'For Melania, it's never ask what Donald can do for you, it's ask what you can do for The Donald.'"

THE MINI-DONALD
Barron Trump, the 21st Century's
Little Lord Fauntleroy

"Those jerks running against my dad are creeps—Cruz is a liar and Hillary is a crook."
—*Barron Trump*

Before giving birth to her first child, Melania posed again for *Vogue*. She was seven months pregnant, but wore a golden bikini.

In March of 2006, she gave birth to a son. Donald suggested the aristocratic first name of "Barron," with Melania supplying the middle name of William.

In the beginning, Barron occupied a crib in his parents' room. "Donald did not change the diapers," his mother said. "He did not view that as a proper role of a man, and I agree."

As he grew older, Barron was given practically a floor to himself on top of the Trump Tower, decorating it according to his wishes. He liked pictures of helicopters and airplanes on his walls.

In a corner of one room was placed a miniature red Mercedes-Benz with "BARRON" on the license plate. "That's a preview of the gift from my father when I get my driving license," said the six-year-old.

Unlike many rich kids, Barron wasn't reared by nannies, Melania preferring a much more hands-on approach. In an interview with *People* magazine in October of 2015, she said, "Donald and I don't like a lot of help raising our boy. We keep it down to a minimum. If you have too much help, you don't get to know your kid."

She claimed that when Donald was off on the campaign trail, she devoted nearly all of her time to Barron. "He is the light of my life. He's also an athlete, liking tennis and baseball. As he grew older, Donald took him with him to the golf course. But we don't have time for that anymore."

The longtime Trump butler, Anthony Senecal, claims, "Young Barron is more like his father than any of his other offspring. He learned to speak at an early age and issued orders when he was three years old to the staff."

Senecal told *Inside Edition* that, "I was serving the tot breakfast. He was sitting in his high chair. He looked at me and ordered, 'Tony! Sit down! We need to talk.'"

According to Melania, "Donald and Barron have a mutual admiration society. Before the campaign, Barron traveled often with us to Mar-a-Lago. Many people think he will grow up to fulfill Donald's shoes. I already call him 'Mini-Donald.'"

He likes suits and ties when he goes out, just like Donald. Of course, we always have to order an array of new suits because he's a growing boy. He is meticulous about his dress."

As Barron entered the pre-teen stage, he became enamored of his mother's skin care products. Every night he generously dips into containers of her caviar skin cream (priced at $150 an ounce). He likes to have baths in her apartment spa, generously pouring perfume from some of the world's most expensive bottles into the bath water.

He is fluent in English and Slovenian, and he also speaks adequate French.

Melania, on *The View*, told Joy Behar: "He's very mature, and he bosses everybody around. He fires housekeepers who anger him. Sometimes, he hires them back…sometimes. They have to learn who's boss. He's just adorable."

People magazine published a feature on Barron, calling him the "Billion Dollar Baby. He has his mom's eyes, his dad's lips, his own floor in Trump Tower, and doting parents. Welcome to the world of Barron William Trump."

***

In 2015, at the beginning of the Republican presidential race, Melania Trump was kept in the background. The other leading candidates quickly established their marriage credentials, Senator Rand Paul of Kentucky citing his 25-year marriage to his wife, Kelly; Senator Ted Cruz of Texas referring to his longtime Heidi, a former employee of Goldman Sachs (he left that out). Next, Senator Marco Rubio of Florida claimed that he'd been married for seventeen years. Then, both Ben Carson and Carly Fiorina made pointed references to their long-term spouses. In contrast, one billionaire candidate said nothing of his wife. "I am Donald Trump, and I wrote *The Art of the Deal.*"

For a while, Donald configured his 33-year-old daughter, Ivanka, as an "unofficial campaign spouse." She made compelling speeches on behalf of her father, and did much to soften his image, as did Melania when she became more involved in the campaign during the months ahead.

Melania kept a low profile, although she was seen at certain events. As autumn came, she had a red or pink overcoat often draped over her shoulders.

During the early years of her dating Donald, she usually wore gowns that displayed an ample bosom. But since she was campaigning as the wife of a Republican candidate, she began to wear clothing that discreetly concealed her upper torso.

"No matter what she wears, she looks glamorous," said image consultant Christina Logothetis.

***

When Donald decided to run for President, he met with Melania and Barron for a family conference. "He talked it over with us, and Barron gave his own opinion," she said.

The boy said that Donald "will make the greatest president ever…and I know he'll win. My dad is not a loser like those jerks I see on TV. Ted Cruz looks like he could play a movie monster."

Reportedly, Barron becomes furious when he hears pundits attack his father on TV. He's also had some arguments at school when his fellow classmates mock Donald. "They probably picked up that crap from their moronic parents. My father is the greatest man in America."

In 2015, when Donald announced for the presidency, Melania said, "I encouraged him because I know what he will do and what he can do for America. He loves its people and wants to help them."

The New York Times asked Melania what kind of First Lady she'd be. "I'd be like Betty Ford and Jackie Kennedy, and support my husband."

If Melania becomes First Lady, she would be the second First Lady born outside the United States. Louisa, the wife of the 6th U.S. president *[John Quincy Adams (1825-1829)]*, was born in England.

"I give Donald my opinions," Melania said. "Sometimes he takes them in. Sometimes he does not. Do I agree with him all the time? No!"

Like Donald, Melania can also be critical of the press, although she expresses her resentment more discreetly. "Reporters talk to people who do not even know me, and then publish their opinions, which often are not true. These people have their fifteen minutes of fame talking about me. They most often distort the facts. Make up stuff really. The press can be very unfair to both Donald and me."

"Donald is not always politically correct, but he tells the truth," Melania claimed. "He is handling everything very well. Everything is not roses and flowers and perfect. He wants America to be great again, and he can make it so. He's a great leader and an amazing negotiator."

Two views of the "Mini-Donald," whose future appears fascinating.

"People had better treat my dad fairly—or else they'll have me to deal with."

Before Donald ran for President, Melania had posed for a series of very sexy photographs of herself, a kind of public flirtation unknown within the histories of any other potential First Lady. As one of Donald's campaign workers said, "You won't see that ugly witch, Heidi Cruz, posting photographs of herself, and certainly not that ugly, aging hippie, Bernie's wife, Jane, showing off all her blubber. And if Hillary ever posed for a magazine centerfold, the publisher would have to make it a three-page spread to take in her elephantine butt."

One reporter who checked out Melania's Twitter images claimed, "There is a touch of Kanye [West] and Kim [Kardashian] to her luxury-streaked romance with The Donald."

Even though she is in her forties, Melania is sometimes asked, "Will you have more children?"

"I don't like to say 'never,' but my life is very busy. We are happy and my hands are full with my two boys—my Big Boy and my Little Boy."

As for her stepchildren, she said, "They are adults. I don't see myself as their stepmother. I am their friend. I am there when they need me. Of course, most of my life revolves around Donald and my remarkable son, Barron. The boy is the center of my life. I taught him to speak Slovenian, and quite a bit of French. Donald remains a monoglot."

Like Ivana, Melania also showed that she could be a business woman on her own. She nets at least one million dollars a year hawking her beauty products or her jewelry collection, "Melania Timepieces and Jewelry."

Lower photo: Interior view of the White House.

After Trump Tower, would its decor be a letdown for the Trumps if Donald wins the presidency, and could Melania and Ivanka fix it?

At its launch in February, 2010, her jewelry sold out in 45 minutes. Donald was the first customer. For the most part, her jewelry consists of cheaper versions of expensive gems from her private collection.

"I like to help women to spend not a lot of money—to feel powerful, elegant, glamorous, to feel good about themselves," she said.

When the distribution outlet charged with her "Melania Caviar Complexe C6" did not, in her view, adequately promote her new skin care product made with caviar, she sued them for $50 million for damages.

In an interview with *Parenting* magazine, Melania said, "It's a lot of responsibility for a woman to be married to a man like my husband. I need to be quick, smart, and intelligent."

"I think the mistake some women make is when they try to change the man they love after they marry him. You cannot change a person."

Were truer words ever said?

RUPERT MURDOCH & DONALD TRUMP
LIKE-MINDED BILLIONAIRES
Marital Woes and Infidelities Among the Insanely Wealthy

The Nude Slovenian Model & "The Lady from Shanghai"
in their Respective Roles as Trophy Wives

Born in Australia in 1931, Rupert Murdoch, who owns both 21st Century Fox and the News Corporation, was destined to meet Donald Trump at some point. With a net worth of more than $5 billion, he richer than Donald, owning some 800 companies in more thatn 50 countries.

As the owner since 1976 of the tabloid, the *New York Post*, Murdoch brought his right-wing politics to Manhattan, introducing British-style tabloid screaming headlines and lots of scandal. His chief rival was the *New York Daily News*.

Later in the 2016 presidential race, the *News* would become the chief media attacker of Donald, aften portraying him as a clown. Murdoch guided the *Post* into right-wing journalism, concentrating on celebrities. Donald became a regular feature as the tabloid revealed his triumphs in business and tales of his marriage to Ivana.

The left wing often attacked the *Post*. Osborn Elliott, dean of the Columbia School of Journalism, called it "a force for evil."

Donald and Murdoch had something in common: Both of them eventually married their "trophy girlfriends," the often scantily clad Slovenia-born beauty, Melania Knauss, for Donald, and Wendi Deng of China for aging Murdoch.

When introduced, Wendi seemed to find Melania charming… and vice versa.

By 1999 the cover story of *Punch*, the satirical London-based magazine, revealed the romance to the world under the headline "MURDOCH'S MISTRESS, THE SECRET LIFE OF THE WOMAN WHO SNARED THE BIG ONE." The story by Steve Vines claimed, "The Viagra-chomping Rupert Murdoch has been dating a Cantonese cutie."

A colleague said, "The boss may be old enough to qualify for a bus pass, but they giggle like lovestruck teenagers.

One of the wealthiest men in the world, the owner of newspapers around the globe, Murdoch met Wendi Deng in China. In her high boots and faux fur, she was called one of the "Shanghai Girls." This burgeoning subset of upwardly mobile young Chinese women were labeled that in the 2010 book, *Shanghai Girls*, by Nina Hanbury-Tenison. It seemed that the goal of these beautiful young women was to succeed at all costs—and that part of

Re: Wendi Deng Murdoch's "endorsement" of Melania.

Is a recommendation from a trophy hunter as notorious as the "Shanghai Girl" Wendi Deng an asset or a curse?

Mr. and Mrs. Rupert Murdoch, the press baron and his estranged "China Doll," Wendi Deng.

the definition of "success" involved marrying a multi-millionaire business-man like Donald Trump or Murdoch.

"Wendi got Murdoch, the ulti-mate, a billionaire with a private jet," said one of her envious for-mer girlfriends. "Oh, what a gold digger. Great success story."

The couple married in a spec-tacular wedding in 1999. He had divorced his second wife just sev-enteen days before. At the time, he was 68, Wendi 30. Together they would have two daughters.

The Murdochs moved in the same circles as Donald and Mela-nia.

Wendi told the press how much she admired Melania. "She's wonderfully supportive of Donald and a lovely person."

As it turned out, Wendi wasn't that loyal to Murdoch, at least not when handsome Tony Blair, former Prime Minister of Britain, was introduced to her.

It wasn't long before she fell for the "sexually insatiable" Blair. Even his own wife, Cherie, re-ported that "sex five times a night...even more," was not un-usual for her husband. "He's al-ways *up* for it."

Wendi apparently agreed. A passionate note surfaced amid the flotsam of a shipwrecked marriage to Murdoch when he divorced her in 2013. She wrote: "Oh, shit, oh shit. Whatever why I'm so missing Tony. Because he is so so charming, and his clothes

Autocratic, egomaniacal Putin (aka"Vlad the Terrible").

Did the Russian dictator chow down on his dose of Viagra for the day?

Tony Blair, the former PM of Britain.

Privately, he was known as "the lover who couldn't get enough."

are so good. He has such good body and has really really good legs. Butt… and what else and what else and what else?"

In her note, she didn't describe that 'what else," but it was obvious to readers what she was referring to.

In 2012, Murdoch endorsed Mitt Romney, hoping he "could save us from socialism."

At first, Donald wanted Murdoch's endorsement. But in October of 2015, the media czar stirred up a controversy after he tweeted, "Ben and Candy Carson terrific. What about a real black President who can properly address the racial divide and much else?"

After that, he tweeted his apologies. "No offense meant. Personally, I find both Obama and Carson charming."

In January of 2016, with Wendi gone from his life, Murdoch announced his engagemenbt to former model Jerry Hall (ex-lover of Mick Jagger). He was just a week short before his 85th birthday, and she was still looking good at 59.

Donald reportedly said, "Rupert is an inspiration for all of us older guys. Will Melania still love me when I'm eighty-five? By then, they'll have something better on the market than Viagra."

WAS MELANIA "TRUMPED" BY THE SHANGHAI LADY?

During his 2016 race for the presidency, Donald was frequently cited in the newspapers for his "bromance" with Vladimir Putin. But his friend, Wendi Deng Murdoch, did him one better. According to rumors, she actually sleeps with the Russian dictator, who has dreams of restoring the former Soviet Empire. She had seen many pictures of the ruler shirtless, so, as Melania reportedly said, "Wendi saw at least half of what she was getting."

What does a 40-year-old woman do when her aging husband divorces her?

Wendi seemed to like seducing powerful men. Rumors circulated that she spent some nights with Eric Schmidt, CEO of Alphabet (the multinational conglomerate created in 2015 as the parent company of Google) at the Beverly Hills Hotel.

Where to go after that? A world leader, like Blair, a media mogul like Murdoch, and even a king of technology like Schmidt were a hard act to follow.

But Wendi, Dahling..Is It True that
Love, or at Least Lightning, with a Mogul Can Strike
FOUR SEPARATE TIMES?

For Wendi, it did. A recent romance with Vladimir Putin was detailed by, among others, *US magazine, Vanity Fair, the Daily Mail,* and *The Mirror.* Putin is freshly single, following a 2014 divorce from his wife of 30 years.

The size of his fortune, like so much about the strange dictator, is perhaps known only to himself. He cites his salary at $100,000 a year. A former fund manager in Russia, however, estimated his net worth at $200 billion. That would make Donald, his partner in bromance, only a poor acquaintance.

Putin is believed to be the richest person on earth, owning a vast network of assets in and (secretly) outside of Russia, nearly 60 airplanes, 700 automobiles (most of them custom made), and countless villas, palaces, and manor houses. Okay, so he's a former KGB spy accused of heinous crimes and unrelenting torture of his victims.

Perhaps one day, Putin and Wendi will be photographed riding together as the sun sets in the West, territory that the dictator…perhaps…would one day want to rule, or so it is said.

" I would be willing to bet I would have a great relationship with Putin. It's about leadership. "

Donald Trump,
interview on Fox News

Chapter Thirteen

POLITICKING & POWER PLAYS:
THIRTY YEARS OF SHIFTING ALLIANCES
Donald, from Divergent Political Allegiances,
Contemplates White House Runs
in 2000, 2004, and 2012

THE REFORM PARTY &
THE BIRTHER MOVEMENT
Warren Beatty ("The Sexiest Man Alive")
vs. "The Skyscraper King of Manhattan."
Which of Them Will Become President?

BUILDING MORE THAN SKYSCRAPERS
"Donald Trump Is the Apotheosis of Our Gilded Age"
On Facebook, Donald's Longtime Butler
Calls for Obama to Be Killed

"The Moral Lepers of the Reform Party insist I give up my live-in mistress if I want to be President."
—Donald Trump

Donald Trump once allowed his long-term butler, Anthony Senecal, to talk to the press. A colorful character, he wears horn-rimmed glasses and has a walrus mustache.

"At Mar-a-Lago, Donald is the king. When he first thought of running for President, I had the bugler play 'Hail to the Chief' when he stepped out of his limousine. If his cap is white, the boss is in a good mood. If it's red, it's best to stay away."

Senecal revealed that Donald is obsessively worried about Islamic terrorist attacks on America.

He recalled the days when Ivana was there. "She liked to swim naked in the pool. But she was horrified that any member of the staff would see her nude. She demanded that all the staff go in hiding when she stripped down for a swim."

He also said that when Donald showed visitors around Mar-a-Lago, he sometimes stretched the truth a bit. "Mr. Trump claimed that the décor in the children's suite was actually painted by a young Walt Disney. Well, we don't know for a fact that he didn't."

Senecal also said that Marjorie Merriweather Post had a well-stocked library. But when the Trumps moved in, the library didn't get much use. "Mr. Trump installed a bar instead and had a large portrait of himself painted in his tennis whites. The portrait, lit at night, dominates the room. The staff calls Mr. Trump 'The King.'"

The butler confirmed what was already known, that Donald is more a "meat-and-potatoes kind of guy than a caviar-and-truffles dandy."

Then he added a tantalizing culinary tidbit: "He likes his steaks so well done that they're like rocks on his plate."

Senecal also revealed that he

facebook

Donald with his opinionated butler, Anthony Senecal. He obviously believes in speaking his mind, calling Hillary "the lying bitch of Benghazi" and Obama "the Asshole of Allah."

TRUMP'S BUTLER IS 'KILL BAM' HATE NUT

● Urges hanging, shooting in tirades
● Lackey, 84, also rants of Hil death

wanted to retire but "Mr. Trump insisted that I stay on at Mar-a-Lago, perhaps as its historian, if nothing else."

"THIS PRICK (OBAMA) NEEDS TO BE HUNG FOR TREASON!"
Or So Says Donald's Butler

In mid-May of 2016, Donald's faithful butler, Anthony Senecal, at the age of 84, became the target of a national scandal after his rantings on *Facebook* were revealed to the world. He was denounced in blaring headlines as a "KILL BAM HATE NUT."

In a series of unhinged and racist online posts, he urged that President Obama "should be taken out by our military" or else "hung for treason." He also denounced Obama as "a pus head."

Then he praised his boss: "Now comes Donald J. Trump to put an end to corruption in government. The so-called elite, who are nothing but dog turds on your front lawn, are shaking in their boots because there is a new sheriff coming to town. I can't believe that a common murderer is even allowed to run ("Killery Hillary") or a commie like Bernie. Come on, America, put your big boy pants on—GET YOURS ASSES OUT AND VOTE!!!"

One of his posts read: "It is time for the SECOND AMERICAN REVOLUTION!!! The only way we will change this crooked government is to douche it!!! This might be the time with this Kenyan fraud in power!!! With the last breath I draw, I will help rid this America of the scum infested in its government--if this means dragging that ball-less dickhead from the White Mosque and hanging his scrawny ass from the portico--count me in!!!"

Another post followed. "If Obama gets hung, then "Sasquatch" (Michelle) does, too. Amen. Two of the most DISGUSTING individuals on the face of God's Green Earth!!! Puke!!!"

He also referred to the former Secretary of State as "the Lying Bitch of Benghazi!" He suggested "she should be in prison right now awaiting the gallows."

Under a photo of Obama, Senecal wrote: "IF ALLAH HAS AN ASSHOLE, IT WOULD LOOK LIKE THIS!!!"

He followed that with another post: "Obama is an unfeeling sack of camel feces. I don't believe he's an American citizen. I think he's a fraudulent piece of crap that was brought in by the Democrats."

"Once the President leaves office, only a FEW Negroes and Josh Earnest will even remember him."

He also had scorn for former Speaker John Boehner and Senate Majority Leader Mitch McConnell. "Both are FUCKING CROOKS and should be run out of D.C. on a rail and covered in hot tar."

1987: DONALD'S FIRST CAMPAIGN SPEECH
"The World Is Laughing at Us"

The date was October 22, 1987, when Donald Trump, future presidential nominee of the Republican Party, made his first political speech.

As twilight fell over southern New Hampshire, his shiny black French-made helicopter landed on a grassy airfield.

He emerged from the craft, a 41-year-old mogul wearing his classic scarlet tie and a well-tailored navy blue suit. He got into a waiting stretch limousine for the seven-mile ride up U.S. 1 to Portsmouth.

There, just before entering a restaurant named Yoken's, where political cronies in Portsmouth had gathered for years, he waved at the crowd, members of which brandished "TRUMP IN '88" signs.

Mike Dunbar, a woodworker (specializing in the crafting of Windsor chairs), novelist, and local Republican party activist, was on hand to greet him. Previously, he had written to Trump, urging him to take on George H.W. Bush and Mike Dukakis in the 1988 presidential election.

At the podium, Donald addressed the crowd and launched into a speech in which he claimed that the United States was on a disaster course. "Other countries such as Japan, Iran, and Saudi Arabia are kicking us around. They're laughing at us. It makes me sick." Unless trade and other policies changed, he predicted a catastrophe for America.

By 2016, this point of view had catapaulted him into a position as the Republican Party's frontrunner.

How it all began: Trump holds a press conference following his speech at a Rotary Club luncheon in Portsmouth on October 22, 1987.

Republican activist, novelist, and furniture craftsman Mike Dunbar listens at left, as Donald states,   "I will not be your candidate in the 1988 race."

Dunbar had hoped that the restaurant would be the venue for Donald's announcement that he was seeking the presidency, but that was not to be. Loudly, the crowd expressed their disappointment when he told them that he would not be a candidate during the Presidential Race of 1988.

With adaptations, the speech that Donald delivered that day would be repeated again and again, especially during Barack Obama's occupancy of the White House. But when he first declared that America was being shoved around by other governments, Ronald Reagan was President.

Later, some staid New Englanders told reporters that they found the New York real estate mogul "brash and egotistical."

Before he headed back in his limo, he told a disappointed Dunbar that he didn't think he could "put up with all the false smiles and red tape that a presidential candidate would have to face."

That relatively unknown speech in New Hampshire in 1987 represented a milestone in Donald's long-running attack on "gridlock and incompetence in government," in which he blamed both the Republicans and the Democrats.

***

Seven months later, in April of 1988, Donald appeared on *The Oprah Winfrey Show*, complaining about America being "a debtor nation."

Oprah asked him if he planned to run for President that year. "Probably not," he told the audience. "But I do get tired of seeing the country ripped off. Right now I don't have the inclination to seek political office."

He later told reporters that if he ever did run for President, Oprah would be the ideal running mate as his Veep. "She's popular, she's brilliant, and she's a wonderful woman."

For years to come, despite a statement to *The New York Times* ["*I believe if I did run, I'd win*"], he would repeatedly deny that he was a presidential candidate.

Dunbar had been among the first to plant a presidential seed in Donald's brain, and he later admitted that. "It was that speech that got the whole thing started," he said.

At the time, Donald was a registered Democrat.

[Dunbar later wrote at least eight romantic/sci-fi/adventure books as part of the "Castleton Series." Aimed at "teenagers, young adults, and the young at heart," they're united with a common theme— "Time travel messes with your mind and your heart." Within some of them, a character named Jack Lincoln is portrayed as the manager of The Sirens, a fast-rising teen band. As part of the story line, after

money started rolling in, Lincoln cheats The Sirens out of royalties that belong to them.

The author admitted that his Jack Lincoln was a "Trump-like figure, bigger than life, one who moves like a bulldozer, and one who has an office that's an entire floor of a Manhattan skyscraper."]

In 2016, when a reporter asked Dunbar if he'd vote for Donald for President, he answered, "The last two—even the last three—Presidents have been so horrible that Donald can't be any worse."

HOT NEWS FROM BUSH COUNTRY (AKA: A REALITY CHECK)
Did "Daddy Bush" Consider The Donald as His Vice-Presidential Running Mate in 1988?

In November of 2015, Donald Trump revealed that way back in 1987, George H.W. Bush ("Daddy Bush") had seriously considered nominating him as his vice presidential running mate, a decision that would have spotlighted him in 1988 at the Republican Convention in New Orleans.

Donald said that Lee Atwater, the former chairman of the Republican National Committee—and the notorious, widely loathed, master of dirty political tricks—contacted him, asking him if he would allow himself to be vetted as a potential vice presidential candidate.

"Lee told me that he thought I would be a great vice president," Donald claimed.

Atwater also held out the possibility that after Bush served eight years, it would be a natural progression that he would pass the Oval Office for another eight years to Donald. "You'd be President in 1996, and you'd do such a fabu-

Lee Atwater, the dirty trickster of the far right: "I'll meet all my enemies when we arrive at the Gates of Hell," he once said, strictly off the record.

lous job you'd be a shoo-in to get re-elected in 2000. That means you'd be America's first President in the 21st Century."

"At the time I was approached, I was in the midst of building my real estate empire, and wasn't raring to devote my life entirely to politics," Donald said. "He was very frank with me, telling me, I'd be a great running mate for George."

"You should go for it, you really should," Atwater said. "I want to talk it over with George, but I'll think he'll go for it big time. George can be a bit dull, and I think you'd provide the high energy needed—call it a big shot of baby-making testosterone."

Donald was disappointed when Bush named a rel-

George H.W. Bush looks skeptical as his vice presidential running mate, Danforth Quayle, delivers one dumb remark after another.

Lee Atwater added his private assessment: "As Greta Garbo said of her co-star (Robert Taylor) in *Camille,* Quayle is so pretty but so dumb."

atively unknown Danforth Quayle as his vice presidential pick. Many insiders told Donald that Quayle was a political lightweight. "He's rather good-looking, but tepid," Atwater said. "He's lily white, very conservative, a homophobe, Blacks won't go for him. Neither will the Jews."

Atwater had told his associates, "Quayle's wife Marilyn is the ball-clanker of the family."

Years later, Donald allegedly told his associates, "I'll never know why Bush picked this guy. He can't even spell potato. A little black kid spelled it correctly, and Quayle told him to add an extra 'e.'"

Atwater died in 1991 at the age of forty from a brain tumor when he was at the height of his

"Had I wanted it, I could have become Vice President in 1988, but I preferred to conquer other worlds—more real estate. And Reality TV lay in my future."

political power.

Donald's claim that he had almost become the Republican's candidate for Vice President at the 1988 Republican Convention was later treated skeptically by Jon Meacham, a Pulitzer Prize winner who was allowed unlimited access to George H.W. Bush. In 2015, he published *Destiny and Power*, a book whose revelations shocked many conservatives. He even provided a critique of George W. Bush's two terms as President—including many of his father's "harsh words for Dubya." ["Dubya," according to the *UrbanDictionary.com*, is a slang term for the most inept President the United States has ever had, i.e., George W. Bush, George H.W. Bush's son.]

As laid out in Meacham's biography, Daddy Bush also fired missiles at Dick Cheney, his son's Vice President, and at Secretary of Defense Donald Rumsfeld.

Meacham maintained that he asked the senior Bush if he had considered running in 1988 with Donald Trump as his vice president.

"What a strange and unbelievable idea," Bush shot back.

According to author John Meacham, when queried, about Trump having been considered as a Veep running mate to Daddy Bush, the ex-President flatly refuted Donald's claim that he'd ever been considered.

***

[Donald's opinion of the Bush vs. the Clinton Dynasty hasn't always been consistent. In one of his books, *Thinking Big* (2007), Donald weighed in with a description of his preference for Bill Clinton over his opponent, Daddy Bush.

"A friend of mine from Arkansas, Bill Clinton, ran and won against the first President Bush. Bill has the ability to think big. His wife, Hillary, is a fantastic person, who also has the ability to think big. That's why Bill Clinton won the election and sent Bush back to Texas. When others were unwilling to tread against Bush's huge poll numbers, Bill had no fear. Bill Clinton is a great guy with courage."

Donald's opinion, of course, would be considerably altered during his 2015-2016 run for president.]

296

DONALD'S HAIR
The Nationwide Rumpus.
Time Reveals the Secrets of His Orange Coif

"Today, no one seems to care if you're a good person.
People only care if you're good looking and rich."
—Dr. Rosalyn Weinman

Donald in his youth was considered a handsome man. He was not only good looking, but very rich and with enormous style and panache—a "babe magnet" as some of his admirers described him.

Although in the eyes of many, his allure continued, with the onset of middle age, he struggled to keep his weight under control. He also, as documented by television cameras around the world, made extraordinary efforts to camouflage a tendency for a condition that's widespread within the general population, male middle age baldness.

His enemies zeroed in on his sensitivity on the subject: "The worst thing a man can do is let himself grow bald," he told Mark Grossinger Estess, one of this casino executives who would die in a helicopter crash.

Donald's coiffure had come under scrutiny and was often talked about—or mocked—on TV. The most notorious assault came from Rosie O'Donnell [*more about that later*].

Donald told *Playboy* in 2004 that he styles his own hair and lets only one person trim it—"My girlfriend, Melania."

For a time, many viewers thought Amy Lasch, veteran of a thirty-year career as a hair stylist for the TV and film industry, was responsible to some degree for Donald's coiffure. (She worked on the set of *The Apprentice* during its first two seasons.) But she later revealed, "Donald wouldn't let me near his controversial mane."

It seemed that everybody had an opinion

In his 2007 book, *Think Big,* Donald wrote about how sweet getting revenge is. His advice: "When somebody screws you, screw them back in spades. When someone attacks you publicly, always strike back. If you want to stop a bully, hit them right between the eyes. Go for the jugular so that people watching will not want to mess with you."

about Donald's hair, and wind-blown photos of his "bad hair days" appeared everywhere. Louis Licari, who colored Ivana's hair for some twenty years, claimed, "I think it's all his hair— but through transplants. I saw him several times in the office of Dr. Norman Orentreich *[a NYC dermatologist known as "the father of hair transplants]* in the early 1980s.

Even the editors at *Time* magazine, who don't usually muck about with such nonsense, made it a point to publicize the secret of Donald's controversial coif. Within its pages, perhaps in an attempt to help other men afflicted with hair loss, "Losi," a well-known men's stylist, described how the look could be replicated:

Upper photo: Donald with Farouk Shami, developer of his favorite hair products. Does the presidential candidate really hate Muslims?

"1. Blow dry the hair forward. Don't confuse this with a classic side-part comb over."

Donald's controversial, even infamous, coiffure, has not only inspired much satire, but also a cottage industry of orange-colored Donald Trump wigs.

"2. Fold and blow the hair back and to the side. That would be in the manner of cartoon character Wilma Flintstone or the TV talk show host, Conan O'Brien."

"3. Sweep and blow the remaining hair on both sides. This maneuver anchors the edifice."

"4. Apply ozone-depleting amounts of hairspray. Voila! Boardroom fabulous!"

The man behind Donald's hair spray, Farouk Shami, claimed, "I like the cut, not the color." The hair guru once sent Donald a box of medium-blonde hair coloring, but Donald nonetheless stuck to orange.

"To get that soft-swerve, he uses an aerosol hair spray," Shami said. "I know environmentalists want to eradicate hair spray!"

At a rally in South Carolina in 2015, Donald said, "They say hair spray is going to affect the ozone. They want me to use a pump spray. But that comes out in big blobs. I want my own hair spray."

He wouldn't name the brand, but it's been said that one of his preferences is Farouk Systems CHI Helmet Head, a humidity-resistant and fast-drying spray.

During the weeks before Halloween of 2015, novelty stores did a rocketing business hawking orange-colored Donald Trump wigs.

Once, during a televised interview on a golf course with a newscaster on Britain's Channel 4, Donald was asked about his hair. Removing his trademark cap, he revealed this not-unattractive "natural look" with the comment, "It might not be pretty, but it's mine."

Men with previous "bad hair" moments everywhere applauded his grace.

BULWORTH AND THE REFORMERS
Warren Beatty's Satirical Overview
of Presidential Politics

"Everybody Should Fuck Everybody Until Everyone Is All the Same Color."
—Warren Beatty as Senator Bulworth

Many pundits compared Donald's flirtation with the presidency to the 1998 movie *Bulworth*, an American political comedy co-written, co-produced, and directed by Warren Beatty, who was also its star. Ironically, Beatty considered declaring a run for the White House in 2000, at the same time Donald was contemplating entering the race.

The madcap film follows the title character, California Senator Jay Billington Bulworth (Beatty), as he runs for re-election while trying to avoid a hired assassin.

His frank but offensive remarks make him an instant media darling and propel him forward in the polls. Along the way, he becomes romantically involved with a young black activist named Nina (Halle Berry).

There are many parallels between the film and the narratives of Donald's campaign. But Bulworth radically departs from the trajectory pursued by Donald when the Senator urges that "everybody should fuck everybody until everyone is all the same color."

At the end, Bulworth is assassinated by an agent of insurance company lobbyists, terrified by the senator's recent push for single-payer health care.

Despite many differences, in hindsight, some aspects of Bulworth seem like an early preview of Donald's campaign for the presidency. The hero (or protagonist) of the film, along with his wife and children, have expressed their deep-seated fears that he might be assassinated. Consequently, both Beatty (as a film character) and Donald Trump are flanked by security guards.

But whereas Senator Bulworth did everything he could to deliberately lose the race by being offensive and wildly inconsistent, the real life Donald found that being offensive only made his poll numbers rise, as did Bulworth's in the film.

Donald proclaimed, "I am the winner, not a loser like the rest of the jerks running against me—Lyin' Ted Cruz, who opposes me, along with Little Marco (Rubio) and Low-Energy Jeb (Bush)."

As a Hollywood actor with a passionate interest in politics, Beatty had made a cinematic impact on progressive politics through his films *Reds* (1981) and *Bulworth*. He also campaigned for two liberals, Bobby Kennedy and George McGovern. Rare for an A-list actor, the Hollywood films he made portrayed socialism in a positive light long before Bernie Sanders arrived on the scene.

On August 12, 1999, *The New York Times* ran a story headlined: "BEATTY REPORTEDLY FLIRTING WITH WHITE HOUSE RACE."

As stated by Beatty: "I have some very strong feelings, the most important of which at the time is campaign finance reform because

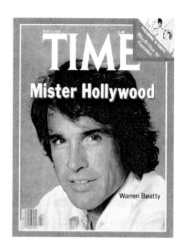

In an "only in America" chain of events that raise eyebrows within the Washington beltway, Hollywood star Warren Beatty gave consideration to a White House run in 1999. The previous year, he'd released a controversial political satire, *Bulworth*. The outspoken senator in that film was later compared to Donald.

Above is the provocative ad for the movie.

its tentacles reach into every other issue. I fear we're getting closer to a plutocracy than we want to, and I believe that deep down the people want to do something about that."

John Bredin, talk show host, educator, and writer, said, "Though Beatty never ran for President himself, he flirted with the idea, and the closest he ever came was in 2000 when he was urged on by Arianna Huffington. I believe he could have won easily—as a charismatic, intelligent, left-wing Hollywood antidote to Reaganism—in the 1980s, 90s, and beyond."

Beatty met with members of the Reform Party to talk about his being their candidate.

[The Reform Party of the United States of America (RPUSA), generally known as the Reform Party USA or the Reform Party, was founded in 1995 by Ross Perot as a viable alternative for independent voters disillusioned with the traditional division of the U.S. Government into the traditional two-party system. In 1992, Perot had famously and feistily run as an independent against (the Republican) George H.W. Bush and (the Democrat) Bill Clinton.

Citing corruption, ineptitude, and waste as incentives for sweeping changes to a government mired in bureaucratic stalemates, the party was most famously associated with Perot himself, the ultra-conservative Pat Buchanan, consumer advocate Ralph Nader, the former professional wrestler, Jesse ("The Body") Ventura, and—if his stories aren't exaggerated—Donald Trump.]

Beatty confessed that he didn't see himself as the best candidate. "There certainly should be someone better. That's not to say that I don't have strong feelings on a lot of things that aren't being spoken."

Biographer Ellis Amburn, author of *Warren Beatty, The Sexiest Man Alive,* wrote:

"Beatty didn't have the time, energy, will, or desire to go directly to the public and ask them to finance his campaign. It was sad, because his platform would have been

For the first presidential election of the 21st Century, Warren Beatty considered a run for the White House.

One of his biographers called him, "The sexiest man alive." But could the actor have turned his sex appeal and chairisma into a successful presidential bid? "I know a Hollywood actor who became President," Beatty said.

good for the nation, espousing campaign finance reform, Medicare for everyone, increasing teachers' salaries, and rebuilding the educational infrastructure, and end, through world trade sanctions, environmental abuse and cruel labor practices."

In September 1999, perhaps terminally discouraged with the political process, Beatty announced that it was "extremely unlikely" that he would run. Several months later, he said, 'I'm not running now.'"

EARLY AND LOUDLY, DONALD PLAYS THE TERROR CARD

"A Terrorist With a Bomb in a Suitcase Could Turn Manhattan into Hiroshima."
— *Donald Trump in his first campaign book*

As he was contemplating his 2000 race for the White House, Donald decided to release another book, *The America We Deserve*. It was to be his "first campaign book" (with many more to follow). To help him write it, he hired author Dave Shiflett, a veteran writer who had previously penned articles for both the *National Review* and *The Wall Street Journal*.

In this book, Donald took lethal aim at many of his rivals from across the political spectrum. He claimed that Pat Buchanan "has totally lost it," and that Al Gore "is an able, underrated man who seems confused."

In terms of its role as a political tract that laid out the scope, scale, and ambitions of a newcomer to a political and electoral setting, some readers compared it to *Mein Kampf*.

In it, he came down hard on America's enemies abroad, especially China, North Korea, and Cuba, and he was "tougher than tough" on crime. The book revealed, as described by reviewer Ron Hogan, a "straight-shooting personality and policy-wonk data points."

Donald praised the "diversity of American culture," denounced the murder of Matthew Shepard, a young gay man in Wyoming, criticized the harassment of Jews and all other hate crimes.

Shiflett later claimed that the platforms Donald espoused in 2015, as opposed to his platforms of 2000, sounded "more like those of a political shock jock than a statesman." But even before the 9/11 attack on the World Trade Center, Donald had expressed fear that "a terrorist with a suitcase bomb could turn Manhattan into Hiroshima II."

In reference to his collaboration with Donald in 2015, Shiflett told *The Wall Street Journal*, "We made a pretty good team. He needed words. I needed money. I have long considered the resulting book my first published work of fiction."

Shiflett likened his 2000 presidential aspiration to a "rich guy out on a lark, bombastic enough to make headlines, not history. It was a short-lived dance through the spotlight—and plenty of fun."

***

The political bug continued to bite deep into Donald's skin. What was a mere flirtation in 1988 had become something of an obsession by 1999, eleven years later.

He told a reporter, "If I decide to run for President, the beauty of it is that I'm very rich."

He commissioned an exploratory committee to determine his chances for victory if he ran as a possible Reform Party candidate in November of 2000 against the Democratic nominee (Vice President Al Gore), or against the Republican nominee (George W. Bush, the governor of Texas).

When the results of the polling came in, Donald was bitterly disappointed to learn that if he participated, he would receive only seven percent of the vote.

***

Despite the miserable prognosis for his chance at election, Donald appointed Roger Jason Stone, Jr. to form a sort of "Trump for President in 2000" Committee.

Stone, a political consultant, lobbyist, and strategist, was noted for his far-reaching use of "destructive opposition research." In other words, he dug up dirt "on the enemy."

The Daily Beast described him as a "self-

Historians are still debating the effect that a rich Texan, Ross Perot, had on the 1992 race for the White House.

At the time, a sitting President, George H.W. Bush, was up against a relatively unknown Democratic governor from Arkansas with a "woman problem."

The question is still being debated: Did Perot's entry cost Bush his re-election?

admitted hit man for the GOP," and *The New York Times* more kindly referred to him as "a renowned infighter and a seasoned practitioner of hard-edged politics."

With Donald, Stone shared his battle plan to advance a candidate: "Attack! Attack! Attack! Never defend! Admit nothing! Counterattack!"

On October 24, 1999, at the urging of Stone, Donald made a TV appearance on *Meet the Press* to announce that he would officially resign from the Republican Party and join the Reform Party. "The Republicans," he charged, "have become too crazy right!"

He was asked if his previous life as a womanizer might harm his chances of becoming President. "I would not run if I believed there was anything in my past that would be an impediment to my winning the race for the White House."

Donald entered the race, giving interviews that outlined his platform. On social issues, he was progressive, supporting gays in the military. "They would not disturb me. After all, I live in Manhattan."

For the Reform Party nomination, he faced opposition from Pat Buchanan, who also wanted to run as their candidate. Buchanan had left the Republican Party in October of 1999, denouncing it as "The Beltway Party."

Donald was supplied

Hatchetman Roger Stone was the attack dog of the far right.

Posters and magazine articles, including rundowns in a the 2004 edition of *Esquire* depicted here, addressed Donald's previous but not-so-serious attempts to run for the White House. In 2000, he would have run not as a Republican or Democrat, but on the Reform Party ticket.

In contrast, a "Trump for President" movement in 2012, in which he would have opposed Obama, was never really launched.

with a detailed background, some of it explosive, on Buchanan and his career. A paleoconservative *[extreme conservative]* political commentator, author, and broadcaster, he had been Director of Communications at the White House under Ronald Reagan. He had also been a senior advisor to Presidents Richard Nixon and Gerald Ford, and was one of the original hosts on CNN's *Crossfire*. He had sought the Republican nomination for President in both 1992 and 1996, and had, each time, lost badly.

In addition to Donald, John Hagelin, a physicist from Iowa whose platform was based on Transcendental Meditation, was also running.

For Donald, Buchanan was just too controversial. "He's to the right of Hitler!" Donald charged. "I guess he's an anti-Semite. He doesn't like the blacks, and he doesn't like the gays."

Buchanan was labeled a "Holocaust Denier." He once wrote that it was impossible for 850,000 Jews to have been killed by diesel exhaust fed into the gas chamber at Treblinka. "It was not a death camp, but a transit camp used as a pass-through point for prisoners," he wrote.

[In truth, some 900,000 Jews were slaughtered at Treblinka.]

The Anti-Defamation League denounced Buchanan as "an unrepentant bigot who repeatedly demonized

If Pat Buchanan — a cultural warrior of the far right—had been nominated as a presidential candidate in 1992, he would have been one of the most controversial men ever to seek that office.

Homosexuals were often his main target, although he was no champion of civil rights for other minorities either.

Even before Donald officially announced he was a candidate for the presidency in June of 2015, he appeared on Fox News, hosted by anchorwoman Megyn Kelly, with whom he would later enter into a well-publicized feud. He was blunt: "This country is a hell-hole!"

Jews and minorities and openly affiliates with white supremacists."

"I can't support such a man," Donald claimed. Consequently, he pushed ahead with his own pursuit of the nomination, running on a platform of fair trade, elimination of the national debt, and universal health care.

His political positions were outlined in *The America We Deserve,* a book released in January of 2000. Dick Morris, former advisor to Bill Clinton, claimed that Donald was only running for President because of the publicity it generated which "might boost his book sales."

MEDIA FRENEMIES & REFORM PARTY ENEMIES
Donald Becomes Politically Notorious

> *"He's a fraud...the greatest con artist."*
> —*NYC Mayor Ed Koch*

As his opinions became more widely publicized, and as his visibility increased, critics lined up to attack Donald. One of them was the outspoken Mayor of New York City, Ed Koch, who called him "a fraud and the greatest con artist when it comes to trumpeting his own name. My gut tells me he knows nothing about policy."

Controversies continued on the Latino front: Donald appeared in Miami and spoke before the Cuban American National Foundation. He denounced Fidel Castro and favored the continuing U.S. embargo against Cuba. He was met with VIVA DONALD TRUMP! signs.

"I have two words for Castro," he told the assembled Cubans. "*Adios, amigo!* Fidel is a killer and should be treated as such."

After he returned from Miami, Donald met with Reform Party leaders who objected to his living openly with his mistress, Melania Knauss. He promised "to remedy the situation."

He was said to have temporarily separated from her, so he would not be charged in the upcoming campaign with having a live-in mistress. "Melania will be missed," he said. But on the day of his withdrawal from the Reform Party, he asked for her to move back into Trump Tower.

That was not the only trouble facing him.

All hell broke loose in the Reform Party when John Hagelin supporters claimed that the party's open primary, which favored Buchanan by a wide margin, was "tainted."

That led to the party holding dual conventions simultaneously in separate areas of California's Long Beach Convention Center. One gathering nominated Buchanan while the other backed Hagelin, with each camp claiming to be the legitimate Reform Party.

Because of all this infighting, Donald planned to withdraw from the party, and Ventura also said he was going to bow out.

Donald gave his reasons to the press. "The Reform Party now includes a Klansman, Mr. David Duke, a neo-Nazi and former leader of the KKK, and Mr. Buchanan, as well as a communist, Miss Fulani."

He was referring to Lenora Fulani, a psychologist and political activist, who became the first woman and the first African American to achieve ballot access in all fifty states. She received more votes in a U.S. general election than any other woman in American history, and ran on a platform of racial equality, gay rights, and political reform.

Lenora Fulani richly deserved her footnote in American history.

This African America liberal ran on the ballots in all fifty states, receiving more votes than any other woman ever had, years before Hillary.

Jesse Ventura may have ended his future in politics when he told *Playboy*, "Organized religion is a sham and a crutch."

When Donald heard that, he said, "There goes the evangelical vote."

Donald officially ended his 2000 campaign and his association with the Reform Party on February 14, 2000 during an appearance with Matt Lauer on the *Today* show. During that interview, he claimed that the Reform Party was "a total mess on the verge of self-destructing."

He did hold out, however, the possibility that he

Jesse ("The Body") Ventura was a pro-wrestler who somehow managed to capture the imagination of the voters of Minnesota, who elected him governor of their great state.

307

might seek the presidency again in 2004.

The Chairman of the Reform Party, Pat Choate, vigorously disputed Donald's claim. "Trump campaigned for the presidency only to smear Pat Buchanan. Trump will be unwelcome to seek our party's nomination in 2004. Actually, I think his campaign was nothing but a Republican dirty trick orchestrated by Roger Stone."

Donald said that "running for President was enormous fun, but doesn't compare with completing one of the great skyscrapers of Manhattan."

***

As a politician contemplating a presidential race, Donald had begun to pick up enemies who opposed him. One of the most vocal was the 85th Governor of Connecticut (1991-1995), Lowell P. Weicker, Jr. He had sought the Republican nomination for President in 1980, but had lost to Ronald Reagan.

Weicker and Donald had conflicted in 1993 when the real estate mogul wanted to expand his gambling empire to Bridgeport. Weicker had vigorously opposed that, telling Donald that he had already entered into a compact with the Mashantucket Pequot Tribal Nation to build the Foxwoods Resort Casino.

Donald challenged the tribal recognition process, claiming, "They don't look like Indians to me."

During a TV interview, Weicker denounced Donald as a "dirtbag and a bigot." Donald reciprocated by calling him "a fat slob who couldn't even get elected dog-catcher."

[In 2015, when Donald announced his bid for the presidency, Weicker, then in his mid-80s, had nothing but disdain for Donald. "I think the man is a total con artist. Maybe it's a reflection of the Republican Party more than Donald Trump if it allows any nut case like Trump to make it as if he were a valid presidential candidate. The party has drifted. The man's a disgrace. But the Republican Party is a disgrace. If I were a Democrat, I'd hope for nothing more than Trump to become the candidate. Do I want an American President to identify with prejudice toward different minority groups? I certainly don't."

J.R. Romano, head of the Connecticut GOP, said, "Weicker is still clueless. Donald Trump has tapped into the angst and anger that many Americans feel toward politicians like Weicker."]

***

By 2004, Donald once again considered challenging George W. Bush for the presidency but ultimately decided not to. He'd been critical of Bush's handling of the Iraq War. For a while, his friend Jesse Ventura, considered running in his place and asked Donald for his support, but the Minnesota governor decided that he, too, would bow out once again.

Donald spoke out on certain issues, suggesting that vaccination might cause autism, and he also criticized advocates of global warming, deriding the claim it was a phenomenon catalyzed by the actions of humans.

In 2009, Donald changed his voter registration from Democrat to Republican, and once again, he considered a 2012 run for the White House, taking on Barack Obama, whom he claimed was one of America's worst presidents. He sharply criticized the President's trade policies, and questioned his citizenship and the authenticity of his birth certificate.

He also questioned whether Obama's grades (and by implication, his intelligence level) had been good enough to warrant entry into Harvard Law School.

Some critics suggested that Donald was toying with the idea of launching a presidential run as a means of gaining free media publicity for *The Apprentice*.

It came as a surprise even to him that a *Wall Street Journal/NBC* poll released in March of 2011 found Donald leading among other contenders for the GOP nod.

As Donald moved deeper into expanding his gambling interests and his role in politics, he made a strong enemy of long-time Republican Lowell P. Weicker, Jr., who served during his long career as a U.S. Senator, a U.S. Representative, and as the former governor of Connecticut.

"He favored the redskins over me," Donald protested, in reference to Weicker's objections to the establishment of a Trump-controlled casino in Weicker's state.

Years later, in an evaluation of his years of public service, Weicker evaluated Trump as "a dirtbag," "a con artist," and "a racist."

A *Newsweek* poll showed him one point ahead of Mitt Romney (too close to call) and just a few points behind President Obama himself.

Executives at NBC gave him a deadline for deciding if he were going to sign a new contract for his hit show, *The Apprentice*. The question was this: Should he run for President and subject himself to a bruising race, or "go for the gold?"

He made a decision: He notified NBC executives that he would sign on for another season of *The Apprentice*. Consequently, on May 16, 2011, in reference to the upcoming 2012 elections, Donald announced, "I will not seek the nomination."

At the time, Public Policy Polling described his race for the White House as "one of the quickest rises and falls in the history of presidential politics."

Even though he donated money for the campaign of Mitt Romney, Donald later mocked him. "He's a small business guy who walked away from some big money from a company he didn't create."

When Romney didn't beat Obama, he denounced the Mormon as "a god damn loser. I backed a loser, and I don't like losers."

***

As each month went by, Donald became embroiled with one media personality after another, usually in response to mocking attacks they'd made on him.

Bill Maher, the very liberal TV talk show host and comedian, offered to donate $5 million to Donald's favorite charity if "he could produce a birth certificate that showed he was not fathered by an orangutan."

Donald then had his lawyers send Maher a copy of his birth certificate with a demand that he receive a $5 million cashier's check. When Maher refused, Donald threatened legal action.

The case never made it to court, like so many other legal suits that Donald used to threaten various

> Donald reportedly told his aides, "David Letterman should be more careful when he suggests that I'm a racist. That could get him into deep shit."

The wildly popular liberal talk show host and atheist, Bill Maher, in a $5 million dollar bet with The Donald.

Maher wanted Donald to prove that his father was not an orangutan.

pundits and media figures.

In another television interview, Donald said, "I would love to be a well-educated black because they have an actual advantage."

Later, David Letterman, the TV talk show host, attacked Donald during an on-air appearance of "Dr. Phil."

"It's all fun, it's all a circus, it's all a rodeo, until it starts to smack of racism," Letterman said. "And then it's no longer fun."

A talk show host himself, Phil McGraw, known as "Dr. Phil," considered Donald a friend. "I don't think Donald is a racist," he said. "Perhaps a bit rash at times. I don't think he always thinks everything through. I think sometimes he's a little from the hip. I don't think he has a racist bone in his body."

Donald watched the program that night. He fired off a response to Letterman: "I was disappointed to hear the statements you made about me last night on your show that I was a racist. In actuality, nothing could be further from the truth, and there is nobody who is less of a racist than Donald Trump."

On April 30, 2011, at the annual White House Correspondents Associa-

Obama, in April of 2011, at the podium for the White House correspondents' dinner, skewered Donald Trump on the eve of the long-plotted death of Osama bin Laden.

Four years later, in 2015, at an equivalent forum, Obama repeated his scathing attacks on Donald.

"I know he's taken some flack lately. But no one is prouder to put this birth certificate issue to rest than Donald, and that's because he can get back to the issues that matter, like, did we fake the moon landing? What really happened in Roswell? And where are Biggie and Tupac?"

tion dinner, both Seth Meyers (a key player and later, host of *Saturday Night Live*) and President Obama ridiculed Donald as he sat grim-faced in the audience. Meyers mocked Donald for claiming, "I have a great relationship with the blacks."

Meyers said he didn't question Donald's statement—"that is unless the blacks are white people."

Meyers didn't let up. "Donald Trump has been saying he would run for President as a Republican, which is surprising because I thought he would be running as a joke."

Obama then rose to the podium. "All kidding aside, we all know about Donald Trump's credentials and breadth of experience. For example—no, seriously, just recently, in an episode of *Celebrity Apprentice*—at the steak house, the men's cooking team did not impress the judges from Omaha Steaks: And there was a lot of blame to go around. But you, Mr. Trump, recognized that the real problem was a lack of leadership. And so, ultimately, you didn't blame Lil' Jon or Meatloaf. You fired Gary Busey. And these are the kind of decisions that would keep me up at night. Well handled, sir. Well handled."

While Obama made these mocking comments, U.S. Navy SEALS were flying in helicopters into Pakistan with the intention of killing Osama bin Laden as a payback for 9/11.

Columnist Maureen Dowd remained a continuing critic of Donald, calling him "The Apotheosis of our Gilded Age, where money, celebrity, polling, and crass behavior in politics and the TV show, *Who Wants to Be a Millionaire*, dominate the culture."

THE BIRTHER BLITZ
Donald Launches New Battles in His War Against Obama

(Did You Know? "Birther-ism" Originated in Hillary's Camp)

Contrary to popular belief, theories about a conspiracy surrounding Obama's birth did not originate with Donald.

During the closing weeks of the Democratic Party's presidential nomination process of 2008, when Hillary Clinton was competing with Barack Obama for the party's nomination, her supporters, in an attempt to revive her then-faltering campaign, sent anony-mous e-mails that questioned the legiti-macy of Obama's U.S. citizenship and his birth certificate.

One e-mail from Hillary's camp claimed, "Barack Obama's mother was liv-ing in Kenya with his African father late in her pregnancy. She was not allowed to travel by plane then, so Obama was born in Kenya. His mother later flew her baby

Politico investigated the charge that the birther issue originated from within the Hillary campaign, and not (at least origi-nally) from Donald's.

"In fact, the claim was first advanced by Hillary supporters as her nomination hopes faded in 2008," *Politico* revealed. "So was the suspicion that Obama was a secret Muslim."

In February of 2008, *The Guardian* re-ported that a Clinton staffer had been forced to resign after forwarding an e-mail that suggested that Obama was a Muslim.

"There is no moral high ground for the Clinton team here; there is only hypocrisy."

Vermont Senator Bernie Sanders, challenging Hillary for the Dem-ocratic nomination, was known as "the Giveaway Candidate," promising free college tuition and everything else.

Economists added up the cost, finding his proposals would levy $15.3 trillion in new taxes, plus another $2 trillion for his health plan.

The economists also claimed that his plans would "slow GDP growth by 9.5%."

Ironically, eight years later, during a February 2016 CNN Democratic Town Hall broadcast from Columbia, South Carolina, Vermont Senator Bernie Sanders referenced the birther movement. Even though it had orig-inated with the Democrats, Sanders charged that, "There is racism inherent in the Republican base. Nobody asked for my birth certificate. Maybe it's the color of my skin."

In February of 2011, Donald spoke at the right-wing Conservative Po-litical Action Conference (CPAC). At that point, he'd become a convert to the Birther movement. "Our current President came out of nowhere. Came out of nowhere! In fact, I'll go a step further. The people that went to school with him never saw him. They don't know who he is. Crazy!"

Although Donald was a Johnny-come-lately to the Birther rumor, he quickly became its most famous advocate.

Later, on Bill O'Reilly's nighttime TV program, the most-watched news show on television, Donald launched what became known as "the Birther Blitz."

He said that he used to believe that Obama was born in Hawaii, "but I have come to have my doubts, since I've seen evidence to the contrary."

Although a right-wing commentator, O'Reilly could also be a tough questioner, and he challenged Donald's claim.

In response, Donald continued: "Now he may have a birth certificate, but there is something on it he doesn't want us to see—maybe religion, maybe it says he's a Muslim. I don't know."

O'Reilly concluded the interview with, "I don't think you believe your charge."

During the weeks that followed, Donald appeared on a number of shows questioning the circumstances of Obama's birth and consequently, his legitimacy as the U.S. President. He even claimed that he had sent a team of investigators to Honolulu to get to the truth of the matter.

The implications of Donald's words were serious, indeed: If it were revealed that Obama had been born in Kenya, it would have invalided his election as a U.S. President. [Only a native son (or daughter), according to U.S. law, is allowed to serve as the nation's President.]

Under more intense questioning, Donald, on another TV show, claimed that Obama's grandmother, who spoke only Swahili, was present at his birth in Kenya: "We have her on tape."

However, it turned out that the tape was a phone interview with Sarah Obama, the President's stepmother. In an interview with Ron McRae, a police officer who became a bishop for the Anabaptist Churches worldwide, Sarah told him that she was present at the birth of Barack Obama and that the birth took place in Kenya.

Later, on The View, Donald said, "I want Obama to show his birth certificate. There is something on that birth certificate that he doesn't like."

That comment led to Whoopi Goldberg defining that remark as, "The biggest pile of dog mess I've heard in ages."

When Donald took up the Birther issue and promoted it, he was accused of racism by both CBS News and The New Yorker.

Rumors can have a devastating effect. Early in 2011, a poll showed that half of all Republicans surveyed by Public Policy Polling believed that the President had, indeed, been born in Africa.

One particularly vicious cartoon widely available across the Internet depicted the Obama family as chimps living in trees. "Now you know why no birth certificate," the caption read.

On April 25, 2011, Donald called for Obama to end the Birther issue by releasing the long form of his birth certificate.

Melania Trump weighed in, too. "It would be very easy if President Obama would just show us the documents. It is not only Donald who wants to see them. It's the American people who want to know the truth."

In a formal move by the White House, Obama released the long form, showing that he was born in Hawaii's Kapiolani Hospital.

Donald, however, did not seem satisfied. "I hope it checks out for his sake. We have to see, is it real? It could be a fake, you know. I am really honored and I am really proud that I was able to get him to do something nobody else could."

On October 24, 2012, Donald offered to donate $5 million to the charity of Obama's choice in return for the publication of his college and passport applications. Obama did not respond to the offer.

During September of 2015, on the campaign trail for the 2016 elections, Donald flew once again to New Hampshire. During a question-and-answer period, an irate New Englander said, "We have a problem in this country. It's called Muslims. We know our current President is one. You know, he's not even an American. Birth certificate, man! We have training camps growing where they want to kill us. That's my question: When can we get rid of them?"

Donald replied, "We're looking at a lot of different things. And you know that a lot of people are saying that bad things are happening out there. We're going to be looking at that and at plenty of other things."

"He dodged the bullet on that question," one reporter claimed.

When pressed on the Muslim question, a Donald spokesman said, "Christians

Right to left: Barack Obama, born in 1961, and Maya Soetoro, born 1970, with their mother Ann Dunham and grandfather Stanley Dunham in Hawaii in the early 1970s.

Obama's mother was born in Wichita, Kansas. She was of predominantly English ancestry, and Wild Bill Hickok was her sixth cousin, five times removed.

need to fear in this country. Their religious liberty is at stake."

Unless some document surfaces somewhere, it now appears beyond a reasonable doubt that the President's father was born in Kenya, his mother in Kansas, and Obama himself saw the light of day in Hawaii.

Il Duce: Donald's detractors began comparing his arrogance to that of Mussolini.

Chapter Fourteen

GOLDFINGER TRUMP
THE MAN WITH THE MIDAS TOUCH
Living Large & Living Loud

TRUMP UNIVERSITY
"Professor Trump," the Big Hair on Campus,
Promises that for $35,000 Any Member of the
"Great Unwashed" Can Become a Millionaire

THE APPRENTICE
"You're Fired!"

DONALD AS THE PAGEANT WORLD'S
"MASTER OF THE UNIVERSE"
The Beauty Industry's Triple Crown:
Miss USA! Miss Universe! Transgenders Can Compete!

In and Out of Court, Donald Feuds with Pageant
Winners & "That Fat Pig," Rosie O'Donnell

In 2004, as one of his worst business decisions, Donald Trump, with two of his associates (Jonathan Spitalny and Michael Sexton), launched Trump University.

At fees ranging from $1,500 to $35,000, it offered courses "taught by experts" in real estate, asset management, and wealth creation. Most of all, it promised courses in entrepreneurship itself "taught by the greatest entrepreneur on earth, who makes more in a day than most people earn in a lifetime."

Promoting Donald as "a professor" was a bit of a stretch. Although prospective students expected to be taught by the master himself, their courses would be delivered via web-based, long distance seminars. Lessons were neither conducted nor taught by "The Donald."

The Trump University website had promised, "In a highly competitive world, the one sure way of being successful is to know everything you can about what you do. And of course, you will have the opportunity to learn directly from Donald J. Trump himself."

For many men and women, dreaming of getting rich, the prospect of learning from "the sorcerer" who spearheaded *The Apprentice* was a formidable enticement.

From the beginning, *exposé* editors at *TheSmokingGun.com* were skeptical—with good reason. The staff noted that Donald had graduated from the Wharton School of Finance. "Perhaps he can lecture on the importance of having a rich father. Or maybe he can offer a somber Founders' Day reflection on how he actually managed to lose money operating a casino?"

If it's one thing that Donald knew how to do, it involved generating free publicity. He boasted that, "Trump University is going to be very big in investment banking and education."

He was heralded in promotional material as a financial swashbuckler, "The Errol Flynn of real estate," or at least a Douglas Fairbanks, Sr.

Trump University (aka Trump Wealth Institute and later Trump Entrepreneur Initiative LLC) was not an accredited university or college, and conferred no college degree.

Those who paid the fees were offered access not directly to Trump, but to Trump U's website, where articles, lectures, and videos about salesmanship were made available. Within some of its videos, they also got some gossip from The Donald himself.

In one sequence, he delivered his thoughts on the pop singer Britney Spears: "She has seen better days. She performed five years ago at the Trump Taj Mahal in Atlantic city, and was great. But today, everything seems to be slipping away from her. Britney, don't let that happen. Keep your shaved head on straight!"

Students also received a primer, a book called *Trump 101*, that featured his picture on the cover. Since he wasn't around to pose for selfies, students had to settle for having their pictures snapped as they stood beside a life-sized, free-standing cutout of the master.

They heard rags-to-riches stories, one instructor claiming that as a young man, he slept on the subways in Manhattan before becoming a real estate mogul.

Trump U coasted under the radar for a few years, but by 2010, a growing coven of dissenters had emerged. The offices of Attorney Generals in six states were bombarded with complaints from former students, and the *New York Daily News* published some of them.

The most serious charges involved allegations that students had been urged "to max out their credit cards to pay for extra courses and seminars." It had also been suggested that graduates of the university

Donald made a powerful enemy over the issue of Trump University. New York Attorney General Eric Schneiderman filed a $40 million lawsuit against him, claiming that students had been defrauded.

Donald fired back, calling the AG "a political hack" and even tying Obama into a so-called conspiracy to bring down lawsuits on him.

would be introduced to powerful tycoons who had made "a killing in real estate."

That never happened.

The most serious challenge to Trump U came in 2013 when Eric Schneiderman, Attorney General for the State of New York, launched an investigation that led to him suing both Donald and Trump U for $40 million on grounds that students had been defrauded. Immediately, Donald dropped the name "university" from his school, renaming it Trump Entrepreneur Initiative. The state required accreditation for any institution calling itself a university.

As was his custom, Donald went on the offensive, charging that no college or university, even Harvard and Yale, ever received complete approval from their students. He told the *New York Daily News* that "ninety-eight percent of Trump U's students praised the courses. Lots of pupils left their seminars with us and became very successful in making big deals with little money."

Vanity Fair ran an article about Trump U by William D. Cohan, headlining Donald as the BIG HAIR ON CAMPUS. The magazine's editor, Graydon Carter, labeled Donald "a short-fingered vulgarian."

He shot back, "Carter is a sleazebag and highly overrated."

Of all the politicians he'd tangled with (up to that date), Eric Schneiderman became Donald's worst enemy, charging him with operating an enterprise "that is nothing short of an out-and-out fraud."

In his suit, during August of 2003, the Attorney General claimed that between 2003 and 2011, Donald and Trump U intentionally misled more than 5,000 students nationwide, including 600 in New York State alone. He charged that Donald made $5 million for his contribution to the "university," a profit that he had promised to donate to charities.

Later, in response, Donald revealed that legal fees had eaten up all the profits, and that there was nothing left to contribute.

Before the New York press,

Graydon Carter, editor of *Vanity Fair*, exposed Donald and Trump University in an article in his prestigious magazine. Donald was ridiculed as the "Big Hair on Campus."

Donald denounced Carter as a "sleazebag."

Schneiderman claimed, "Mr. Trump used his celebrity status and personally appeared in commercials making false promises to convince people to spend tens of thousands of dollars they couldn't afford for lessons they never got."

Appearing on the right-wing TV show, *Fox & Friends*, Donald shot back attacking Schneiderman's character and calling him "…a political hack. The lawsuit was cooked up immediately after he visited Barack Obama at the White House. The two met on Thursday, and he filed the lawsuit on a Saturday. It was a helluva coincidence. Obama wants to get back at me over the Birther issue. I'd had a lot of litigation. I have never heard of a lawsuit being filed on a Saturday."

The response from the AG was immediate. "President Obama and I had more important things to discuss than my busting this penny-ante fraud of Trump University. Donald Trump seems to be the kind of person who goes to the Super Bowl and thinks the people in the huddle are talking about him."

"The Attorney General is a disgusting human being," Donald responded, "a sleazebag and a crook, who is driving business out of New York. He once came to me begging for a campaign contribution, and now he's trying to screw me."

The AG defended himself, as the battle between adversaries was waged in the tabloids. "The fact that Donald Trump has a larger megaphone than most fraudsters is what gets all the attention here. It is true that he did not support me in the primary of 2010, but once I won, he gave me one contribution—and that was it."

Schneiderman attempted to "out-blitz the Blitzer." He wrote an Op-Ed piece for the *New York Daily News*, and appeared on TV talk shows. "Trump's outlandish accusations are not surprising for a showman who has built a career around bluster and hype. But I am not in the entertainment business: I am in the justice business. Instead of going to court, he chose to try the case in the press."

Later, both in and out of court, the AG aired his accusations, asserting that the so-called free seminars "were the first step in a bait-and-switch to induce prospective students to enroll in increasingly expensive seminars starting with the three-day $15,000 fee that led to advanced seminars—the Gold Elite Program—costing $35,000."

"Schneiderman, for tarring me as a fraud, will pay politically for his accusations against me," Donald threatened. "My legal response will blow Schneiderman out of the war."

On the campaign trail in 2016, "Little Marco Rubio and Lyin' Lion's

Head Cruz" (Donald's appellations) repeatedly brought up charges against Trump U and its pending litigation.

"I could have settled for peanuts," Donald said, "but if you give in too easily, then skunks start emerging from the underground to file more lawsuits against you. My lawyers are going to fight this thing, and we will win."

"BLONDE BEAUTIES
—*That's What I Like*"
—Donald Trump

In *The Art of the Comeback*, Donald wrote that Cindy Adams, columnist for the *New York Post*, "knew way back when that I loved beauty. Loved blondes and loved the Miss Universe Pageant."

[That was before he bought a trio of Beauty Pageants.]

At a party, his attorney, Roy Cohn, introduced Donald to Cindy Adams, claiming, "This guy will own New York one day."

She replied, "Oh yeah, pass me the gravy."

She later said, "Who knew he'd own the world some day? His dinner partner that night was a drop-dead gorgeous blonde, with a neckline so low she probably still has bronchitis. And brainy? Couldn't spell CIA. He and I kept talking across Blondie's puffy chest. We laughed all night. Loved one another instantly."

From 1996 to 2015, Donald owned, at least partially, three beauty pageants, of which Miss Universe was the most celebrated. The trio of pageants fell under the baton of the Miss Universe Organization.

The origin of Miss Universe went back to 1926 when it was called the International Pageant of Pulchritude. It flourished for nine years until the Great Depression and war clouds over Europe brought it to a (temporary) halt in 1935.

Revived in 1952, it was spon-

It was a lovefest when the popular gossip columnist, Cindy Adams, met Donald Trump, courtesy of his lawyer, Roy Cohn. They formed a beneficial relationship, and he often gave her insider tips to run in her column.

Ivana meanwhile had won the backing of Cindy's rival columnist, Liz Smith.

sored by Pacific Mills, the California-based clothing manufacturer.

Its chief rivals were Miss World and Miss Earth. Miss Universe drew beauty queens from 190 countries worldwide, and the pageant was seen every year by half a billion TV watchers.

Deep into his ownership of the pageant, Donald claimed that it was worth $40 to $50 million. "I plan to make Miss Universe the world's most dominant beauty show. As far as I'm concerned, Miss America is as dead as the Model T."

"The backers of Miss America don't know what they're doing. It's all fucked up. They're beset with problems. They have this talent contest. Who cares? Beauty pageants aren't about talent. No contestant is a budding Judy Garland. The viewers don't give a shit if a girl can play the piano or the violin. They want to see what she looks like in a bathing suit."

The second pageant he acquired, Miss USA, formed in 1952, is an annual competition that determines America's entrant in the Miss Universe contest. The pageant originated when Yolande Betbeze, winner that year of the Miss America contest, refused to pose for publicity pictures in a bathing suit.

The first Miss USA was Jackie Loughery, who had been Miss New York before any links had been forged between the pageant and the TV networks.

The pageant aired from 1963 to 2002 on CBS. In 2002, Donald brokered a deal with NBC for broadcasting rights to the show, ceding half ownership of the annual event to the network.

Famous hosts of Miss USA had previously included John Charles Daly, Bob Barker, John Forsythe, and Dick Clark.

Since its inception, eight Miss USA titleholders have gone on to wear the Miss Universe crown.

Jackie Loughery, Miss USA 1952.

Modesty in bathing suits was the custom back in the year that Dwight Eisenhower was elected President.

Jackie Loughery became the first Miss New York USA and the winner of the first Miss USA beauty pageant.

Among her husbands were the popular singer Guy Mitchell and the famous TV actor Jack Webb.

When Donald owned the pageants, he gave the winners the use of a deluxe apartment within Trump Place in Manhattan.

Miss Teen USA, formed in 1983 and open to girls ages 14 to 19, was broadcast on NBC until 2007. Since then, the competition has been held at the Atlantis Paradise Island Resort, across from Nassau in The Bahamas.

In a remarkable concession to LGBT rights, Donald showed a noteworthy liberal streak when he allowed transgendered women to compete—if they'd previously won their national pageant—in his beauty pageants. This policy was markedly more liberal than that of the Republican legislators of North Carolina and Mississippi, who, in 2016 passed laws that insisted that a transgendered person must use whichever bathroom corresponded to the gender listed on his or her birth certificate.

Since his acquisition of the pageants, Donald has become involved in some widely publicized feuds, even lawsuits, with his beauty queens, some of which are described in the pages that follow:

ALICIA MACHADO
MISS UNIVERSE 1996
"She's an Eating Machine" Donald Charges

"God, what problems I had with this woman," Donald said, referring to Alicia Machado. As Miss Venezuela, she won the 1996 Miss Universe

Other than his well-publicized pledge to build a wall, what's another reason Hispanics don't like Donald Trump?

It involved his long-standing feud with Alicia Machado, Miss Venezuela, an icon of the Latino world, depicted in all her glory in the three photos above.

competition, becoming the fourth Miss Venezuela to hold that title. Her reign began at around the same time that Donald took over the pageant.

"First, she wins," he said. "Second, she gains fifty pounds. Third, I urge the committee to fire her. Fourth, I go to the gym with her in a show of support. Then she trashed me in *The Washington Post* after I stood by her the entire time. What's wrong with this picture? Anyway, the best part was the knowledge that next year, she would no longer be Miss Universe."

When Donald publicly defined her as "an eating machine," it became a tabloid scandal. More scandal was on the way. In February of 2006, she posed nude for the Mexican edition of *Playboy*, thus becoming the only Miss Universe to pose as a centerfold for any franchise of that magazine.

In 2005, she became engaged to baseball's Bobby Abreu. Then, during their engagement, she appeared on *La Granja*, a Spanish-language reality show, where she was filmed having sex with another character on the show. Shortly after that video surfaced, Abreu abruptly ended their engagement.

TARA CONNER
Should Donald Have Dethroned Miss USA 2006?
(Or Should He Have Given Her Another Chance?)

The belle of Kentucky, Tara Conner, won three beauty contests in her home state before winning the Miss USA crown in 2006.

After her coronation, reports surfaced that she'd been drinking in a setting where she was underaged at the time. Even worse, the tabloids reported that she'd been using heroin, cocaine, and crystal meth.

Some of the pageant's officials wanted to take her crown, but after she agreed to enter a drug rehabilitation program, Don-

Tara Conner, according to the New York tabloids, had gotten into trouble with drugs and alcohol. As owner of the Miss USA contest, Donald wanted to give her a "second chance."

This led to Rosie O'Donell mocking his self-imposed status as "a moral authority." Her ridicule led to one of his most famous feuds.

ald stood by her.

On *The Oprah Winfrey Show*, Donald said he wanted to give Tara a second chance for personal reasons. "My brother, Fred Trump, died of alcoholism. I believe in second chances."

Tara admitted that she had turned to drugs when she was only fourteen in the wake of her parents' separation and the death of her beloved grandfather.

Donald had moved her into an apartment at Trump Place, along with that year's title holders from the *Miss Universe* and *Miss Teen USA* pageants. Tara was alleged, as reported in an *exposé* in the *New York Daily News*, to have invited—in defiance of pageant rules—young men into her quarters. One of her defenders (unnamed in the tabloid) claimed, "Tara is just a small town girl who went wild in New York. She just couldn't handle herself. She was sneaking those nightclub guys in and out of her apartment."

Donald's defense of Tara, and his indulgence in allowing her a second chance, ballooned into one of his most notorious celebrity feuds.

ROSIE O'DONNELL

DONALD: "She's a Degenerate, Ugly, Third-Rate Fatass."
ROSIE: "He's a Gelatinous, Goopy Garden Slug with a Jell-O Orange Comb-Over."

Before her feud with Donald, Rosie O'Donnell knew him well enough for him to invite her to his wedding (to Marla Maples) reception at Mar-a-Lago in Palm Beach.

But after watching him on television granting Tara Conner a second chance, she became furious and attacked him the next day on *The View* when Barbara Walters, its host, was on vacation.

Before millions of TV viewers, Rosie mockingly said, "Donald Trump a moral authority?" Then she tossed her hair to one side to mock his orange coif.

"Left his first wife. Had an affair. Left the second wife. Had an affair. But now he's the moral compass for 20-year-olds in America? Donald, sit and spin, my friend."

She also called him "a snakeoil salesman."

Donald fired back at Rosie in the media, calling her "a slob and a fat pig. I plan to sue her. I look forward to taking lots of money from fat little Rosie."

In an interview with the *New York Daily News*, he told a reporter, "When

I saw that tape of T*he View*, I said, 'you'd better watch out, Rosie, or I'll send one of my friends over to take your girlfriend.' I imagine it would be pretty easy to take her away, considering how ugly fat Rosie looks."

[The TV star was one of a handful of openly lesbian celebrities at the time, living with her partner, Kelli, in a household with four children.]

Donald continued to hit back, claiming that "Rosie was really interested in having some sort of romance with Miss USA herself, Tara Conner." He also claimed that his friend, Barbara Walters, "can't stand Rosie. Fat Rosie hurts the program that Barbara created. I'm worth billions of dollars, and I have to listen to this fatass slob!"

[Since Rosie joined The View, *its TV audience rose some thirteen percent. On her web site, Rosie claimed, "The emperor has no clothes. The comb-over has gone ballistic."*

Gallup took a poll, finding that most of the viewers sided with Donald.

Two views of Rosie O'Donnell.

In the lower photo, she's parodying Donald for his sanctimonious judgments—"As if *he's* a role model!"

In her 2007 memoir, *Celebrity Detox*, Rosie wrote:

"Donald groaned in a strange way, almost salivating over his attack on me. Totally creepy. He was sadistic in a deeply disturbing way. It was like seeing a specimen squirming in a slide in a high school science class. Poke here and it lashes its tail. Add salt to the brine and it shrivels up."

"Donald also reminded me of a lot of garden slugs we used to get on our front steps after rains—gelatinous, goopy slugs, some five inches long, sleek and wet, leaving sticky trails in their wake."

Even Madonna got in on the act. The pop singer had been a friend of

Rosie's since they had starred together in *A League of Their Own* (1992).

Appearing on NBC's *Today Show* for an interview by Meredith Viera, Madonna said she'd heard of the Donald/Rosie feud while vacationing "in the middle of the Indian Ocean."

According to Madonna, she had e-mailed Rosie: "I wanted to hear it from the horse's mouth. Rosie is a stand-up comic, and they're known for talking about provocative things in their monologues. I feel that if every stand-up comic was penalized for saying politically incorrect things, they'd all be hung in the public square."

In her memoir, Rosie wrote that Donald "was not a human being, but a wind-up toy with Tourette's, a man who had allowed himself to get pulled so deeply into capitalism that he had turned his entire being into a product with a price tag on it; he was gift wrapped and stuffed with Styrofoam."

On TV, Donald revealed that he had spoken to Barbara Walters herself, while she was on vacation. He quoted her as saying, "I am no fan of Rosie's." The talk show host had also warned him, "You should never get in the mud with pigs."

Madonna, as she's interviewed by Meredith Viera on the *Today* show, defending Rosie against Donald.

Reporters later suggested that the real reason Madonna dropped by the show was to drum up support for her new film, the animated feature, *Arthur and the Invisibles*, which had received horrendous reviews.

Rosie later wrote, "Trump outed Barbara, dragging this septuagenarian into the fray. He wounded two women, and for what? The worst part of it was that I knew, from the get-go, twisted that he was, I knew in my heart that Barbara had said those things. In one way or another, she had betrayed me. I was Trumped."

CARRIE PREJEAN
Same-Sex Marriage & The Culture Wars

Few beauty contestants have ever been as controversial as Carrie Prejean, recipient of the double-barreled honor of having been crowned Miss California in 2009 and the first runner-up in the Miss USA pageant that same year.

The blonde-haired, green-eyed beauty was reared in an evangelical Christian household in Vista, California. A year after her birth in 1987, her parents separated.

Her opinions about homosexuals were formed when she was growing up during the long divorce proceedings of her parents, who allegedly made homosexual allegations against each other. She heard such false statements as "all men who have mustaches are gay."

As Prejean matured, her modeling career skyrocketed, leading up to her winning the Miss California competition.

She then went on to enter the Miss USA contest, competing with exceptionally beautiful women. The contest was going fine until, in front of millions of TV viewers, the controversial Perez Hilton, who is gay and was one of the judges, asked her to share her views on whether same-sex marriage should be legalized nationwide.

The gay marriage row

How Carrie Prejean lost a beauty pageant and won the Republican Right

Carrie Prejean ater claimed that she lost the Miss USA crown in 2009 for expressing her "heartfelt opinion against same-sex marriage."

Whether that was true or not, she angered millions of viewers, but also won millions of followers from the homophobic far right.

Prejean responded, "In my family, I believe that marriage should be between a man and a woman. No offense to anybody out there. But that's how I was raised."

Before that utterance, which was broadcast across the country, a beauty pageant title holder had almost never become embroiled in the fight over homosexuality.

Hilton, who was known for posting hot gossip across the internet, added a video blog to his website, disparaging her and calling her "a dumb bitch."

"She gave an awful, awful answer," he wrote. He also told ABC News that her Miss California crown "should be taken away because of her homophobia."

She later responded, "I was being dared—in front of the entire world—to give a candid answer to a serious question. I knew if I told the truth, I would lose all that I was competing for: the crown, the luxury apartment in New York, the large salary—everything that went with the Miss USA title. I also knew, or suspected, that I was the frontrunner, and if I gave the politically correct answer, I could be Miss USA."

Donald defended her response, saying, "It wasn't a bad answer. She simply stated her belief. The question was a bit unlucky, and no matter which way she answered, she was going to get killed."

Even the liberal *New York Times* weighed in, stating that her belief was representative of mainstream public opinion on the issue. "While a majority of Americans believe that gay couples should be able to enter into unions with some of the legal protection of marriage, only a minority believe that gays and lesbians should be permitted to 'marry' per se."

[Of course, that opinion would soon evolve in favor of same-sex marriages.]

Prejean's opposition to same-sex marriage endeared her to the right-wing National Organization for Marriage, which used footage of her answer for a TV ad that warned that "same-sex activists want to silence the opposition."

More trouble was on the way. Pageant organizers investigated reports that Prejean had violated the terms of her contract by not disclosing that she had posed for semi-nude photographs. When confronted, Prejean claimed, "It was legitimate modeling."

Donald more or less agreed with her. "We are in the 21st Century. We have de-

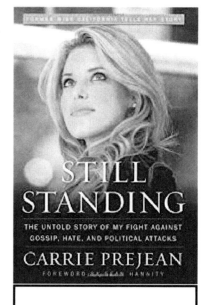

Of course, there was a book deal...of course.

termined the pictures are fine. In some cases, the photos are lovely."

Prejean continued to speak out, doubling down on an incendiary position that she might have been wise to have softened. She went on to assert a statement that many liberals denounced: "Marriage is good. There is something special about unions of husband and wife. Unless we bring men and women together, children will not have mothers and fathers."

[Thus from the mouths of babes emerges "wisdom."]

The tabloids immediately erupted with rumors that Prejean was dating the Olympic champion swimmer, Michael Phelps. He denied it, claiming "I'm not dating anybody. I'm single. My private life stays private."

When quizzed, although Prejean ducked the issue, her grandmother, Jeanette Coppolla, asserted, "Carrie and Michael go on dates—baseball games, dinners. When he's in town, he always calls her and they go out."

Phelps was also asked for an opinion about the same-sex marriage issue. On a morning TV talk show, he said, "I'm not saying I support her. I'm not saying I don't support her."

More trouble was on the way. On June 10, 2009, Donald terminated Prejean's contract, claiming that she had continued to violate its terms.

Prejean fought back, claiming that the producers of the Miss California pageant wanted her to pose nude for *Playboy*. Executives responded that they had merely passed the magazine's offer on to her, as they did all the other offers coming her way.

In August, she sued Miss California USA, charging that she had been both slandered and libeled and was made to suffer religious discrimination. She also alleged that there had been a release of her private medical records.

Pageant officials countersued, seeking profits from a book she'd written in violation of her

The most eligible bachelor of that moment, Michael Phelps, did not want to get involved in the same-sex marriage controversy.

Nor did he want to admit or deny that he was dating Carrie Prejean.

contract. It was entitled *Still Standing: The Untold Story of My Fight Against Gossip, Hate, and Political Attacks.* The pageant also sought a repayment of $5,200 lent to her for breast implants.

By November, a settlement was reached, the terms of which were not revealed. CNN later reported that the settlement was prompted by the alleged discovery of a "sex tape" involving Prejean.

SHEENA MONNIN
MISS PENNSYLVANIA 2012??
A Judge Orders a Miss USA Contestant to Pay Donald $5 Million for Denouncing His Pageant as "Rigged"

A brunette beauty, Sheena Monnin, seemingly made a career out of winning beauty pageants. Her titles, among many others, included Miss Florida USA (2006), Miss Texas USA (2009), and Miss Pennsylvania USA (2012). She was also, amid huge controversy, a (losing) contestant in the *Miss USA Pageant* in 2012.

She later became the founder and CEO of Custom Life Design, an employee assessment and training company. A psychologist, she is also the author of a self-help book, *Hands on the Wheel: Getting Control of Your Life.*

On the night Monnin lost the Miss USA contest, she posted on Facebook the accusation that the pageant was "fraudulent, lacking in morals, inconsistent, and in many ways trashy." She also accused pageant organizers of working from a script in which the final sixteen contestants and the top five finalists were all pre-determined.

Donald called her a "beautiful young woman who had sour grapes because she was not among the final contestants."

In protest, she relinquished her titles of Miss Pennsylvania "rather than compromise my values. I feel the world has a right to know the truth about the pageant. I'm standing up against this

Sheena Monnin...lawsuits, accusations that the contest was rigged, denunciations. "I'm taking a stand against that bully, Mr. Trump."

bully, Donald Trump."

He sued her for $5 million, charging defamation. Because she failed to show up in court on the day of her hearing (based on what was later defined as faulty legal advice from her lawyer) a default judgment was rendered against her for that amount.

"We applaud the judge's very articulate thirty-page decision," said Michael Cohen, Donald's attorney. "We will pursue our rights available to Mr. Trump."

Later, Monnin—after months of inconvenience, expense, and despair— sued her attorney and was able to recover expenses and also resolve the lawsuit.

BIKINIS, BOSOMS, & HIGH HEELS: MISS WORLD GOES TO NIGERIA
(With Death Threats, Decapitations, Mob Violence, & Religious Fanaticism)

In 2002, Donald had set his sights on acquiring the Miss World pageant, which he viewed as the major competition to his Miss Universe Pageant. It was owned by Julia Morley, a Londoner and the widow of Eric Morley, who had organized it in 1951 and controlled it until his death in 2000.

As reported in *Vanity Fair*, Donald's intention was to wrest control of the Miss World Pageant from her at a bargain price.

"Every time I try to put my head up there in the United States, Trump used to try to blow it off," Morley alleged. "He actually took legal action against me for having a Miss World USA contest."

When Judy Bachrach of *Vanity Fair* contacted Donald for his response, he neither admitted nor denied the charge. "He fairly crowed about the hopes of acquiring the Miss World competition," Bachrach wrote.

"Yeah, I'd buy it for almost nothing," he said. "If I did, I would make it better—or maybe I'd shut it down."

He was informed that Morley was trying to make the swimsuits of the contestants more modest.

He chuckled at that: "When I bought Miss Universe, the bathing suits got smaller and the heels got higher—and the ratings skyrocketed."

Weeks later, Donald avidly followed the gory details of the Miss World pageant. It was staged that year in Nigeria, a nation with a large Muslim population, during the holy month of Ramadan.

It was a disaster—a cultural clash of epic (and for the contestants, terrifying) proportions. Some ninety scantily clad beauty queens from around the world were flown to Nigeria's capital of Abuja.

The November pageant with so much naked flesh on display set off a series of bloody riots that led to 250 people dead and thousands injured. Machetes were used to chop off heads; mosques were burned to the ground, and bystanders were "necklaced" with burning tires. Hundreds of protesters attacked others.

"Down with beauty!" was the rallying cry of the day. "Miss World is an abomination! *Allahu Akbar!*"

Julia Morley, depicted above at one of her contests in 2001, operated the Miss World Pageant, but in the mistake of her life brought all that exposed flesh and all those "western decadent" photo-ops to a Muslim nation, Nigeria, during Ramadan.

The result: Mob riots, beheadings, and multiple deaths by "necklaces" crafted from burning tires.

Harrassed and terrified, the scantily clad contestants fled from Nigeria and from Miss World, grateful to escape with their lives.

A Nigerian woman journalist, age 21, who had written about the pageant, had to flee for her life. The young contestants also fled Nigeria. On the way to the airport, their buses passed charred bodies and burning cars. Muslim fundamentalists had been outraged at the provocation of the pageant.

Back in London, headlines screamed SCRAP MISS WORLD.

Morley defended her decision. "To tell the truth, before I left, I thought Sharia was a girl's name. I did! I swear to you. I was totally ignorant. I got into big shit trouble because I hardly realized what I was letting myself in for."

In New York, Donald was no longer interested in acquiring the Miss World pageant. "I was shocked at Morley's decision to fly the girls into Nigeria. The pageant has been so tarnished by the stupidity of going to Nigeria. I wouldn't consider a purchase now. Not unless the price was ridiculously low. You can't go to Nigeria! Everybody knows that!"

UNIVISION
Donald at War with Latino American Television

In September of 2015, in a decision based on Donald's comments in June about illegal immigration, both NBC and Univision, the Spanish language TV network, dropped the *Miss USA* pageant and backed off from their business relationships with Donald.

As part of their settlement, he bought out NBC's fifty percent ownership of the pageant, thereby emerging as its sole owner.

Three days later, he sold the company to WME (William Morris Endeavor), a talent agency founded in Beverly Hills in 2009, and its satellite, IMG, which WME had acquired for $2.4 billion in 2013. Trump then filed a $500 million lawsuit against Univision, alleging defamation and breach of

When Donald made remarks against Mexicans that his partner, Univision, considered racist, the Spanish language TV network withdrew their ties to him, which led to lawsuits.

But the network has long had trouble for broadcasting anti-gay slurs and shows that treated women like disposable objects.

The scene above depicts finals for "Miss Mundial Brasil 2014" on the entertainment talk show *El Gordo y la Flaca*. The show—entitled "Eight Reasons to Fire up the Jacuzzi"— invited guests to take a dip in an on-set hot tub.

contract.

In February of 2016, he and Univision reached a settlement, the terms of which were not made public. Also in 2016, in the void created by the departures of NBC and Univision, Fox signed on to broadcast the *Miss USA* pageant.

Donald told a reporter, "I've exited the beauty contest business. I've got the most beautiful woman in the world waiting for me every night atop Trump Tower."

THE APPRENTICE:
HOW TO BE A WINNER
(aka How Not to Get Fired)

It was a hot day on Venice Beach, south of Los Angeles, as a young man, transplanted to the West Coast from London, hawked T-shirts hoping to eke out a living. One of them was emblazoned with the large message FUCK ME NOW! In his chocolate brown felt Akubra, the young man, known as Mark Burnett, evoked Indiana Jones.

This son of Archie and Jean Burnett, both of them factory workers at Ford Motors, he had enlisted in the British Army at the age of seventeen, advancing into a Section Commander in the Parachute Regiment. He had seen action during Britain's short war with Argentina over the Falklands.

In 1982, he'd emigrated to the United States, where, for a while, he worked as a live-in nanny, looking after two boys for $250 a week. Wanting a bigger slice of "the American pie," he had saved his money and was able to

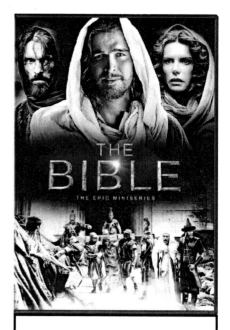

One of Mark Burnett's greatest successes, pre-Donald, was *The Bible*, a ten-hour *History Channel* series seen by millions of viewers.

purchase *Eco-Challenge*, a TV show devoted to competitions. This was the doorway to his career as a TV producer, which, in time, would bring him untold millions.

He continued to work his way up the ladder, and by the summer of 2000, he was producing the hit TV reality show, *Survivor*. By 2009, it had been designated as the Number One reality series of all time.

Burnett's single greatest success was *The Bible*, a ten-hour History Channel series based upon Biblical stories. It was seen by 100 million viewers, becoming in 2013 the top mini-series ever.

[The Bible was developed and produced after Burnett met Donald Trump.]

One day, when Burnett was hawking those $18 T-shirts on Venice Beach, a friend handed him a book called *The Art of the Deal* by Donald Trump, an author he'd never heard of. However, by the following morning, he said., "I have become a Donald Trump fan."

A week later, he called Donald in New York, and the mogul, familiar with Burnett's name because of *Survivor*, took the call. Burnett immediately made his sales pitch, claiming that he wanted to produce another reality show to be entitled *The Apprentice*. "I see you as the star of the series, a kind of businessman's *Survivor*."

"Donald was all ears," Burnett said. "A lot of big CEOs shun publicity. Not Donald. It was obvious to me that he loved the limelight. That was just the kind of celebrity host I needed."

A meeting was set up at Trump Tower. In terms of millions of dollars, this might rank up there with Stanley meeting Livingstone in darkest Africa. "Within fifteen minutes of talking to Donald, I knew he was THE MAN. He

The fine print of this cover of industry magazine *Ad Week* described Mark Burnett (depicted above) as " the man behind *Survivor, Shark Tank,* and *A.D. Now.* "

Burnett was also the genius who pitched the idea of hosting a TV show called *The Apprentice* to Donald Trump.

could make fast decisions, and quick ones at that. He didn't waste time. He gets right to the point. He's a creation of instinct, and his instinct is invariably right. Most of all, he's a natural born showman."

"I wanted this charismatic businessman for my partner," Burnett said. "Ronald Reagan might have been called 'The Great Communicator,' but I found that Donald was even more skilled than the former President. Unless it's inherited wealth, no billionaire is a damn wallflower. It takes intelligence and aggression to get where Donald is."

After reading a synopsis, Donald agreed with Burnett that the New York business world "is a jungle filled with wild flesh eaters."

"There are more snakes here and more things that can kill you than any other jungle in the world. Even Tarzan would get snake bite walking the canyons of Wall Street. A wannabe may be a genius but lack the killer instinct to survive in the dog-eat-dog business world. The city can eat some of these kids alive."

When their meeting ended, Donald and Burnett shook hands. "It's going to be a big hit," Donald said. "I have this gut instinct. Let's go for it."

Before Burnett had walked through his door, Donald had turned down at least seven TV producers who wanted him to go before the cameras with a reality show.

"They wanted to follow me around with cameras, watching me make deals, brush my teeth, and, most certainly, comb my hair. None of this appealed to me. I don't do business that way. Who do they think I am? Anna Nicole Smith?"

A secret deal was worked out between Burnett and NBC. Donald would host the first season, a sixteen-episode series. If *The Apprentice* were moderately successful, with the intention of boosting ratings, they would, for the second season, hire a big CEO name like Microsoft's Bill Gates, or perhaps Virgin Atlantic's Richard Branson to take over for him.

After the first casting call went out, an estimated 215,000 contestants applied from twenty of America's biggest cities. The show was billed as "The Ultimate Job Interview."

After signing the contract, Donald

said, "I was a real schmuck to believe what Mark told me, that the TV show would take up only three hours of my time each week. It ended up taking some thirty hours, but I didn't mind."

He admitted that as the series was launched, he became somewhat of a babe magnet. "All the women on the show flirted with me—consciously or unconsciously. That's to be expected. A sexual dynamic is always present between people, unless you're asexual."

The Apprentice was first telecast on January 8, 2004, and the ratings "went through the ceiling" in Donald's words. An average of some twenty million viewers—he claimed twenty-five million—tuned in. Eventually, it outdistanced the enormously popular CBS hit, *CSI*, which aired during the same time slot.

The first season's finale, which aired on April 15, 2004, was a blockbuster, helping the series emerge as the most highly rated on any network for viewers aged 18 to 49.

According to Donald, "I appeal to millions out there who have dreams of caviar and wishes for the bubbly instead of water."

The degree to which it became a hit came as a surprise. It was one of the highest-rated entertainment shows of the 2003-4 season. Donald was on a roll. The telecast of his Miss Universe Pageant (2004), broadcast from Ecuador, drew an audience of ten and a half million viewers.

Not only that, his 2003 book, *How to Get Rich*, hit *The New York Times'* best-seller list. He subtitled it, "Big deals from the star of *The Apprentice.*"

The so-called "smoochathon" of TV, Robin Leach, who pioneered *Lifestyles of the Rich & Famous*, said, "Donald made rich people not ashamed to be rich and brash. He is the American Dream."

As a billionaire and "household name," he didn't want to stray too far from Trump Tower. "Let the fuckers come to me," he said.

For access to "the boardroom" where many of the scenes were filmed, he had only to take an elevator to one of the building's lower floors for shooting to begin.

Robin Leach made a career on TV of invading the lifestyles of the rich and famous.

His astonishment at "The Donald" is reflected in his open mouth gaping.

In another area within Trump Tower, a studio for filming commercials was installed. Every day, right from his desk, he broadcast to 400 radio stations for the Clear Channel Communications Group.

He was a star and an entertainer, although for a time, he didn't want to play up his status as a TV reality show star, fearing it might turn off some investors who might have preferred a more staid and conservative business mogul with less of a "show-biz" style.

With all of his new-found fame, he was soon inundated with deals calling for him to endorse products at very lucrative terms. *Fortune,* in its April 26, 2004 edition, extolled his status as a TV celebrity. "He's never been hotter," the magazine proclaimed. "Just ask him!"

A month earlier, *Newsweek* had featured him on its cover.

In the 21st Century, a Gallup Poll found that ninety-eight percent of all Americans knew the name of Donald Trump, even some children twelve and below.

After the success of *The Apprentice,* the rap artist and hip-hop star, Jay-Z, boasted, "I am the ghetto's answer to Donald Trump!"

Thousands of business requests flooded into Donald's office. "People all over the world were requesting a job in Mr. Trump's organization," said his chief aide and "gatekeeper," Norma Foerderer.

During these tsunamis of publicity, he claimed, "I'm selling apartments like crazy. And I'm still the biggest real estate developer in New York. I've even been asked to be the grand marshal marching in the annual Israeli parade down Fifth Avenue."

He also like to brag about the success of his books, beginning with *The Art of the Deal,* first published in 1987. "My books sell like hotcakes. I get a great kick at looking at my name on top of all the bestseller lists and telling everybody to go fuck themselves."

He was even picking up endorsements from seasoned politicians who thought that he should run for President of the United States. "Henry Kissinger urged me to do the run, and he told me he suspected I would win. A lot of other big politicos thought the same—I won't name them. I listened

Eliot Spitzer was the former Attorney General and later Governor of New York State before he was disgraced for pursuing—and paying off—prostitutes.

Even he was impressed with the marketing power of the Donald Trump name.

to them, but right now, I love what I'm doing. I don't want to give up my day job."

Eliot Spitzer, the New York Attorney General, said, "Donald has transformed himself, and his name is one of the most identifiable brands in the world. He's not Coca-Cola, but he knows how to capture the imagination of the public. When people see his name, they associate it with good quality and a certain degree of flamboyance. He's part showman."

"If Bill Gates is the quintessential innovator, then Donald is the quintessential deal maker, and part of *The Art of the Deal* is marketing, a certain flamboyance, and tons of self-promotion," Spitzer said. "No one in America knows how to promote himself more than Donald."

"I'm not a celebrity," Donald proclaimed. "I'm a super-celebrity. I showed that money isn't everything. It doesn't guarantee happiness. In real life, money isolates you from other people."

At the conclusion of any year's series, the one person who remained unfired and still standing among the sixteen other wannabes would emerge as the supreme victor and become an apprentice to Donald at the salary of $250,000 a year. He or she would be assigned with managing a project for the Trump Organization, perhaps (but not necessarily) one associated with real estate.

During the run of the show, Donald featured all three of the children he'd fathered with Ivana: Ivanka, Don Jr., and Eric. Melania Trump was also a regular on the show, hawking her fashion and cosmetic products. Ivanka's fashion products were also featured.

Jeff Zucker, president of NBC Universal Television Group, had liked Burnett's proposal. "Donald is a tireless promoter, especially of himself, and Mark—based on the success of *Survivor*—was the ideal producer."

Zucker immediately saw the allure of the "Trump *zeitgeist*. He's the quintessential made-in-America story: He's been up. He's been down. He's been back up again. After all, he wrote *The Art of the Comeback*."

Of course, there were those behind

Jeff Zucker, president of NBC, formed a triumvirate with Donald and Mark Burnett to launch *The Apprentice*. He felt that Donald's flamboyance would be ideal in making the reality show a hit on TV.

There were many naysayers at NBC, many of whom viewed Donald as a "has been," but Zucker's wisdom won the day.

341

the scenes, who objected to the show, citing the fact that "Donald is fodder for the gossip columns, especially tabloid scandal. That might diminish how seriously he would be taken as a business executive."

Zucker disagreed. "He combines gossip, a razor-sharp business brain, and a social presence that could be intimidating on camera. No social figure in New York can top him."

Incredibly, many at NBC initially interpreted Donald as a has-been, belonging to the previous century and "all that debacle with his Atlantic City casinos."

Appearing on *The Larry King Show,* on February 27, 2004, in reference to *The Apprentice,* Donald said, "We have a really good system, where I go into the board room and rattle like a lunatic to these kids, and I leave and go off and build my buildings. And then it gets good ratings, and they pay me. Can you believe this?"

He received enormous praise from people in the industry. Producer Harvey Weinstein called from the West Coast, telling him, "You're the number one star in Hollywood."

Donald's youthful dream of being a mover-and-shaker in the entertainment industry had come true. "In the history of TV, nothing like this has ever happened," crowed Donald. "You know you're a star when Melania and I walk down the street. Taxi drivers slow down and shout at me, 'Trump! You're fired!'"

From Bayonne, New Jersey, to Santa Monica, California, eager contestants arrived to be on his show. Some of them were "token" African Americans and Asians. One black woman, Omarosa Manigault Stallworth, stood out. She was said to air her claws and bring up the charge of racism. Donald himself admitted, "The audiences soon found out she was the Wicked Witch."

One ominously terrifying contestant, when he was fired, gave Trump that same look that Tony Perkins in *Psycho* gave Janet Leigh in the shower before he slashed her nude body. Sometimes, a candidate would beg, "Mr. Trump,

On *The Apprentice,* contestant Jennifer Crisafulli got the boot because of an indiscreet remark she made.

In trying to explain why her team "failed" at their task of opening a restaurant, she said, "It was because of those two old fat Jewish ladies...the pinnacle of the New York jaded old bags."

The next words she heard were, "You're fired!"

342

please don't fire me…pretty please!"

Fired during the fourth episode of the first season, Jennifer Crisafulli appeared on the *Today* show. "What you don't see is there are little ittybitty bullets that come flying, invisible bullets, out of Trump's fingers into your chest, and you're like *pu-pu-pu-pu-pu*. Oh, it was awful, just awful. I got canned in front of forty million people, maybe more. I was devastated."

The 32-year-old bodacious brunette from one of Manhattan's top real estate brokerages had made a slur against "old fat Jewish ladies." That had sealed her fate. After being so politically incorrect, she was shown to the door.

***

"Most people think I'm a fucking flamethrower," Donald said. "Historically, I've had people who stay with me for a long time. There is one exception. If I find an employee stealing from me, I fire them with dragon fire, an act they'll remember the rest of their thieving lives."

After seeing his father perform, Don Jr. told his Dad, "You missed your calling. You should have been an actor."

Donald was no stranger to TV. He had made appearances as a caricature of himself on TV and in films which included *Home Alone 2, Lost in New York; The Nanny; The Fresh Prince of Bel-Air;* and *Wall Street: Money Never Sleeps.* He also appeared in a cameo in an episode of the TV series, *Sex and the City.* A member of the Screen Actors Guild, based on previous earnings and dues paid during the course of his membership, he receives an annual pension of some $110,000 a year.

For the most part, his appearances got rave reviews. Steve Wynn compared his deadpan delivery to the master of deadpan delivery, Jack Benny himself.

Robert Wright, president of NBC, praised Donald's acting ability: "Marilyn Monroe might have required 58 takes to utter three words. But Donald Trump is known as 'one

Omarosa Stallworth was a contestant on the first season of *The Apprentice* and later returned for the TV sequel, *Celebrity Apprentice.*

TV Guide listed her as one of the "60 Nastiest Villains of All Time."

take.' He's better at getting it right the first time than any other actor or performer I've ever met."

Donald also won praise for his on-camera presence from a Hollywood bigwig, Alex Yemenidjian, CEO of MGM. "He has a narcissistic self-confidence that is truly amazing. There's never been a scene-stealer like him since W.C. Fields. He has the strong presence of any of the superstars of Hollywood's Golden Age. I could just hear him as Rhett Butler telling Scarlett, 'Frankly, my dear, I don't give a damn.'"

Competition among the *über*-rich?

Bill Gates: "Compared to Donald, I'm the modest type."

The co-founder of Microsoft, Bill Gates, defined by many experts as the wealthiest person in the world, said, "Unlike the rest of us, Jack Welch and myself, maybe Warren Buffett, we are not braggarts, touting our success. Donald goes against the grain. He flaunts his achievements without shame, certainly without modesty."

"There can be no doubt, present Donald with a microphone or a camera, and he performs," said Regis Philbin, his friend. "He has the look, the reputation, and a ton of charisma."

Russell Simmons, the hip-hop mogul, said, "Donald is a real life Richie Rich. He shares his toys with you. A lot of rich white guys tell you to go to hell as they munch their creamy cakes. They're fucking cake-aholics. That's not Donald. He not only enjoys his toys, he plays with his toys. He is the official bling-bling white guy."

In his book *TrumpNation*, Timothy L. O'Brien wrote:

> *"The Apprentice showcased Donald Trump's one-of-a-kind, carnivalesque traits: The High Plains Drifter glower, the eyebrows that wandered around his forehead like fuzzy Slinkies, the bicycle helmet hairdo, the toughest-guy-in-the-bar swagger, the Day-Glo silk ties, and above all his unfailing on-spot assessments of contestants' strengths and weaknesses — and an unflinching willingness to say exactly what every viewer was already thinking about the ambitious, conniving, befuddled, and aspiring apprentices. Donald, as ringmaster and court jester, was channeling America."*

In trying to explain the success of the show, Burnett said, "People always stop to watch a train wreck. People like rubbernecking on the freeway. On *The Apprentice,* they watched the train wreck in living color."

Jeff Zucker at NBC claimed, "*The Apprentice* is really about making it big in the Big Apple with the Big Guy."

In case anybody didn't already know it, Donald claimed, "In the history of the business world, all the Wall Street Greats, not a single man has ever risen to be the Number One star on television."

For his first season on *The Apprentice,* he was paid $700,000—that's about $50,000 per episode. When the show became a big success, he was paid $3 million per episode, making him one of the highest-paid personalities in the history of the medium. During the summer of 2015, right after he announced his run for the presidency, a press release stated that NBC/Universal had shelled out some $215 million for his fourteen seasons as host of the show. That earned him a star on the Hollywood Walk of Fame.

In spite of the praise for Donald's performance, he came in for his share of criticisms, notably from Jeffrey Sonnenfeld, an associate dean at the Yale School of Management. He called *The Apprentice* a "vulgar show, peddling deception, trickery, and sex. The lesson is that leadership selection is developed in a process similar to musical chairs at a Hooter's Restaurant."

Donald responded to the attack. "That guy claims there's too much sex, that it doesn't exist in the business world. What a laugh! Believe you me, it exists and bigtime. I know from personal experience."

Actually, Donald had to lecture some of

Donald's favorite movies: In *Gone With the Wind,* he could identify with the swashbuckling Rhett Butler as played by Clark Gable holding Scarlett O'Hara (Vivien Leigh) in his powerful arms.

In *Citizen Kane,* he identified with the Orson Welles character, based on the real life William Randolph Hearst, the press baron.

345

his female contestants for "making their hawking look too much like hooking." He told them not to rely too much on mini-skirts and plunging *décolletage*.

In one episode, when male and female contestants were sent out on Wall Street to sell lemonade at a stand as part of their "assignments," the women offered kisses or gave out their phone number to male clients. Donald warned the women that "sex for sale" was more appropriate for a Hollywood casting couch than a Wall Street boardroom.

Penn Jillette, the magician, TV host, and author, attacked the contest as "venal people clawing at stupid, soulless stuff in front of the modern day Scrooge McDuck in order to stay famous. Trump just does what he wants, which is mostly pontificating to people who are sucking up to him."

***

During the second season of *The Apprentice*, one reporter was invited to fly to Palm Beach with Donald where he learned some personal data about him: His two favorite movies were Orson Welles' *Citizen Kane* and *Gone With the Wind*; he liked to devour a package of Oreos while he was watching movies; and his favorite movie star was Clint Eastwood.

"All those Sergio Leone westerns…" Donald said. "Nobody was cooler. He's a Republican, you know."

Donald and Burnett packed each episode with product placements, hawking various Trump enterprises along with Crest toothpaste or Pepsi-Cola. In the first three years of the show's run, this dynamic duo shared $100 million for product placement, the fees averaging some $1.5 million per episode. During the run of the series, Donald raked in an estimated $500 million in entertainment-related income, cashing in on books, speeches, beauty pageants, all of it based around *The Apprentice*.

Forbes magazine jokingly suggested: "Imagine President Donald J. Trump giving his inaugural address on a chilly afternoon in early 2017. Between grand pronouncements, he sips an Aquafina bottle sitting on his lecture—and gets a seven-figure check for his trouble."

The success of *The Apprentice*, where he portrayed "the titan tycoon of the business world" caused him embarrassment.

Although a business genius on TV, in his personal life, he was going through his worst financial crisis, declaring bankruptcy for his Atlantic City casinos.

Many associates, even his own sister, Maryanne Trump Barry, warned about the danger of overexposure. "There is such a thing as the public tiring of a media star," she said to him. "Where Donald Trump is concerned, I wonder if there is such a thing as over-exposure."

In response, Donald answered. "The more famous I get, the more offers pour in."

On August 12, 2004, he starred in a TV ad for a toy company, Hasbro, which had created *Trump...the Game* in which players made Trump-like deals, perhaps earning a million (play-money) dollars in the (fictional) aftermath. He later claimed that the Manufacturers Hanover Bank, which owned Hasbro, had paid him $5 million for his appearance and endorsement.

As a public speaker, Donald was in great demand for appearances at lecture halls as far away as Australia. He was getting $350,000 per speech, the highest speaker's fee in America, far more than Hillary Clinton got. One day, he was offered a deal to present three separate speeches, the first at 10AM and the third and final one scheduled for sometime in the late evening. "Had I accepted, I could have made $850,000 in just one day."

When he hosted *Saturday Night Live,* he told the audience, "Television is just a hobby for me. I'm primarily occupied with my real estate holdings; my best-selling books, and making love to women who have won prizes for their beauty—but not anymore, because I have a girlfriend."

He was referring to Melania Knauss.

On October 15, 2004, Donald made a difficult decision: He would appear at the New York Hilton for a Friars Club roast. He knew it could be brutal, even though the "roasters," for the most part, were his friends.

The zingers delivered that night were devastating. One of the best of them came from Jeff Zucker at NBC. He told the audience that he was unable to attend Donald's wedding, "but I'll catch the next one."

In another swipe, Zucker declared, "Donald has his dating down pat. There's the picking of the ring, the meeting of the parents, the meeting of the grandparents, and then the realization that he went to school with the grandparents."

At the end, struggling to conceal his annoyance, Donald urged the audience, "Go home, go to work, and watch your language."

The New York Times called it "A slash-and-burn salute from a bunch of foul-mouthed comedians lobbing off-color remarks about Trump's career, his looks, his spouse or spouses, his sexual prowess, and even—God forbid—his hair.'"

CELEBRITY APPRENTICE
A Forum Where Nearly Forgotten "Has-Beens"
Can Resuscitate Some Public Recognition

After six seasons, a format for a spinoff series was introduced, *The Celebrity Apprentice,* a variation of *The Apprentice* series. Like its precursor, the show's opening theme song was "For the Love of Money" by the O'-Jays.

Whereas the original version had focused on unknown wannabes striving against each other, this variation on the original theme focused on apprentices culled from among famous, or moderately famous, celebrities who would compete against other celebrities. Frankly, many of these celebrities were has-beens who still had some degree of name recognition. All of them competed to win money for the charitable organizations of their choice.

Celebrity contestants derived from the worlds of sports (Dennis Rodman, for example), or music, radio, reality TV, and dozens of other professions.

British tabloid editor and later talk show host Piers Morgan was once declared the winner for a season. The late Joan Rivers triumphed in the 2009 season. Season three was won by musician Bret Michaels.

MARTHA STEWART
Donald at War with the Doyenne of Domesticity
"Martha Stewart should Stick to Baking Her Cakes"
—Donald Trump

There was yet another spin-off from the original theme. In 2005: *The Apprentice: Martha Stewart,* featuring the lifestyle mogul, was launched. It only survived for a single season.

Stewart had excelled in publishing, broadcasting, merchandising, and electronic commerce, and had written numerous best-selling books (one of the most successful of which had been entitled *Martha).* She had also published and been the creative force behind a magazine called *Martha Stewart Living,* and hosted a TV show, *Martha Stewart Living* (1993-2005).

In March of 2004, based on charges related to the ImClone insider trading affair, she was found guilty of felony charges of conspiracy, obstruction of Justice, and making false statements to Federal investigators. In July of 2004, she was sentenced to serve a five-month term in a Federal correctional facility and a two-year period of supervised release, five months of which were electronically monitored.

After her (hugely embarrassing) stint in prison, she made a comeback in 2005, and launched *Martha*, a TV show that ran from 2005 to 2012.

Both Donald's *The Apprentice* and its short-lived spinoff, *Martha Stewart Apprentice*, were produced by Mark Burnett. From the beginning, her ratings were poor.

Lloyd Allen, her biographer *(Being Martha)*, wrote: "On *The Apprentice*, Martha showed the side of her that is a kinder, gentler boss. The contestants ate off beautiful Martha Stewart plates and slept on Martha Stewart sheets from Kmart."

On the air, whenever she had to fire one of her contestants, in contrast to the "show-no-mercy" tradition of Donald, she let the poor soul down nicely, saying "You just don't fit in."

Originally, or so it was rumored, the executives thought Stewart could be so successful that she might replace Donald altogether. "Millions would watch if Martha came on his show and shouted at him, 'You're fired!'" said the executive.

When Donald heard that rumor, he exploded in anger. "Having Stewart on a spin-off has been a mistake for everybody," he charged. "She's hurt-

Martha Stewart was better at baking cakes than she was in hosting her version of *Celebrity Apprentice*, at least according to The Donald. Her show soon faded from the air.

Appearances can be deceiving. Donald and Martha were not friends—more like jealous rivals.

ing my own ratings. What moron thought she'd be so successful that she could replace me on a hit TV show?"

She shot back, "Donald's criticism of me is mean-spirited and reckless."

When he heard that, he fired back: "Your performance was terrible, boring."

Ostensibly based on its poor ratings Martha's spin-off series was not renewed for a second season.

When she failed, Donald had only kind remarks to make. But before it was over, however, she and Donald tangled. Then she accused him of not wanting her to have a successful series. "You wanted it jinxed," she charged. He denied that.

"YOU'RE FIRED !"

—NBC to Donald about the renewal of his contract for another season of The Apprentice, *based partly on his divisive image, and partly on legalities associated with his upcoming bid for the presidency*

Donald, who had not fully defined himself as a politician way back in 2004, fully supported President George W. Bush for re-election that year.

[Twelve busy years later, in May of 2016, neither Baby Bush nor Daddy Bush would return the favor, announcing they were not going to endorse Donald as the Republican Party's nominee. Both of them harbored ill will toward Donald for continuously trashing their brother and son, "low energy" Jeb Bush, during the Republican Primaries.]

Donald, however, remained friendly with 2004's Democratic nominee, John Kerry.

According to Donald, "He (Kerry) praised my negotiating skills and even suggested that when he was elected President, he might appoint me to be his Middle East envoy."

Kerry allegedly told him, "You'd be the best person to settle the Arab-Israeli conflict."

Donald boasted, "It would take me just two weeks to reach an agreement between these two bitter rivals."

***

Early in 2015, NBC was prepared to proceed with a renewal of *The Apprentice* for its 15th season. But Donald—perhaps tired of the series after such a long involvement—was not ready to sign on. Privately, he was discussing with friends and associates a possible run for the presidency.

Actually, his past and present roles might have, to an increasing degree, been in conflict. When Donald raised the issue about President Obama's birthplace, suggesting that he might have been born in Kenya, some pundits publicly called for NBC to fire him from *The Apprentice*. Liberal political commentator Lawrence O'Donnell led the attack, as did former congressman Anthony Weiner.

Media experts speculated about the extent to which Donald's controversial political statements had contributed to the decline in ratings for *The Apprentice*. It was also noted that after the debut of his campaign for the presidency, many other Trump-associated businesses had a fall-off in sales.

By the end of June, 2015, NBC was deluged with negative reactions to Donald's campaign speech—infamously known as the "Mexican Rapist Proclamation."

In a statement, and in reaction, NBC said, "Due to the recent derogatory statement by Donald Trump regarding immigrants, NBC/Universal is ending its business relationship with him."

There was another problem that made it impossible for Donald to return to his job as the series' host: After he announced his bid for the presidency, he was subject to

When Donald learned that NBC had hired Arnold Schwarzenegger to replace him as host of *The Apprentice*, he reportedly said, "The Terminator will probably end up terminating my hit TV series.

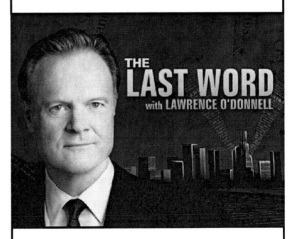

MSNBC's implacable anti-Donald fixture: Lawrence O'Donnell.

a Federally mandated policy requiring that TV stations give equal time to every candidate involved in the same electoral campaign.

In September of 2015, NBC announced that the faded actor, the former Mr. Muscleman and Mr. Universe, and the former governor of California, Arnold Schwarzenegger, would become the host of *The Apprentice* for the 2016-2017 season.

As *Forbes* magazine later wrote, "Should Trump tire of politics, he can take comfort in the fact there's always a place in the entertainment business for washed-up elected officials, as evidenced by his replacement on *The Apprentice*, Governor Arnold Schwarzenegger himself."

Early retrospectives on the Trump campaign, as published by *Mad* magazine and the *New York Daily News* featured insights from *"What, Me Worry?"* Alfred E. Neuman and Sarah (*"la Stupida"*) Palin.

PART TWO

THE SUMMER OF TRUMP

DONALD ANNOUNCES HIS PRESIDENTIAL CANDIDACY

IN THE BEGINNING, with Melania, Donald descended an escalator and moved toward a podium, some microphones, cameras, and news reporters.

Chapter Fifteen

A TV ENTERTAINER & REAL ESTATE MOGUL
Announces His Run for President of the United States

MEXICANS
"They're Bringing Drugs. They're Bringing Crime. They're Rapists!"

MUSLIMS
Donald Pledges to Bar Them from Entry into America

INSULTING HIS GOP RIVALS
"They're Losers! And They're Pathetic.
Especially Low-Energy Jeb Bush."

Although Bloggers and Pundits Predict His Downfall,
Donald Emerges "With More Lives Than Rasputin"

In 2014, supporters of Donald Trump had approached him in his office at Trump Tower and invited him to run for governor of New York. After politely thanking them, he said, "I have much bigger political plans than that. Stay tuned!"

As his political advisor, Roger Stone said, "Donald wanted to climb a higher mountain. How many great hotels, great buildings, great golf courses, can you build?"

Donald Trump singled out Japan, China, and Mexico for taking advantage of the United States. "When do we beat Mexico to the border?" he asked. "They're laughing at us, at our stupidity."

On June 16, 2015, the height of the mountain he wanted to climb was made evident to the world. Hundreds of supporters gathered in the atrium of Trump Tower listening to the sounds of Neil Young's "Rockin' the Free World."

"And now they're beating us economically. They are not our friends, believe me. And they're killing us economically."

Down the escalator descended Donald Trump, preceded by his wife, Melania, in a couture dress. As a former model, she posed as stiff and photogenic as a mannequin.

During a forty-minute speech, Donald made history, as he announced that he was running as a candidate for President of the United States on the Republican ticket, an alliance from which he had bolted so many times before. His goal, he stated, was to "make America great again."

Then he delivered an anti-immigration speech heard around the world.

"America has become a dumping ground for everybody else's problems," he charged. Then he paused a moment to listen to the applause.

"When Mexico sends you its people, these aren't the best and the finest. They're sending people who have a lot of problems, and they're bringing those problems to us. They're bringing drugs. They're bringing crime They're rapists. And some, I assume, are good people."

"It's coming from more than Mexico. It's coming probably from the Middle East. But we don't know. Because we have no protection, and we have no competence, we don't know what's happening. And it's got to stop and it's got to stop fast. As President of the United States, I will build a great wall on our southern border. And I will have Mexico pay for that wall."

As he moved through his stunning diatribe, he pronounced the American dream dead. He attacked President Obama as incompetent, and criticized American trade deals, lambasting Obamacare and the dour U.S. economy. He promised, "I will be the greatest jobs President God ever created. Our country needs a truly great leader, and we need a truly great leader *now*. We need a leader who wrote *The Art of the Deal*."

As for his opponents also seeking the GOP nod, he denounced them as "sweating dogs. How are they going to defeat ISIS? I don't think it's going to happen."

His well-groomed family, each member looking like a model transplanted from the pages of *Vogue* or *GQ*, came under the immediate scrutiny of television cameras. Collectively, they generated a portrait of the American Dream come true: A family who had everything, even good looks (not an ugly one among them). His entourage was the best dressed, the best fed, and the best educated, living a lavish lifestyle. Donald could be safe in the knowledge that his children and their children's children would be provided for during decades to come.

When his speech was over, the sound of the Neil Young song once again blared through the atrium, and Donald and Melania disappeared into their Versailles-like apartments "on top of the world," at the summit of Trump Tower. "The Man Who Would Be King" had officially entered the presidential race.

Although his cheering squad applauded wildly, the worldwide reaction was mostly negative. His anti-immigration rhetoric seemed to appeal to the dark side of millions of Americans.

His hometown paper, the *New York Daily News*, ran a shocking frontpage Photoshopped picture of Donald with a red nose and lips under the "Second Coming" headline: CLOWN RUNS FOR PREZ.

Of course, he would become fodder for late night comedians on television.

Donald had tangled with David Letterman before, but the once popular TV talk show host

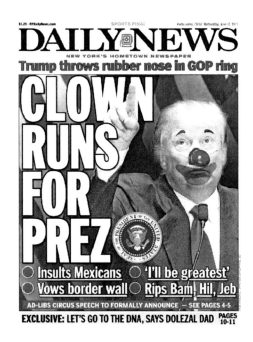

emerged from retirement to present his "Top Ten List of Interesting Facts About Donald Trump." The one that met with the most derisive laughter was the charge that "during sex, Donald calls out his own name."

What came to be known as "The Summer of Trump" descended on America...and ultimately, the world.

***

Immediately, the question arose: Was Donald J. Trump really a Republican? Politically, he'd been called "a nativist," a "populist," a "protectionist," an "America Firster," and an "autocrat." Most voters viewed him as a moderate Republican, although some extreme right-wingers denounced him as "just another Hillary Clinton."

[For the record, Donald had been a Democrat until 1987, switching to the Republican Party from 1987 to 1999, when he was a backer (1999-2001) of the Reform Party. From 2001 to 2009, he came back into the Democratic fold, switching his allegiance to the Republicans again from 2009 to 2011. He registered as an independent from 2011 to 2012, before returning to the GOP in 2012, when he endorsed ("to my ever-lasting regret") Mitt Romney for President.]

During the opening days of that long, hot summer, Donald would launch his campaign, and then proceed to break just about every time-tested political strategy in the rule book. Defying political logic, he went on to dominate both TV news and political gossip in America. His style of campaigning was eventually accepted as "the new normal."

"I plan to be me," he proclaimed.

And so he was. The Republican field was forced to adjust to this new lightning rod, who began to attract supporters who had never voted before.

Whereas some candidates recognized his political allure and tried to channel their own "inner Trump," others chose to remain uncommitted, "laying low," in the futile hope that "The Donald would just disappear," drowning in his own outrageous rhetoric.

But, as history would show, thanks to some degree to his bigger-than-life personality, he would make all the flowers in the garden wilt except one, and that was Donald himself.

In many ways, even from the beginning, he had already outdistanced his competitors. He didn't need to spend millions on political advertising to make himself known. He was already known. As the summer progressed, cable TV news, with its 24-hour coverage, was dominated by his every utterance, no matter how off-the-wall his political proclamations became. Political junkies fell asleep with the television on, awakening hours later as it continued to blast out facts, opinions, and argumentative punditry about Donald.

As a result of the controversies he raised, some of his business contacts withdrew from him. Four TV networks, including NBC's *The Apprentice*, and even Macy's, which carried his clothing line, canceled the marketing partnerships they'd established with enterprises he controlled based on remarks he'd made about Mexicans.

In addition to NBC/Universal, Televisa, Ora TV, and Univision cut ties with Donald. Mexico's largest TV network, Televisa, said that Donald's remarks offended the entire Mexican population. Ora, owned by Carlos Slim, the world's second-richest man, defined Donald's comments as "racist."

"What we've been doing from day one is building something that's much bigger and broader than most people thought and understood," said Corey Lewandowski, Donald's campaign manager.

"Donald likes making history. He likes his name up in lights. And he's having fun," said political advisor Roger Stone.

During his campaign, Donald made frequent references to his ability to self-finance it, citing his "bank full of money. I can't be bought." As events unfolded, he ultimately spent much less on political ads than his competitors (Marco Rubio, Jeb Bush, and Ted Cruz), whose paid ads frequently blanketed the airwaves. In contrast, Donald was the beneficiary of huge blocks of free media coverage, something that TV networks generated in massive amounts in the form of talk shows, interviews, and (supposedly unbiased) news coverage.

Journalists have always found it hard to resist broadcasting details about the wealth (or lack thereof) of a candidate seeking the highest office in the land. Donald claimed he was worth $10 billion, but in September, *Forbes,* the arbiter of American wealth, defined his worth at $4.5 billion.

"I'm worth much more than that," Donald protested.

During his critique of *Fortune's* conclusion, Donald insisted that his 'brand" (that is, the ability of his name to increase the value of entities it promoted) was worth $3

"Doubting the Donald" Trump: What he's really worth. Is it really $10 billion?

billion alone. And as the value of his endorsements have shown, there is, indeed, promotional value—lots of it—associated with his name.

[When Donald's father died in 1999, his estate was valued at $200 million, of which Donald got $40 million.

Forbes estimated that Donald in 1988 was worth $20 million. The Associated Press claimed that by using an S&P calculator, if Donald had invested that money in an index fund [a conservative, not-particularly flashy mutual fund with a portfolio whose components reflect the makeup of a market index, such as the Standard & Poor's 500 Index], he would be worth $13 billion today "and could have just sat back and watched the dividends flow in."]

***

On the campaign trail, polling results revealed that Donald's supporters praised him for "telling it like it is," and they relished his disdain for political correctness. Although frequently defined as a "bully," and denounced as "divisive and "unserious," and despite his inclusion within the much-mocked one percent of rich Americans, he maintained a massive appeal among working class voters. As such, he continued his high-profile attacks on the press, on other politicians (especially Hillary Clinton and President Obama), and also on GOP rivals who challenged him for the nomination. Every morning, he shot off rapid volleys of Twitter comments, lashing out at the critics who had attacked him as recently as the night before.

As a means of pandering to Jewish voters, Donald let it be widely understood that he had Jewish grandchildren, and a Jewish daughter. Ivanka had converted to Judaism before her marriage to Jared Kushner. "I am very honored by that. It wasn't in the plan, but I am very glad that it happened."

[In January of 2013, Donald emerged as a popular figure in Israel, and he owns land there, the Elite Tower Isle, a building site in Ramat Gan, Israel, in which various skyscrapers—including, if and when it's finished, what's conceived as the tallest building in Israel. During the 2013 Israeli elections, he endorsed Benjamin Netanyahu as Prime Minister. Later, however, Netanyahu objected to Donald's proposal to ban Muslims from traveling to the United States.

In March of 2016, when Donald addressed the American Israel Public Affairs Committee—a group that self-identifies as "America's pro-Israel lobby," he received wild applause for denouncing President Obama's lack of support for Israel.]

Those surges of popularity were soon replaced with expressions of mockery and rage. By July, novelty merchants were busy hawking Donald merchandise, regardless of how vulgar, insulting, or obscene.

The most controversial novelty was a butt plug (a rectal dildo) with a cartoon version of Donald's image implanted into it in low relief. Derived from a prototype developed on a 3D printer, it replicated Donald's trademark orange hair, whipped up into a comb-over, and the look of defiance he displayed whenever he came under fire from a rival candidate. It was the creation of Fernando Sosa, a 32-year-old Florida artist, who told the press, "I like the mental picture of Donald going into people's asses."

Although the model portraying Donald eventually emerged as a bestseller, Sosa didn't spare any of Donald's rivals. He also distributed a line of sex toys and dildos that unattractively depicted cartoon images of Ted Cruz, Marco Rubio, and Rand Paul.

In a post-purchase evaluation of the products, a consumer said, "The Jeb Bush butt plug was designed to give you the least thrill of all. As for the Cruz butt plug, a user had to ask, "Are you in yet, Ted?'"

In New York, a street artist named "Hanksy" went even further, depicting Donald in a mural he painted on a wall in Manhattan's Lower East side as a "pile of poop crowned with lemon yellow hair and circled by flies. I started with the fact that Trump kinda rhymes with dump, so I decided to paint him like a giant pile of shit," the artist tweeted.

Horrified that his image would be depicted on a butt plug, Donald wanted to be photographed "looking presidential" for the upcoming cover of *Time*. The photographer assigned to him for that project was Martin Schoeller, who claimed that Donald "was very difficult to photograph. If you asked him to look up a little bit, he says no or he just doesn't do it. He literally has one angle. If I ask him to smile, he puts on a big grin and then goes back to his Zoolander 'blue steel' look."

For one of Schoeller's portraits, Donald agreed to pose with a 27-year-old American bald eagle, named "Uncle Sam." The bird had been transported from Texas to the Trump Tower, even though Donald was hesitant about too close a proximity to a ferociously carnivorous wild bird which can't be trained.

Hit by a car in 1994, Uncle Sam had been evaluated, because of his injuries,

From the sales site of the Donald Trump *"(Don't let him up and into your ass")* butt plug.

361

as "non-releasable into the wild." One of the most widely photographed bald eagles in history, he had appeared in movies, TV shows, and commercials, and had been seen by millions. He posed with Donald and did not attack him, and the subsequent double portrait was incorporated into *Time* magazine's front cover. "Donald is an icon, and Uncle Sam the bald eagle is an icon, so it was a big success," said Jonathon Wood, the bird's owner, a falconer and wildlife rehabilitator.

The bald eagle is an opportunistic carnivore with the capacity to consume a great variety of prey, especially fish. It is both the national bird and the national animal of the United States, and appears on its seal.

It was removed from the U.S. government's list of endangered species in 1995 and transferred to their list of threatened species. As a rule, the bald eagle is a poor choice for up close and person displays, prone to becoming highly stressed, frightened, and unpredictable.

***

In his pursuit of the presidency, Donald not only had to look presidential, but he had to pursue the evangelical vote. At the time, it was being "courted" by Ted Cruz, who more and more was sounding like a messenger sent directly to Earth from God.

Until he ran for President, attracting evangelicals, Donald was not known for expressing his points of view about religion. During an April 2011 interview with broadcasters from the right-wing religion-oriented *700 Club*, he claimed he was a Presbyterian and "have had a good relationship with the church over the years. I think religion is a wonderful thing."

During that interview, he said that he attended Marble Collegiate Church in Manhattan, where he'd married Ivana in 1971. The church later said he was not an active member.

He admitted, "I have not asked God to forgive me of my sins. I think if I do something wrong, I just try and make it right. I don't bring God into the picture."

He went on to assert that "The Bible is my favorite book. Nothing beats the Bible!" He refused, however, to designate his favorite Bible verse—"I don't like giving that out to people that I hardly know."

He said his second favorite book was *The Art of the Deal*.

"EVERY VAGINA IS A POTENTIAL LAND MINE."

—Donald to "Shock Jock" Howard Stern

During the summer of 2015, an anti-Trump movement coalesced and become more vocal. Activists hunted through old television archives for previous interviews he'd delivered in front of cameras. They found that

Donald's political enemies dug into TV archives to replay his provocative and vulgar comments made on *The Howard Stern Show.*

During his interview with Donald, Howard seemed to goad him on, even getting the future presidential candidate to talk about the toilet habits of both Ivana and Melania, his first and third wives.

Donald's scat talk fitted in well with the mode of the Stern show, which often featured Joe Tyler Gold (right photo above) as "Fartman," a fictional superhero who attacks evil using his super-powered flatulence, which allows him to fly through the air.

Fartman even reached the screen in director Tammy Caplan's *Fartman: Caught in a Tight Ass,* which starred Fartman and introduced the evil villain, Tight Ass, who had the ability to squeeze weapons from his ass.

Donald seemed to glide smoothly into this scat world spearheaded by Howard Stern,, although confessing, on the air, "I'm not into anal."

some the most embarrassing of the tapes had been videotaped during Donald's appearances on *The Howard Stern Show* way back in 2004.

On air, he had revealed to Stern that he "felt lucky not to have picked up an STD *[Sexually Transmitted Disease]*. Having sex in the 1980s was dangerous and scary like Vietnam. It was my personal Vietnam. I felt like a great and very brave soldier."

During the same interview, he also admitted that at the age of 22, he had avoided the military draft "because of bone spurs in both of my heels."

Stern chimed in, "A lot of guys who went to Vietnam came out unscathed. And a lot of guys who've gone through the 1980s having sex with different women came out with AIDS and all kinds of things."

Donald also admitted on air that he had arranged for many of his potential sexual partners to get screened for STDs with his own personal doctor.

"Was that a difficult thing to ask a potential partner?" Stern asked.

"The whole romantic process is terrible," Donald replied, "because you meet somebody, and you start getting with that person, and you're really going at it and you say, 'excuse me, we have to stop now.' The 80s are not like...you know, the 70s, which was the best time for sex."

In one bizarre segment with Stern, broadcast widely over the airwaves, Donald discussed the toilet habits of both Ivana and Melania, wives #1 and (eventually) #3. He claimed that Ivana's bowel movements were a "little more normal than Melania's. Melania never poops, not that I know about. She's such an elegant and dainty lady."

He also admitted to what he liked sexually: "I'm not into anal."

World leaders, at news of Trump's ascendency in the American polls, were horrified.

David Cameron (upper photo) in front of #10 Downing Street; Manuel Valls (center); whom the French press had defined as "an adroit leftist;" and movie-star-fabulous Justin Trudeau of Canada each loudly denounced Donald's racist views.

After the show and in private, both Stern and Donald agreed on one concept: "Every vagina is a potential land mind. There is real danger there."

[Sam Clovis, a 25-year Air Force veteran, said, "I was offended by a man who sought and gained four student deferments to avoid the draft and who has never served this nation a day—not a day—in any fashion or way."

Ironically, after denouncing Donald in several e-mails, Clovis went to work for his campaign in Iowa after Rick Perry suspended his pursuit for the presidency.]

DEFIANT DONALD AS POSTER BOY
For Jihadist Recruitment Videos

During 2015's "SUMMER OF TRUMP," in one of his most shocking proposals, Donald called for the exclusion of Muslims attempting to enter the United States "until we can figure out what the hell is going on."

Republican leaders, including Senate Majority Leader Mitch McConnell and Republican House Speaker Paul Ryan, strenuously voiced their objections.

Denunciations also poured in from foreign leaders, including Canadian Prime Minister Justin Trudeau, British Prime Minister David Cameron, and French Prime Minister Manuel Valls.

Reince Priebus, the Chairman of the Republican Party, also protested. GOP leaders argued that banning Muslims violated the party's conservative values and was in violation of both the First Amendment and America's immigrant heritage.

Then *The Washington Post* reported that Donald had been featured as an

Even fellow Republicans made it a point, early and loudly, to denounce Donald and his presidential aspirations.

Top to bottom, Paul (*"I can't hear you"*) Ryan; Mitch (*"the man you'd least want to have a beer with"*) McConnell; and Reince (the oft-horrified chairman of the GOP) Priebus.

enemy of Islam in a new Jihadist recruitment video. Even the U.S. Pentagon issued a statement: "Anything that bolsters' ISIL's narrative and puts the United States against the Muslim faith is certainly not only contrary to our values, but contrary to our national security."

On Fox News, Donald claimed that France and Belgium have been blighted by the failure of Muslims in these countries to integrate. "Living in Brussels is like living in a hellhole because of the dire failure in Muslim assimilation."

Growing ever more provocative, Donald made a public statement in which he advocated police surveillance of mosques in the U.S. "as possible terrorist cells." He cited U.S. General John J. Pershing who, during the Moro Rebellion, allegedly shot Muslim terrorists with bullets that had been dipped in pig's blood as a deterrent to other radicals. [*Most historians cite the pig's blood story as an urban legend.*]

As would be expected, The Council on American-Islamic Relations denounced Donald and his remarks.

[*The **Moro Rebellion** was an armed conflict between indigenous Muslim groups in the southern Philippines (the Moros) and the U.S. military between 1899 and 1913. A bloody incident within a context of four centuries of conflict between the ethnic Muslims and whomever happened to be in control of the Philippines at the time, the Moro Rebellion was not directly associated with other elements of the Spanish-American War of 1898.*]

Hillary issued a response. "Donald Trump not denouncing false statements about POTUS (President of the United States) and hateful rhetoric about Muslims is disturbing—and just plain wrong. Cut it out!"

LATINOS DENOUNCE TRUMP
"He's the American Hitler"

In August, Donald shocked a good deal of the world with a claim that as President, he would forcibly deport more than 11 million illegal immigrants from the U.S. Then he forged forward in his promise to erect a wall along the U.S.-Mexico border, continuing to insist that he'd devise a way to make Mexico pay for it.

Although each of these positions met with ferocious opposition, they added to his legion of hard-core supporters.

Former Mexican President Vicente Fox, in February of 2016, said, "I'm not going to pay for that fucking wall." Felipe Caldéron, another former President of Mexico, said, "We are not going to pay a single cent for such a stupid wall—and it's going to be completely useless if built, which I doubt."

Yet throughout the course of that summer, Donald continued to hit hard on the issue of U.S. border security. At his first town hall campaign rally in Derry, New Hampshire, he said, "On Day One of my presidency, illegal immigrants are getting out and getting out fast."

He also announced that he opposed birthright citizenship, attacking "anchor babies like Ted Cruz, who was born in Alberta, Canada. Anchor babies should not be protected by the 14th Amendment of the U.S. Constitution. All illegal immigrants should be deported but some—the non-criminal element—might be allowed to return if they went through proper channels. But that's not going to happen under my presidency until the border is strengthened."

Figures in the Latino community responded in fury, including singer Ricky Martin, who authored a scathing article condemning Donald and urging Latinos to unite against him. In spite of all these objections and outrage, Donald continued to maintain that he "will win the Latino vote."

Despite the outrage, throughout the course of July, Donald continued to reinforce his claim that Mexican immigrants are responsible for a large number of rapes in the U.S. "There is a mindboggling link between rape and illegal immigration," he said. "Latino immigrants are more likely to perpetrate rape than the wider population." He cited an article that had appeared in *Fusion* magazine, a Paleolibertarian monthly with links to conservative newscaster Glenn Beck. [In 2012, it changed its title to The-Blaze.]

It claimed that "Eighty percent of women crossing the Mex-

Anti-Latino attitudes in the U.S. didn't originate with fans of Donald Trump.

This cartoon by Clifford Berryman first appeared in 1916, and advocated a more aggressive imperialism on the part of Uncle Sam in "disciplining" the rebellious guerillas of Pancho Vila.

367

ican border are raped along the way, often by criminal gangs, traffickers, and corrupt officials."

[There is no centrally recorded government statistics on the ethnicity of convicted rapists in America.]

Hoping to clarify the issue, *The Washington Post* spearheaded an investigation about crime rates among immigrants, later admitting that the present data is incomplete. However, during the course of their investigation, a tantalizing fact emerged: "Crime rates increase as generations of immigrants assimilate into America. Second generation immigrants, who are born in the U.S. (and thereby become citizens), with at least one foreign-born parent, are more likely to commit crimes than first-generation immigrants." It was also pointed out that first-generation immigrants tend to stay out of trouble, hoping to avoid deportation.

At an August 26 news conference in Dubuque, Iowa, tension between Donald and Jorge Ramos boiled over. *[At the time, Ramos was the main news anchor for the Spanish-language media group, Univision, whom Donald was suing at the time because of its refusal to broadcast his Miss Universe pageant. Ramos, whose programs were aimed at Latinos and their role as a critical voting block in U.S. elections, has been called "The Walter Cronkite of Latino America."]*

Employed as a news anchor for Univision, Mexico-born Jorge Ramos is the most powerful newscaster for Latinos. He voiced opposition to Donald's anti-Mexican rants.

But he learned at a rally that disobeying protocols would get him ejected from the sea of Donald's faithful supporters.

Without being formally "recognized," from the podium *[i.e., "granted permission to speak"]*, Ramos began a long, rambling question-cum-political-statement. Refusing to respond, the candidate signaled to his security guards to remove the TV journalist from the audience.

"Don't touch me!" Ramos shouted at the guards marching him out of the room. He was eventually allowed to return and his questions and comments were addressed.

Donald's action was condemned by the National Association of Hispanic Journalists.

He may have been responding to Ramos's earlier declaration, in which he had defined Donald as "the loud voice of intolerance, hatred, and division in the United States."

By August, more and more Latinos attacked Donald, none more vocally than Ricardo Sánchez. Known as "El Mandril" [a name that translates as "a spindle or an axle used to secure or support material being machined or milled"] on his Spanish-language radio show in Los Angeles, he labeled Donald as "El hombre del peluquin" [the man with the toupée]. Other more vocal Latinos compared him to Hitler.

Sánchez claimed that if Donald became President, "It would be like giving a loaded gun to a monkey. But a gun that fires automatic bullets."

During discussions of his anti-immigration stance, Donald cited "Operation Wetback," a program sponsored by President Dwight D. Eisenhower in the 1950s which rounded up and deported illegal aliens. He referenced an article in The Christian Science Monitor:

"Fifty-three years ago, when newly elected Dwight Eisenhower moved into the White House, America's southern frontier was as porous as a spaghetti sieve. As many as three million illegal immigrants had walked or waded northward over a period of several years for jobs in California, Arizona, Texas, and points beyond. President Eisenhower cut off this illegal traffic. He did it quickly and decisively with only 1,075 U.S. Border Patrol agents—less than one-tenth of today's force."

The New York Times launched an attack on Donald's immigration stand. "Because the plan is so naked—in its scapegoating of immigrants, its barely subtextual racism, its immense cruelty in seeking to reduce millions of people to poverty and hopelessness—it gives his opponents the chance for a very clear moral decision. They can stand up for better values, and against the collective punishment of millions of innocent Americans-in-waiting."

In late summer, CNN took a poll of Republicans, finding that 44% of them believed that Donald was the best candidate to handle the immigration issued. No other candidate in the poll even came close.

***

As early as August, Donald launched an attack on Hillary, thinking she would beat Vermont Senator Bernie Sanders in the Democratic presidential primary.

On August 28, he accused her of spilling classified government secrets during her tenure as Secretary of State. To a crowd on August 28 in Massachusetts, he claimed she had misused her private e-mail server and demonstrated a flagrant lack of security standards.

He also attacked her top aide, Huma Abedine. "She, too, is getting classified secrets, and she's married to Anthony Weiner, who's a perv and a sleazebag."

[As a congressman in 2011, Weiner had been caught up in an online sexting scandal. He sent out pictures of himself in tight-fitting, virtually see-through underwear.]

From the campaign trail, Hillary shot back, claiming "The party of Lincoln has become the party of Trump."

She denied that any classified government secrets were on her server. "Material may have been classified later, but it wasn't when I received it in 2009 and 2010," she claimed.

LOATHED BY THE ESTABLISHMENT, & HATED BY THE MEDIA,
Donald Takes Stands on Issues He Claims
"WILL MAKE AMERICA GREAT AGAIN"

As he outlined his views, Donald often found himself opposed to the Republican Party establishment. He was a strong supporter of Social Security, and he called himself a "free trader," though claiming that trade must be reasonably fair. "Right now our political leaders are wimps, allowing other nations like Japan and China to take unfair advantage."

His tax plan called for reducing corporate tax rates to 15%, concurrent with the elimination of various loopholes and deductions. He did not believe the minimum wage should be raised, claiming that it would hurt "the economic competitiveness of the United States."

A CNN poll revealed that Donald was the choice of 45 percent of Republicans who believed he was best able to handle the economy. Jeb Bush, his closest competitor, got only eight percent. Donald also won 32 percent of a CNN poll as the best candidate to handle ISIS, which was double the percentage attributed to Jeb.

The latter came about after Donald had warned that, "We're in danger of the sort of terrorist attacks that will make the bombing of the World Trade Center look like kids playing with firecrackers."

In marked and acrimonious contrast to Hillary and Bernie Sanders, Donald took the opposite point of view on global warming. "This very expensive global warning bullshit has got to stop. Our planet is freezing, record low temps, and our GW scientists are stuck in ice."

He came down hard on China, laying out a series of plans to help make up for the towering trade deficit it faced with that country every year. Declaring China a currency manipulator, he advocated bringing it to the bargaining table. He also stated his goal of reclaiming millions of American jobs and reviving manufacturing by putting an end to "China's illegal export subsidies and lax labor standards." He called for a lowering of the corporate tax rate as incentives to keep American jobs and companies at home.

On health care, he announced his opposition to Obamacare, preferring a free market plan and competition to lower costs. He had stated support for a single-payer system in the past.

He also came out for a strong support of "our veterans who are horribly mistreated," advocating an overhaul of the Veterans Health Administration. He supported satellite clinics for veterans within hospitals in remote rural areas. On education, he advocated support for school choice and local control of primary and secondary schools. He attacked Common Core *[a legally sanctioned educational initiative that defines and standardizes what students in the U.S. should know in mathematics and English language arts at the end of each grade between kindergarten and a senior year in high school]* as "a disaster that must be ended."

To pander to right-wing members of the party, he stated that he supported traditional marriage between a man and a woman, but he didn't really want to make this an issue like Ted Cruz did. Gay activists labeled the Texas senator as "a homophobe like hate-spewing Mike Huckabee."

The June, 2015 Obergefell v. Hodges ruling at the Supreme Court legalized same-sex marriage nationwide. Donald said, "I would have preferred states, you know, making the decision,

A recent gun show in Houston, Texas, displaying weapons for sale.

Among the nations of the world, the United States is often cited as an "armed camp," and the National Rifle Association is accused of controlling the Republican-dominated Senate and House.

371

and I let that be known. But the judges made the decision. So, at a certain point, you have to be realistic about it."

On another social issue, Donald described himself as pro-life, claiming he would ban late-term abortions except in cases of incest, rape, or health of the mother. In previous years, he had defended a woman's right to choose.

He supported the 2nd amendment, and was opposed to gun control in general. He admitted that he has a "New York concealed carry permit for a weapon." He also supported fixing the Federal background check system so that criminal and mental health records are entered into a law enforcement database.

On another front, although he opposed legalizing recreational marijuana, he supported medical marijuana, while being in favor of states' rights on drug-related issues.

Many pundits on the right denounced Donald for "being a traitor to his class"—in other words, they vilified him as a member of the monied elite appealing to blue collar workers, many of whom were without a job. References and comparisons were made between Donald and Franklin D. Roosevelt, another rich, well-connected member of the New York power elite.

Ross Douthat, writing for *The New York Times*, said, "So far, Trump is running against the Republican establishment in a more profound way than the Tea Party, challenging not just deviations from official conservative principle, but the entire post-Reagan matrix. He can wax right wing on immigration on one moment and promise to tax hedge fund managers the next. He can sound like Pat Buchanan on trade and Bernie Sanders on health care."

MELANIA?
A Foreign-Born, Bikini-Clad Fashionista
With Oodles of Sex Appeal and Ample Cleavage

In August, newspapers for the first time began to "discover" Melania Trump, Donald's Slovenia-born third wife, a former model. Pictures of her from her modeling days were published and widely distributed. Most of them showed her tremendous cleavage and bikinis made of so little fabric they barely covered her vital zone. Some of the more provocative ones had been snapped as late as 2011 at Mar-a-Lago, the luxurious Palm Beach estate she shared with Donald.

"She'll make a great First Lady," Donald said triumphantly. "She's got a great heart."

She has a lot of other assets he discreetly opted not to mention.

Nicole Lyn Pesce, writing in the *New York Daily News*, said, "The stunning 45-year-old ex-model looks more suited to *Women's Wear Daily* than the White House, with her figure-hugging designer dresses, mini-dresses, and sky-high stilletos."

Celebrity stylist Philip Bloch, said, "She would be the most stylish First Lady we've ever had, beyond a shadow of doubt—beyond Jackie Kennedy, beyond Michelle Obama."

Melania shares Nancy Reagan's taste for *haute couture,* appearing often in perhaps a slinky gold Alexander McQueen gown or draping herself in a Valentino. She does not shy away from being sexy.

If Donald were elected, it would mark the first time an American President came to power after two divorces. Ronald Reagan had had only one divorce (from movie star Jane Wyman) when he was elected president.

OPPONENTS DONALD DEFINED AS LOSERS

They're Anti-Gay, Anti-Abortion, Anti-Black, Anti-Muslim, and Anti-Immigrant, but They're Fervently PRO-GUN

During 2016s race for the White House, some seventeen major candidates, including Donald Trump, announced they would seek the nomination of the Republican Party.

Noting the crew of dark-suited men and the lone female standing on the stage, one reporter, John Winslow, called the race "a hysterically underwhelming contest of bumblers, second-raters, extremists and religious loonies. You could work your way to the top by not looking obviously demented at first blush to the national media—that is, if you did not use former candidate Michelle Bachmann as your role model."

"Perhaps I'm wrong," Winslow continued, "but Donald Trump showed that having opponents who look demented might advance you in the polls. He surfaced to the top because so many of his challengers held views that put them to the far right of Josef Goebbels, a coven that would make Hannibal Lecter, the serial flesh eater in *The Silence of the Lambs,* look like a Presbyterian deacon."

"All that was missing from this posturing was an open raincoat showing a raging boner," Winslow claimed.

2015, The Summer of Trump: Dirty Linen on Parade
CANDIDATES FOR THE REPUBLICAN NOMINATION FOR PRESIDENT OF THE UNITED STATES

THE LOSERS
First There Were Seventeen
And Then There Were Three,
And Then There Were Two,
And Then, Only The Donald Remained.

Like characters in an Agatha Christie mystery, what began as an overcrowded, seething-with-ambition cast of seventeen eccentric Republicans degenerated throughout 2015s "Summer of Trump" into a brawl that had all parties denouncing one another by autumn.

Although each of the candidates for the Republican Party's nomination brought carloads of ironies and dramas to the summer calendar, we've opted to present a brief thumbnail description of each of them, with apologies for too brief an overview of political careers that, in at least 50% of the candidates, were, indeed, historically brief.

Here, below, therefore are thumbnail portraits of competitors that Donald managed to trivialize into historical footnotes of political careers that might have been but never were.

"Jeb Bush
Is an Embarrassment to Himself and His Family"
—Donald Trump

John Ellis Bush (born February 11, 1953) entered the world in Midland, Texas, where his future sister-in-law, Laura Bush would run through a stop sign at an intersection and kill the high school athlete, Michael Douglas, when she was still a teenager.

Jeb was the second son of former President George H.W. Bush and former First Lady Barbara Bush. He had wanted to run for President earlier, but his older brother, George W. Bush, beat him to it, winning the office after a stint as governor of Texas.

"I had two sons who made it as governor," Barbara said. "Jeb in Florida and George W. in Texas." Privately, she told friends, "Jeb is the smart one."

A graduate of Phillips Academy in Andover, Massachusetts, Jeb later attended the University of Texas, earning a degree in Latin American affairs while becoming fluent in Spanish.

In 1980, he moved to Florida to pursue a career in real estate development. Six years later, he became Florida's Secretary of Commerce until 1988, when he joined his father's successful campaign for the presidency.

In 1994, Jeb made his first run for office, seeking the governorship of Florida, and losing it to incumbent Lawton Chiles. He ran again in 1998 and won, becoming the 43rd governor of the state from January 5, 1999 to January 5, 2007.

As governor, he was viewed as a moderate, at least by Republican standards. That meant he opposed same-sex marriage and abortion, except in the event of rape, incest, or the mother's health. He questioned the arguments for climate change, but then suggested that global warm-

wikimedia commons/gage skidmore

In an attempt to escape from "the curse" of his brother's name and legacy, Jeb ordered his campaign to print posters that avoided any mention of "Bush" and read only JEB!.

Donald said, "When Jeb speaks, the audience falls into a deep coma."

ing might be real. He felt that immigrants should have a path to legal status.

Donald tweeted that "Jeb Bush has to like illegal aliens because his wife, Columbia, is Mexican born."

Jeb campaigned for President, beginning on June 15, 2015, and was viewed as an early frontrunner. To escape the "curse" of the Bush name, he authorized posters to read "JEB," omitting "Bush" as a means, it was surmised, to minimalize an association to the family's (controversial) political past.

From the beginning, he tangled with Donald, attacking his plan to erect a wall along the Mexican border. "It won't work. Part of the border is rugged terrain. What we need is more law enforcement from the Border Patrol. Trump's plan is impossible and would cost hundreds of billions of dollars."

"Low-energy Bush is a weak candidate," Donald charged. "He's a total disaster as a campaigner. He's gone nasty with lies about me. By far, this sad sack has zero chance of winning…a weak candidate."

Ben Carson:
Although He Attacks His Mother With a Hammer and Stabs a Friend, He Becomes a Neurosurgeon and Candidate for the Republican Nomination

Benjamin Solomon Carson, Sr. (born September 18, 1951) came from parents with families growing up in rural Georgia. Sonya was thirteen years old when she married Ben's father, Robert, a minister, who was 28. She later discovered that her husband had another family, for which he abandoned her when Ben was eight years old. His mother, a domestic, had to work two or three jobs at a time to support Ben and his brother, Curtis.

In a memoir, *Gifted Hands,* Carson related that in his youth he had a violent temper and once tried to hit his mother over the head with a hammer because of a dispute over clothing. He also claimed that in the ninth grade, he got into an argument with a friend and attempted to stab him, but the knife thrust was blocked by his intended victim's belt buckle.

Although as a boy, he survived on food stamps, he managed to educate himself, graduating from Yale University in 1973, where he majored in psychology, later receiving his M.D. from the University of Michigan Medical School in 1977. By 1984, he had been appointed the Director of Pediatric Neurosurgery at Johns Hopkins Hospital in Baltimore. His most publicized achievement involved the surgical separation of conjoined twins. Another of his achievements focused on the development of a drastic surgical procedure known as a hemispherectomy, in which part or all of one hemisphere of the brain is removed as a means of controlling severe pediatric epilepsy.

His medical achievements led to his 2008 winning of a Presidential Medal of Freedom Award.

He won the heart of conservatives for his widely publicized speech at the 2013 National Prayer Breakfast, during which he criticized President Obama.

Ben Carson, the soft-spoken African American neurosurgeon who aspired to be President, admited to a violent past, compared Obamacare to slavery, and attacked gays as pedophiles.

He made some of the most controversial statements of any candidate running for the Republican nomination, after announcing that he was seeking the presidency on May 4, 2015. He compared homosexual relationships to pedophilia and bestiality, and he claimed that modern day America is like Nazi Germany. One of his most controversial statements compared Obamacare to slavery.

Donald's campaign managers heard those comments and concluded that, "This Carson wacko will be easy to dissect. Just turn his surgical knife over to us."

Carson claimed, "I have a surgical personality, which means I look very, very carefully before I leap, and I measure the temperature of the water before I put my foot in."

Chris Christie:
Will "Bridgegate" and "Exteme Obesity" Disqualify His Run for the Presidency?

Christopher James Christie (born September 6, 1962), nicknamed "Chris," is the 55th Governor of New Jersey, even though it is a "blue" (i.e., predominantly Democratic) state and he is an ardent Republican.

Born in Newark, he's the son of Sondra, a telephone receptionist, and Wilbur, a certified public accountant. His mother is of Sicilian ancestry, his father of Irish, Scottish, and German descent.

He graduated from the University of Delaware with a Bachelor of Arts in political science in 1984, wining his law degree in 1987 at Seton Hall University School of Law.

George W. Bush appointed him U.S. attorney for New Jersey, a post he held from 2002 to 2008.

In 2009, he filed to run for governor of his state, and, after a tough campaign, defeated Democrat Jon Corzine by winning 49% of the vote.

On many issues, he adopted stances that were more moderate than those of most other right-wing politicos from his party. As would be expected, he opposed abortion, but was soft on immigration. "It is not a crime, but a civil wrong," he said.

He also opposed same-sex marriages, but favored the protection offered by same-sex civil unions. "I believe that homosexuality is innate. If someone is born that way, it's very difficult to say that it's a sin to be gay."

In 2011, there was much speculation that he should seek the presidency of the United States. But he finally decided not to, claiming, "Now is not my time. New Jersey, whether you like it or not, you're stuck with me." He did, however, deliver the keynote address at the Republican National Convention in August of 2012.

When Hurricane Sandy devastated parts of New Jersey later that year, he praised President Obama's aid in Federal disaster relief and hugged him when he flew in to a stricken New Jersey. That act of support subjected Christie to a severe backlash from more right-wing members of his party.

In 2013, Christie ran for re-election as governor and won. That same year, he was also elected Chairman of the Republican Governors Association, succeeding Bobby Jindal of

Pilloried by dozens of cartoonists, both for his obesity and for his alleged pettiness as exemplified by the Bridgegate scandal, New Jersey Governor Chris Christie morphed from Trump's competitor to his attack dog, with mixed results from his increasingly fed-up electorate.

This cover illustration from *The New Yorker* shows a fat child playing in, and disrupting, the traffic across the George Washington Bridge.

Louisiana.

In September of 2013, Christie became involved in a scandal called "Bridgegate." From September 9-13 of that year, two of three strategic and high-volume traffic lanes in Fort Lee were (needlessly and, it was suspected, vengefully) closed. They provided access to New York City via the George Washington Bridge, one of the most heavily traveled routes in the United States.

A massive morning rush hour resulted, and there was outrage in New Jersey, with calls for an investigation of what was believed to have been a deliberate sabotage of Fort Lee's ability to cope with its commuter infrastructure.

It was reported that the lane had been closed by Christie's aides in retaliation against the Democratic Mayor of Fort Lee, Mark Sokolich, for not having supported Christie in his run for a second term. Christie denied all knowledge of the events leading up to the closing of the traffic arteries, but several of his appointees and aides resigned in the aftermath.

Christie formally entered the U.S. presidential race on June 30, 2015.

Based on his potential status as a presidential candidate, the weight and health of the governor became an issue. The columnist Eugene Robinson applied the term "extremely obese" to him, citing medical guidelines of the National Institutes of Health. Christie claimed that in spite of his weight, he was relatively healthy. It was revealed that during February of 2013, that he had undergone "lap-band" *[laparoscopic adjustable gastric band]* stomach surgery, a radical procedure intended to slow the consumption of food.

The Obesity Society, a nonprofit scientific group, issued a statement. "To suggest that Governor Christie's body weight discounts and discredits his ability to be an effective political candidate is inappropriate, unjust, and ong."

Ted Cruz:
"I'm Not the Kind of Guy You'd Want to Have a Beer With"

Two Cubans ran for President in 2015-2016, including one that Donald called "the Anchor Baby born in Alberta" in 1970. He was Rafael Edward Cruz, nicknamed "Ted." A graduate of Princeton University, fellow classmates remembered him as "creepy." Other words used to describe him were "arrogant," "abrasive," "intense," "strident," and a "crank."

He admitted, "If you want someone to grab a beer with, I may not be that guy."

After graduating from Harvard Law School, Cruz, in time, became an advisor to George W. Bush (no great recommendation.).

From 2004 to 2009, he became the first Hispanic and the longest serving Solicitor General in Texas's history. In 2012, he ran for the Senate seat vacated by fellow Republican Kay Bailey Hutchison, and won, becoming the first Hispanic American to serve as a U.S. senator representing Texas. His Senate win was called a "true grassroots victory against very long odds."

Much to his later embarrassment during his campaigns in the Northeast, he was caught on tape saying, "When we used to see a New Yorker in Texas, we'd say, 'Get a noose!'"

A stunning moment that reinforced Cruz's notoriety came in October 2013, when he staged a government shutdown. To make it happen, he delivered a 21-hour filibustering speech in the Senate, with the stated intention of delaying a key vote associated with approval of the federal budget. He orchestrated that (widely denounced) filibuster with the intention of defunding President Obama's Affordable Care Act.

As his months in office went by, he increased the venom of his accusations against President Obama, claiming he was "openly desirous to destroy the Constitution and this Republic." In effect, he was accusing the President of high treason. He followed that with a claim that the 2015 nuclear deal with Iran would define the Obama administration as "the world's leading financier of radical Islamic terrorism."

As a freshman Senator, Cruz also attacked fellow Republicans, calling them a "surrender caucus to Obama. They're squishes on gun control."

John McCain called Cruz a "wacko bird," and Lindsey Graham said, "If you killed Cruz on the floor of the Senate, and the trial was in the Senate, nobody would convict you."

In a heated speech in July 2015, Cruz accused Senate Republican leader Mitch McConnell of telling "a flat out lie" over his intention to reauthorize the Export-Import Bank.

Cruz began campaigning for the presidency as early as March of 2015.

The "Wacko Bird and Anchor Baby," as Donald called him, Texas Senator Ted Cruz is the most hated senator.

He wanted to head the U.S. government, but had only succeeded in shutting it down in an attempt to prevent Obama from providing health care for the poor.

Carly Fiorina:
Can a CEO Who Laid Off Thousands, Botched a Merger, & Departed with a $21 Million "Golden Parachute" Ever Become President?

Cara Carleton Fiorina (*née Sneed*), nicknamed "Carly," was born on September 6, 1954 in Austin, Texas. She attended three different universities, including Stanford and the Massachusetts Institute of Technology, before climbing to the top of the corporate ladder.

She became known primarily for her controversial tenure as CEO of Hewlett-Packard (HP) from 1999 to 2005. She was the first woman to lead a *Fortune* magazine Top-20 company In 2002, she supervised the largest technology sector merger in history, with HP acquiring rival personal computer manufacturer, Compaq, thereby creating, through that merger, the world's largest seller of personal computers. In the aftermath, she was bitterly resented for laying off 30,000 U.S. employees.

By February of 2005, after HP lost half of its value, she was forced to resign. For her failure as a CEO, she was awarded a $21 million bonus, called "a golden parachute." Pundit David Corn called Fiorina "a real American success story—for a corporate Republican."

In *Mother Jones,* Corn wrote: "Her sole claim to president-ish experience is her tenure at HP, and that stint was marked by layoffs, outsourcing, conflict, and controversy—so much so that several prominent HP colleagues recoil at the idea of Fiorina managing any enterprise again, let alone the Executive Branch. She developed a reputation of a manager who knocked heads together—and who chopped them off."

After her ouster, stock prices rose seven percent as Wall Street shouted "hooray."

In 2008, she flirted with politics, becoming an advisor to Republican Senator John McCain during his futile quest for the presidency. However, two years later, she won the GOP nomination for a U.S. Senate seat from California, but lost the general election to the popular incumbent, Democrat Barbara Boxer.

In May of 2015, Fiorina announced her race for the White House on *Good Morning America.* During its broadcast, she claimed, "I'll be the best person for the job because I understand how the economy really works. I'm best equipped to destroy Hillary Clinton, since pundits can't claim a gender bias."

During the coming months, many of her extreme right-wing positions were widely denounced, and her corporate record as CEO of HP was lambasted.

She entered the presidential race at a time when the other candidates, mostly Donald Trump, were demanding that manufacturing jobs to be returned to America.

On *Twitter.com@alecmadrigal*, the "twenty-something" captain of a men's JV varsity basketball team said, "Carly Fiorina looks like Voldemort with a nose."

During her widely denounced tenure as a corporate CEO, Fiorina told more employees "YOU'RE FIRED!" than Donald.

But Fiorina stood as "the poster girl" for an industry campaign aimed at blocking any legislation that would restrict a company's ability to can U.S. employees and hire foreign laborers instead. She argued that an adoption of any Donald Trump's policies about returning jobs to mainstream Americans would seriously imperil the American economy.

"There is no job that is America's god-given right anymore," she announced at a press conference in Washington. "We have to compete for jobs."

That remark led to a massive outcry against her, her critics denouncing her as a "spokesperson for corporate insensitivity."

When Donald heard her remarks, he said. "Let's replay that video clip of Ugly Carly in the Rust Belt. Run her up the flagpole and no one will salute her."

Jim Gilmore:
A Virtual Unknown Marked by 45 Minutes of Fame.

James Stuart Gilmore III (born October 6, 1949), nicknamed "Jim," was the 68th Governor of Virginia from 1998 to 2002. He once served in the U.S. Army as a counter-intelligence agent.

For one year, beginning in January, 2001, he was chairman of the Republican National Committee, promoting the Republican Party's usual stands against abortion. He made the claim, "I represent the Republican wing of the Republican Party."

He entered the 2008 presidential race when it was dominated by John McCain, running against Barack Obama after Hillary lost the Democratic nomination. But on July 14, 2007, Gilmore bowed out claiming it was too difficult to raise campaign funds.

Eight years later, during the 2016 presidential race, Gilmore announced himself as a candidate on a platform to preserve the 2nd Amendment *[the right to bear arms]*. In an anti-immigrant stance, he called for greater border surveillance. He was also opposed to Obamacare, but urged a restoration of the American economy.

It seemed that no one, according to polls, wanted the relatively obscure Jim Gilmore, the former Governor of Virginia, to be President.

Some commentators wondered why he bothered to enter the race.

He struggled but gained no traction. Inevitably, he suspended his campaign on February 12, 2016. Poll after poll indicated that he had garnered virtually zero support. Mostly, he'd been met with the question: "Who is Jim Gilmore?"

The Washington Post wrote: "Like a well-oiled light switch, 'Gilmentum' silently flicked off."

Gilmore appeared at the second debate at the kiddie's table. His 45 minutes of fame came when thousands of Americans googled to find out who he was. His poll numbers later were so low that he did not qualify for inclusion in the second debate.

Lindsey Graham:
The Intelligent, Outspoken and Relatively Moderate Republican Senator from South Carolina

When one of the most controversial senators of all time, the segregationist, Strom Thurmond, retired, Lindsey Olin Graham (born July 9, 1955) ran for his seat and won. It was in 2003. He has held the seat since then.

A reporter for *The Atlantic* described him like this: "Graham is small, wiry, and energetic, with bulging eyes in a round, ruddy face topped with bristly, spit-combed hair. His bared-teeth grin and frenetic manner might give him the effect of a high-spirited French bulldog."

He was born to parents, Millie and Florence James, who ran "The Sanitary Café," an all-inclusive rendezvous that incorporated a restaurant with a bar, pool hall, and liquor store. He received his Juris Doctorate from the University of South Carolina School of Law in 1981. From 1982 to 1988, he served in the U.S. Air Force and was a lawyer before getting elected to the U.S. House of Representatives, serving South Carolina for four terms (1995 to 2003) always with 60% of the vote.

During his second term in Congress, he was more sensible than his fellow Republicans. He was the

Lindsey Graham is a smart, hardworking, sane and rational bulldog from the fiercely independent state of South Carolina.

He was the only bachelor seeking the presidency.

only member of the GOP on the House Judiciary Committee who voted against the impeachment of Bill Clinton, asking his colleagues, "Is this Watergate or Peyton Place?"

Conservative blogs and right-wing radio talk show hosts nicknamed him "Flimsy Lindsey" or "Grahamesty."

He never married and has no children, as far as it is known, which had led to some gossipy speculation in "family values" South Carolina.

As a senator, he managed to remain more reasonable and cooperative than many of his colleagues, often working in a bipartisan fashion with Democrats on such issues as global warming and immigration reform. He's a strong believer in national defense, advocating that the U.S. take a greater leadership role.

On May 18, 2015, he announced his run for President.

Donald denounced him as "all talk—no action. He's a nasty, dumb mouthpiece."

In retaliation, Graham called Donald "a jackass."

384

Mike Huckabee:
Bible Thumping on the Road to Political Oblivion

Michael Dale Huckabee (born August 24, 1955) is nicknamed "Mike," although his critics call him "Hickabee."

He was born in Hope, Arkansas, in the town where Bill Clinton (whom he despised) grew up. He made much of his working class upbringing when he ran for political office, citing his father (Dorsey) as a fireman and mechanic, and his mother (Mae) as a clerk at a gas company.

He read the news and weather on Christian Radio when he was only fourteen years old. He attended schools steeped in Southern Baptist Theology and became an ordained minister, his whole life shaped by "moral absolutes."

He decided to go into politics in 1992, running for lieutenant governor of Arkansas, but lost to incumbent Democrat Dale Bumpers. That was the year that Clinton was elected President. When Clinton resigned as Governor of Arkansas before heading to D.C. as the nation's newly elected president, his lieutenant governor, Jim Guy Tucker, became governor.

In the vacuum created by Tucker's promotion, Huckabee then won the race for Lieutenant Governor of Arkansas, serving in that office from 1993 to 1996. He became the second Republican since Reconstruction to be Lieutenant Governor of that state.

In 1994, Huckabee was re-elected to a full term as lieutenant governor of Arkansas. When incumbent governor Tucker resigned in the wake of fraud and conspiracy convictions, Huckabee automatically became governor in 1996. In 1998, he was elected to a full four-year term and in 2002, was re-elected to a second four-year term.

He ruled the state with a ferociously far right agenda, supporting Intelligent Design and opposing Darwin's theory of Evolution as part of the public school curriculum. He wanted to increase defense spending and urged immigration reform. Of course, he opposed abortion, same-sex marriages, and even civil unions. He outlawed gay marriage in Arkansas and opposed gay adoptions, becoming despised by millions in the LGBT community.

He ran for President of the United States in the 2008 election. On August 11, 2007, backed by evangelicals, he came in second in a Straw Poll in Iowa. Although for a time, he surged forward, winning victories in Alabama,

Arkansas, Georgia, and Tennessee, he finally withdrew from the race for the Republican nomination after John McCain forged ahead to win it instead. For a brief moment, Huckabee was seriously considered as McCain's Veep, until that slot was grabbed by Sarah Palin.

In spite of national poll numbers in his favor, Huckabee announced that he would not be a candidate in the 2012 race. "All the factors say go, but my heart says no."

After four years of reflection, or perhaps boredom, the presidential bug bit him again in time for the 2016 elections. As a candidate, he maintained that he had the political backing of God himself. As regards fundraising, he urged his supporters "to give something in the name of your children and grandchildren."

He was bitterly opposed to abortion, calling for the reversal of *Roe vs. Wade,* and he vigorously continued his attacks on same-sex marriage and Obamacare.

In one of his most notorious maneuvers, earning even more outrage from the LGBT community, he made a well-publicized visit to Kentucky to lend his support to a bigoted redneck county clerk, Kim Davis, who claimed that—based on the teachings of God, and in brazen defiance of Federal law—she could never issue marriage licenses to same-sex couples.

Huckabee was joined in his support of Davis by what some members of the press had labeled as "the other religious nuts." They included Ted Cruz, Rand Paul, and Bobby Jindal.

On September 8, 2015, the day Davis was released from jail, Huckabee was on hand to support a crowd of homophobes, many of them waving Confederate flags. Ted Cruz had made it a point to be there, too, but Huckabee's "goons" pushed him aside so that their man would could stand alone alongside the dour and unattractive Davis, who wore no makeup and whose hair was long and untamed. Davis' husband, looking like a hayseed, also appeared on the platform with her, wearing bib overalls and a straw

MIKE HUCKABEE

God, Guns, Grits, and Gravy

NEW YORK TIMES BESTSELLING AUTHOR OF A SIMPLE CHRISTMAS and DO THE RIGHT THING

Mike Huckabee wrote an autobiography (see above) that proved "what an Arkansas redneck hick he really is," in the words of one reviewer.

In the Republican field, he was the most ardent attacker of same-sex marriage. For a time, he scored big with the most rabid of Bible thumpers.

hat.

Huckabee called Davis "a victim of judicial tyranny."

The next day, a poll of Americans revealed that 65% wanted her to resign for not following the law.

As a role model, Davis herself was seriously flawed. During the course of her life, she had received four marriage licenses during her four marriages to three different men. After a dubious life, she claimed she experienced a religious awakening in 2011.

Her uncompromising right wing stance caused her to be ridiculed across the nation, including a parody on *Saturday Night Live*. She was easy to caricature. Actress Jennifer Lawrence claimed, "She makes me embarrassed to be from Kentucky."

Huckabee was attacked in the press for his endorsement of Davis. One writer claimed that "He seems to think Jesus is coming back to blow up the planet." Another said, "This hayseed from Arkansas thinks Democrats are controlled by a Satanic demon called Jezebel."

"Huckabee is bound to get all the votes of those crazy ass pastors," wrote another journalist. "His campaign theme song is 'Give Me That Ol' Time Religion.'"

But all the "crazy assed

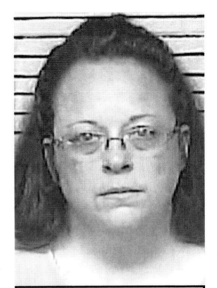

A mug shot of the notorious and grim-faced Kim Davis, a scary fanatic and county clerk from Kentucky.

She defied the rulings of the Supreme Court and refused to issue marriage licenses to same-sex couples.

"It violates my conscience," she claimed, "and it's against the teachings of the Bible."

Hate and intolerance can be taught at a young age, as evidenced by these horrid signs. Obviously, this boy reflected the hostile environment in which he was reared. As a respected Episcopal priest, the Reverend Victoria Duncan, noted in New York City, "God had nothing to do with the bigotry this poster boy was promoting."

votes" in Red-state America weren't enough to propel Huckabee forward this time around. He suspended his campaign on February 1, 2016, throwing his support behind frontrunner Donald J. Trump.

Bobby Jindal:
How an Indian-American "Anchor Baby" Steered
Louisiana Politics "To the Right of Rush Limbaugh"

Piyush Jindal (born June 10, 1971), nicknamed "Bobby," was a former U.S. Congressman and the 55th governor of Louisiana from 2008 to 2016. As governor, he became the first Indian American ever elected to high office in the United States, and he was re-elected in a landslide in 2011, though despised by thousands upon thousands of voters.

His parents, who were from the Punjab region of India, came to the United States shortly before the birth of their child as a means of ensuring their son's citizenship, a situation that forever after marked him in some conservative circles as "an Anchor Baby."

His views against same-sex marriage and abortion were formed when he became a faithful Roman Catholic, later writing about his "spiritual journey."

In March of 2001, George W. Bush made him Assistant Secretary of Health and Human Services for Planning and Evaluation, but he later resigned to return to his native state to

Sycophantic Bobby Jindal, governor of Louisiana and lackluster 2016 candidate for President of the United States, poses with his mentor, George W. Bush in 2008. They try to look like they know what they are doing.

"Dubya" was disgraced for his inept handling of Hurricane Katrina that devastated New Orleans in 2005.

run for governor. He lost, but in time won a seat in the U.S. House of Representatives (2005-2008), becoming the second Indian American ever elected to Congress. In office, he warned of the growth of Medicaid.

Returning to Louisiana once again, he entered the contest for governor, winning the 2008 race. He was re-elected. Nearing the end of his second term, he witnessed a sharp decrease in his popularity, facing a budget deficit and painful cuts in public expenditure.

Throughout his tenure as governor, he always had an eye toward changing his address to 1600 Pennsylvania Avenue. As early as 2008, the attack dog of right-wing radio, Rush Limbaugh, cited him as a possible Veep running mate for John McCain.

On June 24, 2015, Jindal announced that he was a candidate for the Republican nomination for President in the 2016 election. *Time* magazine, in an article entitled "Let's Get the Party Started," claimed that his ethnic background would bring diversity to the GOP.

At that point, however, polls showed that he couldn't even carry the vote in Louisiana. On a national level, he gained no traction at all. On March 3, 2016, he withdrew from the race, announcing that he'd vote for Donald Trump.

John Kasich:
"The Prince of Light & Hope"
Is Hailed as the Only Sane Candidate
in the GOP Primary

The current governor of Ohio, John Richard Kasich (born May 13, 1952), was descended from parents with a mixed Czech and Croatian background.

He was actually born in Pennsylvania in McKees Rocks, an industrial town near Pittsburgh. He later moved to Ohio, where he attended Ohio State University. While enrolled there, he wrote a letter to President Richard Nixon about his concerns for the nation, and,

The only sane adult in the GOP circus. John Kasich, Ohio's finest.

Donald called him "a dummy."

to his surprise, was granted a 20-minute interview. He later said, "He did it for Elvis, so why not me?"

In 1978, he ran a strong campaign for an Ohio Senate seat, and he became the youngest person ever elected to the Ohio Senate, launching a four-year term. He stunned voters by refusing himself a pay raise.

With a Ringo Starr coiffure, he ran for the U.S. House of Representatives and won, serving there from 1983 to 2001. His tenure included eighteen years on the House Armed Services Committee and six years as chair of the House Budget Committee, where he was a key figure in the passage of both welfare reform and the Balanced Budget Act of 1997. The following year, he voted to impeach Bill Clinton, based on the many charges brought against him.

He was married to Mary Lee Griffith from 1975 to 1980, when he divorced her. He knew that if he ever ran for President, he would not be the first divorced man to compete for that office. Ronald Reagan had divorced movie star Jane Wyman before marrying MGM starlet Nancy Davis.

As early as 2003, Kasich formed an exploratory committee to run for President, but when fund raising turned pale, he dropped out. For a while, he hosted a news show on the Fox Network.

In 2009, he ran for governor of Ohio, defeating incumbent Ted Strickland in a close contest. He was viewed as a successful governor, and he won re-election in 2004 with Tea Party support. However, he lost much of that backing when he favored expansion of Medicaid.

In April of 2015, he decided to run for President again, announcing his "New Day in America" campaign. On the campaign trail, he projected himself as "The Prince of Light & Hope." As governor, he was viewed as rather abrasive, but running for President, he evoked a gentler, kinder side. "I won't be an attack dog like Donald Trump," he promised.

However, Donald fired back anyway, claiming that "Kasich is one of the worst presidential candidates in history. He's a dummy falling in Obama's trap for Obamacare."

The New York Times endorsed Kasich's candidacy in January of 2016, attacking Donald and Ted Cruz. "Though a distant underdog, Kasich, a long shot contender, is running unapologetically as a candidate with experience even as others run as outsiders."

Reporter Alan James felt that "John Kasich is the only one of the sixteen candidates seeking the GOP nomination who is not insane. Nor is he a Bible Thumper. Perhaps I should say fifteen candidates, since I don't know how religious Donald Trump is. I got the impression that he likes to spend Sunday morning in bed with some knockout beauty, even his stunning wife."

George Pataki: Donald Claims He Couldn't Get Elected Dog-Catcher

George Elmer Pataki (born June 24, 1945) was an attorney who became the 53rd governor of New York (1995-2006). In 1994, he ran against three-times-incum-

> Patacki's presidential campaign--it seems long ago and far away--with memorabilia destined as tomorrow's quaint collectibles on e-bay.

bent, Mario Cuomo, defeating him in the "Republican Revolution." Pataki was one of only three Republican governors elected since 1923 to serve three consecutive terms. The other two included Thomas Dewey and Nelson Rockefeller.

Pataki had ancestors who came from the old Austro-Hungarian Empire, arriving in the United States to work in a hat factory or to become a mailman and a volunteer fire chief. Born a Roman Catholic, young Pataki grew up to attend Yale University, later earning his law degree from Columbia.

In July of 2000, Pataki's name surfaced near the top of the possible Veep candidates that George W. Bush was considering as running mates. Pataki lost to Dick Cheney, the former Secretary of Defense.

During the next presidential cycle (2004), Pataki was instrumental in bringing the Republican National Convention to Madison Square Garden in Manhattan, which had been viewed as hostile terrain, since the Democrats were to carry 78 percent of the vote that year. Pataki's most famous quote was, "This fall, we're going to win one for the Gipper. But our opponents, they're going to lose one with the Flipper," a snide reference to John Kerry.

President George W. Bush appointed Pataki as a U.S. delegate to the 2007 United Nations Assembly. In 2010, he rejected an offer to run for the U.S. Senate, setting his eye on a presidential bid in 2012 instead.

He later bowed out of the race during the 2012 cycle, but although he re-entered it in 2016, he didn't seem to take his race too seriously, missing filing deadlines in Alabama, Arkansas, Florida, Idaho, Ohio, Oklahoma, Texas, Utah, and Virginia. Ultimately, he failed to gain traction, generating national poll numbers that hovered at around one percent.

As 2015 was coming to an end, he realized how hopeless his Don

Quixote quest for the presidency was and bowed out, endorsing Florida Senator Marco Rubio.

Donald Trump held Pataki's campaign in contempt, claiming he couldn't get elected dog-catcher. "He was a terrible governor of New York… one of the worst."

Rand Paul:

"Donald Trump is an Orange-Faced Windbag."
—*Rand Paul*
"Rand Paul Reminds Me of a Spoiled Brat Without a Properly Functioning Brain."
—*Donald Trump*

Randal Howard Paul (born January 7, 1963), nicknamed "Rand," is a Republican Senator from Kentucky, the son of former presidential candidate Ron Paul. Both father and son are skeptical of big government, advocating Libertarian ideas as channeled through the ultra-conservative Tea Party.

Of the candidates, Paul believes the GOP needs a bigger tent and that they should repair their hostile relationship with Black America. That would include reforms within the criminal justice system.

As such, both Paul and his father picked up thousands of students who supported them, at least until Bernie Sanders took many of them away.

Rand Paul claimed that the GOP had to reach out "to the young, to Hispanics, and to blacks."

The senior Paul had had a compromised relationship with neo-Confederates.

Before becoming a politician, Rand Paul was graduated from the Duke University School of Medicine, and began a private practice of ophthalmology.

In 2010, he entered politics and ran for the U.S. Senate, labeling himself a conservative and a supporter of the Tea Party movement, advocating a balanced budget, term limits, and privacy reform. He stands against gun control.

In other positions, he predictably claimed, "I am 100% Pro-life. He also stated that "same-sex marriage offends me, but I would not support a Federal ban." In spite of his anti-

Rand Paul: a fiercely independent political iconoclast who hated "The Donald" and all of his "outrageous platforms."

gay stance, he contradicted himself by claiming, "The government should stay out of your private life."

Appearing on *The Nightly Show* with Larry Wilmore, Paul denounced Donald Trump as "an orange-faced windbag. A delusional narcissist. Have you ever had a speck of dirt fly into your eye? It's annoying, irritating, and might even make you cry. If the dirt doesn't go away, it will keep you scratching your cornea until eventually it blinds you with its filth. A speck of dirt is way more qualified to be President than Trump."

He also likened Donald to Josef Goebbels, the shrill-voiced Nazi propaganda minister. "I'm not sure I would say Trump is Hitler—Goebbels, maybe."

He later compared Donald to Gollum from *The Lord of the Rings*, referring to the deranged, embittered cave dweller who was abnormally obsessed with a magical golden ring.

Paul's remarks infuriated Donald, who claimed, "Rand Paul is a lowly candidate who's made a fool of himself. Why is he allowed to take advantage of the people of Kentucky? He's truly weird. Reminds me of a spoiled brat without a properly functioning brain."

Rick Perry: From Joke Candidate to Donald Trump's First Martyr

James Richard Perry (born March 4, 1950), nicknamed "Rick," was the 47th Governor of Texas, in office from 2000 to 2015. First elected Lieutenant Governor in 1998, he assumed the governorship when George W. Bush resigned to become President of the United States.

Perry was described as a "tall, perma-tanned Bible-thumping Texan, with the

Rick Perry, the Texas governor with good looks, the body "of a retired underwear model," and a reputation for ultra-conservative politics that made him a demon to most of the feminists of his home state.

He had a history of spectacularly corrupt old-boy favoritism that made him a frequent target of the liberal media.

Perry is depicted here in a detail from his oh-so-patriotic official portrait.

physique of a retired underwear model."

Rolling Stone wrote, "The description of Perry's early political career sounded like the first chapters of true-crime books about serial killers, where nobody notices anything special about the protagonist until the bodies start piling up."

Perry had spent several years denying he had presidential ambitions, even claiming that he would not serve as John McCain's Veep in 2008. "I have the best job in the world—and that's Governor of Texas."

In 2012, he entered the race for President, although early on, he was viewed as "the joke candidate" and considered "not all that bright."

Writing about the GOP primaries, *Rolling Stone* defined the candidates as "a cast of hopefuls who are historically underwhelming, a contest of bumblers, second-raters, extremists, and religious loonies."

At first, Perry seemed to count on his "eelish good looks" and countrified manner to outshine another 2012 frontrunner, Mitt Romney, a Mormon whom Perry fully expected would turn off Southern Baptists and other evangelicals.

During the launch of his 2012 campaign, Perry denounced Social Security as "an illegal Ponzi scheme" and promised that, as President, he would repeal the Federal income tax.

Early polling positioned Perry as a frontrunner, garnering 29% of the vote, with Romney a distant second at 18%.

Perry turned out to be a lousy debater, telling millions of TV viewers that, when he was President, he would eliminate three government agencies. On the air, under pressure, he named two but couldn't remember the third.

[It was the Department of Energy.]

More trouble arose along the campaign trail as embarrassments from his past surfaced. It turned out, and was widely publicized, that his family had once leased and occupied a hunting camp in Texas called "Niggerhead."

He also ran an anti-gay campaign. "There's something wrong in this country when gays can serve openly in the military but our kids can't openly celebrate Christmas or pray in school."

Despite his poor *[some said "catastrophic"]* campaign, *Time* magazine wrote that "Everything is aligned for Rick Perry to be the Republican nominee for President in 2016."

***

True to that prediction, he officially launched his race for the White House on June 4, 2015 in Addison, Texas, to the sound of the Colt Ford song, "Answer to No One."

Only a year before, Perry had been indicted by the Travis County Grand Jury, charged with abuse of office for threatening to veto $7.5 million in funding for the Public Integrity Unit, an Statewide agency charged with prosecuting Corruption in Texas Politics. But by February of 2016, he was cleared of all charges.

In a field heavily laden with candidates, Perry gained no traction, and was an early casualty, withdrawing from the race on September 11, 2015. He was the first in an overcrowded field to drop out, after poor polling deriving from his first debate.

He left his campaign in dire financial straits, having spent nearly four times more money than he raised.

He later endorsed a fellow Texan, "Anchor Baby" Senator Ted Cruz. When Cruz dropped out on May 5, 2016, Perry endorsed Donald for the presidency, having previously denounced "the cancer of Trump-ism, a toxic mix of demagoguery and nonsense."

Previously, Donald had said, "As Governor of Texas, Rick Perry did a horrible job of securing the border. He should be ashamed of himself. He also should be forced to take an IQ test."

Marco Rubio

"A Lightweight like Little Marco Rubio will never make America great again."
—Donald Trump

A Cuban-American, Marco Rubio (born May 28, 1971), an attorney, is the junior U.S. Senator from Florida. His parents grew up in Cuba, but immigrated to the United States in 1956, prior to the rise of Fidel Castro in January of 1959. Neither of his parents was a U.S. citizen at the time of Rubio's birth, leading to some charges that, like fellow Cuban, Ted Cruz, "Little Marco" is also an Anchor Baby."

His later statement that his parents were forced to leave Cuba in 1959, after Castro seized power, was a lie.

After graduating from the University of Miami Law School, Rubio was later elected to the Florida House of Representatives, where, according to *NBC News*, "He aggressively tried to push Florida to the political right." He became Speaker of the Florida House of Representatives at the age of 34, becoming the first Cuban American to ever hold that post.

During his tenure as Speaker, Rubio shared a house in Tallahassee with David Rivera, another representative. After several missed mortgage payments, the bank foreclosed.

In Tallahassee, Rubio became a *protégé* of then-governor Jeb Bush. In 2009, he ran for the U.S. Senate seat from Florida, clashing with Charlie Crist, who had been the incumbent governor of Florida. Since they had opposed many of Crist's policies as governor, the Tea Party endorsed Rubio

Rubio was a critic of Crist's strategy to fight climate change, although many experts predicted that Miami Beach will be under water one day because of rising tides.

On November 2, 2010, during Florida's general midterm election, Rubio was elected Senator with 49% of the vote, in marked contrast to Crist's 30%.

Although he'd just arrived in Washington, a Senatorial newcomer, there was speculation that he might be a potential Republican candidate for the 2012 presidential election. Despite the hype, Rubio opted not to run during that election cycle.

MARCO RUBIO

VOTE ★★★ 2016 ★★★

PRESIDENT

Dream on, Marco...The Florida senator with the big ears promised to restore "the American Dream to the Middle Class," but his race for the White House turned into a nightmare, largely because of Donald's barrage of insults and widely publicized denunciations.

Attacking him as "the Absentee Senator," and a "political lightweight," Donald carried Rubio's home state in the Republican primaries.

Despite Rubio's having stated that he would not run for office again, in the summer of 2016, after his failure to win the Republican party's presidential nomination, he announced that he would run again in a bid for his former Senate seat.

But on April 13, 2015, he officially threw his hat into the ring, becoming a candidate for President in the GOP primaries. That would eventually bring him into conflict with Donald Trump. Rubio's campaign was based on his promise to restore "The American Dream" for the middle class. As justification for his passion, he cited his own background as the son of a working immigrant family living from paycheck to paycheck.

At first, Donald and Rubio refrained from criticizing each other, at least until Donald began to interpret him as a serious candidate. Then, one reporter noted, "They launched World War III."

Donald denounced Rubio as "Dishonest…He's scamming Florida. He treats America ICE [*Immigration and Customs Enforcement*] officers like absolute trash in order to pass Obama's amnesty to criminal aliens guilty of sex offenses. He is the puppet of the special interest Koch brothers."

He also cited Rubio's poor attendance record in the U.S. Senate, asserting that during one year alone, he had missed 35% of the Senate votes because he was out of town.

Rick Santorum:
"I Compare Homosexuality to Bestiality"

If any other candidate had taken a turn as sharp to the right as Rick Santorum, he would surely have run off the road. Richard John Santorum (born May 10, 1958), nicknamed "Rick," represented Pennsylvania in the U.S. Senate from 1995-2007. During his tenure there, in his capacity as "Conference Chairman," he was the Senate's third-ranking Republican.

Self-identifying as a devout Roman Catholic, he became a leading social conservative vehemently opposing same-sex marriage and even artificial birth control. He was also the author of the Santorum Amendment, promoting the teaching of Intelligent Design in schools.

On the foreign front, he favored the War on Terror and declared that weapons of mass destruction had been found in Iraq. He defended the harsh treatment of prisoners in Guantánamo Bay and favored waterboarding during his assault on "Islamic fascism."

On the home front, he lashed out at "radical feminism," comparing pro-choice Americans to Nazis.

He became the major "family values" advocate within the Senate, endorsing only monogamous, heterosexual relationships and traditional (male-female) marriages. He opposed both same-sex marriages and civil unions, too. "I favor laws against polygamy, sodomy, and other actions antithetical to a healthy, stable, traditional family. I compare ho-

Rick Santorum, "family man."

"How?" his legions of haters asked, "did this fanatical, pro-life, anti-gay, semi-permanent fixture at the 'Kiddies' Table' manage to remain in the presidential race as long as he did?"

mosexuality to bestiality."

[In 2015, he signed an online pledge vowing not to respect any law from the U.S. Supreme Court that endorsed same-sex marriage, claiming that such unions were against a "natural created order."]

He went on to describe contraception "as a license to do things in a sexual realm that is counter to how things are supposed to be." He also promised, if elected President, he would get rid of porn, which he claimed "causes brain damage."

Finally, on November 7, 2006, the voters of the very sane state of Pennsylvania wised up about the right wing firecracker, voting him out of office. He lost by more than 700,000 votes to the very sane and rational Bob Casey, Jr.

In 2012, Santorum decided to seek the presidency. He won the Iowa caucuses, getting only 34 more votes than Mitt Romney. He seemed on a roll, winning in eleven state primaries and garnering four million votes, more than any candidate except Romney. But he finally had to concede the race to his rival, whom he endorsed at the Republican National Convention.

In 2015, he decided to run for President once again. But this time he didn't generate any enthusiasm and was assigned to "the kiddies' table" in early debates.

He campaigned as a "culture warrior," and as a "true Christian conservative." Critics accused him of wanting to abolish the tenants of the U.S. Constitution in favor of a "Christian theocracy."

Santorum likened Obamacare to apartheid in South Africa in a Nelson Mandela tribute speech.

One of Donald's campaign workers said, "I've heard of extreme views, and there is Rick Santorum. Up to now, I thought Obama was the worst President in U.S. history. But that's because we won't survive a Santorum presidency. I'm sure he would bring back the Spanish Inquisition."

Santorum ended his campaign on February 3, 2016, endorsing Senator Marco Rubio, although he couldn't really give any good reason for doing so.

Scott Walker:
He Survived a Recall from Voters in His Home State, but Not the GOP Rat Race for the White House

"Scott Walker is not presidential material...He's a not very smart puppet."
—Donald Trump

The 45th Governor of Wisconsin, Scott Walker (born November 2, 1967) received national attention in 2012 when he survived a recall election. Democrats wanted to kick him out of the governor's mansion when he introduced a budget plan that limited collective bargaining among state workers and public employers. The centerpiece of rage and controversy, he became the first American governor ever to survive a recall effort.

Another controversial move was in 2011, when he defunded Planned Parenthood from Wisconsin's State budget. Two years later, he signed a bill that required women seeking an abortion to undergo an Ultrasound so doctors could show the patient the image of her fetus, presumably to shame them into canceling their abortions.

In addition to fighting the unions of Wisconsin, Walker signed a "no-climate tax," opposing any legislation that would raise taxes to combat climate change.

He did not rule out sending U.S. troops to Syria to oppose ISIS, and he said that, if elected President, he would send arms to Ukraine to fight Russia.

He also opposed the U.S.'s growing ties to Cuba, and claimed that he would rescind any prior deal brokered with Iran. He also declined to answer a question about whether he thought Obama was a true Christian.

Walker had not been born in Wisconsin, but in Colorado Springs. He had been reared, however, in both Iowa and Wisconsin before attending Marquette University. He did not graduate, but left school to accept a full-time job with the Red Cross.

He followed that by winning an election to the Wisconsin State Assembly in 1992, a venue where multiple future protests would be lodged against him. Later, he was elected county executive in Milwaukee County, and followed that in minor posts until he decided to seek the governorship in 2006. He didn't make it in 2006. He tried again in 2010, this

Scott Walker during the heady moments of victory in the immediate aftermath of his 2010 victory in the Wisconsin Republican primary.

After a disturbing tenure as a lightning rod for the ultra-conservative Tea Party right, his appeal died fast.

399

time defeating Democrat Tom Barrett.

In late January of 2015, he set up an organization called "Our American Revival," which, in essence, was his first shot at running for President. "Within a month, he'd quickly vaulted into the top tier of likely candidates for the Republican presidential race," or so said *The New York Times*. On July 13, he officially declared himself a candidate for the Republican nomination.

In June, he emerged as a comfortable frontrunner in a *Des Moines Register* poll placing him at 17%, but by the end of August, he'd fallen to 7%. He seemed to wilt during debates, overshadowed by Donald's larger-than-life stage presence. A national survey from Monmouth University that August (2015) had Walker dropping to 3%, in contrast to his 10% in June.

For weeks, despite focused attention from the media, Walker "seemed to walk all over the map, trying to articulate his positions on immigration and other issues, but it was obvious that he was not connecting with the voter," one reporter wrote. "On immigration, he seemed to take three different positions over the period of a month."

Facing declining support, Walker proposed an even more controversial stand than Donald. He suggested that America's northern border with Canada should have a wall built, "stretching from sea to sea." It would be similar to the one Donald was proposing for Mexico.

"It is a legitimate issue for us to look at," Walker said. "Secure the border, enforce the laws. No amnesty," he proclaimed.

His proposal was met with ridicule and scorn. The 5,525-mile-long U.S.-Canadian border is the longest undefended international border in the world, but only a small percentage of illegal immigrant come across it.

Walker and his campaign began a meltdown, plagued with the perception that he would not become a viable candidate, nationally. His campaign funds dried up.

On September 12, 2015, he suspended his campaign, asking other candidates to do the same, so that the GOP could rally around what he defined as the "conservative alternative" to Donald Trump: Ted Cruz. On March 29, 2016, he endorsed Cruz, a senator whose views were even miles to the right of Walker's own ultra-conservative positions.

For doing that, Donald lashed into him, calling him "a puppet, not presidential material. As Governor of Wisconsin, he ran up a massive deficit. He made of mess of jobs, delivering a bad forecast, a mess really. He's not very smart, a dumb fundraiser who hit me very hard—not smart at all."

"I OUTDID ALL THOSE LOSERS"
Donald Trump in Reference to His Performance at His First GOP Debate

The first live broadcast of a Republican National Debate was on August 6, 2015 at the Quicken Loans Arena in Cleveland, the same city in which the Republican Nominating Convention would convene in July of 2016

Broadcast on Fox News Channel, it was watched by 24 million viewers, making it the most-watched event in the history of cable TV.

Because there were so many candidates in an overcrowded race, Fox aired two separate debates.

Candidates at the bottom of the polls were assigned what was derisively called "the kiddies' table." Appearing at 5PM, the low-ranked candidates included Rick Perry, Bobby Jindal, Rick Santorum, Lindsey Graham, Carly Fiorina, George Pataki, and Jim Gilmore, in a debate moderated by Bill Hemmer and Martha McCallum.

The main debate, scheduled for the prime-time TV hour of 9PM, included Donald Trump (prominently positioned as the lineup's centerpiece), and his chief rivals, Ted Cruz, Scott Walker, Jeb Bush, Ben Carson, Marco Rubio, Mike Huckabee, Chris Christie, Rand Paul, and John Kasich. The Moderators included Bret Baier, Megyn Kelly, and Chris Wallace.

Even though he was leading in the polls, many of Donald's Republican enemies demanded that he should not be included in the debate, since he was not viewed "as a serious contender."

In an unrelated grievance, Santorum, Graham, and Fiorina complained to Fox based on their banishment "to the boondocks," The trio claimed that

The lineup for the contenders from the "adults table" at the first Republican debate in Cleveland, August, 2015. It was compared in the press to an "apocalyptic sect of loopy Christian fundamentalists evoking a frat-house dong-measure contest."

their assignment to a second rank position would make them less competitive in the upcoming primaries and caucuses. Fox turned a deaf ear.

A review of the debaters at the kiddies' table noted that Fiorina "was swimming in bright pink in a sea of dark-suited men." Her strong performance catapulted her into the national spotlight, bouncing her up in the polls. Based partly on that, she maintained, "I deserve a prime position on stage with the big boys."

After the early debate that evening, Jindal also got some scant praise, but, for the most part, Pataki, Graham, Gilmore, Perry, and Santorum were punched by critics. The lower tier debate was the first and only one for Perry. His post-debate poll numbers were so dismal that he didn't qualify for inclusion in any future debates. Reacting to that, he decided "to throw in the towel," as he phrased it.

Before going on, Donald had been skeptical, saying, "I'm not a debater, and I don't know how well I will perform. I question the value of debates. Politicians are always debating with little in the way of results."

At the debate, Donald was the chief attraction, being granted the most "voice time" time at 10 minutes, 32 seconds. Jeb Bush trailed at 8:10 minutes. Rand Paul got the least time, at 5 minutes.

Press reaction to the candidates' individual performances was divided. For the most part, Donald was criticized for being "rude and erratic."

In vivid contrast, "his supporters mopped it up," said Ohio voter Greg Benson. "The others were like a Bloody Mary without the vodka."

In post-debate analysis, the press tended to praise Jeb's tolerance, while attacking Donald's harsh rhetoric that called for the deportation of millions. At the debate, Jeb had described immigration as "an act of love," a statement that Donald later mocked.

Donald also clashed with moderators Kelly and Wallace on the issue of

Megyn Kelly: The moderator who became almost as famous as the characters in the news cycle she was covering.

Was the blood coming from her eyes—or from somewhere else? Donald raised that point after her intense probing of him.

sexism and illegal immigration.

Kelly launched into Donald like a tigress smelling fresh kill. She listed shocking derogatory remarks she said the GOP hopeful had made about women, describing them as "fat pigs, dogs, slobs, and disgusting animals."

He reserved his defense for later, trying to escape from her trap, although admitting to a feud he'd previously maintained with Rosie O'Donnell, after she'd attacked him in front of millions of talk-show viewers.

But later, with Don Lemon on CNN, in reference to Megyn Kelly, he said, "There was blood coming out of her eyes, blood coming out of her whatever."

[In a subsequent interview, he backed down, claiming he'd meant blood coming from her nose when he said, "wherever." But audiences knew he was suggesting that she was menstruating.]

He later attacked her as "being highly overrated, so average in so many ways. Crazy, sick, not worth watching, always complaining about me, yet she devotes entire shows to me. Get a life, Megyn! Without me, your ratings would tank. I refuse to call her a bimbo, since that would not be politically correct."

After the debate, polls showed Donald outperforming his rivals. "I was winning at every stage of the debate," he claimed. "*Drudge* put me at the top, and so did *Time* magazine."

In spite of the controversy, many polls showed that Donald was appealing to thousands upon thousands of voters who had never cast a ballot before.

When Kelly appeared in an interview with Charlie Rose that October, she stated her case, claiming that she had not wanted "any sort of war with Trump. He was obviously upset. That's fine: He's running for President. It's not a fun business. There's gonna be ups and downs, and I know he considered that a down. So we just wanted to forge forward and try to put it behind us, not pour any more fuel on that fire."

She defined the feud she and Fox

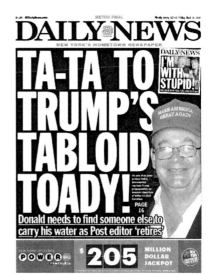

DAILY NEWS

NEW YORK'S HOMETOWN NEWSPAPER

TA-TA TO TRUMP'S TABLOID TOADY!

I'M WITH STUPID!

PAGE 16

Donald needs to find someone else to carry his water as Post editor 'retires'

POWERBALL $ **205** MILLION DOLLAR JACKPOT

Notoriously competitive (some say "mutually vindictive,") the two big tabloids of New York City differed in bloodthirsty ways about virtually everything associated with Donald Trump.

When a Trump fan, a top editor endorsed by Rupert Murdoch at the *New York Post* retired, the *Daily News* exposed and celebrated his departure.

News had had with Donald as "bizarre. I became the story. You know, you never want to be the story when you are a news person."

She told ABC's George Stephanopoulos, "You want to be covering the story so it was like an Alice-through-the-looking-glass experience."

Fox released a statement of its own. "Donald Trump's vitriolic attacks against Megyn Kelly and his extreme, sick obsession with her is beneath the dignity of a presidential candidate who wants to occupy the highest office in the land."

One reporter wrote: "More and more, Trump is sounding like an eight-year-old confused by his feelings for his third-grade teacher and lashing out."

At CNN, Anderson Cooper claimed, "The Kelly-Trump feud fuels the narrative that Trump is a misogynist and too thin-skinned to be President."

Kayleigh McEnany, the conservative columnist, said, "It plays well with the Republican base any time you attack the media."

Kelly claimed that broadcasting news "is a fickle business. Everything is rolling along fine and then you accidentally call Mike Huckabee 'Fuckabee'—and you're gone."

She was asked what her dream interviews would be, responding, "I'd love to interview Putin, Assad, Bill Clinton, Melania Trump, and most definitely Hillary Clinton…and also the Pope."

To Hell with Political Correctness! Donald Trump Is
THE MAN WHO WOULD BE KING

Throughout the "Summer of Trump," Donald received both praise and brickbats. Conservative columnist Ted Wrobleski lauded him, while others used such expressions as "a blowhard," "a TV huckster," a "buffoon," and "a soulless one-per-center."

"He may not be the best person for the job, but Donald Trump has saved us from the play-it-safe, poll-driven, stage-managed, social-media-drenched tedium that passes for presidential politics," Wrobleski wrote. "We can be thankful for that. The political ruling elite can't stand it. American culture and politics are all about

Trumpus Rex

money and celebrity—and Donald Trump's got both."

Talking on Sirius Radio, Chris Spatola, a former U.S. Army captain, attacked Donald. "He is reality TV in an age in which sound bites and sensationalism proliferate. He reflects the public's anger about politics. He appeals to those who feel left behind economically, culturally, and politically. He is not rooted in dogmatic ideology. No one knows what he really believes on policy."

"He plays to a part of the Republican Party that traffics in prejudice and feat. A part that believes immigrants are rapists and drug-dealing criminals, and that homosexuals are corrupting the 'sanctity of marriage'…and yada, yada, yada," Spatola charged.

Finally, he concluded, "Trump is not going to win the Republican nomination."

The Doomsday threat for candidate Donald was also echoed by Chris Cillizza in *The Washington Post.* "The question is what exactly does Trump's popularity (gulp) mean? There is no way he'll get nominated."

The normally savvy Bill Kristol, editor of *The Weekly Standard,* said, "Trump is a mere showman who will not last through the debates. He'll drop out along the way."

Senator Rand Paul, who at first viewed himself as the frontrunner, claimed, "There is no way voters in this country will nominate Trump. He's on every channel, all the time, and people have gone gaga. But it won't last. Trust me."

Donald's attacks in the media swelled into an avalanche. James Fallows, a correspondent for *The Atlantic,* wrote: "He is a novelty, a candidate akin to Herman Cain or Michele Bachmann. He has no experience in appointed or elected office, or in the military. His derisive remarks about Mexicans would not bear scrutiny."

In spite of all these dire predictions, Donald continued to dominate the polls as summer moved toward its inevitable end. On the *National Interest* website appeared this comment:

> *"Donald Trump is egotistical, vain, bombastic, often mean-spirited. He revels in his financial superiority, which he conflates with human goodness. When he contorts his mouth into a kind of tube as he talks, you brace yourself for something outrageous. His likability quotient, at least in terms of public persona, is down somewhere in the single digits and yet, he has just taken hold of the American political system by the neck and doesn't seem inclined to let go anytime soon."*

In late August, Sarah Palin became one of Donald's early supporters, bringing him onto her right-wing TV talk show. "You're bringing back the Silent Majority," she told him. "I need you to set the record straight because I think we're not getting the truth from the White House. The idiots in the press are misrepresenting your positions."

At the end of the interview, she told Trump, "You're a terrific person. Before going off the air, she praised Curt Schilling *[The American major league baseball pitcher, a former video game developer, and right-wing political blogger]* "for comparing Muslims to Nazis."

The political heat wave generated by Donald continued through the dog days of August. Polls showed him beating Carson, Cruz, and Rubio, his chief rivals. He also picked up more support, even from former presidential candidate Pat Buchanan. Buchanan expressed praise for Donald, even though Donald had once compared Buchanan to Hitler.

Donald continued to convert thousands upon thousands of voters to his cause, perhaps based on his rather abrasive approach to politics, a style that was likened to "shooting from the hip—and to hell with political correctness."

He feared no competition from such candidates as Paul, Perry, and Graham. "They spent all summer at the bottom of the polls. I predict all these bottom feeders are losers."

The losers shot back: Paul mocked Donald's credentials as a true conservative; Graham threatened to "beat his brains out"; and Perry compared his politics to a fatal disease. In the polls, Paul came in at 6%, Perry at 1%, and Graham at 0%.

Jeb Bush lost more ground than he'd gained, despite an outlay of millions from his fat campaign war chest. Many pundits had considered Jeb a shoo-in, but as the summer ended, his polls had dropped to 6%. Jeb attacked Donald, calling him "a germaphobe trying to insult his way into the presidency."

Hoping to appeal to Hispanics, the bilingual Jeb often spoke Spanish at campaign rallies.

Donald attacked him for this, claiming, "He should really be speaking English in the United States."

Jeb appeared on ABC News, saying that, "Immigration and multi-lingualism that comes with it contributes to the vitality of America."

"Jeb tries to look cool, but can't make it," Donald said. "He's even dropped those glasses in favor of contact lenses to make him look more masculine. He's spending a fortune in campaign funds to defeat me. But he's a weak, desperate candidate."

As the Trump summer sun continued to blaze, Ben Carson forged ahead in the polls, as did Carly Fiorina.

Carson, Fiorina, and Donald were each "outsider candidates," and the public responded to that, viewing Establishment politicians with disdain. Donald attacked Bush, Cruz, and Rubio as career politicians.

At 18%, Carson rose to second place. Donald attacked Carson as "incapable of understanding foreign policy and illegal immigration. He has never created a job in his life"

He accused Fiorina "of running a dead campaign. If you listen to her for more than ten minutes, you develop a massive headache. She has zero chance." He also attacked her record as CEO at Hewlett-Packard: "She got fired for doing a terrible job!"

During the first months of the campaign, Donald and Cruz were accused of having a "bromance," based on not having mutually attacked each other. In the coming months, however, that would downgrade into "a wild dog fight."

When Cruz was interviewed by right-wing radio talk show host, Hugh Hewitt, the Texas senator said, "I think people are ticked off at Washington, and they want someone who will stand up to the corrupt power elite, someone who will take them on and tell the truth. I think that's why Donald has attracted the early support he has."

In roughly similar phraseologies, Donald, on CNN's *State of the Union* said, "There's a movement going on that's more than me. People are tired of these incompetent politicians in Washington. For that reason, I'm not surprised they're turning to me."

To the shock of many within the Republican Party, Donald went on to attack John McCain, the Arizona Senator who had run for President in 2008. "He was not a war hero," Donald charged. "The war heroes were soldiers who weren't captured. Not only that, he let the public down and didn't defeat Obama in 2008. He's made up pay an awful price for putting that guy in office."

As the first autumn winds blew down from the north, and the dog days of August cooled into early autumn, September unfolded with another big debate.

A pundit, Jimmy Connors, wrote: "For now, we may just have to sit back and marvel as the 'Summer of Trump' comes to an end. We must recognize that it's the real thing…and spectacular. All the naysayers were wrong. Donald Trump, or so it seems, has more lives than Rasputin."

Grigori Rasputin (1872-1916) was the demonically terrifying Russian mystic, priest and confessor to the Empress
Alexandra at the Romanov court of Czar Nicholas II. By
1914, he had become an influential and divisive factor in
Russian politics.

He proved hard to kill, but was done in by a group of
Russian noblemen.

PART THREE

THE AUTUMN OF TRUMP

INCREDULITY

("What the F#@%? Donald Trump?? For President???)

VS. CREDIBILITY

"Donald Trump is here for the duration—and gaining strength and traction by the hour."
—Reporter Paul Solotaroff

Chapter Sixteen

INSULT BY INSULT
Donald Climbs in the Polls

Although Naysayers Insist,
"There's No Way He Can Ever Win"
DONALD KNOCKS OFF
HIS REPUBLICAN RIVALS

POLARIZATION AND PROTESTS
Attacks on The Donald Intensify

"I FINANCE MY OWN CAMPAIGN
And I'm Too Rich to be Bought Like Hillary & Jeb"

BLACK LIVES MATTER
At Pro-Donald Rallies, Protesters Dress Up Like the KKK

By the beginning of September, 2015, many journalists had reconsidered their initial rejection of Donald as a candidate for the White House. Reports cautiously surfaced that "the billionaire frontrunner's demise may be premature." In begrudging admiration, one headline read "THE SUMMER OF TRUMP MAY NOT BE OVER."

One thing, at least, was certain: Donald, his comments, and his points of view made for very interesting reading. His entry into the presidential race had sparked a series of blood feuds, pitting the GOP establishment against dozens of die-hard conservative grassroots movements. As one reporter evaluated the antagonists: "The (Republican) party's nativist constituency is pitted against its globalist elites."

As Donald rose in the polling, it was speculated that he would never be awarded with the actual nomination, but that he might play a kingmaker at a brokered convention. Again and again, it was cited that Herman Cain, Rick Perry, and Michele Bachmann had each been short-term frontrunners in 2012, only to crash, burn, and then fall down from out of the sky.

Nate Cohn in *The New York Times* wrote: "Trump's surge in the polls has followed the classic pattern of a media-driven surge. Now it will most likely follow the classic pattern of a party-backed decline."

On one point, nearly every reporter and TV pundit agreed: Already, although the political season had just started, it had been one of the most unpredictable on record. Donald continued to dominate hour-to-hour media coverage and remained at the top of GOP polls.

"He has seen 'dragon Scott Walker' turn out to be a mere harmless lizard," wrote a reporter in Wisconsin.

Donald needed evangelical support and, with that in mind, tried to show off his theological depths: "When I go to church, and I drink a little wine—the only wine I drink since I shun alcohol—and I eat a little cracker, I guess that's a form of forgiveness."

"Not since Billy Graham," mocked one reporter in response, "have we seen such an uplifting display of Christian sentiment."

***

Through it all, Donald remained witty, provocative, outrageous, and always telegenic, despite makeup that somehow managed to resonate as orange-toned, except for white highlights around his eyes.

Much of the media continued to treat and interpret his candidacy as a

TV reality show.

He glossed over his business failures and highlighted his successes. Even so, David Segal in *The Washington Post* wrote: "The people who know the least about business admire him the most, and those who know the most about business admire him the least."

Reporter Paul Solotaroff wrote: "Since Trump announced his candidacy, he has been mocked and reviled, worshipped and courted, and, till very lately, dismissed as a fever dream of the torch-and-pitchfork segment of the Republican Party. His negatives, however, have been through the roof."

"Even so, he stays on message: 'I am strong. Politicians are weak.'"

"If you're waiting for Trump to blow himself up in a Hindenburg of gaffes or hate speech, you're in for a long, cold fall and winter," said Solotaroff. "Donald Trump is here for the duration—and gaining strength and traction by the hour."

Donald told the world, "I'm tired of the party hacks—the Jeb Bushes, Scott Walkers, and Karl Roves. The people look at these jokers and say, 'This one's owned by David Koch, that one's owned by Sheldon Adelson, and so on. As for me, I'm owned by the people, and I'm going to do right by them."

John McCain, whom Donald had called "not a war hero," spoke up against him during the closing days of August. "Trump has fired up the crazies. It's very hurtful to our party."

The Arizona Senator (the one who had disastrously selected Sarah Palin as his candidate for Veep during his own bid for the presidency in 2008) appeared worried that he

An anti-Trump rally near San Francisco turned into a STOP HATE gathering. A sea of protesters accused Donald of using racism to seize power in America.

Signs also protested his anti-immigration stance and his call for American Muslims to wear special IDs, evoking the Yellow Star that Jews were forced to wear in Nazi Germany.

might lose his own re-election.

In retaliation, Donald shot back: "McCain is all talk, no action. He spends too much time on television and not enough time doing his job."

On September 11, 2015, a poll revealed that Donald continued to appeal to the most extreme members of the GOP—"Those whose views are way out in right field," Sixty-one percent of those polled believed that President Obama was not born in Hawaii. These same voters also felt that Obama was "lying about his religion and was a secret Muslim."

They supported changing the 14th Amendment, which guarantees citizenship to all U.S.-born children, regardless of their parents' immigration status, the so-called "Anchor Babies."

"My Rival Candidates Are Wacko Birds"
—Donald Trump

At mass rallies, Donald jangled the nerves of many in the GOP establishment, who had for years run on the promise of cutting taxes. In contrast, he said he might raise taxes in certain areas, especially on corporations which "do not act in the best interests of America."

He also threatened to impose tariffs on American companies that transferred their factories to other countries to take advantage of "slave labor."

Republicans shot back, claiming that Donald's policies were "antigrowth and would drive the American economy into the ground with huge drops in the G.D.P." Many predicted massive job losses.

In retaliation, he denounced hedge fund managers, defining them as "paper pushers who tend to get lucky on the road to riches."

He also jumped into the health insurance controversy, suggesting that to lower health care costs, insurers should be allowed to sell their policies across state lines. "My plan would eliminate a lot of red tape and lower administrative costs, which would lead to price reductions for the consumer."

His style was loud, pushy, and bombastic, a delivery that seemed to go over with voters. But, almost unnoticed, at first, the soft-spoken Ben Carson was slipping upward in the polls, coasting on his reputation as a Bible-loving Christian with a low-key personality. Polls had him in second place, some having him tied neck-and-neck with Donald.

The two men had completely different styles, with Donald being mad as hell, combative, and unfiltered, and Carson almost professorial.

Carson's campaign advisors told him to backpedal from his highly provocative anti-homosexual views. One observer noted that he went through the summer of 2015 in the shadow of the Trump supernova, and therefore never really came under scrutiny for his many dubious and off-the-wall observations and statements.

Carson advocated a repeal of Obamacare and the imposition of an annual flat tax that could be filed in fifteen minutes. He denounced global warming theories as "irrelevant." He also said that Planned Parenthood opened most clinics in black neighborhoods to control that population.

For most of these statements *The Washington Post* assigned Carson "four Pinocchios," a graphic illustration that implied a low quotient of truthfulness and/or accuracy.

He appealed to the same "hungry-for-change" conservatives that Donald did, but he packaged his message alongside an inspirational life story, aggressively resisting most of Donald's street-fighting tactics.

"He's not going to be a screamer or a bomb-thrower," said Carson's campaign manager, Barry Bennett. "He's in it for the good of the country. Carson by far is the more likable guy."

The unflinching stream of media attacks on Donald continued as columnist Bill Hammond claimed he "was morphing from a sideshow to a virus of the body politic—exposing and exploiting weakness in its immune response to claptrap hucksterism, especially on the Republican side."

Doug Muzzio, a political scientist at Baruch College, claimed, "What Trump says bypasses the cerebral cortex and goes right from the base of his spinal column out of his mouth."

There were reports that Donald's attacks on Mexicans were whipping up hate crimes. After a pair of thugs in Boston beat up a Mexican immigrant, they told police after they were caught, "Trump was right. All these illegals need to be deported."

There was growing concern that if Donald failed in his race to win the Republican nomination, he might establish a splinter party, rejecting the GOP altogether and running as a third party candidate like Ross Perot did in 1992.

Based partly on that possibility, and in light of Donald's notorious unpredictability, the RNC demanded that each of its candidates sign a statement vowing not to run as a third party choice. Reince Priebus, the RNC's chairman, promised to personally negotiate with Donald to get him to sign.

On September 3, Don-

ald signed the pledge. "I see no circumstances in which I would tear up that pledge, although it is not legally binding."

In exchange for signing the pledge, Donald claimed he got nothing from the RNC. A reporter said he "sounded like Marlon Brando at the beginning of *The Godfather*." In a show of one-upmanship, Donald demanded that Priebus fly into New York to meet him at Trump Tower.

One of the first major protests outside Trump Tower was launched on September 3, after he'd signed the pledge to support whatever candidate the GOP ultimately endorsed.

Angered by his comments about immigration, protesters waved signs denouncing Donald as a racist. Many of them wore white hoods and KKK robes. A security guard at the tower was caught on video punching a protester in the face after he ripped up an anti-Trump sign. The guard later claimed, "I was jumped from behind."

It would be the first of many protests to come during the months ahead.

Through it all, Donald's best-funded rival, Jeb Bush, consistently failed to connect with millions of voters. Although he kept snipping at Donald's heels, he remained largely ineffective in bringing him down. Columnist Paul Krugman wrote: "*[Jeb]* Bush may pose as a reasonable, thoughtful type—credulous reporters even describe him as a policy wonk—but his actual economic platform, which relies on the magic of tax cuts to deliver a doubling of America's economic rate, is pure supply-side voodoo."

Although she'd been relegated to the outer fringes of the campaign, Sarah Palin continued to insert herself. During the first week of September, she claimed she'd serve as Energy Secretary in a Trump administration, but followed that pronouncement with the immediate vow to shut down the agency altogether. "I think states should have more control over their lands. Energy is my baby when I was governor of Alaska. I was known for my 'Drill, baby, drill!'"

Donald came under attack from rival candidate Carly Fiorina, who faulted him for not understanding the difference between Hamas and Hezbollah. She cited an interview Donald had delivered to radio host Hugh Hewitt, in which he had confused the Quds Force, a special Iranian military unit, with the Kurds.

Later, he accused Hewitt of asking him "*gotcha* questions," and denounced him as a "third-rate radio announcer."

As his campaign moved forward, Republicans were growing concerned that his inflammatory language would damage their party. There was a real fear that the aggressive tone of his rhetoric would turn off voters, especially Hispanics and African Americans, both of whom, polls showed, viewed him unfavorably at the rate of 80%.

"If we're going to be a majority party in the 21st Century, we're going to have to be a multi-racial, multi-ethnic, and an inclusive party," intoned (Republican) Representative Tom Cole of Oklahoma.

Donald also alienated many in the Black Lives Matter movement, based partly on his calls for law and order, as he defended the police and cited incidences of crime, raising anxiety and prejudice among white voters. He promised he would rid heavily black Ferguson, Missouri, of "gangs and tough dudes. The same goes for Chicago and Baltimore."

He delivered a speech in Nashville, in which he claimed that 99.9% of the police were good. "That first night in Baltimore, officials allowed that city to be destroyed by the blacks. They set back the city 35 years because the police were not allowed to protect people."

Echoing the same sentiment, Ted Cruz expressed a different slant on the assault on cops, blaming Obama for any attacks on the men in blue. Scott Walker also criticized the Black Lives Matter movement, calling for a change in tone "from chants and rallies that fixate on racial division."

With his hawk eye, Donald kept close watch on his competition. Subsequently, he was delighted that Carson, a surgeon and so-called scientist, did not believe in evolution.

Donald heard that Jeb was wounded that Donald found him boring, and promised "to unleash my American animal spirits at the next debate."

"As for Rubio, the high point of his summer was when he hit a kid in the head with a football," Donald told an aide. "As for Christie, he's got the Bridgegate thing, and now he's exposed for taking free plane rides to football games. Cruz seems to be joining himself to me at the hip so no one will look too closely at his wacko bird proposals."

Again and again, many of Donald's detractors stated that they didn't think he'd go over with evangelicals. Carson said, "My faith is a very big part of who I am. I doubt if that is true of Mr. Trump. I don't get that impression from him."

Although for the most part, Donald seemed to defend Planned Parenthood, his did not endorse its platform on abortions. "I would look at the legal aspects of it," he told CNN. His position was in marked contrast to candidates like Cruz, who was willing to escalate another government shutdown as the vehicle that would enable him to strip the organization of its $500 million in Federal funds, none of which went to pay for abortions.

Even Donald's attendance at Marble Collegiate Church in Manhattan came under fire. "That's where this married man met his next mistress, Marla Maples," one anti-Trump campaigner charged.

"Nothing beats the Bible," Donald said. "Not even *The Art of the Deal.*"

David Brody, chief political correspondent for the Christian Broadcasting Network, tried to explain Donald's appeal to evangelicals. "We're sick and tired of being used as political pawns in the Republican leadership's *Game of Thrones.* Along comes Trump, who, for better or worse, is coming across as honest and truth-telling. And evangelicals are loving every moment of it."

When Donald heard that Fiorina, based on her surging polls, would move up from the "kiddies' table" to a prime time position among the main candidates during the upcoming debate, he backed down on his charge about how ugly she was. "I was talking about her *persona*, not her looks," he said, by way of explanation during his appearance on *Fox & Friends* on September 10. "The fact is, I probably did say something about Carly in a jocular manner."

[What he said was, "Look at that face. Would anyone vote for that? Can you imagine that, the face of our next President? I mean, she's a woman, and I'm not supposed to say bad things, but, really, folks. Come on. Are we serious?"

Fiorina had responded, "I'm getting under his skin a little because I am climbing in the polls."]

In spite of the attacks, a CNN poll in September showed Donald's support at 32%, an eight-point gain since August.

Hillary Clinton, perhaps as a preview of how she'd be handling unchivalrous comments from Donald, weighed in on the Trump/Fiorina controversy. At a rally in Washington, D.C., she said, "He seems to delight in insulting women every chance he gets. I must say, if he emerges, I would love to debate him."

To divert attention away from his remarks about women, Donald brought up the subject of foreign affairs: "The Ukraine crisis is rooted in the weakness of President Obama. Vladimir Putin felt free to invade the Crimea because he lacks respect for the President. Obama is not strong."

On September 12, Donald received news that the Texas governor, Rick Perry, had withdrawn from the presidential race. Headlines blared: "TRUMP CLAIMS HIS FIRST VICTIM AS PERRY EXITS." Texas' longest-serving governor had ended his second run with a whimper. *[His first race was in 2012. In July, Perry had declared war on his billionaire rival, accusing him of "being a cancer on conservatism who will destroy the Republican Party if unleashed." In the first weeks of the campaign, the governor had been a leading voice in the anti-Trump movement.]*

When Donald heard the news, he was in Iowa. "Mr. Perry, he's gone. He was very nasty to me. Good riddance!"

Cruz, a fellow Texan, declined to address what Perry's departure meant for the race.

"We have a tremendous field of candidates," Perry said before he left. "Probably the greatest group of men and women. I step aside knowing our party is in good hands, as long as we listen to the grassroots, listen to the cause of conservatism."

Before making his final curtain call, Perry issued one final warning to the GOP, claiming it was experiencing its most serious identity crisis in a generation. He reminded voters that Donald had supported abortion rights, given campaign money to Hillary, and "said good things about Obamacare."

As he bowed out, Perry made a parting shot at Donald on the radio: "Demeaning people of Hispanic heritage is not just ignorant, it betrays the example of Christ."

Donald appeared on *The Tonight Show* simultaneous with its host, Jimmy Fallon. Together, before a conventional sit-down interview, they jointly performed a skit during which Fallon pretended to be Donald's image in the mirror, mimicking his movements, clothing, and hair, responding with approval, at Donald's reflection, to everything he said. As part of his performance (and in the spirit of the late-night venue), Donald, as a good sport, was game for the sendup and used the late-night appearance and interview to promote his image and his brand.

Later, with Fallon, Donald talked about his aversion to apologizing. "I fully think apologizing is a great thing, but you have to be wrong. I will absolutely apologize if I'm ever wrong."

One of his greatest selling points was that, "I'm too rich to be bought, to be, like Hillary Clinton, the toady of the monied interests. In politics, if a man gives, he gets. As a businessman, I gave to many candidates. When they called, I gave, and you know what? When I needed something from them two years later, I phoned them. They were there for me. That's how the system works in this country."

DONALD AT WAR WITH THE GOP
Latino Rage

Just before the second Republican debate *[conducted September 16, 2015, at the Reagan Presidential Library in Simi Valley, California, as moderated by CNN's Jake Tapper, Hugh Hewitt, and Dana Bash]*, Donald stepped up his campaign. Our leaders are babies who are so stupid they stand by helplessly as we become a third world country."

Cruz was also gloomy, citing the "tyranny and lawlessness of jailing a county clerk in Kentucky who refuses to issue a same-sex marriage license." He also condemned Obama for making a pact with Iran. "Americans will die."

These dire doomsday theories seemed to fit in with the grim mood of the country. Polls showed that two-thirds of Americans believed their country was adrift. Pollsters found some of the reasons for the gloom: Slow economic growth, dysfunction in Washington, threats from abroad.

"Conservatives today are more mean-spirited, angry, not optimistic, and much more viscerally divisive," said Matthew Dowd, former top strategist for George W. Bush.

The former President, who, in disgrace, was sitting out the race and in a position where everyone was weighing whether his endorsement would be a help or a hindrance. He was quoted as having said, "Nobody ever bought a product that made them feel worse."

Hours before the debate, the Club for Growth, a deep-pocketed conservative coven of right-wingers, announced the launch of a major ad campaign to take down Donald. The group warned conservatives, "He's really just playing us for chumps. It's astonishing that he's running as a Republican."

On Twitter, Donald shot back, calling the group "little respected," and claiming that as recently as a few months before, its leaders had solicited a $4 million contribution from him. "They are spending lobbying and special interest money."

On September 13, 2015, in anticipation of the feverishly anticipated Iowa caucus, scheduled for February 1, 2016, Donald flew in the Trump jet into Iowa, where he was greeted like a rock star. His arrival was strategically timed to coincide with the most frenetic and most emotionally charged football game in the state, the Cy-Hawk game.

[If you don't follow college sports, the Cy-Hawk game was between perennial rivals the Cyclones from Iowa State University (which is located in Ames) and the Hawkeyes from the University of Iowa (which is in Iowa City).]

As a local reporter claimed, "The star-struck crowd greeted him like a stadium rocker during a sprawling tailgate party before kickoff."

Encircled by his security guards, Donald heard one young man call out, "Donald, you rock!"

The candidate jokingly responded, "Did he take me for Mick Jagger? I don't have that kid's wrinkles."

Not all Iowans were so friendly. One activist compared him "to the bad boy you date over the summer before returning to college."

Noting Donald's rise in the polls, and reflecting a pessimistic evaluation for the wannabe Bush Dynasty, Republican fundraiser John Jordan said, "A lot of Jeb donors wish they had their money back."

In visible contrast to his swell of support in Iowa, Donald's visit included an occasional protester. One of them carried a sign, "MR. HATE, LEAVE MY STATE."

Scott Walker, who had once led in the polls, made a brief appearance in Iowa too, even though he'd promised that if elected, he would "wreak havoc" in Washington." During his time there, he took a swipe at Donald, warning, "It takes more than just talk. It takes action. Action speaks louder than words."

When Iowans told Donald that Carson was moving up in the polls, he took a swipe at him. "I don't think Ben, like Jeb Bush, has the energy to make America great again. Ben is a nice man, but when you're negotiating with China, or Japan, they're going to come against you in waves. They think we're all a bunch of jerks, because our leaders are so stupid, and so incompetent, so inept. We need people that are really smart, that have tremendous deal-making skills, and that have great, great energy, unlike Jeb and Ben."

Many Latino pundits viewed Donald's surge in popularity as perhaps a blessing in disguise, claiming that his anti-Latino rhetoric would propel Latinos into an accelerated involvement in activism and voter registration drives. "We must defend ourselves at the ballot box," said Ben Monterroso, Executive Director of the *Familiar Vota* Education Fund. "We've got to convince Latinos that not participating in civic life has its consequences. In 2016, it showed that nearly 27 million Latinos would be eligible to vote. Mexicans were shown to have been the least likely to naturalize, even though eligible to become U.S. citizens."

Ernest Londoño, an editorialist who has blogged for both *The New York Times* and *The Washington Post*, said that what Trump was really saying was "Make America White Again."

Cristóbal Alex, President of the Latino Victory Project, said, "When you're at-

Even the ultra-conservative *National Review* ridiculed Donald's quest to change his address from Trump Tower to 1600 Pennsylvania Avenue.

tacked, belittled, characterized as being unworthy and subhuman, it has an effect of unifying and leading the collective action. It has folks like Ricky Martin and Gloria Estefan angry. Our job is to take that anger and turn it into action at the voting booth."

Vanna Slaughter, the head of the Dallas chapter of Catholic Charities, said, "Donald Trump can disappear tomorrow, but the damage is done."

On September 13, Donald responded to Hillary's claim that she'd like to debate him. "She's not a natural. I'm not sure she's even going to make it to the starting gate. She'd be easy to beat. So much baggage. When she talks, it's like reading a script written by a pollster."

Comedian Larry Wilmore claimed, "Hillary is getting Obama-ed by an old white guy."

"Sometimes, Hillary acts insulted that she even has to run at all against that communist, Bernie Sanders," Donald was said to have told his aides. "I think she wants a coronation."

Right before the second GOP debate (September 16, 2015), it was revealed that if "Donald doesn't succeed in making America Great Again, he could launch a Trump for Governor of New York campaign in 2018. Then, a spokesperson for realtors in New York chimed in. "Donald has been informed of our plans. Maybe Trump wouldn't be happy living in Albany, but we think he's smitten at being a politician. A governor is not like being POTUS, but at least it would be the Empire State."

Rudy Giuliani, when informed of the real estate mogul's plan, suggested an alternative post. "I think Trump should run for mayor of New York, because a mayor has to be wild and crazy. Ed Koch was. So was I. To be President, you have to be a little bit circumspect."

The Trump campaign did not immediately respond to these suggestions and recommendations.

AS DONALD PLOTS TO TERMINATE HIS RIVALS
"The Terminator" Is Assigned to Take Over
The Celebrity Apprentice

Before this debate, NBC announced that it had signed Arnold Schwarzenneger to take over Donald's hosting role beginning with the upcoming new season (2016-2017) of *The Celebrity Apprentice*. The bodybuilder and movie action hero, of course, had served (2003-2011) as the Republican governor of California.

The 68-year-old former citizen of Austria said, "I'm thrilled to bring my experience to the boardroom to continue to raise millions for charity."

Ostensibly for legal reasons associated with the need to give equal air time to all candidates of a political race, the network had canned Donald's edition of the popular TV series when he entered the presidential race.

The campaign's second Republican debate, scheduled for September 16, 2015 at the Ronald Reagan Presidential Library in Simi Valley, California, was broadcast through a collaboration of CNN with Salem Radio.

Carly Fiorina was moved up to prime time from her previous status at the Kiddies' Table during the first debate in Cleveland. Moderators were Jake Tapper, Hugh Hewitt, and Dana Bash. This prime-time debate drew 23 million viewers, a million less than had tuned into the first debate on August 6th in Cleveland.

[By now, the phrase "The Kiddies' Table" had emerged as an acceptable term in the 2016 election cycle. It had entered the lexicon to describe the first cluster of participants within a doubleheader debate.

It was established as a way to choreograph the large number of participants into a limited time slot. In a two-hour span, each member of the collective horde would barely have enough time to introduce himself or herself.

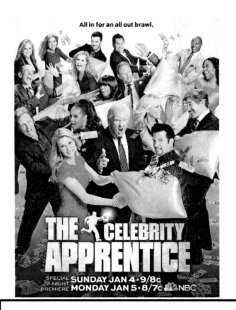 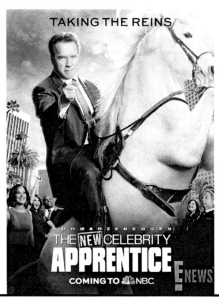

Some aspects of the poster on the left, advertising Donald's *Celebrity Apprentice*, evokes a protest at one of his political rallies. Even the headline at the top (*"All in for an all-out brawl."*) seems to demonstrate the media value of discord, something Donald's enemies were quick to point out in association with his campaign.

On the right, Arnold Schwarzenegger is announced as the new host of *Celebrity Apprentice*. Ironically, as an Austrian immigrant, he had amply demonstrated how far a "New American" could advance. Elected governor of California, and sporting an accent he was never able to lose, he had generated millions and managed the seventh largest economy in the world.

As a solution to that dilemma, it was decided to divide the participants, based on their ranking in the polls, segregated into an early debate for candidates performing badly in the polls. That "Kiddies' Table" debate would be three or four hours before the main event, populated with contenders scoring high in the polls, would be scheduled for prime time, usually at either 8PM or 9PM.

No one had agreed on nomenclature for the first debate in Cleveland, but by the second debate, more and more people were calling it "The Kids' Table" or "The Kiddies' Table." The implication of that term was that these losing candidates had "not yet grown up" enough to be included among the adults debating in primetime.

Polling almost at the bottom of the polls, Lindsey Graham, the feisty Senator from South Carolina, said, "Well, when I'm in the first debate, which is the happy hour debate, at five o'clock, start drinking. By nine o'clock, Donald may make sense to you if you drink enough."]

During the early-hour debate at the Kiddies' Table in Simi Valley, Bobby Jindal said, "Trump is not a liberal. He's not a Democrat. He's not a Republican. He's not an Independent. He believes in Donald Trump."

At the time of the debate, a package of Oreos had been one of Donald's favorite snacks, but he claimed, "I'm weaning myself from them now that their parent company, Nabisco, is moving some of its operations from Chicago to Mexico." He then offered his reporters Tic Tacs, saying "They are made in America."

At the (second) debate, Donald uttered the baseless conspiracy theory that childhood immunization can cause autism. However, he did say he favored vaccines, with the stipulation that their applications be extended over longer periods.

The next day, Alison Singer, president of the Manhattan-based Autism Science Foundation, fired back, claiming, "What he said last night puts children at risk. Trump was reckless in airing this debunked theory in front of millions. We need to put this issue at rest."

Correspondent James Warren wrote: "Donald Trump was a snide, petty, and trashed human being piñata. A sophomoric entertainer. His so-far-winning air of unbridled candor seemed more like peevish arrogance. The prize fight morphed into a rhetorical Ringling Bros. circus."

In post-debate analysis, Marco Rubio was viewed as a strong candidate, and both his and Fiorina's poll numbers increased. Frontrunners like Donald, Jeb Bush, and John Kasich came in for heavy fire, and Rand Paul continued his downward fall.

One journalist described Donald as "Just another face on the crowded stage."

His weak command of several key issues was exposed. Bruce Haynes, President of Purple Strategies *[a PR and communications firm headquartered in Virginia whose name reflects its bipartisan blend of strategies from both*

Columnist Linda Stasi: A pretty face and, when it came to Donald, an acid tongue and a point of view that was ready to rumble.

the "blue" (Democratic) and "red" (Republican) camps], said, "Trump didn't meet the moment. Call it the disappearance of Donald Trump."

Hungry for blood and eager to climb over Donald's wounded body, his Republican opponents attacked him head-on. Fiorina shot back at him for calling her ugly. "Women all over the country heard very clearly what Mr. Trump said," she intoned in a voice loaded with disapproval.

Her words were rewarded with wild applause.

Columnist Linda Stasi wrote: "The debate was sort of like watching a ship of fools slowly sink under the weight of so many whoppers that Burger King should sue for copyright infringement. Hell, these clowns even lied about Hillary's lies, which are so great they can stand on their own."

Carly Fiorina lied about the Planned Parenthood abortion video as part of an emotional anti-abortion appeal later denounced both for its insincerity and lack of accuracy.

The candidate falsely claimed, "Watch a fully formed fetus on the table, its heart beating, its legs kicking, while someone says we have to keep it alive to harvest its brain."

As Stasi phrased it, "I defy her to watch it herself, since the video doesn't exist. Oops."

***

In the wake of the debate, although Ben Carson continued to gain support, a poll of Republicans found that 39% still thought that Donald had the best chance of winning the presidency.

He continued to maintain that he was prepared to spend more than $100 million of his own money in the race to the White House. "I will spend $1 billion if need be. Actually, it's not been necessary to spend a lot of money because of the free media coverage I get."

At a post-debate rally in New Hampshire, a Trump supporter addressed the candidate on stage. "We have a problem in this country. It's called Muslims. You know our current President is one. You know he's not even an American."

Donald chuckled. "We need this question."

The unidentified questioner in a Trump shirt continued. "We have training camps growing where they want to kill us. When can we get rid of them?"

Donald responded with a sense of ominous portent, like a thundercloud looming overhead. "We're going to be looking into a lot of different things. We are going to be looking at that and plenty of other things."

Attacks from Hillary and the White House followed in the aftermath of Donald's Muslim response. Hillary said that she was appalled: "He should start behaving like a President and repudiate the level of hatefulness in such a questioner."

The White House fired back, too, its Press Secretary (Josh Earnest) asking, "Is anybody really surprised that this happened at a Donald Trump rally?"

THE WHITE MAN'S LAST STAND
Donald Responds to Cries from an Anguished, Receding America

Many William Buckley-type conservatives were to an increasing degree lamenting the drift of the GOP during the previous decades. One New York voter, David Carnivale, said: "The hatred the Republicans show toward the Mexicans, blacks, gays, and foreigners has become indistinguishable from the positions of the Ku Klux Klan. Republicans adding science, education, the environment, women, liberals, Muslims, all minorities in general, the poor, the sick, and those in need of welfare to the list of despicable things make the more focused hatred of the KKK seems nearly quaint in their narrow specificity."

Hillary seemed to be on the same page as this voter, charging that Donald was, "Lighting the fires of paranoia and prejudice. When you light those lights, you'd better recognize that they can get out of control. He should start dampening them down and putting them out."

Also at the same time, Ben Carson weighed in, outraging millions, when he said, "I would not advocate that we put a Muslim in charge of this nation."

He also told NBC's Chuck Todd, "I do not believe Islam is consistent with the Constitution."

On September 22, angered by Club for Growth's ads, Donald threatened to sue the political action committee. He attorneys sent them a cease-and-desist letter, accusing them of defamation and libel. Alan Garten, Donald's lawyer, said: "The ads of the pitiful little group were replete with outright lies, false, defamatory and destructive statements, and downright fabrications."

That announcement brought tabloid headlines—POOR LITTLE DONALD WILTS UNDER BLITZ. Pundits claimed, "He can dish it out, but he sure can't take it."

On September, Donald announced that he would not be appearing on any more Fox News Channel programs because the network had not been fair to him. He attacked Megyn Kelly but also news host Bill O'Reilly. He challenged O'Reilly "to have, for a change, guests on his show who were not Trump haters."

Thousands gathered along Fifth Avenue to see the motorcade of Pope Francis arriving in Manhattan.

Donald arrived at Trump Tower, where a large midtown crowd caught sight of him entering the skyscraper. The mostly Hispanic crowd angrily shouted, "Feo! FEO!" [In Spanish, that word translates as "ugly."]

From a second floor balcony of Trump Tower, above the Gucci store, Donald had a panoramic viewing platform from which he watched Pope Francis' motorcade proceed down Fifth Avenue.

In Washington, before a joint session of Congress, the Pope's message was markedly different from Donald's. He said, "Millions of people came to this land to pursue their dreams. We are not afraid of foreigners, because most of us were once foreigners."

Around the time of the Pope's visit, Donald aimed his fire power on "Low Energy Jeb." He was informed that his rival candidate had the backing of a Super PAC which was shelling out $37 million to finance a raft of anti-Trump ads on TV that was scheduled to continue, unrelentingly, until February. "Ads alone can't save a hopelessly drowning candidate," was Donald's response.

Throughout most of August and September, Donald had attacked Bush. But with the advance of autumn, he began to view Marco Rubio as an enemy. In a speech before the Family Research Council Values Voter Summit, he said, "You have this clown, Marco Rubio," That pronouncement was met with boos. Donald looked shocked. His subsequent words were softer: "Rubio is really weak on immigration."

Rubio shot back the next day. "Mr. Trump has had a tough week. Carly Fiorina really embarrassed him." Then he continued his attack, suggesting that Donald would not be capable of being commander-in-chief.

On the defensive, Donald accused Rubio of running up personal credit card debt. "He's got no money! Zero!" He also declared that he had a superior head of hair and attacked Rubio for "sweating too much."

In his speech the following day, a reporter approached Donald about Rubio, asking if Donald viewed him as a threat.

"I think he's a baby," Donald answered.

Author James B. Stewart wrote: "One thing is undeniable. Trump is a master of self-promotion, unrivaled even by the likes of the Kardashians. Whatever the outcome of the current presidential campaign, it has made him as famous, as instantly recognizable, and as talked about as anyone in America. Trump figured out early on that fortune follows fame, which is all but undistinguishable from notoriety."

Seth Grossman, a filmmaker and reality TV producer, said, "I've been working in reality TV for ten years, and I can tell you that Mr. Trump is exactly what we look for in our casting process. He's uncomplicated and authentic. You can understand his entire personality from a 15-second sound bite."

"His buildings are big and bold, shouting TRUMP in all caps. The Donald has absolute confidence even in his most wrong-headed opinions, and doubles down on every mistake, comfortable in the assurance that his wealth provides evidence for his intelligence. He doesn't need to be good in his job—if he fails, he creates chaos, and chaos makes good TV."

At Trump Tower on September 29, Donald laid out his plan for revamping the tax code by reducing taxes across the board on both individuals and corporations while eliminating certain deductions. The tax cuts would include not only the middle class, but billionaires like Warren Buffet, worth $62 billion, and Bill Gates, worth even more at $76 billion.

Denounced by hundreds of critics, the tax proposal, as predictable, won the praise of Grover Norquist, the anti-tax activist. "It's pro-growth, it's pro-fairness."

Most economists predicted that Donald's tax plan, if activated, would add trillions of dollars to the national deficit during its first decade.

"ADIOS, AMERICA—
A Reactionary Land of the Sour Tongue, the Frozen Heart"

Abraham Lincoln, a Republican, said, "America is the last best hope on earth." But as September rolled into October, Donald and the controversial extreme right-wing author, Ann Coulter, envisioned a different America altogether.

Coulter's latest book had been *Adios, America.* In it, she described "the philosophy of the receding roar, the mourning for an America that once was and is now being destroyed by foreign people and ideals."

Donald was hearing this anguished cry across the land. As one columnist described it, "There is now a reactionary attitude toward life. This is an attitude that sours the tongue, offends the eye, and freezes the heart."

ANN COULTER
"ADIOS, AMERICA!" AUTHOR

Ann Coulter is the Darling of the Far Right, and a frequent guest on the O'Reilly Factor on Fox News.

Her latest book was the controversial anti-immigration rant, *Adios, America.* She was also an early supporter of Donald. One reviewer said, "Ann and Donald have something in common—both of them would like to kick ass across the Mexican border."

Entertainment News:
KANYE WEST BACKS DONALD IN 2016
Then Describes His Vision about Becoming POTUS Himself in 2020

At the MTV Video Music Awards at the end of August, Kanye West *[the African-American hip hop recording artist, songwriter, record producer, and fashion designer, who famously married an icon of the social-media industrial complex, Kim Kardashian, in 2014]* announced his candidacy for President in 2020. He delivered this surprise as he accepted the Video Vanguard Award.

He facetiously claimed that after his election, by presidential decree, all future music-industry prizes would have to be cleared through him, with at least half of the prizes going to Beyoncé.

Eugene Craig, chairman of the Young Minority Republican Fund, said, "I don't think there's a better way to reach out to minority voters than to bring Kanye into the fold."

Then there was press speculation about possible cabinet posts, Kanye suggesting that after his occupany of the Oval Office, he would "sex it up," appointing his wife, Kim Kardashian, as Energy Secretary. Perhaps Rihanna as Secretary of State and Taylor Swift as Secretary of the Treasury.

"Pot would become legal and mandatory at all White House dinners," Kayne said.

Donald responded to this with, "Even Kanye West loves Trump. He goes around saying, 'Trump is my all-time hero.' He says it to everybody."

One TV pundit mocked the endorsement. "With Kanye's blessing, Trump is almost moving into the White House."

Donald continued to pick up support from unlikely quarters, even from Quarterback Tom Brady. Although it was not an actual endorsement, Brady called him, "A good friend who has done amazing things. He obviously appeals to a lot of people, and he's a hell of a lot of fun to play golf with."

Brady had met him in 2002, when he was a judge at one of Trump's beauty pageants.

It might be a bit of a stretch, but Richard Nixon was cited as the source of an endorsement of Donald delivered way back in 1987, after his wife, Pat, had praised him to her husband after seeing him on an episode of the *Phil Donahue Show.*

"As you know, Pat is an expert on politics," Nixon later told Donald. "She predicts that whenever you decide to run for office, you will be a winner. Pat was impressed at how you talked about how you could fix America."

A 2016 supporter of Donald Trump for President, the hip hop mogul, Kanye West, was the first to anounce his run for the presidency in 2020.

"America needs another African American President—This time a *real* African American!"

ANTHONY WEINER
& THE SEXTING BROUHAHA
Donald Attacks Him as a "Perv Sleazebag"

Although Hillary and Donald had once been friends—well, sort of—she joined the fray during the autumn of 2015 and attacked him. "His campaign is all about who he's against, whether it's immigrants, women broadcasters, or aides of other candidates. He is the candidate of—you know—being against. He's great at innuendo and conspiracy theories and really defaming people. That's not what I want to do in my campaign."

To answer her charges, Donald decided to fight back by humiliating Huma Abedin, Hillary's top aide. She was married to Anthony Weiner, a former New York congressman forced to resign because of having been caught in a sexting *[text messaging with sexually explicit attachments]* scandal. Donald renewed his attack on Weiner, calling him "the perv sleazebag. And his wife is the chief advisor to Hillary. Is that who we want advising her as President?"

Donald continued: "Abedin was a major security risk, and may have shared classified government secrets with Weiner, who might have included them in his sexting to bimbos he has the hots for."

Donald attacked former congressman Anthony Weiner and his wife, Huma Abedin, who is one of Hillary's closest political advisors.

In a scandal identified forever after as "Weinergate," the congressman was forced out of office when it was revealed that he sent sexually explicit photos of himself to young women. In some, his erect penis was partially concealed by boxer briefs. He'd married Huma in July of 2010 in a ceremony officiated by Bill Clinton.

Donald had heard Hillary admit she made a mistake for channeling her e-mail through a private server when she was Secretary of State. "But I plan to keep after her on her fuck-up," he told aides. "My prediction is, she'll end up not at 1600 Pennsylvania Avenue, but in the darkest jail cell."

"CARLOS DANGER"
The Cinematic Premier of Anthony Weiner

Donald's campaign aides seemingly decided that a way to "get to Hillary's vulnerable underbelly" was to attack Weiner and, indirectly, Abedin. He hoped to demonstrate a lack of judgment on Hillary's part by keeping Abedin as her chief aide, even though her husband was mired in scandal.

His attack was made easier when a feature film *Weiner*, was previewed at the Sundance Film Festival in Park City, Utah, and then sent out to general distribution to theaters across America. The movie was greeted with tidal waves of derisive laughter, which must have brought joy to Donald's heart.

He actually made a cameo appearance in the movie. As part of its its footage, he provides a comment when Weiner dared to run for Mayor of New York City: "We don't want perverts running our city," Donald says. "No perverts!"

The movie focused on the doomed 2013 New York mayoral run. He'd sent revealing cellphone photos of his privates to young women, using the *nom de plume* (or *nom de porn)* of "Carlos Danger."

Almost unbelievably, Weiner, after his resignation, was caught in another sexual scandal, also by sending explicit sexual material via a cellphone. This

In the sexting scandal, newspapers had a field day drawing parallels between Anthony's penis and its nickname, "Weiner."

After resigning from Congress and a "dignified" delay, Weiner entered the 2013 mayoral race in New York City.

Amazingly, seemingly undeterred by the previous brouhaha, he once again transmitted over the internet more sexually explicit pictures of himself for—as it happened—most of the world to see. Obviously, he lost his bid to become the mayor of New York City.

second scandal could not have come at a worse time for him.

Whereas the first scandal had been dubbed in the tabloid press as WEINERGATE, the second sexting scandal—dubbed SEVEN INCHES—broke during his attempt to return to politics by announcing his candidacy for Mayor of New York City.

The news of the second scandal broke in July of 2013 and concerned three young women. Weiner admitted sexting the women. Consequently, he had to confront a call from the editorial board of *The New York Times*, among others, to bow out of the mayoral race, but he refused. He remained in the race until the very end, taking fifth place in the Democratic primary, attracting only 4.9% of the vote.

Donald beefed up his attack on Weiner, emphasizing Hillary's association with him.

Weiner asserted that he will not go to see the film. ("After all, I know the ending.")

He accused its filmmakers, Josh Kriegman (Weiner's former chief of staff) and Elyse Steinberg, of exploiting the fact that his wife, Huma Abedin, 39, is one of Hillary's closest aides. One segment in the film depicts Hillary's campaign workers urging Huma to split from her "deviant husband."

One headline read: "WEINER SHOWS HIS JUNK IN HIS SKIVVIES."

Columnist Andrew Peyser wrote, "He got a sleazy thrill sexting pictures of his engorged manhood to random babes."

During the peak of the controversies that raged, in a dig at Bill Clinton, Weiner said: "I didn't rape anyone, didn't sexually assault anyone, and didn't commit adultery."

Ironically, Weiner's comment about the rape charges that had been brought against Bill Clinton during his presidency provided an excuse for Donald to bring them up again during the presidential campaign.

The news of the Wiener film's upcoming release sparked numerous articles in newspapers across the country. Both "Hillary and Huma," based on unfounded but lurid accusations and insinuations, have faced endless rumors about their own "special friendship."

Donald was made aware of these accusations, and had even read tabloid headlines accusing Hillary of having engaged in lesbian affairs. But, as he told his aides, "We'd better hold off on that for the moment."

Both women have been hailed (even celebrated) for standing by their men. And in Hillary's case, she's been accused of working to destroy her husband's attackers, while simultaneously championing women's rights.

The right-wing *New York Post*, dredging up the scandal yet again in anticipation of the 2016 race, summed it up: "Hill & Bill, Huma & Carlos—

are two political couples mired in sex, lies, and enabling. Not what any presidential campaign wants displayed on the big screen."

Perhaps in response to the unrelenting attacks, Hillary was overheard telling her staffers: "Contrary to popular belief by Trump, I am not the Bride of Frankenstein. Nor do I make lampshades out of human skin. I just want to be a Baby Boomer grandmother lifting Americans out of their current malaise."

In its review of *Weiner,* film critic Stephen Holden, in *The New York Times,* wrote: "This cringe-inducing portrait of an arrogant politician's self-immolation, like John Edwards, Bill Clinton, and Eliot Spitzer, shows that even at the risk of career suicide, the penis will not be denied."

OCTOBER, 2015

"In Politics, It's All About Kicking Ass to Win."
—*Donald Trump*

Donald had driven much of the national news cycle every day during the previous four months with his disruptive presidential campaign.

At Trump Tower, he had time only for crisis-level business emergencies. He told his aides, "That's merely a brush fire. Let Ivanka put it out."

When informed that *60 Minutes* wanted to interview him, he said, "Tell those guys to get in line. Everybody in the whole fucking world wants to talk to me."

By early October, the Rasmussen Report revealed that 58% of Republicans believed that Donald would be their presidential nominee for 2016.

Reporters branched out to determine Donald's unique support among voters. Many of them answered his rallying cry "as a yearning for a great leader to restore a lost swagger."

In the words of reporter Mark Leibovich, "The voters wanted a return to a less complex, less politically correct, and more secure nation. Trump's war on political correctness is especially pleasing to many of the white voters of the GOP, who feel usurped by newcomers and silenced by progressive gains that women, Hispanics, and gays have enjoyed."

In a 70-minute speech in Dallas, Donald ridiculed John Kerry for breaking his leg in a bicycle accident during nuclear negotiations with Iran. "So weak, so pathetic. The people from Iran are saying, 'What a *schmuck.*'"

"Even if I lose, and I won't, but if I did, I'll go back to being Donald Trump, only bigger. I've had more than my 15 minutes of fame," he said.

Occasionally, he mentioned a former Democratic president. "Jimmy Carter used to get off Air Force One carrying his luggage. I don't want a President who is gonna come off carrying a large bag of underwear. We want someone who is going to go out and kick ass and win."

It wasn't just Democrats that Donald ridiculed. He also attacked figures from the Republican Establishment, calling Karl Rove "a totally incompetent jerk."

When it came to criticizing front runner Hillary, he had a lot of help.

A copy of Edward Klein's explosive new tell-all arrived at Donald's office. It is not clear if he read it or even riffled through it, but he was told about it.

The book was *Unlikeable—The Problem With Hillary*. Klein claimed that during her tenure as Secretary of State, she became unhinged and exhibited violent psychotic behavior. He wrote of her confrontations with Obama, during which she accused him of feeding stories about her Email server to the media.

At one point, Klein quoted her as yelling at the Commander-in-Chief, "Call off your fucking dogs."

In another episode, he wrote that Bill Clinton accused his wife of looking old, telling her "to get a face-lift."

Donald also kept a keen eye trained on Vice President Joe Biden, suspecting that he might enter the race competing with Hillary for the Democratic nod. "What's that goof ball saying now?" he asked his aides.

From the sidelines, Biden made an occasional headline, as there was increased speculation that he might enter the race for the Democratic nomination. He was the first to endorse same-sex marriage, long before Obama and Hillary.

Biden was the keynote speaker on October 4 at the Human Rights Campaign's annual star-studded dinner. He claimed, "There are homophobes still left. Most of them are running for Pres-

There was long-standing speculation that Joe Biden, Vice President of the United States, would toss his hat into the presidential ring, challenging Hillary for the Democratic nomination.

Many of Donald's aides feared that the popular Biden might be more serious challenger than Hillary. "We've got a lot of shit to throw at her," said one aide. "Less so at Joe."

ident."

He also threw his support behind allowing transgender people to serve openly in the U.S. military. "All Americans are qualified to serve. Transgender rights are the civil rights of our time."

Biden also said that "Gays and lesbians shouldn't fear those shrill voices trying to undo same-sex marriage and other advances, because Americans have moved so far beyond them and their appeals to prejudice and fear."

Donald was an early riser, and every day, his aides prepared an early-morning dispatch of press comments about himself, both favorable and unfavorable. Sometimes, the negative comments would cause him to explode with fury.

Columnist Nicholas Kristof wrote about the frontrunners in the GOP, many of whom, it seemed, didn't have even the most basic qualifications. "If I wanted a circus ringmaster, I'd hire Trump. If I wanted advice on brain surgery, I'd turn to Carson. Fiorina would make an articulate television pundit. But for President?"

Pundits continued to write columns or analyze the political situation on TV shows, vigorously stating: "Trump as President of the United States? No Way! It's not going to happen! A slow

Throughout the 2015-2016 presidential race, Franki Bruni, columnist for *The New York Times*, wrote some of their most perceptive articles about Donald's race for the White House and the dilemma he posed for the GOP.

He described Donald's campaign as "a carnival."

La divinissima—grand chic of the old-time feminists, Gloria Steinem. The slogan on her T-shirt widely publicized her stand on abortion.

She found Donald a horror. On a scale of one to ten, she had rated him less than a one, especially if he lost all his money.

fade leading to a weak finish in Iowa is possible," wrote Jonathan Bernstein for *Bloomberg View. "Trump is not going to be the GOP nominee, or even come close."*

On October 14, Donald claimed that he needed Secret Service protection, because of the many large crowds he was drawing as frontrunner. He cited presidential hopeful Barack Obama receiving protection during May of 2007, about a year and a half before the November 2008 election that propelled him into office. "Because I'm a Republican, they don't give a shit," Donald said.

Columnist Frank Bruni summed it up: "The slow torture of the Republican primary knows no limit. First, Donald Trump turns it into a carnival, then Ben Carson comes along with his insanity about the Holocaust and guns. Between them, they own nearly 50% of the Republican vote, according to the most recent national surveys."

Donald wasn't the only Republican attacking Republicans. The Texas Senator, Ted Cruz, was becoming a threat. Donald read with glee when George W. Bush told the press, "I just don't like that guy Cruz. He's cynically opportunistic and self-serving."

Cruz had worked as a policy advisor to George W. in his race for the White House in 2000.

Almost daily, Donald uttered something that morphed into a headline. Told that Ben Carson was now leading in the polls in Iowa, Donald said, "Too much Monsanto in the corn creates issues in the brain."

He continued his attacks on Muslims, claiming he was "absolutely certain that he'd close certain mosques—centers of terrorism—and revoke passports from U.S. citizens in our fight against the Islamic state. If a man goes out and fights for ISIS, he can't come back here."

He also claimed that if he'd been President, he could have

WOMAN ESCORTED OUT OF TRUMP RALLY CNN

Across the country and across the world, Muslims turned out at protest rallies with slogans, signs, and rants against Donald's threat to bar them from the United States. In the photo above, Rose Hamid, standing in silent protest wearing a logo that announced "Salam, I come in Peace" was evicted from a Trump rally in Rock Hill, South Carolina.

prevented 9/11. "I am extremely, extremely tough on illegal immigration. I'm extremely tough on illegals coming into this country," he said on *Fox News.*

He told a biographer, "For the most part, you can't respect people, because most people aren't worthy of respect. People are really vicious, and no place are they more vicious than in their relationships with the opposite sex."

Donald aroused fury among the Muslims, but leading feminists also attacked him, including Gloria Steinem, who had been defending women's rights for half a century. The 81-yesr-old author said she was still baffled about Trump saying that model Heidi Klum was "no longer a 10."

"Why did nobody bother to say Trump hasn't ever been a one, much less a ten? If he lost his wallet, how many women would be interested? I just don't understand why what he dishes out isn't equalized and coming back at him."

The bombastic billionaire was said to have become even more bombastic when the latest poll showed that Carson had overtaken him in the race, garnering a 26% approval rating, in contrast to his 22%. This was the first time in more than three months that the real estate mogul had not led in a national poll, a *New York Times/CBS News* survey revealed.

He was skeptical of the polls, suggesting that Carson—"a lot of contradictions"—will face greater scrutiny from the press. "One thing I know about a frontrunner is that he gets analyzed 15 different ways from China. A lot of things about Carson will come out!"

He also questioned Carson's Seventh-Day Adventist faith.

At the Third Debate, GOP Candidates
LASH OUT AT THE MODERATORS
Donald Wins an Endorsement from a Non-Mexican Rapist

The third Republican debate was held on October 28, 2015, at the University of Colorado at Boulder. CNBC moderators included Carl Quinatanilla, Becky Quick, and John Harwood, each destined to endure "a night of hell" before millions of viewers.

The debate was supposed to have focused on the economy, but it quickly disintegrated into a generalized attack on the media, especially as it applied to their propensity for formulating "gotcha" (entrapment) questions.

The two frontrunners, Donald and Carson, each threatened to withdraw if the debate were not trimmed to two hours instead of three. Their wish was granted, even though the shortened venue virtually guaranteed that not every participant would be able to express him or herself within the moments allocated.

The number of participants at "The Kiddies' Table" had by now been reduced to four "losers" (Donald's words). Rick Santorum hopelessly continued his pursuit of the presidency, as did Bobby Jindal, Lindsey Graham, and George Pataki.

The main debate began at 6PM MDT (Mountain Daylight Time, *aka* 8PM on the East Coast), and soon, the candidates, while relatively restrained with one another, became involved in a slugfest with the moderators, calling them biased.

"The questions from the so-called moderators were designed to garner ratings rather than a substantive discussion of the issues," Donald said. "The questions revealed just why most Americans don't trust the media."

Ted Cruz entered the fray, claiming, "A debate should not be a cage match."

Donald also charged that "The Democratic candidates and their moderators get a love fest, while the attack dogs are unleashed on us."

During the commentary that followed the debate, most television pundits defined Ted Cruz, Marco Rubio, and Chris Christie as the winners, primarily because of their take-no-prisoners attack on the moderators. Donald and Ben Carson had no memorable moments, but squeaked to the finish line, unlike Jeb Bush and John Kasich, who delivered lackluster performances.

Cameron Joseph of the Washington Bureau of the *New York Daily News* wrote: "Rubio shined, Kasich punched, Trump squirmed, and Jeb Bush fizzled. Republican candidates spent more time beating up the media than they did targeting each other."

When attacked, which was often, Donald counterpunched, but failed to refute a single charge.

Shortly after the debate, Donald stood next to a microphone facing the press. Alongside him was Mike Tyson, whom Donald had promoted so heavily years before during the boxer's glory days in Atlantic City. The disgraced ex-boxer, who had since then been imprisoned for rape, heartily endorsed Donald's presidency.

As one reporter wrote, "Trump attacks Mexican rapists but accepts the endorsement of an American rapist."

438

CAMPAIGN FEUDS FROM MARRIAGES PAST
Ivana Says That Melania, as First Lady, Would Be
HORRID

In early November, Donald released one of his seemingly endless books, this one called *Crippled America: How to Make It Great Again*. Basically, it was a self-promotional claim that only he could make America great again, and only if he were elected President. Seventeen pages were devoted to "About the Author," listing his properties—and aircraft—and detailing the buildings either developed or licensed in his name. The book opened in seventh place on Amazon's best-seller list.

November also opened with Ivana, "the would-have-been First Lady," trashing Melania, Donald's third wife. Despite Ivana's attack on the woman who had supplanted her, Ivana was supportive of Donald's seeking the presidency. "The problem is," Ivana wrote, "what is he going to do with that third wife of his? She can't talk, she can't give a speech, she doesn't go to events, she doesn't seem to want to get involved."

As for Donald, Ivana claimed, "He was always meant to be a politician."

"Donald's dalliances with Marla Maples while married to me may have derailed his political ambitions for a couple of decades," Ivana said. "At that time, America came to hate him because of how badly he treated me."

NOVEMBER, 2015
"Some mosques are terrorists' cells."
—*Donald Trump*

Potential First Ladies aside, Donald moved into November forging forward with some of his most controversial positons. "I will certainly implement a database to track Muslims in this country," he proclaimed. "There should be a lot of systems beyond databases." That comment came in the wake of an earlier suggestion that, as President, he might have to close down certain mosques used for terrorist cells.

Asked how his database would differ from how Nazis tracked Jews and forced them to wear the Yellow Star, Donald said, "You tell me."

In the wake of enormous backlash, he tweeted, "I didn't suggest a database—a reporter did. Nonetheless, we must defeat Islamic terrorism—

words Obama can't even utter—and have surveillance, including a watchlist, to protect America."

His position drew fire from his rivals, with Hillary calling it "shocking rhetoric," and Jeb Bush attacking Donald "for manipulating people's *angst* and their fears."

Carson, however, seemed to lend his support to Donald's position. "If there's

a rabid dog running around in your neighborhood, you're probably not going to assume something good about that dog. It doesn't mean you hate all dogs, but you're putting your intellect into motion."

To the same degree he attacked Muslims, Donald defended veterans. On November 1, headlines read: "TRUMP WOULD AX BIGS AND REDO FED AGENCY"

[The headline, of course, referred to the U.S. Veterans Affairs Department, the "bigs" being the officers who ran it.]

In a speech in front of the warship *Wisconsin* in Norfolk, Virginia, he outlined his plan to reform the U.S. Veterans Affairs Department. As part of his proposal, he would create a more streamline agency and allow veterans to opt for a private health care provider. "They have earned the freedom to choose."

He revealed no plan, however, about how his new programs would be financed.

OBAMA MOCKS
THE GOP CANDIDATES
Donald Calls Jeb! "Forrest Gump" &
Denounces Dr. Carson's Theories as Bulls..t"

On November 3, 2015, at a Democratic fundraiser, Obama poked fun at the other GOP candidates, claiming that they can't handle the tough questions. "Every one of them says I am weak, and that Putin is kicking sand in my face. But then the Republicans' frontrunner claims he can straighten

Putin out. But then it turns out these wannabe Presidents can't handle a bunch of CNBC moderators."

"If a candidate can't handle those guys, I don't think the Chinese and the Russians are going to be too worried about any of them," Obama said.

At around the time Obama was mocking GOP candidates, so was Donald. Early on the morning of November 4, he unleashed a slew of nasty images targeting Jeb Bush. He compared the former Governor of Florida to a Nazi, mocking his ties to Mexico, and claiming he was intellectually disabled. "ADIOS JEB, AKA JOSE!"

The tweet contained a collage of derogatory pictures, one of them showing Jeb next to a swastika, another depicting him as Forrest Gump. A third jeering cartoon had Jeb in a Mariachi costume and sombrero, standing in a desert studded with cacti.

The following day, Donald released his first batch of ads on radio, mostly a rant against immigrants and the articulation of a "pro-veteran hawkish platform."

"Obama is a total disaster," a voiceover proclaimed. "Donald promises to repeal Obamacare and replace it with something better."

Then, Donald himself chimed in with: "I'll take care of veterans and make our military so strong that nobody will mess with us. I'll secure our borders, and yes, we'll have that wall."

Based to some degree on the distribution of ads like that, the Department of Homeland Security announced that both Ben Carson and Donald would soon have Secret Service protection. Both candidates had requested such security a month earlier.

Some of Donald's aides felt that they didn't need to

Upper photo: Jeb Bush and his overused, never-very-effective campaign logo.

Lower photo: Tom Hanks playing the title role (a slow-witted but kind and well-intentioned child of god), in *Forrest Gump* (1994).

go after Carson since he seemed to be self-destructing with his every utterance.

"WHAT THE TUT?" a headline had screamed when, for seemingly no reason at all, Carson claimed that the Biblical character of Joseph built the pyramids of Egypt to store grain and not as monuments for the burial of the Pharoahs. He made this silly pronouncement, which didn't contain a "grain" of truth, at Andrews University, the flagship educational institution of the Seventh-day Adventist Church, in southwestern Michigan.

Donald denounced Carson's "idiotic theory as strange."

In the same speech, Carson called for transgendered people to have their own bathrooms. "It's not fair for them to make everybody else feel uncomfortable. It's one of the things I don't particularly like about the LGBT community."

Carson's latest prattles included affirmations that the Jews could have prevented the Holocaust if they had been armed, and that men entered prison straight and came out gay.

By the first week of November, Carson's lies on the campaign began to catch up with him. He had previously asserted that he had been granted a prestigious scholarship to West Point, although later, when confronted with facts to the contrary, he backed off from that boast. In the wake of these and a number of other embarrassments, Carson lost his lead in Iowa, receiving 23% of the vote, in contrast to Donald's accumulation of 25%.

The West Point claim had earned Carson the headline: "HE'S FULL OF BULL."

Other stories soon appeared, some of them debunking Carson's rejection of the theory of evolution. Carson, despite his training as a surgeon and scientist, had asserted, "It's a bunch of fairytales encouraged by Satan."

Some columnists concluded, "Carson is about the craziest person ever to seek the presidency."

He continued to get blasted in the media. On November 8, *exposé* articles appeared questioning statements he had made in his autobiography, *Gifted Hands*. In it, he had claimed that he protected white students in his high school the day after Martin Luther King's assassination in 1968. Detroit was riddled with race riots. One of them ravaged the city's Southwestern High School, whose enrollment of blacks exceeded that of whites.

His account was widely discredited by witnesses on the scene at the time.

To defend himself, as it applied to the media's perceived obsession with negative slants on politicians and celebrities, Carson said, "There's got to be a scandal. There's got to be some nurse a candidate had an affair with—

442

there's got to be something. They have gotten desperate. Next week, it will be my kindergarten teacher who claims to the press that I peed in my pants. It's ridiculous!"

On November 8, Donald was thrust into the orbit of millions of Americans when he hosted *Saturday Night Live*. Before his appearance, some 200 protesters rallied to denounce his appearance on SNL, defining him as "a racist piece of shit." The demonstrators massed outside Rockefeller Center in Manhattan, where the broadcast had been scheduled. Protesters included Mexicans whose signs displayed the words, "I AM NOT A RAPIST!"

One of the late-night skits presented on SNL depicted Donald in the Oval Office in 2018, after having defeated ISIS, after having persuaded Mexico to pay for the wall, and after having made Putin cry.

A moment that drew laughs and applause occurred when the show's co-anchor Michale Che, who is black, said "Whenever rich old white guys start bringing up the good old days, my Negro senses start tingling."

Despite its flashes of humor, most reviewers panned the broadcast as "boring."

In the wake of the SNL satire, James Parker, a contributing editor for *The Atlantic,* advocated a new journalistic standard wherein Donald's hair would be defined as off-limits, unsuitable for future satires.

"By all means, lampoon or deconstruct Trump's opinions, which I don't believe are really opinions at all, but random clots and thrombi of rhetorical ectoplasm gathered from the ether with high-end paranormal pooper-scoopers. Yes, make hay with inconsistencies, stick your satirical probes in the hinds of his fascinating and possibly apocalyptic personality. But leave his hair alone."

Donald received a report that Michele Bachmann, the former (notorious and ill-informed) congresswoman from Minnesota, was in Israel, urgently warning its people, much to the consternation of local rabbis, about the imminent second coming of Jesus Christ.

In 2013, Bachmann was under investigation by the House Ethics Committee, the Federal Election Commission, the Iowa Senate Ethics Committee, the Urbandale Police Department and the Federal Bureau of Investigation because of alleged campaign finance violations in her 2012 campaign for President.

"His hair is in the strictest sense powerless. It's doing its best—as hair, as a hairstyle. It lies there and tries and makes no replay. It's quite a nice color. I once described (in print) an actor in a Harry Potter movie as 'sturgeon-lipped.' Why did I do that? Seeking the cheap high of invective, nothing more. Lay off that stuff, is my advice. Going for the hair may not bother him (who knows?) but it's not good for you—or your satire."

Donald was aboard his private plane when it flew into Iowa in mid-November. The rise of Carson in the polls had baffled him. During a 95-minute appearance on an Iowa stage, he used terms like "pathological" to describe his opponent.

He mocked Carson's account wherein he tried to stab a friend only to have his large belt buckle deflect the blade.

Donald stepped from the podium to perform the most unpresidential "show and tell." Thrusting his arm as if stabbing and pulling on his own belt, he asked. "Anyone have a knife you want to try on me?"

The buckle wouldn't have stayed in place!" he said. "Give me a break!" he cautioned the voters of Iowa. "Don't be fools. Don't vote for this irrational man!"

As Donald continued to campaign in anticipation of the Iowa caucus, there were stories about recent developments linked to a former frontrunner for the GOP presidential nomination in 2012. News about Congresswoman Michele Bachmann had popped up during her November, 2015 tour of Israel. The former Republican presidential candidate had asserted her desire to convert as many Jews as possible to Christianity. Her tour of Israel had been organized by the Family Research Council, which she said was in preparation for the Second Coming of Christ. In a (horrified) response, Rabbi Avi Shafran, a spokesperson for Agudath Israel of America, told *The Jerusalem Post*, "Ms. Bachmann's mission should be a reminder of the importance of Jewish education, since the surest defense against missionizing is authentic Jewish knowledge."

THE FOURTH DEBATE
"Ignorance and Arrogance"

Staged in Milwaukee, Wisconsin, on November 10, 2015, the fourth debate was a joint production of the *Fox Business Network* and *The Wall Street Journal*, and as such was aired with the stated intention of focusing on business policies and the economy. The moderators included Gerard Baker, Neil Cavuto, and Maria Bartiromo.

Removed from the debate, based on their low showings in the polls, were Christie and Huckabee. The main lineup featured Donald, positioned front and center in the lineup of the prime-time participants, flanked by Carson, Rubio, Cruz, Jeb Bush, Fiorina, Kasich, and Rand Paul.

At the Kiddies' Table, Bobby Jindal appeared for the final time, just before he ended his run for the White House based on his abysmal showing in the polls.

For the most part, the fourth debate was generally rather staid, and didn't seem to generate many firecrackers. Mostly, the candidate argued with each other over jobs and spending. Many reporters evaluated it afterward as a "snoozefest."

Donald returned to his familiar anti-immigrant stance, praising a Federal court for ruling earlier in the week for the blockage of several of President Obama's executive orders on immigration. He tangled with Kasich over the issue. "I've built a company worth billions of dollars—I don't have to hear from this man," Donald said, casting a bitter look at the Governor of Ohio.

Of the many Republican candidates campaigning in Iowa in anticipation of the much-watched Iowa caucus (scheduled for February 1, 2016), Donald was the only one who kept referring to Vladimir Putin.

"If Putin wants to go and knock the hell out of ISIS, I'm all for it, 100 percent, and I can't understand how anybody would be against it."

Jeb Bush and Donald tangled onstage over foreign policy. There was little love or charity evident between the two candidates. Jeb called Donald's world view "that of a child playing a board game. Monopoly is not how the world works."

In a post-debate evaluation, Bush was described as "still inarticulate" by columnist Charles Krauthammer.

"I suppose Cruz and Rubio did well, which I guess they did if you like illogical

Donald claims that his chief rival, Ted Cruz, was an "Anchor Baby" born in Alberta, Canada, and therefore not eligible to run for President of the United States.

He also learned that in the 1950s, Rafael Cruz, Ted's father, was a Cuban revolutionary who supported the communist overthrow of the Cuban government by Fidel Castro.

economic programs and totally terrifying views on foreign affairs," wrote columnist Gail Collins.

Under the headline "TRUMP MAY TAKE GOP DOWN WITH HIM," Dick Polman of the *Cagle Syndicate* wrote, "If success is measured in ignorance and arrogance, then the winner of the Republican fourth debate was Donald Trump. I can't tell the difference between his real-life *schtick* and his *Saturday Night Live* act."

Reporter Maggie Haberman summed up Donald's dilemma in Iowa: "Mr. Trump's seemingly steady flow of support in those polls could begin to give way, especially as more Republicans turn to more sober-minded candidates with military and national security experience following the terrorist attacks in Paris."

Dave Carney, a Republican political strategist who ran Rick Perry's failed presidential race in 2012, said, "Trump is walking a tightrope. He loves the applause of the crowd 100 stories down. But when you start to make fun of being Born Again and Redemption and Christian faith in our party, you can talk yourself right off the tightrope."

"Trump's attacks on Carson could be the hole in the dike," said Ed Rollins, a veteran GOP consultant.

"Pray for Donald," Carson said in the wake of Donald's denunciation of him based on his many untruths that had been baldly exposed in the press. At one point, Donald had called him pathological and even compared him to a child molester.

"Give me a break," Donald said. "How stupid are the people of Iowa to fall for Carson's crap?"

Donald's voice offered no comfort to the unemployed or to those who were at the lower end of the wage scale, some of them holding down two jobs as a means of supporting their families. "I hate to say it, but we have to leave the minimum wage the way it is," Donald said on the campaign trail. "People have to go out, they have to work really hard and to get into that upper stratosphere."

Columnist Albor Ruiz wrote: "Say what you will about Trump, you have to admire this guy's gall. For a filthy rich guy, born with a proverbial silver spoon in his mouth, poor people are so because they do not work hard enough—and not because despite being overworked, they are paid hunger wages by greedy bosses like him."

Donald might have faced an uphill battle in Iowa, but in New Hampshire, he was clearly the favorite, beating out "JEB!" and "Little Marco Rubio," each of whom were stuck in the mud of single-digit approval ratings. The conclusion of the pundits was this: A New England state that's usually a force for moderation wasn't following that script this time around in going all out for "The Donald."

Whether he used them or not, Donald was supplied almost daily with controversial material and issues he could use against his rivals if he chose to do so. At a point in the campaign where Iowa polls indicated almost equivalent approval ratings between himself and Cruz, he was supplied with information about the background of Rafael Cruz, Ted's father.

In the 1950s, Rafael was said to have been a Cuban revolutionary and a devoted supporter of Fidel Castro. When he opted to emigrate to the United States, although the U.S. government granted him political asylum, he chose instead to move to Alberta, where he became a citizen of Canada. Consequently, the Texan senator (Ted Cruz) was born in Alberta, a fact that later provided ample fodder for Donald's allegations that Cruz, if nominated, would be legally ineligible for election to the nation's highest office.

Trump's Murky Misuse of
BOGUS CRIME STATISTICS

On November 22, Donald tweeted a rant called "USA Crime Statistics—2015."

A photo depicted a dark-skinned man with a bandanna and a mask holding a gun. The abbreviated and loosely defined "statistics" supplied alongside the illustration listed, with very few modifiers, and with no statistical breakdown, the percentages of "Blacks Killed by Whites" (2%); and "Whites Killed by Blacks," (81%). The figures it cited derived, the tweet claimed, from the "Crime Statistics Bureau—San Francisco," an entity that didn't exist.

Some of Donald's tweets—including this ambiguous and confusing attachment demonstrating dubious statistics about perpetrators and their race—were loudly denounced by sociologists as dangerous, divisive, and misleading.

His tweet was expedited just a day after he'd been jeered by a protester wearing a Black Lives Matter shirt. The man was kicked out of a Donald rally in Birmingham, Alabama. In a video, several pro-Trumpers were seen tackling the man, one white man punched him, and a woman kicked him while he was on the ground, CNN reported. From the podium, Donald demanded, "Get him the hell out of here!"

Forced to leave, the protester left, shouting FUCK DONALD TRUMP! No arrests were made.

After his tweet, the press revealed that almost all of the murders happen within a race, the Department of Justice claimed that 84% of white murder victims are actually killed by white perpetrators.

Columnist Shaun King, an African American, wrote: "America has grown to love Donald Trump, not in spite of what we saw as unelectable gaffes, but because of them. Whether we like it or not, the horrific white supremacy of Trump is a reflection of a very real portion of America. Worse than David Duke, he is the most racist, offensive, presidential candidate in modern American history…and he's in the lead."

In the wake of the November, 2015, ISIS terrorist attacks in Paris, in which 130 people were killed, the approval ratings of Donald in national polls increased. Even so, still plagued with the perceived lack of support and cooperation from the "Establishment GOP," he refused to rule out an independent run for the White House in 2016.

On ABC's *This Week*, he was asked what he'd do if GOP opponents "try to take you out."

"I will see what happens," Donald said. "I have to be treated fairly. If I'm treated fairly, I'm fine."

He pledged that he would be "the toughest of the candidates" running for President.

***

One of the most controversial moments in Donald's campaign came when he mocked the disabilities of reporter Serge Kovaleski of *The Washington Post*.

Kovaleski suffers from a disabling malfunction of his limbs. From a televised podium at one of his rallies, Donald delivered a cruel and mocking parody of the man's disability.

Reporters assigned to Donald quickly noted that he often relied on generalities to dodge hard questions about policy. He had an avoidance of specifics, often sidestepping delivery of direct answers in a generalized refusal to be pinned down.

Rich Lowry of *The National Review*, noted, "Trump has an amazing ability to backtrack without incurring any political harm from doing so. His supporters don't seem to care very much about consistency from one interview or statement to the next, as long as he's projecting strength."

Virtually every campaign speech delivered by Donald contained anti-Muslim rhetoric.

One of the low moments for Donald's campaign came in late November when he claimed that thousands of New Jersey Muslims had been televised dancing at the news of the September 11 attacks on the World Trade Center.

When he was challenged to prove that assertion, he said he watched it on television, and he cited a story by reporter Serge Kovaleski in *The Washington Post*.

Kovaleski suffers from a disabling malfunction of the limbs called arthrogryposis *[a congenital defect of the limbs characterized by severe contractures of multiple joints.]*

Kovaleski later came forward to tell the press that the reports of Muslims dancing in the streets after 9/11 were never verified.

[In fairness to Donald, such news was indeed broadcast on television on September 11, and millions of New Yorkers heard it. However, much misinformation was broadcast amid the horrified confusion and consternation of that fateful day.]

When Donald, at a South Carolina rally, heard that Kovaleski was backing down on what he had presented as news within his earlier story, Donald ridiculed him cruelly. "You have to see this poor guy," Donald said, as he flailed his arms around in spastic gestures, mocking Kovaleski's disabilities. It was caught on video, fomenting outrage and denunciations.

He later defended himself. "I would never mock a person who has a disability. I have long donated money to groups supporting people with disabilities. Nobody gives more money to Americans with disabilities than I do. I don't mock people who have problems, believe me."

Appearing with Chuck Todd on NBC, the broadcaster challenged him on the "Dancing Muslims" assertion. Donald stuck by his charge, insisting that he saw this "dance of death" on television.

Near the end of November, Donald became alarmed when polls showed Ted Cruz doubling his support in Iowa, bypassing Carson and nearing Donald's own lead. Cruz stood at 23%, Donald at 25%, newspapers revealed. Carson had surged ahead, but a series of negative stories associated with claims about his past had harmed him with evangelicals.

Voters cited America's foreign policy and the rise of terrorists as the issues that made them favor Cruz. Donald was cited as the candidate best able to deal with economic issues. Carson clearly won out among evangelicals, based partly on his anti-abortion and anti-gay rhetoric.

Before Cruz and Donald launched World War III during the coming year, he praised the rebellious senator from Texas. "He's backed everything I've said. Ted's agreeing with me 100%."

Reporter Cameron Joseph wrote: "Selecting Cruz as his Veep would give Trump someone on the ticket with government experience—even if the highlight of his work history was shutting down that government. The pick of Cruz might shield him—a tiny bit—from charges of racism against Hispanics, as Cruz is half-Cuban."

As for Marco Rubio, in contrast to Donald, who was 69, the junior senator from Florida accented his youth. "If I am your nominee, we will be the party of the future." Whenever he could, he seemed to disparage the grandmotherly Hillary and the grandfatherly Donald as relics of a bygone age. History and voting patterns have shown, however, that GOP primary voters tend to value experience above youth.

Many reporters such as Matt Flegenheimer noted that foul-mouthed terms and language never heard in equivalent settings before were cropping into the campaign, "shit" being a favorite of Donald's in particular.

"The reasons for saltiness seemed varied—a play for machismo, perhaps, particularly as national security becomes a chief focus, or a signal of vitality, rawness, a willingness to break through the din of the overstuffed field of competitors."

As was noted, candidates hoping to outcurse Donald were outmatched. He often called things "political bullshit," and was fond of the expression, "You bet your ass."

He warned his enemies on Twitter, "Treat us fairly or otherwise, I'll tweet the fucking daylights outta ya."

In defense of his penchant for cursing, Donald cited Joe Biden, whose sometimes equivalent epithets were famously called into use during his description and defense of Obama's then newly inaugurated health care law as "a big fucking deal."

PART FOUR
THE WINTER OF TRUMP

THE POPE VS. THE BILLIONAIRE
Pope Francis and Donald Launch a "Holy War of Words"

"DO YOU KNOW WHAT THEY SAY ABOUT A MAN WITH SMALL HANDS?"
Rubio Asks a Crowd of Mocking Voters.
Donald Is Forced to Defend the Size of His Penis

DONALD QUOTES FROM MUSSOLINI
And Gets Offered the Support of the KKK & the American Nazi Party

The GOP vs. THE TABLOIDS
The National Enquirer Assaults Republican Candidates With an Exposé of Porn Links, Gay Parties, & a Police Record of an Arrest in Miami's "Hustler Park."

Chapter Seventeen

VENOM AND DISCORD
"Trumpkins are Mental Midgets and Xenophobic Troglodytes."

"HILLARY GOT SCHLONGED
by Obama"
—*Donald Trump*

REPUBLICAN RAGE & FRUSTRATION
Donald's Rivals, & Their "Long, Bootless Slogs through Alligator-Infested Swamps"

REPUBLICANS ARE AN
Endangered Species

December of 2015 began with what appeared to be a clever political move: Donald Trump would meet with about a hundred black ministers and, after some spirited conversations, would perhaps emerge with their endorsement of his candidacy.

Donald himself had called for such a meeting, hoping that the endorsement of so many black ministers would help dispel charges that he was a bigot.

But despite his intentions, the meeting, as it had been planned, never really materialized. Perhaps bowing to pressure from the Black Lives Matter movement and to other activists, there was much backtracking among the ministers, many of whom refused to appear with him at Trump Tower in Manhattan.

Only a few ministers showed up, and of those who did attend, some seemed out of place. Brebon Hall, a preacher from Toledo, Ohio, told the press, "It appears as if Trump is a possible racist based upon some of the things he's said about black America."

After the "scaled-down" confab, Donald, as was his custom, put a good spin on it, claiming, "There was great love in the room. They liked me, and I liked them."

The discussion had centered on unemployment in the black community, police shootings, and deficiencies in urban education.

Many pastors claimed that al-

By Christmas of 2015, Donald Trump had invaded virtually every aspect of popular culture. Feature writers at Halloween had managed to associate Pumpkins with Trumpkins in the popular imagination to the point where consumers began to confuse the terms.

In the upper photo, a charity "pumpkin carve" in Pennsylvania made special note of the award-winning "Donald Trumpkin."

In the lower photo, artist Jeanette Paras of Dublin, Ohio, locally famous for "pumpkinizing" celebrities and political figures every year since 1988, displayed this image on Facebook ("Paras Pumpkins") as part of her annual "unveiling" of her newest celebrity pumpkin on her front porch.

though they'd been invited, they'd refused to attend. Corletta J. Vaughn, Senior Pastor at the Holy Spirit Cathedral of Faith in Detroit, said "My constituency would murder me if I showed up."

The meeting, even in its scaled-down format, drew fiery denunciations from many African-Americans. The Rev. Jamal Bryant, pastor of the Empowerment Temple Church in Baltimore, called the ministers who went to Trump Tower, "Prostitutes seeking their 15 minutes of fame. My objection to Trump is that he is flagrantly against humanity."

For having said that, The Rev. Darell Scott, who had helped organized the event, sharply rebuked Bryant. "For respectable preachers to be called 'prostitutes on a pole' is very insulting, demeaning,

The much-photographed, shame-inducing sign in front of the hatemongering Harlem congregation of Atlah.

This World Missionary Church is the platform from which the Rev. Manning calls for the death of homosexuals by stoning. He refers to himself as "the sodomite slayer." From the pulpit he rants against Obama, whom he calls Hitler, claiming that he is going "to use gay people to destroy the black community."

He also calls for Harlem to become a "homo-free zone," and maintains that both of the Presidents Bush engaged in anal sex with hundreds of men.

BUT AT LEAST HE LIKES DONALD: Born in North Carolina, where he later picked cotton and pulled tobacco, the Rev. James David Manning, as a young man, burgled some 100 houses and was imprisoned for $3^{1/2}$ years. While in prison, he became his version of a Christian and grew into the most controversial African American minister in the United States.

He reserves his harshest criticism for Ben Carson, whom he calls "a pathetic nigga" and a "demon," and defining Carson's supporters as "closeted sodomites, lesbos, and buttlickers."

He also asserts that Obama and Vladimir Putin will soon be outed as "fags," and that Starbucks puts semen in its coffees. He has also referenced Marco Rubio, Ted Cruz, and George W. Bush as "sodomites and homos." **BUT HE SUPPORTS DONALD TRUMP.**

and misogynistic to say the least. If Trump called black preachers 'prostitutes on a pole,' the entire nation would be in an uproar."

Donald did get another endorsement from the Rev. James David Manning, known as "the Harlem Hate Pastor." He had compared President Obama to Hitler and had accused both George H.W. Bush and George W. Bush of each having had sex with some one hundred men.

There was a sign outside his Atlah Worldwide Church on Lenox Avenue in Harlem that proclaimed: "Obama has released the homo demons on the black man. Look out black woman! A white homo may take your man!"

Manning claimed that "Donald Trump will help black people escape the abyss created by Bill Clinton *and* Martin Luther King, Jr."

Never one to avoid a controversy, the Rev. Al Sharpton said, "I wonder why black religious leaders would seek to bask in the glow of a billionaire while offending their congregants and offending their cloth? I don't know how you preach Jesus, a refugee himself, on Sunday, and then deal with a refugee-basher on Monday."

Donald dismissed Sharpton's rebuke. "Deep down inside, Al likes me a lot. That I can tell you. He's just doing his thing like he always does."

***

Millions of voters-at-large "detested" Ted Cruz, yet by the first of December, approval ratings were moving upward. Donald appraised Cruz's rise with skepticism, noting that whereas Cruz was strong with evangelicals and those defining themselves as "very conservative," among moderate or liberal Republicans *[is there such a thing?]* he drew a low 6%.

As polls showed, the very far right candidates could do well in Iowa because nearly half of the GOP electorate self-defined as "very conservative," standing firmly against abortion and same-sex marriage, among other issues.

America's most famous—some say, notorious—African American pastor, Al Sharpton, inserted himself into the presidential race.

"Black celebrities and luminaries live in a world that is much more engaging to Trump, and parallel to his world, than those of us that have been in politics and civil rights on the ground for a long as Trump has been out there."

"He has little understanding of the lives of the vast majority of African Americans. It's not like there's a Trump building in Harlem."

During the weeks ahead, Cruz would spew a cobra-like venom against Donald. But in December, he seemed to align himself with Donald, perhaps hoping to expand his appeal to voters other than those from the extreme right wing—many of whom had been labeled as "fanatic" in the liberal press.

Columnist Frank Bruni wrote a diatribe entitled *ANYONE BUT CRUZ*.

> *"Cruz is the antithesis of a team player. His thirst for the spotlight in unquenchable. His arrogance is unalloyed. He actually takes pride in being abrasive. His roommate at Princeton said, 'I would rather pick someone from the phone book to be President rather than Ted Cruz.' He never backs down. It's the fruit of a combative style and consuming solipsism that would make him an insufferable, unendurable, President. And if there's any sense left in the election, and mercy in the world, it will undo him soon enough."*

***

The final month of 2015 had hardly begun when headlines exposed the dilemma of the Establishment: "Fellow Republicans want Trump pushed out, as long as someone else does the pushing," wrote one journalist. "The fear was that

Darth Vader from Hollywood's *Star Wars* trilogy incited frustration and teror as the most destructive force in the Universe.

Because of his destructive after-effects of (among others) the government shutdowns he engineered, Cruz's enemies made frequent comparisons.

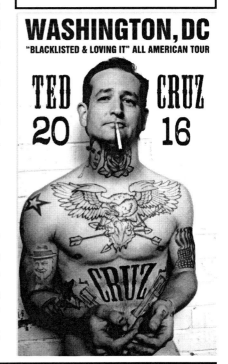

Ted Cruz's electoral campaign was said to have generated more weird commercial products than any other candidate. Among them was this poster, as crafted by the conservative artist Sabo, on sale for $50 through Cruz's websites, likening him to a "blacklisted and loving it" tough guy who'd wreak havoc in Iran.

if Donald were the standard bearer, he would imperil the political careers of other "downticket" Republicans.

The end of the year poll conducted by *ABC News/The Washington Post* revealed that Donald's unfavorable rating derived from 65% of women and 74% of nonwhite voters.

"Trump would be a disaster," said Senator Lindsey Graham of South Carolina, who wanted the GOP presidential nomination for himself. "If you're a xenophobic, race-baiting, religious bigot, you're going to have a hard time being President, and you're going to do irreparable damage to the party."

Many in the GOP seemed equally horrified that if not Donald, then Ted Cruz would be an even less desirable standard-bearer.

Donald was growing less fearful of Ben Carson in the wake of the carnage inflicted by terrorists on innocent people in Paris. Tied with Donald in November, polls in December showed the mild-mannered, soft-spoken Carson slipping as terror reshaped the race.

A new national poll from Quinnipiac University revealed that the neurosurgeon had slipped seven points. Republican strategist Ron Bonjena said, "Carson is failing the commander-in-chief test that Republican primary voters require, especially around national security."

Carson made a highly visible, much-reported gaffe when he claimed that China was engaged in a military incursion in Syria when he meant Russia. He also called Syrian refugees "rabid dogs."

MANY JEWISH VOTERS DISMISS DONALD
As a "Meshuggina Goy"

Both Carson and Donald hoped to rally Jewish voters to their respective causes. *[There are some Jews, believe it or not, who are not Democrats.]* As such, both candidates appeared at a rally of wealthy, influential Jewish Republicans.

Carson, with dismal results, misspoke several times during his speech. He mispronounced Hamas, pronouncing it like "hummus," which, of course, is a food product made with garbanzos. His attempt at a joke about Jews and money was greeted with boos.

The major insight he proffered involved telling his hip Jewish audience that, "The Middle East is complicated." He expressed that with ominous portent, as it had been a revelation, sharing it with a group whose members were far better informed about the Middle East than he was.

Carson revealed that he had just returned from Israel where "I feared I might be shot."

"That went over like a coven of Tennessee evangelical snake-handlers shouting the glory of Jesus Christ at a convention of rabbis," said Bernard Goldstein from Dallas.

Donald fared better than Carson, but then almost any candidate could have done better. However, Donald was jeered when he refused to answer a question about whether Jerusalem should be split into two.

Like Carson, he seemed to associate Jews with money, bringing up the link three times. "Stupidly, you want to give me money," he said. "But Trump doesn't want your money."

As one of the donors in the audience later said, "That remark went over like a Jew drinking a pint of pig's blood."

During his speech, Donald promised to fly to Israel for a meet-

Benjamin Netanyahu after a "working dinner" with Hillary Clinton in 2009.

Netanyahu seemed to shy away from an endorsement for Donald, who avidly sought the support of Jewish voters, frequently asserting that his daughter, Ivanka, had converted to the Jewish faith.

Since "Bibi" presides over a country whose population is 20% Muslim, he did not extend a welcome for Donald, as a presidential hopeful in the heat of a contested campaign, to visit Israel.

ing with Prime Minister Benjamin Netanyahu, but the highly publicized trip was canceled. It was speculated that Donald's mere presence with the prime minister at holy sites could have caused domestic turmoil. "Bibi," as he is called, presides over a country that is one-fifth Muslim.

Donald told the press that he would schedule a visit with Netanyahu after he became President.

A New York stockbroker later told the press, "Jackie Mason, Trump isn't. *Oy gevalt!* 'Billary' Clinton he isn't either. What he is, however, is a *ganze macher (larger-than-life schemer/arranger who can make things happen)*. He's dismissed by the *chochem (clever people or wise guys)* as a *meschuggina goy (mad, crazy, or insane non-Jew)*."

"THE WORST PRESIDENTIAL RACE
In the History of the Republic"

Since the early 1970s, the Iowa caucuses have been the first major electoral event of the nominating process for President of the United States. As such, they're frantically pursued by candidates because of the massive media attention they generate during U.S. presidential election years.

In 2016, they were scheduled for February 1, and as their preludes began to heat up, candidates, including Donald, turned to the relatively cheap medium of radio to get their messages across.

Consequently, hour after hour, motorists driving along highways were pummeled with appeals. Whereas some chatter dismissed Marco Rubio as "no more than a pretty face," other broadcasts droned on, calling Cruz "the worst kind of politician."

Since the media seemed intent on giving him hour after hour of free exposure, Donald didn't purchase any TV ads. But he did buy radio ads.

On December 2, as more and more voters began to interpret Donald as a possible strong military leader, he revealed that he "sometimes felt bad for not having served in the military. *[He had used four college deferments to avoid being shipped off to Vietnam. His final rejection was based on bone spurs in his foot.]*

Many former military men criticized him, including retired Marine Lt. Col. Orson Swindle. "I just find Trump to be a huckster, and he's very good at it. Such comments he's made are distasteful to veterans." *[Swindle had been shot down during a jet fighter mission in 1966 in Vietnam and had spent six years as a prisoner of war.]* "Trump took the easy way out," he said.

With support for Donald mounting, in spite of critics, columnist David Brooks weighed in. "Trump is what GOP voters want at the moment. He reflects their disgust with the political Establishment. He gives them the pleasurable sensation that somebody can come to Washington, kick some tail, and shake things up." He suggested that when voters face the final decision about who to put in charge with having their finger on the nu-

PRESIDENT OBAMA CALLS FOR END TO BIGOTRY IN IMPLICIT REBUKE OF DONALD TRUMP

clear trigger, it would not be Donald.

"In contrast to Carson, Trump, even when he misspeaks, voters see him as someone who projects strength and confidence," said Ford O'Connell, a GOP strategist who was on John McCain's campaign team in 2008.

Whereas only 5% of GOP voters in Iowa thought Carson would be best at handling terrorists, an impressive 30% thought Donald was the man for the job.

Columnist Mike Lupica called the 2016 presidential race "the worst in this country's history."

"Donald Trump is the angry face of it all, able to out-talk everybody on radio and television, and out-tweet them, and shock the world with his theories about Muslims. But Trump isn't alone. He's just the one with the biggest bullhorn, able to out-shout even the bullhorn media."

Hip-hop impresario Russell Simmons, who has been a pal of Donald's for more than three decades, told him, "It's time to find a new rap. You seem to be like a one-man wrecking ball willing to destroy our nation's foundation of freedom. Stop the bullshit! Stop fueling fires of hate."

On December 9, President Obama appeared to use the 150th anniversary of the constitutional amendment abolishing slavery to challenge the incendiary rhetoric of Donald. At a ceremony at The Capitol, he rebuked Donald for saying that as President, he would bar Muslims from entering the United States. "Our freedom is bound up with the freedom of others," he said, "regardless of what they look like, or where they come from, or what their last name is, or what faith they practice."

Even the best-selling author of the Harry Potter series, J.K. Rowling, voiced her view, comparing Donald to her evil and scheming (fictional) villain, Voldemort.

During an interview with Barbara Walters, Donald denied he was a bigot. "Probably the least of anybody you've ever met. I just have common sense."

After White House spokesman Josh Earnest denounced Donald "as a carnival barker." even David Cameron, the prime minister of the U.K. weighed in, calling Donald's remarks "divisive, unhelpful, and quite simply wrong."

In the aftermath of J.K. Rowling's designation of her fictional character of Voldemort (portrayed above in one of the *Harry Potter* movies by Ralph Fiennes) as "worse than Donald," the internet witnessed a sudden burst of Voldemort images sporting orange wigs, mocking Donald.

Establishment Republicans were among his loudest critics: House Speaker Paul Ryan (R-WI) told the press, "This is not conservatism."

Columnist Linda Stasi wrote that "Donald is a bald-faced liar—even if he's not bald-headed. What he is and what Trump has always been is the greatest showman since Michael Jackson. If The Donald really believed the disgusting, incendiary, and nut-job things he said about Muslims, Mexicans, and everyone who isn't him, he would have stayed in Palm Beach with all those other white, WASPy types!"

Yet in spite of the outrage he'd generated, Donald's "shoot-from-the-hip" style of proclamations only seemed to enhance his poll numbers.

As a potential warning (some said "threat") to such GOP critics as Rand Paul and others, Donald tweeted: "A new poll indicated that 68% of my supporters would vote for me if I departed from the GOP and ran as an independent."

Reporter Patrick Helay wrote: "While many candidates appeal to the passion and patriotism of their crowds, Trump appears unrivaled in his ability to forge bonds with a sizable segment of Americans based on anxieties about a changing nation, economic insecurities, ferocious enemies, and emboldened minorities (like the first black President, whose heritage and intelligence he has all but encouraged supporters to malign)."

At times, Donald seemed to threaten his antagonists, vowing to attack his political opponents "ten times harder than they criticize me." He even evoked the horrors of Hiroshima, when he said, "We'll bomb hell out of our enemies."

Many pundits claimed that in using fiery language to win favor from frightened Americans, Donald was following in the tradition of Barry Goldwater, George Wallace, Joseph McCarthy, Huey Long, and Pat Buchanan.

Jennifer Mercieca, a political

Even the tabloids suddenly became models of righteous good citizenry.

Here, one of the biggest tabloids in Donald's home town denounced his implicit potentiality as an autocrat.

expert at Texas A&M, said, "Trump's entire campaign is run like a dema-gogue's, a language of division, his cult of personality, his manner of cate-gorizing and maligning people with a broad brush."

It was noted that Donald seemed to believe in what Vince Lombardi once said: "Winning is not everything. It is the only thing."

THE GOP'S RHETORIC GETS HOTTER
"Homicidal Maniacs Are Trying to Kill Us!"

Two massacres, one in France, another in California, strongly affected the style of Donald's race for the White House. Each became a controversial topic in his continuing anti-Muslim rants.

On November 13, a series of coordinated terrorist attacks occurred in Paris and its northern suburb, Saint-Denis, in which 130 innocent people were slaughtered, 89 at the Bataclan Theater. Another 368 people were in-jured. Three suicide bombers struck targets in Paris' Saint-Denis, followed by suicide bombing and mass shootings at cafés, restaurants, and a music venue. ISIL and the Is-lamic State of Iraq claimed responsibility.

On December 2, fourteen people were slaughtered and 22 se-riously injured in a terrorist attack (a mass shooting and an at-tempted bombing) on the Inland Regional Center in San Bernardino, Califor-nia. Within a rented banquet hall, the as-sassins, Syed Rizwan Farook and Tashfeen Malik, a married cou-ple, carried out the barbaric act. They fled in a rented SUV but,

Tashfeen Malik and Rizwan Farook were the perpetrators of a terrorist attack in San Bernardino, California on De-cember 2, 2015. The homicidal husband-and-wife team killed 14 civilians and injured 22 others. Both of them died in a shootout with police later that same day.

The FBI concluded that they were "homegrown violent ex-tremists inspired by foreign terrorist orgaizations." Their enormous stockpile of weapons led investigators to con-clude they they intended to inflict further terror attacks as part of their "Hate America" campaign.

four hours later, police pursued their vehicle and killed them in a shootout.

The FBI revealed that the perpetrators were "homegrown violent extremists" inspired by foreign terrorist groups and trained through lessons on the Internet. The murderous duet had stockpiled weapons, ammunition, and bomb-making equipment within their home.

In the wake of the shootings, Obama urged Americans to avoid a war on Muslims. "ISIL does not speak for Islam. They are thugs and killers, part of a cult of death."

When Donald heard those words, he tweeted, "Is that all there is? We need a new President—and FAST!"

In the wake of the massacre of Americans by Islamic terrorists in San Bernardino, GOP candidates ranted and raved. Some, including Ted Cruz, blamed Obama "for failing to protect lives."

He also warned of the "gathering storm of homicidal maniacs who want to kill us."

Donald was the least hysterical among the field of GOP hopefuls, calling for a "moment of silence for the victims."

When the GOP battleground relocated to New Hampshire, he became harsher in his rhetoric, blaming Obama's failure to stop "radical Islamic terrorism." He warned voters that "something really dangerous is going on with Muslims in mosques. There is also something going on between Muslims and the President we don't know about."

Although accused of being inconsistent in his positions, he remained steadfast in talking about "you" and "we," while attacking the "dangerous them."

Shortly before his death in June of 2016 at the age of 74, Muhammed Ali came out swinging one final time.

"I am a Muslim and there is nothing Islamic about killing innocent people in Paris and San Bernardino or anywhere else in the world. True Muslims know that the ruthless violence of so-called Islamic jihadists goes against the very tenets of our religion."

THE GOP IS DEAD

What if this slogan is true, that the Republican Party died because of a changing demographic and intolerance (or stupidity, or self-interest and/or greed) on the part of its ruling elite?

464

On December 7, in the wake of the husband-and-wife attack in California, Donald delivered his strongest counterattack yet.

In a widely publicized speech, he endorsed a platform calling for "a total and complete shutdown of Muslims entering the United States," not just immigrants and tourists, but even Muslims who are U.S. citizens, but who travel abroad.

At a rally in Mount Pleasant, South Carolina, he cited the danger posed by Muslims, and said they wanted to be governed by *sharia* law.

Donald's call for an anti-Muslim ban was not universally condemned. Many talk radio hosts defended his position. "Anyone who thinks Trump's comments will hurt him doesn't know the temperature of the American people," said radio host Laura Ingraham.

In the wake of widespread criticism, Donald weakened his stand. "If a person is a Muslim, goes overseas, and comes back, they can come back," he said. "They're a citizen. That's different."

Many newspaper editorials condemned Donald's stance against Muslims. As the *New York Daily News* phrased it, "a creature of ego, overweening ambition, barstool intellect, and vision that extends further than the mirror, Trump, the inquisitor, made a lie of American exceptionalism. Never could he take the oath of office to preserve, protect, and defend the Constitution without committing perjury."

Donald's attacks on Muslims had catalyzed the special outrage during the second week of December, with some headlines greeting him with: HATE YA BACK, DON. GOP HAS TO SHUN HIM OR SUFFER. HIS BIG LIE HAS SINISTER NAZI ECHO.

A response came fast from Nihad Awad, the executive director of the Council on American-Islamic relations. "Trump sounds more like the leader of a lynch mob than a great nation like ours."

In spite of his anti-Muslim attacks, or perhaps because of them, mid-December polls put Donald in a strong lead ahead of his rival GOP candidates. Those voters who had cited security as their top reason for voting seemed overwhelmingly to approve of Donald.

However, the situation in Iowa was different. For the first time, the firebrand Texas senator, Ted Cruz, became the frontrunner, registering a 24% approval rating to Donald's 19%. As recently as October, Ben Carson had led the pack at 32%.

PAYING THE PRICE
Donald's Anti-Muslim Rants
Cost Him Millions in Middle Eastern Deals

Donald's call to bar Muslims from entering the country threatened to diminish his brand's golden appeal in the Middle East, including in such countries as Dubai. The Dubai-based Landmark Group, responded to his threatened ban by removing all Trump-derived products from the shelves of its Lifestyle retail stores.

Before his denunciations, the name Trump was synonymous with American luxury and bigtime success. In the Middle East, his name had been applied to golf courses, residences, home accessories, and, in Turkey, some major hotels.

At the Trump Towers in Istanbul, a complex that housed both upmarket stores and luxurious condos, resident Melek Toprak said, "I feel ashamed to live in a building associated with such a vile name."

The business world estimated that Donald's incendiary remarks had cost him millions of dollars, if not tens of millions, in lost licensing and other deals.

But he said he was unbowed, that he had many friends in the Middle East, and that they had told him he had addressed a difficult problem that other world leaders had studiously avoided.

Business leaders were quick to point out that Donald had worked with Muslim investors in the Middle East for years. A $325 million investment in 1995 from a Saudi prince had helped him refinance ownership of the Plaza Hotel in

New billionaire Hussain Sajwani has transformed the skyline of Dubai with luxury apartments, deploying extreme marketing strategies. He is now called "The Donald of Dubai."

In one of his most lavish gated communities, he made a golf course bearing the Trump name as its centerpiece. "We made a deal with the Trump Organization," Sajwani said. "They know how to run golf courses. We stay away from politics."

But Donald's comments about Muslims had a ripple effect. Damac Properties, owned by Sajwani, removed the Trump name from a stone wall in front and also replaced images of Donald and his daughter, Ivanka, from a billboard nearby.

Their images were replaced with an enormous photo of Marlon Brando as Vito Corleone in *The Godfather*.

466

Manhattan. And in Dubai, Donald already had a fully operational golf course and another under development.

Ironically, his Muslim partner in the United Arab Emirates was Hussain Sajwani. Together, they were building a massive luxury complex seven times bigger than the Pentagon.

NEO-NAZIS AND HATE GROUPS
Feel Emboldened by Donald

As another result of Donald's anti-Muslim tirade, he breathed new life and new energy into the KKK and the American Nazis. Many white supremacy covens suddenly felt emboldened and even legitimatized.

In an article in *Politico*, Don Black, founder of *Stormfront*, a white supremacist group, spoke out: "Demoralization has been the biggest enemy, and Trump is changing all that. He's certainly creating a movement that will continue independently of him even if he does fold at some point."

Donald had also suggested that Black Lives Matter activists "deserved to be roughed up" for disrupting free speech rallies.

In August, he received the endorsement of David Duke, the former imperial wizard of the KKK. "How come it's against American values to want to preserve the heritage of this country?" Duke asked. "I'm for Donald Trump."

HAIL DONALD TRUMP—the ULTIMATE SAVIOR, was positioned as one of the headlines in the neo-Nazi website, *The Daily Stormer*.

The Southern Poverty Law Center's Intelligent Project said that Donald's words had contributed to a resurgence of the "main-streaming of hate."

George Lincoln Rockwell (1918-1967) was the godfather of the American Nazi Party, and his beliefs and writings have continued to be influential among white nationalists and neo-Nazis in the 21st Century.

On August 25, 1967, Rockwell was assassinated in Virginia by a member of his own group. He threatened that if he came to power in the United States, he would execute at least ninety percent of all Jews.

To counter the Black Panthers rallying cry of "Black Power," he started calling for "White Power,"which later became the name of the party's newspaper and the title of a book he wrote.

DONALD AS A GUERRILLA FIGHTER

*Popping In and Out at Rallies Along the Campaign Trail
Attacking "Lyin' Ted," "Little Marco," & "Crooked
Hillary,"*

"I'll be the most high-energy guy ever to occupy the Oval Office."
—*Donald Trump*

As 2015 entered its final weeks, Donald's method of campaigning was different from that of any of his GOP rivals. He was light on travel and heavy on media time. At least once a day he was interviewed on camera or over the phone for a "call-in chat," often provocative.

When he did leave his home base in New York, he flew on a private jet, touching down in such places as New Hampshire, Florida, and South Carolina, among other stops. He'd appeared at pro-Trump rallies, greeting hundreds of supporters, mired only by protesters, some of them violent.

Characterizing his travels as "pop in, pop out," he managed to keep his national lead in the polls, although Cruz and even Marco Rubio "seemed to be breathing down my neck with their bad breath," he told aides.

His wife, Melania, admitted, "Donald is a homebody who prefers to sleep in his own bed."

At a rally in Orlando, Florida, he said, "I came in, I spoke for twenty minutes, and then I got the hell out."

Two primary battles that especially concerned him included New Hampshire—"a more advanced electorate"—than in "evangelical Iowa." In contrast to his lackluster performance in Iowa, the New Jersey governor, Chris Christie, was surging ahead in New Hampshire, and "Little Marco Rubio" and "carpet bomber," Ted Cruz, were showing strong wins there, too.

In Iowa, Donald looked upon Rubio with great skepticism as he "became another Bible thumper," appealing to the evangelicals. "Not many evangelicals come out of Cuba," he said, seemingly disbelieving Rubio's "Ol'-time" religious credentials. To Donald, they evoked a cynical ploy to attract right-wing voters.

He read a confidential report about Rubio's much-vaunted religious background. Born a Roman Catholic, he converted to Mormonism, like Mitt Romney, before returning to the Catholic fold. At present, he seemed to be attending both a Southern Baptist Church and a Catholic one.

To appeal to the evangelicals, Donald threw his support behind those who felt same-sex marriages were being forced upon them, in spite of their religious objections. Or, as John Kasich jokingly said, "These people think they might have to serve a gay person a cupcake."

Both Donald and Rubio were supplied with polls that showed that 70% of white evangelical Protestants opposed same-sex marriages, whereas only 39% of the general voting public opposed such unions.

In the middle of his campaign in Iowa, Rubio encountered unwelcome headlines: KISS OF DEATH: BILLIONAIRE WHO FUNDED SAME-SEX MARRIAGE ENDORSES RUBIO.

The reference was to financier Paul Singer, a high-profile contributor to efforts to legalize same-sex marriage. For reasons known only to himself, he was a strong supporter of Rubio.

Perhaps to counter the negative publicity, Rubio hired Eric Teetsel, an anti-gay conservative activist, to join his campaign. TV ads appeared in Iowa attacking Rubio. "Can anyone think of anything Marco Rubio has ever done in the few times he's shown up on the Senate floor—anything at all except amnesty. He looks good on TV—and that's

What do Donald Trump and David Duke have in common? Both are interpreted as heroes by American Nazis.

about it."

For a change of pace, for a while, at least, Donald stopped attacking his GOP rivals and aimed heavy ammunition at Hillary instead. He outrageously accused her of being responsible for the Syrian refugee crisis. "And she calls me dangerous."

Not letting up on her, on December 11, at Manhattan's Plaza Hotel, which he had once owned, he addressed the annual luncheon of the Pennsylvania Commonwealth. It was here that he adopted a new nickname for his major Democratic rival, calling her "Crooked Hillary," a moniker he'd maintain in the public conscience throughout the remainder of his campaign.

Inside the hotel, a small group of protesters interrupted his speech and had to be escorted out. One woman who refused to budge was thrown to the floor. Outside, Marnie Halasa, dressed in a red, white, and blue uniform, carried a sign that read—"Trump Makes America Hate Again."

Within two days after his appearance at the Plaza, Donald loaded his verbal arsenals and went after Ted Cruz. In the latest national poll, Donald still commanded a lead at 27% but Cruz was moving up at 22%, a 12-point gain since October. Carson seemed to have lost his footing and fallen from his mountain peak.

"BRUISE CRUZ" screamed a headline as Donald went after the Texas senator, calling him "a maniac. Look how he's dealt with the Senate. I don't think he's qualified to be President. You can't walk into the Senate screaming and calling people liars and not be able to cajole and

Nikki Haley began her tenure as Republican governor of South Carolina in 2011, the first woman to serve in that capacity in that red state.

In 2016, she endorsed Marco Rubio for President, angering Trump supporters. In the call for attendance to an upcoming Republican debate, depicted above, a heavily muscled superman (with Donald's head superimposed onto its torso) is seen overpowering Haley after she denounced him.

get along with people." He delivered that attack on *Fox News* to Chris Wallace.

At every event, Donald was met with protesters, and often there was violence. At a rally in Las Vegas, a black protester, pastor Ender Austin, interrupted Donald's speech. Police grabbed Austin, who sat defiantly on the floor, almost defying security to drag him out of the building.

One Trump supporter shouted, *"Set the motherfucker on fire!"* Another screamed *"Shoot him!"* Yet another yelled out, *"Kick his ass!"* One Trump supporter was caught on camera barking the Nazi salute, *"Sieg heil!"*

The GOP Establishment was building its own wall against Trump, but many celebrities he'd known stepped forward to either endorse him or to speak kindly of him.

Quarterback Tom Brady didn't exactly endorse Donald, but had kind words for him and called him a good friend.

For that, Brady was denounced, the *New York Daily News* splashing out in "Second Coming Headlines" that "BRADY HAS NO BALLS!"

An active player in Republican politics and a Marco Rubio supporter, Paul Singer is an American hedge fund manager, activist investor, and philanthropist, and a financial supporter of GLBT rights.

Since his son came out as gay in 1998, he has sought to persuade other Republicans to support gay marriage. "The fact that gay couples want to marry is a kind of a lovely thing and a cool thing and a wonderful thing."

It's estimated that Singer has donated $10 million to gay rights.

Donald had come to Brady's defense during the "Deflategate Scandal," in which the football player was linked to charges involved letting some of the air out of footballs used in high-stakes games.

Amara Grautski, a reporter, wrote: "Patriots' quarterback Tom Brady went from deflated balls to no balls. The four-time Super Bowl champ turned big-time chump when he fumbled a perfect opportunity to condemn his good friend, Donald Trump, for his dangerous demagoguery and racist rhetoric."

As Donald came to be perceived more and more as a serious candidate, investigative reporters delved into his past, and revelations appeared.

Reporter Isabel Vincent came up with an *exposé* about Donald and his charities. She discovered that the last check Donald had written for his foundation had been way back in 2008 for the amount of $35,000.

"He hasn't coughed up a dime for his charitable foundation in six years, but has used the donations of others to give to the private school attended by his son, Barron. The Donald J. Trump Foundation doled out half a million dollars in 2014, $50,000 of which went to the Columbia Grammar and Preparatory School at which Barron was a student.

More and more was being learned about Donald's personal life and even his eating habits. He constantly battled a weight gain, since his preferred foods were steaks, hamburgers, pastas, and French fries. This unhealthy diet seemed to have little effect on his health. "I am fortunate to have been blessed with great genes—both from my parents who led long and very productive lives. If elected President, I would be the healthiest holder of that office in the history of America."

To back up his claim, his doctor, Harold Bornstein, a specialist in internal medicine and gastroenterology, claimed that his patient's health was "astonishingly excellent. Only positive results from many tests such as for high blood pressure," the doctor maintained. "He's lost fifteen pounds. His physical strength and stamina are extraordinary."

Tom Brady, a football quarterback for the New England Patriots, took a beating in the press for his having touted his friendship with Donald Trump. Brady is considered among the greatest quarterbacks of all time.

The football player and Donald have played several rounds of golf together, and Donald stood by Brady when he was alleged to have played a role in the "Deflategate" scandals. Charges were filed that there was evidence of "football tampering" by letting some of the air out of the balls used in the game.

BURNING BUSHES:
THE COLLAPSE OF A DYNASTY

"You're not going to insult your way into the presidency!"
—Jeb Bush, shouting, to Donald onstage

The fifth GOP debate was held on December 15, 2015 at the Venetian Resort in Las Vegas. This was the second debate to air on CNN, with Wolf

472

Blitzer being the chief moderator along with Dana Bash and Hugh Hewitt.

The debate was split into primetime and pre-primetime, with the Kiddies' Table occupied in their hopeless quest by Mike Huckabee, Rick Santorum, Lindsey Graham, and George Pataki. For Pataki and Graham, it would be their last hurrah, as each would suspend their respective campaigns before the end of the month.

Eighteen million people watched as Donald, Cruz, Rubio, Carson, Bush, Fiorina, Paul, Christie, and Kasich squared off. The audible coughing heard from onstage during the debate came from the only medical doctor among their ranks (Ben Carson), who had suffered from a lingering infection for the previous few weeks. At the debate, he seemed to be "sharing his cough" with the candidates close to him.

Donald and Rubio became prime targets during the debate, which focused on toughness, with immigrants and foreign intervention showing glaring divisions among the candidates.

From the beginning, one of the top contenders, Cruz, went aggressively after Rubio, questioning his conservative credentials and his judgment on national security and immigration. The Texas senator accused Rubio of lining up with liberals in favoring amnesty for immigrants.

Bush tore into Donald for his anti-Muslim rants, hoping to move his lackluster campaign forward in spite of, or because of, his famous name. Yet despite strenuous efforts and mountains of cash, he seemed to be failing to connect with the voters.

"Donald, you are not going to be able to insult your way into the presidency," Bush said. "That's not going to happen. Leadership is not about attacking people and disparaging them."

"With Jeb's attitude, we will never be great again," Donald said. "That I can tell you." His remarks were greeted with loud boos.

THE GOP'S FINEST, LIVE FROM LAS VEGAS! Donald decimated all of them.

Columnist Frank Bruni described "the sparring and preening, the puffed chests and sound bites over nuanced policies and earnest reflection. Cruz was the defining figure, his certainty verging on cockiness, his ambitions transparent, his attempts to tap into some warmth a mesmerizing exercise in futility."

Cruz claimed that his position on immigration, and that of Rubio's, was "like suggesting the fireman and the arsonist have the same record because they were both at the scene of the fire."

Donald, as anticipated, came in for his share of brickbats, and Rand Paul compared him to "totalitarian governments" because he supported monitoring the Internet for suspicious activity. Bush entered with his own bricks tossed at Donald, saying, "Trump is not a serious candidate, but merely great at one-liners."

"He's a chaos candidate," Bush said, "and would be a chaos President."

"Jeb doesn't believe I'm unhinged," Donald shot back. "He said that very simply because he has failed in this campaign. It's been a total disaster. Nobody cares."

In the lower tier of candidates, Huckabee and Santorum, among others, valiantly chased after an elusive dream. Desperate to attract attention, Santorum said, "We have entered World War III. We have a leader who refuses to identify it and be truthful to the American people," a libelous reference, of course, to Obama.

Huckabee seemed to agree. "We have an enemy out to kill us, and we have a government we don't trust any more." The former New York Governor, Pataki, called Donald "the know-nothing candidate of the 21st Century."

In some corners, the most hated man in America, and the bane of many local police departments, Wayne LaPierre, CEO of the NRA.

Lindsey got in his licks, claiming that Donald's stand on the Muslims "has made us less safe." Asked if he would support him if he were the nominee, he said, "Like Bob Dole, I may sleep late that day" [i.e., the day he'd have to cast a vote].

With more bluster than details, each of the upper-tier candidates, including Carly Fiorina, tried but failed to convince voters that they

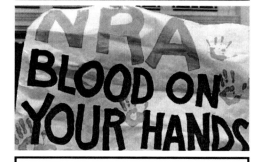

Although Jeb (and most of his Republican candidates) extolled the direct links between gun ownership and their lobbyists definition of freedom, many thousands of voters heartily, even passionately, disagreed.

would "make us safe." But as the evening ground on, it degenerated into tedious, even puerile, bickering.

Reporters ridiculed Cruz for equating Obamacare to "Nazi appeasement." As one reporter wrote, "There are those who say Cruz is smart. But how dumb can you get, comparing Nazis killing millions of people to Obama trying to give everyone some form of health insurance to save their lives? Smart? Sounds like an idiot to me."

Columnist Linda Stasi wrote: "Donald is bombastic and boorish, but Cruz? Now you're talking a bully without respect for the very government he claims to love for all his slimy, sweet words. His spoiled brat screaming and stomping his feet helped shut down the government which cost the U.S. economy $23 billion."

A New York Republican, Peter King, referred to Cruz and his Tea Party as "government terrorists."

With devastating accuracy, Stasi attacked and ridiculed Cruz's Senate filibuster, wherein, for hour after hour, as a means of blocking a timely Senate approval of the budget, he had droned on, overnight about "'Green Eggs and Ham;' delivered a Darth Vader impression; and spoke of 'The Little Engine that Could' and other nonsense."

Many persons in the media attacked the candidates' weak stands on gun control. In 2000, Donald had favored a ban on assault weapons. But in 2015, he pledged to veto gun controls. In reference to recent schoolyard shootings, he said, "You're going to have these things happen, and it's a horrible thing to behold."

Jeb Bush, a so-called "moderate," addressed the National Rifle Association and declared, "The sound of our guns is the sound of freedom."

In the wake of the debate, the newspaper offices were flooded with letters to the editor, some quite articulate, as in the case of John Amato of New York City: "The debate was full of sneers, weird looks, anger, teeth-grinding, and verbal explosions. It looks like who is left standing next November will win. It's kind of like a 'third

Regardless of what was happening on the campain trail, radio's bombastic Rush Limbaugh could always be counted on to weigh in with an opinion. Although he rarely had a kind word for Donald, his pronouncements could sting his rivals too.

Limbaugh entered the anti-immigrtion fight by claiming, "Rubio was part of the 'Gang of Eight' trying to secure amnesty and wishes now that he hadn't done that."

world' country during a *coup d'état*."

One of Ted Cruz's memoirs came up for scrutiny at the time. Published in 2015, it was entitled *A Time for Truth*. As many reviewers pointed out, "Truth had nothing to do with it."

An excerpt from it was shown to Donald, in which he learned that Cruz had described himself as "a geeky kid." In his self-appraisal, Cruz had claimed that he changed his name to Rafael Edward Cruz *[nicknamed Ted]* when he was a teenager.

At school, his classmates had ridiculed him when he was first known as "Rafaelito" and as "Felito."

"The problem with that name was that it seemed to rhyme with every major corn chip on the market," Cruz wrote. "Fritos, Cheetos, Doritos, and Tostitos."

For two years, Rafael, his born again Christian father, refused to call him Ted, viewing the Anglicization of his name as a rejection of both him and his heritage.

When the final verdict on the Las Vegas debate came in, it was generally assumed that Donald had established his alpha dog dominance over the other candidates in the overcrowded field. It was noted that many of the weaker candidates were afraid to take him on because he was known for his venomous push-backs.

Bush's assault against Donald was seen "as a long, bootless slog through the alligator-infested swamps associated with virtually everything about Donald and his candidacy."

One caller, speaking on a talk-show radio program in Las Vegas, called Cruz "Donald's pussy," suggesting he was afraid to really take him on. That, of course, would change during the weeks ahead.

The "bromance" between Vladimir Putin and Donald Trump reached the tongue-kissing stage in a now notorious mural that was spread to millions through social media. Evaluated as a political masterpiece, it brought world-wide attention to a barbecue restaurant in Vilnius, Lithuania, on the NATO border with Russia.

Locals have been using the mural as a backdrop for romantic kissing photos of their own.

Up until then in the campaign, Cruz showed, or at least pretended, respect for Donald, probably with hopes that he might avoid as many direct confrontations until much later in the campaign.

All of that was about to change.

The more viable Cruz appeared, as reflected by increasingly favorable polls, the stronger became the attacks on his character (or lack thereof).

Reporter Jennifer Steinhauer wrote, "It is the hate that dare not speak its name. Since his arrival in 2013, Ted Cruz has managed to alienate, exasperate, and generally agitate the plurality of his 99 colleagues in the Senate. He stands out for this widely held reputation for putting Ted first."

After the debate, Rubio struggled in third or fourth place, coming under fire for having made a big bet on immigration overhaul. He now seemed to try to back away from it. But Cruz wouldn't let him.

***

Newspapers continued to play up the "BROMANCE OF DONALD AND VLAD."

According to Donald, as expressed on MSNBC's *Morning Joe*, "Putin is at least a leader, unlike what we have in this country. "

Larry McShane, a reporter, wrote: "The two men—despite matching egos—remain an unlikely mutual admiration society. Trump all sculpted hair, tailored suits, and golf clubs; Putin all toned pecs, shirtless photo ops, and hunting rifles."

CARPET BOMBINGS VS. MAGIC CARPETS
Just Imagine If Aladdin Had Had a Nuclear Weapon!

Some polls seemed deliberately to mock Donald's supporters, including one conducted by Public Policy Polling. When presented with whether they'd be in favor of bombing the city of Agrabah [*"the (fictional) city of mystery and enchantment," aka, the home of Aladdin and his true love, Jasmine, "Princess of Agrabah," as depicted in Disney's animated film,* Aladdin (1992)], results indicated that 41% of people self-identifying as Trump supporters claimed they were in favor of bombing it.

[*According to Justin Mayhew, a communications specialist for PPP, the polling group that conducted the survey, "We made the question intentionally vague. We wanted to see how far this would go."*]

In the aftermath of the survey's (horrifying) implications, headlines shouted "WATCH YOUR ASS, AL-ADDIN!"

Only 13% of Trump supporters opposed the bombing. Among Democrats, 19% favored the bombing.

At around the same time, Katrina Pierson, a spokeswoman for Donald, appeared on Fox's *The O'Reilly Factor,* and seemed to encourage the use not only the bombing of some (vaguely defined) point in the Middle East, but a full-out nuclear strike. "What good does it do to have a good nuclear triad if you're afraid to use it?"

Abdel-Rahman is currently serving a life sentence at the Butner Medical Center which is part of the Butner Federal Correctional Institution in Butner, North Carolina. Formerly a resident of New York City, Abdel-Rahman and nine others figured into a prosecution derived from investigations of the World Trade Center bombing of 1993.

Abdel-Rahman was accused of being the leader of *Al-Gama'a al-Islamiyya* (also known as "The Islamic Group"), a militant Islamist movement in Egypt that is considered a terrorist organization by the U.S. and Egyptian governments. He, with his alleged cohorts, were convicted of seditions conspiracy, which requires only that a crime be planned, not that it necessarily be attempted.

How did Aladdin become an issue in the 2016 race for the White House?

Aladdin, of course, is the hero of a Middle Eastern folk tale that appeared in *The Book of One Thousand and One Nights,* and was revived in 1992 as part of a Disney animated film. In the yarn, Aladdin becomes rich and powerful with the aid of "the Genie of the Lamp," and goes on to marry the Sultan's daughter.

In a survey, nearly half of Donald's supporters favored the U.S. bombing of Agrabah, Aladdin's home town, not realizing it was fictional.

LET ME ENTERTAIN YOU

"I Watched Every Episode of The Apprentice.
That Trump is One Hell of an Entertainer"
—*A Trump Fan at a Rally*

Hoping to revive his campaign, Bush arrived in New Hampshire, where he didn't seem too articulate, or at least very artful. "I've got to get this off my chest. Donald Trump is a jerk!"

A Granite State poll conducted near the time of his arrival put Donald in first place at 26% of the vote to Jeb Bush's 10%.

Despite that success, the Trump camp felt that its ground plan wasn't working as well as they wished. Demographics revealed that his supporters were younger and without a college degree.

A disturbing element was cited in as a result of the polling. Although hordes of people were turning out at Donald's rallies, the survey showed that many of them had never voted before—and it was not certain if they would in 2016.

Another factor emerged as expressed by rally attendee Phil Beaton: "I'm not political, and I don't plan to vote. I came to be entertained. I watched every episode of *The Apprentice*. That Trump is one hell of an entertainer."

A retired Jersey City police captain, Peter Gallagher, on December 21, entered the fray over whether Muslims did hail and celebrate 9/11. He told the press that Muslims in New Jersey had celebrated 9/11 on rooftops and in street parties until they were dispersed by "disgusted cops," thereby backing up and corroborating Donald's much-disputed comments.

"Some men were dancing, some held kids on their shoulders. The women were shouting in Arabic in the high-pitched wail of Arabic fashion."

Other witnesses also came forth to back up Donald's previous claims, including yet another police officer, who claimed that he witnessed "a jubilant Arab celebration" on John F. Kennedy Boulevard. That was near the Masjid Al-Salam Mosque, where the 'blind sheikh," Omar Abdel-Rahman, screeched his sermons of hate before the 1993 bomb attack on the World Trade Center.

During his fielding of the rage generated by his widely refuted charges associated with Muslims who celebrated 9/11, Donald, campaigning in Michigan, stumbled into yet another controversy, based entirely on comments he (unchivalrously) delivered in front of thousands of his supporters.

At a rally, he commented on Hillary's battle against Obama for the Democratic nomination during the 2008 race.

Evaluating the outcome of that competition, Trump told his audience, "She got *schlonged.*" Of course, as every New Yorker knows, *schlong is* a (Yiddish) word for penis.

Someone at the rally who was unfamiliar with the word asked a supporter what it meant. "It means Hillary got fucked by Obama," the Trump supporter in a red cap bluntly extrapolated.

TRUMP SUPPORTERS
Perceived as "Peasants in Revolt"

In spite of their differences, Hillary and Donald, according to a Gallup Poll, each ended up among the most admired men and women in the world. Obama and Hillary tipped their respective lists, but Donald came in second, tying with Pope Francis.

Donald and Hillary certainly didn't admire each other. Their holiday spirit didn't last long. The Christmas season's last broadcast of "Jingle Bells" was played as Donald went on the attack, citing Bill Clinton "as a notorious philanderer. He's fair game in this campaign. Bill was a liability that Hillary suffered during her 2008 campaign against Obama, and this time around, it will be no different."

More and more talking heads on TV were claiming that without the support of African American voters, Donald could never win the presidency. A poll conducted by Quinnipiac University revealed that 88% of black America viewed Donald unfavorably.

The Rev. Jesse Jackson claimed that Donald's speeches on the campaign trail were "devastating, painful, and hurtful." The pastor was asked if he felt that Donald was a racist. "I don't use that kind of language."

Donald and Jackson had known each other for some three decades, and he had given Jackson free office space in one of his building in the Wall Street district.

During the course of his business career, Donald had known many African American celebrities, such as boxer Mike Tyson and his wife, Robin Givens, as well as the king of pop, Michael Jackson. Don King, Tyson's former promoter, said, "Donald's my man. That's who he is. As for those outlandish remarks, that's Donald. This is not a presidential endorsement. It is

GETTING SMEARED (OR WAS IT SCHLONGED?) BY DONALD

Here we go again. Donald Trump, as part of a smear campaign, decided to revive the most notorious sex scandal of Bill Clinton's presidency.

Monica Lewinsky and Bill were all smiles when this photograph on the White House grounds was taken, but soon they would not have anything to smile about.

A French newspaper (in English translation) wrote: "Only in America can the act of fellatio at the U.S. presidential palace lead to the impeachment of a sitting president. In Paris, we are far more sophisticated about such matters."

In lashing out at Hillary, some of the points Donald made about the sexual embarassments of the Clintons were true.

Blood Moon's award-winning biography *Bill & Hillary, So This Is That Thing Called Love* lays out—in a style equivalent to this overview of Donald Trump—most of the embarrassments , scandals, compromises, and pain associated with the Clintons.

a humanistic endorsement."

For the most part, Obama stayed out of the campaign, but right before Christmas, he blasted Donald for exploiting the fears of the working class man—"Joe Sixpack"—claiming that much of the contempt he faced was for being the first black commander-in-chief.

The President also asserted his belief that the relentless charges about being born in Kenya, and that he was therefore not an American, or the lie that he was not a Christian, were all tied in with the fact that he was the first black President.

***

With his wife Melania, and his son, Barron, Donald flew to Mar-a-Lago in Palm Beach for the Christmas holidays. For one day, he quit tweeting attacks on his enemies.

But on the night before Christmas, 2015. Hillary and Donald weren't singing Christmas Carols, but exchanging barbs instead. She claimed that Donald had "a penchant for sexism," and would not be the best candidate to advance women's rights.

Blasting back, he accused her of "playing the woman card." On Twitter, he wrote, "Be careful, Hillary, as you play the war-on-woman-being-degraded card. When you complain about a penchant for sexism, who are you referring to? I have great respect for women."

Without saying so, he was actually threatening to introduce her husband's 1990s reputation—"his abuse of women"—into the 2016 race,

"The Mini-Donald," as Melania called him, appeared at Christmas in a matching blue suit and tie, as he made the rounds of the various tables at Mar-a-Lago. "A future President in the making," said one of the guests. Another guest at a nearby table called Barron "the best dressed nine-year-old in America."

After dinner, when Barron retired for the night, Donald and Melania went to a midnight service at the Episcopal Church of Bethesda-by-the Sea, where they had been married in 2005.

"Hillary has some nerve to talk about a war on women and other bigotry toward women when she has a serious problem with her husband," Katrina Pierson, a Trump spokesperson said on CNN. "I can think of quite a few women who have been bullied by Hillary in an attempt to hide her husband's misogynistic sexist secrets."

She was getting stabbed on all sides, both by Donald's forces and by her aging rival, Senator Bernie Sanders of Vermont. On CBS's *Face the Na-*

tion, he revealed that he might also be Donald's worst enemy, as he planned to win over much of his constituency in his support of a $15-an-hour wage, the creation of new jobs, and his making college tuition free.

At year's end, economists began to analyze not only Sanders' give-aways, but also those among the GOP frontrunners. Shockingly, it was determined that the Trump plan would increase the U.S. deficit by $12 trillion over ten years.

His chief rival, Cruz, had a plan that called for a flat tax rate and the elimination of all payroll taxes used to fund Social Security and Medicare. Most economists denounced this plan as "irresponsible fantasy."

Back on the campaign trail, Cruz proved himself to be the major "culture warrior" of the GOP, unless one counted the losing evangelical, Mike Huckabee. The Texas senator continued with his anti-gay chant, insisting that as President, he would be under no obligation to accept the Supreme Court's decision on same-sex marriage.

***

Despite her pregnancy, Ivanka had been on the campaign trail advocating for her father. Right after Christmas, she posed for a picture of herself as a pregnant mother.

A business woman, Ivanka was set to give birth to her third child.

She leveraged the occasion into a vehicle for the promotion of "Daddy Don," claiming that he was one of the campaign's greatest advocates for women. "He 100% believes in quality of gender."

The 34-year-old daughter was asked about political ambitions of her own. "At this point, I would never contemplate it, but that doesn't mean when I'm fifty, I might have a change of heart."

***

Now famously pregnant, and, as headlined by *Town and Country*, "in charge of a growing American Dynasty," the cover girl was once again Ivanka, by now an overexposed regular with some mileage under her belt.

In the throes of a show-stopping *haute mode* pregnancy, the press headlined her situation as "Trump and Bump."

483

Many members of the Republican Establishment, including both John McCain and Mitt Romney—each a failed presidential candidate in his own right—continued to express their total contempt for Donald and his campaign. Yet despite ferocious opposition from the Old Guard, poll after poll continued to document his amazing depth and breadth of his support.

His attackers trivialized his supporters as "Trumpkins." In the words of journalist Michael Walsh, they were "mental midgets and xenophobic troglodytes who've crawled out from their survivalist caves to destroy the Beltway Establishment."

A headline read THE PEASANTS ARE REVOLTING, as national polls put Donald at 40% in the GOP race, with Cruz trailing at 8%.

Rick Wilson, writing in *The Daily Beast,* said that Trump supporters "put the entire conservative movement at risk of being hijacked and destroyed by a bloviating billionaire with poor impulse control and a profoundly superficial understanding of the world."

One conservative writer concluded, "The Trumpkins are sick of winning and having nothing to show for it, and their vengeance will be terrible."

Spy magazine dubbed Donald "the short-fingered vulgarian—neither a real Republican nor a real conservative."

Donald's hometown newspaper, the *New York Daily News,* awarded him its annual "New York Knucklehead of the Year Award for his superstorm of stupidity." The paper stated that the award was "to identify people who make asses of themselves with acts of vanity, ambition, and plain stupidity at levels far beyond those of mere morons."

Donald was determined not to let the year end without dredging up discord associated with the embarrassments of "Bubba" Clinton, appearing on the *Today Show* to bring up the old charges of his infidelities that marred his presidency in the 1990s.

"There was certainly a lot of abuse of women," Donald charged. "You look at whether it's Monica Lewinsky or Paula Jones or many of them, and that certainly will be fair game, certainly if they play the woman card with respect to me."

"I like the fact that Bill Clinton is out campaigning for his wife. He failed badly in 2008, really badly. He did a poor job of campaigning, if you wanna know the truth."

When Bill Clinton as president was mired in scandal in 1998, Donald appeared on CNN. He told the audience, "Bill is probably got the toughest skin I've ever seen. I think he's a teriffic guy."

After the Clintons left the White house, Donald pitched the idea to them of settling into one of his gilded properties in Manhattan. But instead, they moved to Westchester County, into a verdant suburb north of the city.

Donald even praised Bill's golfing abilities (or lack thereof). The former President is only a so-so golfer known for taking mulligans.

He also claimed that Hillary "would be the worst president ever."

However, back in 2008, Donald had said, "I know Hillary, and I think she'd make a great President or Vice President."

On December 29, GOP presidential candidates temporarily slowed their attacks on Donald, firing instead upon Marco Rubio. Recent polls had indicated that he was running in second place to Donald.

Governor Chris Christie slammed Rubio for repeatedly not showing up for work. Ads attacked Rubio for attending big fund raisers and missing key Senate hearings that had been scheduled after terrorist attacks in Paris and San Bernardino. One ad claimed, "Over the last three years, Rubio has missed important national security hearings and missed more total votes than any other senator."

The year of 2015 might be labeled "The Year of the Polls." When Civis Analytics, a Democratic data firm, released the results of its latest survey, it indicated that Donald was strongest in the South, in Appalachia, and in the industrial North. He showed his greatest strength among Republicans who are less affluent, less educated, and less likely to turn out to vote. Donald was particularly upset over that latter revelation. His most ardent fans were new Republicans, some of whom were nonetheless registered as Democrats.

His most loyal state was West Virginia, followed by New York. He fared well in Florida, in spite of the fact that two of that state's sons, Rubio and Jeb Bush, were also in the race.

His strength faded as the survey moved west, with an especially low approval rating in staunchly Republican Utah.

As 2015 ended, columnist Timothy Egan summed up the GOP state of affairs. "The Republican Party is now home to millions of people who would throw out the Constitution, welcome a police state against Latinos and Muslims, and enforce the religious test for entry into a country built by people fleeing religious persecution. This stuff polls well in the party, even if the Bill of Rights does not."

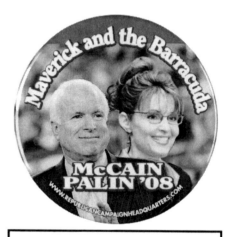

Mitt Romney, the GOP nominee for President in 2012: "I will not endorse Donald Trump."

John McCain, the GOP nominee for President in 2008: "I will not endorse Donald Trump."

Chapter Eighteen

CAMPAIGN VITRIOL
Boiling with Hatred

THE POLARIZATION
OF AMERICAN VOTERS
Enraged, Mutually Antagonistic Candidates
Upgrade Their Arsenals and Intensify Their Venom

THE GOP IS HORRIFIED
and Trapped Between a Bomb and a Kamikaze

"You can't make Châteaubriand out of cowpies, or chicken salad out of chicken shit."
—Linda Stasi, in reference to Ted Cruz

Donald Trump opened January of 2016, the year of the presidential election, attacking President Obama for taking time out from his duties to attend a special screening of *Star Wars: Episode VII – The Force Awakens* (2015). Seizing the opportunity as a sound bite, Donald accused him of prioritizing *Star Wars* over the War on Terror. The attack came in an ad posted on Instagram. "He prefers to watch the latest installment of the storied sci-fi franchise instead of using the force to fight ISIS," Donald charged. "We are in a serious war."

The ad ended with a film clip wherein the President ends a press conference with the words, "OK, everybody, I gotta get to *Star Wars.*"

The Trump video left out a major point: Obama was going to a special event for Gold Star families, those who had lost loved ones in the Iraq War. At his press conference, the President had tackled the subject of terrorist threats, global climate change, and Guantánamo Bay.

Donald revealed that he planned to spend $2 million of his own money over the upcoming months on ads in early primary or caucus states such as Iowa, New Hampshire, and South Carolina. He was still leading in the national polls, although evangelicals were converging around Ted Cruz, who had spent a lot of time campaigning in Iowa in anticipation of feverishly anticipated February 1 caucus.

Dr. Ben Carson, who had once been a frontrunner in Iowa, began 2016 with deep rifts in his campaign staff, as evidenced by the resignation of its manager, Barry Bennett. Carson's spokesman, Doug Watts, also resigned after multiple fumblings by Carson, many of them exposing his *naïveté* in foreign affairs. Despite strenuous efforts to stop it, Carson's campaign continued its downward spiral.

As America moved into 2016, arch conservatives, such as columnist Peggy Noonan, was asking, "Will Donald Trump unite or divide the GOP? We could see a great party split. The question is whether his race will play out over the next few cycles, or turn abrupt and fiery. Some in Washington speak giddily of the prospect, wondering aloud if the new party's logo will be a lion or a gazelle."

Other columnists, such as Ross Douthat, weighed in on the strange turn the GOP had taken. He admitted, "I underestimated Donald Trump. I sold him wildly short, and his entire campaign to date has proven it. Trump has had a very easy time turning his celebrity fan base into a meaningful constituency."

Douthat also wrote, "I'm not completely humbled. Indeed, I'm still proud enough to continue predicting, in defiance of national polling, that there's still no way that Trump will actually be the 2016 Republican nominee. Trust me: I'm a pundit."

Donald's major competition was also being examined, and not faring well, either. According to odds makers and prediction markets, Marco Rubio, the "absentee" senator from Florida, was a probable nominee, even though he was still a distant third behind Donald and Cruz in the polls.

As columnist Frank Bruni noted: "For those who could not stomach either Cruz or Donald as the nominee, Rubio was the flawed, rickety lifeboat they clung to, the amulet they clutched. Trump is too perverse, Cruz too cruel."

Unattractive episodes from Rubio's past emerged. During his tenure as majority whip in the Florida House of Representatives, he used Statehouse stationery to write a letter of support for the issuance of a real estate license for his sister's husband, who had served twelve years in a Federal prison for distributing $15 million worth of cocaine.

Rubio was often called "The Republican Obama," owing to his youth (age 44) and his elevation to a presidential contender while still a first-term senator.

But one GOP strategist called him "the Republican Bill Clinton, a Slick Willie who straddles ideological divides carrying the Tea Party banner while still cozy with Wall Street donors."

Journalist Eleanor Clift claimed, "He is triangulating," a Clintonian verb used to describe Rubio's evolving position on the issues. He was often denounced as "fuzzy."

Donald continued his assault on his GOP rivals, but saved much of his fire to burn Hillary. He made outrageous accusations against her, suggesting she caused tremendous deaths in the Middle East and that she was the chief architect of the migration of millions of refugees from Syria. He blamed her for voting for the war against Iraq and for the U.S. intervention in Libya that resulted in the killing of Moammar Khadafy in 2011, followed by a civil war. He further blamed her for the deaths of four American citizens at the U.S. consulate in Benghazi.

"The entire world has been upset by her wrong judgments," Donald charged. "She did a terrible job as Secretary of State."

At a rally in Mississippi, he accused both Hillary and Obama of being the "twin founders of ISIS." He claimed that their "reckless decisions" inspired the birth and survival of the terror group, which burns men in cages and beheads others. He called for Hillary to end up "behind bars for her misuse of her private email system. She should be in jail for what she did. What she did with those emails is a disgrace."

His New Year's celebration was brief, and by January 3, he was admitting to the press that, "I feel guilty. My campaign for the White House has cost me so little. I was going to have to spend some $35 to $40 million by now. But I have spent almost nothing. That's why I feel guilty." He made these remarks on CBS's *Face the Nation*.

He claimed that thousands of supporters were attracted to him because he was self-funded and wasn't a "bought candidate like Jeb Bush or Marco Rubio." He survived on endless appearances on TV and call-ins on talk radio shows, and—lest we forget—his provocative tweets. *[Melania confessed around this time that she wished "he wouldn't tweet so much."]*

As he moved deeper into his campaign, comparisons were inevitable with the communist witch hunter, Senator Joseph McCarthy, who, in the early 1950s, had terrified (and sometimes ruined) liberals and leftists.

Top photo: Detail from an anti-Rubio poster distributed widely during the caucases.

Lower photo: Donald Trump attached this illustration directly to his Twitter feed with this (devastating) message:

"Little Marco Rubio, the lightweight no show Senator from Florida is just another Washington politician."

Columnist Richard Cohen said, "Trump is not quite ready yet to fill McCarthy's boots. He has the late senator's gift for exaggeration and self-worship, and he needs the spotlight the way a vampire needs blood. We've been down this road before. But this time, instead of a demagogue on his knees like McCarthy shooting craps ('Come on babies, Papa needs a new pair of shoes!'), we've got one who owned the gaming tables in Atlantic City."

A poll released January 6 was deeply disturbing to leaders of the Republican Party. In essence, voters said, "It's Donald Trump—or nobody."

In the latest NBC/Survey Monkey Poll, he grabbed 35% of the voters, with Ted Cruz trailing at 18%. Most of Donald's supporters said they'd vote for him because they saw him as a strong leader. The majority of voters claimed that if Donald failed to get nominated, they would sit out the presidential election in November.

Despite Donald's sizable lead, he turned on Cruz, his closest rival. "The fact he was born in Alberta, Canada, is a big problem. He was, in fact, an Anchor Baby."

McCarthy with attorney Roy Cohn during Senate hearings.

In the 1950s, the gay attorney was "the brain" behind McCarthy. He later became Donald Trump's "take-no-prisoners" lawyer.

Donald had once demanded a forensic audit of Obama's birth certificate. Now he predicted an equivalent problem for Cruz. "The GOP may be tied up in court for two years if Cruz wins, because he was born to an American mother and a Cuban father in Canada. I would not call that a 'natural born' U.S. citizen."

Every day from his campaign trail, Donald promised to "Make America Great again." In defiance, outside his rallies, protesters sometimes carried signs—"AMERICA WAS NEVER GREAT!"

Many older voters recalled a time half a century ago when non-Hispanic whites made up more than 83 percent of the population. By 2016, that figure had fallen to only 62% of the demographic. It was predicted that Hispanics might be in the majority in 20 or 30 years, far outnumbering African

Collusion, collaboration, and betrayals from the then-president of the Screen Actors Guild, Ronald Reagan.

491

Americans. The ongoing shift in voting power deeply alarmed many of Donald's most ardent supporters.

Columnist Eduard Porter wrote: "The reaction of whites who are struggling economically raises the specter of an outright political war along racial and ethnic lines over the distribution of resources and opportunities."

"Racial animosity in the U.S. makes redistribution to the poor, who are disproportionately black, unappealing to many voters," wrote economist Alberto Alesina.

The eminent sociologist, William Julius Wilson, said, "White taxpayers have opposed welfare because they see themselves as being forced, through taxes, to pay for stuff for blacks that many of them could not afford for their own families,"

In-depth surveys showed that Donald appealed to this white voter, who feared he or she would soon be disenfranchised by the rising tide of minorities.

The Immigration Wars: HATING RUBIO and (ANCHOR) BABIES

Some Donald supporters said, "DON'T LOOK NOW, BUT IT ISN't JUST TED CRUZ WITH THE ELIGIBILITY PROBLEM."

This illustration appeared on the conservative website patriotretort.com with the caption BABY MARCO: "EL CUBANO."

Throughout most of his campaign, Donald had avoided an outlay of cash for expensive ads, having concluded that the daily 24-hour news cycle, as broadcast on cable TV, usually spotlighted him as the lead-off news event.

His monopoly of the nation's daily news cycle was defined as a "chokehold" by some pundits.

But in the first week of January, he launched his first-ever TV ad campaign, an anti-immigration video that, before 2PM on the day of its release, made him an international laughing stock.

On TV, swarms of desperate refugees were depicted running (presumably) toward the U.S. border, as a voice intoned, "Donald will stop illegal immigration by building a wall on our southern border that Mexico will pay for."

It was later revealed that the immigrants depicted in the video were not racing from within Mexico toward the U.S. border. The refugees depicted were Moroccans attempting to flee from their native land into Mellila.

[Mellila, along with nearby Ceuta, are autonomous Spanish ports, much-disputed remnants from Spain's imperial age, on the Mediterranean coast of Morocco.]

"I'M NO BIMBO"
—*Melania Trump*

At a chic party in Miami's Design District, Ivana, the "dumped" first wife of Donald, continued her rather catty attack on Melania, suggesting she might be too ill-informed, too shy and retiring, to make a suitable First Lady. However, she totally endorsed Donald's candidacy.

She didn't say so, but the inference was that he'd need a First Lady like herself, with an energy and capability equivalent to how she'd supervised the restoration of the Plaza Hotel in Manhattan and a major Trump casino hotel in Atlantic City, to help him run the country.

These remarks seemed to push Melania out of the shadows and into the light. At the beginning of the campaign, she'd chosen to remain within Trump Tower with her beloved son, Barron, as Donald flew in and out of Manhattan. She told the press that when they were separated, she spoke to him at least five times a day.

She told a reporter for *Harper's Bazaar* that, "I have chosen not to go political in public. That's my husband's job. They say I'm shy. I'm not shy."

"I also am not behind in the issues," she said, "as some of my critics have suggested. Behind closed doors, I am very political. Between me and my husband, I know everything that is going on. I follow politics from A to Z."

"I have my own mind, my own opinions," she maintained. "I am my own person. I think my husband likes me for that."

Her increased visibility on the campaign scene earned her big headlines, including one in

The increased visibility (and perhaps the increasing defensiveness) of Melania made its way into increased media exposure.

"Growing up as a little girl in Slovenia, never in my wildest dreams did I ever think I might be a candidate for First Lady of America."

493

MEANWHILE, IN THE U.K....
"If Britain Bans Donald,
Would He, as President, Carpet Bomb London?"

Throughout the campaign, and during the spring months to come, Donald generated headlines virtually every day. Some of them were unexpected, as when the House of Commons in London debated whether he should be banned from the British Isles. Members of Parliament were responding to a petition that had circulated and had garnered some 580,000 signatures, calling for a blockage of his presence from the U.K., based on his call to ban Muslims from entering the United States.

"If Trump came to visit our country, he'd unite all of us against him," said the British Prime Minister, David Cameron, who had previously expressed his widely distributed distaste for the GOP frontrunner.

In reference to Donald, among the bizarre letters the PM received was one from a British survivor of World War II: "Are you considering breaking off diplomatic relations with the United States if voters put Mr. Trump in the White House? Please remember that the Yanks helped us in World War II...and be kind, won't you?"

Donald answered his detractors in England, those who had objected to his suggestion that America seal its borders as a response to the global threat of terrorism.

George Osborne, Chancellor of the Exchequer, denounced Donald's "hate speech" but rejected the call to bar him from entering the U.K., asserting that his "nonsense" views must be defeated through debate rather than banning him. "Bloody hell! He might be the next President of the United States."

Many Londoners were angered when Donald told *MSNBC* that "Parts of London are so radicalized that the police are afraid for their lives." Boris Johnson *[London's Mayor from 2008-2016]* dismissed that assertion "for being simply ridiculous. The only reason I wouldn't go to some parts of New York is the real risk of meeting Donald Trump."

In the House of Commons, lawmakers attacked Donald as "a demagogue," "an idiot," and "a joke."

Jack Dromey, a Member of Parliament, said, "It would be dangerous and deeply divisive" to let Trump fly into London."

It was even suggested that he might fear for his life if he wandered into Birmingham, based on that city's large Muslim population.

"Donald Trump is free to be a fool, but he's not free to be a dangerous fool in Britain," said Tulip Siddiq, another member of Parliament who labeled Donald's words as "poisonous. They are not comical."

Not every lawmaker agreed, some of them pointing out that barring Donald might make him a martyr. Time and time again, lawmakers kept pointing out that the United States was Britain's major ally and barring a U.S. President from its borders was "unthinkable."

One member of Parliament asked, "What if the Queen invited The Donald for tea at Buckingham Palace?"

"His mother, a fine woman, was born in Scotland," another member pointed out. "British blood flows through his veins."

The Trump Organization eventually issued a statement: "We will pull back from plans to invest about $1.03 billion, or £700 million, in Scotland if the government votes to bar Mr. Trump from entering Britain. Barring Mr. Trump will alienate millions of Americans who wholeheartedly support him."

Mark Hughes of Edinburgh said, "Trump threatening to pull millions out of Scotland and abandon his planned golf course near Aberdeen, I say good riddance. We're just fine without whatever vulgar monstrosity his money would build."

Jeanetta Baratta tweeted, "Go then, pull out: No one wants you in Scotland anyway."

One of Donald's most ardent supporters, Glenn Forrest, of Chicago tweeted: "When he's elected President, Mr. Trump would be justified to carpet bomb London to bring back memories of the Blitz."

Many American columnists, such as Ted Wrobleski, chided the Brits for

Whereas Donald will be indelibly associated with NYC and its idiosyncracies, across the pond in London, Boris Johnson—in terms of *braggadoccio* and media swagger—is a more-than-adequate counterpart.

Donald-isms that made him unpopular in the U.K., some of them uttered as early as 2012, included: "Wind farms are a disaster for Scotland like Pan Am 103, an abomination, only sustained with government subsidy."

Boris' coif has been compared to Donald's.

their anti-Trump rants. "BUTT OUT ON TRUMP!" headlined one of his columns. "Let Americans deal with the stuff on our side of the pond. After all, we won the Revolutionary War. It's not your country anymore. On migrants, Trump's position was better safe than sorry. What if they banned him if he were the U.S. head of state? What are we to do? Break off all diplomatic relations with us? Close the embassies? Drive us back into the arms of the French?"

Eventually, despite the fiery British rhetoric, both in and out of Parliament, the House of Commons, as it turned out, discreetly opted not to hold a vote about barring, or not barring, Donald from the U.K.

"DONALD PREFERS A POTTY-MOUTH TO A SILVER SPOON—
This Is a Campaign Worse Than Voters Have Ever Seen"

With alarming frequency, polls revealed just how polarized America had become, and as he continued his campaign, it seemed that Donald was making it even worse. For the first time in history, polls demonstrated that both of the frontrunners, both Donald and Hillary, were unpopular by record-breaking margins. "We're given a choice," said Brett Halper. "We'll have to vote for Hillary or Donald and decide which one we hate the least."

As he neared the end of his administration, Obama, as evaluated in the words of writer Ed Criscoll, had presided over "the hateful eight years." As America's first black President, he had been the single most polarizing President in American history.

However, many savvy politicians said Obama would soon lose that label, transferring it onto his successor after the November 2016 elections. "Take your choice: it's either Donald or Hillary. Talk about polarizing," wrote one GOP activist.

Pollsters found the public "ready to lay down their switchblades and switch to howitzers," in the words of one reporter. Donald's latest disapproval rating had him at 57% opposed, with Hillary a close rival.

Donald's other rival, Ted Cruz, "did not come across as a day at the beach," in the words of *MSNBC's* Chris Matthews.

Columnist Kyle Smith wrote: "Cruz is worse than a used-car salesman. He's more like a used car salesman's lawyer. GOP candidates are chasing the most extreme, stubborn, and confrontational members of their party. It'll be a campaign season nastier than anything you've ever seen. There won't even be a pretense of playing to our better instincts. Forget hope and change. It's time for nope and rage."

Most of Hillary's supporters seemed unmoved by Donald's onslaught. "Same old, same old," said Ann Poe, a Democratic City Councilwoman in Cedar Rapids, Iowa.

David Brock, founder of the pro-Clinton Super PAC, *Correct the Record*, said, "These are desperate moves by Trump to appeal to the right wing. He's throwing red meat at his conservative base."

Donald was not satisfied in going after just Hillary. Once Bill Clinton hit the campaign trail, he attacked the former President "as an abuser of women."

Hillary shot back at Donald. During one of her interviews on CBS's *Face the Nation,* she said, "Talk about my husband's infidelity is a dead end, a blind alley for Trump."

In an appearance in Cedar Rapids, Bill Clinton didn't snap at the bait tossed by Donald. Instead, he brushed aside issues associated with his former dealings with women. "I'm in this campaign only to help Hillary, not to answer Trump's ridiculous charges. I have no response. He says a lot of silly things."

When not either joining in the assault on Hillary, or firing shots at Donald, the other frontrunners went after each other. Jockeying for position from way behind, Chris Christie told Laura Ingraham, the right-wing radio talk show host, that "Hillary Clinton would pat Rubio on the head and then cut his heart out if they squared off in a general election. That guy's been spoon fed every victory he's ever had."

Competing for the evangelical vote, Rubio and Cruz each began a tirade about which of them was the most religious. Cruz presented himself as a man so devout that he seemed to wake up to the sound of "Onward Christian Soldiers" with trumpets blaring. "Put on the full armor of God," he exhorted his campaign volunteers.

Later that day, he told a rally in Iowa, "Any President who doesn't begin every day on his knees isn't fit to be commander-in-chief."

He was speaking at a convention of Faith & Freedom, screeching about "religious liberty." Translated, that meant the freedom to refuse gay people's access to same-sex weddings.

As one LGBT activist said, "In other words, these people wanted their freedom while denying it to millions of others. What bullshit!"

Back on the east coast, *The New York Daily News* took a dim view of both Trump and Cruz. One of its blaring front page headlines read "DROP DEAD, TED." Inside, another headline proclaimed "WAD AN ASS HE IS."

In one of its editorials, it claimed, "Cruz and Trump are sorry specimens. Neither is blessed with the character of a New Yorker."

The paper concluded that, "Trump is one white guy even Al Sharpton can't bamboozle or threaten with a racial demonstration—the kind that can end with Sharpton getting a nice fat seat on whatever board he's threatening with racism at the moment."

On January 13, Cruz's finances were exposed by *The New York Times,* the paper claiming that the candidate solicited and received a loan of more than $1 million from Goldman Sachs and Citizen's Bank. *[His wife, Heidi, worked for Goldman Sachs.]*

According to the paper, whereas he had spent the money to finance his 2012 Senate race in Texas, he had failed to disclose the loan on his campaign finance report.

Ted and Heidi had decided at the time to liquidate their entire net worth to finance their campaigns. A spokesperson for Cruz claimed, "The failure to report the loan was inadvertent."

Early in January, Donald daringly decided to invade Burlington, Vermont, staging a bigtime rally in the hometown of Bernie Sanders, who had once been its controversial "commie mayor." For fans or detractors hoping to get into the rally, security was told to "eliminate the riff-raff" and invite only Donald's faithful. "I'm planning to take care of my people—not the morons voting for Bernie or the undecided," Donald said.

Donald's rally in Burlington unfolded within the Flynn Center for the Performing Arts, attracting a heady mix of supporters, protesters, and the merely curious. His speech was interrupted by protesters who had lied about their loyalties to security guards at the entrance. "Confiscate their coats," Donald urged from the platform. "Turn those loose outside where it's ten degrees below zero."

After they were removed, he told the faithful. "Oh, I would like to run against Bernie. A dream come true."

When Sanders heard that, the socialist said, "And I would love, love, love to run against Trump."

As the campaign moved forward, Donald became increasingly known for his tweets, which at times became notorious. He even tweeted that he would "kick the ass of drug lord El Chapo."

Surprisingly, from somewhere deep within Mexico, El Chapo tweeted back. "Keep fucking around, and I'll make you eat those god damn words, you fucking whitey."

In January, the drug lord was captured at his hideaway in Mexico.

The "oily" Ted Cruz, as some members of the press had dubbed him, also tweeted anti-Trump messages. "Can that kind of slime [*a reference to Donald*] even be showered off with a firehouse?" he asked.

On January 10, Donald appeared on *MSNBC's Meet the Press*, hosted by Chuck Todd. He was told that once again he had been compared to Kim Kardashian or else to circus king P. T. Barnum. By this point in his campaign, the association of Donald with that entertainer and impresario had become widespread. The *National Review*

RAFAEL EDUARDO CRUZ

★★★   ★★★

EL CUBANO DE CANADÁ

Reaction against Cruz from across the internet was swift. This went out to thousands of Twitter accounts from Cruz opponents across the political spectrum.

Some of them included the twittered message "Cruz for PM (Prime Minister)."

had called Donald "the P.T. Barnum of American politics," and in a roughly equivalent phraseology, *Salon.com* had deemed him "the Second Coming of P.T. Barnum."

Donald opted for and seemed to cheerfully endorse the Barnum comparison. "We need a little bit of Barnum," he said, "because we have to build up the image of this country. We have to be a cheerleader for America. Obama is not. He's the great divider."

As tension increased, more and more Old Guard Republicans like John McCain expressed fears that a lasting split along class divisions might erupt because of provocations from mavericks like Donald and Cruz. "I haven't seen this large a division in my career," said McCain. "Ronald Reagan and Gerald Ford were tense in 1976, but not like this."

Political strategists within the GOP claimed it might be hard to suppress the passions of an angry, hard-core, anti-immigrant base in the future. It appeared that the nativists weren't going away early; if anything, they appeared to be becoming more feverish.

Columnist Frank Bruni wrote: "If you're not with them, you're a loser (Trump's words) or godless (Cruz's words). The duo markets name-calling as truth-telling, pettiness as boldness, vanity as conviction. And their tandem success suggests a dynamic peculiar to the 2016 election. A special rule prevails: Obnoxiousness is the new charisma."

David Von Drehle in *Time* magazine wrote, "The GOP has awakened to find itself in bed between a bombshell and a kamikaze."

Many analysts concluded that Independents—and not traditionally defined Republicans or Democrats, who seemed to be running neck and neck—would decide the outcome of the general election in November, and that Independents appeared to be far from sold on the GOP frontrunners, Cruz or Donald.

In the 2012 election, 41% of all voters had self-defined as moderate, with 29% weighing in as conservatives.

In contrast, polls also showed that Donald's unfavorable ratings were higher than those of any candidate in the GOP field.

Ted Cruz didn't fare much better. According to Dean Stroker, a Hillary campaign aide, in reference to Cruz, "'That wacko bird,' [a label coined by John McCain], seemed to have stuck to his [i.e., Cruz's] slimy feathers like tar."

In 2016, in response to Donald's negative comments about Mexicans, "El Chapo" ("Shorty," aka Joaquín Archivaldo Guzmán Loera), depicted here after an arrest in 1993, sent a threat to "whitey Trump."

Identified by U.S. officials as Public Enemy no. 1, he was, at various periods of his saga, the most powerful drug trafficker in the world, a billionaire kingpin responsible for the transport of some 500 tons of cocaine into the United States.

CHARLESTON:
THE DARKEST OF THE GOP DEBATES

Resembling a Cartoon Sideshow, It Features a Texas Ideologue with a Professional Hatred for New Yorkers and an Agenda to the Right of Attila the Hun

PLAYGROUND BULLIES AT WAR

When Donald Defines Cruz as a "Canadian Anchor Baby," Cruz Rips Donald's "New York Values"

"WE DON'T WANT YOU!"

Horrified Canadians Lash Out at Bible-Thumping Cruz

The sixth GOP debate was held on January 14, 2016 in North Charleston, South Carolina, by the Fox Business Network at that town's Coliseum. Moderators included Neil Cavuto and Maria Bartiromo. In the prime time debate, Donald occupied center stage, adjacent to such other "mainliners" as Ted Cruz and Marco Rubio.

The 5PM "Kiddie Table debate" had featured Mike Huckabee, Rick Santorum, and Carly Fiorina. Rand Paul had been invited, but he had bowed out, resenting his demotion from prime time "to the losers' debate." In spite of, and in defiance of, his low poll numbers, he insisted he was a first tier candidate running a first tier campaign.

Voters did not agree. One voter in South Carolina said, "I sort of like Donald's hair, but I find Rand Paul's hair a big turn-off for me."

Other polling of South Carolina voters showed that many opinions were based on very personal reactions. "I was for Ted Cruz," said a garage mechanic from Charleston, "because I think he believes in Jesus. Then I saw that wife of his, this Heidi thing, on TV. I found her disgusting. If there's one thing I hate, it's a god damn Texas broad."

The rising heat of the debate was fueled by acidic exchanges between Cruz and Donald, as they engaged in bitter rivalry, their former "bromance" long buried with the ashes of yesterday. Donald questioned the Texas senator's eligibility to run for President, calling him an Anchor Baby born in Alberta, Canada, to a Cuban father from Castro's communist island of Cuba.

"You might drag the party into a legal fight with Democrats since you were born outside the United States," Donald said. "That's the question mark over your head. The Constitution calls for a natural-born citizen. Alberta is not part of the United States. Neither is Kenya for that matter."

Cruz, who had frequently touted his credentials as a constitutional lawyer, angrily shot back. "I'm not taking legal advice from Donald Trump.

I recognize that Donald is dismayed that his poll numbers are falling in Iowa."

Cruz then assailed Donald for having so-called "New York Values," reminding his audience in contemptuous tones that "not many conservatives come out of Manhattan. I think most people know exactly what New York values are. Everyone understands that the values in New York City are socially liberal."

In Donald's best moment throughout the debates, he eloquently defended New Yorkers. "When the World Trade Center came down, I saw something that no place on earth could have handled more beautifully, more humanely. That was a very insulting statement Cruz made."

That debate was one of the darkest of the campaign. Each of the candidates depicted America suffering through a great malaise, declining economically and militarily, its once lofty position as leader of the Free World fading.

Rubio tried to slip an occasional comment into a debate otherwise virtually monopolized by Donald and Cruz. "I hate to interrupt this episode on *Court TV*," the Florida senator said to laughter and applause. But when he eventually got to speak, Rubio offered little that was new, for the most part referencing canned, overused, overexposed comments from the campaign trail.

Several candidates attacked Donald's endorsement of a 45% tariff on all goods entering the U.S. from China. He denied having ever made that comment.

"During the mutual hatred that by now was obvious between Donald and Jeb, Hillary was mentioned too. Jeb! charged that if she were elected, she would spend the first 100 days of her office going back and forth between the White House and the courthouse, facing charges about her improper use of e-mails.

Rubio joined in the assault, claiming, "Hillary would be a disaster as President. She is not qualified to be the commander-in-chief. Someone who cannot handle intelligence information cannot be in charge. Nor can someone who lies to the families of those victims in Benghazi."

After the debate, which was widely watched in Cruz's native-born Canada, most Canadians were horrified by Donald's suggestion that Cruz should return north to run for Prime Minister.

Canadian newpapers were inundated with letters to the editor. Everad Soares wrote: "Please, Americans, do us a favor and keep him. We're enjoying watching your soap opera—what a script!"

"We don't want this jerk who has already rejected his Canadian citizenship," claimed Michael Reece. "Get lost and stay lost, Cruz!"

"The last thing Canada needs is another politician who sounds like he's on crack," claimed blogger John Ignatowicz.

Nothing generated more anti-Cruz hostility than his attack on "New York Values."

Columnist Mike Lupica wrote, "Cruz really must think he can get the nomination of his party by simply working the slower-thinking precincts, sharing a world view that could fit inside a shot glass."

Lupica ended his tirade by claiming, "It is the other party who has a donkey as its mascot. But Cruz is the one who is a jackass."

By the thousands, New Yorkers fired back at Cruz. Even Hillary said, "Just this one time, I applaud Donald Trump for defending New York. New Yorkers value hard work, diversity, tolerance, resilience, and building better lives for their families."

New York's Mayor, Bill de Blasio said, "On behalf of all New Yorkers, I'm disgusted at the insult that Ted Cruz threw at this city and its people."

"What are New York values?" tweeted Scott Wooledge of Manhattan. "We dominate the world of finance, medicine, science, fashion, art, music, theater, publishing, media, and hospitality."

New York State's Governor, Mario Cuomo, said, "If the jerk has any class at all, and I suspect he doesn't, Cruz should apologize to the people of New York."

Even the conservative *Wall Street Journal* weighed in on Cruz's assault on New York, "The problem with the Princetonian's anti-New York riff is that it echoes Sarah Palin's 2008 disdain for the part of the country that she said wasn't the real America. Cruz is playing the same kind of polarizing politics to win over conservatives in Iowa, by showing contempt for half the country. This is not the way to build a conservative majority."

These "Second Coming" tabloid frontpages made Ted Cruz as welcome in New York as the Second Coming of the Bubonic Plague.

In an analysis of the debate, columnist Gerald F. Seib wrote: "After months of dancing around each other in crystallizing anti-establishment anger, the two (Trump and Cruz) now know they are fishing from the same pond with less than three weeks to go before voting in Iowa begins."

Cruz emerged as a slashing, skilled debater, even if he wandered down some dark backwoods road in the rotting sagebrush wastelands of Texas. For most of his career in the Senate, he had been dismissed as a "cartoon sideshow—an ostrich boot-wearing ideologue."

Reporter Michael Barbaro wrote: "Cruz just didn't dominate much of the debate, he slashed, he mocked, he charmed, and he outmaneuvered everybody else on stage, but none as devastatingly and as thoroughly as this campaign's most commanding performer, Donald J. Trump."

At the time of the debate, news broke that Donald had picked up the dubious backing of White Nationalist Groups, including the Ku Klux Klan. Members were leading the "Bias Bandwagon," agreeing with Donald's proposed crackdown on illegal immigration—"those Mexicans coming here to rape our women and take our jobs."

Voters in Iowa were bombarded by robo-calls. Many of them encouraged voters to turn out for Donald, "The Great White Hope to Save America."

Jared Taylor, founder of *American Renaissance*, a webzine sometimes described as a white supremist publication, said, "We need smart, well-educated white people who will assimilate to our culture. Vote Trump! We don't need Muslims in this country!"

Donald also picked up support from other white supremacist groups for having tweeted inaccurate crime statistics used by various KKK sympathizers. He suggested that Black Lives Matter activists deserved to be "roughed up." He was also receiving signs of support

As Trump's insults and rhetoric got hotter, so did the implicit threats of violence to come from gun advocates and/or members of the Tea Party.

Trump fans called the act of affixing this bumper sticker to the backside of their cars an act of honest polical activism.

Opponents defined it as another incentive for road rage.

from virtually every Islamaphobe in America.

GOP candidates, especially Donald and Cruz, shifted to the right as it applied to their point of view about climate change, as the campaign trail became studded with rocks. In 2008, Rubio had backed a cap-and-trade program to combat climate change, but in a ploy to win the right wing, he shifted to the side of those who denied climate change, opposing remedies like cap-and-trade. "It will hurt the U.S. economy," he maintained.

Ironically, Republicans had once championed market-based systems to control pollution as a way to avoid more direct regulations.

But now, as part of a concentrated effort to thwart their (black) President and his Democratic supporters, the GOP took the night train out in another direction, questioning scientists, and perhaps the scientific process itself, in an attempt to win votes among the ill-informed.

As the days of January moved forward, Donald appeared to be losing in Iowa, yet nationwide, he was still the favorite among the Republican electorate. He actually went up in polls in December and January, as Cruz voters seemed to be leveling off.

"I smell blood on the battlefield," Donald told his aides. "Tainted Cruz blood."

"Brashness Becomes Boorishness, Peacockery Becomes Peevishness"

Tea Party rally in Hartford, Connecticut, in 2009.

The movement's nascent roots went viral, just in time to feed the fires of Donald's rhetoric.

Holy War, Tea Party Style

In Sioux Center, Iowa, just before the all-important Iowa caucus in early February, Donald delivered one of his most controversial statements: "I could stand in the middle of Fifth Avenue and shoot somebody, and I wouldn't lose my loyal voters."

[Surprisingly, that remark was uttered at—of all places—Dordt College, a private, Christian, liberal arts college that's closely affiliated with the Christian Reformed Church in North America.]

He used the speechifying venue there to bash radio talk show host Glenn Beck for having appeared at GOP rallies hyping the dubious candidacy of his rival, Ted Cruz. "Beck is a loser and sad sack," Donald proclaimed.

Many pundits had been recently evaluating the Republican campaign as if it had evolved into a contest exclusively dominated by Cruz and Donald. Charles Krauthammer, who appeared frequently on TV talk shows, wrote: "The 2016 race had turned into an epicontest between the ethno-nationalist populism of Donald Trump and traditional conservatism, though in two varieties; the scorched-earth fundamentalist version of Ted Cruz, and a reformist version of Marco Rubio—and articulated most fully by non-candidate Rand Paul and a cluster of productive thinkers and wonks dubbed 'reform-icons.'"

As the Republicans of Iowa were still trying to make up their minds about which candidate to endorse, columnist Michael Walsh summed up the race as a "cage match" between Donald and Cruz. "Brashness becomes boorishness," he wrote of Donald. "Peacockery becomes peevishness, and ostentation becomes obnoxiousness. A decisive loss for Trump in Iowa might mean a reversal of fortune to rival that of Oedipus. But betting that Trump will implode on his own accord has been a fool's game since he announced in June of 2015."

Walsh also wrote that, "The prickly charm of Cruz lacks Obama's easy charm, and as the 'first half-Cuban President,' that just doesn't have the same ring to it that the first black President has. Further, he lacks Marco Rubio's boyish earnestness, and the kind of urban *machismo* exemplified by Chris Christie. That doesn't fit the Harvard debater. Cruz is going to have to keep the knives out until he's the last man standing. There is no other way for him."

Columnists across the country kept writing about the GOP's Holy War, especially those aspects launched and perpetrated by Cruz and Rubio. At one rally, an evangelical conference, Cruz paraded onto the stage after a right-wing preacher, a real nutbag, talked about the death penalty, "according to the Bible," for gay people.

The Texas senator came out and pointedly did not renounce the horrendous "Biblical mandate." His strategy for changing his address to 1600 Pennsylvania Avenue hinged on evangelical support. He seemed shocked that the thrice-married Donald was capturing a lot of his voters.

On the campaign trail, Cruz hit harder against abortion and same-sex marriage. Many observers claimed that his so-called political rants were nothing more than "hell's fire sermons," with constant invocations of God or Jesus Christ, with whom Cruz seemed in constant Facebook contact.

Jeb Bush even questioned Donald's professed faith. Rubio referenced "Judeo-Christian values," so frequently that many voters began to wonder if he knew that there was, within the constitution, a separation of church and state.

"If Rubi gets elected," wrote one reporter, "Muslims and Asians will have reason to fear for their future in Born Again America."

Hustling to South Carolina on his private jet, Donald addressed a Tea Party rally at Myrtle Beach.

From the podium, he lit into Cruz with rattlesnake venom. "Nobody likes Ted Cruz. Nobody in Washington likes him. He didn't report his bank loans from Goldman Sachs, and he's got bank loans from Citibank—and then he acts like Robin Hood. His wife worked for Goldman Sachs, which helped fund his Senate race. He's beholden to rich campaign donors...*Nasty Ted!* Nobody likes him anywhere once they get to know him. He's a hypocrite."

Donald's opinion of the nastiness of Cruz was echoed by many, some of them attacking him with better skills than Donald had.

One of the best of the New York columnists, Linda Stasi, wrote: "Ted Cruz is as disingenuous as he is despicable. You can't make Châteaubriand out of cowpies, any more than you can make chicken salad out of chicken shit. So from New York to Texas Ted: Screw you and the horse you rode in on. *Yeehaw!*"

Donald continued to label Cruz as an

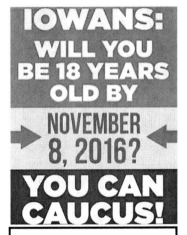

Pundits from all sides of the political spectrum denounce the Iowa Caucus as irritating, misleading, and undefinitive.

But as a PR tool and bellweather for heartland America's political groundswells, each of the 2016 candidates threw themselves into it with something approaching passion.

"Anchor Baby," citing his birth in Alberta.

Retaliating, Cruz referred to his American "roots," asserting, "As an expert on the Constitution, I say there is no issue at all about my right to seek the Presidency."

Actually, he was misleading his followers. Other scholars of Constitutional law claimed that the definition of "natural born" had, in its 230-year history, never been fully resolved by the Supreme Court.

Although he'd been born in Calgary, Cruz claimed U.S. citizenship through his mother. He had moved to Houston when he was four, and "didn't realize" (his words) that he was still a Canadian citizen until the *Dallas Morning News* pointed it out to him in 2013. Subsequent to that, he renounced his Canadian citizenship in 2014.

The Constitution (and Cruz knew it) states that "No person except a natural born citizen of the United States shall be eligible to the office of President." The interpretation hinged on the phrase "natural born." [*In a twist on an example that Cruz's fellow Republicans had been chanting in reference to Obama for years, Cruz's opponents were saying: "If Cruz's mother had given birth to him in Kenya, or in Canada, would he therefore be a "natural born" U.S. citizen?"*]

On the campaign trail, Cruz continued to hammer Donald relentlessly, accusing him of "being nothing but a deal-maker who will capitulate to the Washington Establishment."

The 1996 Republican presidential nominee, Bob Dole, had never liked Cruz. He told reporters, "The GOP would suffer cataclysmic and wholesale losses if Cruz were the Republican nominee. Trump would fare better."

Dole, a former senator from Kansas, also questioned Cruz's allegiance to the Republican Party. "I wouldn't call him a conservative. Extremist is the word. Trump probably could work with Congress because he's a kind of deal-maker. Cruz has falsely convinced Iowa voters he's a kind of mainstream conservative."

Dole's favorite candidate had been Jeb Bush, but even he had to admit, "Jeb has trouble gaining traction."

Jerry Falwell, Jr., President of Liberty University, gave what history will record as the single most over-effusive, over-the-top introduction of Donald Trump in the history of academia.

508

"Donald Trump Embodies the Best Qualities of Jesus Christ and Martin Luther King, Jr."
—Televangelist Jerry Falwell, Jr.

At around the same time, even Donald became a "Bible Thumper," as demonstrated at his rally at Liberty University, a prominent evangelical Christian institution in Lynchburg, South Carolina.

He had pledged to defend Christians "under siege," citing a reference from "Two Corinthians 3:17." [*That phraseology raised eyebrows among the many Bible students in attendance, who knew that the book he was citing was almost universally referred to as "Second Corinthians."*]

Jerry Falwell, Jr., [*son of Jerry Falwell (1933-2007), the ultra-conservative founder of Liberty University, a megachurch in Lynchburg, Virginia (The Thomas Road Baptist Church) and the political activist organization "Moral Majority"*] compared Donald favorably to both Jesus Christ and the Rev. Martin Luther King, Jr.

The pastor also said that, "Donald is a wonderful father and a man who I believe can lead our country to greatness again."

However, other evangelists, including those ardently supporting Cruz, feared, "Donald is like a wolf in sheep's clothing, invading the flock."

As January deepened, polls showed Donald still out in front, often winning over more and more evangelicals who might have otherwise supported Cruz. The Texas Senator, in the words of one reporter, was practically conducting "holy-roller revivals."

A *New York Times/CBS* poll had Donald, a Presbyterian, dominating the field with 42% of the evangelical vote.

A retired police officer from Oklahoma City claimed, "Trump is the only one who can pull America back from the abyss."

Along the way, Donald picked up a number of controversial endorsements, not just from the KKK. He won praise from America's most controversial sheriff, the immigrant-hating Joe Arpaio of Maricopa County in Arizona.

He also won praise from sources that included ultra-conservative author Ann Coulter; boxing champion Mike Tyson; Minnesota governor and previous pro wrestler Jesse Ventura; actors Stephen Baldwin and Gary Busey; wrestler/stuntman Hulk Hogan; and basketball star and "bad boy" personality Dennis Rodman when he wasn't extolling the virtues of North Korea's crazy dictator.

Another Trump endorsement came from gun advocate and rock guitarist Ted Nugent, who, on the warpath against Obama, referred to the President's supporters as "Pimps, whores, and welfare brats, soulless supporters electing a President to destroy America."

Then, a dubious "for Donald" endorsement came in from the New York-hating, has-been pitcher, John Rocker. In 1999, he had said, "The biggest thing I don't like about New York are the foreigners. How the hell did they get into this country?"

"You can walk the entire block of Times Square and not hear anybody speaking English. Donald Trump is my guy."

"Imagine having to take the subway to the ballpark," Rocker said: "It's like you're riding through Beirut. You sit next to a kid with purple hair on one side. On the other, some queer has AIDS. They get off and new passengers come on. The seat is taken by a dude who just got out of jail for the fourth time. On your right is a 20-year-old welfare mom with four kids—fathers unknown. It's depressing."

Editorial writers across the country continued with barrages, the *National Review* writing: "Donald Trump is a menace to American conservatism who would take the works of generations and trample it underfoot on behalf of populism as heedless and cruel as 'The Donald' himself."

Others disagreed, including John Feehery, a Capitol Hill lobbyist. "Trump won't do long-lasting damage to the GOP coalition. Cruz will."

Back in Donald's hometown of New York, the *Daily News* continued to mock Donald with its tabloid covers depicting him as a clown. The paper lamented the fact that Donald was still running strong and then editorialized, "The latest polls are a horrifying Rorschach test of the mentality of the GOP base. If only forced medication were available on a mass scale."

Although subjected to mounting criticism from around the world, Donald continued to win new voters every day. "I'm running my campaign from the heart—and the brain," he told the press.

However, Peter Wehner, a former White House adviser to the Bushes, said, "Trump's style degrades people and public discourse. His keen sense to go for the jugular and play to the Kardashian culture is effective, but dangerous for failing to offer a positive vision for the country."

"A lot of times I sound negative, but I'm really positive," Donald maintained. "Make America Great Again is a very positive campaign. I'm either going to get this campaign right, or else I'm not going to do it at all."

Chapter Nineteen

MAMA GRIZZLY ENDORSES DONALD
Sarah Palin Emerges from Her Troglodyte Cave

"BIRD BRAINS FLOCK TOGETHER"
Media reaction to Palin's endorsement of Donald Trump

PALIN BLAMES OBAMA
After Her Violent Son Is Arrested for Abuse of His "Gal Pal"

CHRISTIE
"LOOKING LIKE A HOSTAGE"
ENDORSES TRUMP
Then Eviscerates Rubio

Early in 2016, Sarah Palin, "the rogue Vice Presidential candidate" who helped John McCain lose his Republican bid for the presidency in 2008, emerged from the snow drifts of Alaska (from whose vantage point she could see Russia) to endorse Donald Trump. In Ames, Iowa, on January 19, she threw her Tea Party credentials behind him.

From a podium at Iowa State University, the wilting Venus's flytrap, by now beloved only by the Republican Party's most extreme right-wing fanatics, pumped up an audience with, "Are you ready to vote for the leader to make America great again? Are you ready to stump for Trump? I'm here to support the next President of the United States."

Then, repeating her faded, much-discredited signature phrase, she said, "He's been going rogue left and right!"

Columnist Gail Collins noted the half-smile on Donald's face as he stood uncomfortably next to her onstage, hearing her sing his praise as she warbled off-key and off-message.

According to Collins, it was "hard to tell if it were a half smile of self-satisfaction or the look of someone trapped at a dinner party next to a stranger who's describing how she met President William Henry Harrison in a past life."

Previously, Palin had thrown her endorsement to Ted Cruz during his run for the Senate of Texas. As payback for having switched allegiance, Cruz supporters later stigmatized Palin as a "deserter" and a "Trump turncoat."

Donald used his pulpit at the Iowa rally to denounce Cruz as "worse that Hillary Clinton. He didn't disclose his bank loans from Goldman Sachs," he continued, "because that greedy Wall Street firm owns him."

Palin's contract as an analyst with Fox News had ended (and pointedly not been renewed) in 2015, and since then, she had maintained a relatively low profile.

Cynics claimed that she had opted to endorse Donald as part of a cynical ploy to propel herself back into the media spotlight during the 2016 presidential race. Some pundits went on to speculate that she was seeking a cabinet position, or perhaps—although this was far-fetched—a nomination as his vice-presidential running mate.

Negative reactions to Palin's association with, and endorsement of, Donald were loud and immediate. One headline blared "A TRUMP/PALIN TICKET?—WHAT IS AMERICA COMING TO?" Columnist James Hyland wrote: "It's hardly surprising that a nattering nabob of narcissism like 'The Donald' would easily win the endorsement of another self-infatuated public celebrity—that nattering nemesis of the caribou, Sarah Palin. Perhaps she's gunning for the job of energy secretary in a Trump administration."

Most *politicos* pondered if Palin's backing would make a dent in the Trump campaign. "Palin's brand among evangelicals is as gold as the bathroom faucets at Trump Tower," boasted Ralph Reed, chairman of the ultra-conservative extreme right-wing Faith and Freedom Coalition, a group he defined as "a bridge between the Tea Party movement and evangelical voters."

Palin's endorsement of Donald could not have come at a worse time for the failed Veep candidate, who had been derisively nicknamed "John McCain's idiot Alaskan squaw" during the 2008 race for the White House.

Palin's eldest son, Track, an Iraq war veteran, was arrested by the police at Wasilla, Alaska, at the Palin family home. He was jailed overnight following an alleged attack on Jordan Loewe, 26, a woman whom newspapers labeled as his "gal pal."

The battered young woman charged that Track had punched her in the head and kicked her before grabbing a rifle and holding the barrel "just a few inches from my face."

Reportedly, he had yelled at her, "Do you think I am a pussy? Do you think I won't kill you?"

The following day at another Trump rally in Tulsa, Oklahoma, Palin said, "I guess I have to address the elephant in the room," referring to her son's arrest, details of which had been splashed all over newspapers and featured on cable news.

She began by attacking Obama, asserting that he "wore political correctness like a suicide vest. He's the weak-kneed capitulator-in-chief. He causes us to bend over and say thank you to our enemies."

Sarah Palin *en famille* in 2008, photo courtesy the Alaska governor's office.

Palin family photo shows then-Alaska Governor Sarah Palin (center) surrounded by her tribe.

From left to right, back row: son Track and husband Todd; second row: daughter Willow, Governor Sarah Palin, daughter Bristol; at front, daughter Piper.

Commentators suggested that she was hinting that the United States "was getting rectally fucked by its enemies."

"With Donald Trump as President," she shouted, "there will be no more pussy-footin' around! Our troops deserve the best!"

Reporters noted that perhaps for the first time in American political history, three figures prominently associated with the political news cycle—Donald (in New Hampshire), Track (in Alaska), and Sarah (in Tulsa)—had each, within a short span of time, invoked use of the word "pussy" as an insult and putdown.

At the Tulsa rally, Palin claimed that the domestic violence incident associated with her son was the result of post-traumatic stress based on his previous tour of military duty in the Middle East. "My son was changed by the horrible experience he endured while serving his country. Track, like the sons of so many other mothers, came back a different person, a bit hardened. He and his fellow soldiers and airmen, and every other member of the military, came back wondering if their country appreciated the sacrifices they'd made for our freedom."

"Everything stops at the top, and Obama is the commander-in-chief. Look at how bad he runs the Veterans Administration. Just hear Donald talk about how awful our vets are treated. My son is a victim of Obamacare, or the lack of care. His weak veterans' policy is the reason Track got off-track."

BLAME OBAMA
Yes We Can!
Politifake.org

I SCREWED YOU ALL

BUT THANKS FOR BLAMING IT ON THE BLACK GUY

Columnist Gail Collins claimed, "Republicans are currently okay with blaming the President for anything, even sunspots. But some of them may have found Sarah Palin's latest charge a little creepy."

She blamed Obama for her son's death threats and reported assault upon his girlfriend.

ENTER MICHAEL BLOOMBERG
Richer than Donald,
Could this Republican "Gazillionaire"
And Three-Term Mayor of New York City
Banish Donald to His Lair in the Trump Tower?

In January, word leaked that Michael Bloomberg, the three times Republican Mayor of New York City, was contemplating a run for the White House. The stony-faced, self-made "gazillionaire" had been one of the most liberal high-profile Republicans of his era. As mayor, he had championed same-sex marriage and was pro-abortion.

Described as "rich as a double chocolate fudge cake," he had a lot more money than Donald and could finance his own campaign. It was speculated in some quarters that the White House could be within the reach of this "short, Jewish, divorced billionaire."

Early in the race, he had hired a team to formulate plans for his potential run as an independent in the already overcrowded presidential race. Some of his aides, speaking off the record, said, "Mike didn't think Donald Trump or Bernie Sanders would make a good President—perhaps each of them would be a disaster."

In years past, Bloomberg had also contemplated a run, but rejected the idea, saying, "I can't win."

On January 24, Donald uttered a completely insincere statement. "I would welcome the entrance of Michael into the race. We've been friends over the years. I don't know if we are friends anymore. If he runs, I think I would do well against him."

But behind the scenes, he feared a run from Bloomberg, predicting it would siphon off much needed votes.

When Bloomberg's wealth was reported at $37 billion, Donald scoffed at that entry as it appeared in *Forbes* magazine, evaluating the former mayor's media tech company as "very fragile."

"His is a technology company, which in a short time could be easily replaced. I think real estate is a far more secure bet."

Bloomberg set a March deadline for an announcement of whether he'd become a candidate. For a potential candidate, March was the final date access could be granted to the ballots in all fifty states.

His backers studied previous third-party runs. It was rumored that the former mayor would have been willing to spend $1 billion of his own fortune to finance his presidential campaign.

Bloomberg, aged 73, was four years older than Donald, and he said that he had no personal *animus* against him. He did express his fear that Donald might have a "devastating lasting hold on the GOP field."

An aide said that Bloomberg strongly disagreed with Donald's political positions, especially his stance on immigration.

Bloomberg feared that Hillary's personal scandals, including the notorious private e-mails she sent during her tenure as Secretary of State, might seriously harm her candidacy.

The founder of the financial news and information provider, Bloomberg, LP, had been a political novice when he launched an unlikely bid for mayor in 2001. A longtime Democrat, he became a Republican as a vehicle for entering the race, although he later listed himself as Independent.

Jonathan Lemire, writing for the Associated Press, said, "Bloomberg oversaw a gilded age in the nation's largest city, as Manhattan shed its gritty image to become a sparkling star of film and television. Record numbers of tourists arrived, as did young professionals seeking their future. But critics noted the growing gap between rich and poor."

Michael Bloomberg: Well-informed, well-connected, sometimes visionary, and sane.

Bloomberg also became the nation's most vocal proponent of gun control, and used his vast fortune to bankroll candidates who clashed with the National Rifle Association.

"Liberals found fault with his cozy ties to Wall Street," Lemire wrote, "and also his unquestioned support for the New York Police Department, which drove down crime during his tenure, but engaged in tactics that a Federal judge later ruled discriminated against minorities."

MEGYN KELLY
Donald Engages in What the Press Calls "A Pissing Match" With a Premier News Anchor at Fox

The seventh debate had been announced for January 28 in Des Moines, Iowa. Donald had announced that he would not appear. "Let's just see how much money Fox is going to lose in advertising revenue with me not showing up," he told reporters.

He said that "Roger Ailes and Fox News think they can toy with me, but I don't play games."

"I don't like being used by this lightweight," Donald said of Kelly.

"She's trying to use attacks on me to win ratings. I have zero respect for her as a reporter. She is totally biased against me."

Ted Cruz mocked Donald's refusal to join his opponents in the latest GOP debate. "He's such a fragile soul," Cruz said in his most mocking, sarcastic voice. "You know if Kelly asks him mean questions, his orange hair might stand on end."

Three miles away, Donald staged his "dual screen" rally at a packed auditorium at Drake University, claiming that his one-man show was staged to raise much-needed money for veterans.

"We have to stick up for ourselves as a people, and we have to stick up for our country when we're being mistreated," he said.

Right before he appeared, word had leaked that he might be in the GOP debate after all. It was broadcast, but unconfirmed, that Fox News had apologized to him for Kelly's "excessive questioning." That apparently turned out not to be true.

Donald discounted the rumor, saying, "Once this ball started rolling, we can't stop it." He claimed that his rally had already solicited $5 million in contributions to veterans' charities, and he was definitely going through with his competing event.

"I plan to out-Fox Megyn," he said. "I will not call her a bimbo, since that is not politically correct. However, I can safely say she's a bad reporter."

Before going onstage at the rival rally, many of the candidates mocked Donald's boycott. The mean-spirited Cruz, "the man everybody loves to hate," referred to him as "Ducking Donald," and called for a *"mano-a-mano"* contest with Donald.

When he heard about that, Donald responded, "Can we stage such a debate in Canada?" Of course, he was drawing attention to the senator's birthplace in Alberta.

In a review of Donald's one-man act, columnist Michael Barbaro wrote: "Trump put on a show all right—and it was entirely about him: His hurt, his feelings, his vanity, and his revenge."

Looking sheepish, Rick Santorum showed up at Donald's event, although he refused to be photographed in front of a TRUMP FOR PRESIDENT sign. He said, "I'm supporting another candidate."

Mike Huckabee also showed up at Donald's rally, and this "guns, grits, and gravy" losing candidate had kind words for Trump, suggesting a possible future endorsement.

In references to Donald's rally, many veterans claimed they would not accept any of his charity. Paul Rieckhoff, founder of the Iraq and Afghanistan Veterans Association, told the press, "If offered, we will decline donations from Trump's event in Des Moines. We need strong policies from candidates. We will not be used for his political stunts."

***

At 8PM on January 28, the seventh GOP debate opened in Des Moines, minus Donald. Sponsored by Fox News Channel, it was moderated by Bret Baier, Chris Wallace, and the controversial Megyn Kelly. Fox had refused Donald's request to have her removed.

The 5PM debate at the "Kiddies' Table" was significant in that it marked the final appearances of losing candidates who included Carly Fiorina, Jim Gilmore, Mike Huckabee, Rand Paul, and Rick Santorum. In February, all of these candidates, whom Donald always referred to as "the losers," would suspend their presidential bids. When Donald learned about this, he said, "They didn't have a chance. I ripped them to shreds."

IRAQ AND AFGHANISTAN VETERANS OF AMERICA

To Donald Trump: "Keep your money. We won't be used as a political pawn."

Depicted above: US soldiers on a successful rescue mission near Baghdad in 2003.

The debate opened with Kelly "addressing the elephant in the room"— that is, the absence of the leading candidate.

In a burlesque, the Texas senator said, "I'll stand in for Donald." He then pretended to be him, saying: "Ted Cruz is a maniac, and everybody on this stage is stupid, fat, and ugly. Ben Carson, you're a terrible surgeon."

Then, slipping back into his own character, he said. "Now that we've gotten Donald Trump out of the way..."

The audience roared with laughter.

Cruz and his arch rival on stage, Marco Rubio, filled the void left by Donald, clashing over immigration and other issues. Trying to get a word in, Rand Paul of Kentucky questioned Cruz's authenticity, claiming he had "a shifting sands stance on immigration and amnesty."

Although Cruz was condescending to Rubio, he avoided any reference to the nickname ("Little Marco") Donald had assigned to him.

"I like Marco," Cruz said, barely concealing his hostility.

An Iowa reporter would later write: "At least Cruz didn't say that both of them were Cuban refugees trying to take over the control of the U.S. government, as if we didn't have enough native homegrown boys who could do the job better."

When an opportunity arose, the other candidates on the stage tried to work in a word or two. But Jeb Bush, Carson, John Kasich, and Rand Paul delivered lackluster remarks, and failed to win any traction with the already biased audience, many of them Donald's supporters.

During his time in the spotlight, Christie directed most of his fire at Hillary, claiming, "She'll never get within ten miles of the White House. Do you want a white Obama in the Oval Office?"

Both Cruz and Rubio appeared as "holier-than-thou" preacher-politicians. In a last-ditch appeal to evangelicals, Rubio claimed that if he were elected, his faith would play a great role in his administration, assuring his audiences, "Jesus Christ came down to earth to die for your sins."

"The Florida senator said those words as if the all-Christian audience had never heard that theory before," said a TV newscaster in Des Moines. "What does he take us for? A pack of heathens? Perhaps he's stayed out in the Florida sunshine too long."

The candidates weren't the only ones attacked. Kelly came in for her fair share of criticism. One sarcastic late night radio caller labeled her "a true bimbo!"

Another unidentified caller on radio said, "What on God's earth convinced these pathetic jackals on stage tonight that either of them could be President of the United States? I hope Donald Trump, when he becomes President, deports Rubio back to Castro's little Commie island of Cuba, and sends Ted Cruz back to Alberta where he'll probably freeze his balls off—that is, if he has any. As for Jeb Bush, he reminds me of my third-grade English teacher. ISIS would laugh at him before they caged him, doused him with gasoline, and lit a match. As for the others, ISIS, when it invades Washington, would probably toss them off some very high rooftop. That fat boy, Christie, would probably splatter into a million pieces of blubber."

Another call-in to the station asked, "Where is Donald Trump now that we need him"? Instead of Donald making us great again, we were treated to a third-rate vaudeville show at the last GOP debate."

The state has long suffered from jokes decrying it as the corniest state in the union. It's quiet around here UNTIL the every-four-year hysteria of THE CAUCUS.

"TRUMP DIVIDES GOD'S VOTERS"

—Headline in a Des Moines Newspaper

In the wake of the debate, editorial writers and reporters went into high gear dissecting what had taken place.

Under a banner headline, "TRUMP DIVIDES GOD'S VOTERS," a reporter wrote, "Evangelicals still wield power, but both their unity and influence have faded by 2016. Once, the faithful voted overwhelmingly for Michele Bachmann, Mike Huckabee, and Rick Santorum. But no more. This coven of homophobes and anti-abortion avocates have lost their allure."

Author Sarah Posner said: "Many evangelicals are abandoning Cruz and Rubio to support Trump, who is unabashedly ignorant of biblical imperatives that form the foundation of evangelical culture. Polls show Trump attracting a quarter to a third of white evangelical support."

Columnist Steve Hewitt wrote: "Trump doesn't really seem to give a damn about religious issues. As for the fight over providing insurance coverage for contraception, Trump would probably say 'Get a fucking condom, god damn it! There are enough starving kids in the world already."

In-depth polling discovered that the far-right wing of the Republican Party was not appealing to the millions of more moderate or independent Americans. That discontent was expressed by Walter Bennett of Shenandoah, Pennsylvania.

"Domestically, all the Republican debaters wanted to repeal the Affordable Care Act, casting millions back to uninsured status, and slash domestic spending, creating an ever wider gap among the haves, have-at-least-a-little, and having nothing at all. Most Americans will be in the latter two categories."

"The GOP rivals want to set fire to the social compact of this nation at home while marauding in search of conflicts to exacerbate wars abroad," Bennett said. "Oh, and Rand Paul wants to declare every fetus a citizen. By his very absence, Donald Trump proved that without him, the choice is 'none of the above.'"

***

Around the nation and abroad, everybody seemed to have formed an opinion about The Donald, including both his former wife, Ivana, and a Holocaust survivor in Amsterdam.

In honor of Holocaust Memorial Day, Auschwitz survivor Eva Schloss, the stepsister of Nazi victim Anne Frank, told the press, "Donald Trump is acting like another Hitler. If he becomes President of the United States, it will be a complete disaster. Like Hitler, he would incite racism, maybe not against the Jews but against Muslims and Mexicans."

At a chic party in Palm Beach, First Wife Ivana was taking credit for Donald's run for the White House, claiming that it was she who had first suggested that he enter politics.

Married to Donald from 1977 to 1992, she seemed to have regretted that she had lost her chance to become First Lady.

A so-called friend, who did not want her name used, said, "I think Ivana was asked to stop attacking Melania—perhaps by Donald himself, but she has continued to dish her. She can really pile it on about what a terrible choice Melania would be as First Lady. Real pissy stuff. She endorses Donald but not Melania."

Several of Ivana's friends thought that with her business background and proven track record of "getting things done," she would have been a far better choice as First Lady.

One of her critics disagreed: "As First Lady, Ivana would be a loose cannon."

FEBRUARY, 2016
From the Granite State to the Palmetto State, Donald Deflowers "Pussy Boy Cruz"

"I haven't left my house in days. The best election commentary I've heard so far. I watch the news channels incessantly. All the news stories are about the election. All the commercials are for Viagra and Cialis. Election…erection…election…erection…Either way, we're getting fucked."

—Bette Midler

***

Donald Trump began the month of February by presenting his favorite tabloid, *The National Enquirer*, with a ten-point plan to fix America.

"We're being laughed at by the rest of the world," he claimed. "I'm running for President because I see no one else capable of doing the job! "When I was growing up, I saw the respect that other countries had for us—but not

521

anymore. When Ronald Reagan was President, we were respected. But today it's much different. People in this country feel we are the whipping post for other countries."

In a nutshell, he promised to:

1. *Protect the U.S. from ISIS and radical Islamic terrorism.*
2. *Find the next General Douglas MacArthur.*
3. *Reopen the debate about Obamacare and replace it with something that benefits everybody.*
4. *Create jobs.*
5. *Rebuild the country's infrastructure.*
6. *Save Medicaid, Medicare, and Social Security.*
7. *Renegotiate foreign trade deals.*
8. *End Obama's executive actions on immigration.*
9. *End border crossings from Mexico, and*
10. *Build a "great, great wall" along the U.S.'s southern border.*

In its same issue, the *Enquirer* revealed that "hefty Hillary" had gained more than thirty pounds and had started to waddle. "She has been gorging on all manner of fatty, high-calorie foods," claimed the article. "Soon, she will have to be rolled down the campaign trail."

The magazine went on to claim that in addition to gorging on pizza, hot dogs, tacos, and Dairy Queen ice cream, she "continues to hit the bottle with reckless abandon after a long day."

The *Enquirer* also ran a tabloid headline about a possible blip in Rubio's sexual background. The writer suggested that the Florida senator had a "zipper problem," and predicted some "shady lady" might surface to ruin his run for the presidency. It was alleged that when Rubio was Speaker of Florida's House of Representatives in Tallahassee, he paid this mystery lady's expenses, charging them to his American Express card.

When contacted, the woman told the *Enquirer*, "The allegations that I had an inappropriate relationship of any kind with Marco Rubio are absolutely false. Expenses were incurred when I worked for the GOP House campaigns in 2007."

***

Celebrities from movie stars to leading feminists backed certain candidates. Deserting Hillary, Susan Sarandon threw her support to Bernie

Sanders.

Meanwhile, Gloria Steinem pronounced Donald a "total fraud." She told *Women's Health* magazine, "He was, as they say, born on third base, but thinks he hit a home run. His father was a very successful developer, and nothing makes money as successfully as already having it. The buildings outside of New York that bear his name, he didn't build. He is not competent in understanding social issues."

Steinem, as expected, came out for Hillary, claiming "She represents the interest of women very well, very fiercely, and very devotedly."

CORNSTALKERS
IN "A CORNFIELD CRUCIBLE"
Hustling Voters in the Hawkeye State
Before the Iowa Caucuses

Late in January, newspapers photoshopped Donald, Rubio, and Cruz, along with Hillary and Sanders as "cornstalkers" hustling the voters of Iowa. At the time, candidates were blitzing the Hawkeye State before its caucus on February 1.

To demonstrate how religiously observant he was, Donald attended a nondenominational church (the First Christian Orchard Campus in Council Bluffs) with his wife Melania. As part of a minor gaffe, during a ceremony where communion wafers were passed among the congregants on a silver tray, Melania correctly took a communion wafer from the silver plate when it was passed. But in what some observers described as a "cringeworthy moment," Donald mistook the communion plate for the collection plate. Digging some money from his pocket, he tried to put in an offering, something which *The Daily Mail* reported he later laughed off to members of his staff.

Polls showed that in the Iowa Caucus, Cruz would be his chief rival. Reacting to these polls, Donald attacked him as a "total liar" on ABC's *This Week.*

At a Cruz rally, someone rose from the audience shouting, "Ted Cruz looks so weird!"

To that, Cruz shot back, "Is that Donald Trump out there?"

Right before the caucus, a former Iowa staffer for the Trump campaign filed a sexual discrimination lawsuit. She alleged that during her stint with the Trump campaign, she was paid less than the male staffers, and she also had to endure crass comments from Donald about her looks.

In her complaint to the Civil Rights Commission, Elizabeth Mae David-son, 26, said that when Donald met her and a female volunteer, he said, "You guys could do a lot of damage."

Davidson was fired on January 14. She stated that the alleged discrimination caused her to suffer "lost wages, mental anguish, and damage to my career."

During an interview with *Bloomberg Politics*, Donald denied her accusation, defining her as "a disgruntled employee who wanted to come back to the campaign, but she didn't do a good job."

Hours before the Iowa caucus, the candidates were still slinging mud and trying to outmuscle each other. Races on both the Democratic and the GOP sides seemed too unpredictable to call. Bradley Todd, a veteran GOP strategist, said, "Betting on the caucuses would be like divining chicken bones."

Before the voting began, Iowa reporters ran articles headlined CAN CRUZ TRUMP TRUMP? and WILL RUBIO SNEAK BY BOTH?

The night before the caucus, whereas bombastic Trump had the lead at 30%, with Cruz trailing at 24%. Rubio racked up only 15%.

Reporter Alan Rappeport wrote: "Candidates have munched on pork chops in the heat of summer and hunted game in the dead of winter. Spouses and children have been dispatched as surrogates across the plains of Iowa."

In the final hours, candidates were leaving nothing to chance, furiously crisscrossing the state and making direct appeals to voters.

Iowa was hardly a microcosm of America, since it is mostly rural, overwhelmingly white, and very evangelical.

It seemed that the battle in Iowa had evolved into a two-way race between Cruz and Donald. At best, Rubio could only hope for a third place finish in Iowa, and Jeb Bush and Chris Christie had more or less moved on, focusing on the next battleground, New Hampshire.

No one worked harder for votes than Cruz, who visited all 99 of the state's counties, sounding like a hell-raising preacher on the stump. At one point at a town hall meeting, he asked the audience to get down on its knees and pray that the Supreme Court would not recognize same-sex marriage. Fortunately for the GLBT community, God opted not to grant his prayer.

The New York Times labeled Iowa "THE CORNFIELD CRUCIBLE" in one of its headlines.

On the campaign trail in Iowa, Donald notoriously suggested that the primary voters of that state were "stupid," and to prove his case, evangelical voters turned out in droves to give Senator Cruz an unexpected victory. If anyone read the results of previous contests, this surge of support for this extreme right-wing candidate should have come as no surprise. After all, these were the same evangelicals who had awarded victories to both Rick Santorum and Michele Bachmann.

Humbled by his defeat in the cornfields of Iowa *[which many sociologists have concluded do not represent the voting preferences of large swaths of the rest of the U.S.]*, Donald made it clear that he did not like to lose.

Despite the limited conclusions the Iowa caucus provides, many reporters, failing to take into account that the fanatical religious right does not represent the scope of the United States at large, claimed that the Cruz victory brought into question the depth of support for Donald's unconventional candidacy.

In Iowa, Cruz won 28% of the vote, with Donald getting 24%. Rubio was breathing down Donald's neck, winning 23%. Ben Carson, who had once been a frontrunner, suffered the biggest setback, receiving only 9% of the vote.

In defeat, Donald demonstrated his gracious side, claiming he was deeply honored by the support he received. In a salute to Iowa, he said, "I think I might come here and buy a farm—I love it."

That's what he said: What he must have thought was, "Get me the hell out of this cornfield. I want to go back to Fifth Avenue."

During his acceptance speech, Cruz sounded like an old-time Elmer Gantry. "Let me first of all say, to God be the glory."

Reacting to its shameless pandering, some of Cruz's enemies asserted that that remark "libeled God's good judgment."

In a dig at Donald, Cruz said, "No one personality can right the wrongs done by Washington."

Meanwhile, Rubio, boasting about his strong third place showing there, said, "The people of this great state have sent a very clear message—after seven years of Barack Obama, we are not waiting any longer to win our country back."

Polls showed that evangelicals made up 62% of Iowa's electorate.

Right before voters turned out, a rumor spread that Carson had quit the race for the Republican nomination, and that he was flying back to his home in Florida.

The most embarrassing (and most widely publicized) defeat was suffered by Jeb Bush, who despite vast expenditures and a lot of on-site campaigning, had garnered only 3% of the vote—a humbling rejection, perhaps of the Bush dynasty itself.

Columnist John Podhoretz wrote: "The voters of Iowa did not fall for Trump's vainglorius and solipsistic blather about making America great again. In fact, 75% of the voters rejected his nonsense, not wanting to place their party in the hands of an insult comedian character assassin."

In 2008, the Protestant pastor, Mike Huckabee, had been declared as the winner in that (long-ago) Iowa caucus. But voters had, since then, grown disenchanted with him. He won a meager 1.8% of the vote and subsequently suspended his disastrous campaign.

As for the Democrats, in their own neck-and-neck contest, the Vermont senator, Bernie Sanders, rode a wave of support from young and first-time Iowa caucus-goers. Hillary Clinton, however, by the narrowest of margins (mostly winning voters aged 45 and older), carried the state. Even though her margin of victory had been narrow, she was at least able to avoid the embarrassing rejection she'd suffered in 2008, when she had lost to both Barack Obama and to the soon-to-be-disgraced John Edwards who had come in second.

The third contender among the Democrats was Martin O'Malley, perhaps the finest—and most sane—of all the candidates. But Iowa voters rejected him, granting him only one-half of one percent of the vote. Consequently, his campaign leaked news that he would drop out of the "rat race" even before all the votes had been tallied.

The morning after the caucus, headlines blared that Donald had been "CRUZ-IFIED," but he showed no letting up, no change in his tactics, as he, along with Hillary, rushed onward to the next battleground, New Hampshire, a state

Martin O'Malley, running for President on the Democratic ticket, might have scored victories in a different time and place. In a field of extreme views or candidates who carried "too much baggage," he was a fine and decent man.

Confronted with the Black Lives Matter movement, he dared say, "All lives matter," and was booed off the stage.

markedly less conservative than Iowa.   In New Hampshire, Donald expected to win big. In contrast, Hillary—based on that state's close links to Bernie's home state of Vermont—anticipated losing.

During the Iowa campaign, many of the GOP candidates had made many false statements. Donald nailed Cruz on several of his off-key messages, calling him a "liar." Perhaps the biggest lie of all was spread by Sarah Palin, who accused the Republican Congress of giving Obama "a blank check."

In point of fact, GOP members of Congress had opposed virtually everything the President had proposed.

Before leaving Iowa, perhaps never to return, Donald privately was heard chiding primary voters for picking candidates who had not won the nomination in sixteen years. "They pick losers. That's why they went for Lyin' Ted."

"PUBLICITY
IS THE DONALD'S COCAINE
and Right Now, in New Hampshire,
He Has the Biggest Pile of Blow in His Life"

—Fortune Magazine

During the first week of February, Donald's battleground moved to New Hampshire, where his rivals felt energized after his defeat in the Iowa cornfields.

Jeb Bush, as he continued his spectacular descent, attacked Donald as "a man of deep insecurity and weakness."

Former New Hampshire governor, John Sununu, branded Donald "a loser because of his string of business failures, especially in Atlantic City."

Chris Christie sarcastically called him, "Donald the Magnificent."

Bleary-eyed and "dog tired," Rubio flew into Manchester and encountered an "army" of campaign volunteers willing to stump for him, many asserting that he was the best-equipped candidate to unite the splintered Republican party.

527

Soon after his arrival in Milford, New Hampshire, Donald won the "male beauty vote," as one female reporter noted. Scott P. Brown, former nude model and ex-Senator from Massachusetts, endorsed him. In 2012, as incumbent Senator, he had lost his bid for re-election to his first full term to Elizabeth Warren. *[After that defeat, he moved to New Hampshire where, two years later, as an obvious transplant, he ran unsuccessfully for the New Hampshire Senate, eventually losing to Democrat Jeanne Shaheen.]*

"Donald Trump is the one person who has the independence and can be the change agent to get Washington working again," Brown claimed.

In Windham, New Hampshire, Cruz said, "Six weeks ago, Trump was saying every day that I was his friend, that he loved me. That I was terrific, and that I was nice. And now I'm an Anchor Baby from Canada."

Those words, although intended as a put-down, would be

SCOTT BROWN

In attacking Donald, Elizabeth Warren, the outspoken senator from Massachusetts, and the bitter rival of Scott Brown, delivered the sharpest attacks on Donald, even more cutting than Hillary's.

In retaliation, mocking her claim to have Cherokee blood, Donald labeled her "goofy-looking," and "Pocahontas."

Former Massachusetts senator, Scott Brown, threw his "weight" behind Donald Trump.

The former nude model, on this *resumé*, gave vital statistics, but left out his penis size, which became a topic of debate during the GOP race.

His *resumé* did reveal that he had "excellent hands" and that he wore a size ten shoe, if that provides any clue.

the last kind remark Cruz would make about Donald in the coming weeks. "The Texas rattler was released spewing his venom," said one of Donald's aides.

In the wake of his terrible defeat in Iowa, Ben Carson shot back, accusing Cruz's campaign of spreading false rumors about him, claiming without any formal authority that he was quitting his campaign. The neurosurgeon denounced the rumors spread by Cruz aides as "lies and dirty tricks."

Minutes before voting had begun, Rep. Steve King, Cruz's campaign co-chair, tweeted, "Carson looks like he is out. Iowans need to know that before they vote. Most of his supporters will switch to Cruz, I hope."

E-mails from Cruz's campaign urged precinct captains to be aware that Carson had withdrawn from the race. "Spread the word," they urged Republican voters.

In a look back at Iowa, Donald blamed his loss on his boycott of the most recent debate. Nonetheless, he insisted that he'd have done the same thing over again, since he had raised a reported $6 million for veterans that night.

Once again, Donald warned potential supporters of Cruz, "If you guys get the nomination, the Democrats are gonna sue the ass off this Canadian Anchor Baby."

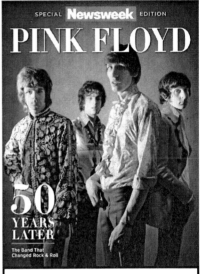

"Ohio" John Kasich, ethical and relentlessly hard-working, canvassed every county in Iowa prior to the caucus, and always reflected his basic sanity in a field of sometimes bizarre eccentrics.

Admittedly, his idea—if he became president, as expressed on a TV interview—to bring back Pink Floyd was sort of eccentric.

Under the headline "POLLSTERS—YOU'RE ALL FIRED," it was revealed that thirteen polls in Iowa had pre-determined the winner as Donald days before voting began.

In New Hampshire, Rubio even thanked Jesus for the Second Amendment [*i.e., the right of the people to bear arms*]. In response, a pundit said, "After all, Jesus loved nothing more than a good, American-made assault weapon to kill people in greater numbers."

Another columnist noted, "Pretty boy Rubio thanked 'My Lord and Savior Jesus Christ.' He ignored all the Jewish, Hindu, and Muslim voters, to name just a few. Oh, screw 'em if they won't come to Jesus."

Although Cruz had emerged as the victor in Iowa, he came under devastating attack from many newspapers. The *New York Daily News* wrote, "On issue after issue—guns, taxes, gay rights, foreign policy—Cruz offers himself as an uncompromising zealot. The architect of one government shutdown desperately wants another. In his long, rambling victory speech, he saluted the 'heroes who rushed into burning buildings in the wake of 9/11.' Those are the same heroes Cruz turned his back to by refusing to support the bill offering health care and financial assistance to responders who served on the smoldering pile after 9/11."

In New Hampshire, failing candidate John Kasich, the governor of Ohio, came up with a vote-winning idea. He promised that, if elected President, he would reunite the iconic rock band, Pink Floyd, for a musical concert.

"I'll get the group at least to play a couple of songs," he vowed. "Since we have so many troubles in America about finances, I'll ask the band to start with a little song they created called 'Money.'"

Under a provocative headline "HERE'S NOBEL PEACE OF CRAP," a News Wire Services story broke the revelation that Donald had been nominated for a Nobel Peace Prize, thereby elevating him into a position alongside Pope Francis and Nadia Murad.

[*Nadia Murad was a 21-year-old Yazidid tribeswoman who escaped from ISIS terrorists and brought the story of her plight as a sex slave ("ISIS forced us to pray - then raped us") to the attention of the international community, the United Nations, and, through broadcasts in Egypt, to the Muslim world.*]

Nobel Watcher Krist-

Many of his fans believe that the Nobel Peace Prize, whose Medal is depicted above, should be awarded to Donald Trump.

In the words of one of his sponsors, "They gave it to Barack Obama in 2009, and Donald deserves it more than he ever did."

ian Berg Harpviken said that Donald's nomination letter cited "his vigorous peace through strength ideology, used as a threat weapon of deterrence against radical Islam, ISIS, nuclear Iran, and Communist China."

Ever the Voice of Enlightenment, Cruz mocked Donald claiming that "if he became President, he would throw a fit and nuke Denmark."

In a moment of restraint, Donald said, "I'm trying to be a little bit more understated and statesmanlike. Some people like that."

But within moments, Donald found his inner Machiavelli and accused Cruz of stealing the Iowa caucus. He demanded a "do-over."

"Lyin' Ted Cruz didn't win Iowa, he illegally stole it," Donald charged. "That's why all of the polls went so wrong and why he got more votes than anticipated." Then he lashed into the Cruz campaign for fomenting what Trump and Carson supporters described as a choreographed conspiracy to mislead voters. It involved the dissemination of a false rumor that Carson had dropped out of the race. "Based on the fraud Cruz committed, a new election should take place and the present results nullified. And this liar calls himself a Christian!"

***

With schoolyard insults and a chest-thumping *machismo*, Donald trudged through the snows of New Hampshire. It was a radically different political terrain from that of Iowa. As regards the hot-button issue of abortion and birth control, polls showed many Republican women there supported a woman's right to choose.

Some 35% of male voters were for Donald, but only a quarter of the women planned to vote for him.

Clara Frechette, a tax analyst, said, "I don't think Trump really cares about women's issues, and their being equal to men. As for Cruz, he'd be looking at the Bible and quoting it, 'The man should be the head of the household and the women should do what the men say.'"

Cruz continued with his anti-gay hysterics, calling into the radio show of Tony Perkins. *[For reasons known only within the darkest recesses of his soul, Perkins is the most vehement opponent of gay rights in America.]*

During that call-in, Cruz lamented, "Our heart weeps for the damage to the traditional marriage that has been done." Quoting Biblical scripture, he addressed an audience of homophobes, exhorting them, "To be as wise as serpents and as gentle as doves."

Yet when Cruz, with his hand out for money, visited the Manhattan office of a supporter of same-sex marriage, he cooled his rhetoric. He told the billionaire mega-donor, Paul Singer, "If New York politicians want to legalize it, that is their business."

That wasn't enough to convince Singer, who later endorsed Rubio, even though he, too, opposed same-sex marriage.

When the Supreme Court, by one vote, legalized same-sex marriage, Cruz told a conservative rally that the decision "was one of the greatest threats to our democracy we have seen in modern times."

"And people call Cruz educated," said Ernest Bellows, a Trump supporter. "Cruz sounds just like any other redneck rodeo cowboy. Time his horse tossed him onto the dusty ground."

Sensing Rubio as one of this major rivals, Governor Christie attacked him. "Let's get the boy out of the bubble. His appearances are scripted. One New Hampshire reporter compared Rubio to a computer algorithm designed to cover talking points.

"Rubio is not really progressive," said reporter Julie Fleming. "He's so far right of Ted Cruz, if such a thing is possible, only he conceals it. He's anti-choice even for victims of rape and incest. He's against Obamacare. He was part of the infamous 'Gang of Eight,' pushing for immigration reform. Now he *hates* amnesty. His ads in Iowa were about the 'free gift of salvation' offered by Christ. Perhaps if he fails as a politician, he could become a fire and brimstone preacher. He plays both sides, a Baptist one week, a Catholic the next."

Both Cruz and Rubio were attacked by a fellow *latino,* Jorge Ramos, the Univision anchor, who said, editorially, to an audience that included thousands of *latinos*, in reference to these *(latino)* candidates' anti-immigration stances, "There is no greater disloyalty than the children of immigrants forgetting their own roots. That is a betrayal."

On February 4, it was announced that Megyn Kelly, Donald's nemesis, who had, to wide acclaim, emphasized Donald's designation of women as "fat pigs, dogs, slobs, and disgusting animals," had won a victory. It

To the GLBT community, at least those who bothered to find out who this man is, Tony Perkins, president of the co-called Family Research Council, is the most hated man in America.

He's hysterical on the subject of same-sex marriage, defining such unions as a symbol for the collapse of Western civilization.

was reported that HarperCollins had offered her $10 million for a memoir.

Reaction from the public was generally unfavorable, one TV viewer claiming, "Kelly will never contribute anything of value to society—just a dressed-up doll sucking up the money."

[Kelly anchors the Fox News Channel program, The Kelly File. Her show is the no. 2 rated cable news program.]

"Low Energy Jeb" continued to hustle for votes in New Hampshire. He hoped to win supporters who wanted to censor some of the things coming out of "the bloviating billionaire's potty mouth."

"Enough with the cursing," said Bush at a campaign rally. "I'm tired of the profanity, tired of the vulgarity. There are kids listening to him, for crying out loud."

"Bush was responding to Donald's dropping 'shit bombs' along the campaign trail and crowing that he'll "kick ISIS' ass," wrote one reporter.

Meanwhile, Donald eased up on his war on Megyn Kelly, claiming that he would appear at the next Fox debate, scheduled for March 3 in Detroit.

On February 5, Bush unveiled his "secret weapon," calling for the assistance of his formidable mom. Consequently, a frail Barbara Bush showed up in New Hampshire, looking every bit –and more—her ninety years on this earth.

She retained a bit of her famous spark, tearing into Donald in a TV interview. Like her son, she attacked Donald's foul language. "I don't know how women can vote for someone who said what he said about Megyn Kelly. It's terrible. Money doesn't buy everything. It's incomprehensible to me why people are voting for this man."

Appearing on *This Morning,* she said, "I don't advise Jeb, but if I did, I would say, 'Why don't you interrupt like the other people in the debates?'"

Two years before, Barbara had candidly admitted that America "had had enough Bushes." But she came around. Or did she?

Detail from the official White House portrait of stern, no-nonsense former First Lady, Barbara Bush, *grande dame* of the Republicans.

She hated Donald Trump for, among other reasons, his attacks on Jeb!

Perhaps she spoke the truth originally. Voters in New Hampshire and Iowa seemed to agree.

Barbara was also opposed to Hillary. She received a copy of the latest Edward Klein book, *The Problem with Hillary*. In it, an alleged quote was attributed to Bill Clinton. Reading it, the quote must have warmed the cockles of Barbara's tired heart.

"Trump is a generational challenge," Bill said, "and a challenge for the Hispanic vote. We've got to destroy him before he gets off the ground."

"Maybe the Clintons will do Trump in and allow Jeb to move up," Barbara told one of her son's campaign workers.

But as Marco Rubio surged in the polls, Barbara watched with dismay, noting that Rubio had once been a *protégé* of her son. "Jeb did so much for him."

She was surprised at the young women who flocked to Rubio's rallies, although their numbers didn't surpass the number that Bernie Sanders attracted.

Many young women, flocking to a Marco Rubio rally, seemed more interested in his "male beauty" than they were in his campaign.

A female Rubio aide said, "When Marco speaks, young women swoon, old women faint, and toilets flush themselves."

Barbara Bush told a Jeb supporter, "Here's one old woman who won't faint. And I'll flush my own toilet, thank you!"

JAWS OPEN WIDE IN NEW HAMPSHIRE
Otherwise Known as "the Shark," Chris Christie Begins
DEVOURING "LITTLE MARCO"
As Donald Tells Jeb! To Shut Up

The eighth GOP debate was held at Goffstown, New Hampshire, on February 6, and this time, Donald showed up to star in the middle of the stage at the event organized by *ABC News* and the *Independent Journal Review*. The debate at St. Anselm's College Institute of Politics was the first not to feature a "Kiddie Table." (The losers had dropped out.) The moderators were relatively unknown: Josh McElveen, Mary Katherine Ham, David Muir, and Martha Raddatz.

The debate opened with mishaps. Kasich's introduction was inadvertently skipped, and Carson missed his cue.

To winnow down the field and perhaps to score a lethal blow at Rubio, Chris Christie led an all-out assault as only a native of New Jersey can do. He hammered Rubio as "callow, ambitious, and lacking in accomplishment."

It was the fiercest attack the Florida senator had ever suffered, and he seemed to wither in the spotlight. He gave his best "deer-in-the headlights" look, and seemed rattled. He pushed back with scripted lines, but failed utterly under Christie's prosecutorial glare.

As if Christie needed any help (he didn't), both Bush and Donald sliced Rubio into ribbons, but they were weak compared to Christie's personal derision. "He cut into Rubio with a beheading machete," observed a New Hampshire reporter.

Rubio at one point became so flustered he repeated the exact sound bite four times, thereby confirming Christie's point.

"There he goes," Christie

"IMPOSSIBLE TO HEAR TRUMP OVER CHRISTIE'S EYES"

After New Jersey governor, Chris Christie, dropped out of the race, he threw his considerable weight behind Donald Trump's.

On CNN, as Donald delivered his standard anti-immigrant, anti-foreign trade speech, a gloomy Christie looked on as if in a trance.

Rumors spread that he was too unpopular to get re-elected as governor of New Jersey, so his hope for a political future hinged on Donald naming him as his Veep or at least appointing him Attorney General.

Before politics took its toll, there was a time when bearded Chris Christie looked relaxed, relatively thin, and not like a shark.

Here, he is, younger and perhaps happier, long before his entanglements in Bridgegate and his entry into the orbit of Donald Trump.

said. "The memorized 25-second speech."

He attacked Rubio for taking credit for policies "although he skipped out on the vote. That's not leadership! That's truancy! You do nothing but utter your rehearsed sound bites. How many times in one night all you can say over and over again is that Obama is leading the nation to disaster?"

Columnist Frank Bruni wrote: "Christie's last-gasp strategy was to turn Rubio into a limp, soggy, chew toy, and the New Jersey governor was all jaws."

Despite Christie's strong and very macho performance, it would ultimately be his curtain call. The New Jersey governor suspended his campaign four days later after finishing sixth in the New Hampshire primary.

Donald attacked Jeb Bush: "He wants to be a tough guy, but it doesn't work very well." Bush tried to interrupt him, but Donald told him. "QUIET!" The audience booed Donald, but he claimed they were just Bush donors and special interest lobbyists.

No review of Donald's performance in the New Hampshire debate was as devastating as that of columnist John Podhoretz. "He was awful, so horrible, so disgusting in the debate—his lies, his distortions, his deceits, and his libels thicker and fouler than they've yet been. The man some Republicans want for their President is a disgusting jerk they somehow believe will have their backs when the only backs he'll ever have is his own."

The acid tongue of columnist John Podhoretz turned on Donald with lacerating venom, defining him as "a disgusting jerk, a comedian character assassin, and a mouthpiece of vainglorious and solipsistic blather."

Chapter Twenty

JOHN WAYNE, FROM THE GRAVE
*How a Dead, Slow-Drawling Movie Icon Endorsed
The Donald*

"BERNIE'S LOVE CHILD"
Is Exposed and Publicized in the Tabloids

One of their Former Aides Accuses Jeb! and Dubya of
"IMPORTING AND USING COCAINE"

DONALD INSULTS THE POPE

By February, the lives of all the candidates—as exposed by some of that month's editions of *The National Enquirer,* had heated up to the point where even the snows of New Hampshire seemed on the verge of melting.

One of the stories that widely circulated involved a Donald endorsement supposedly derived from the film star and icon of the far right, actor John Wayne (1907-1979), a tough-as-nails Republican diehard, who, along with his faded career, had retired to "Boot Hill" thirty-seven years before.

Aissa Wayne, the actor's daughter, a California attorney speaking at the John Wayne Museum near her father's birthplace in Winterset, Iowa, had said, "America needs help. We need a strong leader. We need someone like Mr. Trump with leadership qualities, someone with courage, someone who is strong like John Wayne."

Aissa told Donald, "My father would be very proud of you right now."

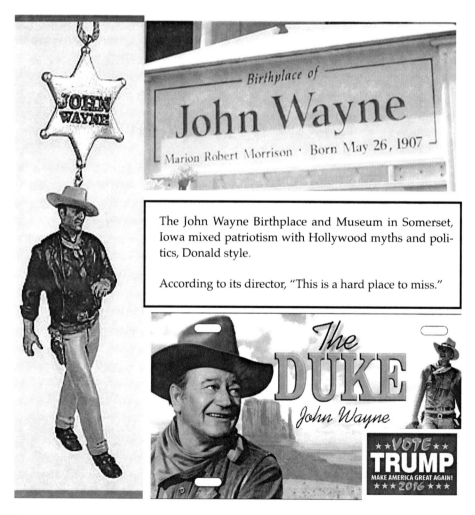

The John Wayne Birthplace and Museum in Somerset, Iowa mixed patriotism with Hollywood myths and politics, Donald style.

According to its director, "This is a hard place to miss."

Donald once met Wayne, and was impressed. At the museum, posed in front of a fake desert background, a horse saddle, and a gun-toting effigy of the actor, he claimed, "He represented real strength—an inner strength you don't see very often. That's why his endorsement means so much to me."

The *National Enquirer* also revealed that one of the White House wannabees, Vermont Senator Bernie Sanders, was alleged to have fathered "a love child."

On his website, the socialist presidential hopeful had revealed that he had four children and seven grandchildren.

Actually, three of his kids are stepchildren born to his wife, Jane, from her previous marriage. Sanders was said never to have wed the mother of his only biological child, a 46-year-old son named Levi.

The senator, according to the tabloid report, was reported to have fallen in love with Levi's mother, Susan Campbell, during the sexual revolution of the 1960s. Reporter Sharon Churcher wrote: "Levi sometimes went hungry and lived in the dark in a rental apartment where the electricity was frequently turned off. Bernie wouldn't pay the bills."

In the same issue, in an "equal opportunity" exposé of the Bushes, the legendary CIA drug smuggler and pilot, Barry Seal, revealed that he had "orchestrated an elaborate sting at the Miami-Opa Locka Executive Airport in which the DEA got a videotape of Jeb and his brother, George W., bringing a kilo of cocaine into Florida for resale."

This exposé came from Roger Stone's book, *Jeb! And the Bush Crime Family.*

In it, Stone alleged that Jeb snorted coke the night his father, George H.W. Bush, was elected President in 1988.

It also made the claim that Jeb, during his tenure as governor of Florida, had snorted cocaine because he found the slow pace of Tallahassee "so boring."

The book was co-authored by Saint John Hunt, son of the notorious Watergate figure, E. Howard Hunt. Jeb was criticized for his war on drugs, the book labeling him a hypocrite "since he was a heavy drug user himself."

DONALD CALLS FOR TORTURE
of Terrorists Using Methods
"Worse Than Waterboarding."

GAWKER'S
Compilation of Derogatory Names for Donald

To live up to his John Wayne toughness, Donald, on February 7, doubled down on his call for harsh interrogation techniques of suspected terrorists. "I want to go a lot further than waterboarding."

"In the Middle East, you have people chopping off other people's heads. This hasn't happened since medieval times. There's never been anything like this." Donald was speaking on NBC's *Meet the Press*.

"Believe me, going beyond waterboarding in terms of getting information would really work. Enhanced torture wouldn't bother me a bit. Look, when terrorists fly planes into the World Trade Center and kill thousands of people, you can't handle psychos like that with kid gloves made of unborn lamb."

On the eve of the New Hampshire primary, Donald called Cruz a "pussy," based on his objections to tough stances on waterboarding "or something even more horrendous."

It all started when a woman in the audience rose up at one of Donald's rallies. She was the first to accuse Cruz of being "a pussy" for opposing waterboarding.

"She just said a terrible thing," Donald told his audience. "OK, you're not allowed to say it—and I never expect to hear that from you again. She said, 'Ted's a pussy!'"

Hoping to ambush Bush "coming around the pass," Donald also fired at him, too. "Jeb is just desperate, even though he called on his mammy to bail him out in New Hampshire. He's a mama's boy. This sad person had

Trump's "Ted Cruz is a pussy" comments helped catalyze TV funny guy Jon Stewart to showcase his own promotion of the newest Donald Trump lawn ornament, one of his own design, as part of a relentless late-night anti-Trump ridicule campaign.

As Trump's campaign continued to churn out raw material for late-night comedy commentary, Stewart said, "I want to thank Donald Trump for making my last six weeks my best six weeks."

gone absolutely crazy. The guy's a nervous wreck. He's having some kind of breakdown."

When Jeb heard that, he told the press, "Donald Trump is not just a loser. He's a liar and a whiner."

Indeed, the real estate mogul called Cruz a pussy, a name never before uttered with such abandon in association with a presidential campaign, but in context, it was only one of an armada of names his opponents had associated with The Donald.

In an attempt to document some of them, *The Gawker,* a web and blog site focusing on political and entertainment industry gossip, rounded up an array of names that Donald had been called by his enemies. They included, in no particular order:

"Off-Brand Dr. Seuss villain."
"Fan-mail order meat salesman."
"Delusional cheese creature."
"Orange-tufted sentient troll doll."
"Flopped-over traffic cone."
"Cheeto-dusted bloviator."
"Hot pork balloon."
"Brightly burning trash fire."

And, as Donald faced New Hampshire voters in that state's upcoming primary, he was assigned yet another new name: "Fossilized meatball!"

"DAWN OF THE BRAIN DEAD

...Mindless Zombies Turn Out in Droves to Make Donald the New Hampshire Winner"

No tabloid in America was harsher than Donald's hometown newspaper, the *New York Daily News,* which featured his February 9 win in the New Hampshire primary. He was depicted on the cover in clown makeup with vastly overpainted scarlet lips.

A second headline read: "CLOWN COMES BACK TO LIFE IN N.H."

Under his Photoshopped caricature was this caption: "Like a Chucky doll, this monster just won't go away. Donald Trump won the first-in-the-nation New Hampshire GOP primary handily—and scarily."

[Iowa had been a caucus, not a primary.]

More than three out of ten Granite State GOP voters had flocked to the

DO ZOMBIES SUPPORT DONALD?

The New York Daily News compared Donald's supporters in New Hampshire to "mindless zombies."

The upper photo shows a gone-viral photo still from the 2004 horror-comedy *Shaun of the Dead*. Currently, zombie culture and its spinoffs is a market estimated to bring more than $5 billion to the U.S. economy every year, according to *24/7 Wall St*, a financial analyst agency.

Pop authority Steven "The Zombie" Uden, one of the participants in World Zombie Day, said, "Everyone can be a Zombie. We have no prejudice, we are unselected. Zombies, differently from vampires, do not have a beauty pattern. You can be tall, small, thin, or fat—that does not matter for zombies."

polls to give Donald a spectacular win, with 34% of the vote. Ted Cruz came in with 12%. And in a surprise move, it turned out that John Kasich, the Ohio governor, won second place with 16% of the vote.

At his victory rally, Donald announced, "We're going to beat China, Japan, Mexico. We're going to beat all those countries. The world is going to respect us again, believe me."

In fourth place, Jeb Bush polled only 11%. Donald at this point seemed

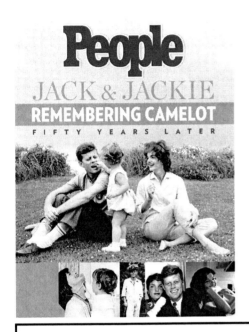

DON'T LET IT BE FORGOT

From reports, Donald and Melania want to bring "Camelot" back into the White House, but if they try, they'll face some stiff competition from previous residents.

"Camelot" is often used as a reference to the presidency of John F. Kennedy. The Lerner and Loewe Broadway musical was in vogue following JFK's assassination in 1963, and his widow Jackie quoted its lines in a history-making interview with the press:

"Don't let it be forgot, that once there was a spot, for one brief shining moment, that was known as Camelot," adding that "there will be great Presidents again, but there'll never be another Camelot again… It will never be that way again."

On stage on Broadway, in the musical version of the legend that inspired Jackie's quote, Richard Burton (lower photo, left), starred as the tragic King Arthur, with gay actor Roddy McDowall playing a treacherous courtier.

to crush his rivals as badly as he had promised to eradicate ISIS.

The most embarrassing loss was suffered by Rubio, probably based on his utter failure during the New Hampshire debate. He received only 1% of the vote.

On the Democratic front, Bernie Sanders scorched Hillary in the New Hampshire Democratic primary. He won 69% of the vote, compared to her paltry 39%.

Polls showed that an astonishing two-thirds of New Hampshire voters agreed with Donald's proposal to temporarily bar Muslims from entering the United States.

Christie had hoped for a surge in New Hampshire, but like Rubio, he was greatly disappointed. He finished in a distant sixth place. He had little money left in his campaign purse, and a slim chance of being eligible for the next GOP debate. He told his few supporters that he was returning to New Jersey "to take a deep breath."

Despite strenuous efforts to humiliate Donald with a crushing debate, the opposite happened. "I left all of them in a snow bank," he proclaimed. "Now, it's on to South Carolina and another sweeping victory."

The GOP was left to muddle on with Cruz and a severely weakened Rubio, Kasich, and Jeb!

CAMELOT?

In a 21st Century Replay of Jack & Jackie, Donald and Melania Discuss the Glam Quotient of Their Presidency

After a thundering victory in New Hampshire, Donald returned briefly to his estate, Mar-a-Lago, in Palm Beach.

There, he discussed re-defining it as a "Winter White House," with his *fashionista* wife and former model, the Slovenia-born Melania.

"It'll be like the Kennedy compound in Palm Beach, only far greater in size, elegance, and culture," Donald predicted. "Of course, I'll have to retro-fit the 90-year-old estate to accommodate Secret Service agents. I'll pay off the expenses myself, saving the taxpayers money."

It was surmised that the commissioning of Donald's very large portrait hanging in the building's main hall had, in some way, been clairvoyant of his upcoming presidency. In it, he was depicted in a white tennis sweater with a full head of hair like JFK. It was described as "very Kennedyesque, oh so WASPY, and so young." The staff already referred to it as "Mr. Trump's presidential portrait."

In the meantime, Melania was reported to be rehearsing her role as the future First Lady, and said to be consulting "image coaches" about how to act, speak, and behave.

"She's modeling herself as Jackie Kennedy," an insider told the press. "She's been trying out hair extensions similar to those worn in the early 1960s by Jackie."

Ted Cruz and the Porn-Industry Star of
DEVIANT WHORES

"Lyin' Ted" Mistakenly Casts "A Woman With a Past" Into One of his Political Ads.

In February, a skin-flick babe, a former actress in the soft-core porn industry, starred in a political ad for holier-than-thou Ted Cruz, the (ostensibly) God-fearing candidate of the Republican Right.

A thirty-second TV and internet ad, entitled *Conservatives Anonymous*, had featured the body beautiful Amy Lindsay. Before her "Cruz gig," she had starred in such soft-corn porn films as *Deviant Whores; Carnal Wishes;* and *Timegate: Tales of The Saddle Tramps.*

[Other, more mainstream gigs had included an appearance in Star Trek: Voyager *and a secondary role in the 1996 film adaptation of Henry James'* The Portrait of a Lady, *starring Nicole Kidman.]*

When Cruz was told of this, he ordered his staff to halt distribution of the

Soft porn queen Amy Lindsay, pictured in the revealing photo above, was selected by the Ted Cruz campaign as the star of a TV ad aimed at "Onward Conservative Christian Soldiers."

545

ad immediately. It had featured actors cast as a group of dismayed, ex-Marco Rubio supporters gathered together in a group therapy session. Lindsay told *Buzzfeed* that she had not yet made up her mind about how to vote: Donald or Cruz?

She claimed that she had not duped the Cruz campaign, saying she thought they were aware of her previous porn work. She thought the Texas senator wanted to get rid of his "stuffy image."

"I didn't think they wanted some old white Christian bigot, but a cool, open-minded woman like me."

DONALD SHOOTS SOME VIAGRA
Into Low Energy Jeb! and Publicly Asserts that Dubya Should Have Been Impeached for the Iraq War

George W. Bush was not on stage at the next Republican debate staged on February 13, 2016 at Greenville, South Carolina. But he emerged as the hot topic at the debate, nonetheless.

Organized by *CBS News*, it was moderated by John Dickerson in Greenville's Peace Center for the Performing Arts starting at 9PM and lasting for 90 minutes. This would mark the ninth and final debate appearance of Jeb Bush, who suspended his hideously expensive and ill-fated quest to follow his brother and father into the White House.

During the debate, the name of the 43rd President of the United States was invoked multiple times, with varying degrees of reverence and/or scorn, as the tensions erupted between Jeb and Donald, the debate's chief combatants.

Provocatively, Dickerson asked Donald if he stood by his previous position that "Dubya" *[George W. Bush, son of George H.W. Bush]* should have been impeached for leading the country into the Iraq War.

"Obviously, the war in Iraq was a big fat mistake," Donald said. "We spent $2 trillion, thousands of lives. Iran is taking over Iraq with the second largest oil reserve in the world. George Bush made a mistake. We can make mistakes, but that one was a beauty. We should have never been in Iraq."

"You can do whatever you want, call it whatever you want," Donald continued in his assault on the former President. "I want to tell you, they lied. They said there were weapons of mass destruction. There were none, and they knew there were none."

Jeb sprang to the defense of his (disgraced) older brother.

"Here's the deal. I'm sick and tired of Barack Obama blaming my brother for all of the problems he's had. And frankly, I could care less about the insults that Donald Trump gives to me. But I am sick and tired of him going after my family. My dad is the greatest man alive, in my mind. And while Trump was building a reality TV show, my brother was building a security apparatus to keep us safe. And I'm proud of what he did."

"The World Trade Center came down during your brother's reign, remember that?" Donald interjected.

His remark, though completely accurate, was met with loud boos from the right-wing audience, which was overwhelmingly packed with diehard Bush dynasty fans and (according to Donald) their paid lobbyists.

"My mom is the strongest woman I know," Jeb continued.

"So she should be running," Donald tartly responded.

In spite of Dubya being one of America's worst Presidents, he was absurdly defended by other Republican candidates. Rubio chimed in with, "I thank God, all the time, that it was George W. Bush in the White House on 9/11 and not Al Gore."

At that, Ohio Governor John Kasich interjected "This is just crazy. This is just nuts. Jeez, oh man."

The Bush family was still popular in South Carolina, a state that has a high concentration of veterans, at least those not killed in Iraq. The crowd loudly booed Donald any time he denigrated Dubya, but applauded any candidate who defended him. The vitriol seemed to take Donald by surprise as he had never been so pummeled at a debate before this.

As expected, the debate centered at times on the recently deceased, notoriously conservative Supreme Court Justice Antonin Scalia, as a battle raged over his successor. Beloved by archconservatives, he opposed abortion,

Donald's attacks on "Low Energy Jeb" was reflected in political ads. Upper photo is from an ad from the Trump campaign suggesting that Jeb's speeches could put a potential voter to sleep.

Viagra was recommended as a means of correcting Jeb's "E.D."—in this case, "Electoral Dysfunction."

gun control, and same-sex marriage.

As for gay rights, he had charged that "homosexual activists are trying to eliminate the moral opprobrium that has traditionally been attached to this perversion."

That claim, and countless other prejudicial utterances, earned him the loathing of millions of Americans. On the other hand, millions on the far right praised his three decades on the Supreme Court as the "voice of conservative Renaissance."

As was noted, Justice Clarence Thomas followed Scalia's every pronouncement "like an Uncle Tom heeding his master."

Donald criticized Chief Justice John Roberts, a usually conservative Dubya appointee who had been vilified for his role in two recent decisions whose outcome had upheld Obama's Affordable Care Act.

Onstage, Donald contemptuously said to Jeb, "Your brother wanted Roberts on the Court. He twice approved Obamacare. Good going, man!"

Donald then continued his assault on Dubya, claiming that he should have been impeached for his role in inaugurating America's involvement in the War in Iraq.

During the debate, Donald did not ignore his most serious rival, Ted Cruz. In fact, Donald lost his cool when Cruz charged that if Donald were President, he'd nominate a liberal to fill Scalia's seat. He also told the audience that Donald had once endorsed abortion.

"You are the single biggest liar," Donald shot back. "This guy will say anything. Nasty guy. Now I know why he doesn't't' have a single endorsement in the Senate."

Donald repeated his

After the unexpected death of Anthony Scalia, the ultra-conservative Supreme Court justice, conspiracy theories abounded. They inluded commentary from across the political spectrum, including the right-wing Breitbart (upper photo) to a headline from the *National Enquirer* (lower photo).

On the campaign trail, Donald fanned the flames, spreading his suspicion that Scalia may have been murdered by a lethal injection into his butt from a hooker.

charge that Cruz had undermined Ben Carson's race in Iowa.

"I will say it is fairly remarkable to see Donald defending Ben after he called him pathological and compared him to a child molester."

Even Dickerson, the debate's moderator, seemed to turn on Donald, asking him why he used language that many voters found offensive.

"On occasion, in order to sort of highlight something, I'll use a profanity," Donald said.

Ted's wife, Heidi Cruz, of course, was not on stage for the debate. However, on the radio in South Carolina, she made a claim that would even cause the right-wing evangelist, Pat Robertson, to blush: "Ted is running to show us the face of God that we serve. The God of Christianity is the God of freedom, of individual liberty, of choice and of consequence."

Earlier, Ted's father Rafael, had claimed, "It is the Holy Ghost who has called on my son to run for President."

Before the debate, Bible-thumping Ted himself said, "We can win if we awaken and energize the body of Christ."

So far, there is no evidence that either God or Jesus ever endorsed Ted's candidacy—far from it.

"TED CRUZ

Is mentally unstable & the biggest liar I've ever come across"
—Donald Trump

"DONALD TRUMP

is a creature from the fever swamps of the far left."
—Ted Cruz

The war between Donald and the Bush dynasty did not end on the evening of the South Carolina debate. "If Dubya had gone to the beach during his presidency, we would have been better off," Donald said.

After heavy losses in Iowa and New Hampshire, losing candidate Jeb had summoned the Bush family to his political deathbed in South Carolina. Dubya arrived with his wife Laura, the former First Lady. Prior to the debate in upstate Greenville, Laura showed up in Charleston to inform a rally about what a fine and decent man Jeb was.

Addressing that same rally, her husband, the former President, told the crowd, "There seems to be a lot of name-calling going on. But my father told me that labels were for soup cans. My brother Jeb has a deep and genuine faith that reveals itself through good works, not loud words."

To retaliate, Donald at a news conference, mocked Dubya's widely ridiculed "Mission Accomplished" appearance aboard the *U.S.S. Abraham Lincoln* in May of 2003. "The country was not safe during this jerk's presidency," Donald charged. "The worst attack on this country came during 9/11."

A former President was not the only one butting into the South Carolina primary. A sitting President, Barack Obama, also mocked Donald. "Being President is a serious job. It's not hosting a talk show or a reality TV show. An inexperienced man like Donald Trump is unworthy of handling nuclear codes.'

In California, Obama said, "I continue to believe in the American people, and I think they will not elect Donald Trump President."

Donald dismissed Obama's attack, accusing him of doing "a lousy job. He has set us back so far. You look at our budgets, at our spending. We can't beat ISIS. Obamacare is terrible. Our borders are like Swiss cheese."

Obama is lucky I didn't run the last time when Mitt Romney ran—or else Obama would have been a one-term President."

Desperate for a win in South Carolina, the Christian Warrior, Ted Cruz, continued his Holy War against Donald, attacking him for claiming that George W. should have been impeached, and referring to Donald as "a creature from the fever swamps of the far left."

He made the unproven charge that Donald, if elected President, would replace Scalia with a choice "that would be indistinguishable from those of Hillary Clinton and Bernie Sanders."

Despite his self-avowed status as defender of the Constitution, he decided that, as a Senator, he would not fulfill his constitutional duty.

"I will block anyone—I mean, anyone—Obama names to the Supreme Court. Let me repeat: Any nominee Obama might name."

In one of his biggest attacks on Cruz to date, Donald charged, "He's a mentally unstable individual and the biggest liar I've ever come across. It's hard to believe that a Christian could be so dishonest and tell that many lies."

On February 15, Donald stunned an audience of supporters, saying that he might have to renege on his pledge not to run as an independent, and denouncing the GOP élite for not playing fair with him.

Early on the morning of February 17, Donald woke up to shocking news. The latest polls by *NBC* and *The Wall Street Journal* revealed that Cruz was polling ahead of him at a rate of 28% to 25%.

The Texas senator had endorsed ads revealing remarks that Donald had made during his so-called liberal past. One ad depicted Donald endorsing abortion. To answer that charge, Donald reconfirmed and reinforced his credentials as an anti-abortion candidate.

His attorneys sent Cruz a "cease-and-desist" letter, warning him to stop airing those ads.

At a CNN-sponsored town hall rally, Cruz told Anderson Cooper, "I laughed at his threat. I have practiced law for twenty years, and his letter was one of the most ridiculous and frivolous I've ever received."

The tension between the two rivals increased, markedly, during the weeks ahead.

Both Marco Rubio and Jeb Bush tried to gain traction in their obsession with toppling the frontrunners. Rubio hauled out Nikki R. Haley, the Indian-American governor of South Carolina and a rising star in the GOP. Before the cameras, she endorsed the Cuban-American, emphasizing their respective immigrant backgrounds. Haley herself was the daughter of Sikh immigrants from India.

It was also noted that both of them shared youth as a trait in common. "We are the future of the GOP," Haley declared. "Rubio is the best chance for Republicans in November."

Jeb! was not to be outgunned. Currently in sixth place in pollings, he posed with a gun bearing his name on it, plus the short caption, "AMERICA." His sudden macho posturing and swagger "triggered" a fusillade of mockery. On Twitter, a random outsider chided him with "Suicide is never the answer, Jeb!"

He was also criticized in countless tweets for not having engaged the safety device on the FNX-25 pistol, something that was obvious to gun aficionados from the photo. The pistol had been a gift from a gun maker, FN Manufacturing, in Columbia, SC.

Outside scrutiny heated up, too. Reporters such as Joe Nocera explored

Christian warriors and Trump haters, Heidi and Ted Cruz appear at a rally in Houston.

Alleged to be intelligent, Cruz continued to make one dumb remark after another. "If Trump becomes President, the Second Amendment will be written out of the Constitution."

Donald's business background, concluding, "Trump made real estate blunders that turned billions in potential profits into mere millions. His foray into Atlantic City brought him close to personal bankruptcy. He claims about owning a sprawling business empire, but what he actually runs these days is a licensing company that slaps the Trump name on everything from buildings to steaks to an education company that's being sued for 'persistent fraud, illegal and deceptive conduct.' My conclusion—

Smiles and brilliant PR prevailed from the Obama camp during most of the Pope's visit, as shown by this assemblage on the balcony of the White House. In this official White House photo, Michelle, Francis, and Barack wave to their adoring fans.

(P.S. The Pope has a long tradition of waving from balconies.)

and I say this as a grizzled veteran of business journalism—is that Trump's business acumen (not to mention his net worth) has been widely overstated, by Trump himself. His core business skill is self-promotion."

A poll of potential Trump supporters in South Carolina revealed to Donald the political priorities of his supporters.

At least 70% believed that the Confederate flag should fly over the South Carolina State Capitol; 38% wished that the South had won the tCivil War, and a stunning 80% supported his ban on Muslims. At least 31% thought that homosexuality should be outlawed, and another 56% wanted the practice of Islam made illegal in the United States.

Donald avoided a direct answer when confronted with the astonishing and bigoted results of those pollings.

"All I can say is that my supporters are strong believers in what they believe. Good Christians, each and every one. Evangelicals love me!"

"KID DONALD"
VS.
THE POWER OF THE PAPACY
Pope Francis Suggests Wall Builders Are Anti-Christ

By mid-February, a "Holy War" of sorts was waged between Pope Francis, during a visit to Mexico, and Donald Trump on the campaign trail.

Time magazine claimed that the war that erupted "could not involve more polar opposites. Trump's name is synonymous with billions of dollars. Francis chose to be named after the patron saint of the poor, Francis of Assisi."

Both men, who tied for second place in a poll of "the world's most admired men," have an uncanny knack for getting their different messages across.

Near the end of his historic tour of Mexico, Pope Francis arrived in Ciudad Juárez, a city that's a hellhole of drug violence, poverty, and crime. He visited a prison filled mostly with criminals imprisoned on drug-related offenses, often murder, and later prayed at the border between Mexico and the United States. He lamented and prayed for the migrant dead, and condemned the "grave injustices" inflicted upon those who were forced by poverty and violence to cross illegally into America's great Southwest.

Il Papa waited to make his incendiary remarks when he was on the papal plane *en route* back to Rome and the Vatican. "A person who thinks only about building walls, wherever they may be, and not building bridges, is not Christian."

The Pope was responding to a direct question from a reporter. He'd been asked about Donald's claim that, as President, he would build a very high border wall.

"This is not in the gospel," the Pope said.

Within the hour, Donald had been alerted to the Pope's point of view. In the broadest sense, Francis' statement could implicate the religious tenets of such Republican candidates as Ted Cruz, who is evangelical, and it might have had implications for Jeb Bush, a Catholic, and Rubio, a sometimes Catholic, and even for John Kasich, who was reared as a Catholic and once considered becoming a priest before he entered politics.

But it was Donald, as was his custom, who fired back. Almost no major political candidate in the history of the Republic had ever directly confronted a sitting Pope before. "I think it is disgraceful for a religious leader to question a person's faith," he charged. "I am proud to be a Presbyterian. I am not a Catholic, but a Presbyterian. As President, I will not allow Christianity to be consistently attacked and weakened."

When reporters contacted Cruz, he stayed out of the confrontation, unwilling to get dragged into it. "I'm not going to come between Donald and the Pope," he said.

Privately, he told an aide, "Let those two duke it out."

Donald's rebuttal of the Pope's statement was conveyed to Francis, who by then was safely within the walls of the Vatican. Diplomatically, he responded that he wanted to give Donald the benefit of the doubt because he had not heard about his border plans independently.

Donald, however, didn't let up. He called the Pope "a pawn and an instrument of the Mexican government. I don't think the Pope understands the problems we have with our border. I don't think he understands the danger of an open border with Mexico. He has been fed only Mexico's propaganda."

Then one of Donald's senior advisers, Dan Scavino, claimed, "The pontiff's words were startling, considering the Vatican is 100% surrounded by massive walls."

When informed of Donald's latest shot at him, Francis said, "Aristotle defined a human person as *'animal politicus.'* So at least I am a human person."

Donald wasn't letting up in the Holy War. "If and when the Vatican is attacked by ISIS, which as everyone knows is ISIS's ultimate trophy, I can promise you that the Pope would have only wished and prayed that Donald Trump would have been President because this would not have happened. My opponents are using the Pope as a pawn for their policies. They should be ashamed of themselves for doing so, when so many lives are involved and when illegal immigration is so rampant."

In his final statement, *Il Papa* tried to elevate the conversation. He urged the faithful to see migrants as brothers and sisters. At no point did he recommend that Catholics should withdraw their support from Donald. "Let us together ask our God for the gift of conversion, the gift of tears. Let us ask him to give us open hearts. Nor more death. No more exploitation. There is still time to change. There is still a way out and a chance, time to implore the mercy of God."

"I don't like fighting with the Pope," Donald said. "He's got a lot of personality...very different. But that wall around the Vatican is very, very big."

Pundits compared and contrasted the two world famous leaders, concluding that whereas Donald lived in a gilded marble palace in New York, the Pope lived in a gilded marble palace in the Vatican.

Reporter Carl Campanile wrote: "Trump makes shocking statements in the most bombastic way possible, and *Il Papa* makes shocking statements in the meekest way possible."

In the wake of the conflict between The Donald and *Il Papa*, the most recent poll showed that 78% of possible Republican voters favored a wall between the U.S. and Mexico.

Reporter Patrick Helay wrote: "Politicians rarely rebuke the Vatican so forcefully for fear of alienating Catholic voters. Trump's attack on Pope Francis reflected a political calculation that criticizing the Pope would not hurt him with conservatives. Some Southern evangelicals take a dim view of the Catholic church."

A Vatican spokesman, the Rev. Frederico Lombardi, denied that the Pope was trying to tell Catholics how to vote. "It was not a slap at the GOP presidential candidate. The Pope's opposition to the border wall is his general view, which is very consistent with his courageously following the indications of the Gospel offering welcome and solidarity."

Perhaps as a last word, Donald said, "If I ever meet the Pope, perhaps as President of the United States, I will enlighten him about our side."

Columnist Ross Douthat provided the most satirical overview of the "Clash of the Populists," referring to "The Donald" vs. Pope Francis.

Douthat wrote: "*The Book of Daniel* predicted it. *The Book of Revelation* confirmed it. The Necronomicon *[the fictional textbook of magic appearing in the horror stories of H.P. Lovecraft]* spelled it out in language too terrible for human ears to hear. And if you read Trump's *The Art of the Deal* backward in the original Sanskrit, you'll find it foretold there as well: Before the Seventh Seal is opened, before Famine and Pestilence are loosed, the Man in White must do battle with the combed-over Titan, amid the ravening shrieks of Twitter and beneath the unblinking eyes of Cable News."

Douthat also noted that the two men often shared a certain rhetoric. Whereas Donald preferred phrases like "low energy," "liar," and "loser;" *Il Papa* preferred "Pharisee or self-absorbed Promethean neo-Pelagian, though he might also use "whiner" or "sourpuss."

In the meantime, gossip columns were filled with endorsements and rebuttals from various celebrities, many of whom weighed in on one side or another. Joe Pantoliano *[the actor who interpreted the character named "Joey Pants" in* The Sopranos*]* joined in the attack on Donald, claiming "I'm with Pope Francis 100%. Trump promotes bigotry, exclusivism, racism. He's like Raid. You spray it in the corners, and all the cockroaches come out."

"Y'ALL CRAZY!"
Journalists Assert:
"Dixie Ding-Dongs Go for Trump as Jeb! Quits"

On February 21, the *New York Daily News* conveyed the results of the South Carolina primary to its readers. Reporter Denis Slattery was blunt: "The piggish voters of South Carolina gobbled up the slop that Donald Trump served, handing the bloodthirsty billionaire his second straight Republican presidential primary."

Throughout the course of the race in the Palmetto State, Donald had tangled with Pope Francis over the border wall; called Ted Cruz a "maniac" and a "liar," and promoted a story about his support of a U.S. general shooting renegade Muslims with bullets dipped in pigs' blood.

At a rally of his supporters, Donald delivered his victory speech. "It's rough running for President. It's mean, it's nasty, it's vicious…and it's beautiful."

With most of the precincts reporting, Donald had made off with 33% of the vote, with most of the evangelicals going for him—and not for Ted Cruz or Rubio, each of whom came in with about 22% of the vote.

An emotional Jeb Bush, on the verge of tears, came in at fourth place. Soonafter, he announced that he was dropping out of the race.

"Poor little mama's boy," Donald said mockingly, referring to the aging Barbara Bush showing up in South Carolina to urge voters to support the losing campaign of her second son.

The former First Lady and Jeb's older brother, "Dubya," had hoped to play on their lingering popularity in South Carolina.

The elusive Melania, Donald's wife, made a rare appearance, telling the crowd of beer drinkers (from plastic cups) that, "My husband Donald will make the best President ever." It can be assumed that her knowledge of previous American presidents was limited.

Donald's triumph in South Carolina was on the dawn of the "Ides of March." In just nine days, the nominating race would be fought in a dozen states stretching from Massachusetts to Texas.

Privately, the Trump campaign had more or less written off Texas, fearing it would go to that state's Senator, Cruz. However, Donald had hoped for a sweep through most of the other contests.

Newspapers continued to attack him as fact checkers reported that his campaign speeches "departed from the truth" at the rate of 77%. Just 6% of his statements were judged to be "true or mostly true."

Economists attacked his threat to impose a 45% tariff on goods from China, predicting that such a hostile act "would punish the world with a devastating trade war."

Even though Donald, still on shaky ground, was far from assured of the GOP nomination, he was eagerly devouring news from the Democratic battleground. Sanders was mounting a robust challenge to Hillary, attracting young voters by "offering them a lot of free stuff such as college tuition."

Donald followed the returns from Nevada, noting that Hillary had "Berned the Bern" in that state's caucuses. She had swept to victory over the "grumpy old man" (as his enemies called Sanders), garnering massive political support from workers in the Las Vegas casino hotels. Her fans and allies, often in reactions against Donald's candidacy, included blackjack dealers, pit bosses, cooks, room maids, janitors, and others who catered to the high rollers who flocked to this gambling mecca in the West. In the aftermath, among the Democrats, Hillary won 52% of the vote, with Sanders drawing less than 47%.

With the South Carolina results in, both Cruz and Rubio realized that each of them had to knock out the other before taking Donald on. An embittered Cruz did not take defeat lightly, labeling Rubio a "Donald Trump with a smile. Rubio and Trump are both liars, although Rubio lies with a smile."

On the campaign trail in South Carolina, Rubio sounded like a deranged Pat Roberson, running a "holier-than-Thou" campaign in his attempt to woo evangelicals from both Cruz and Donald. Rubio constantly repeated invocations of God and attacked the Supreme Court for legalizing same-sex marriage.

Since all three frontrunners were shouting about their commitment to religion, pollsters set out to determine why voters preferred one "priestly candidate" over the other.

A resident of Columbia, Betsy Bullis, said, "I voted for Rubio because we both love HBO's *Ballers,* and Rubio, like myself, thinks Batman could win a war against Spiderman. He told his supporters that."

Jack Daven, of Greenville, said he had been a Cruz supporter but that at the last minute had switched his vote to Rubio. "When Ted Cruz at this rally broke into this silly song, telling us how he serenaded his wife, Heidi, while courting her, it made my rebel blood squirm. He also said he wakes up scared every day and prays to God for mercy. I didn't want a little coward like that in the White House."

Theresa Kostrzewa, a former fundraiser for Jeb Bush, predicted that his backers would now throw their support behind Rubio. "I've talked to voters who want fresh blood. South Carolina is like the parting of the Red Sea. Republicans, this is your sign from God."

So far, the backers of Rubio and Cruz had spent a staggering $220 million for attack ads during their campaigns, with pitiful results. Bush had spent the most money, to no avail.

One of his wealthy Florida backers, who did not want to be named, said, "I put a ton of money on his ass, and he let us down. I think the 'Bush Dynasty' had ended not with a blast, but with a whimper. Good riddance, I say."

Katie Packer, a GOP strategist, said, "Our hope is that the field will winnow and conservatives will coalesce behind one candidate who is a real conservative."

Columnist Paul Krugman wondered why the GOP establishment viewed Rubio as a moderate and a sensible candidate. "Not long ago, someone holding his policy views would be considered a fringe crank. His statements on foreign policy are terrifying, as is his evident willingness to make a bonfire of civil liberties. His tax cuts would be almost twice those of George W. Bush. That means that millionaires like Mitt Romney would pay precisely zero in Federal taxes. It's not a fight between a crazy guy (Donald) and someone reasonable (Rubio). It's idiosyncratic, self-invented crankery vs. Establishment-approved crankery—and it's not at all clear which is worse."

February was moving toward an inglorious end on the campaign trail as one event after another provided fodder for the tabloids and cable TV news.

In a surprise move, Cruz fired his top adviser, Rick Tyler. Tyler had been asked to resign after a video was released with a false quote by Rubio, who was depicted as saying, "The Bible doesn't have all the answers."

The Cruz campaign had also spread the (patently false) rumor during a key voting moment that Ben Carson was dropping out of the race in Iowa. A Photoshopped, cobbled-together photograph of Obama with Rubio, shaking hands, was distributed suggesting that the Florida senator should drop out of the race for actually having shaken the hand of the President of the United States.

Donald also came in for his share of issues associated with dirty tricks and doctored videos. Cruz campaign aides arranged for audio clips from Donald's speeches to be inserted into visual scenes from the hit TV series, *Game of Thrones*. Donald talks about torturing people with the blunt brutality of a medieval king.

He was portrayed as a member of Night's Watch, a fraternal order whose members had been assigned to deflect any assault on a massive wall under siege by a "race of outsiders."

In this sword-and-sorcery fantasy epic, Donald is portrayed as saying,

"Our enemies laugh at us. They protest our waterboarding, but they chop off heads...We need to build a wall and build it quickly."

Whereas attacks on Donald continued, Cruz and Rubio received a barrage of charges thrown at them, too. Columnist Frank Bruni claimed, "Ted Cruz makes angelic claims that are diabolically hypocritical. The Texas senator is some piece of double-talking, disingenuous work. His dirty tricks do stand out in the context of his flamboyant claims of rectitude and righteousness. He directs you to his halo as he surreptitiously grabs a pitchfork."

"The Bible talks about if someone treats you unkindly, repay them with kindness," Cruz told a rally in South Carolina.

In the Senate, Cruz had likened GOP senators who claimed it was logistically impossible to defund Obamacare to "Nazi appeasers."

Quote after quote attributed to Cruz depicted him as a bit unhinged, as in 2012 in a presidential debate when he claimed, "Mitt Romney actually French kissed Obama."

Throughout the campaign, Cruz continued to rant about same-sex marriage, calling it "the greatest scourge of our time." He seemed to view such unions as catalysts for the doom of civilization.

Even though he had by now already trounced both of his Cuban American competitors (Cruz and Rubio), Donald continued his attacks. He'd already accused Cruz of being a Canadian anchor baby. Now, he questioned Rubio's credentials to run for President, sowing seeds of doubt about his place of birth. "Ted Cruz and Marco Rubio are ineligible to run for President, Donald tweeted. "Cruz was born in Canada. I don't know where Rubio was born."

An unnamed aide to Donald made an outrageous charge. "I heard it on good authority in Miami that Rubio was born in Havana, and may have been the bastard son of Castro."

Donald chimed in: "I was told that Rubio's parents were not U.S. citizens when he was born. They were citizens of Castro's communist island of Cuba."

The latest poll showed Donald leading in ten of the next fourteen states to vote in the GOP primaries or caucuses. He was leading in Nevada, Alabama, Georgia, Alaska, Massachusetts, Tennessee, Virginia, Oklahoma, Minnesota, and Louisiana. As expected, Cruz was ahead in Texas, and Donald also trailed him in Arkansas, Colorado, and Kentucky.

In New York, Donald's fellow New Yorkers had a keen eye focused on the GOP race. In Albany, Governor Mario Cuomo signaled that he was ready to run for President if a Democrat failed to win in November. A source said, "Mario is seeing the light of a rapid leftward turn of the grass roots.

His entire future rests on the defeat of a flawed Hillary and "the Abominable Snowman of Vermont" (i.e., Sanders).

In New York, Donald's fellow billionaire, Mike Bloomberg, was disheartened at a recent poll that revealed that his fellow New Yorkers weren't ready to vote for him for President, although they had already elected him mayor three times.

Nearly 60% of the voters claimed they preferred other candidates.

Another former New York Mayor, Rudy Giuliani, once a presidential candidate himself, revealed that he was an adviser to Trump's campaign. "People like that Donald tells it like it is. I like that he is eschewing political correctness."

Super Tuesday loomed for Donald. He told his aides, "After that, we could almost have the nomination locked up."

***

One by one, the once-leading candidates for the GOP presidential race began to fade from the radar screen. Perhaps in an attempt to regain more exposure, Ben Carson, who had distinguished himself as a neurosurgeon, continued to stir up controversy with his bizarre opinions.

Donald reacted with amusement when he heard Carson's views on President Obama. Carson claimed America's first black President didn't understand African Americans "because he was raised white." He was, of course, referring to the commander-in-chief's white mother.

"He grew up in white America," Carson said. "That doesn't mean there is anything wrong with that. It's just that when a claim is made that he represents the black experience, it is not true."

Carson's rebuke of Obama brought the strongest satirical attack of the neurosurgeon from Linda Stasi, who continued to swing the sharpest ax among columnists.

"Ben Carson needs to drop out of the race—the human race—and return to Mars, or whatever planet he came from. You don't have to be a brain surgeon to know that the guy is one step away from a tinfoil hat."

It was with trepidation that many GOP leaders, such as Senate majority leader Mitch O'Connell, watched as the candidates, mainly Donald, headed west to Nevada to compete in the races leading up to Super Tuesday.

Republican leaders faced a dilemma, privately proclaiming "anyone but Trump."

However, the party's second frontrunner, Ted Cruz, seemed to be loathed even more by party leaders, and hardly emerged as the proper can-

560

didate for voters to rally around.

Rubio was a possibility, although it was feared that he was too far to the right to attract moderate Republicans, Independents, or "Reagan Democrats."

In Nevada, where Donald owned a hotel, he was widely viewed as the favorite.

The caucus in Nevada, on February 23, turned out to be a voting disaster. Its procedures and its integrity were widely denounced on radio, TV, and in print. Voter fraud was alleged, along with insufficient ballots and general pandemonium at the precincts. Some fights broke out between Donald's supporters and those promoting the candidacy of Cruz. There were also allegations that many of Donald's supporters had cast ballots multiple times. Some Trump supporters showed up at the voting precincts wearing KKK robes.

As the results poured in, Donald, receiving the lion's share of the vote in Trump-friendly Las Vegas, became a new "American Idol," winning 33% of the vote, taking another giant step toward becoming the Republican nominee.

Rubio trailed at 24%, with "God's anointed," Cruz, getting only 21%.

In the wake of his provocative comments, Carson got 6.6% of the vote, with John Kasich, viewed as the most sensible of the candidates, receiving a meager 3.8%. The so-called "voice of reason" emanating from the Ohio governor had not seemed to resonate.

At a "watch party" at the Treasure Island Hotel in Las Vegas, Don-

After years of suppression, Adolf Hitler's *Mein Kampf* was republished in Munich in 2016 and became a bestseller.

A copy of the *Führer's* manifesto was rushed to Donald.

Throughout the campaign, Donald was frequently compared to Adolf Hitler (left).

From the campaign trail, he also quoted from Mussolini (right). "A good quote is a good quote, even if Mussolini said it," Donald insisted.

ald received thundering applause. There were screams of joy and delight. "Thank you, Nevada," he said. "We will make America safe and great again."

ADOLF HITLER'S *MEIN KAMPF*
After Someone Sends Him a Copy,
Donald Gets an Endorsement from the KKK

A scholarly edition of Adolf Hitler's infamous autobiography, *Mein Kampf,* first published in 1925 and filled with the Nazi dictator's anti-Semitic and genocidal rants, was outlawed in Germany for many years after World War II. It was republished in Munich in 2016 and became a bestseller.

One neo-Nazi in Munich sent Donald a copy of the *Führer's* manifesto, with a note: "Read it! There are lessons to be learned. Don't go after the Muslims. Go after the Jews! The *Führer* got it right."

Around that time, Hitler had re-entered the news cycle when his recently uncovered medical records were revealed. It had long been known that one of his testicles had never descended, but recently, he'd been exposed for having a "teeny tiny Wiener."

"Poor Eva," wrote a journalist in Stuttgart, referring to Eva Braun, Hitler's longtime mistress, who actually had wanted to go to Hollywood to become "another Lana Turner."

On February 24, Donald received an endorsement from a coven of admirers, who might also have supported Hitler had they lived in Germany in 1933. David Duke, the former Grand Wizard of the KKK, and once a presidential candidate himself, announced his support of Donald.

"Not voting for Trump would be a treason to your heritage," Duke claimed over the radio, addressing his followers. Duke implored them to volunteer to rustle up some votes for the New York billionaire.

"Voting for him is a strategic action. I hope he does everything we hope he will do." Duke urged KKK members to "Get off your duff. Get off your rear end that's getting fatter and fatter for many of you every day on your chairs. Among other Trump volunteers, you're going to meet the same kind of mindset you have."

Many politicians and civic groups called upon Donald to disavow the KKK's controversial endorsement. "I disapprove," he said at the time, and then changed the subject.

Duke had come out for Donald before, especially when he promised that a wall would be built during his administration to keep out Mexican rapists, and had called for a ban on Muslims entering the United States.

"I praise the fact that Trump has come out on the immigration issue," the former "Wizard" said. "I'm beginning to get the idea that he is a good salesman."

DENOUNCING DONALD

Cruz and Rubio Attack Donald at the Houston Debate As "An Empty Suit Without a Plan" and "a Bloviating Billionaire"

The tenth GOP debate, in Houston, had been heralded as a "do-or-die" for the remaining candidates in the race. At this point, whereas Cruz and Rubio remained as Donald's only serious competitors, Kasich and Carson would be onstage as well.

The debate was conducted on the evening of February 25 on Cruz's home turf in Texas, broadcast by CNN from the University of Houston. It had been scheduled just five days before Super Tuesday (March 1, 2016), a day when either primaries or caucuses would be held in fourteen states.

It was to have been sponsored by *NBC News,* but the RNC chairman, Reince Priebus, had previously denounced the network for having "bad faith" during the October 28, 2015 debate in Boulder, Colorado. That debate had drawn "dragon fire" from Donald, who didn't like the tough, often embarrassing, questions the moderators asked.

During the debate in the Lone Star State, all five remaining candidates—Donald, Cruz, Rubio, Carson, and Kasich—were invited for their input. This would represent the tenth and final debate for Carson, who skipped the following (March 3) debate in Detroit, and then dropped out of the race the following day.

As in a Hollywood rendition of a boxing match, perhaps one starring Sylvester Stallone, Rubio came out swinging, giving his most aggressive performance after his embarrassingly robotic debate in New Hampshire. He lit into Donald with a verbal assault weapon, ridiculing his health care proposal, immigration deportation plan, and even deriding him for inheriting millions from his father, Fred. The billionaire was depicted as a blowhard—"an empty suit without a plan."

"You're the only person on this stage who's ever been fined for illegally hiring people to work on your building projects," Rubio said.

"No! No! No!" Donald shouted back, "I'm the only one on this stage who's hired people. You haven't hired anybody."

"Donald hired workers from Poland and had to pay a $1 million fine for doing so," Rubio claimed."

He wouldn't let up on Donald, as he attacked his business acumen. "If you built that wall between the United States and Mexico, like you constructed Trump Tower, you'd be using illegal immigrants. If you hadn't inherited $200 million, you'd be selling watches on the streets of Manhattan."

When he finished his blitz against Donald, Cruz entered the fray to deliver some "sucker punches."

"When I was fighting against amnesty, where was Donald? He was firing Dennis Rodman on *Celebrity Apprentice*." Cruz uttered that charge with a smug mockery as Donald glared at him.

Both Cruz and Rubio bitterly attacked Donald for an impending lawsuit in which former students of Trump University were charging fraud and demanding refunds of their tuition.

Never at a loss for words, Donald called Rubio "a choke artist" and denounced Cruz as a "liar. Ted Cruz lacks the ability to get along with anybody." Then he turned to his Texas challenger. "You should be ashamed of yourself."

Inevitably, the subject of Hillary came up, with Cruz reminding Donald that polls showed that she could beat him in the November election.

"Hell, she would really kill you," Donald countered.

The debate degenerated into indecipherable shouting and name-calling.

Showing the ravages of their respective ages, Barbara Bush sat in the auditorium with her husband, former U.S. President, George H.W. Bush.

Despite the exit from the race of their son, Jeb, they were on hand to watch what Barbara later described as "a horror show." Their faces reflected their disillusion not only with the candidates, but perhaps with the state of the Republican race as well.

The weatherbeaten pair, survivors of many a political brawl, had never participated in something like this. There was a bitterness reflected in their faces as they looked on in disgust, still licking the wounds of the GOP's repudiation of their son, Jeb, during his spectacularly expensive and ill-fated quest for the presidency.

The next day, television's talking heads and many editorial writers awarded the debate to Rubio, claiming that he had stung Donald with his quick jabs and sharp denunciations. Rubio appeared to have benefitted from debate training, perhaps with coaches. Conveying a kind of desperation, he was sweating profusely as his chance of becoming America's first Cuban-American President faded.

Reporters described him as "newly pugnacious," as he tore into Donald, even attacking him for outsourcing the manufacture of his clothing line, including those "tasteless ties," to China.

When Donald protested, Rubio outshouted him. "Make them in America!"

Rubio may have won the debate, but many editorial writers agreed: "The Florida senator did not look or sound very presidential."

"NO MORE TIME FOR CLOWNS
& Dancing Bears"

—Ted Cruz, After the Tenth Republican Debate

In an almost desperate last-ditch effort to defeat Donald in the Super Tuesday GOP primaries, Cruz and Rubio stepped up their fire power. Campaigning hard in Texas, where polls had him in the lead, Cruz drew upon the massacre at the Alamo in 1836. "America is besieged," he claimed. Some Texas reporters claimed, "If Cruz loses Texas, he's a dead coyote on the trail"

Appealing to evangelicals, he claimed, "Texans will not give up their freedom quietly." He never spelled out exactly what freedom Texans had lost during the Obama years. "The time for the clowns and dancing bears has passed," he said, in an insulting reference to Donald.

Rubio also didn't let up, calling Donald a "con artist." He mocked his misspelled words in his endless tweets and even claimed he got "so flustered by my attacks during our last debate that he wet his pants."

"Donald Trump is Mr. Meltdown and can't spell. He writes 'chicker' instead of choker, and 'honer' instead of honor. A third grader could have done better."

Donald fired back: "Lightweight choker Marco Rubio looks like a little boy on stage—not presidential material."

Cruz also sent out tweets, one of them cringe-inducing: "Trump called me a soft, weak little baby. Hope he doesn't eat me."

One columnist responded to that: "I can only hope he does."

The homophobic Cruz didn't seem to realize that "eat me" in gay parlance referred to a blow-job.

The anti-Trump forces were marching as to war, with the Cross of Jesus going on before. Sometimes, however, Rubio quit claiming he was the candidate of Christ and reverted to character assassination.

At a rally in Kennesaw, Georgia, Rubio mocked Donald's appearance. "He likes to sue people. He should sue whoever did that orange face of his. It's the worst spray tan in America."

Donald responded with: "Little Marco applies makeup with a trowel before a debate."

Rubio might have found his voice, but Donald never lost his own. "Little Marco has a fresh mouth, and he's a very nasty guy. I see him starting to sweat. Thank God he has really large ears, the biggest ears I've ever seen, since they protect him from the profusion of sweat running down."

"Unlike Little Marco and Lying Ted Cruz, I won in Nevada with the young, I won with the old. I won with the highly educated. I won with the poorly educated. I love the poorly educated."

No one had ever accused Donald of being a Christian soldier, a Bible thumper like his chief rivals, Cruz and Rubio. Those two Cuban attack dogs had entered the race, hoping to divide the evangelical vote between them. It was estimated that 72% of the GOP electorate in the primaries consisted of "Born Again evangelical Christians." However, Rubio and Cruz were surprised to see Donald appealing to evangelicals, even in Texas.

Writing for *Bloomberg View*, Francis Wilkinson said, "Unfortunately for those two senators, many conservative evangelicals have concluded that they don't need a candidate who shares their values. They can tolerate, even embrace, a candidate who is profane, greedy, vain, shifty, and thrice married with a loud history of sexual conquest."

He suggested that evangelicals were "nostalgia voters, eager to return to an idealized, socially conservative, and white-dominated past."

In-depth surveys of Tea

Realizing that they were each losing their race for the nomination, both Ted Cruz and Marco Rubio reverted to cruel mockery of Donald in their campaign speeches.

At one point, Cruz compared Donald's rally speeches to the kind of entertainment you'd expect from "circus clowns and dancing bears."

Party diehards, most often evangelicals, discovered that they had strong, hardcore beliefs. They seemed convinced that Obama was not an American citizen, having been born, they claimed, in Kenya.

They were also convinced that he supported Islamic terrorists and was not a Christian, "but a Muslim tyrant, with a goal to turn the United States into a godless communist nation."

As one of Trump's most ardent supporters in Dallas told a pollster: "Trump will put the white man on top again, like he used to be, like it was before all the niggers, queers, Jews, Islamic terrorists, Hillary lesbians, and Mexican rapists steal our country forever."

The swiftness of the cultural change disturbed many evangelicals, who longed for a return to a perhaps illusionary golden yesteryear. "We now have gays in the military," said one evangelical from Fort Worth. "In the good old days, like in the Eisenhower era, faggots could not serve in the military. Homosexuality should be made illegal like it was back then. These guys should be put in prison along with the nigger murderers and Mexican drug dealers. Now there is talk of even letting transgendered people, whoever the fuck they are, serve in the military. Faggots have never served in the military and shouldn't now. Trump will see to that."

[In point of fact, thousands upon thousands of gay men and women fought and died during World War II, many of them heroically.]

As Rubio continued with his assault that Donald "had urinated in his trousers," Donald mocked Rubio's excessively parched throat. At one rally, he brandished a plastic water bottle, mocking "Senator Choke." Once, Rubio was caught on camera reaching desperately for a bottle of water, which he proceeded to noisily gulp down as millions laughed at him on TV.

Waving a water bottle at a Texas rally, Donald poured half of its contents onto the floor before ostentatiously gulping from it in a mocking imitation of Rubio. "That night, he looked like he had survived five days in the Sahara without benefit of a single drop," Donald said.

Cruz also claimed, "*ABC, CNN,* and multiple news reports have cited Trump's dealings with S&A Construction, which was owned by 'Fat Tony' Salerno, who is a mobster, who is in jail."

Appearing on *Meet the Press,* Cruz brought up Donald's alleged ties to the Mafia. "The reason he won't release his income tax forms is that it would reveal his link to organized crime," Cruz charged.

Just when American voters thought the GOP primary cat-and-dog fight could sink no lower, Rubio became the "bottom-feeder." Even the Queen of England reportedly asked, "Just what is happening to the United States?"

On February 28 at a rally at Roanoke College in Virginia, and on a Christian Sunday, no less, a smirky Rubio told the crowd, "Donald's hands are the size of someone who is 5 foot 2. And you know what they say about a man who has small hands."

Then he paused, as the crowd mockingly laughed. As if to protect himself, he added, "That is, you can't trust 'em."

He knew exactly why the crowd was laughing. "Small hands, small dick," was the reference, according to the (tired, old, and frequently disproved) urban myth.

Donald did not immediately defend the size of his penis. That would come later.

***

To recover from the onslaught of attacks from his two bitter rivals, Rubio and Cruz, Donald won the endorsement of a former rival on February 26. The governor of New Jersey, Chris Christie, endorsed him as the best GOP candidate to beat Hillary in November.

At a campaign stop in Fort Worth, Texas, Christie, who had already dropped out of the race, claimed, "There is no one better prepared to provide America with the strong leadership it needs than Donald Trump."

Donald gushed over the endorsement, and there was speculation that the losing candidate, Christie, wanted Donald to name him as his vice-presidential running mate.

Only a year before, Christie had told Fox News anchorwoman Greta Van Susteren that, "I don't think Donald is suited to be President of the United States."

Many greeted the endorsement with ridicule. On Twitter, David Kochel cracked, "New lessons, kids. Sometimes the best option for the fat kid is to hand over his lunch money to the schoolyard bully!"

On the campaign trail, Christie vowed, "We're gonna kick Obama's ass out of the White House. We're going to show up at 1600 Pennsylvania Avenue with an eviction notice."

Back in his native New Jersey, a local *politico* tweeted, "The bright lights are going out for our disgraced governor. He's got troubles at home. But right now, he's become the opening act for the star of the show…Donald Trump."

One newspaper headline read: "I HATED DONALD TRUMP. NOW I LOVE HIM"—CHRISTIE.

In the wake of his weak showing at the debate in Houston, Donald, in the words of one reporter, "fought back like a wildcat."

Columnist Rick Lowry wrote: "Now Trump has a prominent wingman who shares his taste for no-holds-barred political combat."

The acerbic columnist, Linda Stasi, couldn't resist jumping into the fray. She noted that Donald had been called a "carnival barker/jackass/a cancer/loser/narcissist egomaniac/pants wetter/bully."

But Christie, "traveling a bridge too far," had forgiven Donald all his failings and was now his chief surrogate.

"Peter only denied Jesus three times, and he went down in history as one of the world's biggest hypocrites," Stasi said.

Facing Super Tuesday, Donald continued to reveal just how thin-skinned he was. On February 26, he claimed that he would reverse the First Amendment when he became President. In a threat to the news media, he said, "We're gonna open up those libel laws, folks, and we're gonna sue you like you've never been sued before."

That his patience was wearing thin was obvious.

[Around the same time, Donald's adversary, Bill Clinton, also had his nerves tested in South Carolina by a heckler, a retired marine sergeant in Bluffton. "We had four lives in Benghazi that were killed," the man said. "And your wife tried to cover it up."

The crowd booed the heckler, and the former President of the United States said: "Shut up and listen to my answer."

Donald couldn't have done it better.]

In Washington, Hillary told the press, "It's been surprising to me to see

"Small hands, small dick," or so goes the disproven American myth.

At a contentious debate, Donald held up his hands to show the world, "They're not that small." He also told voters that "I'm more than adequate down there, too."

Rubio of the big ears also revealed his hands, showing that they were larger than Donald's, thereby suggesting that he was better hung.

Actually, women who have gone to bed with either man confided that both candidates are "far larger than average," without providing exact measurements.

somebody who was affable and was good company, and had a reputation of being kind and bigger than life, really traffic in a lot of prejudice and paranoia like Donald Trump. He doesn't fit into what I thought I knew about him."

News reached Donald on February 27 that Hillary had demolished her rival, Bernie Sanders, in the South Carolina primary, thereby reinforcing her frontrunner status as the Democratic nominee. An overwhelming turnout of African American voters propelled her to victory, as she defeated the aging Vermont senator by 47 points.

Meanwhile, Karl Rove went on the offensive. During the administration of George W. Bush, he had been called "Baby Bush's brain." The President in power at the time had a name for him: "Turd Blossom," inspired by a wildflower that thrived in decaying cowpiles in the grasslands of Texas.

At a luncheon of Republican governors gathering in Washington on February 19, Rove told his fellow right wingers that nominating Donald would be catastrophic for the GOP. "It's not too late to stop this onslaught," Rove predicted. Last-ditch efforts to block Donald's inexorable advance were energetically debated.

Perhaps in desperation, many members of the Republican Establishment seemed to think that "Little Marco" might be their man, although during the previous few months, millions of dollars had been spent on ads touting his glory. As one donor said, "We ran the flag up the pole and found few voters ready to salute it."

The baby-faced 44-year-old was told by the power brokers to continue "with his slash-and-burn night of the long knives, cutting into Donald with his recently sharpened vitriol." As the Old Guard of the GOP fumed and fussed over the emergence of Donald, he and Rubio continued in their sarcasm.

"If elected President, Donald would be flying 'Hair Force One,'" Rubio said, mockingly.

"Little Marco is too dim to have attended my Ivy League *Alma Mater*," Donald charged.

Rubio shot back, "Donald brings to mind the lunatic North Korean dictator with nuclear ambitions."

Satire ruled the day, none better than that of Frank Bruni who, in *The New York Times*, came out with a gender-bending appraisal:

"Imagine for a moment the presidential candidacy of a rich, brash, real estate magnate and reality TV star named 'Donna Trump.' Quizzically coifed and stubbornly sun-kissed, she's on her third marriage. There's clear evidence that

infidelity factored into the demise of her first. One of her children was conceived out of wedlock."

"Her sexual appetites had been prodigious, at least according to her frequent chants and claims and vulgar cants. She has a tendency to talk about men as sirloins and rump roasts of disparate succulence. She denigrates those who displease her on cosmetic grounds. So-and-so used to be a 9, but, with that male-pattern baldness and desperate comb-over, is down to a 6. So-and-so thinks he's covering up that fat around the waist with baggy suits, but we know better."

Bruni went on to predict that "Donna Trump" would not have a chance in the race for the White House.

Donald had hoped that he could move on with a quick disavowal of his KKK support, but at the very last day of February, it returned to haunt him when he appeared on CNN's *State of the Union*. The subject of David Duke was brought up again.

"I don't know anything about David Duke," Donald said on camera, even though millions watching him knew that he did. "I don't know anything about white supremacists."

For that, he was severely attacked from many quarters for not having denounced Duke and the KKK. Cruz immediately tweeted, "You're better than this, Donald. We should all agree that racism is wrong, the KKK is abhorrent."

Then, one of New York's (Republican) Congressmen, Peter King, weighed in, telling Jake Rapper on CNN, "Donald says he doesn't know who David Duke is or what the white supremacist group stands for. If his statements are true, it means Trump is genuinely dumb. If he is lying, that is shameful. In any case, he should not be running to lead the United States."

Of course, the Rev. Al Sharpton had to weigh in too. "How can Trump not know who David Duke is if he is saying to people he has enough knowledge to run the Free World?"

Reporter Adam Edelman pointed out, "Trump's dumb act was particularly odd because the real estate mogul had once condemned Duke. In 2000, he said he would not run for President on the Reform Ticket because the party included Duke as a member."

To make matters worse, Donald tweeted a quote from Benito Mussolini. The Italian fascist had once said, "It is better to live one day as a lion than 100 years as a sheep."

Asked to defend having been inspired by a fascist, Donald responded,

"It's a very good quote. It's a very interesting quote. I know who said it, but what difference does it make whether it's Mussolini or someone else?"

TV host Chuck Todd asked him if he wanted to be associated with a fascist.

Donald demurred. "No, I want to be associated with interesting quotes."

***

Donald's detractors weren't confined just to the United States. He was attacked around the world. Reporter Dan Bilefsky wrote, "Trump has been depicted as a snarling demagogue in France, equated with Donald Duck in Spain, and described as worse than Lord Voldemort in Britain. With his series of election wins, the reaction has become one of befuddlement, outrage, and panic, along with admiration in some unlikely quarters."

El Pais, one of the most influential newspapers of Spain, even published an imagined quote from the grave of Philip I, Spain's ascetic, empire-building 16th-century king. *El Pais'* editors wrote that if Philip had been alive, he'd have suggested that Donald should define himself as the agent who'd bring back the Inquisition.

In Germany, the front cover of *Der Spiegel* depicted Donald with the American flag behind him engulfed in flames. Its headline blared: "MADNESS: AMERICA'S AGITATOR."

Support for Donald came from surprising quarters, including from *Mlada fronma Dnes*, the leading newspaper of the Czech Republic. It seemed that Donald had evolved into a sort of folk hero among the disillusioned populace of Eastern and Central Europe. Many citizens equated Donald's rise to that of Ronald Reagan.

Fans were drawn to his showmanship and swagger. "To many Czechs, Trump signifies American values like show business and working hard to achieve success," wrote editor Jaroslav Plesi.

Donald also enjoyed massive popularity among the Russians, who wrote of his "budding 'bromance'" with Putin. The Russians took delight in Donald's lack of political correctness, as when he referred to the "protruding nipples" of the gay former Congressman, Barney Frank.

The newspapers consistently quoted the new legend that Putin and Donald were part of a mutual admiration society.

TRASHING DONALD'S COMPETITORS
What They're Hiding: The Enquirer Reveals All

On the last day of February, 2016, *The National Enquirer* released an exposé that shocked millions of Americans.

The headlines read: "WHAT THEY'RE HIDING!"

The tabloid ran pictures of Marco Rubio, Hillary Clinton, Donald Trump, Bernie Sanders, and a gloomy-looking Ted Cruz, followed by subheads blaring, "Gay Sex Arrest," "Rape Cover-up," "Child Sex Scandal," and "Suicide Shocker."

The paper did not identify which of those headlines belonged to which candidate—and with the intention of avoiding libel, we don't want to either. To play it safe, it was suggested that we replicate the words as they appeared.

Inside, a photo was published that was alleged to be of Rubio "wallowing in bubbles at a guys' foam party in Miami" when he was a young man. Yet another photo purported to be his image at a dance bar "in the swing with other topless men."

Reporter Sharon Churcher wrote that Rubio was hiding a "secret gay past."

Political blogger Wayne Madsen claimed, "People in the gay community have told me it was well known that Rubio frequented gay nightclubs. And foam parties were almost exclusively gay events."

The Enquirer also revealed (allegedly) official records that Rubio had been arrested, along with two other men, at 9:37PM on May 23, 1990, in Miami's crime-plagued Alice C. Wainright Park.

A homeowners' association newsletter stated that the park was "a haven for gang warfare, gunfire, prostitution (gay and straight), drug deal-

ing, and muggings.

Police major Delrish Moss said, "It was very dark and had lots of trees. People went there to smoke illegal substances, have sex, and drink."

Charges made against the men were later dismissed. *The Enquirer* quoted Rubio aide Todd Harris, who claimed that the young men were merely caught drinking beer after hours.

The tabloid also headlined a story with "SUICIDAL WIFE DRIVEN CRAZY BY HIS RUTHLESS AMBITION!" It was an *exposé* of Cruz and his wife, Heidi. The two had met while working on George W. Bush's presidential campaign in 2000.

On August 22, 2005, in Austin, policemen discovered Heidi sitting "with her head in her hands" on the grass near an expressway. An officer later alleged that "she had walked away from her home after having two sips of a margarita an hour before dinner."

He also said she was in danger, as she was sitting in despair only ten feet from the rushing traffic."

Cruz's campaign admitted that his wife "experienced a brief bout of depression."

Bernie Sanders came in for his share of scandal. The paper had already reported that he was alleged to have fathered a love child during the hippie era.

Now, the tabloid claimed that he had written smutty essays when he had a stint as a freelance journalist in the 1970s. He wrote

In a blatant attempt to win the support of the most "redneck of redneck voters," Ted Cruz "The Commander" (right) donned a hunter's "black face" camouflage for a duck hunt with the controversial Phil Robertson, a reality TV star, a noted homophobe, and a personality that his detractors perceived as gauche, menacing, unlikable, utterly without humor, and to some, terrifying.

Cruz believed he'd earn the votes of *Duck Dynasty* fans as a camera recorded his plot to penetrate and kill, with shotgun pellets, some harmless duck, which had—until this ad was shot— been flying freely through the air.

At the end of this gruesome and utterly distasteful ad (entitled "Cruz Commander,") voters were urged to "JOIN THE FIGHT TODAY!"

of a man who goes home and masturbates to fantasies about being with a woman on her knees, a woman tied up, and a woman abused.

One woman, as described in one of Sanders' essays, was said to have fantasized "about being raped by three men simultaneously." He also wrote an article advocating that six-month old babies should be allowed to romp naked on the beach so "they can see each other's sexual organs—and maybe even touch them."

According to the article, Sanders also confessed to a fascination with stories about sexual assaults on kids. He was said to have written, "Do you know why porn magazines sell so well if they run such articles as 'Girl Raped by 15 Men?'"

As Congressman from Vermont, in 2003, Sanders opposed measures that cracked down on pedophiles who traveled overseas to such countries as Thailand to prey on kids. He also voted against outlawing some Internet child porn.

The allegations in that edition of the *Enquirer* against Bill and Hillary had been (frequently) aired before—that her "horndog husband" engaged in a series of affairs not only with Monica Lewinsky, but was accused of molesting Kathleen Willey, a volunteer at the White House, and of an actual rape of Juanita Broaddrick when he was governor of Arkansas. Hillary was accused of turning a blind eye to her husband's indiscretions, even though an advocate of women's rights.

Cruz had accused *The Enquirer* of being kind to Donald, and indeed, his biggest "scandal," as reported by that edition of that publication, was a glowing endorsement from has-been singer Pat Boone, who said, "Donald would make a great President. He would tell it like it is."

Our Media Age:
CELEBRITIES & CELEBRITY-DRIVEN POLITICS
TV Icons, Dubious, Ill Qualified, or Indifferent, Weigh in with Endorsements

The tabloid also reported that other entertainers, including Wayne Newton and Gary Busey, had endorsed Donald.

Other celebrities supporting various candidates were revealed to include Jennifer Lopez and Michael Douglas, each of whom supported

Hillary. ("I think it's time for a woman," Lopez said.

Bernie Sanders won endorsements from Danny DeVito and Will Ferrell; and his fellow Canadian, Justin Beiber, endorsed Cruz.

Marco Rubio picked up the support of actor Orson Bean and Olympic hero Kurt Angle.

Ben Carson drew support from Mickey Rourke and Kelsey Grammer, with NBA Hall of Famer Charles Barkley wanting another Bush (Jeb!) in the White House.

In a TV ad, Cruz picked up a controversial endorsement from the so-called "redneck of all rednecks," Phil Robertson, a reality TV clown, star of *Duck Dynasty*. He endorsed Cruz at a rally in South Carolina.

At one point, Robertson had been temporarily suspended from his A&E TV show after making homophobic comments. He said, "I just can't understand why they prefer a hole to a pussy."

PART FIVE

2016: THE SPRING OF TRUMP

"NEVER TRUMP"
Republicans Rage & Scream
About Their Party's Presumptive Nominee

TRUMP REVEALS
How He'd Get Mexico To Pay for the Wall

DONALD SWEEPS TO VICTORY
IN THE NORTHEAST

DONALD TRUMP
Is a *"Pathological Liar, Narcissist, & Serial Philanderer"*
—*Failing GOP candidate Ted Cruz*

Chapter Twenty-One

EUROPE PONDERS THE QUESTION "IS TRUMP WORSE THAN DRACULA?"

Journalists Wonder If America Is On the Road to Fascism

"THIS DEBATE MARKS THE DEMISE

of the Dignity of the American Political Process"

—*The New York Daily News, in reference to the March 3, 2016, Republican Debate in Detroit*

DEMOCRATIC STRATEGISTS DEBATE HOW THEY CAN CASTRATE A CANDIDATE

"Whose Cojones Are Made of Steel

"The Hot, Hot, GOP Race Has Devolved Into a Yuuge, Balls-Out, Pissing Match"

March came in with a blast, as Mexico unveiled its strategy to counter slurs from Donald Trump. All of this followed in the wake of the billionaire's plan for a massive wall to divide the two nations. Both Marco Rubio and Ted Cruz had also proposed building a wall along America's southern border.

Mexico was greatly offended to have endured its immigrating nationals designated as "drug runners and rapists," and it was horrified by Donald's call for a mass deportation of eleven million undocumented immigrants.

In Mexico City, Francisco Guzman, the chief of staff to President Enrique Peña Nieto, said it was time "to push back." He announced a major public relations campaign to highlight the rewards of U.S./Mexican relations, both to the U.S. economy and its people.

Until March, the Mexican government had avoided any direct confrontations with Donald, although some of its diplomats had labeled his projected policies "ignorant and racist." But now, Vicente Fox and Felipe Calderon each denounced Donald, comparing him to Hitler.

Guzman said, "With our top trading partner (the United States), we need more bridges and fewer walls. America is the destination for about 80% of our exports. We also share many cultural and family links. I want the man or woman who becomes President in November to view Mexico not as a threat but as an opportunity."

Donald's harsh language against Latinos, especially Mexicans, was leading to a massive incentives for Latino immigrants to become naturalized U.S. citizens so—in the event he received the GOP nomination, they'd be able to vote against Donald in the November election.

Overall, according to Federal figures, applications for naturalization jumped 14% beginning in January. Nearly nine million legal residents had been able to naturalize, which would, it was surmised, contribute to an increasingly significant voting block if the subjects continued the process of becoming citizens. The majority of Latinos in the U.S. are Democrats. Naturalization drives were particularly effective in Colorado, Florida, and Nevada, states likely to be fiercely contested in November.

IN EUROPE,
DONALD IS DENOUNCED
As "The World's Most Dangerous Man"

Mexico was not alone in sounding alarms against Donald. Headlines on the Continent blared—UNITED STATES EMBRACES LATTER-DAY MUSSOLINI.

In Rome, readers were warned, "Donald Trump could become Silvio Berlusconi with nukes," a reference to that country's disgraced ultra-conservative prime minister.

In Europe, Donald was labeled as "the anti-Obama, the loud mouth that spews hatred." The influential German news magazine, *Der Spiegel*, wrote that Donald was "the most dangerous man alive," before waxing nostalgic for George W. Bush. "Faced with the choice of Trump, we could suddenly discover a soft spot for Dracula," wrote one columnist.

From London, David Cameron attacked Donald, claiming that he "fuels hatred." In contrast, the French rightist and ultra-nationalist, Jean-Marie Le Pen, sang his praises.

Nearly all newspapers noted that Fascism had flourished on European soil during the mid-20th Century. "Could it possibly be coming to America in the 21st Century?" asked one Italian journalist.

Although at first, Donald had been dismissed as part of America's "lunatic fringe," by March, Donald was being taken seriously by Democratic campaign strategists.

Matthew Dowd, chief strategist for George W. Bush, said, in reference to her vulnerability, "Hillary has built a large tanker ship, and she's about to confront Somali pirates."

She launched her campaign on the high ground, saying, "Instead of building walls, we need to be tearing down barriers. Trump's rants do not represent American values. Racism, sexism, bigotry, discrimination, inequality are not American values."

She faced a problem with white men who were marching under Donald's banner by the millions.

David Pfouffe, architect of Obama's 2008 campaign and its calls for hope and change, said, "Today, it's more like hate and castrate."

Before the end of the month, Democratic strategists had concluded that despite intense opposition, Donald was now a formidable candidate. As his power grew, so did his opponents: As one Hillary campaign aide pondered, "What blade can we use to castrate him? His *cojones* seemed made of steel."

YANKEE CARPETBAGGERS
(Donald & Hillary)
EACH SWEEP TO VICTORIES
IN THE SOUTH
Blacks for Her, Whites for Him

At long last, Super Tuesday, March 1, dawned.
*[**Super Tuesday** refers to one or more Tuesdays early in the presidential primaries when the greatest number of U.S. states hold caucuses or primary elections. Because greater numbers of delegates to the presidential nominating conventions can be won on one of these election days than on any other single day of the primary calendar, they are fraught with competitive emotion and intensely scrutinized by pundits.]*

Donald, according to polls, showed a 33-point lead over his nearest rivals, Cruz and Rubio.

Some 49% of Republican voters in the CNN/ORC poll gave him a giant lead, with Rubio trailing at 16%, and Cruz a tardy 15%. Cruz, however, appeared set to "steal" Texas with its whopping 155 delegates. The only poll that put Rubio ahead was Minnesota at 23% of the vote. But that was a statistical three-way since Cruz got 21%, Donald 18%.

On the Democratic side, Hillary appeared in a strong position to topple Bernie Sanders, having drawn hordes of African Americans to the polls. Like Rubio, Sanders was "banking on Minnesota."

Super Tuesday produced a massive turnout for both Hillary and Donald. His victories swept across the South and New England, although Cruz carried his home state of Texas. Donald scored big in Alabama, Georgia, Tennessee, and Massachusetts, with narrow victories in Arkansas, Vermont, and Virginia. He showed he had broad appeal, even in the Evangelical Deep South and the more moderate, secular Massachusetts.

At his Mar-a-Lago estate in Palm Beach, he proclaimed, without justification, "I am a unifier. Once I knock down my rivals, I am going to go after one person: Hillary Clinton."

His strongest support came from low-income white voters, especially men and those without college degrees.

Whereas Cruz boasted of victories, not only in Texas but in Oklahoma, Rubio suffered grievous setbacks. As

predicted, Rubio limped along, scoring only in Minnesota, which is not known for deciding presidential elections.

On his home turf in Miami, the greatly weakened candidate urged voters "not to give in to the fear and anger, by listening to sham artists and con artists who try to take advantage of your suffering."

In Palm Beach, Donald trivialized that advice by tweeting, "The Little Absentee Senator has spoken."

Hillary proved that she could pull together widely diverse voters, scoring wins over Bernie Sanders in both Texas and Virginia, and showing very strong support across the Southern states. She overpowered Sanders in predominantly black and Hispanic districts of the country. She also swept Massachusetts.

In Miami, she shouted to a rally, "America never stopped being great." She won sizable victories in Arkansas, where she was once First Lady, as well as in Alabama, Georgia, and Tennessee. Sanders carried his home state of Vermont.

Hispanics helped Hillary carry Texas with 66% of the vote, as opposed to Sanders getting 33%. However, Sanders swept to victory in neighboring Oklahoma, with 53% of the vote as opposed to her 42%. Sanders also beat her in Colorado, with 58% of the vote to her 41%. As anticipated he carried Minnesota with 60% to her 40%.

Cruz won Alaska, but no one seemed to notice except Sarah Palin, its former governor. She would later desert Cruz and back Donald in the presidential race.

Charles Krauthammer reacted with: "Cruz didn't have the great night he needed to put away Rubio and to emerge as Trump's only remaining challenger."

Donald's win embittered the GOP's Old Guard, even to the point that many of them vowed to quit the party and vote for Hillary. "I signed up for the party of Lincoln, not the KKK," said Ben Sasse, Republican Senator of Nebraska.

Donald's strong showing in the South was summed up by one voter, Mark Harris, 48, of Canton, Georgia. "He's not afraid to get in the trenches and fight for you. He's going to be a bully, and he's going to tell them what he thinks, and he's going to push to get it done. He don't care who he makes mad in the process."

At Mar-a-Lago, in reference to Rubio's attempts at humor, Donald said, "Little Marco decided to become Don Rickles, but Rickles has a lot more talent."

Stunned by Trump's strong approval ratings, many Americans threatened to move to Canada or elsewhere if the bombastic billionaire were elected President.

Al Sharpton said, "I'm planning on leaving if Trump becomes President...but only because he'd probably have me deported anyhow."

Samuel L. Jackson, the Washington, D.C.-born actor, said, "If that motherfucker becomes President, I'll move my black ass to South Africa."

Columnist Leonard Greene summed it up: "Donald Trump is to racism what Chris Rock is to a monologue on Oscar night. And Chris Rock killed it. Trump is to bigotry what Stephen Curry is to a jump shot, what Adele is to a song, what guns are to the NRA."

Entertainment News:
DONALD CONTRACTS AIDS
(But Only on Film)

Writer-producer-star Sacha Baron Cohen opened *The Brothers Grimsby* in the United States, although its distributor, Sony Pictures, limited the marketing of this satiric comedy. As a plot device within its script, Donald gets AIDS in one gasp-inducing scene.

The world premiere for this film was in London, where that macabre scene was met with loud cheering from the audience. Elsewhere in Europe, at the end of that scene, there were standing ovations.

In Hollywood, Sony had protested the scene to Cohen, and wanted it removed, but he refused. Studio executives were nervous about angering the vengeful and litigious Donald.

Sacha Baron Cohen continued with his satiric range of movies with the release of his latest, *The Brothers Grimsby*. Appearing in a black thong, he announced his character in the movie as a "brand new tool."

But what brought audiences to their feet cheering was when the character playing Donald Trump contracted AIDS.

Ryan Grim, writing for *The Huffington Post*, said, "Trump, with his perfectly balanced combination of bluster, hypocrisy, and ignorance, is almost a lampoon version of the 'ugly American,' the loud, brash, U.S. tourist whom much of the world loves to hate."

IT'S ALIVE!!
Conservative Republicans React with Horror
to the Frankenstein They Created in their Hate Labs

Anti-Trump Republicans spent much of March figuring out ways to deny him the nomination, fearing he might taint the public image of their party for decades to come. They began to spend millions of dollars on attack ads in Florida, which they hoped would propel Florida's native son, Rubio, into the lead.

In reference to the ads, Hope Hicks, spokeswoman for Donald, said, "This is yet another desperate attempt by the out-of-touch Establishment élites and dark money people, who control the weak politicians, to maintain control of our broken and corrupt system."

Jeff Berkowitz, a former RNC official, said, "The best case scenario for the NEVER TRUMP backers is to throw the convention into disarray, either by ensuring that Trump does not reach the eight-state threshold so the rules have to be changed, or by changing the rules even if he does."

"In failing to confront the most divisive forces of the *[tea party]* movement, Speaker Paul Ryan may have set the party up for its current crisis," wrote reporter Jenifer Steinhauer

Donald said, "Paul Ryan, I don't know him, but I'm sure I'm going to get along great with him. And if I don't, he's going to have to pay a big price."

Ryan faced a dilemma: Whereas he wanted to remain true to the values he had spent his career promoting, he confronted a Republican frontrunner who repudiated them.

Frankenstein. IT'S ALIVE! Harry Reid, the Democratic Senator from Nevada, said, "Donald Trump is appealing to some of the darkest forces in America. It's time for Republicans to stop the Frankenstein they created in their hate lab."

A small but influential group of Republicans met together, emerging from their huddle to suggest that a third-party option might spare voters "the odious choice of Hillary or The Donald."

"I would sooner vote for Josef Stalin than I would vote for Trump," said Max Boot, a foreign policy advisor to Rubio.

Columnist Mark Cunningham claimed that the Republican Party had invited "a hostile takeover by The Donald. Ever since the Reagan years, the GOP regulars have been aiming for the Gipper's 'second coming' merely by imposing ever-stricter ideological tests. Today, the main alternatives to Trump are Ted Cruz and Marco Rubio—each a specialist in pushing one or another set of right-wing buttons."

"Cruz's best moment," Cunningham claimed, "came when he talked about trying to get his sister out of that crack house—everything else is a rehearsal performance."

Emerging from the lunar dust of his failed 2012 presidential bid, Mitt Romney made headlines again in March. He led the charge of the Old Guard in attacking Donald, whom he seemed to despise, even though Donald had supported and contributed money to his dismal campaign.

Romney claimed that a Donald nomination would "imperil the GOP. He's a fraud and a phony who would drive the country to the point of collapse. He's playing American voters for suckers. He has neither the temperament nor the judgment to be President."

One reporter, after hearing this, whispered sarcastically to a colleague, "Mitt should tell us what he really thinks."

Donald counterattacked, deriding Romney as a "failed candidate, a choke artist, and a loser for his defeat by Obama."

Then, Senator John McCain of Arizona, another failed presidential hopeful, also denounced Donald. He called him "ignorant of foreign policy who has made dangerous utterances on national security."

These warring factions, as noted by

Mitt Romney, the failed 2012 GOP candidate for President, was all smiles, but not when he vigorously attacked Donald.

In a bit of head-scratching *double entendre,* Donald zapped back with: "In 2012, he was begging for my endorsement."

"I could have said, 'Mitt, drop to your knees—and he would have.'"

columnists, were forcing the GOP to the point of rupture. In Salt Lake City, stronghold of his fellow Mormons, Romney continued his assault, claiming that Donald "embodied a brand of anger that has led other nations to the abyss."

Romney also blasted Donald for his "affairs and for lacing his speech with vulgarities. "Dishonesty is Trump's hallmark. He commits offenses—the bullying, the greed, the showing-off, the misogyny, the absurd third-grade theatrics."

In a *New York Times* editorial entitled, "The GOP's Monster in the Mirror," appeared this indictment:

"It is an excellent thing that Republican leaders have noticed the problem they've fostered, now embodied in the Trump candidacy. But until they see the need to alter the views and policies they thave promoted over the years, removing Trump will not end the party's crisis."

NEW CHAPTERS IN THE SIZE WARS
America's Fascination with Sex
"Prickly" Donald Continues to Defend the Size of His Penis
Against Assaults from "Little Marco"

On March 3, the eleventh GOP debate took place at the Fox Theater in the center of economically depressed Detroit. It was the third debate hosted by Fox News, with anchors Bret Baier, Chris Wallace, and the controversial Megyn Kelly, who had previously been denounced by Donald.

When the conservative news anchor arrived in the auditorium, a Trump supporter yelled at her, "Brought any Kotex, Megyn?" Of course that was a reference to Donald having suggested that she had been menstruating at the last debate.

This reunion of Kelly with Donald was the first since their televised feud six months before.

Body language expert Susan Constantine, said, "The body language of both Trump and Kelly was clearly adversarial. The language was loud and clear: Those two can't stand each other."

The Detroit debate was a prelude to the upcoming primaries in Maine, Kansas, Kentucky, Louisiana, Michigan, Mississippi, Idaho, and Hawaii.

Rubio and Cruz, Donald's leading competitors, were in a fight for their political lives. Behind the scenes, Rubio had announced to his aides,

"Tonight the gloves come off. It's going to be a bare-knuckled prize fight."

The following morning, the *New York Post* carried the tabloid headline—"PRICKLY DON RIPS BELOW THE BELT—SIZE MATTERS."

During the debate, Donald mounted a defense of his lower anatomy to score points against Rubio.

"I called Rubio a lightweight," Donald said. "I would like to take that back. He's really not much of a lightweight. And he referred to my hands. If they are small, something else must be small. I guarantee you, there is no problem there."

That line drew the most boisterous laughter of the evening.

Then Cruz rebuked both Rubio and Donald for bringing up such a subject. "I don't think the people of America are interested in a bunch of bickering school children."

Turning to Rubio, Donald called him, "Little Marco."

The Florida senator shot back in mocking tones, "*Big* Donald."

A reporter later wrote, "Donald defended the size of his male member before ten to twenty million of his fellow Americans. For the real truth, we need to interview perhaps 24 of his former bathing beauty contestants, get their estimated measurements before arriving at a general consensus. For example, if one beauty says 10 inches, another claims 6, we'll average that out to a studly 8 inches."

An editorial in the *New York Daily News* said, "Mark the time at approximately 9:06PM on March 3, 2016, when the dignity of the American political process expired. Trump's insinuation in a presidential debate that he is well-endowed genitally unpardonably demeaned the office he seeks and the nation he hopes to lead."

[After the debate in Detroit, since the size of Donald's penis had become the topic of a national debate, some researchers weighed in with their comments.

Although to some it reeked of "junk science," a study in 2011 by the Asian Journal of Andrology claimed that men with shorter index fingers than ring fingers were not as well endowed as men with bigger

A national landmark, the 1928 Fox Theater in downtown Detroit was selected as the venue for the eleventh Republican debate.

The anchor and namesake of a neighborhood nicknamed "Foxtown," the movie palace is the largest surviving of the great cinema showcases of the 1920s. Long before Donald mounted the stage here, the theater hosted Elvis Presley and Frank Sinatra.

index fingers. The study was carried out on patients who had been hospitalized for urological surgery. While they were sedated, scientists measured their manhoods, later reporting their findings to the world."

The Detroit debate did not consist exclusively of penile measurements. Megyn Kelly, perhaps setting herself up for a renewed menstruation attack from Donald, brought up a killer question, almost deliberately trying to provoke him once again. "I understand that your Trump University got a 'D' from the Better Business Bureau and not the 'A' you had claimed. In fact, the Attorney General of New York likened Trump U's plaintiffs in a civil case against you as 'Bernie Madoff victims."

Enraged, but controlling his temper, Donald denied her accusation but Rubio, sensing fresh blood, moved in.

"The students *[at Trump University]* signed up because they believed that Trump was this fantastic businessman who was going to teach them the tricks of the trade," Rubio said. "When they finally realized it was a scam, they asked for their money back."

Moderator Baier tried to embarrass Donald by claiming that top military brass would refuse to administer the harsh measures he demanded (i.e., water boarding and/or killing the families of terrorists) because their enforcement, despite direct orders from the President, would violate the law.

"If I say to do it, they're going to do it," Donald responded, defiantly.

He frequently interrupted his rivals, which brought a "schoolteacher rap" from Cruz. "Donald, learn not to interrupt. It's not complicated. Count to 10, Donald. Count to 10."

Under heavy fire, Donald seemed to back down from previously stated political positions. He claimed that the United States needed highly skilled people, and that he would allow such immigrants, even if Mus-

Bernard Lawrence "Bernie" Madoff (born 1938) is an American investment advisor and fraudster, the admitted organizer of the biggest financial fraud in American history. It defrauded an estimated $65 billion from thousands of investors.

In 2009, Madoff was sentenced to 150 years in prison, the maximum allowed.

Both of Madoff's sons were implicated. One was sentenced to ten years in prison, the other committed suicide by hanging.

After Madoff's arrest, the SEC (Securities and Exchange Commission) was lacerated for its lax and/or inept oversight of improprieties on Wall Street.

lim, into the country on an as-needed, case-by-case basis.

He also changed his position on assault weapons, stating that he no longer supported a ban. He refused to authorize *The New York Times* to release a recording of an off-the-record interview he gave that newspaper. During that session, it was alleged that he said he would be "flexible about an immigration policy."

"You could resolve this issue very quickly just by releasing the tapes," Cruz chided him.

"I've given my answer, Lyin' Ted," Donald snapped.

Columnist Rick Lowry noted how often GOP candidates "paid *obeisance* to Ronald Reagan. But Trump has set out to kick down the door of the House of Reagan; a structure teetering on the brink of collapse. Much more decrepit than anyone noticed. Someone just old enough to cast his first vote for Reagan in 1980 would be 54 years old today. Trump will, on occasion, reference Reagan, although all he seems to know about him is that he used to be a Democrat—just like you know who."

"HEY, MITT! KISS MY BLUEGRASS!"
Shrugging off Romney's Thunder,
Donald Grabs Kentucky and Louisiana

As the election results came in, it became increasingly obvious that Mitt Romney's venomous attacks on Donald had hardly "dented his fender" with voters. He had eked out victories in both the "Bluegrass State" of Kentucky and in Louisiana, edging out Cruz.

"If loser Mitt had devoted that same energy to winning the presidency four years ago, as he is now trying to destroy our party, he would have won the election," Donald charged. "Republicans such as him are eating their own."

Margins were close, however: Donald won Kentucky with 35.98% with Cruz trailing at 31.65%. In Louisiana, Donald got 41.4% of the vote, with Cruz behind at 37.8%

In the Midwest, Cruz scored an upset in Kansas at 48.2% of the vote, with Donald a distant second at 23.8%. "God Bless Kansas," said a jubilant Cruz, invoking God's intervention once again: "The scream you hear coming from Washington is one of utter terror at what we, the people, are doing together."

Cruz also carried Maine, with 45.9% of the vote, with Donald at 32.6% In Palm Beach, Donald cattily said, "I expected Cruz to do well in Maine.

After all, it borders Canada, his birthplace." Donald also used the occasion to attack the politicians in Washington, assailing them for their "incompetent leadership. Those eggheads—half of them can't even tie their shoes."

Hammering home his victories, Cruz urged Rubio and Kasich to drop out of the race.

More and more, "Little Marco" was living up to Donald's characterization of him as a loser. He finished a distant third in Kentucky, Kansas, and Louisiana, coming in fourth in Maine.

As shown by his wins in Louisiana and Kentucky, Trump showed that he could still mix populism and pugnacity, his appeal to the working class seemingly growing month by month.

"Our machine keeps rolling on and on to victory," he proclaimed.

From the Democratic war zones, Bernie Sanders notched a surprising win over Hillary in Kansas, a 36-point lead in the caucus there. He did better in caucuses than in primaries.

"The grumpy old man," as his enemies referred to him, also scored a 12-point victory in the caucus in Nebraska.

But it was a different story in Louisiana as voters turned out to give Hillary a stunning 47-point lead over Sanders.

"Everyone's trying to figure out how to stop Trump," Donald said at a rally in Florida.

In the wake of the latest election, many columnists wrote articles claiming "ONLY CRUZ CAN STOP TRUMP."

But the establishment faced serious reservations about their second-tier candidate, "and not because he's hideously ugly," said Janet Hope, a Republican voter in Lawrence, Kansas, trying to make up her mind which GOP candidate to back. "Trump is too narcissistic; Rubio is cute but dumb; and Kasich's candidacy is a joke."

Columnist Jonah Goldberg wrote: "Cruz's fellow senators don't like him because they don't like him. They say he's arrogant and condescending, a terrible listener and completely uninterested in actually getting anything done that doesn't further his own interests."

Goldberg concluded, "Cruz missed one

Poa pratensis is commonly known as Kentucky bluegrass. The name derives from its flower heads, which are blue when the plant is allowed to grow to its natural height of two to three feet.

When Donald swept to victory in the Kentucky primary, the fact that "bluegrass" rhymes with "ass" gave headline writers a field day.

thing: The black swan known as Donald Trump. Cruz brilliantly made his bed, and Trump leapt into it when Cruz wasn't looking."

Donald's Enemies Rip
With a Litany of
NAME-CALLING

A well-known journalist, Joe Klein, appeared on *Morning Joe,* hosted by Joe Scarborough and Mika Brzezinski. Klein claimed that Donald was "operating out of his lizard brain."

Donald's political enemies came up with a litany of unattractive names to call the candidate—"Hitler, a buffoon, a phony, a potty-mouth, pompous, narcissistic, nasty, and ignorant."

But the most vicious was to label him "a junkyard dog with rabies."

Scarborough accused him of suffering from "Trump derangement syndrome," without explaining what he meant.

Mika and Joe had been working hard, overtime. The previous evening, they had hosted an hour-long town hall meeting with Trump.

"It was a classic Trump performance filled with nastiness and ignorance," Klein claimed. "He said he opposed the Trans-Pacific trade deal because of Asian currency manipulation, apparently not knowing that China was not part of the deal. He also said that Germany and South Korea should be forced to pay for American troops protecting them, when they already do pay a share."

***

Reporters across the country set out to investigate why Donald, in spite of his well-publicized flaws, continued to gain support from a wide range of voters across America, and the answers they got were as diverse and eccentric as the American demographic itself.

Billy Fletcher, a GOP voter in New Orleans, said, "Trump is a junkyard dog, and I have no illusions about his character. But I'm 100% behind him. He goes with his gut, and I like that. Rubio is too prissy, Cruz is a lunatic, a religious nutbag. What choice is there? Hillary Clinton? You've got to be kidding!"

Longtime Republican stalwart, Peggy Noonan, wrote in her column: "We are more or less witnessing the end of the GOP as we knew it."

Among American newspapers, the *New York Daily News* remained Donald's chief editorial adversary. On March 6, it ran a column headlined, "TRUMP IS HITLER." That coincided with the assessment of Louis C.K., a standup Manhattan comedian:

"Trump is an insane bigot," the entertainer said. "He is dangerous. The guy is Hitler. Do you think the Germans in the '30s saw that shit coming? Hitler was just some hilarious and refreshing dude with a weird comb-over who would say anything at all. Hitler was hilarious until he became terrifying."

Louis C.K. wasn't the only critic equating Donald with the *Führer*. Similar opinions had been expressed by comedian Bill Mahler, as well as by Chris Christie, former New Jersey governor Christie Whitman, and Philadelphia mayor Michael Nutter.

Donald was also criticized by such luminaries as Michael Chertoff, the former secretary of homeland security. Robert Zoellick, the former deputy secretary of state, said, "There's something heartbreaking about the prospect that America's next commander-in-chief may be a global joke, a man regarded in most world capitals as a dangerous buffoon."

Columnist Nicholas Kristof wrote that Donald was "pugnacious, pugilistic, preening, and puerile," and asked for other words to describe him. He claimed that the results poured in like a deluge: "Petulant, pandering, pathetic, peevish, prickly, pernicious, patronizing, Pantagruelian, prevaricating, phony, presumptuous, potty-mouthed, provocative, pompous, predatory, and so many more, including the troubling 'probably president.'"

The popular journalist, Joe Klein, drew the comparison of Donald with a lizard brain. What did he mean?

"Lizard brain" is a common phrase for the ancient knob of reflective low-brain cells (the brain stem, cerebellum, and basal ganglia) perched atop the spinal cord. These parts handle basic body functions like breathing, balance, and coordination, and simple survival urges like feeding, mating, and defense.

These contrast with the frontal lobe of a human's brain, the seat of thought and reason.

"WE SHOULD EXECUTE THAT TRAITOR, BOWE BERGDAHL,

& Find the Whore Who Injected Poison Into Justice Scalia's Butt"

—Donald Trump

Throughout his campaign, Donald took some unscripted and alarming" detours way off the political trail. Sometimes in defiance of his handlers, he issued opinions that made headlines.

Such was the case when he called for the "execution death" of Army Sergeant Bowe Bergdahl, who had deserted his military post in Afghanistan in 2009 and was subsequently captured by the Taliban.

"Bergdahl was a traitor," Donald said. "He should be put to death. He endangered the lives of his fellow soldiers."

Attorneys for the disgraced sergeant sent a letter to Donald, requesting an interview in advance of Bergdahl's arraignment for desertion. They expressed their concern that his scathing remarks might deprive their client of a fair trial, to which he was entitled. In an attempt to contain the damage he might have caused, these lawyers were considering either deposing Donald or calling him as a witness.

The electorate's attention soon shifted to another issue. As one reporter noted, "Bergdahl was small fry when Donald found even bigger fish to fry." By then, Donald had interjected himself into the mystery surrounding the February 13 death of Antonin Scalia, the 79-year-old right-wing justice of the Supreme Court.

Rumors surfaced that the CIA had carried out his murder by hiring a $2,000-a-night hooker, who injected the judge's buttocks with the

Donald Trump wants this man dead! Bowe Bergdahl deserted his post in 2009 in Afghanistan and was held captive, caged and tortured, by the Taliban. He was released in 2014 as part of a prisoner exchange for five Taliban members.

In December of 2015, Bergdahl was ordered to face a general court-martial charge for desertion, which could impose a life sentence in prison. His trial is set for February, 2017.

poisonous contents of a syringe.

Donald claimed that he was shocked by allegations of a cover-up. "As President, I will get to the bottom of this," he promised. "I suspect that something fishy is going on about the judge's death. Let's face it: Scalia's passing is big stuff. It really affects the balance of the court."

William J. Bennett, host of *Morning in America,* a radio show, said, "Trump is the perfect man to expose any conspiracy because he's not part of the good old boys' club. These run-of-the-mill establishment politicians are all puppets owned by big money. But there's one man who isn't beholden to anyone—and that's Donald Trump."

Bennett's suggestion, widely broadcast over the media, was that Donald, as President, could get to the bottom of a possible conspiracy and expose exactly who murdered Scalia.

RABBLE-ROUSING HIS TROOPS
With Free Publicity

Instead of paying for expensive political ads, Donald—thanks to the ratings he generated—received huge amounts of free publicity, agreeing to one controversial (and unpaid) TV or radio appearance after another. On March 6, he appeared as a guest on CBS's *Face the Nation,* calling for new laws on torture.

"I think we are weak. We cannot beat ISIS. We should be at them very quickly. General George Patton would have had ISIS down in about three days. We have to beat the savages!"

He had previously called for a return to waterboarding and other tortures.

"We have to play the game by their rules if we're going to win. You're not going to win if you're soft. I think we have to change the present laws because they are not working. They're killing our soldiers when they capture them. They're laughing at us right now. I would like to strengthen the laws so that we can compete."

In the first week of March, Donald blitzed the "Rust Belt States," campaigning at stops that included Warren, Michigan, where he lamented the loss of American manufacturing jobs that caused many blue collar workers to lose their homes.

He noted that former businesses that used to produce useful products, such as brooms, had been shipped overseas, leaving the American worker stranded with no income.

He delivered speeches in factories which had been shut down in the Middle West.

His appeal was to "Reagan Democrats," who felt their former alliance with Democrats no longer protected their economic interests. "They seem more interested in promoting affirmative action and welfare aimed at minorities," said one discharged factory worker. "We are white, the forgotten class in America."

Columnist Ted Wrobleski wrote of an America infected with "Trumpocalypse," and then evoked for his readers the horror of a Trump presidency:

"What will happen if he gets elected? Rips in the space-time continuum? Seismic disturbances in the Force? Isn't this how *The Walking Dead* starts? Few presidential elections in recent memory have been this divisive this early. It's husbands against wives in some places. Brother versus sister. Kids against moms and dads. Our new Civil War approaches."

Linda Stasi, the "hot, hot" columnist, wrote, "This GOP election has devolved on the world stage into a literal, *yuuuge*, balls-out, pissing match. It has friend and foe, all alike, laughing at America and making us all look, yes, not great."

By now, "Zombie Apocalypse" is a familiar phrase and concept.

But Donald's political enemies created a new word to describe the consequences of a possible Trump presidency.

The illustration above depicts what a "Trumpocalypse" would actually mean.

Chapter Twenty-Two

BRITISH PUNDITS INSIST THAT A TRUMP PRESIDENCY WOULD LEAD TO MAJOR GLOBAL DISASTERS

DONALD REBUTS GOP ATTEMPTS

*to Designate One of their Own as a Third-Party Independent,
Threatening Violent Protests in Cleveland
if Republicans Sabotage His Nomination.*

SEXUAL POLITICS

Cruz Denies Any Association with $1,000-a-Night Hookers

*Despite Opposition, Surveys Reveal that
Millions of Americans, Especially Members of the Military,*

ADORE DONALD TRUMP

"MAKE AMERICA HATE AGAIN"

Protesters Mock Trump and His Campaign Slogans

The presidential campaign, such as it was, of Michael R. Bloomberg, three times mayor of New York, began with a whimper and ended, on March 7, with a sigh. He decided not to enter, claiming that a three-way race might lead to the election of Donald J. Trump.

He attacked Donald's "divisive and demagogic campaign," and claimed that if he were elected, it would "compromise the moral leadership of America around the world."

"As it stands now," Bloomberg said, "my candidacy could lead to the election of Trump or Ted Cruz. That is not a risk I can take in good conscience. Trump and Cruz are zealots who would weaken our unity and divide our country."

With his fellow New York billionaire out of the race, Donald could continue his onward march toward the nomination.

On March 8, a densely scheduled evening for primary elections, Donald hit two more home runs, winning both Michigan and Mississippi, where he scored his most decisive victory, wining 47% of the vote, as compared to the deeply evangelical Cruz, who won only 36%.

Cruz, however, carried Idaho with 44% to Donald's 28%.

As the East Coast went to bed, polls were still open in Hawaii.

Trump would later carry Hawaii, Obama's native state, where he had once promised an investigation into "the birther issue."

Rubio was a big loser that night.

As for the Democrats, although Sanders won with a narrow margin in Michigan, Hillary "clobbered" him in Mississippi, taking 83% of the vote. During her campaign there, she accused Sanders of orchestrating an "artful smear" by insinuating that she'd been bought by Wall Street.

After the most recent primaries, Donald set his sights on "destroying" Rubio in the eyes of his home state of Florida. "Little Marco is sweating," Donald told a rally. "It's pouring down."

At a rally in Warren, Michigan, Donald said, "Rubio is going down, and because I wanted to show off what a good athlete I am, I wanted to show with the size of my hands how I could grab him. I didn't want him to get hurt hitting his head going down."

Polls showed Donald leading by twenty points in Florida,

"You know, in Florida, they hate Little Marco so much because of the fact he never shows up to vote in the Senate. He conned the people of Florida into voting for him."

On the campaign trail after Minnesota, Rubio scored a second victory by winning the GOP primary in Puerto Rico. Popular with Hispanics there, he captured all of that troubled island's twenty-three delegates.

By now, Donald had instructed his staff to compile printouts of the barrage of attacks that appeared online and in the press about him every day. These he avidly consumed, often with his morning coffee.

Some of the editorials irritated him more than others. One particularly incendiary piece had been written by Heather MacDonald, a Thomas W. Smith fellow at the Manhattan Institute.

"Instead of engaging with his opponents' ideas, Trump invariably sneers at his rivals' appearance and launches *ad hominem* insults. Mocking the size of Marco Rubio's ears and bragging about one's sexual organ may be uproariously funny to a seven-year-old boy, but such sandbox tactics should be inconceivable for someone who aspires to the office once occupied by George Washington, Abraham Lincoln, and James Madison."

"Trump is the consummate bully, delighting in kicking people when they are down," MacDonald continued. "Long after Rick Perry and George Pataki were lifeless corpses and of no possible threat to his presidency, Trump continued to entertain audiences by gratuitously mocking Perry's eyeglasses and intelligence, belittling Pataki's political stance, and gloating about how he routed both from the race."

The GOP elite continued on their hopeless quest to stop Trump, spending some $10 million on hostile ads in the crucial state of Florida. These TV spots depicted Donald as a "liberal," a "huckster," and a "draft dodger." On military matters, he was denounced as a "poseur."

Tom Hanton, a former POW in Vietnam, claimed, "Trump would not have survived as a prisoner of war. He would probably have been the first to fold."

To fight back, on March 6, Donald unleashed a savage assault of his own, a 60-second ad denouncing Marco Rubio as "corrupt," accusing him of misusing a Republican credit card as a means of lining his own pockets.

In the ad, a narrator claimed, "As a legislator, the corrupt Marco Rubio flipped on a key vote after making a quick $200,000 deal selling his house to the mother of one of the bill's lobbyists."

The ad also accused Rubio of using the GOP's credit card "to live it up in Las Vegas," and to pave the driveway to his home.

There was more: "Rubio has spent years defrauding the people of Florida," the narrator charged. "The lightweight is a dishonest person. He's a no-show for having missed key Senate votes."

"With these ads, I am doing the people of Florida a great favor by exposing this crook," Donald claimed.

To retaliate, Rubio's forces prepared an ad attacking Donald for using profanities in his speeches to various rallies. Although the actual profanities could not be broadcast on TV, it was clear to viewers that they included "pussy," "shit," "fuck," and "mother-fucker."

The ads were timed to run before the March 15 primary in Florida, which was also the date that voters in North Carolina, Illinois, Missouri, and Ohio would go to the polls.

Publicly Rubio Expresses Remorse For
TAUNTING DONALD
Who Says, "I'm Not Politically Correct."

"UNLEASH THE GENERALS ON ISIS"

On March 10, at Coral Gables, Florida, the twelfth GOP debate, the fourth and final one for CNN, had been scheduled just before the all-important primaries in Florida, Illinois, North Carolina, Missouri, and Ohio.

Moderated by Jake Tapper, and co-sponsored by *The Washington Times*, the debate was staged at the University of Miami's BankUnited arena. Other moderators included Dana Bash, Hugh Hewitt, and Stephen Dana.

Going into the debate, both Donald and Rubio, Florida's native son, pre-

As President of the United States, Donald claimed he would destroy ISIS.

He denounced Obama for his failure to use the words "Islamic terrorists," and in his speeches, he noted the tide of young people heading to the "caliphate" in Iraq and Syria to become radicalized before returning to the United States and other Western countries.

"These recruits are some of the most dangerous and fanatical adherents to radical Islam," he claimed. "They plan to kill us!"

dicted victory in that state's primary. For Rubio, losing his home state could be the death knell of his presidential campaign.

As it turned out, it would be his final debate, as he would suspend his campaign in its aftermath. Or as one commentator said, "For Marco, it was too much, too soon. You don't just arrive in town and start running for President."

Instead of making the debate too personal, as in previous cases, Donald tried to stake out some policy positions: "We have to knock out ISIS. Get rid of it, and then come back and rebuild our country, which is falling apart. I would listen to the generals. Right now, they're not allowed to fight. We're not knocking out the oil because we don't want to create environmental pollution in the air. We used to fight to win."

He also defended his stand against Muslims. "I don't want to be politically correct. We have a serious, serious problem of hate. All across the Middle East, you have people chanting, 'Death to the US of A.' That does not sound like a friendly act to me."

The worst personal jab of the evening came from Cruz. "If you nominate Donald Trump, Hillary Clinton wins."

Most newspapers characterized this debate as low energy. Others referred to it as "surprisingly calm."

"We're all in this together," Donald said in an appeal for party unity. In spite of the moderators pressing him for more details about his policies, he demurred.

Bash pointed out that Social Security was heading toward insolvency in 22 years. Donald claimed he would keep it afloat by cutting fraud and abuse.

Then, Bash raised the point that such measures would save, at the most, only $3 billion out of an expected deficit of $147 billion. Donald then said, "I'd cut foreign aid."

Cruz chimed in, "Your solutions don't work, Donald."

After the debate, Rubio told reporters that he regretted "my schoolyard taunting of Trump." *[As witnessed by millions, he had ridiculed the brash, suntanned real estate mogul as "small-handed" (i.e., small-dicked) and made fun of his "orange face."]*

It's not something I'm proud of,"

Donald appealed to older voters, such as retirees in states ranging from Florida to Arizona.

He promised to save Social Security, in spite of warnings that the system was heading for insolvency.

Rubio told MSNBC. "If I had it to do over again, I wouldn't. If taunting is what it takes to become President of the United States, I don't want to be President."

Donald ended his appeal to Florida voters by saying, "The Republican Party has a great chance to embrace millions of people that it's never known before. We should seize the chance!"

PRO-DONALD ENDORSEMENTS
From a "Pathological" Surgeon and from the Country's Most Famous Transgendered Celebrity

Celebrity approval arrived unexpectedly from a woman who was new on the media scene.

Caitlyn Jenner (previously known as Bruce Jenner) emerged to claim, "Donald would be good on women's issues. As for Hillary, she's a fucking liar."

"Because of Donald Trump's macho attitude," Jenner continued, "some say he would not be a good candidate for women to support. Actually, I think he would be very good for women's issues. I would never vote for Hillary. If she becomes President, the country is over. She's a political hack."

On March 11, the retired neurosurgeon, Ben Carson, who had already dropped out of the race, appeared before reporters in the ballroom of Mar-a-Lago to endorse Donald.

Carson's endorsement came as a surprise. At one point in the campaign, Donald had said that the soft-spoken doctor had "the pathological temperament of a child molester."

At Mar-a-Lago that day, Carson told the press, "Donald and I have buried the

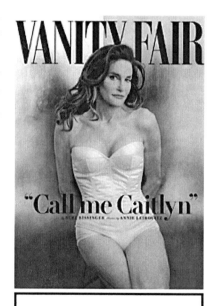

Donald entered a new frontier in the culture wars based on the use of public toilets for the transgendered.

He promised that if Caitlyn Jenner visited Trump Tower, she could use any bathroom she preferred.

hatchet."

Then he announced that he would be joining Donald on the campaign trail. "if the Republicans lose in November, we're surrendering the country to the socialists."

Later, on *Fox News*, Carson said, "There are two Donald Trumps. There's the Donald Trump that you see on television and who gets up in front of a big audience, and there's the Donald Trump behind the scenes. They're not the same person. One's very much the entertainer, and one is actually a thinking individual."

Cruz must have looked on all this with disdain, as later that day, he defined Donald's supporters "low information voters." One reporter said, "In other words, Cruz thinks Donald's fans are dummies."

Cruz, too, had an endorsement to tout, claiming that he had won the support of Utah Senator Mike Lee, the only member of that body to endorse him, since all the others, including Lindsey Graham, had no kind words to say about the Texas senator.

Around the same time, Cruz picked up yet another endorsement, this time from Carly Fiorina, who had lost her bid to become the presidential nominee. She once said, "That guy (Cruz) would say whatever he needs to get elected."

Now, she sang a different song, one in favor of the man she had previously competed against: "Cruz has fought for religious liberty and is a leader and a reformer," she said.

[Reportedly, she had detested Donald ever since he'd publicly mocked "her ugly face."]

As Donald staged and appeared at rallies across the country, some of his supporters engaged in violent confrontations with protesters.

At a rally in North Carolina, a 78-year-old man, John McGraw, sucker-

At Mar-a-Lago, the retired neurosurgeon, Dr. Ben Carson, appeared before the press to bury the hatchet.

Donald had once made odious charges against the surgeon, but now, with Carson's backing, he hoped to strengthen his position among the more right-wing conservatives and evangelists.

punched a black protester (Rakeen Jones) at a Trump rally. Whereas security then roughly removed Jones (the victim) from the arena, McGraw then calmly sat down, receiving applause and congratulations from Trump supporters.

"Next time we see him, we might have to kill him," McGraw later told *Inside Edition* in reference to Jones. "We don't know who he is. He might be a terrorist."

At another rally, Donald seemed to brazenly encourage, even solicit, a violent response from his protesters. A man rose from his seat in the auditorium and, in reference to a nearby protester, started shouting toward Donald, "I'd like to punch that one in the face myself."

In response, Donald said. "If someone punches him [*i.e., the protester*], I'll pay his legal bills if he gets into trouble."

From the podium, he spoke fondly of the "good old days when the police could rough up protesters without fear of a backlash."

These conflicts took place in Fayetteville, North Carolina, a rally that was disrupted seventeen times, mostly with shouts coming from African Americans, some of whom were handcuffed and forcibly removed from the arena.

On March 10, at a rally in Jupiter, Florida, Donald's campaign manager, Corey Lewandowski, was seen grabbing the arm of Michelle Fields, a reporter from *Breitbart News*. She had left the confines of the "corral" designated for the Press Corps, and started to advance toward Donald as he was exiting from the Trump National Club. The campaign manager grabbed her arm, bruising it, and nearly yanked her to the floor.

On March 11, Fields lodged a criminal complaint against Lewandowski. A Trump campaign aide said Fields' allegation was "entirely false. I did not witness any such encounter, and I was right there."

However, the event had been caught on video, indicating some sort of physical confrontation between the two antagonists.

Although it was widely publicized in

Anthony Cage, bloodied in front of the Peabody Opera House in St. Louis.

An activist, Cage learned the price one paid for attacking Donald's candidacy at one of his rallies.

the media, the case was later thrown out of court.

En route to an event in Chicago, Donald and his aides flew to St. Louis, where a rally turned bloody. The clashes occurred in front of the city's Peabody Opera House, leaving one man bloodied and another charged with assault. Pictures of Anthony Cage, a black activist, with his face bloodied, appeared on frontpages around the country.

Before entering the opera house, Trump supporters screamed profanities and racial slurs at the group of largely black protesters gathered outside. Inside, protesters frequently interrupted Donald's campaign speech.

He lamented that police officers were "too kind" in evicting the protesters. "These bad dudes realize there is no consequence for protesting and interrupting our free speech rally."

That night, the St. Louis Police arrested 28 people for disturbing the peace.

"These troublemakers should go home to mommy," Donald said. "They should get a job. They contribute nothing."

The following day, R&B singer Chris Brown issued a call to African Americans to travel in large numbers to Trump rallies to fend off violent attacks from Trump supporters. "Man," Brown said in a video he posted online. "This shit is getting crazy. Black people getting assaulted at fucking rallies where you're supposed to talk at. What you need to start doing? Go together—40, 50 deep. See what they do then!"

Protesters in Chicago shut down Donald's scheduled rally there when violent confrontations broke out on the sidewalks between pro-Trump and anti-Trump brigades, the latter of which was composed predominantly of Latinos and African Americans.

It soon became apparent that Chicago's battle-toughened men in blue were no match for the volatile crowds gathering at the University of Illinois.

Reporter Michelle Fields broke out of the "barrier" where the press had been assigned and headed toward Donald as he was exiting from a rally.

His campaign manager, Corey Lewandowski, perhaps fearing that she might be planning to cause the candidate harm, grabbed her arm to restrain her.

The incident, part of which was recorded on a security camera, became notorious and led to a court case in Jupiter, Florida.

Donald and his aides met with the police, and determined that for the safety of tens of thousands, it was better to cancel the rally.

One Donald supporter, Kevin Anand, said, "This is so wrong. Everyone has a right in America to speak. If you don't like Donald Trump, you don't have to vote for him. But some of us want to hear what he has to say. Why should some ugly mob shut us down in a country where free speech is supposed to be guaranteed?"

Reporters noted that the city of Chicago has been run for decades by Democrats and populated by nearly equal thirds African Americans, Latino, and whites, seemingly a volatile mixture as it pertains to any form of politics.

**

Another disturbing incident occurred on March 12, when Donald was addressing a rally in Dayton, Ohio. A protester, Thomas Dimassimo, 22, charged over a fence at the back of the outdoor stage and rushed toward Donald. Four Secret Service agents blocked his access, wrestling him to the ground.

Startled at first, Donald soon regained his composure, telling his audience, "I was ready for him," he said, flashing a double thumbs-up. "But it's much easier for the cops to do it."

Dimassimo was later revealed to be a Bernie Sanders supporter and part of the Black Lives Matter movement. He was charged with inducing panic and disorderly conduct.

Before his attempted attack on Donald, an overview of his Twitter account revealed him sticking out his tongue and tweeting "FUCK YOU, BITCH DONALD TRUMP."

Outside the rally, in Dayton, protesters held up signs that read, "IF YOU SUPPORT TRUMP YOUR DICK MUST BE SMALL." Others proclaimed: "TRUMP IS HITLER'S CHILD."

The Sunshine State Didn't Shine on
MARCO RUBIO
As Near Tears He
DROPS OUT

In Ohio, Buckeye Democrats Turn the Tide for GOP's
JOHN KASICH

On March 12, Cruz won the most delegates from the state of Wyoming. In Washington, D.C., Rubio narrowly beat Governor John Kasich before the upcoming make-or-break primaries in five large states that included their respective home states of Florida and Ohio.

RepuFjoblicans are relatively rare in the nation's capital. Their ranks consist mainly of lobbyists, attorneys, and/or Capitol Hill staffers.

In reference to Rubio's strong showing in D.C., reporter Jason Horowitz wrote, "Rubio's victory amounted to what might be the Establishment's last roar at the angry anti-Washington masses, who have dominated the electorate so far. "Rubio carried 37% of the vote with Kasich breathing down his neck at 36%." Cruz and Donald were buried in the Potomac," wrote one reporter.

Wyoming was not a priority on Donald's campaign agenda, as they had written it off from the beginning. "I'll turn over that state to Cruz and his ostrich-skinned cowboy boots," Donald said. "He'll probably look more like a city slicker than a real cowboy."

On March 13, with only two days remaining before the big GOP primaries, polls showed Donald enjoying a safe lead in Florida, but in a dead heat with Kasich in Ohio, where he remained a popular governor.

Before voting began, Kasich claimed, "I will not take the low road to the highest office in the land," an inference that Donald, Cruz, and Rubio would.

In Palm Beach, Ivana, Donald's first wife, voted for her former husband, denouncing Rubio as "a silly boy."

"He is too young, too inexperienced. Hillary just lies a lot. Donald will run the country like a business."

Though it had been about a month since Marco Rubio's defeat, he still looked depressed & mournful during this ABC interview.

Friends of the youthful candidate speculated that this son of refugees from Castro's Cuba would seek the presidency once again in 2020.

Contradicting previous statements attributed to her, Ivana said, "I have no trouble with Melania as a possible First Lady. Right now, I'm juggling three boyfriends."

In Florida's "winner-take-all" GOP presidential primary, Donald swept to victory, leaving "Little Marco to cry in his Gatorade."

Donald went on to capture the delegate lead in North Carolina and Illinois. On election night, Missouri was too close to call.

With results from Florida pouring in, Donald was declared the winner, with 46% of the vote. (Rubio received only 27%. Cruz trailed at 17%.)

In North Carolina, Donald won 40% of the vote, with Cruz in second place with 37%. In Illinois, Donald led with 39% of the vote, with Cruz at 31%.

At Mar-a-Lago, Donald told supporters, "This is a great evening. We have to bring our party together. We have something happening that actually makes the Republican Party the biggest political story in the world. Millions of people are coming out to vote."

In Florida, the country's most sought-after swing state, Donald walked off with 99 delegates.

In Ohio, thousands of Democrats crossed over to vote in the Republican primary so they could cast a vote for their popular governor. About 7% of the voters identified themselves as Democrats. A majority of those Democrats, some 53%, voted for Kasich, with 40% supporting Donald.

Corey Lewandowski, Donald's campaign manager, boasted that the Democratic defectors represented a national trend. "A lot of voters are changing their party affiliation to vote for Donald. This is a pattern we've seen in state after state. It's a good sign for Donald's campaign and a good sign for the Republican Party."

From the Democratic side of the war zone, Hillary swept to victory in primaries in Florida, North Carolina, and Ohio, bounding back from her upset loss to Bernie Sanders in Michigan.

At this point, she had netted so many more delegates than the Vermont senator that she was ahead by three times what Barack Obama had achieved at this point in the presidential race back in 2008.

We're going to win and go on winning," Donald said. "Win, win, win! Don't worry, Marco. You've got a great future. But it wasn't your time, kiddo."

Then, to the disappointment of his supporters in Miami, Rubio announced that he was bowing out of the race. "America is in the middle of a real political storm—a real *tsunami*—and we should have seen it coming. This may not have been the year for a hopeful and optimistic message."

After dropping out, Rubio blamed attack ads that had deluged voters in Florida. "I was blitzed," he claimed.

As it turned out, Donald carried Missouri, but only by the slimmest of margins, winning 40.9% of the vote, as opposed to Cruz, who garnered 40.7%.

The day after the results came in from Missouri, Donald issued a warning to the GOP elite. "There will be riots in Cleveland if I am denied the GOP nomination. I think the establishment will have problems like they've never seen before if they deny my supporters. I think bad things will happen."

House Speaker Paul Ryan criticized Donald for suggesting there might be riots in Cleveland in July, but he rejected a proposal that he, personally, should enter the race for the GOP nomination as the party's "anti-Trump alternative."

Donald's swelling roster of victories came with ominous warnings. British analysts predicted that a Trump presidency would be one of the world's ten biggest global risks. *The Economist Intelligence* unit claimed that a Trump-led government might endanger the world economy, creating chaos in America and abroad and increasing the risk of terrorism across the planet.

***

As more and more politicos perceived that Donald was successfully "locking up" the GOP's nomination in July, there was talk of who he'd pick as his vice presidential running mate.

Polls came up with suggestions: Sarah Palin, the former governor of Alaska; Joe Arpaio, at the age of 83, "America's toughest sheriff;" New Jersey's Governor Chris Christie; his campaign rival

Donald's ardent supporters recommended various "Law and Order" candidates as his vice presidential running mate.

Choices included the widely discredited Sarah Palin, who had run unsuccessfully with John McCain in 2008, and Rudy Giuliani, the former mayor of New York City.

A surprise choice was Joe Arpaio, the anti-immigrant Arizona sheriff sometimes cited as the toughest law enforcer in America. He backed Donald's call for a wall along the southern border.

Ted Cruz; and former New York City Mayor Rudy Giuliani. Rubio was conspicuously absent from the list.

As campaign tensions mounted, and Donald's enemies grew into the millions, there were death threats delivered to Trump Tower, some of them serious enough to merit investigation by the Secret Service.

As could be predicted, Donald's children also received threats. Such was the case when handwritten letters filled with white powder were delivered to the Manhattan condo of Eric Trump and his wife, Lara, on Central Park South.

Lara opened the envelope and white powder spilled onto her kitchen floor. She summoned help, and the powder was analyzed. It turned out to be lemonade mix.

The letter, signed "X," had been mailed from Massachusetts. "If your father does not drop out of the race, the next envelope will not be fake," its writer threatened.

Then the battleground shifted to a widely publicized confrontation between failed presidential candidate (and former governor of Massachusetts) Mitt Romney and Donald.

Romney announced, in a highly visible snub to Donald, that he would vote for Ted Cruz in the Utah caucus. Romney went on to urge Republicans not to vote for John Kasich, asserting that such votes would only help Donald.

Donald was quick to respond: "Failed presidential candidate, Mitt Romney, the man who 'choked' and let us all down, is now endorsing Lyin' Ted Cruz."

On that same day, *Fox News* blasted Donald for his "crude and sexist" trashing of their network's news anchor, Megyn Kelly. Donald had called for his supporters to boycott her nightly TV newscast. Donald had tweeted that Kelly was "overrated" and "sick...Her show is not worth watching," he charged.

Fox defended its anchor. In a statement, it charged that "Trump's vitriolic attacks against Megyn Kelly and his extreme sick obsession with her is beneath the dignity of a presidential candidate who wants to occupy the highest office in the land."

In Arizona, a state with 58 delegates to offer its GOP nominee, former governor Jan Brewer endorsed Donald. So did that state's infamous anti-immigrant sheriff Joe Arpaio.

Meanwhile, dozens of columnists nationwide continued to hit Donald in editorials. Linda Chavez wrote: "Donald Trump seems to believe that the way you deal with dissent is to crush it—not with compelling ideas or more reasoned speech, not with dignity in the face of foul threats, but with punches that will see the protesters 'carried out on a stretcher' as they were in the 'old days.' If he keeps predicting violence, he'll likely get it—and the results for our country will be very ugly."

Anti-Trump GOP leaders, minus the war paint, worked behind the scenes to deny him the nomination. A coven of leaders met in Washington to map out a 100-day campaign of attack ads and other means to mow him down, beginning with the April 5 primary in Wisconsin.

They also planned a delegate-by-delegate lobbying to rally anti-Trump forces in the hinterlands. Their tactics were referred to in the press as "guerilla fighting" or "desperate measures."

It was also put forward that another means of defeating Donald would involve the very risky backing of another presidential candidate to run on an Independent ticket. The former governor of Texas, Rick Perry, was evaluated as a possible candidate, as was Tom Coburn, the former senator from Oklahoma.

In an exclusive, an investigative team from the *New York Daily News* discovered that many members of the military, along with their families, living on or near military bases in the United States, overwhelmingly favored Donald's presidency.

"I love Trump," said a sailor at Camp Pendleton in California. "He's brutally honest, and I like brutal honesty." The sailor also agreed with Donald's policy to bring back torture.

In North Carolina, an Army specialist at Fort Bragg, the nation's largest military base, said, "In my profession—infantry—we're hard-ass, alpha males, get to it, get it done. That's what Donald Trump is."

Even though Donald had growing support in Arizona, and prominent endorsements, he still faced trouble at a Trump rally at Fountain Hills, a suburb of Phoenix. In a scene evocative of a showdown in the Wild West, anti-Trump protesters parked their vehicles in the middle of the rally's access route—in this case, a three-lane highway. Some of the event's more ardent participants chained themselves to their cars in an effort to thwart police officers charged with clearing the blockade. Violence erupted in the searing heat, including an episode involving a Trump supporter who knocked a protester to the ground and then stomped on his body, kicking him.

Back in Manhattan, Trump haters clashed with the police at Trump Tower after marching through Midtown with anti-Trump slogans. The most popular signs were clustered around Columbus Circle and urged protesters to FUCK TRUMP. A shoving match between screaming protesters and men in blue broke out along Central Park South. Cops responded to the refusal of protesters to back down by pepper-spraying them. After in-your-face entanglements with police officers, several of the protesters were handcuffed and arrested.

MELANIA TRUMP'S BREASTS
Who Should Be Cited as a Role Model?
Jayne Mansfield or Grace Kelly?

As Donald's candidacy began to be taken more seriously, attention focused on his wife, Melania, as a potential First Lay. Many newspapers in their Sunday Styles sections, wandered down memory lane and came up with provocative pictures of her snapped during the early years of the 21st Century. She had been photographed multiple times in outfits with plunging *décollétage* that exposed virtually all of her breasts except the nipples.

She was not afraid to show off her legs, either, in gowns whose slits practically climbed to "Mount Everest." In 2000, she had provided photographers with a "leg bomb" in a gown years before Angelina Jolie wore an equivalent garment at the Oscars.

In a separate incident, based on an outfit she wore to a gala at the Waldorf Astoria in Manhattan, *fashionistas* labeled her dress a "baby doll" as her breasts seemed ready to pop out of her shocking pink frock.

In distinct contrast, in February of 2016, voters at a GOP victory party in South Carolina were introduced to a "New Melania." She wore an Antonio Berardi bubblegum pink shift dress that didn't conceal her figure, but kept her breasts safely tucked away.

During a colder month, in Colorado, she was attired in a white and pink dress that covered her upper torso. To emphasize her revised modesty quotient, she'd draped a Christian Dior coat across her shoulders.

In years past, she'd been called "Donald's sex kitten," especially when she posed nude and alluringly positioned on a bearskin rug for the British *GQ.*

She had also posed in a *va-va-voom* Hervé Leger dress while hawking her jewelry collection on QVC.

Patsy Cisneros, a corporate image consultant, said, "All that cleavage is well and good when you're the third spouse of Donald—but not so acceptable for a presidential hopeful's wife. Melania has become more demure as his campaign's chances have gotten better."

"If Donald wins, designers will be more than eager to dress his wife," Cisneros continued. "If he's elected, there's going to be enormous visibility for designers who dress her. Everyone is going to be throwing clothes at her for her appearances."

***

On March 21, at the Verizon Center in Washington, D.C., at the annual rally of the American Israel Public Affairs Committee, one of the largest pro-Israel lobbying groups in the world, Donald promised he'd bring peace to the Middle East if he were elected President. Then, as part of his speech, he unleashed a verbal broadside against Iran.

"My number one priority is to dismantle the disastrous deal with Iran," he told the audience of 18,000 Jews. "The deal is catastrophic—for America, for Israel, and for the whole Middle East." He also denounced Iran's recent missile tests and spoke of that country's threats against Israel.

The mogul received some of his biggest cheers when he disparaged Obama. He praised Prime Minister Benjamin Netanyahu and endorsed the idea of moving the U.S. Embassy from Tel Aviv to Jerusalem.

He also told the assembly that "my daughter Ivanka is about to have a beautiful Jewish baby."

Earlier that day, he had spoken with the editorial board of *The Washington Post*, saying that the United States should cut back its funding of NATO. We certainly can't afford to do this anymore. We're spending a lot of our money protecting our so-called Allies."

The next morning, many Jewish leaders attacked Donald's speech before thousands of Jews. Rabbi Shmuel Herzfeld, leader of the oldest synagogue in Washington D.C., the Ohev Sholom congregation (aka The National Synagogue) said, "This man is wicked. He inspires racists and bigots. He encourages violence. Do not listen to him."

***

On March 27, a newspaper headlined a blessed event in the Trump clan as "HEIR TO THE HAIR IS BORN." That was its way of announcing that Ivanka, Donald's 34-year-old daughter, had given birth, with her husband Jared Kushner, to her third child.

The latest grandkid tally is now number eight for "Grandpa Donald." Ted Cruz did not send congratulations. Instead, he launched a savage

613

attack on the once-again grandfather on *Fox News*. "Donald is completely ignorant on foreign policy. He's out of his depth, not smart enough to handle America's role in foreign affairs. His presidency would be a disaster for the nation. He just doesn't understand the issues—and I do."

Or so he said.

REPUBLICAN VOTERS EVALUATE THEIR OPTIONS FOR FIRST LADY:
A Beautiful Nude? or "Screeching Harridan from Hell?"

A Super PAC, *Make America Awesome,* produced a series of Facebook ads targeting conservative Mormon voters in Utah, a state that is about 60% Mormon. The ads assumed that Mormons would be repulsed by direct access to Melania's immodest photos from GQ.

The text associated with this photo trumpeted "Meet Melania Trump, your next First Lady. Or you could support Ted Cruz on Tuesday."

Columnist Seth Mandel weighed in. "People keep saying that this election is a battle for survival for the GOP. Maybe. But if this is how the party of faith and family values fights for its life, it's dead already."

Enraged, Donald blasted back: "Lyin' Ted Cruz just used a picture of Melania from a *GQ* shot and used it in a campaign ad," Donald tweeted. "Be care-

The *New York Post*, among other Republican-leaning newspapers, thought Melania Trump would make a "model First Lady," a reference to her former life as a model who, depending on the circumstances, wasn't afraid to disrobe.

One reader wrote in that he was voting for Donald because "Melania has Lincoln Bedroom Eyes."

614

ful or I will spill the beans on your wife."

In anger, Cruz responded, "Donald, if you try to attack Heidi, you're more of a coward than I thought. Classless."

Cruz denied that he personally was responsible for the controversial ad that went out to voters across Utah.

Then, Donald's aides launched a counterattack. They ran a grotesque picture of Heidi Cruz, making her look, as described by a reporter, "like a screeching harridan from hell." The photograph was run alongside one of an elegant and serene depiction of Melania.

Heidi responded to the attack ad: "I have one job on this campaign, and it's to be helping Ted win the race," she said.

In a voice filled with rage, and an expression contorted with hatred, Cruz lashed back at Donald. "I don't get angry often, but you mess with my wife, you mess with my kids—that'll do it every time."

"Good ol' Texas boy, Ted, practically shit his pants," said a Wisconsin farmer who attended a Cruz rally.

Although Donald had not directly attacked Cruz's two daughters, a cartoon had recently depicted them as monkeys.

Donald's campaign manager, Corey Lewandowski, told the press, "This is Cruz's effort to gain attention to try and stay relevant in the race that he has lost."

A rival candidate, Ohio governor John Kasich, weighed in, calling for families of presidential candidates to be "off limits. We cannot allow these attacks on families," he said on NBC's *Meet the Press.* "There's got to be some rules, and there's got to be something that gets set there. Some decency."

Lindsey Graham appeared on NBC's *Today* show. "Hey, guys, knock it off. The world is falling apart. Man up!"

Cruz tried to toss in the final word: "Donald, real men don't attack women. Your wife is lovely, and Heidi is the love of my life."

Then an avalanche of attacks from Democrats poured in: "What in hell does Cruz mean?" asked one voter in Los Angeles. "His whole campaign was launched with attacks on Hillary. The last time I checked, she was a woman. So you attack her. That means, in your

In one of the more lurid *exposés* during the campaign for the GOP presidential nod, the *National Enquirer* ran an article charging that Ted Cruz patronized $1,000-a-night hookers.

The Cruz campaign vehemently denied the charge.

own words, you're not a real man. But I knew that all along, you bastard!"

Another tweeted, "Heidi should be attacked. What poor judgment. She married a loser like Ted Cruz. Pathetic!"

In the wake of the Melania nude photo scandal, the GOP "rat race" devolved into a true mudfight when *The National Enquirer* came out with an exposé linking Cruz to a string of hookers (aka, "a carnal quintet").

The supermarket tabloid headlined its feature story "FIVE ROMPS THAT WILL DESTROY TED CRUZ." In a two-page spread, Cruz was accused of having sustained five extramarital affairs, including one with a $1,000-a-night hooker, a teacher, and three co-workers.

"The story is bullshit," Cruz said, fighting back and blaming Donald for enlisting his so-called friends at the *Enquirer* for these startling revelations. They were especially damaging since Cruz had more or less depicted himself on the campaign trail as a "Messenger of God."

"Trump demonstrated that when he's scared, when he's losing, his first and natural resort is to go to sleaze and to go to the slime," Cruz said at another rally in Wisconsin. "And truth has nothing to do with it."

Donald denied that he was behind this "bimbo eruption" suddenly swirling around Cruz's head. The context echoed the sexual revelations associated with Bill Clinton when he was President.

One of Donald's employees at Trump Tower defended his boss, but in a very roundabout way. "If I were married to a dog like Heidi, I'd pay a hooker, too."

Cruz continued to defend himself, "I have never veered to the wrong side of the Ten Commandments. These attacks are garbage. There is no low where Donald won't go."

Instead of being confined to a supermarket tabloid, the exposé made its way not only into the campaign, but into the mainstream press. The *Enquirer* story detailed one "torrid tryst" inside a closet at a state Republican convention, and another inside the private Republican Capitol Hill Club.

Cruz continued to lament the attacks, calling them "an utter lie, a tabloid smear." He then delivered a strange statement. "Donald may be a rat, but I have no desire to copulate with him."

In a Facebook posting, Cruz wrote: "The *Enquirer* report is completely bogus and totally unnecessary. They're offensive to Heidi and me, and offensive to our daughters. Trump's consistently disgraceful behavior is beneath the office we are seeking, and we are not going to follow."

The exposé launched at least two million reactions, mostly from Cruz's many enemies. Whether it was true or not, a Washington hooker tweeted, "Ever since he reached Washington to shut down the government, Ted became known as a reliable, $1,000-a-night trick."

A former female aide who had campaigned for him in Houston tweeted, "In the Lone Star State, Cruz has long been known as the Texas horndog."

Donald's camp indulged in some "revenge porn" of their own. An aide discovered that their boss's nemesis, Megyn Kelly, had also posed for *GQ*, not nude, but wearing a short blackslip dress and red high heels. "A real hooker-like pose," an aide said.

Jennifer Weiner, author of the novel *Who Do You Love?* wrote: "The would-be first ladies (Melania and Heidi) will survive nudity and mockery, but both of them will be diminished, stripped of their personhood, and reduced to objects. They have been flattened into human baseball cards, to be rated and traded, compared and assessed, and their worth depends not on who they are or what they do, but on how good they look, and how much their husbands love them."

An informal poll in New Orleans, a late night talk show, asked listeners to call in with answers to a question: "Would you like to bed either Melania Trump or Heidi Cruz?"

The one-hundred callers, all of them male, cast every vote for Melania.

***

Ted Cruz had loudly predicted he'd win Arizona—at least until the results were announced. Donald had "scorched" Cruz under the Arizona sun, picking up 46.2% of the vote, as opposed to Cruz's paltry 22.4%.

As one Phoenix merchant said, "In Arizona, we're much smarter than Texans. They were dumb enough to vote for Cruz."

Donald garnered all fifty-eight delegates in that state's winner-take-all primary. He appealed to the voters' anger over immigrants crossing the Mexican border illegally into their state.

As for the Democrats, Hillary (with 60% of the vote) easily won over Sanders, who received only 37.1% of the vote,

***

Based partly on Mitt Romney's endorsement, Cruz was hoping for a win in Utah.

In the wake of the terrorist attack in Brussels, Cruz said, "We need to empower law enforcement to patrol and secure Muslim neighborhoods before they become radicalized."

His remark drew fire from New York City Police Commissioner Bill

617

Bratton: "Stick to running your long-shot campaign—and shut your big mouth. You don't know what in hell you're talking about."

Meanwhile, snoopers from all ends of the political spectrum were working around the clock researching embarrassments to discredit Donald. At the time, he was on the warpath against China's "unfair" advantage in trading with the United States, and was prominently promoting his promise to bring manufacturing jobs back to America.

Made in China

OH DONALD!

Say that it isn't so!

Then, a reporter made a discovery in Bloomingdale's in Manhattan that would make Donald turn orange in the face: *Gawker.com* published a photo showing stacks of boxes piled up at the store with Ivanka's footwear brand. Printed on the boxes were the words "Made in China."

Rick Wilson, a die-hard Republican, was a strategist for Rudy Giuliani's short-lived Senate campaign against Hillary. He was in a quandary when faced with a choice of Hillary or Donald.

"Hillary's foreign policy record as Secretary of State may be a disaster, stretching from China to the 'Russian reset' to Benghazi. But on these things she's merely wrong, not unhinged. She'll make a lot of wrong decisions, but they'll be wrong because of caution, calculation, and philosophy, not because of ignorance and instability. It makes a difference."

"Equally important," Wilson wrote, "Clinton will teach Trump's troll party, currently riding a high that they can tell everyone to go to hell and get away with it, a hard lesson. Furious voters' national hissy has finally given them what they want—a pure, blindly stupid avatar of their rage and dissatisfaction."

On March 23, in Palo Alto, California, at Stanford University, Hillary attacked Donald and Cruz, denouncing their reckless rhetoric. "If Trump gets his way, it will be like Christmas in the Kremlin. It will make America less safe and the world more dangerous." Then she vigorously assaulted both of them, claiming their stated goals "will alienate America's closest allies, demonize Muslims, and empower Russia."

The popular columnist Gail Collins summed up the state of affairs for the GOP. "How can things get worse for them? Jeb Bush turned out to be a terrible candidate. Marco Rubio turned out to be an annoying twit. Donald trump is a nightmare. Something had to be done, and so the solid, steady moderate elite decided that best strategy was to rally around...Ted Cruz. Welcome to worse."

Another missile aimed at the GOP was revealed in a poll released by *USA Today/Rock the Vote Poll*. It revealed that the Republican Party faced lasting damage by having lost the youth vote—52% would go to Hillary, and only 19% to Donald.

On March 23, Jeb Bush (showing no enthusiasm) endorsed Cruz, calling him a "consistent, principled conservative. For the sake of our party and country, we must overcome the divisiveness and vulgarity of Donald Trump, or we will certainly lose."

One voter, mostly in jest, asked him, "But what do you really think, Jeb?"

A disturbing poll released that same day by Monmouth University revealed that 27% of Trump's supporters would not vote for a different Republican nominee. Many claimed, "If Trump isn't the GOP nominee, we won't even bother to vote in November."

The poll positioned Donald's favorability ratio at 43%, with Cruz at 29%.

Columnist John Podhoretz weighed in on the unlikely possibility that an alternative to Donald would magically appear at the Cleveland convention:

"Cruz has yet to demonstrate that he has a national constituency. Alas for him, the movement he wanted to lead—conservative white people—had its candidate. His name is Trump. Kasich has a following of people who still cry when they listen to 'Eleanor Rigby' and its invocation of 'all the lonely people' and who want a hug because their Aunt Minnie has the shingles."

As Donald increased his wins, millions of American Muslims were said to be "watching the growing horror, fearing for their status in America."

Accordingly, many became alert to the benefits of increasing the numbers of American Muslims who voted. Muslim organizations increased their efforts to add voter registration facilities to their mosques and community centers. "The fear and apprehension in the American Muslim community has never been at this level before," said Ibrahim Hooper, a spokesman for the Council on American-Islamic Relations.

Before September 11, 2001, the majority of Muslims had voted Republican. But during the presidency of George W. Bush, they shifted more or less to the Democrats, with 70% self-defining as Democrats, 11% as Republican.

On March 26, Donald delivered his harshest attack on U.S. allies, who, he insisted "must start paying for their protection." He claimed he would boycott oil from Saudi Arabia and from other oil-producing allies unless they provided troops or funds to fight ISIS. "If Saudi Arabia was without the cloak of American protection, I don't think it would be around."

He also threatened that, if elected President, he would remove American forces from both South Korea and from Japan if they didn't pay more. "It's getting expensive defending the Free World," he said.

In a move designed to anger his campaign manager, Corey Lewandowski, Donald hired the controversial Paul Manafort to oversee the "delegate-corralling" and media strategy aspects of his race.

This New Englander was battle toughened, having worked on the campaigns of six different Presidents, including Ronald Reagan.

He was also nototious for having lobbied for shady and controversial foreign dictators, including Ferdinand Marcos of the Philippines and Jonas Savimbi, the leader of the Angolan rebel group UNITA.

"We have been disrespected, mocked, and ripped off for many, many years by people who were smarter, shrewder, and tougher," he claimed.

He also said, to the shock of many, that he would allow Japan and South Korea to develop their own nuclear programs and not depend on America to protect them from China and North Korea. "I would use nukes as a last resort."

Columnist Frank Bruni took a close look at the "Anyone But Trump" movement, especially those "holding their noses and turning to a grotesque choice: Ted Cruz."

"Attila the Hun? True, he was truculent, but what can a spirit do? Torquemada? A tad rigid, yes, but that's what righteousness sometimes looks like. Cruz has gone from the insufferable nemesis of Republican traditionalists to their last best hope. The likes of Mitt Romney, Lindsey Graham, and Jeb Bush have now given him endorsements—or approximations thereof—that will go down in political history as some of the most constipated hosannas ever rendered."

Ann Curry, the former *Today* anchor, spoke of the media-making Trump: "He is not just an instant ratings, circulation/clock clicks goldmine, he's the mother lode. He stepped up onto the presidential campaign stage precisely at the moment when the media is struggling with deep insecurities about its financial future. The truth is, the media has needed Trump like a crack addict needs a hit."

In a shrewd move, Donald hired Paul J. Manafort to lead his delegate-corralling efforts. The 66-year-old strategist was one of the most experienced in managing nomination fights. He was known for having managed the 1976 Gerald Ford convention in a showdown with Ronald Reagan.

In an about-face, Manafort had performed in a similar capacity for Reagan in 1980. He had also played a leading role in the nominations of George H.W. Bush in both 1988 and 1992.

In a Statement That Enrages Millions of Feminists, Donald Calls for Some Form of PUNISHMENT FOR WOMEN WHO ABORT

In one of the worst missteps of his presidential race, Donald offended millions with an abrasive comment about criminalizing women who submit to a legal abortion.

"If abortion were illegal," he said, "and a woman went ahead and had one, there would have to be some form of punishment." That was his answer to MSNBC's Chris Matthews after he was presented with a hypothetical question.

"I haven't determined what the punishment should be," he said. "The woman is a victim, as is the life in her womb."

The fallout was instantaneous, beginning with Cecile Richards, president of Planned Parenthood. "His stance, vile and stupid, is about controlling women."

Trump recanted his remarks hours later, after facing immediate, hostile attacks from both the GOP and Democrats.

Then he fine-tuned his original statement with another statement, "The doctor or any other person performing this illegal act upon a woman would be held legally responsible, not the woman."

"Trump's remarks would drag the country back to the days when women were forced to seek illegal procedures from unlicensed providers out of sheer desperation," said Debbie Wasserman Schultz, chairwoman of the Democratic National Committee.

Jeanne Mancini, President of the March for Life Education and Defense Fund, said, "No pro-lifer would ever want to punish a woman who has chosen abortion. We invite a woman who has gone down this route to consider paths to healing, not punishment."

Columnist Nickolas Kristof wrote: "Maybe Trump in his flip-flopping wavering about women's issues can at least remind us of a larger truth. Whatever one thinks of abortion, criminalizing it would be worse."

>> BREAKING NEWS
TRUMP TO MSNBC: "SOME FORM OF PUNISHMENT" FOR WOMEN IF ABORTION ILLEGAL

Appearing on MSNBC with TV anchor Chris Matthews, no friend of Donald's, the candidate fell into a trap.

Provocatively, Matthews asked him if abortion were made illegal, would there be some form of punishment for the mother who aborted her child?

Donald shocked millions—and not just women—when he said that there should be "some form of punishment." His casual remark caused outrage across the country.

Meanwhile, the Democrats Were Raging, Too

The remarkable Debbie Wasserman Schultz is a congresswoman from Florida and the chairperson of the Democratic National Committee. She is pro-choice, and a supporter of gun control legislation and the LGBT community.

She was the first Jewish congresswoman elected from Florida, and was the co-chair for Hillary Clinton's unsuccessful run for President in 2008.

Although she's done a remarkable job in all offices she's held, Bernie Sanders demanded that she be removed as chairperson of the Democratic National Committee, because "she unfairly favored Secretary Clinton over me."

Chapter Twenty-Three

Hothead Cruz Gets Denounced by the Former
Speaker of the House as
"LUCIFER IN THE FLESH...
A MISERABLE SON OF A BITCH"
and the NY Daily News Nicknames Him
"KING TURD" and "BEELZEBUB"

Donald Threatens to Cut Off the Flow of
BILLIONS OF DOLLARS TO MEXICO
And calls for a Massive Buildup of the U.S. Military

"NEVER TRUMP" GETS BURIED
As Donald Scores Big in the Northeast

The Daily News, NYC's Most Anti-Trump Tabloid, Devotes
EQUAL TIME TO HATING CRUZ

After Riots in California, Radical Billionaire Charles Koch,
One of the Staunchest and Most Implacable Conservatives in
the World, Denounces Donald Trump and Ted Cruz and
THREATENS TO SUPPORT HILLARY

"Donald Trump's candidacy is not only fracturing the Republican Party...it's putting more stress on more friendships than any other political development in my experience."

—Peter Wehner

April Fool's Day arrived with a dismal forecast for Donald's campaign aides. If the GOP candidate won the presidential nomination, he would be the most disliked candidate in the thirty-two years since such a poll existed. According to the *Washington Post/ABC News* poll, Donald registered a whopping 67% unfavorable rating.

Before Donald, in 1992, President George H.W. Bush had been the most disliked candidate, receiving a 57% unfavorable rating in his race against Bill Clinton.

Surveys revealed that Donald's misogyny and fear-mongering had offended or turned off millions of voters.

His unfavorability rating among women was even higher, registering 75%. Among Hispanics, some 85% claimed that they disliked him intensely, mainly because of his stance against Mexicans.

In contrast, although it was nothing to brag about, Hillary received a dismaying 52% unfavorable rating among voters-at-large.

Although she had tended to ignore Donald's attacks on her, she slammed him at a closed-to-the-press Lower East Side fund-raiser in Manhattan. Its guests included one of his worst enemies, Rosie O'Donnell, who said, "Really, I feel like we are watching an id—an id with hair," she said at the event for LGBT supporters.

"I'm hoping," Rosie continued, "that his campaign keeps going until they have insulted every American in every group in every part of the country. We could have a landslide."

Donald had previously pub-

Of the many rappers whose lyrics have been inspired by Donald Trump, none burst onto the media scene as decisively as Mac Miller, whose hit song, "Donald Trump" sold millions beginning in 2011. Donald threatened to sue him.

When Miller learned that Donald was running for President, he said, "Oh fuck! This is horrible. I have a fucking song with this dude's name and now he's being such a douchebag."

Donald's response? "Little Mac Miller is an ungrateful dog."

licly insulted here. O'Donnell took the opportunity to strike back at Donald as a loser, comparing him to the Harry Potter villain, Lord Voldemort.

Around the same time, she told the press, "I'm done with marriage." The former host of *The View* made the comment after finalizing a divorce from her second wife, Michelle Rounds.

It wasn't just the Democratic Party who wanted to stop Donald. Among the GOP, the NEVER TRUMP movement was growing daily, almost with every controversial utterance he delivered. As one editorial writer described it, "The Never Trump group is trying to sell Republicans on a dangerously reactionary senator (Cruz) as an improvement over a dangerously reactionary businessman."

The NEVER TRUMP movement organized and paid for tens of millions of dollars' worth of last-ditch negative ads. Their tenets were embraced by GOP senators and governors, as well as big money donors, political strategists, and grassroots activists.

Senator Lindsey Graham of South Carolina best expressed their dilemma: "Having to chose between Trump and Cruz is like deciding between getting shot and getting poisoned."

Columnist Michael Goodwin suggested that Donald was his own worst enemy on the campaign trail. "His suicide-by-media efforts are of a different sort. He foolishly agrees to long interviews with news organizations that already declared him unfit to be President, and gives them what they want. In his *hubris*, he provides the rope to lynch mobs."

At long last, Bob Woodward, writing in the *Washington Post*, revealed how Donald would force Mexico to pay for a border wall. He declared that if elected President, he would cut of the flow of billions of dollars in payments that immigrants sent back, through banking channels and wire transfers, to their home country.

"That would decimate the Mexican economy," he said. "My proposal would jeopardize a stream of cash that would be vital to Mexico's struggling economy."

Woodward went on to speculate that the daring (and legally horrifying) proposal would test the bounds of a President's executive power.

According to Donald, his threat would be withdrawn if Mexico made a one-time payment of $5 to $10 billion for construction of the 1,000-mile border fence.

"Nearly $25 billion was sent home by Mexicans living in the United States in 2015, mostly in the form of money transfers." Donald said, "The majority of that comes from illegal aliens."

Several columnists set out to unravel the confounding candidacy of Donald Trump. Eduardo Porter wrote: "The most solid appeal among Repulican primary voters may be what it says about the waning role of religion in American politics. His popularity is a sign that Americans are finally losing their religious spirit, following the long trend in other advanced nations. Trump is not just the least religious Republican in the field, he is perceived as less religious than Hillary Clinton."

A poll by Pew Research Center revealed that less than half of the Republican voters viewed him as religious, given his three marriages and his multiple positions on abortion.

IVANA SAYS:
"Donald is The Best Ex I Ever Had"

In a satirical, media-savvy adaptation of Marla Maples' famous remark ["Donald is the best sex I ever had"], Ivana, his first wife, told the media that he was the "best ex I ever had."

Years after her nasty divorce, she had softened her position on Donald, claiming that her "woman-loving ex would be good for America."

She gave an interview from within her opulent seven-story townhouse on Manhattan's Upper East Side, which she had purchased for about $3 million in 1998.

She also asserted her role as a political adviser to her former husband. "We speak before and after his appearances, and he asks me what I think."

"Donald is a fantastic businessman, unlike Obama, who cannot make a decision if his life depended on it."

Although once an immigrant herself, she opposed immigration. She cited an example of a pregnant Mexican girl crossing illegally into the United States. "She gives birth in an American hospital, which is free. The child automatically becomes a U.S. citizen. She then brings the whole family. She doesn't pay taxes. She doesn't have a job. She gets the free housing, she gets the food stamps. Who's paying? You and me."

In her delicate way, Ivana weighed in on the controversy about Donald's small hands.

"Speaking of hands—and other body parts—Donald does just fine in that department," she said. "If there was a problem there, Donald would not have five kids."

TRUMP GETS "CREAMED"
IN DAIRYLAND
As Evangelical Cruz Milks the Wisconsin Cow

No good news came out of Wisconsin in the days before the primary there as the state's governor, Scott Walker, endorsed Ted Cruz and right-wing radio hosts flayed Donald.

Cruz was ahead by ten percentage points in the polls, and the STOP TRUMP movement was scoring points.

One highly placed Wisconsin state senator said, "Don't get the wrong idea. We hate that Texan windbag Cruz. But we hate Trump even more. Call our voting for the Texan a marriage of convenience, about as sexually unfulfilling as a lesbian married to a gay male."

However, polls showed that Donald still had a lot of support among white working class voters.

The Wisconsin primaries had been scheduled for April 5. As anticipated, Cruz trounced Donald, getting some 48% of the vote, in contrast to Donald's 34%. Pundits defined it as a major setback for the Trump campaign.

At a victory rally in Milwaukee, Cruz told cheering supporters, "Tonight is a turning point. It's a rallying cry. We have a choice, a real choice."

Hope Hicks, Trump's spokesperson, assailed the winner as "'Lyin Ted.' He's worse than a puppet—he is a Trojan horse, being used by (Republican) party bosses attempting to steal the nomination from Mr. Trump."

On the Democratic front, Bernie Sanders scored his sixth straight victory in the nominating race.

Ted Cruz carried the primary, beating Donald in the dairylands of Wisconsin.

One local reporter wrote, "I'm not surprised. Cruz is a cowpie himself."

***

627

On his home turf, New York City, Donald was hoping to sweep to a decisive victory, but his rivals had other plans. At a rally on Long Island, he was greeted with cheers and jeers, a mixed reaction from a crowd filled with nervous unrest in a cavernous film studio peopled with many white, blue collar voters. "It's great to be home!" he said to the raucous crowd.

At this point, both Cruz and Kasich had more or less abandoned hopes for any significant wins in the five boroughs of metropolitan New York, hoping instead for gains upstate where they would meet greater numbers of conservative Republicans.

Even Cruz had enough sense to know he couldn't win New York City, since he'd made his distaste for the place known.

His campaign recognized that Cruz didn't necessarily have to beat Donald on the mogul's turf, and probably wouldn't succeed even if they tried. Instead, in game of "wait and see," Cruz and his cohorts opted to continue amassing the delegates needed to keep him from accumulating a majority of committed delegates before the Republican convention in July.

"THE MYSOGYNISTIC, HOMOPHOBIC, RACIST VULGARIAN"
(No, We're Not Talking About Donald!)
IS DEFEATED IN NEW YORK

After attacking Donald in a debate, berating him for his "New York values," the brazen Texas senator, Ted Cruz, got the Bronx cheer as his unappetizing presence arrived in a city he loathed.

He was derided for "crawling back into town seeking votes but also begging for cash."

"Ted Cruz is a hypocrite," said Ruben Diaz, Jr., the Bronx Borough President. "He not only offended New Yorkers, he offended Bronxites, and now he's here looking for money and votes."

When it was announced that Cruz would address the Bronx Lighthouse College Preparatory Academy, students threatened a boycott. In a letter, he was denounced as "misogynistic, homophobic, and racist, a man who uses vulgar language, gestures, and profanity."

In the "Battle for New York," that city's *Daily News*, the most anti-Trump newspaper in the nation, gave equal time to hating Ted. After a string of critical headlines from that publication, Cruz spoke to reporters on his way out of a Brooklyn synagogue. "It's tabloid reporting," he said. "I'm much more interested in the people of New York than what journalists think."

Oih vey! Shamelessly pandering to Jewish voters in Orthodox Brooklyn, Ted Cruz tries to make a matzo ball.

After shaking countless hands, he didn't even wash his own hands before handling the dough.

For Donald, April 7 was both a good day and a bad day. The good news involved former mayor, Rudy Giulinai, who announced that he'd vote for him.

The almost simultaneous bad news involved headlines trumpeting: "DON DROOLED FOR BABY DAUGHTER—WHAT A BOOB." It was revealed that he once commented on his one-year-old daughter, Tiffany, whom he had conceived with his second wife, Marla Maples.

In a recycled segment from a 1994 episode of *Lifestyles of the Rich and Famous,* its host, Robin Leach, asked, "Donald, what does Tiffany have of yours, and what does she have of Marla's?"

"I think that she got a lot of Marla's," Donald replied. "She is a really beautiful baby, and she's got Marla's legs. We don't know whether she's got another part yet, but time will tell." Then he had gestured toward her unformed breasts.

On April 9, hoping for a big win in the New York primaries, Donald traveled the four miles from the glitzy Trump Tower to visit Ground Zero, the memorial to 9/11 in Lower Manhattan. It was his first-ever visit to the memorial.

He was accompanied by his wife, Melania, who was attired in a tight-fitting black pants suit and high heels whose height seemed to equal that of the Trump Tower from which she had descended.

Donald racked up another first, giving $100,000 to the memorial.

After spending a half hour at the site, he left without speaking to reporters.

Although he had prepared for a sweeping victory in the New York primary, he nonetheless blasted the "corrupting" nominating system of the state's Republican Party.

On radio, Donald said, "I guarantee New Yorkers could forget about the Federal government if Cruz is nominated. I won in Louisiana, but lost the delegate race to Cruz because of the nonsense going on, real shenanigans. The system is corrupt."

His delegate wrangler, Paul Manafort, on NBC's *Meet the Press*, played the Nazi card against Cruz: "He's using Gestapo tactics to wrest the nomination from Trump."

As the New York primary neared, it was revealed that more than half of the record spending on negative advertising was aimed at candidate Donald. More than $132 million had already been spent. Of that amount, some $70 million of it had been configured with the intent of preventing Donald from getting the nomination. Three GOP Super PACS had already defined "taking Trump down," as one of their primary goals.

[In contrast to the mega-spenders, Donald would spend just over $16 million on TV ads.]

The anti-Trump PACS were helped by Hillary, who joined in the onslaught on Donald with negative ads of her own. Most of them highlighted his stances on immigration and abortion.

Medusa

Despite the negative screams, Donald's campaign rolled inexorably onward, earning him the name "Teflon Don."

On April 12, House Speaker Paul Ryan ruled himself out for a presidential bid, squashing speculation that he would emerge at a brokered convention to topple Donald. Pundits speculated that Ryan actually hoped that Donald would be the nominee—and lose—so that he could step in and grab the nomination in 2020, without having a sitting Republican President to run against.

"I will not accept the nomination of our party," Ryan said, echoing the words of Lyndon Johnson in 1968 when he bowed out of that year's presidential race.

The spectacularly non-charismatic

Days before the New York primary, Newspapers wrote about Ted Cruz's "friendemies."

Columnist Johan Goldberg said: "Like Perseus pulling Medusa's head out of a sack to petrify his enemies, Cruz has been able to dangle the prospect of a President Trump to strike fear in the hearts of even his biggest detractors."

Senate leader, Mitch McConnell, whose appearance had been likened to that of a stern Presbyterian deacon, seemed to be reconciling himself to the fact that the Texas senator might be the only one to stop Donald.

"These guys [*i.e. the Republican Establishment*] are only using Cruz to shut down Donald before they stab Cruz in the back this summer," said Erick Erickson, a right-wing talk show host.

***

To their chagrin, just as the GOP elite was thinking the unthinkable—that is, the nomination of Cruz as the Republican Party's nominee for President—the senator from Texas became the centerpiece for an avalanche of mocking headlines about "BAD VIBRATIONS."

On April 13, it was revealed that Cruz had once defended a Texas law banning the use of sex toys. As part of his struggle for state-wide fame and approval from conservative voters, he had argued that there was no constitutional right to stimulate one's genitals.

In reaction to that revelation, one provocative late-night talk show host told his listeners, "I'm sending Cruz a 12-inch dildo and telling him where to stick it."

Even Cruz's former long-ago roommate from Princeton, Craig Mazin, insisted that Cruz did not always feel that way about sex toys. Without directly saying so, the suggestion was that Cruz had used sex toys himself.

Days before citizens of New York were scheduled to vote in that state's primary, yet another poll revealed that Donald was the most unpopular candidate to run for President in some three decades, and that he was viewed unfavorably by 67% of Americans. Only David Duke, the KKK leader, beat him with an unfavorability rating of 69%.

Ted Cruz didn't win any popularity contests either, re-

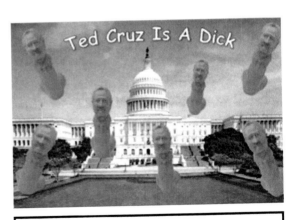

Ted Cruz always claimed that he was a strict believer in following the exact wording of the Constitution.

"At no place does this wonderful document grant citizens the right to use sex toys to stimulate one's genitals. I'm calling for a statewide ban in Texas!"

flecting a 53% unfavorable rating, despite his allegations that Jesus Christ, even God, had endorsed him.

Republicans who publicly asserted that they would vote for Donald were often inundated with hate mail. Such was the case with Craig Dunn, the Republican chairman of Howard County, Indiana.

On the air, after being asked if he would support Donald, he replied, "Only if Satan was one vote away from the nomination."

He soon found out how ardent Donald's supporters could be. Almost immediately, he was showered with hate mail, one Donald fan refering to Dunn as "the biggest traitor since Benedict Arnold."

A typical message to Dunn read, "You sorry motherfucker, I hope the worst for you and your!"

Dunn later evaluated that period of his life like this: "My life became a living hell. I received hate email to my business and political accounts. People left hateful messages on my home and my office phones."

The irony is that, as a pledged delegate from Indiana, based on the fine print of Indiana's election laws, Dunn was obligated to vote for Donald, at least on the first ballot.

***

Garry Kasparov, chairman of the New York City-based Human Rights Foundation, released an article suggesting that Donald represents the worst of a great city.

"It's tempting to rally behind him, but we should resist. Because the New York values Trump represents are the very worst kind. He exemplifies the seamy side of New York—the Ponzi schemers and the Brooklyn Bridge sellers, the gangster traders like Bernie Madoff, and the celebrity gangsters like John Gotti—not the hard work and sacrifice that built New York and America. He stands for fake values, debt instead of cash, appearance over substance, gold paint instead of the real thing."

On April 19 as New Yorkers went to the polls to place their votes in the primaries, Donald made history. The results came in a few seconds after voting ended at 9PM.

Donald had swept to victory in his home state, receiving the approval of 89 of the 95 delegates. In a surprise move, with the exception of Manhattan where he lived, he had won every county in the state. [Ironically, it was Kasich who picked up the three delegates from Manhattan.]

In vivid contrast, Cruz—either because of his attacks on the great people of a great city or because most sophisticated urbanites simply couldn't stand him—didn't win any delegates. Not even one.

In the Democratic race, Hillary knocked out Bernie Sanders. He had been born in Brooklyn, but deserted it for the wilds of Vermont. She had been born in Chicago, but ultimately selected New York State as her home address.

During his victory speech at Trump Tower, Donald sounded almost presidential. "Our jobs are being sucked out of our states," he told the faithful who had gathered to cheer.

Then the Queens-born mogul declared his love for his home state to the sound of Frank Sinatra singing "New York, New York."

[Donald had trounced "that right-wing fanatic" as Cruz was known, winning 83% of the vote. His closest competitor was John Kasich with 25%. New York-hating Cruz scored a paltry 15% Cruz supporters were denouncd as "fools" in some quarters, usually because of the candidate's widely publicized distaste for the Empire State.]

For New York, it was a historical moment. The last time the state had been home to each of the two leading presidential candidates was a face-off in 1944 between an ailing Franklin D. Roosevelt and Republican Thomas E. Dewey, who was ridiculed for looking like the tuxedo-clad groom on top of a wedding cake.

***

In the Colorado caucuses, Cruz swept to victory, capturing that state's thirteen right-wing delegates. Donald's people had had no organized national campaign in operation there, virtually giving the state to Cruz.

The losses for Donald were reported as "troubling," although some of his aides diagnosed their loss with: "Cruz appeals to the redneck West more than a city slicker like Donald."

Donald was labeled a sore loser when he complained about it to social media: "The people of Colorado had their vote taken away from them by phony politicians. This will not be allowed."

On AM970's *Cats Roundtable Radio Show*, as moderated by John Catsimatidis, a former mayoral candidate for New York City, Donald said, "This guy hates New York. He voted against appropriations for New York, for Hurricane Sandy, for other things. Now he's trying to pretend like all this stuff never happened."

CRITICS EQUATE DONALD'S BELLOW & BLUSTER SCHTICK WITH "BIGOTRY & BUFFOONERY"

But He's Cited for Allowing Jews and Blacks into Waspy Palm Beach

After his colossal sweep of the GOP primary in New York, the Trump campaign seemed at a crossroads. Whereas he had abundantly proven that he could get votes in popular elections, there now rose a crucially important issue of whether those votes would translate into approval from the Republican Party's convention delegates.

[EDITORIAL NOTE: Election by-laws vary widely state-to-state, but generally, the Republican Party, unlike the Democratic Party, allows each state to decide whether to use the winner-take-all method or the proportional method of voting in a winner in a primary election. In the winner-take-all method the candidate whom the majority of caucus participants or voters support receives all the delegates for the state.

Based on the arcane and extremely complex nature of state party election by-laws—a system that Donald repeatedly and perhaps accurately condemned as being "rigged"—the approval of delegates and their pledges of (voting) support for an individual candidate is as important (perhaps more so) than the approval of popular voters.]

Beginning in mid-to-late April, Donald began to focus not just on GOP primary voters—many of them rabidly right wing—but on convention delegates. Cruz was winning the allegiance of some of them by "clod-hopping" across such states as Wyoming.

"This is a multi-level audience play," said conservative talk show host Laura Ingraham. "Trump's message to the voter is that the system is corrupt and has to be changed, and he's the real outsider. To the delegates, he's playing a 'you-better-watch-it' game—because the people are on to you."

It had become clear that Donald was facing a pivotal moment in his quest to reside at 1600 Pennsylvania Avenue. Reporter Jonathan Martin wrote: "Installing political veterans atop his campaign, committing to an eight-figure budget, and at least trying to impose a measure of discipline on himself, Trump appears mindful that if he does not improve his performance, he risks having the nomination snapped from his grasp."

To his rage, Donald tended to be outmaneuvered at grassroots Republican events where insiders, based on arcane election statutes, seemed to delight in thwarting his advances.

"Lyin' Ted Cruz showed he was adept in these little side shows," Donald said. "Stealing delegates doesn't necessarily make him qualified to take over the government. Up to now, he had only succeeded in shutting down the government."

As the campaign went on, more and more political analysts continued to watch Donald's rise and to document his many failures. It was obvious that he was defying Washington consensus to help attract voters, thousands of whom had never supported a Republican ticket before. Yet there were ominous signs, and headlines warned that "TRUMP'S TRIAL BALLOONS CATCHING UP WITH HIM." Pundits concluded that "a style long on gut instincts is finally taking its toll."

Late in March, he had suggested that it might not be a bad idea if Japan and South Korea had nuclear arms.

President Obama ridiculed that remark, and the South Koreans and Japanese feared an arms race.

Since then, Donald had changed his tune, saying that he did not want the two American allies to actually get "the bomb."

He also backed down on other headline-generating positions, including his suggestion that women should face some sort of punishment for aborting a child. He also softened his previous statements on torture, agreeing—after a horrified reaction from the media—to respect the law as regards the interrogation of suspected terrorists.

Despite his implied retraction of a few of his earlier positions, Donald's blunt rhetoric continued to attract record-breaking crowds, as many as 25,000 at a rally in Alabama.

He was also drawing unprecedented swarms of protesters. Polls showed that 31% of Republican women claimed they'd be upset if he became the nominee. Nationwide, 73% of women viewed him unfavorably. Threats poured into Trump Tower, as a half dozen Secret Service men stood ready to protect him.

In spite of all his derogatory "fat pig" comments about women, his grip on the nomination seemed to get stronger. On March 26 he tweeted, "Nobody has more respect for women than Donald Trump."

By mid-April, in spite of dire predictions to the contrary, he had won twenty of 32 nominating races. "I'm the biggest story in politics—forget what's his name, that crazy socialist, and fat Hillary."

"Donald is a showbiz guy and reality TV star, and his talk is his *schtick*," said Christopher Ruddy, a friend. Critics called his "bellow and bluster *schtick* bigotry and buffoonery."

"People label him as racist," said one Palm Beach socialite who did not want to be named. "But he's opened up Waspy Palm Beach to the Jews. He's even friendly with the blacks."

***

Back on the campaign trail, Donald's chief rival, Ted Cruz, kept "sliming" New York again, hoping to appeal to the rural voters of Pensylvania. "Let me tell you what Trump and his media want to convince everybody: That Pennsylvania is a suburb of Manhattan. Manhattan has spoken, and Pennsylvania will follow obediantly. At least that's what Trump wants you to do."

Donald tweeted his response: "Ted Cruz is mathematically out of winning the race. Now all he can do is be a spoiler, never a nice thing to do. I will beat Hillary."

The "old" Donald Trump resurfaced at a rally at the Indiana State Fairgrounds in Indianapolis. He was back in "red meat form," attacking "Crooked Hillary" and "Lyin' Ted Cruz," whom he likened to a lion's head.

When protesters interrupted his speech, he bellowed to the guards, "Get 'em out! I love waterboarding!"

Was he suggesting that the guards subject the protesters to torture?"

***

The May issue of *Fortune* revealed that Donald's net worth is $3.72 billion, far less than the $10 billion he claims. The figure was also below the $4.5 billion cited by *Forbes* the previous October. The lower water estimate of $2.9 billion was set by *Bloomberg Politics* in May, which caused a lot of speculation about just how rich Donald really was.

In the same edition, *Fortune* ran a photo of Donald from 2008. In it, as he's talking on the phone, he's clearly "flipping the bird," a universal "fuck you" sign, to a photographer.

While on the subject of money, economists in late April released a report of what "Trumponomics" would look like, revealing that if Donald became

President, his tax cuts would benefit the very rich with an average reduction of 12% or perhaps $275,000 each. The bottom 20% of wage earners would see that tax bill reduced by "a hair under 1%." The richest of the rich, they estimated, including Donald himself, would save a staggering $1.3 million annually in taxes.

TOILETS FOR THE TRANSGENDERED
"Where," Republicans Raged, "Should Caitlyn Jenner Squat?"

All of Cruz's hopes were riding on Indiana, where he made crude jokes about new bathroom by-laws that determined where the transgendered, based on new laws in such states as North Carolina, could use only a toilet associated with the gender they were documented with at the moment of their birth.

"What's next?" Cruz lamented. "Donald dressing up like Hillary to get into the little girl's room? Not with my daughters!"

Known for changing his positions, Donald weighed in on the transgender bathroom issue, breaking from mainstream Republican rhetoric endorsed by, among others, Cruz, who was terrified that men dressed as women would invade women's toilets and assault the little girls they found inside.

In marked contrast to his Republican rivals Donald said that transgender people should be allowed to use whatever bathroom they felt comfortable in, including those at Trump Tower.

"Leave it the way it is now," he said. "There have been very few complaints, if any."

He also admitted that the Trump Organization "probably employs some transgendered."

Cruz quickly pounced on him: "Trump is no different from politically correct leftist elites. Today, he joined them in calling for grown men to be allowed to use litle girls' public restrooms."

***

It could safely be said that Donald, of all the candidates seeking the GOP nomination, was the most tolerant to members of the LGBT community, as influenced, no doubt, by his being a native of a very tolerant New York City. But as

ALL GENDER RESTROOM

Anyone can use this restroom, regardless of gender identity or expression

the campaign deepened, he leaned more to the right on the issue, no doubt to appease and placate his homophobic supporters.

Back on December 21, 2005, Donald had sent congratulations to Elton John and his lover, David Furnish, when they entered into a civil partnership in London.

"I knew both of them, and they got along wonderfully," he said. "It's a marriage thats going to work. I'm very happy for them, If two people dig each other, they dig each other."

As *The New York Times* pointed out, "Trump is far more acepting of sexual minorities than his party leaders have been."

His rivals, including Ted Cruz and especially Rick Santorum and Mike Huckabee, had made their horrified opposition to same-sex marriage widely known. Marco Rubio, too, had frequently emphasized that he opposed same-sex marriages.

As the nation's (Democratic) Vice President Joe Biden quipped: "There are still a lot of homophobes around, and most of them are running for the Republican nomination."

In 2000, Donald and Rudy Giuliani had been captured on video in a playful "gay mood" when the then-New York City mayor had dressed in drag for a skit at a political roast. Donald pretended to be turned on by "Sexy Rudy," and nuzzled his neck, getting excited at the smell of his perfume.

As late as 2011, Donald, a sophisticated urbanite, had said, "I know many, many gay people. Tremendous people."

As evidence of his tolerance, he was believed to be the first owner of a private resort in Palm Beach (in this case, Mar-a-Lago) to openly welcome a gay couple.

However, as the 2016 campaign deepened, he moved to the right on same-sex marriage, claiming that he believed that the bonds of matrimony should be confined exclusively to a man and a woman. However, he thought it should be left to the States to decide.

[Legal authorities have pointed out that if that were the case, the associated legal and personal complications would be chaotic, unclear, and overwhelming.]

***

Simultaneous with defending the "squatting rights" of Ms. Jenner, Donald took a politically incorrect position. He didn't want to see the engraving of Andrew Jackson removed from the face of the U.S. twenty-dollar bill. He went on to denounce "pure political correctness" the proposal of putting

an image of the black civil rights pioneer, Harriet Tubman, in its place.
"I don't like seeing it," he said. "She might be better off on the little-seen $2 bill."

[A former slave, abolitionist and Union spy, Tubman (died 1913) led hundreds of African Americans to freedom on the Underground Railroad. It was announced by Treasury Secretary Jacob J. Lew that Tubman's image will replace Andrew Jackson's on the bill, and that a series of other bills would likewise be revised to include images of seminal feminists and human rights activists who will eventually include Eleanor Roosevelt, Elizabeth Cady Stanton, and Susan B. Anthony.

The New York Times *described this development as "the most sweeping and historically symbolic makeover of American currency in a century."*

"DONALD KICKS TED CRUZ'S ASS OUT OF NEW ENGLAND"

On April 26, victory parties were hosted for Donald in Pennsylvaia, Maryland, Connecticut, Delaware, and Rhode Island.

Both Donald and Hillary had dominated that round of primary contests. He had swept through five eastern states. On the Democratic front, Hillary had won four. Only tiny Rhode Island, usually a bastion of liberalism with a high percentage of college-age and twenty-something voters, had allied itself with Sanders.

Donald scored the best of all the candidates, with more than thirty percentage points over his rivals, Cruz and Kasich. After the vote, Donald seemed close to his goal. To the horror of his critics, a sudden aura of invincibility shone like a halo around his orange comb-over.

Appearing before adoring hordes at Trump Tower, he said, "When a boxer knocks out the other boxer, you don't have to wait around for the decision."

Peter Wehner, a senior fellow at the Ethics and Public Policy Center, claimed, "The candidacy of Donald Trump is not only fracturing the Republican Party, it is breaking up friendships as well. His candidacy is putting more stress on more friendsips than any other political development in my experience. The dynamic is playing out in public, too. Glenn Beck and Sarah Palin, while not lifelong friends, were once close. No more."

Trying to look presidential Donald gave his first foreign policy speech, with calls for "America First. We will no longer surrender this country, or its people, to the false song of globalism."

He attacked Hillary and Obama as "reckless, rudderless, and aimless." He also called for easing tensions with China and Russia, the defeat of ISIS, and a massive buildup of the military.

***

The battle for the primary voters of Indiana and California intensified. Stopping first in Indiana, Donald renewed his attacks on Hillary, claiming, "She couldn't even get elected to a seat on a city council if she didn't play 'the woman card.'"

The next day, when challenged, he stood by his statement. "In a national election without the woman card, she would get only five percent of the vote."

It was on to California, where he hoped to solidify his quota of committed delegates so he could win on the first ballot at the upcoming GOP convention in Cleveland in July.

An angry mob broke through the steel barricades outside the Hyatt Regency Hotel in Burlingame, near the San Francisco International Airport, in an attempt to disrupt one of his rallies. Donald had to be smuggled in through the rear entrance, under heavy guard.

Outside the Hyatt, protesters threw eggs at the police and shouted obscenities, such as "FUCK TRUMP!" Some illegal aliens, fearing deportation if he became President, waved Mexican flags.

The riot at Burlingame took place the day after another rally, and an almost equivalent protest, in Orange County, near L.A. There, some twenty protesters had been arrested after clashing with the police. Cops appeared in full riot gear to control the angry mob.

In a surprise announcement, the staunchly conservative billionaire, Charles Koch, who had spent millions backing Republican candidates, faced the press. He said that he was "disgusted at the current GOP presidential races. I will not spend a

Kansas-born Charles de Ganahl Koch, owner of "Dixie Cup" and other products, is the sixth richest person in the world and a major contributor to the Republican Party.

He has expressed his disappointment in the chief rivals seeking the GOP nomination, both Ted Cruz and Donald Trump.

cent on any of the contenders—and that includes Ted Cruz and Donald Trump."

Then he threw out the shocking suggestion that in a desperate move, he might even support Hillary Clinton.

***

In Indiana, during the twilight of his failing campaign, Cruz seemed desperate. As evidence of that, he took the strange position of naming his vice presidential running mate. It was Carly Fiorina herself, a former rival and failed candidate who had previously denounced Cruz when she was running against him.

In October, she had told CNN, "There is no honor in charging up a hill that you know you can't take, only encountering casualties. Cruz is a total phony. He says one thing in Manhattan, another in Iowa. He says whatever he needs to get elected."

In Indiana, in revised circumstances, she was singing a different tune: "The Republican Party is in a struggle for the soul and future of the nation."

Donald's aides ridiculed her selection as a running mate for Ted Cruz. One of them quipped, "The former Hewlett-Packard executive began her failed administration by telling 30,000 employees, 'You're fired!' She even had to steal that line from Donald's hit TV show, *The Apprentice.*"

The most hellish attack on Cruz came not from Donald, but from John Boehner, the former (deeply frustrated and oft-humiliated) Republican Speaker of the House. Now retired and free for the first time to reveal what he really thought, he said, "Ted Cruz is Lucifer in the Flesh...I've never worked with a more miserable son of a bitch!"

This statement, widely dispersed across the nation, was delivered at Stanford University.

In contrast, the speaker said that he had a great affection for Donald. "We regularly hit the links together and are texting buddies."

Now that John Boehner is no longer the Republican Speaker of the House, he is free to speak his mind.

And so he did, ripping into Ted Cruz, "that miserable son of a bitch who was a pain in the ass and shut down our government."

Cruz shot back. Demurring with false innocence, he said: "The truth of the matter is, I don't know Boehner. I've met him only two or three times in my life."

That statement was so blatantly false that Donald said, "Now I know why I call him 'Lying Cruz.'"

Boehner's attack drew its sharpest fire from an unlikely source, the Satanic Temple. A blog site with which it's associated (the "Friendly Atheist,") posted this comment: "Cruz's failures of reason, compassion, decency, and humanity are products of the Christian faith."

[Based in NYC, with a branches in Detroit and California, The Satanic Temple is an atheistic, humanistic, and intensely political group that uses Satanic imagery to promote social justice, egalitarianism, and the separation of church and state.

The group's public statements have attacked fundamentalist Christian organizations that it believes interfere with personal freedom.

Some critics have questioned whether the Satanic Temple is a prank, a satire, or a genuine Satanic cult. Officially, at least, it does not believe in a supernatural Satan, as its associates believe that this encourages superstition that will prevent their ability to remain "malleable to the best current scientific understandings of the material world."

***

Back in Manhattan at Trump Tower, Donald met with his aides. "After the voters go to the polls in Indiana and California, the race for the nomination will be all over for Lucifer in the Flesh. The press will be on his devil's tail as he, with pitchfork in hand, races back to the Gates of Hell."

THE SATANIC TEMPLE

As reviewed by the New York Times, "*The Satanic Temple*, with only a website, some legal savvy, and a clever way with satire, this new, mostly virtual religion has become a sharp thorn in the brow of conservative Christianity."

Supporters cite its founders' most visible success as their creation of a faith-based organization that met all of George W. Bush's "White House Office of Faith-Based and Community Initiatives" criteria for receiving government funds.

Understandably, the group's criteria were repugnant to most of the conservative Christians who had to evaluate them.

In the aftermath, many legal arguments arose that rebutted the Bush Administration's sanction of public funding for conservative Christian lobbying groups.

Chapter Twenty-Four
(May, 2016)

DONALD TRUMP BECOMES THE PRESUMPTIVE REPUBLICAN NOMINEE

In the GOP's Battle Against Hillary
Donald Mocks Her for "Feeling the Bern"
From Sanders, Who Won't Give Up His Campaign

"UNHINGED, RANTING, & RAVING"

Ted Cruz is Banished to the GOP's "Elephant Graveyard"
As Trump Triumphs in Indiana

DONALD WANTS TO KNOW:

What Was Ted Cruz's Father Doing With Lee Harvey Oswald?

"Running as Trump's Veep Would Be Like Buying a Ticket on the Titanic"
—Senator Lindsey Graham

On May 1, columnist Maureen Dowd released her summary of candidate Donald: "He exudes macho, wearing his trucker hat, retweeting bimbo cracks, swearing with abandon, and bragging about the size of his manhood, his crowds, his hands, his poll margins, his bank account, his skyscrapers, his steaks, and his beautiful wall. He and his pallies, Paul Manafort and Roger Stone, seem like a latter day Rat Pack, having a gas with tomatoes, twirls, and ring-a-ding ding."

As the month began, possible GOP vice presidential running mates were falling all over themselves, fleeing from invitations to be included with Donald on the Republican ticket.

"No chance," said John Kasich. Wisconsin Governor Scott Walker was said to have expressed a viscerally negative reaction to Donald. South Carolina Governor Nikki Haley bowed out without ever having been asked, as did Senator Jeff Flake of Arizona.

"Hahahahahahahaha," wrote Sally Bradshaw, senior advisor to Jeb Bush.

Also indicating a complete lack of interest was Marco Rubio, Senator from Florida, although he's been known to change his mind.

Nonetheless, some potential candidates for the VP slot emerged. They included Chris Christie, Governor of New Jersey, and Senator Jeff Sessions of Alabama. Ben

HIDE
IF ESCAPE IS NOT POSSIBLE

Running for Cover

Fearing disastrous consequences for their political futures, many politicians who otherwise might have been considered as candidates for Donald's vice presidential running mate reportedly went into hiding.

Ducking out were such prominent politicians as Nikki Haley, Jeff Flake, Scott Walker, Marco Rubio, and most definitely, Jeb!.

Could it be Newt?

The notoriously controversial former House Speaker Newt Gingrich would have been willing to run as Donald's Veep.

"If he needs me, it would be very hard for a patriotic citizen to say no."

Carson said he might consider it.

From the beginning, most columnists had not taken Donald's candidacy seriously, claiming he'd be "buried" in early primaries by the likes of Scott Walker, Jeb Bush, and Rick Perry.

Of course, that didn't happen. Columnist Michael Walsh gave his forecast, claiming that Donald would be the GOP nominee "absent an alien invasion, the zombie apocalypse, or the sudden re-annexation of California by Mexico."

"Can he beat Hillary Clinton?" Walsh asked. "You're darn right he can."

TED CRUZ & THE INDIANA PRIMARY
Was it Custer's Last Stand? Or the Battle of the Alamo?

The fight to win the "red" [*i.e., mostly Republican*] state of Indiana suddenly became scalding hot and bitterly contentious. Cruz and Donald forgot about national issues and dug up every personal scandal that had ever been unearthed, using them as weapons in their attacks on each other.

At a rally, Cruz lambasted Donald as "an amoral narcissist and a pathological liar."

"Donald Trump is a serial philanderer and he boasts about it. I want everyone to think about your teenaged kids. The President of the United States talks about how great it is to commit adultery, how proud he is. He describes his battle with venereal disease as his own 'personal Vietnam.' That's a quote, by the way, from *The Howard Stern Show.* Do you want to spend the next five years with your kids bragging about infidelity?"

Donald immediately zapped back with slurs about "Lyin' Cruz."

MEMORIES OF CAMELOT IN CUBA
And Associations with the Murder of JFK

On May 2, the *National Enquirer* ran a frontpage exposé—"TED CRUZ FATHER LINKED TO JFK ASSASSINATION."

Rafael Cruz, now a pastor, was reported to have once been a supporter of the Cuban dictator Fidel Castro. But he fled Cuba in 1957 and later disavowed communism.

The tabloid hired photo experts to examine a photo reportedly of Rafael Cruz, which was snapped alongside JFK's assassin, Lee Harvey Oswald, in August of 1963, just months before the President was shot in Dallas. At the time, Oswald was working on behalf of a pro-Castro group, The Fair Play for Cuba Committee.

More than a half-century later, on the campaign trail in Indiana, Donald brought up the question: "What was Rafael Cruz doing with Lee Harvey Oswald?"

As voters went to the polls in Indiana, Cruz became almost unhinged, repeating, loudly, his familiar accusations: "Trump is a pathological liar. He doesn't know the difference between truth and lies. It's a pattern straight out of a psychology textbook. He accuses everyone of lying. He is utterly amoral, a narcissist at a level I don't think this country's ever seen. He's also a serial philanderer. His campaign can't run a lemonade stand."

Donald rejoined with: "Today's ridiculous outburst only proves what I've been saying for a long time. That Cruz does not have the temperament to be President of the United States. Wow, Lyin' Ted really went wacko today. Made all sorts of crazy charges. Not very presidential. Sad."

This picture was dug up of Lee Harvey Oswald, the 1963 assassin of John F. Kennedy, and Rafael Cruz, the father of candidate Ted Cruz.

Cruz's campaign denounced the photo and article as "another garbage story."

"Trump is detached from reality," Cruz charged, "and his false, cheap, and meaningless comments every day indicate his desperation to get attention and a willingness to say anything to do so."

Seizing advantage, Donald Trump, Jr. said, "That was an impressive meltdown by Cruz. Desperate but impressive. Reminded me of my three-year-old coming off a sugar high."

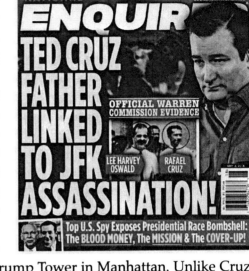

Late on election night, after 93% of the states' precincts had submitted their tallies, it was announced that Donald had won the Indiana race. He had 54% of the vote, as compared to 37% for Cruz, with Kasich trailing at a paltry 8%.

Donald addressed his supporters with a victory speech at Trump Tower in Manhattan. Unlike Cruz, he showed a certain grace in his triumph: "I don't know if Cruz likes me or if he doesn't like me, but he was one hell of a competitor...a tough, smart guy. We're going to love each other."

Veteran GOP strategist Ed Rollins had predicted, "Indiana was Cruz's last stand. There are no more back doors at the Alamo. If Trump wins, you'll see the air go out of Cruz's balloon. You'll see people jump on the Trump bandwagon."

A national poll showed Donald having a two-point lead over Hillary, 41% to her 39%.

"I will defeat Crooked Hillary," he boasted.

In Indiana, after his defeat, Cruz announced, "I'm leaving the field. We gave it everything we got. But the voters chose another path. With a heavy heart, but with boundless optimism for the long-term future of our nation, we are suspending our campaign."

Then, in an clumsy attempt to reach for and embrace his wife, he accidentally jostled her with his elbow, another graceless moment in a graceless campaign.

Meanwhile, despite his horrible turnout, Kasich's campaign claimed that their leader was "still in the running"

On the Democratic front, upstart Bernie Sanders had beaten Hillary, sweeping to victory in Indiana and promising "more victories in the weeks to come."

Our favorite columnist, Linda Stasi, released her assessment of the Indiana primary under the headline "Even God could not help Cruz." Then she labeled him "a narcissist who had the balls to call Donald the ultimate narcissist."

As for Cruz's family circle, in a style evoking that of God himself Rafael Cruz had announced to his son's followers that "Jesus personally has anointed my son."

Stasi challenged John Boehner's label for Cruz as Lucifer. "Damien the Omen, son of Satan and a jackal, yes. Lucifer, no."

The columnist then noted that Carly Fiorina, named as Cruz's Vice Presidential running mate, was a bad omen herself. Exiting from the podium after announcing Cruz as "the next President of the United States, she fell off the stage, dropping faster than Cruz's chance at the nomination."

Cruz ignored the fallen, floundering diva, conspicuously failing to come to her rescue.

Some reporters speculated that Cruz lost the basketball-loving Hoosiers when he referred to a basketball hoop as a "ring."

During his abortive campaign attempts for his son, Rafael Cruz had claimed that "gay marriage is a socialist conspiracy" and that "Obama should be forcibly returned to Kenya."

As the results of the Indiana primary came in on May 3, Donald won that state's fifty-one delegates. The Indiana win gave him a delegate count of 1,047. He needed 1,237 to win, so the Indiana victory put him within striking distance of the nomination.

As the *New York Daily News* trumpeted on its frontpage: "Dearly beloved, we are gathered here today to mourn the GOP, a once-great political party, killed by the epidemic of Trump." It pictured an elephant in a coffin under the head: "REPUBLICAN PARTY: 1854-2016."

The only moderate in the GOP race, John Kasich, Governor of Ohio, also ended his long shot quest for the presidency on May 4, after the Indiana primary. He had portrayed himself "as the only adult in the GOP primary."

He ended his bid for the Republican nomination in Columbus, Ohio. "I have faith that the Lord will show me the way forward and fulfill the purpose of my life." He had presented himself as an optimistic candidate in a gloomy race where his rivals spoke of despair, and Cruz had warned that the nation was going over an "abyss"

Kasich had carried only one state, his own, Ohio.

On May 4, the day after the Indiana primary, Kate Bradshaw wrote: "Ted Cruz, the 'adorably' unlikable teabagger the Republican establishment pushed as a viable alternative to Trump, as it held its nose, dropped out after losing the Indiana primary Tuesday night. Trump was just the sideshow in a GOP clown car stuffed to the gills with nearly 20 others, but now he's the main character."

After Trump carried Indiana, *Time* magazine's Philip Elliot asked the big question: "Does he emerge as this century's Ronald Reagan, who remakes the party's image for a generation, or as someone more akin to Barry Goldwater, who lost 44 states in 1964?"

Donald himself released a pithy opinion: "If I was presidential, only about 20% of you would be here, because it would be boring as hell."

[Apparently, he saw being unpredictable as an asset, shrewdly appreciating the rowdy nature of his rallies, where music from the Rolling Stones sometimes cranked away on the soundtrack.

In May of 2016, in a statement to Time *magazine, a spokesperson for the band said, "The Rolling Stones have never given permission to the Trump campaign to use their songs and have requested that they cease all use immediately." The spokesperson went on to say that neither Trump nor anyone from his campaign had asked for permission to use the songs.*

Rolling Stones' songs played at Trump rallies had included "You Can't Always Get What You Want," "Sympathy for the Devil" and "Brown

Mick Jagger—not the typical Republican.

Sugar."

In February, one of Trump's campaign volunteers told a reporter from The New Yorker *that Trump had personally curated the playlist.]*

On May 26, it was revealed that a survey showed that Donald had already bagged the 1,237 delegates he needed to win the GOP nod.

In a delegate count, the Associated Press reported that Donald "was over the top" with 303 delegates at stake in the June 7 primaries. He'd become the presumptive nominee of the Republican Party.

He reacted to his good fortune by chiding Hillary "who can't close the deal," a reference to her ongoing, still inconclusive race with Bernie Sanders.

***

With Donald firmly ensconced as the presumptive GOP nominee, elements from his complicated past resurfaced to haunt him. He had played a supporting role in a 1989 Bo Derek movie, *Ghosts Can't Do It,* an enigmatically suggestive title.

A box office failure, the film was widely panned by movie critics. It did, however, sweep the Razzle Awards, winning trophies for "Worst Picture," "Worst Actress," and "Worst Director" of the Year. For his role in that film, Donald won a Razzle Award as "Worst Supporting Actor."

According to *The New York Times,* the plot "involves a main character dying and becoming a ghost, and his wife drowning a young man so that the spirit of her dead husband can inhabit his earthly body and engage in carnal pleas-

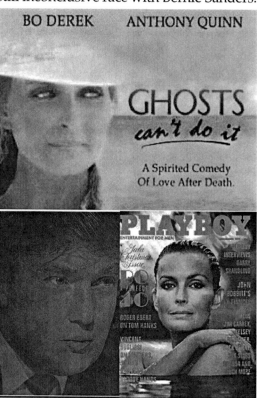

Donald Trump had a small supporting role in one of the worst films ever made, *Ghosts Can't Do It,* a so-called comedy starring Bo Derek, depicted above on the 1994 cover of *Playboy.*

As one reviewer wrote, "Trump purses his lips like a condescending sex offender. All two of his scenes are with Bo Derek, and he looks her right in the eye and vows to destroy her. In short, it's not his fault this movie sucks, but he doesn't make it any better."

ure—again—and also complete a business deal with Trump."

"*Oih vey!*" audiences said before staying away in droves.

Before Cruz bowed out of the race, he alerted his supporters that Donald had also inspired a character in *Back to the Future II*. Its screenwriter said that he based the character of "Biff Tannen" on Donald Trump—"a caricature of a braggadocious, arrogant buffoon who builds casinos with giant pictures of him wherever he looks."

HATE CRIMES INCREASE
As Donald Steps Up the Pace of His Anti-Muslim Assaults

In early May, Georgetown University's Center for Muslim-Christian Understanding documented an upsurge in violence against Muslims in the United States. The crimes dated back to the end of 2015, the year in which Donald had demanded a ban on Muslims entering the United States.

This came as no surprise to President Obama, who spoke of the "threats and harassment Muslim Americans faced."

Cited were the murders of three university students in Chapel Hill, North Carolina. "Islamophobia now has lethal effects," the report claimed. Yet GOP polling showed that a large majority of his party's primary voters endorsed the Muslim ban.

Donald came under fire from London's newly elected Muslim mayor, Sadiq Khan. Son of a Pakistani bus driver, he had promised to be "a mayor for all Londoners."

Khan told reporters that he'd vote for Hillary if he were a U.S. citizen. He also stated that "Islam is perfectly compatible with Western values," although millions would disagree with that assessment.

Then he accused Donald of "playing into the hands of extremists. He is ignorant about Islam."

Donald stuck by his ban on Muslims entering the United States, although he said that he might make an exception for Khan, based on his election as London's mayor.

Sadiq Khan, the newly elected Mayor of London, attacked Donald for threatening to bar Muslims from entering the United States.

Donald suggested he might make an exception for the Lord Mayor. But Khan responded, "I have no desire to be an exception."

651

Khan responded, "I have no desire to be an exception."

Unintimidated by his critics, Donald renewed his attack: "I think Islam hates us," he told CNN's Anderson Cooper. "There is an unbelievable hatred of us. We can't allow people coming into this country who possess this hatred of us."

Donald then told *Fox & Friends* that he might ask New York's former mayor, Rudy Giuliani, to lead a terrorism commission that would block non-citizen Muslims from entering the United States.

"MEXICAN EX-PRES LOSES HIS COJONES"
—*New York Daily News*

Vicente Fox, former President of Mexico, once emphatically stated that his country would not "pay for that fucking wall."

But on May 5, he apologized. "If I offended you, I'm sorry," he said to the presumptive GOP nominee. He even invited Donald to Mexico to see "what our country is all about. Forgiveness is one of the greatest qualities that human beings have. It is the quality of a compassionate leader. You have to love thy neighbor."

No word emerged from the Trump camp regarding a possible visit South of the Border.

In Washington, Donald celebrated *Cinco de Mayo* and showed his "love for Hispanics" by tweeting a photo of himself grinning over a *faux-Mexicano* dish while bragging about his business. At the Trump Tower Grill, he claimed that the chef made the best taco bowls around.

The following day, it was revealed that even though Donald may "love Hispanics," he'd hired an Irish chef to make the taco bowls.

In the wake of the Trump posting, hordes

Vicente Fox, proud *Mexicano*. The former president of Mexico issued a public statement that his country would not "pay for that fucking wall." But he later apologized for the expletive he had included in his remark.

That led to press attacks that Fox "has no balls" or *cojones*, as they're called South of the Border.

poured into Trump Tower to sample the taco bowl. Before that onslaught, the dish had been featured only on Thursday.

The chef, reporters discovered, was a big white guy named Chris Divine, who claimed, "I'm as Irish as they come."

At the same time that Donald was tweeting expressions of his love for Hispanics, he sent a different message to bankrupt Puerto Rico: "DROP DEAD."

The presumptive GOP nominee didn't think America should bail out the little island nation staggering toward bankruptcy. *[Technically, according to some experts, although the island territory is barred from declaring bankruptcy because of a quirk in U.S. law, the financial situation of its crushing debt was dire, indeed.]*

"They have far too much debt. Don't forget. I'm the king of debt. I love debt," he told CNN.

Despite his bluster, he offered no solutions to the island's financial predicament, which had catalyzed massive unemployment, driving hordes of islanders to the U.S. mainland, especially to central Florida.

***

By now, more and more Republicans were denouncing their presumptive nominee. On May 5, Senator Ben Sasse of Nebraska called for someone to run against both Hillary and Donald, labeling them "dishonest liberals less popular than dumpster fires." Although insisting, "I'm not the guy," he pushed for a third party option to take on Donald.

"Why shouldn't America draft an honest leader who will focus on 70% solutions for the next four years? You know...an adult."

Sasse said he didn't want to be away from his young children. Most strategists claimed that at this point in the race, a third party run was "a mere pipe dream."

John McCain, the senior U.S. Senator from Arizona who had been the GOP nominee in 2008, said he would not attend his party's convention. As justification for that radical decision, he cited his fears for his own chances at re-elec-

Looking like a "good ol redneck country boy from the wilds of Nebraska," as an Omaha reporter described him, Senator Ben Sasse didn't think either Donald or Hillary were suitable to be President of the United States.

tion: "If Donald Trump is at the top of the ticket, here in Arizona, with 30% of the vote being Hispanic, no doubt, this may be the race of my life."

On May 5, House Speaker Paul Ryan issued an extraordinary statement. The nation's highest-ranking Republican, third in line to step in as President, announced that he was "not ready" to endorse Donald. Ironically, he had already been designated as Chairman of the upcoming GOP convention in July in Cleveland, where Donald seemed likely to receive the nomination of the Republican Party.

Those who presumed to know what Ryan was thinking claimed that he viewed many of Donald's remarks as a "toxic brew."

Donald, within an hour, issued a biting rejoinder: "I am not ready to support Ryan's agenda. Perhaps in the future we can work together and come to an agreement about what is best for the American people."

On CNN, Ryan called for "a standard bearer who shares our principles."

[In modern times, a party nominee has never failed to gain the support of both the House Speaker and the Majority Leader of the Senate.]

Then, Donald issued a threat to the Speaker, warning Ryan, "You'll pay a big price if you don't support me."

"It'll be a hot time in the old town today," predicted a newscaster, in reference to the escalating tensions between Donald and key figures within the party that seemed barely able to contain him.

On May 12, Donald was flying to Washington to "woo the reluctant bride," a reference to Ryan.

Many editorial writers described Ryan's dilemma. He faced a splintering GOP with his arch-conservative politics in peril.

Complicating matters, it was speculated that Ryan had a long-term plan to run for President himself in 2020. Forecasters had suggested that during that upcoming election cycle, he might face off against either Ted Cruz and/or Marco Rubio.

Ryan might also have to face Ben Sasse, a "NEVER TRUMP" kingpin. A female staffer who works for Congress gave her opinion. "Ryan looks like that jerk in high school who begged you for a date, whereas Sasse is your

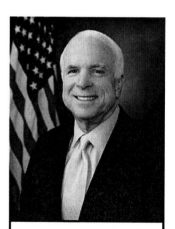

Ever since Donald attacked John McCain, claiming he was not a war hero since he'd been captured, the Arizona senator made his disdain for "The Donald" known.

The 2008 GOP nominee announced that he was going to boycott the Republican convention.

real boyfriend."

After meeting with House members in reference to the screams emanating from Republicans about what was described as the impending civil war within the Party, , Ryan said, "To pretend we're unified as a party would lead us to go into the fall at half sprint."

In response, Donald defiantly told the press, "I have no intention of reinventing myself for Mr. Ryan," and announcing that he had "a mandate" to lead the Republican Party.

Then he compared his campaign razzmatazz to the showmanship of Broadway openings and championship baseball games.

"Success begot success and it would be foolish of me to change my behavior now. A lot of voters, millions of them, want Donald Trump to be Donald Trump."

Guy Cecil, chief strategist of Priorities USA, the Super PAC supporting Hillary said, "Trump's rally rants and Twitter brawls are meant to dominate media coverage and public conversation, so that Democratic challengers have less space to break through all the noise. He doesn't want people to talk about his record or positions."

"I have been victorious in twenty-nine states, most recently in Nebraska and West Virginia," Donald said. "People are tired of trade deals that are ripping our jobs apart and taking their wages."

Did the Washington frost eventually melt between Trump and Paul Ryan?

In a chilly meeting, they confronted each other. Donald, however, did not emerge from their meeting with an endorsement. Ryan referred to Donald as "warm and gentle" (perhaps he met an imposter).

In the wake of their meeting, he told the press, "A process of reconciliation is underway." It was reported that behind closed doors, Donald had backed down on his threat to remove Ryan as Chairman of the Republican National Convention in July.

In a wishy-washy statement, Ryan said, "It is important that we discuss the principles that tie us together."

Ryan and Donald met for 45 minutes, with Reince Priebus "as their chaperone."

One aide reported, "Paul and Donald did not come to blows."

Anti-Trump protesters in Washington confronted the line of cars hauling Donald and his aides to his meeting with Ryan. Donald faced a cabal of undocumented aliens, a coven of women from the protest group Codepink, and a lone man holding a "RABBIS AGAINST TRUMP" sign. Many brandished signs asserting "ISLAMOPHOBIA IS UNAMERICAN."

***

He might have been holding his nose, but Reince Priebus, the embattled, world-weary Chairman of the Republican National Committee, then launched a defense of the GOP's most likely candidate.

Appearing on CBS's *Face the Nation,* he said: "Donald Trump has rewritten the traditional playbook of politics. And I don't know if anyone else could have pulled off what he's pulled off over the past year." He suggested that voters didn't really care about his boorish behavior toward women, or his refusal to release his tax returns.

"Voters only care that Trump will create an earthquake in the nation's capital," Priebus continued. Then he admitted that it was "a bit odd" that Trump had pretended to be a public relations rep named "John Miller" and, having adopted that as a persona, had talked about his own exploits, sexual or otherwise. "This is not a big issue with the electorate. All these stories that come out—and they come out every couple weeks…People just don't care."

Columnist Mike Lupica summed it up. "The whole world can scream about prevarication—or even past fornication—and it only makes his supporters scream louder."

Another columnist, Richard Cohen, wrote: "I have concluded that Priebus has no pride, no shame, and, almost certainly, no future. After Donald Trump loses the presidency, the name Priebus will, like Quisling, take on a separate meaning. Poor Priebus bobbed and weaved his way from TV studio to TV studio, on May 15, on a trudge of abasement, a rite of shame."

Donald later commented on his meeting with Ryan. "We talked about the success I've had. Paul said to me that he has never seen anything like it because I'm a non-politician and I beat very successful politicians. He was really fascinated by how I'd won. I said, 'It's just like I have good ideas and I've bonded with people and my people are very loyal.' They will

Throughout America, this sign appeared on various lawns of Republicans, Democrats, and independents alike.

It was a voter's way of expressing disgust at all Washington politicians, most notably Hillary Clinton and Donald Trump.

stay through thick and thin, whereas the people that support Little Marco and Lyin' Cruz wouldn't. And if Jeb sneezed, they'd leave."

"CROOKED HILLARY" VS. "DANGEROUS DON"
Pundits Predict that It Will Evolve into the Ugliest Political Race In Modern Times

In a May 7 editorial, *The New York Times* wrote: "There's ample reason to expect *Clinton vs. Trump* to be the ugliest, most cringeworthy contest of the modern era. It promises to be a half year long slog through the marital troubles, personal peccadilloes, financial ambitions, social media habits, and physical appearances of 'Dangerous Don' and 'Crooked Hillary,' two labels that the campaign and their allies are already deploying."

JFK never admitted to marital infidelity, and Bill Clinton had denied everything. But long before he ran for President, Donald, on *The Howard Stern Show* and in other interviews had admitted to "erotic escapades."

Columnist Frank Bruni wrote: "Trump isn't just any libertine. He's a retro rascal, a throwback to an era and ethic of big suits, paneled boardrooms, thick billfolds, and buxom arm candy. In the context of the pansexual, gender-fluid, Molly-popping millennials who make conservatives shudder, he's a musky whiff of nostalgia, a stubborn ember of patriarchy, a vintage stripe of a sybarite. He's promiscuity steeped in chauvinism and misogyny: More old-fashioned, and more comforting."

***

From a stage, in a swing through the Pacific Northwest during the second week of May, Donald asked a rally in Washington State if they'd noticed how much "nicer" he'd become. Then he ridiculed Senator Lindsey Graham as "a total dope who is constantly on television."

He then proceeded to trash Hillary: "She's married to a man who hurt many women. Bill Clinton was impeached for lying about what happened with a woman. Hillary treated these abused women horribly."

Danielle Allen, a political theorist at Harvard, said, "Trump wants to rumble with Hillary in a battle of the sexes because he believes that it will be losing terrain for her. This is the terrain on which the NEVER TRUMP campaigners largely fought him, and they failed."

"I look forward to debating this crooked woman politician," Donald said.

The snarling candidate also attacked "liberal darling Elizabeth Warren: She's goofy, a fraud, and weak and ineffective. I hope corrupt Hillary chooses her as a running mate. I will defeat both of them."

Warren shot back. "There's more enthusiasm for Trump among leaders of the KKK than from leaders of his own political party. You can beat a bully—not by tucking tail and running, but by holding your ground."

Columnist Maureen Dowd asked Donald about his Twitter feud with Senator Warren.

"You mean, Pocahontas?" Donald asked.

[Warren had claimed that she has Native American blood.]

DONALD AND
THE PINOCCHIO QUOTIENT
Politico Reveals a Misstatement of Facts
At Least Once Every Five Minutes, Yet Polls Reveal That
Trump Fans Seem to Universally Hate Hillary

On the campaign trail, Donald consistently accused Ted Cruz and Hillary of being liars. But *Politico* examined one week of his speeches and found that on the average, he misstated the facts at least once every five minutes.

Since his designation as the GOP nominee, polls showed him running even with his likely challenger, Hillary, who couldn't shake Bernie Sanders from her tail. A Reuters/Ipsos poll placed her at 41% among likely voters, Donald at 40%.

By now, an alarming trend had surfaced: The majority of voters didn't trust either candidate. Some polls revealed that both of them were among the most hated candidates ever to seek the presidency.

As a means of breaking this standoff, as part of a strategy cooked up from somewhere within Donald's campaign, he decided to not only attack Hillary, but to zero in on Bill Clinton's widely known charges of rape and sexual assault.

In an attack ad, what Juanita Broaddrick had alleged against Bill Clinton in 1998 (about a rape that allegedly occurred in 1978) were resuscitated.

In addition, the charges of sexual harassment from Kathleen Willey, a former White House volunteer, were also fanned back into flames. Accompanied the "news" were photos of the former President sucking on a cigar. (One of the more revolting charges aired by Monica Lewinsky was, as a result of those references to cigars, also revived.)

The pro-Trump ad asked, "Is Hillary really protecting women?"

Of all the candidates running for President, Donald was often awarded with as many as "Four Pinocchios" for his statements (and mis-statements) at various rallies.

Max Boot, senior fellow at the Council on Foreign Relations, wrote: "All politicians spin and twist facts to some extent, but Trump's lies are so epic and recurring as to put him in a whole other universe of dissembling—a place where facts are meaningless and the truth can be anything he wants it to be at that particular moment."

"Nobody in this country was worse than Bill Clinton with women," Donald charged. "He was a disaster. Hillary was a total enabler."

DONALD ENDORSES THE NRA
"Gun Nuts Back Nut"
—*New York Daily News*

On May 20 in Louisville, Kentucky, Donald warned that Hillary would be a great risk if she were elected President. "She would let violent criminals out of prison and disarm law-abiding citizens."

Then he gleefully accepted the endorsement of the notorious National Rifle Association.

Although he had not been a staunch supporter of guns in the past, he stated his new position, claiming that the November election would be a referendum on the Second Amendment.

"Crooked Hillary is the most anti-gun, anti-Second Amendment candidate ever to run for office."

In January, he had called for "ending gun-free zones in school," a position widely denounced as "extremely dangerous." Some reporters called it "time for a playground shootout."

Donald told an NRA rally that he had a permit to carry a gun. "Nobody knows that," he said, "Boy, would I surprise someone if they hit Trump," speaking of himself in the third person.

"Heartless Hillary wants to disarm America's grandmothers, leaving them defenseless against murderers and rapists."

Donald left the NRA convention after promising its members that he would repeal Obama gun controls "in the first hour that I am the President."

He also spoke of his big game-hunting sons, Donald Jr. and Eric, "who are both avid hunters and gun owners."

His sons had recently been photographed with their (dead) big game trophies in Africa within a context that evoked the bravado of super-macho Ernest Hemingway in the days prior to his suicide.

"My boys have so many rifles, so many guns, that even I get a little concerned, "Donald said.

He attacked limitations on gun control. "It will never stop an armed killer, a rapist, a genocide tyrant, or terrorist mass murderer with a rolled-up newspaper."

Right-wing NRA boss Wayne LaPierre took the occasion to "belch fire about transgender bathrooms," which in some way he viewed as a terrible threat to all those gun-toting he-men.

JERSEY BOY, CHRIS CHRISTIE
Trump's "Mister Big"

During the GOP debates, no other candidate had been as effective in attacking Hillary as Chris Christie, the governor of New Jersey. It came as no surprise on May 9 when Donald named him as director of his transition team. Headlines announced Christie as "TRUMP'S MISTER BIG," referring, of course, to the rotund governor's massive waistline.

There was speculation that this was the first step to maneuver Christie into position for a top job in Trump's post-election administration, in the event that he would win the November election.

Rumors raged that Christie might be designated as either his vice presidential running mate, or else be named as U.S. Attorney General during the formation of Trump's post-victory cabinet.

Then another potential vice-presidential candidate signaled his interest in running as Donald's VEEP.

On May 22, billionaire Mark Cuban, owner of the Dallas Mavericks, a self-described Independent, revealed that he'd be amenable to being named a vice presidential running mate to either Hillary or Donald.

"Absolutely," he told NBC's *Meet the Press*.

"I think Donald has a real chance to win, and that scares a lot of people. But what's scary about it to me is that you can see him now trying to do what he thinks is right to unify the party."

Cuban also said that he was considering a run for the White House himself one day.

Like father, not like son: Charles Kushner (left) ended up in jail. Not so his son Jared (right).

In an Orthodox Jewish ceremony, Jared married Ivanka and became the father of her three children and the son-in-law of Donald Trump.

When Jared learned that Donald was considering Chris Christie as a possible Veep running mate, he was horrified. It was Christie, then attorney general of New Jersey, who had sent Jared's father, Charles, to jail.

***

Christie's hastily defined duties involved assessing and assembling a team of experts on domestic and foreign policy, and the setup of the nucleus of a new administration to replace the one presently administering the White House.

Naming Christie to the transition team involved the Trump clan in some very awkward moments. On the same team was Jared Kushner, Ivanka's Orthodox Jewish husband, Donald's son-in-law.

A decade before, in his capacity as the U.S. Attorney in New Jersey, Christie had put Jared's father in jail. Charles Kushner had pleaded guilty to eighteen felonies after hiring a prostitute to seduce his brother-in-law as a means of blackmailing him in 2005.

At the time, Christie had attacked Kushner for his "outrageous criminal conduct" and had sought the maximum penalty behind bars.

"Oh, to be a fly on the wall when Jared and Fatso came together in the same room," said a Trump aide who didn't want to be named.

Donald, speaking of his son-in-law, said, "He's a whiz in real estate, but lately, I think he's showing more interest in politics. Perhaps one day he— and not Bernie Sanders—will be the first Jewish President of the United States. Ivanka would be the greatest of all First Ladies."

Hoping to win supporters, Donald became a political chameleon, reversing his positions on the minimum wage and higher taxes for the rich.

On November 10, 2015, on the Fox Business debate, he'd said: "Taxes are too high, wages too high. We're not going to be able to compete against the world. I hate to say it, but we have to leave it the way it is."

But on May 8, 2016, on *Meet the Press*, he said: "I don't know how people make it on $7.25 an hour. I would like to see an increase of some magnitude. But I'd rather leave it to the states."

In September of 2015, he outlined his tax plan. "Highest tax bracket would be reduced from 39.5% to 25%. Americans will get a simpler tax code with four brackets: 0%, 10%, 20%, or 25% instead of the current seven."

But also on May 8, speaking to *This Week*, he said, "I am willing to pay more, and you know what? The wealthy are willing to pay more."

As a means of addressing Donald's wavering policies on amending the tax code and coping with the deficit, on May 22, Maya MacGuineas, president of the Committee for a Responsible Federal Budget, released an editorial with some alarming statistics:

"Donald Trump has promised to pay off the debt in eight years. That would require $28 trillion in savings over ten years. He has also promised to balance the budget, which would require a still hefty $8 trillion in savings. There's a big problem with these promises: His plans to date would cost—not save—$12 trillion. His plans so far are utterly unworkable. There is no painless way to get rid of our debt."

[The United States' debt stands currently at 75% of the GDP. That is the highest it's been at any other time other than World War II. The debt, experts agree, is expected to grow to just under 86% of the GDP by 2026, exceeding the size of the entire American economy within the next 20 years.]

ENRAGING GREENPEACE
Donald Denies Climate Change and
Trivializes the Environment

In a May 24 frontpage exposé, the *New York Daily News* ran a story headlined "EARTH, WIND, & LIAR"

"Trump plays GOP for suckers—calls climate change bullshit, then submits plans for a wall to protect his golf course in Ireland from global warming," the paper claimed.

Previously, Donald had defined climate change as "a con job, or else a fiendish plot by the Chinese."

But in Ireland, it was announced that he wanted to build a two-mile-long seawall at his golf resort to keep out rising tides. Rising sea levels caused by climate change had unleashed storms that had battered the Irish coast where sat Trump International Golf Links and Hotel in County Clare. Resort officials had said that the beach had been disappearing at the rate of about three feet a year because of rising waters.

***

Hoping to arouse passions in chilly North Dakota, Donald flew into Bismarck, the heart of that region of the country's oil and gas boom. At a rally, he called for "more fossil fuel drilling and few environmental regulations."

He also vowed to cancel the Paris Climate Change Agreement, which committed nearly every nation to curb climate change.

He also vowed to rescind Obama's signature climate change rules and revive construction of the Keystone XL pipeline, which would bring petroleum from Canada's oil sands to the refineries of Texas and Louisiana's Gulf Coast.

In another switch, Donald turned to the very reluctant Republican Party to raise money for the upcoming fall election. Up to now, or so he claimed, he had spent $40 million of his own money on the primaries, although that was much disputed.

He claimed that he would need $1.5 billion as a war chest for the electoral battles to come. For that bundle, he would need fat-cat GOP donors—"no more self-financing."

Many of the major-league donors who had financed Mitt Romney's 2012 run privately told associates, "We're sitting this one out."

MAKING UP IS HARD TO DO
In a Tepid Resolution of Their Feud,
Megyn Goes Soft On Donald

During a broadcast on May 17, Fox's TV anchor, Megyn Kelly, and Donald tried to make up...sort of. Some reporters called it "a lovefest," but it really wasn't. Body image experts claimed that both of them artfully concealed it, but they obviously held each other in contempt.

The interview was her first sitdown with Donald since the now notorious August GOP debate, when she had grilled him about "vile remarks he'd made about women." The May 17 interview itself was too tepid to generate many headlines.

Donald still insisted that her original question was unfair. "I was caught off guard because I'd never actually debated before. I don't really blame you because you're doing your thing, but from my standpoint, I don't have to like it."

She pressed him about any regrets he might have had.

"I could have done certain things differently...I could have maybe used different language in a couple of instances. If I hadn't fought back in the way I fought back, I don't think I would have been successful," he said.

In a statement not confirmed, it was reported that after leaving the interview, Donald said, "I think Kelly is just using me to gain more exposure. With my friend Barbara Walters retiring, Kelly's trying to become the next Barbara Walters."

For the most part, Kelly got bad reviews, including an attack from Jennifer Rubin, writing for the *Washington Post*. "She wasn't newsy. It was the sort of gauzy, non-confrontational and unrevealing celebrity interview. In essence, she conceded that Trump had won in her feud with him. Kelly now risks becoming yet another chess piece in Trump's game of intimidation."

REPUBLICANS COALESCE AROUND DONALD
*But Popularity Polls Rank Lice and Dumpster Fires
Ahead of Both Candidates*

Hillary wasn't the only one firing at Donald. During a commencement address at Rutgers University, Obama labeled many of his plans "just plain stupid," decrying the anti-intellectual tone coming from his Republican enemies. "Ignorance is not a virtue. It's not cool not to know what you're talking about."

From the 50,000 people in the audience, Obama drew raucous applause when he said, "Building walls won't change the world, which is more interconnected than before. When you hear someone longing for the good old days, take it with a grain of salt."

He was referring to the time when homosexuals were subject to arrest for being gay, and when civil rights were denied to African Americans, and when women, for the most part, were confined to the kitchen.

In another development, the always outspoken congressman, Long Island's Peter King, wanted to break up the "bromance" between Donald and Vladimir Putin.

On CBS's *Face the Nation*, King publicly begged Donald to end his infatuation with the Russian dictator. "I'm supporting Trump, but I still have real questions with him as far as national security is concerned."

Facing the inevitability of a Trump nomination in July, many very conservative Republicans, both individuals and groups, were slowly coming around to lend their support. When faced with a choice of Donald or Hillary, many adamantly supported Donald all the way.

As Penny Nance, President of Concerned Women for America put it, "Trump is not my first choice. He's not my second choice. But any concerns I have about him pale in contrast to Hillary Clinton."

Privately, many Republicans, not going on record, said, "I would prefer the Bitch of Buchenwald to Hillary Clinton," naming the Nazi matron of horror who made lampshades out of human skin.

More and more, GOP members were starting to coalesce around their presumptive nominee. However, many qualified their support, saying they did not agree with all of his positions, such as gay rights and abortion rights.

Perhaps the most bizarre poll ever taken, a real eye-popper—revealed that Americans would choose lice over having Trump as President. In popularity rankings, he ranked along with such stomach churners as root canals, traffic jams, and jury duty. In a Public Policy polling survey, voters had a higher opinion of used car salesmen.

Donald's unfavorable rating stood at a whopping 61%. However, the news wasn't all bad for him. He won out over hemorrhoids.

Those who still had a favorable view of Donald went 65% for the theory that Obama was a Muslim. Only 7% agreed that Bible-thumping Rafael Cruz (Ted's father) had been involved in the assassination of JFK. One of the four voters with favorable views of Donald held the view that Supreme Court Justice Antonin Scalia had been murdered.

Occasionally, amid the whirlpool of publicity generated by Donald, Ivana occasionally spoke her mind.

As the mother of three of his children *[Donald Jr., Ivanka, and Eric]*, she said, "The campaign is very hard for them because they all have families," she told the Fashion Institute of Technology. "Don Jr. has five kids and a wife; and he has to be on the campaign trail. Ivanka has three kids. She just gave birth to another baby. And Eric has a wife. It's very, very stressful for them, because they have to follow Donald and support him."

Ivana said she didn't know about Donald's grandchildren, whose ages ranged from eight months to eight years. "They are very young, they understand their grandfather is very important and wants to make a difference, but I am not sure what they think otherwise."

***

Donald's campaign and his missteps made him vulnerable to satire, as columnists devoted oceans of ink to mocking him.

Thomas L. Friedman wrote: "OK, it's easy to pick on his foreign policy. But just because he recently referred to the attack on the World Trade Center as happening on 7/11—which is a convenience store—instead of 9/11, and just because he held 'a major event' in Russia two or three years ago—The Miss Universe contest, which was a 'big, big, incredible event'—doesn't make him unqualified. I'm sure you can learn a lot schmoozing with Miss Argentina. You can also learn a lot eating at the International House of Pancakes. Perhaps he never understood Arab politics until he ate hummus—or was it Hamas?"

***

In May, despite increased pressure, and despite having boasted that he paid "the lowest possible tax rate," Donald steadfastly continued to refuse to release his tax returns.

On *Good Morning America*, he promised to release his tax returns after they were audited. "You'll learn very little from my returns," he claimed. He told ABC host George Stephanopoulos "My taxes are none of your business. You'll see it when I release them."

If he doesn't release his returns, he will be the first presidential nominee in a half-century who refused to do so. Ted Cruz claimed, "He won't release his returns because they will reveal his business dealings with the Mob."

As May moved on, the attacks on Donald continued. *The Wall Street Journal*, in an exposé, claimed that despite Donald's claim of being worth $10 billion, he didn't have enough liquid assets to self-finance the fall election. The paper wrote, "His pretax income in 2016 is likely to be about $160 million."

A spokesperson for Trump denied the *WSJ's* assessment. "It did not take into account cash held by Trump properties."

***

Near the end of May, Donald was on the campaign trail in California. He told a raucous and wildly cheering crowd in Fresno that "I can't stand to hear Hillary screaming into the microphone."

Once again, the police had to escort hecklers from the auditorium. Outside, protesters clashed with Trump loyalists.

"Hillary is a disaster," he told the partisan audience. "She has bad judgment. That was said by Bernie Sanders. He's given me some of my best lines. Crazy Bernie charged that she wasn't qualified to be President. Do you think Hillary looks presidential?"

The crowd responded by roaring its disapproval of her.

***

During the course of May, speculation briefly focused on "the debate that never happened,"despite many headlines that trumpeted: "TRUMP'S 'BERNING' DESIRE TO DEBATE."

Trump demanded that the networks shell out as much as $15 million for charity before he'd agree to a showdown with Bernie Sanders.

"Bernie and I would get high ratings in a big arena somewhere," Donald said. "And we could have a lot of fun."

"We are ready to debate Trump, and I hope he doesn't chicken out," said Sanders spokesman Jeff Weaver.

Hillary was skeptical, publicly doubting whether "The Donald" and "Giveaway Bernie" would ever confront one another in a one-on-one debate.

As it happened, the lady was right.

But even though the energy behind the "non debate" fizzled out, Donald relentlessly egged Sanders on, daring him to run as an independent.

"Of course he'd say that," Hillary responded. "I think Ted Cruz should run as a third-party candidate, Marco Rubio as a fourth-party candidate, and John Kasich as a fifth-party candidate."

The Trump camp was in a jubilant mood as a fourth national survey, conducted by the *Washington Post* and *NBC/Wall Street Journal*, positioned Trump at 43% and Hillary at 46%, respectively The numbers revealed on 11% surge toward Donald since the results of the previous survey had been announced in March.

In contrast, polls continued to show that many Americans (57%) seemed to dislike both candidates with equally intense fervor.

The same polls showed Bernie Sanders trouncing Donald 54% to 39%.

Perhaps Sanders summed up the dilemma with the greatest precision. As he stated during an interview with *ABC News Sunday*, "We need a campaign, an election coming up, which does not have two candidates who are really very, very strongly disliked."

Chapter Twenty-Five
June and early July, 2016

"HILLARY CLINTON MAY BE THE MOST CORRUPT PERSON EVER TO RUN FOR PRESIDENT"
—Donald Trump

DONALD FIRES HIS CAMPAIGN MANAGER
Ivanka Tells Dad "It's Him (Corey Lewandowski) or Me!"

AN ASSASSINATION ATTEMPT
On Donald Is Blocked By Policeman

June got off to a bad start for Donald Trump, as the lawsuit against his Trump University entered another phase. Judge Gonzalo P. Curiel of the United District Court ordered that documents related to the case be unsealed. That led to unwelcome headlines, some calling the school "SCREW U." Others announced "HOW 'SCHOOL' SOLD TRUMP SNAKE OIL."

The presidential candidate was fighting a California lawsuit in which his school venture was charged with misleading thousands of students who paid up to $35,000 for seminars to learn about his real estate investment strategies.

Documents unsealed revealed that one enticement "script coercion" read: "Do you enjoy seeing everyone else but yourself in their dream house and driving their cars with huge checking accounts? Those people saw an opportunity and didn't make excuses, like what you're doing now."

At a rally on May 27 in San Diego, Donald had attacked the case's presiding judge. "I have a judge who is a hater of Donald Trump. He was appointed by Barack Obama, and I believe he is a Mexican."

The son of Mexican parents, Curiel had been born in Indiana, making him an American citizen.

Legal scholars claimed that by impugning the honesty of the judge in a pending case, Donald could be held for contempt of court.

The promoters of Trump U. told customers that they should "max out" their credit cards to pay the high tuition fees.

The California lawsuit added to Donald's legal woes. At the time, he was also being sued for issues associated with Trump University in New York. That state's Attorney General, Eric Schneiderman, had filed a $40 million suit against Donald in 2013, alleging that the billionaire swindled more that 5,000 students through his school.

For a brief time, Gonzalo P. Curiel became the most controversial judge in America.

Donald Trump accused him of a "conflict of interest" presiding over a Trump University Class Action Lawsuit because of his Mexican heritage.

He was born in Indiana to Mexican immigrants.

In one of the documents, instructors were told how to deal with students who complain about the cost of "tuition." Remind them that Trump is the BEST!" the document instructs.

The controversial for-profit university had been shuttered since 2010. In the ensuing months and at other rallies, Donald continued to attack Curiel, bringing up his "Mexican heritage."

In court testimony, former Trump U managers testified that the business school relied on high pressure sales tactics, hired unqualified instructors, made deceptive "get-rich quick claims, and exploited vulnerable students of varying ages." One struggling couple was urged to charge $35,000 on credit cards, even though it would endanger their economic future.

The "University" had been established in 2005, with Donald owning 93 percent of it.

His lawyers fought back, claiming that complaints were emanating from only a small number of former students. "The vast majority of pupils gave us positive reviews," Donald claimed.

At the time of the Trump U documents release, Donald, during the final days of May, unleased a vitriolic attack on the media, who had been "pestering me with

Gary Johnson President 2016

A native of North Dakota, Gary Johnson is the Libertarian Party nominee for President in the 2016 election.

Starting as a door-to-door handyman, he developed a multi-million-dollar construction firm.

He became the fiscally conservative Governor of New Mexico in 1994 where he was known as "Governor Veto."

JILL STEIN GREEN PARTY

Born in Chicago to Russian Jewish parents, Jill Stein is the 2016 nominee of the Green Party for President of the United States, having sought that same office in 2012.

A medical doctor, she is an activist for clean energy, health care, and local green economies. In her articles she calls for "Healthy People, Healthy Planet." Stein has also developed multiple musical albums with co-star Ken Selcer in the folk-rock band "Somebody's Sister."

questions about veterans. He called an ABC reporter "a sleaze."

In January, in a feud with Fox, he opted to boycott the GOP debate, which had led to lower ratings for the network. In lieu of attending the debate, he participated in a competing event, a televised fund-raiser nearby, where he announced that he had raised more than $6 million (a sum that included, he said, a personal donation of $1 million) for veterans.

After an investigation, the *Washington Post* reported that he had not made the charitable donation. To show that he had, he produced a photocopy of a check he'd written. It was suggested by many reporters that Donald had been "forced to make the belated donation" after his failure to do so had been exposed in the press.

***

In early June, it was revealed that two minor third and fourth-party candidates might tip the outcome of the incredibly close election. They included Jill Stein, who was running as the Green Party candidate; and former New Mexico governor, Gary Johnson, the Libertarian hopeful.

The question undecided was if the involvement of either or both candidates would benefit Donald or Hillary. Johnson was running with another governor, William Weld of Massachusetts. Donald attacked Johnson's running mate, suggesting that "he hits the bottle."

***

Speaking at a Democratic rally in San Diego, Hillary approached the podium with guns blazing, all of them aimed at Donald. She claimed that electing him President would be a "historic mistake." She charged that he was "hopelessly unprepared and temperamentally unfit to be commander-in-chief."

"He is a reckless, childish, and uninformed amateur, who has played at the game of global stagecraft. This is not someone who should ever have the nuclear codes. It's not hard to imagine Donald Trump leading us into a war just because somebody got under his thin skin."

He was sending nasty tweets about her even as she spoke. "Bad performance by Crooked Hillary Clinton," he tweeted. "She doesn't even look presidential. A terrible performance...pathetic."

Columnist Paul Krugman ridiculed Donald on the same day that Hillary attacked him: "No doubt Trump hates environmental protection in part for the usual reasons. But there's an extra layer of venom to his pro-pollution stances that is both personal and mind-bogglingly petty. He has repeatedly denounced restrictions intended to protect the ozone layer because he claims they're the reason his hair spray doesn't work as well as it used to. The Republicans are rallying around this rich guy who worries about his hairdo."

Around this time, Donald was in California, addressing a rally in San Jose that turned violent. As Trump supporters filed into the auditorium, some were pelted with eggs and attacked with heavy objects. Victims showed off their gashes before photographers. Water balloons were thrown, as steel barriers were toppled. Cops in riot gear prevented a full scale attack.

On CBS's *Face the Nation*, Donald admitted that he not only would consider a Mexican judge prejudiced against him, but he also feared bias if the judge were Muslim. He claimed that Judge Curiel should recuse himself from the Trump University case.

Even fellow Republicans, such as the usually friendly Newt Gingrich, claimed that Donald's comments about judges "is one of his worst mistakes yet."

Speaker Paul Ryan said, "I completely disagree with Trump's comments about Curiel."

Mitch McConnell said, "Trump should be working on unifying the party, not on settling scores and grudges."

One lawyer, who did not want to be named, said, "Donald is right. What is all this protest? Of course, judges are some of the most biased people in America—take Clarence Thomas, for instance. Some judges in the South have made their intolerance for homosexuals or African Americans all too obvious."

Even though he'd just attacked Donald for his comments about the Mexican judge, news leaked out on June 3 that Ryan had finally came around and endorsed Donald, although seemingly with great reluctance. "I feel confident that he would help us turn the ideas in our agenda into laws. He would help other people's lives. That's why I'm voting for him this fall."

Ryan said that "Trump's Mexican judge rant is the definition of racist, but I still support him."

HILLARY MAKES HISTORY
Just as her GOP Rival Faces Headlines Labeling Him as "Deadbeat Don"

Monday, June 6, was a date that will live in American history. Hillary Clinton became the first woman to capture the presidential nomination of a major political party.

After a bruising fight with Bernie Sanders, who was still refusing to abandon the race, she appeared on the brink of an unprecedented moment.

She clenched the Democratic nomination with the support of hundreds of super-delegates. The Associated Press was the first to declare that she had reached the golden number of 2,383 needed to secure the nomination. Advisers to Sanders took a dim view of the AP tally.

At a rally in Brooklyn, Hillary appeared before her most ardent supporters. "Tonight caps an amazing journey—a long, long journey. We all owe so much to those who came before and tonight belongs to all of us." Her victory came nearly a century after women won the right to vote nationwide.

Until now, Obama had remained on the sidelines in the Democratic race between Sanders and Hillary. Now, in a move to unite the two warring factions of the Democratic Party, he came out and emphatically endorsed her. In contrast to Sanders' venomous campaign assaults upon her, Obama said, "I don't think there's ever been someone as qualified to hold the office. She's got the courage, the compassion, and the heart to get the job done."

During some closed-door meetings in the Oval Office, Obama presumably tried to channel Sanders' forceful energy into uniting—not dividing—the Democratic Party.

Perhaps he urged him to "cool it with his attacks on Hillary," in the heat of which he'd claimed she was not qualified to be President.

While Hillary, during her moment of triumph, was in her glory, Donald became the focus of negative headlines, including one which read "DEADBEAT DON STIFFED US."

A report listed hundreds of instances in which people working for the Trump organization did not get paid or else were "shortchanged or stiffed" from previously agreed-on wages or fees. It was reported that Donald's organization had violated the Fair Labor Act two dozen times at the Trump Plaza Casino in Atlantic City, based on its failure to pay minimum wage or overtime.

Included among the shortchanged were hundreds of workers, real estate brokers, bartenders, waiters, and other employees, many of them deeply resentful.

Within a climate permeated with bad publicity for Donald and good publicity for Hillary, newscasters opted to release additional polling results.

674

A *Fox News* poll of independent voters found 32% in favor of Donald, 22% in favor of Hillary, and 23% in favor of Gary Johnson, the Libertarian candidate.

However, in a general election poll of all voters, Hillary maintained a three-point lead. The poll showed an overall drop of support for Donald. Of all the voters polled, 72% reported, "We're angry as hell at Washington, and we're not going to take it anymore."

A PYSCHOTIC MUSLIM MADMAN
Massacres 49 in Gay Club in Orlando—
Worst Mass Shooting in U.S. History

A psychotic American-born Muslim and ISIS supporter, 29-year-old madman Omar Mateen, cackled as he opened fire on patrons at a gay night-club early Sunday morning, June 12 in Orlando, killing 49 of them and wounding many others. It was the deadliest mass shooting in U.S. history. "This guy wanted to kill all of us," said survivor Jeanette McCoy.

The mostly Latino, mostly celebratory night of dancing to salsa and merengue at the Pulse nightclub ended in blood and mayhem.

"The gunman behind the massacre was a bloodthirsty homophobic bigot who was unhinged and unstable," as reported by Daniel Gilroy, and ex-Fort Pierce policeman who worked with him as a private guard. "I never heard him refer to anybody who was black or gay as anything else but niggers and queers," Gilroy said.

The *New York Daily News*, in a front-page headline, trumpeted, "THANKS, NRA. Because of your continued opposition to an assault rifle ban, terrorists like this lunatic can legally buy a killing machine and perpetrate the worst mass shooting in U.S. history."

Donald seized the moment, claiming, "I said this was going to happen, and it is only going to get worse." He criticized Hillary for what he claimed was her desire

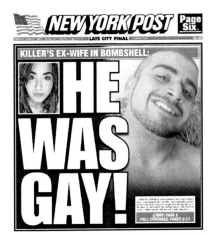

Perpetrator of the Orlando massacre, Omar Mateen.

But will this headline, as it appeared on the front page of the *New York Post*, ruin his chances of entering Jihadists' Paradise?

"to dramatically increase admissions from the Middle East."

"Referring to militant Muslims, he said, "We will have no way to screen them, pay for them, or prevent the second generation from radicalizing. The rampage in Orlando is just the beginning."

Donald used the blood-soaked occasion to renew his attacks on Obama, accusing him of not cracking down on Islamic terrorists "because he doesn't get it, or else because he sympathized with them. Look, we're led by a man that either is not tough, not smart, or he's got something else in mind. There's something going on. Why can't he utter the words, 'radical Islamic terrorists?'"

Then, in an unusual show of temper and anger, President Obama denounced Donald's remarks after the Orlando massacre, calling them "a dangerous mind-set that recalls the darkest and most shameful periods in American history. We hear language that singles out immigrants and suggests entire religious communities are complicit in violence. Where does this stop? Are you going to start treating Muslim Americans differently? That would make us less safe."

Donald used the Orlando massacre as a herald call for more guns in society. "If some of the great people who were in that club that night had guns strapped to their waist or ankle, casualties would have been lower."

Then, rather unconvincingly, Donald also claimed that he would be the best friend that the LGBT community ever had in the White House.

As he made those remarks, Sacramento pastor Roger Jimenez, in reference to LGBT people, preached from his pulpit, "The tragedy is that more of them didn't die. I'm kind of upset that he didn't finish the job, because these people are predators."

Responding to that, a journalist wrote, "Sir, you are a predator of Satan disguised as a follower of Jesus."

Then the blowhard Lieutenant Governor of Texas, Dan Patrick, posted "Man reaps what he sows," referring to the gays of Orlando.

***

In discussing the Orlando massacre, Donald veered from the GOP party line, calling for people on the terror watch list to be barred room buying firearms. His tweet could be interpreted to support some of the measures being pushed by Democrats opposing Republicans in Congress at the time.

In the wake of the massacre, a new poll reflected how disenchanted the electorate continued to be. Only 29% had a favorable view of Donald, as opposed to 43% for Hillary.

According to Bill Cunningham, a New York-based political consultant, "Trump is new to the scene, and he said things that time and time again offended different groups of people. This will be the most negative, vitriolic, mud-throwing campaign ever. It will be negative, negative, negative."

When this poll was released, Donald was at a rally in Dallas staged at Gilley's honky-tonk ballroom, where John Travolta rode a mechanical bull in the 1980 film *Urban Cowboy*.

"Where's the horse?" Donald called out. "I want to get on that horse."

The occasion marked the first anniversary of his presidential campaign launched from Trump Tower.

He attacked Obama for failing to defeat ISIS, and then promised his adoring fans that, when he became President, that was one of the first things he'd do.

"We'll plaster MAKE AMERICA GREAT AGAIN on a cowboy hat."

His speech was interrupted several times by protesters who were drowned out by his supporters.

Outside the rally, many of his fans came fully armed with assault weapons, which was their legal right. Anti-Trump protesters mocked and/or trivialized them. One young man walked up to an armed Trump supporter and, in a gesture reminiscent of the Flower-Power Hippy protests of the 1960s, placed a daisy in the barrel of his rifle.

Donald Trump had turned 70 on June 14, and astrologers predicted that "surprises by the bucket load" awaited him in the upcoming year. "They will be good surprises," claimed astrologer Sally Brompton. She advised him to "surround yourself with people whose lust for life is as strong as yours."

Donald had celebrated his birthday quietly with Melania and their son Barron at Ralph Lauren's Polo Bar near Trump Tower.

If elected in November, Donald would be the oldest President ever sworn into of-

Donald Goes to Texas

At Gilley's, Dallas' most famous honky-tonk, Donald wanted to ride the mechanical bull made famous by John Travolta in *Urban Cowboy*.

He also claimed he'd trade in his trucker's cap for a cowboy hat if it had his campaign's rallying cry.

fice. Before that, it had been Ronald Reagan, who was still a "baby" (aged 69) at the debut of this presidential administration.

In another "birthday development," it was revealed that Russians had penetrated the "Trump file" at the Democratic National Committee's headquarters. The file contained "sensitive private and personal information" which presumably was delivered to the Russian President Vladimir Putin.

During the previous few months, polls had revealed that Donald was doing well with white male voters, many of whom felt disenfranchised and were often out of work. The majority of them were not college educated.

In mid-June, publicity associated with the release of a new book, *The End of White Christian America,* revealed how the white demographic had changed during the last few years.

Author Robert F. Jones released it after going through mountains of surveys to write this "obituary" to the nation's shrinking population white Protestants, who had dominated the United States since its inception.

Based on eye-popping data, it revealed that in 1993, when Bill Clinton became President, 51% of the U.S. population had identified themselves as white Protestants. By 2014, that figure had declined to just 32% of the population.

Donald's success with such voters, especially those who self-identified as evangelicals, came as a surprise to many. "Although he stumbled through Biblical passages such as 'Two Corinthians,' he seemed to have mastered the more important scripture of the evangelicals." Jones claimed. "He did so by calling towns like Ferguson, Missouri, one of the most dangerous places on earth."

The "obituary" of White Christian America has been written by author Robert F. Jones.

He claims that the population of those who identified themselves as white Protestants has shrunk to just 32% of the population.

678

Anti-Trump attacks reached new lows on June 18 when a political action committee, Americans Against Insecure Billionaires with Tiny Hands, released a mocking new video ad:

In a voiceover, a woman asks, "If the White House phone rings at 3AM, could his little hand even pick up the receiver?"

The ad, analyzed and discussed as a news item on MSNBC, also called for Donald "to release his official hand measurements,"

Another woman in the ad then asks, "How can he create jobs if his hands are too small to shake on the deal?"

Then a man questions, "When he decides to launch his nuclear war, will his stubby fingers even be able to push the button all the way down?"

Nicknamed "Jeff," Jefferson Beauregard Sessions III sounds like a name left over from the Civil War.

The Junior U.S. Senator from Alabama was the first senator to endorse Donald Trump, and was considered a possible VEEP nominee.

As a senator, he is loathed by the LGBT community, based partly on his demands for a constitutional ban on same-sex marriage.

***

In mid-June, news leaked out that delegates who were scheduled to attend the GOP convention in Cleveland were planning a mutiny to stop Donald from ever receiving the nomination. As reported by the *Washington Post*, their campaign, code-named "Anybody But Trump," would involve a change in the party rules a week in advance of the convention.

One of the components of their plan involve passing a "conscience clause," allowing a delegate to vote for whomever they wanted during a floor tally.

"I think any attempt to overturn the will of the delegates would result in a rebellion," predicted Senator Susan Collins of Maine, who has yet to endorse Donald.

When he got whiff of it, Trump himself defined this cabal of delegates and their plot as "an illegal act."

"Any attempt to dump Trump would be a disaster," said one of his strongest supporters, Senator Jeff Sessions of Alabama.

Speaker Paul Ryan, however, granted his fellow Republicans a free pass to dump Trump "if voting for him violates their conscience."

In his rise to power, Donald sometimes benefitted from the gaffes and shortcomings of his Republican opponents. Maureen Dowd, in a June 19 column in *The New York Times* asserted that for decades, she had seen Donald as a New York celebrity, "not the apotheosis of evil uttered in the same breath of Hitler or Mussolini."

She then referred to Cruz as "a crazy nihilist, a creepy, calculating ideologue;" to Rubio as "a hungry lightweight;" to Chris Christie as "a vindictive bully;" and to Jeb Bush as "a past his sell-by-date scion."

Then she noted: "Trump's obnoxious use of ethnicity only exposed the fact that the Republicans have been using bigotry against minorities and gays to whip up voters for decades."

"YOU'RE FIRED!"

—Donald to Corey Lewandowsky

"YOU'RE HIRED!"

—Donald to Paul Manafort

A major shakeup in Donald Trump's campaign for President occurred on June 22, when his reporter-grabbing campaign manager, Corey Lewandowski, was abruptly fired. Caught unaware, he was brusquely escorted out of Trump Tower by two security guards.

Michael Caputo, a Trump adviser, almost immediately tweeted, "DING DONG THE WITCH IS DEAD!"

Behind the scenes, it was alleged that Ivanka was threatening to distance herself from the campaign if her father didn't ax Corey.

His departure left campaign chairman Paul Manafort in charge. But by now, was he the undisputed leader?

Ivanka was said to have been distressed ever since Corey grabbed reporter Michelle Fields by the arm at a Florida event. An item appeared in New York newspapers that Corey had also gotten into a shouting match on a Midtown Manhattan street with Hope Hicks, the campaign's spokeswoman.

That wasn't all. Ivanka was said to have encountered the final straw when Corey was "caught red-handed trying to plant a negative story about her husband, Jared Kushner."

Donald's oldest son, Don, Jr., admitted that his siblings played a major role in Corey's firing. He told *Bloomberg Politics*: "We're involved in talking with our dad about this, sure. But in the end, my father's always going to make up his own mind."

Donald issued a statement, praising Corey for his past services. "He's a good man, but it's time for a change. I think it's time now for a different campaign. We ran a small, beautiful, well-unified campaign. It worked very well for us in the primaries. But we're going to be a little bit different from this point forward. A little different style."

After his abrupt dismissal, Corey sat for an interview on CNN, in which he had nothing but praise for Donald. He also claimed that he had a "great relationship with Kushner," and had never tried to plant a negative story about him.

Paul Manafort had been in operational control of the campaign since April 7.

An aide claimed that in the past three weeks, Corey with a baseball bat had been walking around campaign headquarters. "He tapped people on the shoulder with that bat. The guy is fucking nuts. Corey was down to just the interns and the airplane."

Ryan Williams, a Trump critic, said, "The dismissal of Lewandowski shows donors, activists, and party officials

A failed candidate for political office himself, Corey Lewandowski was Donald Trump's first campaign manager.

A pond hockey player from Lowell, Massachusetts, he is veteran of a number of nasty political campaigns.

Lewandowski first met Donald in April of 2004 at a political event in New Hampshire. Donald was impressed with his aggressive style of campaining, and hired him as his campaign manager in 2015.

Until he was fired, he operated Donald's campaign based on a policy he widely enforced as "LET TRUMP BE TRUMP."

In 2016, the controversial Paul Manafort became Donald Trump's campaign manager, replacing Corey Lewandowski.

A veteran of numerous presidential election campaigns, Manafort, a native of Connecticut, is a notorious lobbyist whose clients around the world often include brutal dictators dominating governments and political factions in Nigeria, Somalia, Zaire, Kenya, and Pakistan.

that Trump is willing to make significant changes, even if it means parting ways with a trusted political aide."

The grandson of a union printer, Corey had had a long political background, having been a worker on various campaigns. He had twice run unsuccessfully for office himself, once in Massachusetts and again in New Hampshire.

He met Donald in April of 2014 at a political event in New Hampshire. Summoned to Trump Tower in January of 2015, Donald hired him at a salary of $20,000 a month. From the beginning, Corey's motto was "Let Trump Be Trump."

Donald said, "He leaves me alone, but he knows when to make his presence felt."

After he won in Corey's home state of New Hampshire on February 9, 2016, Donald acknowledged the important role Corey had played.

Donald praised Corey as a family man. He'd met his future wife, Alison, when he was in the ninth grade and she in the eighth. She married his best friend in 1998, but he died on a United Airlines flight on 9/11. Corey married her four years later and became the father of their four children.

In April of 2016, another veteran GOP operative, Paul Manafort, was hired. The following month, he was named campaign chairman. It seemed inevitable that Corey and Manafort would clash.

Before linking up with Donald, Manafort had been as adviser to the presidential campaigns of Gerald Ford, Ronald Reagan, George H.W. Bush, Bob Dole, George W. Bush, and John McCain. He was also a lobbyist, having previously worked for such foreign dictators as Ferdinand Marcos, the deposed despot of the Philippines.

Many of Manafort's associations with dictators have been sharply criticized. His company was listed among the top five lobbying firms receiving money from human rights-abusing regimes. Collectively, they were called "the Torturer's Lobby."

One of Manafort's more controversial links involved his previous role as an adviser to Ukrainian president Viktor Yanukovych, even as the U.S. opposed him because of his ties to Russia's Vladimir Putin. In February of 2014, Yanukovych was overthrown by violent protesters, and he fled to Russia.

JARED KUSHNER

Donald's Son-in-Law, a Man With Many Secrets, Also Rises

The real power behind the throne in the Trump campaign is said to be Jared Kushner, a business man and real estate investor heading Kushner Properties, which also owns *The New York Observer*. He is the son of the real estate developer Charles Kushner. Married to Ivanka, Jared spent at least $7 billion on New York real estate from 2007 to 2016.

Reared in an Orthodox Jewish family, he attended Harvard.

His father, Charles, was once arrested on charges of tax evasion, illegal campaign donations, and witness tampering in 2004 He was eventually convicted on all of those charges.

The flagship acquisition for the Kushners is the office building at 666 Fifth Avenue, which father and son purchased.

Kushner joined Donald's campaign initially as a speechwriter and was charged with working on a plan for a White House transition team, should his father-in-law be elected in November. Donald later assigned the transition team roundup to Chris Christie.

As *The New York Times* phrased it, "Kushner has become involved in virtually every facet of the Trump presidential campaign, so much so that many insiders seek him as a *de facto* campaign manager." There is a certain irony there. For decades, the Kushners bankrolled Democrats seeking office.

The New York Times also pointed out that Jared is now "at the center of a campaign that has been embraced by white nationalists and anti-Semites."

"Jared and I are extremely close," Donald said. "He is an amazing son-in-law, a big and bold thinker."

***

As for Lewandowsky, out of a job, he landed on his feet when it was announced that he'd been hired as a political commentator for CNN. That network's boss, Jeff Zucker, said he was "drooling" to sign up Donald's former campaign manager. For his new gig, CNN was reported to have signed Corey for a fee of half a million annually. A CNN spokesperson denied that figure.

Then it surfaced that Corey had signed a non-disclosure agreement with Donald, making revelation of information about both him and his campaign a violation of his contract.

In the wake of hiring Corey, many CNN staffers were upset to have him join their ranks. Once source asked the question, "Will CNN tell its viewers that before Corey speaks, he is legally prohibited from criticizing

Trump?"

It was also reported that CNN anchor, Anderson Cooper, didn't want Corey on his show.

HarperCollins offered Corey a $1.2 million book deal for a revealing insider's look at the Trump campaign. After failing to provide the publisher with his non-disclosure agreement, HarperCollins was said to have withdrawn its offer.

BRITISH GUN-GRABBER ATTEMPTS TO ASSASSINATE DONALD TRUMP

At a June 18 Donald Trump rally at the Treasure Island Casino in Las Vegas, Michael Steven Sandford tried to grab a police officer's gun so that he could kill Donald.

Reportedly, the unarmed 20-year-old Brit, in the United States on an expired visa, approached a police officer and politely asked him if he could get an autograph from Donald.

Trying to distract the officer, he then reached with both hands and tried to pull a gun from the cop's holster so he could use it to shoot at Donald, who was speaking.

Sandford appeared in leg irons that Monday in the U.S. District Court in Nevada to face a charge of potential violence on restricted grounds.

According to a Secret Service reporter, the deranged would-be assassin had driven from Hoboken, New Jersey, all the way to Las Vegas, where he parked his car on June 16. His first priority after checking into a hotel was to visit a shooting

Michael Steven Sandford, British would-be assassin of Donald Trump in Las Vegas, perhaps had dreams of entering the history books as a clone of Lee Harvey Oswald.

A total misfit in life, Sandford, if convicted, could face up to ten years in prison for confessing to a Secret Service agent that he had plotted to assassinate the presumptive Republican nominee.

range for his first-ever lesson in how to fire a gun.

An employee at the range told police that Sandford had fired twenty rounds from a 9mm Glock pistol.

From the Secret Service report, it was revealed that the unhinged Brit said that if he were released from custody, he would make yet another attempt to assassinate Donald. In his possession, a ticket was discovered to Phoenix, where Donald was scheduled to appear the next day.

In England, Sandford's father was interviewed in Portsmouth, where he lived. He told the local paper, the *Portsmouth News*, that for the past three months, he had become alarmed about his son and his whereabouts. He also revealed that his son was autistic and suffered from Asperger syndrome.

In court, it was exposed that he had suffered from obsessive-compulsive disorder and anorexia. When he was fourteen, he had been hospitalized, but escaped.

It was noted that he had fallen in love with a young woman, a native of New Jersey, and had become "lovesick." He was so depressed that his father gave him money to fly to the United States to live close to the object of his obsession.

His father had not been able to reach him. "My son doesn't talk much and never about his private life. His attempt on Trump's life came as a total surprise, because he never showed the slightest interest in politics." He also revealed that his son had dropped out of high school at the age of fifteen.

"He has always been a polite and very peaceful boy. I can't believe that he's become radicalized. Maybe he's been blackmailed or something. It's against my boy's nature to do anything like this. Maybe somebody got hold of him and put him up to this. I'm mortified. He's a good boy, but with problems."

DONALD IS CHARGED IN RAPE OF A 13-YEAR-OLD GIRL

Who Alleges, "I Was His Sex Slave"

As if Donald's campaign didn't have enough trouble, a bizarre lawsuit emerged in a California court in May.

A "Katie Johnson" filed a bombshell $100 million lawsuit in which she claimed she was repeatedly raped by Donald in 1994 at one of "billionaire pedophile's" Jeffrey Epstein's "sex parties" at a mansion in Palm Beach.

The suit claimed the GOP nominee "took my virginity and that he and Epstein treated me as a sex slave during a horrific four-month period."

Johnson was said to have offered her story to the tabloids, along with photographs of herself, for $25,000. As reported by *Radar Online*, Epstein's infamous "little black book" did not contain the name of Katie Johnson.

Johnson charged that she and her family were threatened with harm if she didn't give in to sexual demands. The suit further alleged that Johnson and another sex slave, also 13, gave naked Donald and Epstein sexually charged massages in the same room at Epstein's Manhattan residence. The plaintiff said she was enticed with promises of money and a modeling career.

The complaint that was filed stated that a woman, identified in court papers only as "Tiffany Doe," reportedly an employee of Epstein, could confirm Johnson's allegations.

In one alleged encounter, Johnson claims she was tied to a bed by Donald and "forcibly raped." The suit also claimed that he refused to wear a condom, despite her pleas.

"Defendant Trump slapped the Plaintiff Johnson in the face with his open hand and angrily stated that he would do whatever he wanted and that he was in charge," the suit maintained.

It also stated that, "After achieving sexual orgasm, Defendant Trump put his clothes back on, and when the plaintiff Johnson sobbed about being afraid that Defendant Trump had impregnated her, he angrily threw some $100 bills at her and screamed at her 'to get a fucking abortion' with the money."

The complaint

Aquazzura Wild Thing Shoe

Trump Hettie Shoe

WHAT DIFFERENCE DOES IT MAKE?

About $640 retail, per pair, and a boatload of ill will for Ivanka from the Italian fashion industry and from an electorate already convinced of the Trump empire's greed.

Aquazzurra's *Wild Thing* (left) vs. Ivanka's *Trump Hettie* (right). You be the judge: Did Ivanka steal the design of the Italian shoe manufacturer?

also claimed that she had been sexually assaulted by Epstein on three different occasions during that same four-month period, including "one savage attack during which I was beaten, raped, and sodomized by Epstein."

In 2006, Epstein was arrested and accused of sexual abuse by some forty different women, some of whom claimed they were teenagers at the time. None of these women implicated Donald in any wrongdoing.

In February of 2016, Donald publicly referenced Epstein and then went on to drag Bill Clinton into this seedy mess. "Clinton has a lot of problems coming up in my opinion with that famous Caribbean island with Epstein. A lot of problems." He made these remarks at the Conservative Political Action Conference, where he distanced himself from the financier.

Donald allegedly banned Epstein from the Mar-a-Lago Club after he was accused of propositioning an underage teenage girl.

Eventually, after a widely publicized court procedure, Epstein drew a sentence of eighteen months for a misdemeanor—soliciting an underage girl. He was released after thirteen months for good behavior.

In California, Donald's lawyer, Alan Garter, claimed that an investigation produced no evidence that "Katie Johnson" actually existed. He cited her address and phone number as false. He also denounced charges associated with Donald's alleged involvement at Epstein's sex parties as completely false.

"The allegations are disgusting at the highest level and clearly framed to solicit media attention, or more likely are politically motivated." Garten said. "To be clear, there is absolutely no merit to these claims, and based on our investigation, no evidence that the person who has made these allegations actually exists."

The case was dismissed by a Los Angeles Federal Judge in May, but resurfaced in Manhattan Federal Court in June.

Katie Johnson's lawyer claims that his client "remains traumatized by the abuse."

The case, as of this writing, remains uncertain.

FOOT FETISHES & LITIGATION NEWS
Aquazzura's Wild Thing Vs. Ivanka's Trump Hettie

Her father might be facing charges of rape, but daughter Ivanka, on June 22, was sued by an Italian designer for ripping off his design for a high-end, fringe-toed, and tassel-strapped pair of stiletto high heels. Filed in

Manhattan Federal Court, the case alleged that the Trump fashion maven appropriated a popular Aquazzura shoe.

Ivanka's lawyers shot back, "The case is about generating publicity."

"One of the most disturbing things in the fashion industry is when someone blatantly steals our copyright design and doesn't care," claimed a lawyer for Aquazzura, referring to their popular shoe which they had marketed as, "Wild Thing."

Whereas the exclusive Italian original retails for $785, Ivanka's knock-off design, marketed as "the Trump Hettie," sells for only $145 at Bloomingdale's in Manhattan.

Hillary Says:
"DONALD WILL NUKE THE U.S. ECONOMY AS BANKRUPTER-IN-CHIEF"

All political strategists from both parties were aware of how crucial the African American vote would be in the upcoming presidential election. A Quinnipiac University poll found that Donald's support among "the blacks" (his words) was almost nil, with less than 1% of the vote in a national election. This was in contrast to the 6% that Mitt Romney had garnered in 2012.

In distinct contrast, Hillary polled 91% of the black vote.

With white males, Donald trounced Hillary, winning 56% of their support as opposed to her meager 25%.

At the start of June, Hillary has amassed a fortune of $41 million in her campaign's war chest. On June 23, it was revealed that Donald had only $1.3 in his campaign fund. That was the worst financial report of any major party nominee in recent history.

In another assessment, it was also revealed that Donald had only seventy members on his campaign staff, as opposed to Hillary, who had assembled an army of 700.

At this point in June, the *Clintonistas* had spent $26 million in attack ads, whereas Trump staffers had not spent anything.

In response to his campaign's low bank accounts, Donald said he might have to tap into his personal fortune to keep his forces parading along. He claimed that he had spent $50 million of his own money during the primaries.

Campaign filings, as required by law, revealed that he had shifted a lot of campaign money back into to his own staff or properties. It was shown that he had reimbursed at least $1.1 million to his businesses and family members for campaign travel costs they had incurred.

Some financial experts raised eyebrows at the numbers and the transactions he claimed. They included $423,000 which had gone to Mar-a-Lago, and more than $170,000 paid out to Trump Tower, in their respective roles as campaign headquarters.

***

Meanwhile, among the Democrats, although Bernie Sanders was still biting into Hillary's flesh, she avoided—for the sake of party unity—attacking him, since she knew she would need the "young Turks" who supported him.

Instead, she aimed her fire directly at Donald, predicting a "recession and global panic" if he ever became President. She outlined a list of his business failures and bankruptcies, with a special emphasis on his dealings in Atlantic City.

She also attacked his suggestion that the United States, as a way out of its debt crisis, might opt to default on its debts, a path of action that could set off a world depression.

"Alexander Hamilton, our first Treasury Secretary, might be rolling over in his grave," she charged. "Maybe we shouldn't expect better from someone whose most famous words are, 'You're fired!' she said. "He's written a lot of books about business. They all seem to end at Chapter Eleven."

In a surprise reaction, Donald threw stones at Hillary's commitment to her religious faith. Speaking at a meeting of evangelical leaders, he said, "There's nothing we know about her faith, or lack thereof, even though she's been in the public eye for years. It's going to be an extension of Obama, but worse. At least with Obama, we had our guard up. With Hillary, you don't know."

In a speech at the Marriott Marquis at New York City's Times Square, he warned evangelicals that the Democrats under Hillary might "sell Christianity down the tubes. Evangelicals especially are under siege."

In all their speeches, Hillary and Donald continued to exchange gunfire. In a speech at the once-robust former steel town of Monessen, Pennsylvania, Donald charged, "The wave of globalization had wiped out totally, totally, our middle class. You can blame Hillary and her trade deals for that."

She shot back at him: "He's one to talk about globalization of American manufacturing jobs." At a rally, she held up a Trump shirt. "It's made in Bangladesh!"

AFL-CIO President Richard Trumka also attacked Donald for "crying crocodile tears about lost jobs and shuttered factories. He embodies everything that is wrong with our current trade policies. He has consistently sent American jobs overseas to line his own pockets with cheap labor."

At another rally, Donald promised that as President, he would withdraw the United States from NAFTA, impose high tariffs on foreign goods, and start a currency war with China. He also promised to scrap the Trans-Pacific Partnership, a twelve-nation trade deal among the United States and its Pacific Rim allies.

He always left his rallies with a promise—"It's time for the American people to take back their future."

***

Since House Speaker Paul Ryan had been critical of Donald, the mogul reportedly took delight when the media compared the conservative Republican to his lookalike, the fictional TV character, "Eddie Munster," from the classic hit TV show, *The Munsters,* from the 1960s.

In a scathing article in the *New York Daily News,* Andy Parker blasted Ryan and the other "gutless wonders" of the GOP for failing to take action on gun control. Parker's daughter, Alison, had been a reporter for Virginia TV when she was shot to death on live TV the previous August.

"It was probably snarky of me to compare Paul Ryan to Eddie Munster, but forgive me for being one pissed-off dad doing what I can to save another from the soul-crushing agony I live with every day. Given Ryan's action of the course of the last 24 hours, I'm not sorry I said it. Like the rest of his colleagues in the GOP leadership, Ryan is a coward and an obstructionist and a tool for the National Rifle Association."

"HERE LIES HILLARY *(and Lies & Lies)"*
—New York Post

As time marched on, Donald seemed to lose his footing at times. He even delivered several self-inflicted wounds. He attacked a Federal judge, issued a self-congratulatory boast after the terror attack in Orlando, and stepped up his oral assaults on Hillary.

In Manhattan, he appeared at the Trump SoHo Hotel, where he called her "a world class liar," and charged that "she is the most corrupt person ever to seek the presidency. She would destroy the last scrap of our independence. We'd be under her total and complete control."

He also blamed her for all the turmoil in the Middle East. His critics pounced on his remarks, calling them "a patchwork of cable-news-ready sound bites as opposed to the presentation of new ideas."

At another rally, he accused Hillary for the invasion of Libya and "handing the country over to ISIS, the barbarians." He also assailed her for "getting rich by cutting deals with brutal foreign regimes that donated millions to her family's foundation or paid for Bill Clinton's speeches. "She has perfected a politics of personal profit and even theft."

Many pundits claimed that that speech marked the unofficial debut of the general election campaign.

In one of his more outrageous accusations, he claimed that Hillary was probably the victim of blackmail from the Chinese who had gained access to her e-mail account while she was Secretary of State.

Hillary was not the only woman Donald attacked. Elizabeth Warren, the Senator from Massachusetts, assailed Donald in speech after speech. He went after her, stating that to get into Harvard, she had falsely stated that she had Cherokee blood, thus benefitting from Affirmative Action awarded to Native Americans. She said that she was five percent Indian, but was not able to prove that.

In retaliation, Donald mocked her as "Pocahontas." In response, Native Americans attacked him for "using that racist assault."

To retaliate, Warren, campaigning with Hillary in Cincinnati, called Donald "a bigot with a goofy baseball hat."

"Pocahontas is one of the least productive of U.S. senators," he rejoined.

BREXIT

When The British Said "Cheerio" To The European Union,
DONALD SAID:

"With a weakened Pound, more people can afford to stay at my golf hotel."

On June 24, news about Britain's decision to exit from the European Union shocked much of the world. A historic decision known as "Brexit," it carried world-shaping consequences, including the possibility of a global economic crisis.

It rattled financial markets and rocked political regimes worldwide. As David Cameron announced his upcoming resignation, the value of the British pound plummeted on financial markets. Britain had brought on itself the dubious honor of being the first country to break from the painstakingly assembled 28-member bloc.

Reporters caught up with Donald in Ayrshire, Scotland, where he had deserted his U.S. campaign trail for promotion of his new golf course and resort on that country's southwestern coast.

Purchased in 2014, Trump Turnberry is a luxury golf course and resort dating back to the 1900s.

"Our friends over here have voted to take back control of their economy," Donald claimed. "Take back their politics and their borders. I was on the right side of that issue, while Hillary, as always, stood with the elite. So did Obama."

Donald pledged that when he became President, he would reverse "the worst legacies of the Clinton era."

He tried to turn the anti-EU vote in Britain into a good sign that might help elect him President. "I think there are great similarities between what happened here in Britain and my campaign in America." He told reporters. "People on both sides of the ocean want to take their country back." He attacked both Hillary and Obama for urging Britain to stay in the EU.

Donald was in Britain, at his newly opened golf resort in Scotland, at the time of the Brexit vote. In a referendum with worldwide implications, Britain had decided to end its association with the European Union.

When he learned that such a move had led to the immediate and historic decline in the value of the British pound, he told reporters, "A weakened pound will make rates at my golf resort more reasonable, and we should benefit financially from the more affordable rates."

The British media responded with fury.

"The American people are tired of seeing stupid decisions and having Swiss-cheese borders," he said.

In Scotland, he faced the inevitable protesters, some of his opponents flying Mexican flags. During the opening ceremonies for Donald's golf course, British comic Lee Nelson held up golf balls emblazoned with swastikas as news cameras spinned.

***

July arrived for Donald Trump like the blast of a firecracker. A *Fox News* poll had him favored to beat Hillary Clinton by a margin of 43% to 39%. He'd been trailing her by five points.

He held a 14-point lead among men, but trailed her among women voters by 6%. And whereas the candidates were tied among voters under 40, the mogul beat her among older voters.

Meanwhile, Bill Clinton and Attorney General Loretta Lynch came under fire on June 30 for holding a private meeting on a plane at the Phoenix Airport. The parlay came in the wake of an FBI investigation of Hillary's e-mail server, with the implication that Bill Clinton had somehow unduly influenced (or coerced) the Attorney General in the case pending against Hillary.

The impromptu and probably accidental meeting was widely denounced by Donald, even though Lynch emphatically and repeatedly insisted that all that they talked about golf and their grandchildren.

"Their meeting was terrible," Donald said, "and it was really sneaky. It was something they didn't want publicized as I understand it. Wow. I just think it was terrible. The meeting was so out of bounds even the liberal media's making it a big story."

***

An ad from Donald's campaign machine. But is the Star of David, in association with allegations of corruption and cash something that might offend Jews?

The media immediately questioned the judgment of whomever approved the ad.

And although the Trump children's "hipness quotient," as worldly Manhattanites, is said to be off the charts, didn't they know that this might offend?

On July 3, agents of the FBI intensely grilled Hillary over the use of her private e-mail server, which she'd used during her tenure as Secretary of State. Meeting voluntarily with her probers in Washington, she reportedly answered all the questions put to her.

In an unconfirmed report, CNN announced that no charges would be brought against her. That immediately provoked an attack from Donald. In the past, he'd called for her to go to jail. He tweeted, "Like I said, the system is rigged!"

"It is impossible for the FBI not to recommend criminal charges against her," he tweeted. "What she did was wrong. What Bill did was stupid!" By that, he referred to Bill meeting Loretta Lynch on the tarmac of the Phoenix airport.

***

In an informal survey, *The New York Times* revealed their "readers' pick" for who consumers would most like to see designated as Donald's vice-presidential running mate.

The most favored choice for the no. 2 spot was Sarah Palin. [*As noted by* The Times, "*She hates the Establishment and, like Trump, considers herself a maverick.*"]

Other readers wanted Tennessee Senator Bob Corker because of his much-needed foreign policy experience. Michele Bachman was also a leading contender. [*"She's a Trump woman and attractive, with strong Tea Party and evangelical support."*]

Chris Christie was an obvious choice for second banana. Ben Carson, Donald's former rival, was described as "capable, steady, classy, and intelligent."

Even though she'd said she didn't want the job, South Carolina's Governor Nikki Haley was also cited. [*Haley is "living proof that Donald is not a racist, a misogynist, and a xenophobe," wrote a reader.*] The name of Condoleezza Rice bubbled up from obscurity to appear on the list. [*An odd choice, she was described by participants in the survey as "honest and charming."*]

Newt Gingrich was a heavy favorite [*"...a true Washington insider"*]. Also cited was Jeff Sessions, the senator from Alabama. Near the bottom of the list was Mary Fallin, the charismatic governor of Oklahoma. The oddest choice was Ivanka Trump [*"...smart as a whip and someone Donald will listen to."*]

It seemed inevitable that Donald couldn't advance further into July without generating unwanted headlines. On July 2, he ignited a firestorm when he called Hillary "the most corrupt candidate ever" and tweeted an illustration that positioned her face next to a Star of David over a pile of money. He cited a *Fox News* poll that showed that 58% of respondents thought she was corrupt.

His tweet drew angry responses from around the country, some of them accusing Donald of being an anti-Semitic white supremacist. Moving swiftly, within a few hours, he, or someone on his campaign staff, had replaced the Star of David with a red circle.

He later tried to escape criticism, claiming that viewers had misinterpreted the tweet. "It wasn't the Star of David but a sheriff's star."

No one seemed to be buying that.

***

On the campaign trail, Donald had attacked the presidency of George W. Bush, especially when he was debating Jeb!. He accused the former President of misleading America into its involvement in the disastrous war in Iraq, costing taxpayers trillions of dollars—not to mention the horrible loss of American lives.

In early July, the publication of Jean Edward Smith's new biography, *Bush*, backed up Donald's complaints against the 43rd President. The first sentence of the book reads: "Rarely in the history of the United States has the nation been so ill-served as during the presidency of George W. Bush."

The biography concludes: "Whether George W. Bush was the worst President in American history will be long debated, but his decision to invade Iraq is easily the worst foreign policy decision made by an American President."

***

On July 5, the FBI director, James B. Comey, recommended that no criminal charges be filed against Hillary Clinton for her handling of classified information when she was Secretary of State.

The announcement came some two hours before she boarded a familiar carrier, Air Force One, with Barack Obama to take her to the crucial voting state of North Carolina, then absorbed over a controversial law about transgenders' use of bathroom facilities.

The FBI found no evidence that she had intentionally transmitted or willfully mishandled classified information, elements necessary to warrant a criminal charge. But although he recommended that no charges be filed, Comey nonetheless rebuked Hillary for her use of a private e-mail address and server.

In his testimony before a Congressional committee—the majority of whose members were hostile Republicans—Comey may have damaged Hillary more than all of Donald's previous attacks on her. The FBI director called into question her ability to function as Commander-in-Chief.

Comey charged that Hillary "was extremely careless in her handling of very sensitive, highly classified information."

Instantly, Donald's campaign went to work preparing attack ads, claiming that Hillary was incompetent to hold down the highest office in the land.

He responded to the FBI director's charges. "Our adversaries almost certainly have a blackmail file on Hillary Clinton. Her lawyers and Bill Clinton have been up to no good. Mr. Comey's findings disqualify her from running for the presidency. Her judgment is horrible. Look at her e-mails."

On August 29, 2015, in Minneapolis, Hillary responded: "I have said repeatedly that I did not send nor receive classified material, and I'm very confident that when the entire process plays out, that will be understood by everyone."

To contradict her, the FBI discovered that of some 30,000 e-mails returned to the State Department, 110 e-mails in fifty-two e-mail chains were determined to contain classified information.

In the wake of the FBI director's testimony, Donald claimed, "The FBI did me a favor. I would rather face Crooked Hillary than Crazy Bernie. Why? Because Hillary is corrupt. The decision to give her a pass is a total miscarriage of justice."

In another development, it was announced

James Comey is the seventh and current director of the F.B.I. In 2013, he was appointed to the post by President Obama.

He received widespread condemnation from Republicans when he announced the results of Hillary Clinton's e-mail controversy.

He said he was recommending to the U.S. Department of Justice that no criminal charges be filed against the former Secretary of State.

that the GOP's fund raisers had raised $51 million to add to Donald's war chest. He chipped in another $3.8 million He claimed that voter disgust over Hillary's escaping prosecution had generated millions to his campaign fund.

"People are sick of the constant scamming of all of us by the Clintons," he charged. He also took the occasion to blast New York Mayor Bill de Blasio, calling him a "maniac, the worst mayor in the history of New York."

Then, in another reckless charge, Donald, on July 6, charged that Hillary offered Loretta Lynch a bribe by promising to reappoint her as attorney general. [*There is no evidence whatsoever of this.*]

As he attacked Hillary for allegedly trying to bribe her with a cabinet post, reporters continued to press him on his choice of a vice presidential running mate.

"I have a lot of choices," he said, "but at the moment, I don't know, although the time is soon coming where I will have to make a decision."

He named Wisconsin governor, Scott Walker, as a possibility. Scott himself had been an early frontrunner for the GOP nomination, but soon dropped out of the race, using the occasion to attack Donald's suitability as a candidate for the presidency.

IN PRAISE OF DESPOTS
Some of Donald's Ideas on Foreign Policy

To the horror of the State Department, and perhaps to the consternation of his handlers, Donald was quick to enunciate controversial opinions about some of the planet's most notorious autocrats. Some of his comments enraged many listeners who marveled that he had actually gotten away with uttering them.

Saddam Hussein,
the "Butcher of Baghdad"

Donald: "He was a bad guy, right? Really bad guy. But you know what he did well? He killed terrorists. That was good. He didn't read them their rights. They don't talk. They were terrorists. It was over."

[*In contrast, Paul Ryan called Hussein "one of the most evil figures of the 20th Century. He committed mass genocide." And many national security experts have sharply contested whether the citizens of Iraq murdered by Hussein were terrorists, or merely citizens who protested his authority.*]

Vladimir Putin,
Corrupt Dictator and "Curse of Russia?"
Donald: "We can work together. We'll get along fine."

Mohammar Khadafy,
"The Terror of Libya" and a Former International Terrorist
Donald: "Libya would be so much better off if he were still in charge."

Kim Jong Un,
the Brutal and Probably Psychotic Dictator of North Korea,
Who Threatens the West with a Nuclear Attack
Donald: "Ya gotta give him credit. It's incredible. He wiped out his uncle. He wiped out this one, that one…"

"BUT HE'S EASY TO GET ALONG WITH"
Donald Butts Heads With Republican Senators

On July 7, Donald flew into Washington, holding a testy meeting on Capitol Hill, where he "picked fights," according to the press, with some of the leaders of the GOP.

One encounter was with Senator Jeff Flake, Republican of Arizona.

"You've been very critical of me," Donald said to him.

"Flake responded, "Yes, I'm the other senator from Arizona—the one who didn't get captured." *[Flake was referring to Donald's charge that John McCain, a prisoner of war in Vietnam, was not a hero.]*

He also met with Mark Sandford, Republican senator from South Carolina. Sandford told the press, "I wasn't particularly impressed."

Ben Stasse, Senator from Nebraska, and Mark Kirk of Illinois, each announced that they were not endorsing the GOP nominee.

Donald lashed back, calling Kirk "dishonest and a loser."

Kirk shot back, "He's an Easterner, a privileged bully. Our bullies are made of better stuff in Illinois."

"It was a great meeting that will help Trump unify the GOP," said Rep. Lee Zeldin of Long Island, in his evaluation of the contentious exchanges that took place.

It was???

***

On July 8, Micah Johnson, 25, a heavily armed gunman who had served in the U.S. military in Afghanistan, mowed down five police officers in Dallas, allegedly as a "payback" for the shooting of two black men in Louisiana and Minnesota.

A black racist with a hatred of white people, he set out to kill as many policemen as he could. His Facebook profile revealed that he supported the new Black Panther Party, a coven of African Americans who advocated violence against whites and Jews.

At his home in Dallas, police found bomb-making materials, ammunition, ballistic vests, and a personal journal of combat tactics.

The worst mass killing of police officers since 9/11, the massacre *seguéd* instantly into the political campaign. Donald called the brutal killings "an attack on our country. We must stand in solidarity with law enforcement, which we must remember is the force between civilization and total chaos. Every American has the right to live in safety and peace. We will make America safe again."

The cop killer's Facebook profile shows him dressed in an African dashiki and holding a clenched fist in the familiar stance of a Black Power salute.

AMERICA'S ELITE GETS VOCAL
Ruth Bader Ginsburg Denounces Trump as
Rudy Giuliani Supports Him

In the days leading up to the Republican convention in Cleveland, famous American figures, including the oft-revered Supreme Court Justice Ruth Bader Ginsburg and former NYC mayor Rudolf Giuliani, spoke out on controversial, hot-button issues.

Rare for a Supreme Court Justice, Ginsburg said, "I can't imagine what this place would be—I can't imagine what this country would be—with Donald Trump as our President. For the country, it could be four years. For the court, it could be—I don't even want to contemplate that."

She even suggested that with a Trump presidency, it might be time "to move to New Zealand."

She went on to speak about the stalled nomination of Judge Merrick B. Garland. Republican senators had continued to refuse to bring his nomination to the floor.

"I think Mr. Garland is about as well-qualified as any nominee on this court. Super bright and very nice, very easy to deal with. And super prepared. He would be a great colleague."

***

On another issue, Rudy Giuliani, who had once sought the presidency himself on the Republican ticket, denounced the Black Lives Matter movement, accusing it of ignoring black-on-black crime, for inciting violence against the police, and for promoting racism.

"When you say Black Lives Matter, that's inherently racist," he said on CBS's *Face the Nation*. "White lives matter. Asian lives matter. Hispanic lives matter."

"They sing rap songs about killing police officers, and they talk about killing police officers, and they yell it out at their rallies and the police officers hear it."

"When there are sixty shootings in Chicago over the Fourth of July and fourteen murders, Black Lives Matter is nonexistent. Do black lives matter or only the very few black lives that are killed by white policemen?"

Giuliani went on to accuse the Black Lives Matter movement of "painting a target on the back of police officers." On MSNBC, Giuliani said that the swell of protests and demonstrations in response to black men being shot and killed by cops has

Revered for her scholarship and contemporary savvy: Ruth Bader Ginsburg.

The U.S. Supreme Court Justice set off a firestorm when she made her distaste for Donald Trump known.

Former New York City Mayor Rudy Giuliani, a politician legendary for his oratory and political showmanship.

His rhetoric angered African Americans. "The police are the ones saving black lives," he said. "Black lives matter is not saving black lives. It's the police officers doing it."

led to "divisiveness and anti-police rhetoric. I think the reasons there's a target on police officer's backs is because of groups like Black Lives Matter that make it seem like all police are against the blacks. They're not."

"The police are the ones saving black lives," he said. "Black Lives Matter is not saving black lives. It's the police officers doing it."

BUT DONALD, ON GAY RIGHTS, WHERE ARE YOU, EXACTLY?

"Does an "Urban Sophisticate" Like Donald Trump
Really Care Who Someone Marries
or Where They Go to Take a Piss?"
—a GOP Delegate from New York

Although gay rights was a hot-button issue for the GOP, Donald seemed to want to avoid getting involved. Social conservatives opposing same-sex marriage and abortion rights, had dominated GOP platforms of the past, as in 2012.

Donald himself has claimed, "tremendous friendship with the gay community." Gays, in fact, have not been singled out for attack in his speeches, and thousands in the GLBT community supported him. At times, Donald has also criticized all those laws trying to prevent transgendered people from using the public restrooms of their choice. In fact, he received a supportive call from Caitlyn Jenner, the former Olympic athlete previously known as Bruce Jenner.

Many GOP delegates argue that their party can no longer afford to alienate people by taking intolerant positions on gay rights.

But these moderate voices face almost hysterical opposition. Cynthia Dunbar, delegate from Virginia, has compared the gay rights movement to Nazism.

A rival delegate said, "Ms. Dunbar should sit down and read a book about the history of the Nazi party."

A delegate from Missouri, Hardy Billington, went so far to take out an ad in his hometown newspaper, claiming that homosexuality kills people at two to three times the rate of smoking. *[Of course, this was ridiculous.]*

Mary Frances Forrester of North Carolina suggested that "the homosexual agenda is trying to change the course of western civilization." Perhaps she confused gays with ISIS.

Lanhee J. Chen, who led Mitt Romney's platform efforts in 2012, said:

"The bigger problem for the Trump people and the Republican National Committee is the fact there are these major disagreements between where Trump is on some of these issues and where the activist base of the Republican Party is."

Of course, Donald could take the position of Bob Dole, the Republican nominee in 1996. When he was asked about the official platforms and ideologies endorsed by party members during that election cycle, he said, "I never read it."

The Race Wars: Donald Self-Defines as
"THE LAW AND ORDER" CANDIDATE

On July 11, at a campaign rally in Virginia Beach, Donald responded to the killing of two black men by the police in Minnesota and Louisiana, and of five police officers gunned down in Dallas.

Lacking his usual fire-and-brimstone approach, Donald said, "We must stand in solidarity with law enforcement, which we must remember is the force between civilization and total chaos. I am the law-and-order candidate," he declared, echoing a campaign slogan that put Richard Nixon into the Oval Office in the tumultuous election of 1968, in the wake of the assassination of Martin Luther King, Jr. and Robert Kennedy.

Hoping to sound presidential, Donald said, "The attack on our Dallas police is an attack on our country. Our whole nation is in mourning. Yet we have also seen increasing threats against our police and a substantial rise in the number of officers killed in the line of duty."

"We must remember the police are needed the most where crime is the highest." He cited Chicago as a case of a violence-plagued city with a high crime rate where blacks often murder fellow blacks.

"Every kid in America should be able to securely walk the streets of their own neighborhood without harm. Everyone will be protected equally."

His ardent supporter, Chris Christie, backed him up. "We need a President who once again will put law and order at the top of the priority of the presidency of the country."

Christie also used the occasion to get in some digs at Hillary. "She is weak, ineffective, pandering and—as proven by her recent e-mail scandals, which was an embarrassment not only to her, but to the entire nation as a whole—she's either a liar or grossly incompetent. It's probably both."

On July 12, Donald, on TV, watched with great skepticism as Vermont Senator Bernie Sanders endorsed Hillary as the Democratic nominee for President. In spite of that, she faced angry Sanders supporters who held up signs, "NEVER HILLARY." Both candidates, even though they might not really like each other, seemed to unite against a common foe: Donald Trump.

"I intend to do everything I can to make certain she will be the next president," Sanders said.

"There goes Crooked Hillary and Crazy Bernie trying to trick voters," Donald said.

"We are joining forces to defeat Donald Trump," Hillary proclaimed.

Donald also took the occasion to denounce Justice Ruth Bader Ginsburg as a "disgrace" after she voiced her criticism of him. "I think she should apologize to the court. I couldn't believe it when I saw it."

He predicted that her comments against him would backfire, giving him the election. "It's so beneath the court for her to be making statements like that. It only energizes my base even more. I would hope that she would get off the court as soon as possible."

ANGRY CAUCASIANS DEFEND TRUMP
The Donald, Last Stand of the White Man

In a rare frontpage lead story in the July 14 edition of *The New York Times*, Nicholas Confessore wrote an article headlined "TRUMP MINES GRIEVANCES OF WHITES WHO FEEL LOST."

Sounding more like an editorial than a straight news story, he claimed: "In countless collisions of color and creed, Donald J. Trump's name evokes an easily understood message of racial hostility. Defying modern conventions of political civility and language, Mr. Trump has breached the boundaries that have long constrained America's public discussion of race."

The article revealed work done by Michael J. Norton, a professor at the Harvard Business School. He suggested that "whites have come to see an anti-white bias as more prevalent than anti-black bias, and that these people think further black progress is coming at their expense."

In another study by Michael Tesler, a political scientist at the University of California, it was revealed that many whites believed that "blacks play the race card or else are racist themselves."

"GOP CAVES IN TO TRUMP'S WALL OF SHAME

Porn's a Health Crisis, but Coal Is Clean"

—*New York Daily News*

On July 14, it was announced that the platform committee of the GOP had drafted a list of controversial, far-right proposals, which were a non-binding document that had to be approved at the Republican Convention in Cleveland.

Many editorial writers found the proposals more appropriate for a convention in 1948.

According to the draft of their official platform, the GOP approved a wall "covering the entirety of the southern border."

Donald gloated over their endorsement of his wall, claiming "It will make America safe again."

The proposed platform did not say how the wall would be financed.

Other proposals called for "special scrutiny" of people entering the United States from "regions associated with Islamic terrorism."

Appealing to the most conservative of Republicans, the document also warned that pornography is a "public health crisis."

At the same time that porn was defined as dangerous to one's health, the use of coal was deemed "a clean energy source."

The committee also adopted measures that supported the teaching of the Bible in public schools, and a measures rejecting Charles Darwin's theory of the Evolution of Species as a scientific theory for presentation there either.

In spite of the Supreme Court's legalization of same-sex marriage, the platform stripped virtually all support and rights from America's gay community. It supported adoption agencies which refused to work with gay couples, and also endorse the rights of parents to seek the widely discredited tenets of "conversion therapy" for their gay children.

In Springfield, Illinois, Hillary said that "the party of Lincoln has now become the party of Trump. His campaign adds up to an ugly, dangerous message to America."

Epilogue

PRELUDE TO CLEVELAND
Donald Trump Claims That as President,
He'll Urge Congress to Declare
WORLD WAR III

Donald Veers to the Extreme Right & Names
EVANGELICAL HOOSIER,
INDIANA GOVERNOR MIKE PENCE
As His Veep Running Mate

THE ODD COUPLE
A Homophobic, Bible-Thumping Misogynist is
Donald's Choice as
The Man Who's a Heartbeat Away from Being President

At last, on July 15, the world learned that Donald J. Trump had named Tea Party favorite, Michael Richard Pence (called "Mike") to be his vice presidential running mate in the 2016 presidential election.

Newspapers noted that in 1988, George H.W. Bush had named another Hoosier, Danforth Quayle, as his Veep. A former radio talk show host, Mike called himself "Rush Limbaugh on decaff."

In his selection of this Born Again Christian, Donald had more or less abruptly rejected two highly visible and highly competitive finalists, New Jersey governor Chris Christie and former House Speaker Newt Gingrich.

To accept the invitation from Donald, Pence had to end his re-election campaign as governor of Indiana. Polls showed that he would have lost the race anyway because earlier and very expensive errors in judgment he had made during his administration of his state.

The liberal press had a field day writing satirical headlines about "Magic Mike." They included:

THE DONALD'S RUNNING WITH STUPID!

~

TRUMP-PENCE MATCH MADE IN HATER HELL

~

DONALD, PICK THE TEA PARTY FANATIC AND
LOSE MORE SUPPORT

~

REMEMBER: A PENCE IS WORTH ONLY A PENNY

~

MIKE PENCE WANTED TED CRUZ TO BE PRESIDENT

~

POLL SHOWS NINE OUT OF TEN AMERICANS WANT TO KNOW:
"WHO IN HELL IS MIKE PENCE?"

~

THE GREAT WHITE DOPE AND THE HOOSIER HOMOPHOBE

~

A RIGHT-WING TRIFECTA—
RACIAL HATRED, RELIGIOUS HATRED, AND SAME-SEX HATRED

~

PARTY OF GOP SWITCHES INITIALS TO BIFF:
BIGOTS, IDIOTS, FASCISTS, AND FOOLS

***

It was July 14, Bastille Day, in the French Riviera city of Nice. Revelers were parading along the seafront promenade enjoying the fireworks when suddenly, a crazed 31-year-old Muslim fanatic from Tunisia started driving a large ice truck down the crowded boulevard. He massacred eighty-four men, women, and children, and injured another 100 or so along the length of his deadly mile-long path. He killed them with an automatic rifle and also by crushing them under the wheels of his truck. His slaughter of innocents came to an end when French police assassinated him.

The resort's waterfront esplanade was transformed into a field of bloody, twisted bodies, pulverized beneath the wheels of this death machine.

In New York, Donald had been set to announce his vice presidential running mate at 11AM at Trump Tower, but postponed his appearance to honor the victims in Nice.

Speaking to the press, Donald claimed that as President of the United States, he would go before Congress and ask for a declaration of World War III to battle the Islamic terrorists. "I would, I would," he vowed. "We're dealing with people without uniforms. I'll also focus on restricting immigration and getting NATO more involved."

Angry that his choice for Veep had been prematurely leaked, he finally got around to formally designating Mike Pence, the controversial governor of Indiana, as his vice presidential running mate. He denied reports that almost up until the last minute, he "kept wavering in his choice."

A poll revealed that nine out of ten Americans had never heard of Pence. These same people would soon be filled in on stands he had taken both as a congressman and as an unpopular governor.

One of the first polls taken after the announcement discovered that only 12%of voters claimed that Pence's name on the ticket would make them more likely to vote for Trump. Most of this support came from evangelicals who didn't find

Shortly after Trump's announcement of Mike Pence as his Veep nominee, *The Advocate* described their campaign banner—superimposed next to Pence delivering a speech during his less-than-spectacular stint as governor of Indiana— as "curiously sexual," based on how the shaft of the "T seems to penetrate the hole in the "P."

Donald Trump "all that religious" in spite of his protestations.

None of these evangelicals had ever doubted the faith of Pence. As a congressman, he used to read passages from the Bible to either an empty chamber, or perhaps to an audience of only two or three fellow congressmen.

The Hillary Clinton campaign certainly knew who Pence was, and its administrators were shocked that Donald had made a selection of such a "right-wing nutbag, the most extreme pick in a generation." As a comparison, Barry Goldwater in the 1964 campaign against Lyndon B. Johnson was cited. *Clintonistas* attacked Pence's extremist views on abortion, gun rights, immigration, the LGBT community, and the minimum wage.

John D. Podesta, Hillary's campaign manager, said, "Trump has reinforced some of this most disturbing beliefs by choosing an incredibly divisive and unpopular running mate known for supporting discriminatory policies against millions of Americans and his failed economic policies as governor of Indiana."

"As a politician, Pence has a rich history of marginalizing women," said Mary Stech, spokesperson for "Emily's List," a pro-choice group. "As regards women, he shares something in common with Donald Trump. Together, they are a perfect storm of classic out-of-touch GOP extremism. For the very few women still not convinced that Trump isn't a threat to women, Governor Pence should do it—these two men are not to be trusted."

To the LGBT community, Pence was among the most loathed politicians in America. Not since the Third Reich went down in flames in the spring of 1945 had such anti-gay rhetoric been heard in America

In 2002, Pence stated, "Congress should oppose any effort to recognize homosexuals as a discreet and insular minority entitled to the protection of anti-discrimination laws similar to those extended to women and ethnic minorities." As it was assessed at the time, he wanted to strip away the rights of millions of tax-paying American citizens.

Gay activist Paul Bristol said, "This corn-fed Hoosier boy really hates our guts and holds us in utter contempt. History may one day record that Donald J. Trump took leave of his senses in nominating this Midwestern psycho. The Trump children should have known better even if daddy was an idiot. They were said to have vetted Pence. Could they be as stupid as dear ol' dad?"

"In choosing Pence," wrote one reporter, "Donald Trump selected a politician who has scars from the kinds of ideological fights that electrify social conservatives. He has support from evangelicals who aren't sure they can stomach Trump."

Lynn Evans, who had campaigned against Pence in Indiana every time he'd run for office, said, "If Trump becomes President and is assassinated, and Pence becomes President, and is informed of an imminent nuclear attack, instead of retaliating, he'd probably get down on his knees and ask Jesus to save America."

"Pence dodged the bullet in our state," wrote one reporter. "Had he run for re-election as governor of Indiana, he would have gone down in flames. He and Danforth Quayle could go out and get drunk together—no, not that. Pence avoids places where alcohol is served, viewing it as some kind of devil's brew."

Although Pence's selection as a potential Veep was viewed with mounting horror by millions, the Tea Party defined him as a hero. Senate Leader Mitch McConnell said Pence was "a great choice. We look forward to enthusiastically supporting the ticket."

Ironically, in December of 2015, Pence had opposed Donald's call to ban Muslims from entering the United States. The governor referred to it as "offensive and unconstitutional."

House Speaker Paul Ryan said that he rejoiced after hearing that Donald had picked a "good movement conservative. Clearly Mike is that. No one will challenge his conservative principles."

Ryan's backing of Pence was to be expected. As a former congressman, Pence had favored Ryan's plan for America—low taxes on the rich, free trade, and a trimming of the Social Security net.

In newspapers across the country, "Letters to the Editor" boxes were flooded with e-mails. Michael G. Sivler of New York wrote: "Pence is the obvious choice, given the Republican platform. He's anti-women, anti-gay, anti-poor, and anti-immigrant. He is not merely right wing. He's cruel, racist, and uncaring."

S.C. Palepu, also of New York, claimed that "the choice made sense since Donald didn't want a running mate to steal the limelight from him like Newt Gingrich or Chris Christie might have done. Mike Pence has the personality, the charisma, and the star wattage of a rutabaga."

Many pundits claimed that Donald's selection of such a staunch anti-gay, anti-abortion social conservative at least would be a complicated gamble, attracting the most extreme of evangelicals but alienating millions upon millions of moderate and independent voters.

Columnist David Brooks mocked Donald's endorsement of Pence: "With his selection, Trump launched his verbal rocket ship straight through the stratosphere, and it landed somewhere on the dark side of Planet Debbie. It was truly the strangest vice presidential unveiling in recent political history. Ricocheting around the verbal wilds for more than twice as long as the man he was introducing, Trump even refused to remain on stage and gaze on admiringly as Pence flattered him. It was like watching a guy lose interest in a wedding when the bride appeared."

The press had been mocking Christie as "Trump's lap dog." Apparently, according to some reporters, he'd made a last-ditch plea to Donald to name him, but was rejected. He'd been one of Donald's earlier backers, having dropped out of the race for President himself.

"He tried so hard to get the Veep nod, but ended up not just losing badly in the presidential stakes, but looking so much weaker than before," said Ed Rollins, longtime GOP strategist.

"Christie's rejection was death by humiliation," said Andy Borowitz, the *New Yorker* humor columnist. "Slow, twisting, and played out in public, like a reality show elimination."

At the time of his loss of the Veep nod, Christie's approval rating as governor of New Jersey had sunk to a dismal low of 26 percent.

As for Newt Gingrich, he reportedly said "I knew all along that I was too smart for Donald. He feared that as his Veep, I would outshine him on the campaign trail."

Donald told the press he might find a position for both Gingrich and Christie in his new government.

As a side note, Haskel Lookstein, was the prominent New York rabbi who had supervised the conversion of Ivanka Trump to Judaism before her marriage to Jared Kushner. It had been announced that he would deliver one of the opening prayers at the Republican Convention in Cleveland. But when criticism of his involvement with Donald's campaign increased, he withdrew his offer of a public appearance, asserting that the preannounced invocation "had become too political. Politics divides people. It does not bring them together."

Throughout the campaign, reporters had called Donald, among other labels, "borderline pathological" or even "the Michelangelo of Deception."

For decades, he had been known for exaggerating money claims. For example, appearing on a TV interview with Larry King, he claimed he was paid $1 million for a speech. Actually, he got $400,000 for that speech, an impressive enough figure.

As one reporter noted, "With all the lies he's told, he has the *cojones* to call Hillary a liar. Compared to him, she's the Goddess of Truth."

The *Washington Post* fact-checked forty-six of Donald's statements. They determined that there was something misleading with 70% of them, an error rating worth four Pinocchios, an abysmal record.

710

One liberal newsman, a cynical one at that, wrote: "On July 15, as Trump announced what a great guy and governor Mike Pence of Indiana was, he told the greatest lie yet. Pence is great all right, if you go in for a homophobic, Bible-thumping misogynist to the right of Joseph Goebbels."

So Ya Wanna Unify the GOP?
PUNDITS SLAM
THE VOTING RECORD OF
MIKE PENCE

Sometimes, His Stands Were So Far Right That They're Incompatible with Positions Endorsed by Donald

"Just who is this Mike Pence?" voters wanted to know.

Born in Columbus, Indiana, one of six children, Mike Pence was the son of a gas jockey. His grandfather had emigrated from Ireland through Ellis Island to become a bus driver in Chicago.

Pence earned a law degree from Indiana University in 1986 and later became a right-wing radio talk show host, adopting Rush Lindbaugh as his role model, but without Rush's bite. "He talked about the weather and how the chickens were laying," wrote one critic.

He spearheaded two unsuccessful campaigns for Congress—in 1988 and again in 1990, but was trounced by longtime Democratic incumbent Phil Sharp. Eventually, he won a congressional seat in November of 2000 and was re-elected four more times by safe margins. He campaigned on "a return to the GOP values of the 1994 Republican Revolution." In 2009, he was elected to become the Republican Conference Chairman, the third highest ranking GOP leadership post.

Deserting Congress, Pence ran and won the Republican governorship of Indiana in 2012.

He continues to maintain that he is "a Christian, a conservative, and a Republican in that order." The former altar boy had once considered entering the priesthood.

A champion of traditional family values, he married his wife, Karen with the jet black hair, in 1985 and they have three children—Michael, Charlotte, and Audrey. When Pence was a congressman, the family lived in Arlington, Virginia.

A Democratic strategist in Indiana (who did not want to be named) said,

"As First Lady, or Second Lady, as the case may be, Karen Pence would adhere to the political beliefs of Grace Coolidge and Lou Henry Hoover. But instead of being a fashion maven like Jacqueline Kennedy or Nancy Reagan, she would follow the dress code—not the politics—of Bess Truman, actually more like Mamie Eisenhower."

Politically, Donald and Pence are miles apart. That's why the press consistently referred to them as "The Odd Couple" [*a reference to a 1968 film starring Jack Lemmon and Walter Matthau about two incompatible divorced men living together*].

Most often, Pence's political stances are based on ignorance. Long after the government confirmed that cigarette smoking could cause cancer, he mocked their alarm. In 1998, he announced the statement as "hysteria—smoking doesn't kill. Time for a quick reality check." Perhaps he was the one needing the reality check.

As one reporter from Indianapolis wrote, "Pence wants us to get lung cancer."

After announcing Pence as his Veep, Donald praised his accomplishments in Congress, earning even more Pinocchios.

During a twelve-year career in Washington, Pence did introduce 90 controversial bills and resolutions. Not one of the Pence bills ever became law. Even his fellow GOP congressmen rejected them.

In 2003, he launched a ferocious attack on the LGBT community, calling for "an audit to ensure that Federal money not be given to organizations or any group that celebrated and encouraged the types of behaviors that facilitated the spreading of the HIV/AIDS virus." Shockingly, he advocated that Federal money be directed instead toward the discredited "conversion therapy" programs aimed at turning homosexuals into heterosexuals.

He also called for the removal of gays and lesbians from the military. "Homosexuality is incompatible with military service because the presence of homosexuals in the ranks weakens unit cohesion." In 2010, he urged that the policy of "Don't Ask, Don't Tell" not be repealed, again citing unit cohesion as his motivation. He also opposed the 2009 Matthew Shepard Hate Crimes Act, claiming that by endorsing it, President Obama wanted to advance a radical homosexual agenda. He wanted pastors to be free to express Biblical views on the issue of "homosexual behavior," which, in essence, called for their deaths.

Of course, he opposed same-sex marriage and advocated a nationwide constitutional ban on it, or else an overturn of the 5-4 Supreme Court Ruling. He also opposed civil unions and any government recognition of homosexuals at all.

He continued with his rants that no Federal funding should be used to aid people with HIV/AIDS unless programs were established to "change the sexual behavior of these people."

One columnist asked, "Exactly what does Pence advocate? Praying away the gay at some Nazi concentration camp? The Nazis found the gas chamber quicker."

Pence detested gay people, but loves guns. The NRA gave him an "A+" for his votes against any form of gun control. In Congress, he voted to ban lawsuits against gun manufacturers and to loosen regulations on Interstate gun purchases, including on assault weapons.

He also endorsed a Trans Pacific Partnership and other trade pacts such as NAFTA that Donald has consistently campaigned against.

As for NAFTA, Pence said, "I believe it's the only thing Bill Clinton has ever done that I agree with. Trade means jobs."

In striking contrast, Donald had defined NAFTA as "the worst economic deal in the history of America."

In Congress, Pence had defied his fellow GOP members when he attacked such signature programs as "No Child Left Behind" and a Medicare prescription drug benefit.

As one critic said, "He attacks women's rights to control their own bodies, tells gays who they can love, and now he wants poor people who can't afford much needed drugs to die. What a guy!"

As a congressman in 2006, Pence had proposed an immigration compromise by creating a guest worker program. He faced intense opposition from his fellow Republicans, and the bill died like a plucked wildflower. Instead of a wall, he advocated building a fence along the Mexican border.

Pence has been one of the leading attack dogs opposing Planned Parenthood, advocating that the government refuse Federal funding in spite of the good work they do providing reproductive health care and saving women's lives in their health clinics. His stance was based entirely on the subsection of their organization that focuses on abortions, even though no Federal funding was used for that purpose.

At one point, and with a sense of outrage, he cited video footage which purported to show a Planned Parenthood clinic "harvesting body parts of a fetus."

It turned out that such footage was a fake: The videographers who tampered with the footage and faked it were later indicted on a charge of tampering with a government record. Pence did not apologize to Planned Parenthood.

Pence stirred up an even bigger uproar in March of 2016 when, as governor, he advocated a stringent abortion measure. The law that he advocated would have barred abortions motivated solely for reasons associated with the fetus's race or gender. It would also have barred the availability of an abortion based on the diagnosis that the fetus suffered from a disability such as Downs syndrome.

It also would have made the receipt, sale, or transfer of fetal tissue a felony.

For these and for other positions he adopted, Pence came under fire from women's groups. Subsequently, a Federal judge issued a preliminary injunction to block the proposed law as endorsed by Pence.

On March 26, 2015, Pence was introduced to millions of Americans for the first time when he signed into Indiana law the notorious so-called Religious Freedom Restoration Act. Critics called it "freedom to discriminate against gay people." News about its negative implications almost instantly went viral.

The statewide law was condemned nationwide by everyone except evangelicals.

Companies doing business in Indiana not only denounced the bill, but threatened to withdraw business from the state. The mayors of Seattle and San Francisco each announced their respective bans of state business travel to Indiana.

Powerful CEOs notified Pence that they were pulling their conventions out of Indiana, citing the new laws as insulting and injurious to the well-being of their employees and/or customers. Ultimately this wave of cancellations and bad publicity cost the state economy some $60 million in lost revenues. *Angie's List* announced it would cancel a $40 million expansion at its headquarters in the state.

Visitors were urged to boycott the state of Indiana after Governor Mike Spence signed a law (the Religious Freedom Restoration Act) that made it legal for businesses to turn away LGBT customers.

As a result of that boycott and the tsunamis of negative publicity for Indiana that followed, the state lost $60 million in revenues, and set an example for how NOT to run a state government.

The fallout and negativity generated by Pence was so severe that pundits who had traced his political career predicted its imminent

714

demise.

Bowing to the pressure, he agreed to "fix" the bill, revising the law so as not to discriminate against the GLBT community. Evangelicals attacked him for backing down. In the meantime, Indiana still has laws that discriminate against LGBT people in unemployment benefits and housing.

"Pence's Law," as it came to be known, generated so much attention that Obama mocked it at the annual 2015 White House correspondents' dinner. He joked that he and Joe Biden had become so close that if they came to Indiana, chances were that they would not be served a pizza.

***

As the Republican nominee for Veep, Pence will offer no comfort to millions of people who fear the oncoming devastation of global warming.

As governor of Indiana, he threatened to disobey the Federal government's orders to lower carbon emissions. "The government rules will raise electricity costs for Hoosiers," he claimed. "That will result in less reliable electricity and impede economic growth and prosperity in Indiana and the rest of the country."

He also claimed that the Clean Power Plan was "ill conceived and poorly executed." He further accused the Environmental Protection Agency of going beyond its legal authority in enacting the rules of the plan. He announced that as Governor, he'd join several other Red states in trying to block the Clear Power Plan in Federal courts.

Pence and Donald appeared uncomfortable in each other's presence as they faced a joint appearance on CBS's *60 Minutes* where they were interviewed by journalist Lesley Stahl. She immediately zeroed in on foreign policy and how Donald had condemned Hillary for voting for the war against Iraq and how she had urged U.S. intervention in Libya.

Ironically, Pence—of whom Donald seemed to abundantly approve—had advocated almost exactly the same positions.

When challenged with this, Donald seemed to duck the question, as Pence squirmed.

Stahl then said, "In other words, Hillary is to be condemned and Pence is given a pass?"

Pence not only endorsed the U.S. military intervention in Iraq, but, as a member of the Foreign Affairs Committee, had made annual visits to both that country and to Afghanistan. In 2007, he was ridiculed for a remark he made while visiting a market in Baghdad. "It reminds me of a normal outdoor market in Indiana in the summertime."

Only months before, men, women, and children had been blown apart in a bomb attack at that very market he visited.

However, Donald and Pence were on the same page when the governor tried unsuccessfully to prevent Syrian refugees from settling in Indiana.

On *60 Minutes*, Donald said, "We're going to declare war on ISIS. We have to wipe it out." He also stated that he would use "brains and brawn" to defeat Islamic terrorists. "We'll need very few troops on the ground. We're going to have unbelievable intelligence, which we need right now and don't have."

He blamed Hillary for the rise of ISIS. "She invented these terrorists with her stupid choices. She is responsible for ISIS. She led Obama because I don't think he knew anything. I think he relied on her."

"As Bernie Sanders claimed, she's got bad judgment," Donald charged. "So bad. She's got bad instincts."

He also said he would call on Turkey to play a larger role battling ISIS. "Ankara alone could eliminate ISIS."

In announcing his choice of Pence as a "job creator," Donald failed to call attention to the announcement by Carrier, Inc., a manufacture of air conditioning and refrigeration units, that it was pulling its manufacturing facilities out of Indianapolis and moving them to Monterrey, Mexico. That meant a loss of 1,400 American jobs.

Chuck Jones, the head of the union representing the steelworkers who will lose their jobs when Carrier moves beginning in 2017, was asked for an opinion about the Trump-Pence ticket.

"Those 'job creators,'" he said. "All that duo needs is a circus tent."

During a Pence interview on *60 Minutes*, he blamed Hillary and Obama for the attempted military coup in Turkey, with its subsequent loss of life. "The larger issue here is declining American power in the world."

William Kristol, the editor of the conservative *Weekly Standard*, said, "Pence and Trump will probably conceal their differences on the campaign trail and stick to about the only thing they agree on—that Obama was a horrible President and Hillary was a horrible Secretary of State."

***

In all the hysteria surrounding the Pence selection on the eve of the convention, Donald still had time to comment on other personalities making news.

He defended the Fox media mogul, Roger Ailes, against charges of sexual harassment brought by former anchor Gretchen Carlson. She claimed in a court document that she had to refuse his sexual advances.

In an interview with the *Washington Examiner*, Donald said, "Trust me, Ailes is no perv. I think the accusations against him are unfounded, based on what I've read. Totally unfounded."

He took delight when Ruth Bader Ginsburg, Justice of the Supreme Court, apologized for her criticism of his candidacy. She told the press her comments against him were, "Ill-advised—and I regret making them."

On July 17, as Republican delegates were packing their bags and heading for Cleveland, news erupted about an ambush against police officers in Baton Rouge, Louisiana. That city had been the scene of daily protests following the shooting of a black man, Alton Sterling, reportedly at point blank range while he was being restrained by local police.

On that sleepy Sunday morning, a deranged African American, a former Marine, shot and killed three policemen and wounded three others.

The killer, Gavin Eugene Long, wore a Ninja-like black mask as he went on his murderous rampage. It was later revealed it was his 29th birthday, and he was a self-described member of the Nation of Islam.

Campaigning as the law-and-order candidate, Donald declared that "America has become a divided crime scene."

President Obama issued a call for calm in the wake of the shootings by police officers of two African American men and the subsequent massacres of police officers in both Dallas and Baton Rouge.

After listening to the President, Donald tweeted, "He doesn't have a clue. How many law enforcement people have to die because of lack of leadership in our country? We demand law and order!"

***

Hours before the convention opened in Cleveland, Donald reportedly threw a "temper fit" over his "showbiz plans" for the gathering. He had wanted the flamboyant boxing promoter, Don King, to address the convention, but his proposal was vetoed. The chairman of the Republican National Committee, Reince Priebus, reminded Donald that King has once stomped a man to death and had been convicted of manslaughter. Donald finally gave in.

He also wanted Tom Brady, the New England Patriots' quarterback, to address the convention, but Brady, it appeared, was not available. Nor interested, perhaps. Donald was also said to have requested Bob Knight, Indiana University's men's basketball coach, but he didn't make the GOP speakers' lineup either.

Donald also wanted Kathleen Willey to appear and to recite her claim that in the 1990s, while in the Oval Office, Bill Clinton allegedly groped her.

Nikki Haley, governor of South Carolina, was said to have turned down an invitation to speak as well.

One highly visible competitor who agreed to speak at Donald's party was "Lyin' Ted Cruz," perhaps hoping that he could be the Republicans' nominee in 2020.

***

On the day the convention opened, Donald proclaimed, "It's going to be the classiest, the greatest, and most amazing convention in the history of conventions—like a real spectacle with a showbiz edge."

"Hillary might have Barbra Streisand or possibly Meryl Streep, but we've got Antonio Sabato, Jr., Scott Baio, even Willie Robertson *Duck Dynasty.*"

Whatever Donald did, he didn't plan to re-invite Clint Eastwood, who appeared in 2012 and delivered a rambling speech to an empty chair that he pretended held Obama. It was a sad spectacle and was ridiculed across the nation. The GOP was seen as a party of "cranky old white men yelling at ghosts," in the words of reporter James Poniewozik.

FASHION & THE CULTURE WARS

What Trump Fans Were Wearing in

Cleveland

DAY ONE

Of the Republican National Convention
Monday, July 18, 2016

GOP DELEGATES CONVENE
IN CLEVELAND

"An Alamo of Aggrieved Counterattacks
As Custer Seeks Revenge"

RANCOR AND HARD-EDGE RHETORIC
"LOCK HER UP!"

Launch Fiery Gathering as Protesters Rant Outside

MELANIA TRUMP—WOULD-BE FIRST LADY—
Is Charged with Plagiarism, Stealing Words and Phrases from
Michelle Obama.

GOP ADOPTS ITS MOST HOMOPHOBIC PLATFORM
IN HISTORY—
"Gays Should Be Stripped of All Rights Except Taxation"

"It Was Like Putting Lipstick on a Pig"
—the Ghostwriter of Donald's *The Art of the Deal*

The timing could not have been worse for The Donald. On the eve of the Republican Convention in Cleveland, Ohio, the author who "ghosted" *The Art of the Deal* for Donald attacked the presumptive GOP nominee for President of the United States.

Donald had long maintained that his famous book, which had roosted on *The New York Times* bestseller list for 51 weeks, was his second favorite book after the Bible.

His ghost writer, Tony Schwartz, admitted that he felt deep remorse for "putting lipstick on a pig." He claimed that he regretted portraying the real estate mogul in a positive light, stating a firm belief that the election of Donald as President of the United States "might lead to the decline of Western Civilization."

Donald had split the $500,000 advance in royalties from Random House with Schwartz. During its preparation, a period that lasted about eighteen months, Schwartz had met frequently with Donald.

"The money came as a huge windfall for me," Schwartz said. "But I knew I was selling out. Literally, the term was invented to describe what I did."

Today, Schwartz, who runs a consulting firm, recalled his frequent meetings with Donald—in his office, in his Manhattan apartment, in Palm Beach, and in his private helicopter. He claimed that Donald suffered from an at-

In August of 2015, Donald Trump insulted and embarrassed John Kerry and Barack Obama by saying that they should read and learn from his book, *The Art of the Deal,* as an antidote to screwing up their negotiations with Iran and the rest of the world.

Lower photo. Just before the convention in Cleveland, ghostwriter Tony Schwartz, who wrote the book in Donald's name, forcefully rejected the book's premises and announced publicly, "I would have titled the book *The Sociopath.*"

tention deficit disorder. "He could not focus for long on any subject other than his own self-aggrandizement for more than a few minutes. If, as President, he had to be briefed on a world crisis in the Situation Room, it's hard to imagine him paying attention for very long."

The author admitted that he wrote a memoir which was "a fable of fame and fortune woven mainly from falsehoods or euphemisms that Trump created."

"Donald Trump is a hateful, one-dimensional blowhard, who is pathologically impulsive, obsessed with publicity, self-centered, and so cold he pisses ice water."

"Lying is second nature to him. More than anyone I have ever met, he has the ability to convince himself that whatever he is saying at any given moment is true, or sort of true, or at least it ought to be true."

Schwartz admitted that he'd made a "Faustian bargain" in ghosting the book for the mogul. "I was caught between the Devil and the higher side."

While researching the book, Schwartz spend days listening to Donald on the phone, often fighting with attorneys, bankers, or reporters. "The experience was draining for me. Even more draining was trying to make Trump appear as a sympathetic character. Rather than the just hateful or, worse yet, one-dimensional blowhard that he was." He deliberately left out unflattering details

After the great success of the book, Donald offered the author a chance to write a sequel for a third of the profits. Schwartz turned down the "second ghost job."

In the *New Yorker*, Donald attacked Schwartz. "Wow! That's great disloyalty, because I made Tony rich. He owes me a lot. I helped him when he didn't have two cents in his pocket. It's great disloyalty. I guess he thinks it's good for him—but he'll find out it's not good for him."

Schwartz, appearing on *Good Morning America*, said, "I feel it is my civic duty to speak out against Trump" He also claimed that he was pledging all of his 2016 royalties due him to charities supporting immigrants and victims of torture. "I like the idea that the more copies that *The Art of the Deal* sells, the more money I can donate to the people whose rights Trump seeks to abridge."

It was later announced that Donald planned to sue Schwartz in a suit that demanded the return of all the royalties paid out so far.

***

The city of Cleveland was tense on the night of Sunday, July 17. The

Cleveland Republican National Convention was set to open the following afternoon.

The theme of Monday's confab of delegates on the first night was to "Make America Safe Again."

Outside the Quicken Loans Arena, the atmosphere felt anything but safe. At least part of the fear was based on Ohio's controversial open-carry law, allowing people to walk around fully armed.

Police chief Calvin Williams had appealed to Ohio's governor, John Kasich, to issue a temporary ban on that state law. But the former presidential candidate claimed that he lacked the authority to suspend the law.

Newspaper headlines proclaimed "LET THE CIRCUS BEGIN—ANYTHING CAN HAPPEN."

"Bring 'em on," said Cleveland Mayor Frank Jackson. "Have no fear. The people of Cleveland are not strangers to unrest and demonstrations and protests."

The forecasts were dire: "BLOOD WILL FLOW IN THE STREETS OF CLEVELAND."

Agitation from at least 10,000 protesters, both pro- and anti-Trump, had been anticipated. Groups ranged from those calling for a communist overthrow of the government to Bible-thumping Born Again right-wing religious zealots, some of them predicting the fast-approaching End of the World.

The controversial Black Lives Matter movement was expected to show up in full force, denouncing cops as "fat pigs who should be fried like bacon."

"All these gun-toting protesters piling into our city is total insanity," said Steve Loomis, head of the Cleveland Police Patrolmen's Association.

In June, Cleveland's mayor, Jackson, took out a $50 million insurance policy, a precaution to protect his city in case of massive destruction of property.

Members of the KKK supporting Donald were expected to arrive, as were the rather threatening new Black Panther Party, a radical nationalist coven. The Oath Keepers, another radical anti-government group, were due to arrive as well. This cabal was composed mostly of heavily armed former members of the military.

Motivated by images of the terrorist attack which had recently devastated Nice, in France, the city had taken precautions to prevent a massacre. Police officers placed barriers or barricades along key streets and intersections leading into the downtown neighborhoods near and around the Arena.

More than 3,000 Ohio policemen would be on the scene, outfitted with state-of-the-art gear and body cameras. This force was beefed up by 4,000 security officers from various government agencies, including hundreds from the FBI. Officers arrived from locations ranging from Florida to California.

The pugnacious former Senator from New York, Alfonse D'Amato, predicted that the officers were needed to prevent a calamity. "Some of the hooligans will be armed," he said. "So I think we are going to have riotous conditions caused by these absolute degenerates who don't give a damn about the values of this country and are trying to rip us apart."

In an appearance on *Fox News* on July 17, RNC chairman Reince Priebus was more optimistic: "Every convention has its share of problems and protests," he said. "Obviously, this has been a pretty politically charged environment over the past year. So we are taking extra precautions to prevent violence in Cleveland."

Before the convention opened, Paul Manafort, Donald's chief adviser, attacked Kasich for refusing to support Donald after he won the nomination. "Kasich is embarrassing our party in Ohio. It's a disgrace he's not showing up for the Republican convention in his own state."

As anticipated, the evening was marked by fiery speeches, beginning with venomous attacks on Hillary Clinton. One delegate from Delaware said, "Don't print my name, but Hillary is getting blamed for the massacres of police, the Nice slaughter, all the earthquakes or volcanic eruptions, any loss of jobs, for all poverty, for any terrorist attacks against U.S. citizens, for her husband's infidelities, and for secret deals with some of the most horrible dictators on the face of the planet. I never realized she had such power."

The #NeverTrump movement, still mostly aligned with the failed candidacy of Ted Cruz, staged chaos on the convention floor. The insurgent delegates tried to push forward a roll call vote to overturn previously agreed-upon rules supported by pro-Trump forces. It would deny Donald's enemies a chance to stir up a fight during prime time TV at the first night's session. Most of the fight was over whether delegates would be "bound" to vote for Donald based on previous elections and caucuses. These rebels wanted to be cut free of any obligations forged during the primaries. "We want to be allowed to vote our conscience," became their oft-repeated, anti-Donald rallying cry.

The pro-Trump forces booed the anti-Trump insurgents, and the Republican National Chairman hastily denied insurgents' demand for a roll call with a voice vote.

Dissidents had submitted petitions from nine states, which, according to party rules, would have, in most "normal" circumstances, forced a roll call vote. That tactic didn't work. When their requests were denied, the Colorado delegation stormed out in protest, followed by angry delegates from both Virginia and Utah.

BENGHAZI...AGAIN
"I Blame Hillary Clinton Personally For the Death of My Son"
—Patricia Smith

The tumultuous night led off with speeches by emotional parents who had lost their offspring at the "murdering hands" of illegal immigrants. That was followed by Marine Corps veterans who had fought in the attack on Benghazi in Libya and lived to tell about it.

The most emotional speech of the evening came near the beginning. It was delivered by the nearly hysterical Patricia Smith, the mother of Sean Smith, one of the four U.S. soldiers who had died during the attack on the U.S mission in Benghazi in 2012.

"I blame Hillary Clinton personally for the death of my son," she claimed, even though the charge was outrageous. Nonetheless, she brought tears to many delegates, as one representative from Georgia later said, "Ms. Smith was preaching to the choir, and most of us knew that Hillary was not personally responsible. Only a fool would believe that, but we cheered her on anyway because all of us hated Hillary."

"The entire campaign comes down to a single question," Smith said. "If Hillary Clinton can't give us the truth, why should we give her the presidency?" She paused to notice a hand-painted sign in the audience urging its reader to "LOCK HER UP!"

"That's right," Smith said. "Hillary for prison. She deserves the stripes!"

Midway through Smith's vengeful rant for her dead son, Donald interrupted the Fox News broadcast and spoke personally to Bill O'Reilly, the leading Fox News anchor. He was later criticized for interrupting Smith's speech, since most Republicans around the country were watching the Fox News broadcast of the convention instead of MSNBC's or CNN's.

STUMPING AND TRUMPING
Prime Time Blahs at the RNC
THE REPUBLICANS ANNOUNCE THEIR KEYNOTE CONVENTION SPEAKERS:
D-List Entertainers from Show Biz's Dead Zone Breathlessly Witnessing to Millions About Donald: A Calvin Klein Underwear Model, and a Has-Been from Happy Days.

Donald had promised convention-goers that exhibitions of "show biz star power" would be sizzling onstage and rooting for him at the Convention, but all the big names in Hollywood, including Barbra Streisand, seemed to have run away in droves and in many cases, migrated toward Hillary. So instead of super stars, Donald rounded up what the *New York Daily News* headlined as "HAS-BEEN D-LISTERS TO KICK OFF SIDESHOW CONFAB."

Sabato

Antonio Sabato, Jr., whom aging female delegates and the few log cabin gays remembered for his provocative "underwear revelations" for long-ago Calvin Klein ads, came onto the stage, still looking good after all these years.

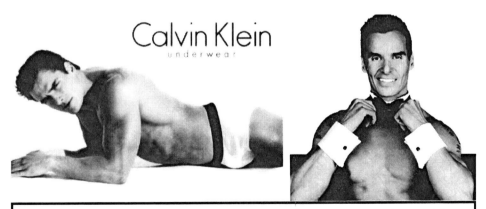

Hillary Clinton could persuade and enlist A-list legends such as Barbra Streisand or Meryl Streep to promote her candidacy.

In contrast, for "star power" of his own, Donald had to turn to former Calvin Klein underwear model Antonio Sabato, Jr. On the right, he appears as a Chippendale dancer.

He was remembered for his role in the soap opera, *General Hospital*, and he has also appeared in reality shows, including *My Antonio*, in 2009. In the latter, various young women competed to be his girlfriend.

From the podium, he spoke of his immigrant status, asserting that he'd arrived in the U.S. from Rome in 1985, the son of an Italian father and a mother from what was then known as Czechoslovakia. He'd been granted citizenship in 1996. "I took no shortcuts—it was legal," he proclaimed, as he invoked the teachings of Jesus Christ, with a call to protect the future of the nation's children.

He went on to attack the previous eight years of the Obama administration, making the claim that the rights of Americans had been trampled upon.

Baio

Remembered by older delegates from the time he was 16, actor and TV director Scott Baio also made an appearance. He'd been cast as The Fonz's cousin, Chachi Arcola, in the hit TV series, *Happy Days*, which went off the

Front cover, April, 1979, of *Tiger Beat* magazine, documenting the peak years of teen idol and boy band hottie Scott Baio, one of whose big hits was "How Do You Talk to Girls?" Baio made two records, the second and final of which was released in 1983.

At the Cleveland Republican Convention, this refugee from the long defunct TV series, *Happy Days*, vigorously endorsed the candidacy of Donald Trump.

So a decades-old TV gig on *Happy Days* and an unchivalrous use of the C-word makes you a celebrity?

Depicted above is Scott Baio's Twitter—the one that attracted the attention and approval of Donald Trump. It propelled him from show biz obscurity to prime time as a keynote speaker at the RNC.

air in 1984. He had also played a role in the TV sitcom, *Charles in Charge,* which premiered on CBS in 1985 and ran for 126 episodes.

Born in Brooklyn in 1960, Baio was a political conservative. He had campaigned for Ronald Reagan at a young age, and had also attended his state funeral.

In 2012, he'd endorsed Mitt Romney, claiming, "I can't tell whether Obama is dumb, a Muslim, or a Muslim sympathizer."

Baio said, "America is an easy place to get to, but it's important to know what it means to be an American. It doesn't mean getting free stuff."

That charge was met with wild applause from delegates who loathed the welfare system and food stamps. "Being American means sacrificing, winning, losing, failing, succeeding, and sometimes doing things you don't want to do, including hard work, in order to get where you want to get."

Baio had attracted Donald's attention when he sent out, via Twitter, a now-notorious photograph of Hillary. She was shown in front of a banner which read "COUNTRY."

Her body covered up the "O" in the banner, and the two final letters of "COUNTRY" were cut off. That left her in front of wide letters that collectively spelled "CUNT."

[Below the photo, a caption read: "So There's a Letter Blocked. What Difference Does It Make?"]

Robertson

Also as a speaker at his convention, Donald invited a quasi-celebrity, Willie Robertson, of the hit TV show, *Duck Dynasty.* As one reporter said, "Bearded Willie was hauled out to appeal to the hicks and the rednecks, or are those two terms redundant?"

Giving an embarrassing speech attacking political correctness, Robertson said, "Heck, I don't even know if they know how to talk to people in real America." No doubt, he was referring to Hillary and Obama. "They don't hunt and fish and pray. They just don't get it. Today, in a lot of ways, America is in a bad spot, and we will need a President who will have our back."

Clarke

It was to be a night promoting Donald as the candidate of Law and Order, with appeals to the mostly all-white audience. For the sake of appearance, Donald had tapped two African Americans to rebuke black protesters—specifically the Black Lives Matter movement.

David A. Clarke, Jr., the sheriff of Milwaukee County in Wisconsin, and a sometimes commentator on the Fox network, attacked the Black Lives Matter movement, proclaiming, "Blue Lives Matter."

He praised police officers around the country. "So many of the actions of the Occupy Movement and the Black Lives Matter transcend peaceful protest and violate the code of conduct we rely on." That remark brought cheers from the floor.

Clarke also received a robust round of applause when he praised the acquittal in Baltimore of Lt. Brian Rice in the alleged manslaughter death of Freddie Gray, which had led to nights of rioting, burning, and looting in that city.

Glenn

Belonging to that rare breed, an African American Republican, Colorado delegate Darryl Glenn, in a race for the Senate, said, "Someone with a nice tan needs to say too, 'All Lives Matter.'"

McCaul

Texas Rep. Michael McCaul, a member of the House Homeland Security panel, asked the delegates, "Are you safer today than you were eight months ago?"

Manigault

In a bizarre appointment, Donald named Omarosa Manigault, his director of African American outreach for his campaign. She had been the most controversial and outspoken guest on the first season of *The Apprentice,* making two appearances. She lost both times.

A reporter confronted her with the awful "near zero" support Donald had among African Americas. She admitted that the Trump campaign for the black vote "will be an uphill climb."

Cotton

Senator Tom Cotton of Arkansas came on stage to deliver his own military credentials and those of his family. He claimed that America "needs a commander-in-chief who calls the enemy by its name and enforces 'red lines' ruthlessly."

Giuliani: "Blue Lives Matter"

The most impressive law-and-order speaker of the night was Rudy Giuliani, who delivered the fiery speech of this career, the evening's biggest hit.

He, too, endorsed Blue Lives: "What I did for New York in lowering crime, Donald will do for America. The police don't ask if you're black or white, they just come to save you. We reach out with love and compassion to those who have lost loved ones in police shootings, some justified and some unjustified. People fear for themselves. They fear for their police officers who are being marked instead with a target on their backs. We pray for our police officers in Dallas and Baton Rouge and their families, and we say thank you to the Cleveland Police Department for protecting us."

He attacked Obama for his failure to identify Islamic terrorists. "Our enemies see us as weak and vulnerable because of him."

Delivering a full throated endorsement of Donald, Giuliani said, "In the last seven months, there have been five major Islamic terrorist attacks on us and our allies. We must not be afraid to define our enemy. It is *Islamic Extremist Terrorism*. The vast majority of Americans do not feel safe. They fear for their children."

A consummate showman, the former mayor built to a crescendo, as he shouted and waved his arms, getting the delegates to rise to their feet.

Although lauded by most of the delegates, Giuliani did not receive universal praise from newspaper columnists. Mike Lupica wrote: "The former New York mayor looked as if he were some cartoon, exploding head-ring announcer on *Monday Night Raw.* It was as if he thought he could arm-wave and stammer and shout himself back into political relevance with this bogeyman speech, at one point screaming, 'They're coming here to kill us!' It is always reassuring to hear this guy act like some expert at protecting anybody from terrorism. The next time he does that for anybody will be the first time."

MELANIA LOOKED GOOD…
Until Two Hours Later

At the end of Giuliani's speech, Donald himself appeared in a blue-tinged theatrical fog, like Batman in a movie. He was back-lit in silhouette as he showed up to the sound of Queen's "We Are the Champions." It was a precedent-breaking move, as most nominees in the past didn't appear until their acceptance speech in the final night of their respective conventions.

He told the clapping delegates, "Oh, we're going to win. We're going to win big."

He had come onstage to introduce the guest speaker of the evening, his stunning ex-model wife, Melania Trump. Beautifully made up and coiffed, she appeared in a white *haute couture* gown.

Her appearance would be the highlight of the evening. A headline the next day read:

"DONALD TRUMP'S WIFE MORE ELEGANT THAN MERYL STREEP."

She had come to praise her husband. "I know he will make a lasting difference," she told the delegates who seemed awed by her beauty and regal poise. "Donald has a great and deep and unbending determination and a never-give-up attitude. If you want someone to fight for you and for your country, I can assure you he's the guy."

"My husband offers a new direction, a welcoming change, prosperity, and greater cooperation among peoples and nations Donald intends to represent all of the people. That includes Christians and Jews and Muslims. It includes Hispanics and African Americans, and Asians and the poor and middle class."

"As First Lady, I will help women and children who need it."

Then she returned to praising Donald again. "He has a kinder, gentler side. That kindness is not always noted, but it is there for all to see. That is one reason I fell in love with him to begin with."

Her carefully rehearsed speech was met with a standing ovation except from the still bitter Ted Cruz faction. As one Colorado delegate complained, "Donald has a pretty wife, and Ted does not. But Donald is not extreme enough for most of us. He wants to deport illegal aliens. I'd prefer to round them up and shoot them. It's cheaper that way. Don't quote me."

It was approaching 11PM when the "Pig Castrator from Iowa," Senator Joni Ernest, appeared. In her attack on Hillary, she spoke to a half-empty arena.

"Hillary Clinton cannot be trusted," Ernst charged. "Her judgment and character are not suited to be sitting in the most powerful office in the world."

As she made those remarks, Hillary had just concluded addressing the

NAACP's annual convention. Donald had rejected an invitation to address the assembly of African Americans.

"There is no justification for directing violence at law enforcement," Hillary said. "As President, I will bring the full weight of the law to bear in making sure those who kill police officers are brought to justice."

In the meantime, a reporter was doing some fact-checking. Parts of Melania's speech had a familiar ring. She thought she'd heard it before.

A national scandal was about to erupt.

THE GOP's OFFICIAL 2016 PLATFORM
"Terrifying, Out of Date, and to the Right of Atilla The Hun"

The official platform adopted by the Republican delegates seemed to pass quietly under the radar screen, but it was one of the harshest and most socially conservative ever written, with homosexuals coming under the same heavy fire as the terrorists who threatened the safety of the United States.

The platform stated, "Five unelected lawyers robbed 320 million Americans of their legitimate constitutional authority to define marriage as the union of one man and one woman."

The bigoted report also stated: "The Court twisted the meaning of the 14th Amendment beyond recognition. To echo Scalia, we dissent. We, therefore, support the appointment of justices and judges who will respect constitutional limits on their power and respect the authority of the states to decide such fundamental social questions."

The platform endorsed traditional families over "modern families. Every child deserves a married mom or dad." The report also endorsed the application of widely discredited "conversion therapy" procedures as "therapy" for gay minors. It granting any parent the legal power to subject a young son or daughter suspected of becoming a gay man or lesbian to medical and psychological treatment in an attempt to alter their sexual orientation. *[Widely discredited by, among others, the State of California, this form of coerced behavior alteration has often ended in suicide.]*

In another assault, the Republican platform endorsed the right of any business to discriminate against gays and refuse to grant them services if that conflicted with a business person's religious views.

As anticipated, the platform drafters came down hard on the right of a woman's right to choose, granting almost no ground for a woman to abort a fetus, even if giving birth might lead to a woman's death.

The platform also called for the Bible to be taught in public schools, and asked for state or national legislators to use the Christian religion as a guide in lawmaking.

It also advocated that female soldiers be removed from combat, and rejected any need for gun control.

The platform adopted its most extreme position on the use by transgendered person of public toilets.

The "social and cultural revolution" being imposed on America by the Obama administration was attacked. Obama was accused of "wrongly defining sexual discrimination to include sexual orientation and other categories." It called for states' rights in determining the use of restrooms, locker rooms, and other facilities. The government was accused of drafting a mandate that was "at once illegal and dangerous, ignoring privacy issues."

The platform attacked Obamacare and criticized the "radical anti-coal agenda advocated by Democrats."

It also endorsed Donald's controversial call for building a wall along the southern border with Mexico.

The extreme right-wing advocacy of the platform drew fire from the liberal press, and even from the more enlightened conservative press, too.

The editorial board of *The New York Times* came down hard on the GOP platform, labeling it "one of disruption and damage. It rivals Donald Trump for shock value. It goes with the most extreme version of every position and is tailored to Trump's impulsive bluster. Ideologues pushed through a raft of plans to banish any notion of moderation. The planks of 2016 have been fashioned as underpinnings for Trump jingoism. The GOP used to insist it was a "big tent" open to one and all. Now, it's a Big Wall party braced by a destructive platform out of touch with American lives and devoid of the common sense the nation needs for any form of political progress."

DAY TWO

Of the Republican National Convention

Tuesday, July 19, 2016

GOpers "CLINCH THE DONALD DEAL"

As Don Jr's. Symbolically Defining Vote
"Throws Dad Over the Top"

SHOWTRIALS: "LOCK HER UP!"

Chris Christie, Puts "Lying Hillary" on Trial, without
Representation, at a Televised Kangaroo Court,
as Thousands of Agitated Republicans Scream for Blood

Within an hour of delivering her speech before the convention, Melania came under fire. Ugly charges of plagiarism arose, with allegations that she had borrowed complete passages of the speech that First Lady Michelle Obama had delivered at the Democratic National Convention in 2008.

It's not definite, but Jarett Hill, an out-of-work journalist watching the convention on his laptop from a Starbucks in L.A. may have been the first "detective" to note the similarities in the two speeches.

Most of the plagiarized passages concerned the importance of hard work and honesty. Sometimes, a complete paragraph was used with only minor changes or else a repetition of three words repeated verbatim as in "integrity, compassion, and intelligence."

Reporters at the *Huffington Post* discovered the similarities and tried to reach the Trump campaign for a comment. Their queries went unanswered.

It was not clear how much of the speech Melania had written herself.

She was known to speak five languages, of which English was her fifth. Sometimes, in TV interviews, she had made such errors in grammar as "he don't."

Hours before delivering her speech, she was interviewed by Matt Lauer aboard the Trump jet. Standing beside her husband, she made the claim that, "I wrote most of the speech myself with as little help as possible."

By Tuesday morning, the day after her worldwide mega-exposure, Melania's plagiarism had become the story of the day, even "Trumping" the news of Donald's nomination. But instead of headlining that triumph for which he'd struggled for months, *The New York Times* devoted its lead story to the plagiarism charge.

It seemed that Ivanka's husband, Jared Kushner, Donald's son-in-law, had originally commissioned veteran speechwriters John McConnell and Matthew Scully to write the remarks for Melania. They had written George W. Bush's speech to the nation that he delivered on September 11, 2001.

Their draft was delivered to Melania, and the two men heard nothing. When they watched her on TV, they admitted that almost none of their original draft had been used.

Reportedly, Melania had been disappointed in the speech they had crafted and wanted it reworked.

It appeared that she had turned to a different writer for help.

When confronted with charges of plagiarism, the Trump campaign aides buckled down and went into denial, at first admitting nothing.

Stuart Stevens, who had written speeches for Mitt Romney in 2012, commented on the charges. "It's like some guy trying to paddle across a river in a rowboat who shoots a hole in the boat."

Experienced speechwriters sometime avail themselves of several programs which are available online and, in some cases, free—including DupliChecker—which are capable of catching a plagiarism. Yet such computer applications were not used by Melania or her associates.

Chris Christie, the former attorney general of New Jersey, stated that had such a case come before him, he would not bring charges of plagiarism against Melania. "Ninety-three percent of the speech was original," he claimed.

Jeffrey Lord, a Trump supporter, appeared on CNN shifting the blame away from Melania. Overall, however, he downplayed the controversy. "Let's face it: This is not Benghazi."

Jason Miller, a spokesman from the Trump campaign, defended the integrity of Melania's speech. "Her team of writers took notes on her life's inspiration, and in most instances included fragments that reflected her own thinking. That included her immigrant experience and her love of America which shone through in her speech, which made it such a success with the convention."

His statement was followed by a supportive tweet from Donald himself. "It was truly an honor to introduce my wife, Melania. Her speech and demeanor were absolutely incredible. Very proud!"

Sean Spicer, RNC's chief strategist, shrugged off the charges. "The phrases in question are so pedestrian, they're used in the throwback cartoon *My Little Pony.* They're also used by singers Kid Rock and John Legend, so were talking about seventy words."

Campaign manager Paul Manafort weighed in, too. "There's no cribbing from Michelle Obama's speech," he said on *CNN.* "To think that she'd be cribbing from Michelle Obama is crazy."

Donald's former campaign manager, Corey Landowsky, who had been fired, stated that if Manafort had vetted Melania's speech, and approved it, he, too, should be fired.

Don Trump, Jr., took a different slant from Manafort. "Melania's speech writers should not have done it," he said, virtually admitting there was plagiarism after all.

Many newspapers published side-by-side extracts from Melania's speech on Tuesday night at the Cleveland convention, and Michelle's speech from 2008.

MELANIA: "You work hard for what you want in life. Your word is your bond and you do what you say and keep your promise. You treat people with respect."
MICHELLE: *"You work hard for what you want in life. Your word is your bond and you do what you say and keep your promise. You treat people with dignity and respect."*

MELANIA: "We want our children in this nation to know that the only limit to your achievements is the strength of your dreams and your willingness to work for them."
MICHELLE: *"We want our children — and all children in this nation — to know that the only limit of your achievement is the reach of your dreams and your willingness to work for them."*

Reports that Melania had stolen from Michelle set off a series of angry tweets from African Americans.

"All the Trumps do is attack Obama, and now they're caught swiping from Michelle," wrote Elija Yett of Ohio. "The next thing we'll hear is Melania giving the 'I Have a Dream' speech."

Yasmin Yonis wrote, "I'm not surprised that Melanie *(sic)* plagiarized from Michelle. White women have spent centuries stealing black women's genius, labor, babies, and bodies."

One musician tweeted, "It's totally predictable. White people always steal from blacks. Elvis Presley got his entire sound from Little Richard."

Many reports noted that even Donald's campaign slogans of "America First" and "Make America Great Again" were stolen from Pat Buchanan and Ronald Reagan.

Press criticism of Melania's speech was often negative, as reflected by this comment in the *Washington Post.* "Melania's speech was so platitudinous—a gauze collection of assurances that her husband, Donald Trump, is 'kind and fair and caring' and will 'never, ever let you down'—it could have been delivered by any spouse about any candidate."

LOCK HER UP!
Vindictive and On Stage
The Spurned Governor of New Jersey Depicts
Hillary in Kangaroo Court as a Murderous Ma Barker
...or Lizzie Borden

Chris Christie waddled onto the stage, barely recovered from his rejection as Donald's vice presidential running mate. Since he couldn't attack "the main man" he decided instead to light a fire under Hillary Clinton and to "convict" her in a mock trial.

The former Attorney General from New Jersey, himself involved in a raft of upcoming litigation for Bridgegate, Christie once again became a prosecutor, indicting the former Secretary of State for all her alleged crimes. Delegates, like members of a bloodthirsty mob, were asked to call out GUILTY OR NOT GUILTY from the floor at the end of each of his indictments.

Of course, in every case, the delegates shouted "GUILTY" followed by a roars from the Republican faithful to "LOCK HER UP," a phrase which became the oft-repeated rallying cry of the evening.

In reference to Hillary, Christie charged, "She cared more about protecting her own secrets than she did about protecting America's secrets. And then she lied about it over and over again."

"We're going to present the facts to you tonight sitting as a jury of her peers, both in this hall and in your living rooms across the nation. He then followed with a distorted list of her professional and personal failures.

He mocked her for "cozying up" to Vladimir Putin and for supporting the brutal murderer and dictator, Syria's Bashar al-Assad. "She set the stage for the rise of ISIS during her tenure as Secretary of State," he claimed.

He brought up her e-mail scandal, drawing on the testimony of the FBI director, James Comey, who had re-

The overnor of New Jersey, Chris Christie, conducted a kangaroo court trial that judged and convicted Hillary Clinton *in absentia* from onstage at the GOP convention in Cleveland.

The verdict screamed repeatedly from the floor from the rowdy delegates?: A lifetime in prison for her.

cently appeared on "the hot seat" before a congressional committee. After presenting the evidence, Comey said the FBI would not recommend that she be indicted.

"Let's look around the world at the violence and danger of every region that has been infected by Hillary's flawed judgment," Christie said.

Listening to Christie's rants on TV, Hillary was not amused at the mock trial in absentia, where she could put up no defense. She hit back with a snarky tweet about the governor's Bridgegate-derived legal troubles. "If you think Chris Christie can lecture anyone on ethics, we have a bridge to sell you."

***

After a tumultuous campaign, with charges and countercharges and threats by the "Dump Trump" delegates, the time had come for the actual nomination. It had for some time been made clear that Donald had the 1,237 delegate votes needed to make him the nominee. Nonetheless, there were many attempts to sabotage the count.

That brought an element of suspense to the tense evening, as the media watched to see what disgruntled delegates from Colorado or Alaska would do.

The controversies were shot down as Donald was formally crowned as the GOP's presidential nominee.

In honor of the nominee's home state, the delegates from New York were allowed to cast its votes out of order. That way, New York would be credited as the entity that provided its bombastic native son the 1,237 votes needed. As head of the New York delegation, Donald Trump, Jr., cast the deciding vote that "threw Dad over the top."

From the floor, Don Jr. smiled at his siblings, Ivanka Kushner and Eric Trump, before making his announcement. "Congratulations, Dad, we love you."

As he said that, the house band broke out in a jazzy rendition of Frank Sinatra's "New York, New York." Overhead, the Jumbotron displayed fireworks.

"It's not a campaign anymore," Don Jr. said, "It's a movement." Then, #1 Son pledged to put New York, which had not voted Republican during a presidential election year in 32 years, in play. But the road to the presidency, of course, would be an uphill battle.

Not everyone was rejoicing. Donald's chief rival, Ted Cruz, perhaps with an eye to a presidential bid in 2020, met with donors and activists at a reception across the street from the arena.

The roll call reflected discontent. In normal times, the Ohio governor, John Kasich, would have visibly and triumphantly positioned at the head of his state's delegation. But he was conspicuously absent, having refused to endorse Donald for President.

Senate Majority Leader Mitch McConnell of Kentucky appeared on stage a number of times, but his presence was met with scattered boos. After all, he represented the Washington Establishment which Donald was running against.

House Speaker Paul Ryan, third in line to assume the presidency, was viewed as the GOP's bright hope for 2020. He, too, appeared, reminding the delegates of his past arguments with Donald. Nonetheless, he was on hand, appearing ready to endorse him, claiming, "Democracy is a series of choices."

After the roll call, it was learned that 721 delegates had cast their votes for other candidates, mostly for Ted Cruz, but also for Marco Rubio and John Kasich. The convention showed the most discontent since 1976 when Ronald Reagan's forces battled the sitting President Gerald Ford, who assumed the position after Richard Nixon had resigned over the Watergate scandal and Vice President Spiro Agnew had stepped down after being exposed for having accepted bribes.

At the conclusion of the vote, Donald appeared on the screen. "Today has been a very, very special day watching my children put me over the top earlier," he said. "I'm so proud to be your nominee for President of the

United States, and I look forward to sharing my thoughts with you on Thursday night about how to build a brighter future of all Americans."

After the vote, many Cruz supporters walked out of the building. Kendal Unruh, one of the anti-Trump leaders, said, "It's just not me who's going to take this defeat personally. There is so much discontent here tonight."

Before the evening ended, Ryan returned to the stage to deliver a passionate plea for unity within his fractured party. "Let's see this thing through," he shouted at the delegates. "Let's win this thing. Let's show America our best." His appeal had many delegates rising to their feet, at least those who had remained in the arena.

***

The most electrifying moment in the hall came when Don Jr. was presented as the featured speaker of the evening. He delivered a rousing speech that savaged Hillary and heaped praise onto dear old dad.

"When people tell my Dad it can't be done, it gets done. When people tell him something is impossible, that triggers him into action. For my father, impossible is just the starting point."

"You want to know what kind of President he'll be?" Junior asked. "Let me tell you how he ran his businesses, and I know because I was there with him by his side at the job sites, in conference rooms from the time I could walk. Dad didn't hide behind some desk in an executive suite. He spent his career with regular Americans."

The 38-year-old went on to say, "He hung out with the guys on construction sites, pouring concrete and hanging sheetrock. Dad listened to them and he valued their opinions as much and often more than the guys from Harvard and Wharton locked away in offices away from the real work."

"We didn't learn from the MBAs. We learned from people who had doctorates in common sense. It's why we're the only children of billionaires as comfortable in a D10 Caterpillar as we are in our own cars."

Speaking in a rapid-fire dialogue, as was his custom, Don Jr. got the loudest applause of the evening.

He took the usual GOP positions, attacking Obamacare and gun control, as he called for American energy independence.

He falsely claimed that as President, Hillary would "Take away the guns of Americans." He also mocked present gun control laws. "Just look at how effective these laws have been in such inner cities as Chicago. Seventy people were murdered last month alone and over 3,400 American lives were lost there since the Obama administration took office in 2009."

Donald's second daughter, Tiffany *[the daughter derived from the union of Donald with his second wife, Marla Maples]* spoke next.

At the podium, addressing Republican delegates and the nation at large, she was "all blonde, sweetness and sugar," in the words of one delegate. Her job involved revealing he personal side of her formidable father.

"He wrote sweet notes on my report cards and words of advice," she claimed. "I always look forward to introducing him to my friends," She claimed that "he was always there for me when I needed him."

After the roll call, Donald ended up with 1,725 delegates. Just weeks before the convention, pundits had predicted he would not get the 1,237 needed, and that it would be an "open convention." They were wrong.

Donald announced, "Together we have achieved historic results with the largest vote total in the history of the Republican Party. This is a movement, but we have to go all the way."

"God Will Abandon America if Hillary is Elected President."
—Ben Carson

The evening was peppered with dull speeches, with sober discussions of conservative principles interspersed with attacks on Hillary.

Ben Carson, the African-American neurosurgeon who had dropped out of the race to back Donald, charged that Hillary was "attempting to deceive poor blacks. She would continue with a system that denigrates the education of our young people, puts them in a place where they're never going to be able to get a job, where they're always going to be dependent, and where therefore they can be cultivated for their votes. This is not what America is about"

As anticipated, Carson provided no real evidence against the former Secretary of State to back up his claims.

Fred Brown, who chairs the National Black Republican Council (yes there is such a group), spoke to the press. He said he'd been a regular at GOP conventions since the 1970s. "I think the 2016 convention in Cleveland is the whitest in my memory."

Meanwhile, at his ranch in Texas, George W. Bush watched the convention with dismay. He told friends, "I am worried that I will be the last Republican President. History may record that."

He feared that Donald's inflated ego and bizarre stands would cause irreparable harm to our party. "We might just disappear like the Whigs."

DAY THREE

Of the Republican National Convention

Wednesday, July 20, 2016

As Trumpkins Boo and Wife Heidi Flees Convention Hall

TED CRUZ REFUSES TO ENDORSE DONALD

"LYIN' TED" STICKS IT TO DONALD

Dashing Unity Hopes for the GOP

"Cut & Paste" Aide, Falling On Her Pen, Accepts Blame for

MELANIA'S PLAGIARISM

NATO

*Trump Announces that He May Not Defend America's
"Deadbeat Allies" Unless They Pay Their Fair Share*

LACKLUSTER INDIANA GOVERNOR

*Mike Pence & Other Second Bananas
Promise to Make America First Again*

In one of the more reckless decisions of the Donald campaign, the embittered senator from Texas, Ted Cruz, was allowed—apparently without restrictions—to address the assembled delegates at the Republican National Convention on Wednesday night, July 20.

At first, he was cheered by the Trumpkins, who erroneously believed that he'd come to Cleveland to throw his support behind Donald, that he would "bury the hatchet" after the carloads of venom each had unleashed upon the other during the course of the tumultuous campaign.

But as his speech unfolded, the early days of the campaign when Cruz had locked Donald in a bear hug quickly became a distant memory.

Treachery from Inside the Convention:
Ted's Final, Prime-Time Effort to

CRUZ-I-FY DONALD

He opened with rambling rants about the U.S. Constitution and the need for evangelicals to discriminate if they didn't want to serve a homosexual.

He didn't phrase it that bluntly, relying instead on code words such as "religious liberty," but his followers knew what he meant.

In vain, however, the Trumpkins kept waiting for "red meat" as his speech neared its end. Many of them were expecting a triumphant conclusion in the form of a resounding endorsement for Donald.

None ever came. Instead, in an astonishing anti-climax, the defiant Cruz urged delegates to "vote your conscience," and the anti-Trump cabal knew what that meant.

Immediately, Trumpkins turned on him, almost booing him from the stage with their cadenced chants of "TRUMP! TRUMP! TRUMP!"

The loudest and most intense rage came from the New York delegation, which had been strategically positioned close to the podium. With a wry smile, Cruz sarcastically said as the live television cameras whirled, "I appreciate the enthusiasm of the New York delegation," [*What he probably really meant to say, but opted not to, was, "I hope you'll all be delivered instantly to the Gates of Hell."*]

"Freedom matters, and I was part of something beautiful," he said.

[No he wasn't. He ran a vicious smear campaign against Donald, calling him names which had included "pathological liar."]

Fearing for Heidi's safety amid the hostile crowd, security guards rushed her from the arena. One delegate screamed in denunciation "GOLD-MAN SACHS" at her, a reference to the Wall Street firm she'd been associated with. Other less tactful delegates called her a "Texas bitch" or "a Texas cunt."

As Cruz ranted, the Trump siblings sat in stone-faced silence as they watched "the man they loved to hate" grandiosely fall short of endorsing their father.

As Cruz neared the end of his speech, the boos increased in volume and intensity.

At this point, as a means to sabotage his rival's domination of the moment, Donald made an dramatic appearance in the arena. As he advanced toward his seat in the VIP section, he delivered a "thumbs up" to the chanting crowd, many of whom cheered his authoritarian entrance, contributing to a confusing medley of boos and cheers simultaneously permeating the arena.

Peter King, a Congressman from Long Island, was the first to launch a post-speech attack on Cruz. "He's a disgrace. He's a self-centered liar and fraud. *Lyin' Ted!* I never trusted him. I never liked him, and I think he's disqualified himself from ever being considered as the Republican nominee for President."

Backstage, two security guards had to restrain a man who wanted to physically assault Cruz.

Expressing his contempt for Cruz, one delegate said, "What we needed was a pitchfork and some torches. Perhaps we should have tarred and feathered him"

Laurie Powell, a delegate from North Carolina, had been a Cruz supporter, but after his speech she turned against him, yelling, "Cruz is an asshole! He's not our nominee! What he needed to do tonight is get behind our nominee. He put himself above our party. As far as I'm concerned, the jerk's political career is over and done."

A Cruz alternate delegate from the senator's home state of Texas, Toby Walker, defended the failed candidate with some soothing platitudes: "What they did to him was really cruel. I think he did a great job trying to unite the party."

[He did such a great job that the next day, one newspaper headlined the night as "CIVIL WAR."]

Walker continued his defense of Cruz: "My heart breaks for him, and his campaign and his wife and two little girls. The boos aren't fair. His speech was exactly what we needed from him to unite the party."

[Many reporters analyzed Cruz's speech as the opening gambit of his campaign for the presidency in 2020.]

Gingrich

In a limp explanation, in an attempt to camouflage the depths of the insult to Donald, former House Speaker Newt Gingrich, who was the speaker scheduled after Cruz, told the delegates, "You misunderstood the senator. Ted Cruz said you can vote your conscience for anyone who will uphold the Constitution. In this election there is only one candidate that will uphold the Constitution." And in that phrase, there was no doubt that he was referring to Donald Trump.

No one was buying Gingrich's attempts to soften the blow. Unity of party was the last thing they heard in Cruz's bitter rant.

What Cruz did succeed in doing was to take the spotlight off the evangelical Indiana Governor Mike Pence. Tomorrow's headlines would focus mostly on Cruz, with only minor copy about the uncharismatic Pence.

Walker

Another failed presidential candidate, Scott Walker, governor of Wisconsin, came onstage to address the delegates. He spoke in a very loud voice, perhaps hoping to sound decisive and forceful. He didn't want to be accused of being a low-energy candidate like Jeb!. Walker, too was rumored to be looking for another run for the White House in 2020.

"Trump knows there is a better way forward," he said with absolutely no sincerity. He veered into the delegates' favorite subject, an attack on what a "criminal" Hillary Clinton was. He claimed that if she were more of a Washington insider, she'd be in prison. The delegates rose to their feet to cheer that remark, even though it made no sense.

"America, you have the choice," Walker said. "You decide. You deserve better."

Perhaps that was a chastisement for the voters having rejected him."

Rubio

Another failed candidate, Marco Rubio of Florida, didn't bother (or wasn't asked) to fly to Cleveland for the convention. Instead, he sent a videotaped, pre-vetted address to the delegates, throwing his weight behind Donald, and telling his fans that it was "time to unite."

What he meant, wrote a Miami reporter, was that the time to unite would be in 2020 when he ran once again for the presidency.

From the Podium, In Anticipation of the 2020 Elections, A NEW CROP OF AMBITIOUS CONSERVATIVES SPIN FOR RECOGNITION

In addition to the likes of Scott Walker and Ted Cruz, many Republican politicians appeared on stage not so much to sing the praise of Donald, but as a preview of their own run for the White House in 2020.

Such was the case with Senator Tom Cotton of Arkansas. "I'm the only politician here this week that married a girl born in Iowa."

He later admitted he was pandering, knowing that Iowa was the first state to select a candidate for President in the 2020 race.

One reporter said, "There were so many hopefuls waiting in the wings for the 2020 race. The convention was filled with not so subtle wooing and chit collecting. Many delegates privately told me that they suspected that Hillary would win the White House for the next four years. Would daughter Chelsea get her old room back? That was the question."

Laura Ingraham

Conservative talk show host Laura Ingraham fared better, receiving at one point a standing ovation. "All you boys with wounded feelings and bruised egos, we love you, but you must honor your pledge to support Donald Trump." She was chastising not only Cruz, but Jeb Bush and Ohio governor John Kasich for their refusal to support the GOP nominee.

Talk show radio host Laura Ingraham gave the Nazi salute at the Republican Convention. Or was it a wave goodbye?

The convention probably wasn't the best venue for such a gesture, since many of Trump's fanatics had been yelling *"Sieg Heil!"* that night.

Rick Scott

Florida governor Rick Scott, with his Yul Brynner coiffure, also addressed the delegates. "Perhaps I know that some of you have reservations about my friend Donald Trump," he said. "Sometimes, he's not polite. He can be a bit rough, and to some people, he can be a little direct. But this election isn't about Donald Trump or Hillary Clinton. It's about the very survival of the American dream. Any candidate is better than a Democrat. It's time for Americans to put down their partisan banners and do the right thing for this country."

"Instead of the 16 or 17 candidates who ran for the GOP nomination in 2016, I suspect there will be at least thirty candidates in the 2020 Race for President.

All the 2020 hopefuls seemed to be racing to court Sheldon Adelson, the Las Vegas magnate who invests millions in GOP political campaigns.

Even Mark Cuban was discussed as a possible candidate FOR 2020. He is the wealthy owner of the Dallas Mavericks. David Carney, a GOP strategist, said, "Donald Trump has given the Mark Cubans of the world a road map."

Paul Ryan

Of all the possible candidates for the Republican Party's presidential nomination in 2020, House Speaker Paul Ryan appeared to be a favorite. He told the delegates, "The Republican Party is a ship floating on populism right now. I stand opposed to those of us who profit off anger, outrage, and dark emotions for short-term goals."

That appeared to be a dig at Donald's candidacy.

Ryan's reluctant and wavering support for Donald turned off a number of voters. Eric R. Carey of Arlington, Virginia, said: "A once promising politician, Paul Ryan has lost his way. Given that his entire public career has been one of shameless advancement of his incoherent budget policy, migration of wealth to the already rich, and, above all, himself, an accurate assessment of him would be of a transparent, valueless self-promoter who found his place in an equally empty political home."

Eric Trump

Eric Trump also addressed the convention. Although his speech was not memorable, many delegates found him more personable than his older brother, Don. Jr. Eric seemed the most charitable of the Trump children, since he runs the Eric Trump Foundation, which helps finance St. Jude's Hospital.

Eric provided specifics about how his father had rescued failing government projects, citing his rescue of Central Park's derelict Wollman Rink, site of a famous ice-skating scene in the hit romantic drama *Love Story* (1970).

Eric told the delegates: "Throughout my father's career, he has been called upon by government to step in and save delayed, shuttered, and grossly over-budgeted public projects, everything from the exterior of Grand Central Terminal in Manhattan to the iconic old post office in Washington, D.C."

"It's time for a President who has always been the one to sign the front of the check—not the back," Eric said.

One delegate from New Hampshire said, "I thought Eric gave a great speech, although I don't really remember what he said. One thing I do recall. He said Donald was his best friend."

All that a delegate from Minnesota recalled was that Eric said that he and his relatively new wife were considering raising a family. "He's very good looking," she said, "and very rich."

In contrast, Don Junior's speech had made him a star. Some members of the New York delegation told him he should follow in the footsteps of Rudy Giuliani and run for mayor of New York City, taking on the sitting mayor, Democrat Bill de Blasio.

Manhattan GOP leader Adele Malpass said, "I like the sound of 'Mayor Trump.' Perhaps the sound of 'Governor Trump.'"

"For Don, Jr., the sky is the limit," said John Antoniello, who heads the Republican Party on Staten Island.

More About Melania

Although Cruz's non-endorsement dominated the nation's headlines the following morning, commentary about Melania's plagiarism of Michelle Obama's 2008 speech to the Democratic convention continued to generate headlines. As had been predicted, a member of the Trump Organization stepped forward "to fall on the sword."

Taking the blame was Meredith McIver, 65, a former ballet dancer who had joined the Trump Organization in 2001. Since then, she had become Donald's favorite author, ghostwriting—in his name—such Trump-centric hits as *Trump: How to Think Like a Billionaire,* and *Trump: How to Get Rich.*

McIver issued her *mea culpa* and told the press that although she had offered to resign, Donald had instructed her to stay on. "I feel terrible for the chaos I have caused," she admitted. "I apologize to Mrs. Obama. No harm was meant."

"Melania and I discussed many people who inspired her and messages she wanted to share with the American people," McIver said.

The writer claimed that during phone conversations with Melania, Mrs. Trump had read passages to her from other writings that had inspired her. "I wrote them down and later included some of the phrasing in my draft that ultimately ended up in the final speech. I did not check Mrs. Obama's speeches. That was my mistake."

Donald himself has never been sued for plagiarism in any of the books he wrote. However, he once threatened to sue Barack Obama for "stealing my words."

He was talking about 2011, when Obama "used my tough talk about trade relations with China."

On *Fox News,* Donald had threatened to sue the President. "It was almost my language he used in a speech, grounds for a lawsuit. A lot of people have said that Obama's talk was almost taken word for word from my playbook."

"Incidentally, Joe Biden is an admitted plagiarist," Donald charged.

He was referring to the Vice President's admission that he lifted lines from a speech by Neil Kinnock, the British politician. Biden had confessed to the plagiarism after a speech he delivered during his unsuccessful run for the presidency in 1988.

Magic Mike

During its advance planning, Day Three of the RNC had been choreographed as a showcase for Mike Pence, a world-class opportunity for the prospective Veep to introduce himself to millions of Americans who had never heard of him before.

But ironically (and anti-climactically), it would not be Pence, but Cruz who dominated the headlines the next day.

Pence was aware that he was not a charismatic figure. Seeming to admit how dull he was, he announced from the podium, "Trump is a man known for his large personality, colorful style, and lots of charisma. So I guess he was looking for some balance on the ticket."

Columnist Kyle Smith would later write, "Pence is the Superego of Donald's Id."

"Donald Trump is someone who doesn't quit," Pence lauded from the podium. "Trump is tough. He perseveres. How about his amazing children? Aren't they something?"

Although Pence was said to have spent twelve hours locked away in his hotel suite working on his speech, it contained no surprises. He got the biggest applause when he attacked Hillary, using the refrain that she would, if elected President, "be giving Obama a third term in office."

Rhetorically, he announced that the GOP ticket for 2016 represented a "rendezvous with destiny." Then he added a word of caution: "None of us should think for one second that this should be easy. You know this won't be America's first glimpse of the Clinton machine in action, as Bernie Sanders can tell you. Democrats are about to anoint someone who represents everything this country is tired of," Pence said.

***

In an evaluation of the convention, one editorial writer said, "All week, speaker after speaker has painted a vision of a country imperiled by black nationalists, cop killers, immigrant murderers, Muslim terrorists, and criminal Democrats. Other than that, a good time was had by all until Lying Ted Cruz took the microphones."

Several thousand Trumpkins at the convention had vengefully screamed "LOCK HER UP!," lacerating Hillary for her alleged criminal activity.

An adviser to the Trump campaign, Al Baldasaro, a New Hampshire state representative and a Marine Corps veteran, had an even harsher punishment in mind. He called for Hillary to be executed for treason.

"She should be put in the firing line. She is a disgrace for the lies that she told those mothers about how their children got killed over there in Benghazi. She also dropped the ball on over four hundred e-mails requesting backup security. Hillary Clinton is nothing but a piece of garbage."

As always, columnist Linda Stasi summed up the dynamic of the convention with the most acid evaluation ever:

"Air kissing and ass kissing, airheads and heirheads, cheeseheads and cheeseballs, the Joker & the Dark Knight, countless white supremacists and eighteen black delegates. Nazi salutes and thumbs up, hip grabbing and back slapping. Make America Great Again and lock her up. Christie's kangaroo court and elephants acting like asses, Lucifer in flames and Trump in fog, Muslim banning and Muslims for Trump. Damn! I'm going to miss the Republican National Convention—this is the best show since *Hamilton*."

DAY FOUR
Of the Republican National Convention

Thursday, July 21, 2016

Gloom and Chaos as the Convention Nears Its Final Moments
DONALD ATTACKS IMMIGRATION & CRIME
"I AM THE VOICE OF LAW & ORDER!"

"LUCIFER—HE'S BACK!"
—John Boehner, in reference to Ted Cruz's Atomic Fallout

Gay Republican Delegates from Washington, D.C. Swim in
A SEA OF HOMOPHOBES

THE TRUMP QUINTET
& A NEW GENERATION OF REALITY TV
Donald's Children Emerge as Convention Celebrities
With Comparison to the Kennedy Clan of the 1960s

As the month of July sweated its way to the dog days of August, and as the four-day GOP Convention in Cleveland unfolded, "The Impossible" happened. Against all odds, Donald J. Trump was going to become the Republican nominee for President of the United States.

Although there would be hopeless last minute attempts to block his candidacy, it seemed inevitable that Donald battle Hillary Clinton for the presidency.

Of course, a war chest was needed, but that was beginning to happen. During the previous month, the Trump coffers of gold had grown from a low of $1.3 million to $26 million in campaign contributions, as reluctant Republican donors were beginning to dig deep.

Nearly every major newspaper in America articulated an ominous concept associated with this most problematic of elections: Both Donald and Hillary carried too much baggage, too many negatives. Negative ratings, in fact, for both candidates had reached an alltime high.

Most voters were presented with the repellent choice of voting for whichever candidate they hated the least. It would be a case of picking the lesser of two evils to move into 1600 Pennsylvania Avenue on the 240th anniversary of the Republic.

Finally, as the fourth day of the convention opened, Thursday, July 21, delegates heard speaker after speaker, including Rudy Giuliani, who mostly expressed variations of the same theme: All of them despised Hillary, viewing her as "corrupt" and a "criminal deserving a lock-up."

Ranting demands to confine her in leg irons were heard throughout the Quicken Loans Arena in Cleveland.

America was no longer Ronald Reagan's shining city on a hill. If you believed the convention's speakers, the Republic was mired in a swampland of gloom, doom, and chaos run by inept leaders who were born in other countries, perhaps darkest Africa.

To warm up the crowd, Rudy Giuliani, the former mayor of New York, appeared before the crowd to deliver an impassioned and fiery speech. Surpassed only by Chris Christie, he became the second most powerful voice demanding the imprisonment of Hillary. Naturally, he brought up her e-mail scandal.

"If the Republicans take over the White House, we'll reopen the case. I'm really sick at what the Clintons have gotten away with."

"If Donald Trump becomes President, we'll bring her to trial. It is not double jeopardy. The statute of limitations is not up yet."

Giuliani, a ferocious former prosecutor, told delegates, "I'd like to be the attorney selected to prosecute her for high treason in giving away America's secrets to its deadliest enemies."

***

The surprise guest speaker of the convention's fourth and final evening was Peter Thiel. The billionaire co-founder of PayPal stunned the convention with: "Every American has a unique identity. I am proud to be a gay man. I am proud to be a Republican. But, most of all, I am proud to be an American."

His comments, to the shock of many watching from far away, were greeted with loud applause from the floor.

"I don't pretend to agree with every plank in our party's platform," Thiel said. "But fake culture wars only distract from our economic decline, and nobody in this race is being honest about it, except Donald Trump."

Then the 48-year-old billionaire likened himself to Donald, claiming, "We are not politicians, but both of us are builders. And it's time to rebuild America."

In addition to his self-defined status as a gay male, Thiel also belonged to another minority group: He was a Trump supporter from Silicon Valley. That made him what was called "a species of humans so endangered it might be called extinct."

"If a vote were taken tomorrow in the Silicon Valley, I bet Hillary Clinton would win about 95% of the vote," said one executive who did not want to be named.

Thiel had recently made national news when it was revealed that he had provided the financial support for Hulk Hogan's legal fight against Gawker Media, which bankrupted that exposé media firm.

"Techies" tended to view most of Donald's positions as abhorrent. Although he runs a notorious (and very sophisticated) Twitter campaign, most men and women who work in Silicon Valley viewed the GOP nominee as "an ignoramus." It was reported that most techies also evaluated Donald as a "kind of kryptonite."

Out, loud, and proud computer techie Peter Thiel, one of the only people from Silicon Valley to stump for Trump.

Donald claimed that as President, he would enlist Microsoft founder Bill Gates to help him close down and deny casual access to essential parts of the Internet. He also promised to force Apple to manufacture iPhones in America, and he also threatened Amazon with an antitrust investigation.

It seems that most techies are Democrats. In fact, one Mozilla CEO was forced out of his position when it was revealed that he had contributed to a campaign opposing same-sex marriage.

Thiel's remarks were mostly warmly received by the nineteen delegates representing Washington, D.C. A third of the delegation from the nation's capital were either gay or lesbian. They were still voting with the Republican party even though it had just written a platform attacking gay rights, gay parenthood, and transgender issues.

These delegates had wanted some language inserted into the platform condemning discrimination against gays and acknowledging that they were often targets for murder from the Islamic Caliphate. All of their requests for revisions to the Republican platform had been rejected.

In high-profile contrast, the Democratic Party Platform, since 1980—the year that Ronald Reagan, no friend of gay people, had risen to power—had consistently called for general civil rights for the LGBT community.

The Washington, D.C. delegates applauded Thiel as one of their won, but most of the arena broke into shouts of "USA! USA! USA!" that were intended as a sign of their approval for the gay tycoon.

Christian Berle, an environmental policy analyst from Washington, D.C., said, "The GOP is becoming more and more narrow and more and more spiteful. I had to struggle to remain a Republican, as most of my gay friends have left the party. I have to ask myself every day: "Why am I a Republican?"

Jose Cunningham, the chairman of the Washington, D.C. delegation at the convention, said: "I'm gay, Latino, American, pro-life, and evangelical. Why didn't Trump put me on the stage?"

***

Much of the news on Thursday (the convention's last day) and Friday continued to focus on Ted Cruz's notorious campaign speech and his failure to endorse the GOP candidate for President. A reporter caught up with the disgraced and booed candidate as he headed back to Texas on a plane. "I won't vote for Hillary Clinton," Cruz said, "and I'm not going to endorse Donald Trump like some servile puppy dog. He targeted both my wife and father during the primary race, and those insults I can't forgive."

At a breakfast meeting on Thursday, July 21, the final day of the convention, with delegates from Texas, Cruz was booed by many in the audience, some of whom frequently interrupted his remarks chanting "TRUMP! TRUMP! TRUMP!"

Charles Krauthammer, the popular columnist and *Fox TV* talking head, defined Cruz's convention speech as "the longest suicide in American history."

Carl Paladino, former New York gubernatorial candidate, tweeted a picture of Donald talking into the ear of the Texas senator. It was captioned: "After I move to the White House, I'll hire you to mow the lawn."

Paladino said, "Cruz could have blown the roof off the building, attained statesman status, and be appointed to the Supreme Court under a Donald Trump administration. But he chose to implode with self-love."

Jeff Roe, Cruz's campaign manager, appeared on the *Chris Stigall Show* on Philadelphia radio. He claimed that Chris Christie had "lost his political testicles" when he endorsed Donald. That was a counterpunch for the New Jersey governor's denunciation of candidate Cruz on a previous night.

Most voters appeared disgusted with Cruz's campaign speech, as reflected in "Letters to the Editor" columns in newspapers across the country.

John Guonagura wrote: "Cruz is a modern-day Benedict Arnold—a traitor to his party. Politics is a dirty game, and Cruz is as low as it gets. The Texas battle cry was, 'REMEMBER THE ALAMO!' Now it should be 'FORGET TED CRUZ!'"

Marie Giovanniello wrote, "How sad that Ted Cruz has lived up to his pathetic shortcomings."

Nicholas A. Langworthy, chairman of the Erie County (NY) Republican Party, said "Cruz slit his own throat. He is finished in national Republican politics."

The Daughter Also Rises

With her straight blonde hair, her winning smile, stunning looks, and lovely pink frock, Ivanka Trump addressed the convention before Donald came out. Positioned as "the crown jewel of the Trump campaign," Donald had saved her appearance for last, thinking she would be the most impressive of his speech-making children.

The 34-year-old, the recent mother of her third child, she had converted to Judaism when she married real estate mogul Jared Kushner.

From the podium, as broadcast to millions, Ivanka claimed Donald would be "a boon to women. As President, my father will change the labor laws that were put in place during a time in which women were not a significant part of the work force. He will focus on making quality child care affordable and accessible for all."

"At our family's company, there are more female executives than male. Women are paid equally for work that we do and, when a woman becomes a mother, she is supported—not shut out."

For fifteen minutes, Ivanka spoke lovingly of Donald to loud applause. "Politicians talk about wage quality, but my father has made a practice at his company and throughout his career fighting for equal pay for equal work, and I will fight with him."

She had been positioned as a vital component in the evening's lineup, a speaker who would trumpet the best aspects of Donald to women voters. His favorability rating among women at the time was near a low of 24%.

Throughout her speech, Ivanka referred, frequently and repetitively, to "my father."

"I grew up constructing Lego skyscrapers at the feet of a man who was building the real thing," she said.

"Like so many of my fellow millennials, I do not consider myself categorically Republican or Democrat. More than party affiliation, I vote based on what I believe is right for my family and my country. Sometimes, it's a tough choice. That is not the case this time. Come January, 2017, all things will be possible again."

After listening to both Eric and Ivanka speak on different nights, it was obvious to delegates that brother and sister were on the same page about recognizing what a magnificent builder their father was.

When not at the convention hall, Ivanka and her husband, Jered Kushner, were often seen at the fourth floor hotel suite of billionaire casino magnate Sheldon Adelson. He always had a banquet of kosher food spread out—no pigs in a blanket, no lobster rolls.

After four of Donald's children had addressed the delegates, many reporters emphasized their similarities to images of the Kennedy clan in the 1960s.

DONALD'S CONVENTION ADDRESS
Thursday, July 21, 2016

Addressing a rocky and divisive convention in Cleveland on its final night, Donald Trump proclaimed, "I'll be a strongman!" Crime and violence that today afflicts our nation will soon come to an end," he promised. "Beginning on January 20, 2017, safety will be restored."

"The problems we face now—poverty and violence at home, war and destruction abroad—will last only as long as we continue relying on the same politicians who created them. A change in leadership is required to change these outcomes. There can be no prosperity without law and order. Hillary Clinton is proposing mass amnesty, mass immigration, and mass lawlessness."

He painted an America dipped in blood, a misdirected country that had suffered from a 50% increase of policemen killed in the line of duty during 2016 alone. He blamed it on "the rollback of criminal enforcement by Obama."

He also used the occasion to attack Hillary for her "legacy of death, destruction, and weakness."

"America is a nation of believers, dreamers, and strivers that is being led by a group of censors, critics, and cynics."

He accused Obama of "using the pulpit of the presidency to divide us by race and color. He has made America a more dangerous environment for everyone."

He also vowed to champion the cause of "The Forgotten American" and to destroy Radical Islamic Terrorism.

When he spoke of illegal immigration, there were chants of "BUILD THE WALL! BUILD THE WALL! BUILD THE WALL!"

He received massive approval when he spoke about recent killings of police officers. "I have a message to every last person threatening the peace on our streets and the safety of our police. When I take the oath of office next year, I will restore law and order to our country."

In many ways, Donald reminded voters of a President delivering a speech during wartime.

"It is time to show the whole world that America is back—bigger and better and stronger than ever."

In the Quicken Loans Arena, with a thicket of U.S. flags stanchioned behind him, he seemed to portray himself as a Messianic figure who would rescue America from three principal evils—illegal immigration, Global Radical Islamic Terrorists, and urban crime "which makes it unsafe to walk the streets of America."

"I can fix it," he boasted, a comment that would later be mocked by Hillary for suggesting that he could do it alone.

David Gergen, an adviser to four U.S. Presidents, said: "Trump puts forward the same iron fist of Richard Nixon. But Nixon clothed his in a velvet glove. Trump, however, threw away that glove."

The 70-year-old mogul used dark imagery in his portrait of a rotting America. At times, his voice was filled with anger when he spoke of an

America humiliated around the world. "Any politician who does not grasp the danger is not fit to lead the country."

Yet he shocked many delegates from Red states when he transgressed the Republican's homophobic platform and vowed to use his power to protect LGBT citizens from "violence and oppression of a hateful foreign ideology," referring to the execution of gay people in the Muslim world. "Many times, they were beheaded, stoned to death, or thrown from tall buildings."

Amazingly, the audience applauded, in contrast to when a gay American soldier, addressing delegates via a videotaped recording, was booed at the convention that nominated Mitt Romney in 2012.

"I have to say, that as a Republican, it is so nice to hear you cheering for what I just said," Donald said, in reference to his remarks about protecting gays.

In his self-portrayal as a savior for his people, he said, "Every day I wake up determined to deliver a better life for the people all across the nation that have been ignored, neglected, and abandoned."

**

Many editorial writers were disappointed that he didn't use the occasion to present a detailed plan for change. "As always, it was an empty sales pitch," claimed one reporter.

The ever critical *New York Times* lashed out against him: "He has sought advantage by playing to disaffected people's worst instincts, inventing scapegoats and conspiracy theories, waging and inciting vicious attacks on those who disagree with him. He is a poisonous messenger for a legitimate demand: That an ossified party dedicate itself to improving working people's lives, instead of serving the elite."

Even after such a forceful speech, many delegates left the arena still hesitant about a vote for Donald. As Governor Gary Herbert of Utah put it, "I'm going to vote for Mike Pence, and Donald Trump comes along with the package."

Before the delegates filed out of the convention all that fateful evening, Donald delivered a ringing all to protect the American children of the future: "To every parent who dreams for their child, and every child who dreams for the future, I say these words to you tonight. I'm with you, I will fight for you, and I will win for you."

In his closing remarks, Donald said, "To all Americans tonight, in all our cities and town, I make this promise:

We Will Make America Strong Again.
We Will Make America Proud Again.
We Will Make America Safe Again.
And We Will Make America Great Again."

On July 23, just two days after Donald's grim message to American voters on the final night of the RNC in Cleveland, his arch-opponent, Hillary Clinton, announced her running mate for Veep, former Virginia governor, now Senator Tim Kaine.

A New Phase in The Donald Wars Had Begun.

POST-CONVENTION POSTSCRIPT

For The Donald, for His Entourage, for the Republicans, & for the Nation:

Chaos, Confusion, Turmoil, Rage, & Despair

"I'm told every day to be nicer. But is that what America really wants?"
—Donald Trump

On the front cover of its edition of August 22, 2016, *Time* magazine, with a banner headline saying "MELTDOWN," depicted a dripping wax effigy of Donald Trump.

The article claimed, "Since the convention in Cleveland, Trump has done almost nothing right by traditional standards. He has picked fights with senior Republicans and Gold Star parents, invited Russian spies to meddle in U.S. democracy, and appeared to joke about gun enthusiasts' prematurely removing a U.S. president from office. He's shuffled campaign messages like playing cards and left GOP elders fretting that he lacks the judgment to be Commander-in-Chief. During a dismal two-week stretch, he surrendered a narrow lead over Democratic nominee Hillary Clinton and now trails by an average of eight points in recent nationwide polls."

One senior Hillary adviser said, "Trump can set himself on fire at breakfast, kill a nun at lunch, and waterboard a puppy in the afternoon. And that doesn't even get us to prime time."

In the wake of the GOP convention, Donald was at the center of one spectacular misstep after another.

In a bizarre rant on July 27, from a podium during a televised speech, he extended an invitation for Russia to commit espionage against Hillary and her Democrats, and to hack her e-mails. "Russia, if you are listening, I hope you are able to find the 30,000 Hillary e-mails that are missing. You'll find some beauties."

His phraseologies were immediately denounced as "treasonous" by security experts, and as a "new low" by news industry pundits.

761

House Speaker Paul Ryan immediately condemned the rant, denouncing Russia as a "global menace led by a devious thug. Putin should stay out of American elections."

On editorial writer suggested that the invitation he had extended to the Russians for the continuation of their espionage would be defined as grounds for impeachment if Donald Trump were elected President: "This is something a lot more serious than Bill Clinton getting a blow-job in the Oval Office."

With avid interest, Donald had watched the Democratic convention in Philadelphia. Although he was infuriated by nearly everything he saw, he had been enraged by one testimonial more than by any other: that of Khizr Khan, the Muslim father of a 27-year-old soldier killed in Iraq. Khan had ripped into Donald with, among others, the accusation that whereas military families had made ultimate sacrifices and endured oceans of suffering, "You, Mr. Trump, have sacrificed nothing."

The Khan family's son, Captain Humayun Khan, had been killed in 2004 by suicide bombers in Iraq after he'd waved his soldiers back and away from harm. For his bravery, he'd (posthumously) earned the Bronze Star and Purple Heart.

At the Democratic National Convention, at the podium, Khizr's wife, Ghazala, clad like a conservative Muslim woman, in a blue headscarf, had positioned herself silently and supportively beside her husband.

Khan's emotional denunciation of Trump was one of the highlights of the final night of the Democratic Convention. The event was climaxed by Hillary's address to the nation wherein she accepted her historic nomination for President.

Khan had articulated the feelings of Muslim Americas who had been repeatedly outraged by Donald's anti-Muslim pronouncements and rhetoric.

Shortly after the Khans' address to the nation, Donald reacted with white-heated venom, belittling and publicly trivializing them: "The father did all the talking because the mother was forbidden to speak because of her religion," he charged.

Khan shot back that his wife had not spoken because she was too overcome with grief at the death of her son.

As national coverage of the incident intensified, Governor John Kasich of Ohio—long an outspoken opponent of the Republican nominee, lashed out once again with, "There's only one way to talk about Gold Star parents: With honor and respect."

As July neared its end, Donald continued to horrify and amaze. When he appeared on ABC-TV's *This Week* for an interview with George

Stephanopoulos, he made a spectacularly embarrassing foreign policy gaffes:

"Putin is not going into Ukraine, OK, just so you understand. He's not going into Ukraine, all right? You can mark it down. You can put it down."

[Donald's lack of understanding of the situation horrified insiders throughout the diplomatic community. Way back in 2014, in a move condemned by the Free World, and based on directives emanating directly from Putin, Russia had already invaded the Crimea, and had, since then, effectively annexed it from Ukraine.]

As the very hot month of August roared in like a fiery lion, so did campaign rhetoric. In an unusual move for a sitting President, Obama urged GOP leaders to withdraw their endorsements of Donald, describing him as "unfit to serve as President."

The month wasn't looking good for Donald. Stories appeared that described how Republican leaders were looking for ways "to replace loudmouth on the ticket," although it was not immediately made clear just how that would be accomplished. Loyal staffers were reported to be "almost suicidal," based on the potty-trail of gaffes perpetrated by their autocratic boss.

[A defender for Donald emerged at around this time in the form of 86-year-old Clint Eastwood. In Esquire *magazine, he said he supported Donald — "The good, the bad, and the ugly." Eastwood then went on, in print, to bash America's "pussy generation."]*

***

As if matters weren't complicated enough, simultaneous with the harshest of the backlashes against Donald, Melania's past suddenly came roaring back to haunt her.

It was revealed that way back in 1995, the would-be First Lady had been an undocumented and illegal worker. She had posed for nude fetish-industry photos on the fringes of the sex industry. This discovery was in marked contrast to her previous claims that she had arrived in the U.S. for the first time in 1996.

This new information, and the unearthing of these erotic, now widely distributed photos, revealed that her previous statements had been untrue. Had Donald's immigration policies been in effect at the time the photos had been snapped, she would have been deported.

In a daring *exposé*, the usually pro-Trump tabloid, *The New York Post*, in its edition of July 31, 2016, ran, on its front cover, a nude photo of Melania snapped in Manhattan in 1995. The nipples of her ample breasts are covered with blue paste-on stars, and she uses both hands to cover her (otherwise naked) vagina, with some pubic hairs showing.

On page 3 of that same edition, *The Post* had positioned a view of Melania's *derrière*. She's wearing only high heels.

The racy photos were taken by French fashion photographer Jarl Alé Alexandre de Basseville.

[Describing himself as "The Prince of Normandy, and a descendant of the 1st king Harald of Norway," he was born in Bordeaux, France, on July 8th, 1970. In a statement he made to the press, he said, "I am completely against this world, and I don't understand why girls fuck with old guys to afford a Chanel, Louis Vuitton, or Hermès bag. The fashion industry has become the biggest pimp ever."

Was he referring to Melania? Actually, he praised her, calling her "a super great and fantastic personality."]

The Post, in its edition of the following day, ran additional, even more shocking erotic photos, depicting Melania as a player in a lesbian romp with an also-naked Emma Eriksson, a gorgeous Scandinavian nudie. From the rear, she embraces Melania with arms that encircle her torso at a point just below her breasts. In another photo, the Viking goddess is depicted wearing a low-cut long robe designed by the notorious John Galliano. She raises a whip as if preparing to beat Melania, who's dressed in a skin-tight gown and high heels.

***

Around August 7, as the dog days of midsummer caused landscapes across the country to shimmer with perspiration and heat, Donald's poll numbers plummeted. Predictably, Donald went on the offensive.

As if he could see clairvoyantly into the future, he claimed that if he lost the presidency in the upcoming November election, it would be based on it having been "rigged" in favor of Hillary.

Trump advisor Roger Stone predicted *[or threatened, depending on your point of view]*, "The government will shut down if they *[the Democrats]* attempt to steal this and swear Hillary in."

John Pitney, a former GOP operative, also weighed in: "Given the history of Trump rallies, there is some potential for violence if Hillary is elected."

On the campaign trail, Donald had taken to calling the Democratic nominee, "Hillary Rotten Clinton."

"The voter ID situation has turned out to be a very unfair development. We may have people voting ten times. It's inconceivable that you don't have to show identification in order to vote."

Another blow hit the Trump campaign on August 8, as fifty of the country's top GOP national security officials signed a pact claiming that Donald "lacks the character, values, and experience to be President of the United States. He would put at risk the country's national security and well-being," the document stated. "He would be the most reckless President in American history."

As this document was released, Donald flew into depressed Detroit to deliver a speech outlining his economic agenda and tax changes. He claimed that his plans for the economy would spur economic growth and bring new jobs. He called Hillary "The Steward of Stagnation." His plan included deep tax cuts for the rich, himself included. He then went on to promise the disruption of long-standing trade agreements with other countries…"We can't fix a rigged system by relying on the people who rigged it in the first place."

***

As August deepened, Hillary's attacks on Donald grew ever harsher. Frequently and publicly, she questioned his mental and emotional stability, asserting that it would be dangerous to turn over America's nuclear codes to such a deranged personality. "Imagine him in the Oval Office facing a real crisis," she said. "A man you can bait with a tweet is not a man you can trust with nuclear weapons!"

***

In defiance of the Republican National Committee virtually screaming for Donald to become more presidential, he delivered a suggestion [or was it a threat?] that echoed, instantly around the world.

The *New York Daily News,* on its front page, summed it up like this: "When Trump hinted gun-rights supporters shoot Hillary, he went from offensive to reckless. He must end his campaign. If he doesn't, the GOP needs to abandon him."

During a speech in the crucial "swing state" of North Carolina, Donald had delivered a jaw-droppingly enigmatic remark that horrified virtually everyone:

"Hillary wants to essentially abolish the Second Amendment. By the way, and if she gets to pick Supreme Court Judges, [there's] nothing you can do, folks.

765

Although the Second Amendment people...maybe there is. I don't know."

Reporters interpreted his remark as a suggestion that gun advocates should aim (and shoot) their weapons at Hillary. True loyalists in the crowd applauded, but others among his supporters appeared shocked. Of course, the National Rifle Association quickly tweeted its continuing endorsement of their combustible candidate.

Literally millions of Americans, led by Senator Elizabeth Warren, condemned Donald's call to arms: Warren tweeted, "Donald Trump makes death threats because he's a pathetic coward who can't handle the fact that he's losing to a girl."

Anti-Trump groups, including the Democratic Coalition Against Trump, demanded an investigation by the FBI, arguing that Donald should be arrested for attempting to incite violence, perhaps even an assassination of his opponent.

Regardless of the outcome of the November 8 elections,

There Is One Thing On Which All Voters Will Agree:

Donald J. Trump has earned a permanent and deeply entrenched position in the pages of the history of the Republic. He stands out as a unique and historically important figure, vital to an understanding of the American Experience.

God Bless America.

Donald Trump, The Man Who Would Be King

DARWIN PORTER

As an intense and precocious nine-year-old, **Darwin Porter** began meeting movie stars, TV personalities, politicians, and singers through his vivacious and attractive mother, Hazel, an eccentric but charismatic Southern girl who had lost her husband in World War II. Migrating from the Depression-ravaged valleys of western North Carolina to Miami Beach during its most ebullient heyday, Hazel became a stylist, wardrobe mistress, and personal assistant to the vaudeville *comedienne* **Sophie Tucker**, the bawdy and irrepressible "Last of the Red Hot Mamas."

Virtually every show-biz celebrity who visited Miami Beach paid a call on "Miss Sophie," and Darwin as a pre-teen loosely and indulgently supervised by his mother, was regularly dazzled by the likes of **Judy Garland, Dinah Shore,** and **Frank Sinatra.**

It was at Miss Sophie's that he met his first political figure, who was actually an actor at the time. Between marriages, **Ronald Reagan** came to call on Ms. Sophie, who was his favorite singer. He was accompanied by a young blonde starlet, **Marilyn Monroe.**

At the University of Miami, Darwin edited the school newspaper. He first met and interviewed **Eleanor Roosevelt** at the Fontainebleau Hotel on Miami Beach and invited her to spend a day at the university. She accepted, much to his delight.

After graduation, he became the Bureau Chief of *The Miami Herald* in Key West, Florida, where he got to take early morning walks with the former U.S. president **Harry S Truman**, discussing his presidency and the events that had shaped it.

Through Truman, Darwin was introduced and later joined the staff of **Senator George Smathers** of Florida. His best friend was a young senator, **John F. Kennedy.** Through "Gorgeous George," as Smathers was known in the Senate, Darwin got to meet Jack and Jackie in Palm Beach. He later wrote two books about them—*The Kennedys, All the Gossip Unfit to Print,* and one of his all-time bestsellers, *Jacqueline Kennedy Onassis—A Life Beyond Her Wildest Dreams.*

For about a decade in New York, Darwin worked in television journalism and advertising with his long-time partner, the journalist, art director, and distinguished arts-industry socialite **Stanley Mills Haggart.**

Stanley (as an art director) and Darwin (as a writer and assistant), worked as freelance agents in television. Jointly, they helped produce TV commercials that included testimonials from **Joan Crawford** (then feverishly promoting Pepsi-Cola); **Ronald Reagan** (General Electric); and **Debbie Reynolds** (Singer sewing machines). Other personalities appearing and delivering televised sales pitches included **Louis Armstrong, Lena Horne,** and **Arlene Dahl,** each of them hawking a commercial product.

Beginning in the early 1960s, Darwin joined forces with the then-fledgling **Arthur Frommer** organization, playing a key role in researching and writing more than 50 titles and defining the style and values that later emerged as the world's leading travel guidebooks, *The Frommer Guides,* with particular emphasis on Europe, California, New England, and the Caribbean. Between the creation and updating of hundreds of editions of detailed travel guides to England, France, Italy, Spain, Portugal, Austria, Hungary, Germany, Switzerland, the Caribbean, and California, he continued to interview and discuss the triumphs, feuds, and frustrations of celebrities, many by then reclusive, whom he either sought out or encountered randomly as part of his extensive travels. **Ava Gardner** and **Lana Turner** were particularly insightful.

It was while living in New York that Darwin became fascinated by the career of a rising real estate mogul changing the skyline of Manhattan. He later, of course, became the "gambling czar" of Atlantic City and a star of reality TV.

Darwin began collecting an astonishing amount of data on him, squirreling it away in boxes, hoping one day to write a biography of this charismatic, controversial figure.

Before doing that, he penned more than thirty uncensored, unvarnished, and unauthorized bioraphies on subjects that included **Peter O'Toole, James Dean, Marlon Brando, Merv Griffin, Katharine Hepburn, Howard Hughes, Humphrey Bogart, Michael Jackson, Paul Newman, Steve McQueen, Marilyn Monroe, Elizabeth Taylor, Frank Sinatra, Vivien Leigh, Laurence Olivier, the notorious porn star Linda Lovelace, the Gabor sisters, Tennessee Williams, Gore Vidal,** and **Tru-**

man Capote.

Darwin Porter is also the author of *Love Triangle,* devoted to the Hollywood careers of **Ronald Reagan** and his two actress wives, **Jane Wyman** and **Nancy Davis.**

As a departure from his usual repertoire, Darwin also wrote the controversial *J. Edgar Hoover & Clyde Tolson: Investigating the Sexual Secrets of America's Most Famous Men and Women,* a book about celebrity, voyeurism, political and sexual repression, and blackmail within the highest circles of the U.S. government.

In time for the 2016 race for the White House, and in addition to the Donald Trump book *(The Man Who Would be King),* Darwin also wrote *Bill & Hillary—So This Is That Thing Called Love.*

Porter's biographies, over the years, have won at least a dozen first prize or runner-up awards at literary festivals in cities which include Boston, New York, Los Angeles, Hollywood, San Francisco, and Paris.

Darwin can be heard at regular intervals as a radio and television commentator, "dishing" celebrities, pop culture, politics, and scandal.

A resident of New York City, Darwin is currently at work on history's first comprehensive biography of **Lana Turner,** *Hearts and Diamonds Take All,* because, in his words, "Her story, with its carloads of intrigue and its status as an insight into the American Experience, has never really been told."

DANFORTH PRINCE

The co-author of this book, **Danforth Prince** is president and founder of Blood Moon Productions, a firm devoted to salvaging, compiling, and marketing the oral histories of America's entertainment industry.

Prince launched his career in journalism in the 1970s at the Paris Bureau of *The New York Times.* In the early '80s, he joined Darwin Porter in developing first editions of many of the titles within *The Frommer Guides.* Together, they reviewed and articulated the travel scenes of more than 50 nations, most of them within Europe and The Caribbean. Authoritative and comprehensive, they were perceived, before the collapse of the travel industry in the aftermath of the Great Recession of 2008, as best-selling "travel bibles" for millions of readers.

Prince, in collaboration with Porter, is also the co-author of several award-winning celebrity biographies, each configured as a title within Blood Moon's Babylon series. These have included *Hollywood Babylon—It's Back!; Hollywood Babylon Strikes Again; The Kennedys: All the Gossip Unfit to Print; Frank Sinatra, The Boudoir Singer, Elizabeth Taylor: There is Nothing Like a Dame; Pink Triangle: The Feuds and Private Lives of Tennessee Williams, Gore Vidal, Truman Capote, and Members of their Entourages;* and *Jacqueline Kennedy Onassis: A Life Beyond Her Wildest Dreams.* More recent efforts include *Peter O'Toole—Hellraiser, Sexual Outlaw, Irish Rebel;* and *Bill & Hillary—So This Is That Thing Called Love.*

His latest book, co-authored with Darwin Porter, is *James Dean, Tomorrow Never Comes.*

Prince is also the co-author of four books on film criticism, three of which won honors at regional bookfests in Los Angeles and San Francisco.

Prince, a graduate of Hamilton College and a native of Easton and Bethlehem, Pennsylvania, is the president and founder of the Georgia Literary Association (1996), and of the Porter and Prince Corporation (1983) which has produced dozens of titles for Simon & Schuster, Prentice Hall, and John Wiley & Sons. In 2011, he was named "Publisher of the Year" by a consortium of literary critics and marketers spearheaded by the J.M. Northern Media Group.

Publishing in collaboration with the National Book Network (*www.NBNBooks.com*), he has electronically documented some of the controversies associated with his stewardship of Blood Moon in at least 50 documentaries, book trailers, public speeches, and TV or radio interviews. Most of these are available on **YouTube.com** and **Facebook** (*keywords: "Danforth Prince"* or *"Blood Moon Productions"*); on **Twitter** (*# BloodyandLunar*); or by clicking on **BloodMoonProductions.com**.

An animal rights activist, Danforth makes it a point to adopt unwanted feral strays from the sidewalks of New York City, at least three of which have evolved into treasured companions and pets.

Of special merit, and greatly missed, will be CAESAR, his "celebrity" Rottweiler-Pit Bull. Beloved by neighbors, and eventually configured as a therapy dog for members of his church, Caesar (aka César, aka Cesár) died during the compilation of the final pages of this book.

LANA

Beautiful and Bad, Cult Goddess of the 40s, 50s, and Beyond

HER FULL STORY HAS NEVER BEEN TOLD

All of that will change on Valentine's Day, 2017, when Blood Moon will release THE DEFINITIVE BIOGRAPHY of Hollywood's "Other" Most Notorious Blonde.

Lana: "I'd like to think that in some small way, I've helped to preserve the glamour and beauty and mystery of the movie industry."

Lana: "They won't forget"

LANA TURNER, Hearts and Diamonds Take All

by Darwin Porter & Danforth Prince;   Softcover, 528 pages, with photos
ISBN 978-936003-53-2   Available everywhere on Valentine's Day, 2017

LOVE TRIANGLE

RONALD REAGAN, JANE WYMAN, & NANCY DAVIS

Unique in the history of publishing, this scandalous triple biography focuses on the Hollywood indiscretions of former U.S. president Ronald Reagan and his two wives. A proud and Presidential addition to Blood Moon's Babylon series, it digs deep into what these three young and attractive movie stars were doing decades before two of them took over the Free World.

Hot, Unauthorized, and Unapologetic!

LOVE TRIANGLE
RONALD REAGAN,
JANE WYMAN
& NANCY DAVIS

DARWIN PORTER & DANFORTH PRINCE

***

As reviewed by Diane Donovan, Senior Reviewer at the California Bookwatch section of the Midwest Book Review: *"Love Triangle: Ronald Reagan, Jane Wyman & Nancy Davis may find its way onto many a Republican Reagan fan's reading shelf; but those who expect another Reagan celebration will be surprised: this is lurid Hollywood exposé writing at its best, and outlines the truths surrounding one of the most provocative industry scandals in the world.*

"There are already so many biographies of the Reagans on the market that one might expect similar mile-markers from this: be prepared for shock and awe; because Love Triangle doesn't take your ordinary approach to biography and describes a love triangle that eventually bumped a major Hollywood movie star from the possibility of being First Lady and replaced her with a lesser-known Grade B actress (Nancy Davis).

"From politics and betrayal to romance, infidelity, and sordid affairs, Love Triangle is a steamy, eye-opening story that blows the lid off of the Reagan illusion to raise eyebrows on both sides of the big screen.

"Black and white photos liberally pepper an account of the careers of all three and the lasting shock of their stormy relationships in a delightful pursuit especially recommended for any who relish Hollywood gossip."

In 2015, LOVE TRIANGLE, Blood Moon Productions' overview of the early dramas associated with Ronald Reagan's scandal-soaked career in Hollywood, was designated by the Awards Committee of the **HOLLYWOOD BOOK FESTIVAL** as Runner-Up to Best Biography of the Year.

LOVE TRIANGLE: Ronald Reagan, Jane Wyman, & Nancy Davis
Darwin Porter & Danforth Prince
Hot, scandalous, and loaded with information about their Hollywood careers
that the Reagans never wanted you to know.
Softcover, 6" x 9", with hundreds of photos.   ISBN 978-1-936003-41-9

THE KENNEDYS

ALL THE GOSSIP UNFIT TO PRINT

A Staggering Compendium of Indiscretions Associated With Seven Key
Players in the Kennedy Clan; A Cornucopia of Relatively Unknown but
Carefully Documented Scandals from the Golden Age of Camelot

Darwin Porter & Danforth Prince

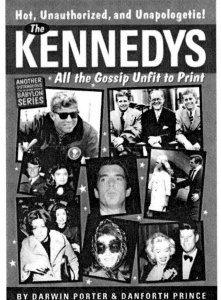

*The great enemy of truth is very often not
the lie—deliberate, contrived, and dishonest, but the myth—persistent, persuasive,
and unrealistic."*
　　　　　　　　　　　—John F. Kennedy

*"Pick this book up, and you'll be hard-
pressed to put it down"*
　　　　　—Richard Labonté, Q-Syndicate

The Kennedys were the first true movie stars to occupy the White House. They
were also Washington's horniest political tribe, and although America loved their
humor, their style, and their panache, we took delight in this tabloid-style documentation of their hundreds of staggering indiscretions.
Keepers of the dying embers of Camelot won't like it, but Kennedy historians
and aficionados will interpret it as required reading.

Hardcover, with hundreds of photos and 450 meticulously researched, highly detailed, and very gossipy pages with more outrageous scandal than 90% of American voters during the heyday of Camelot could possibly have imagined.

ISBN 978-1-936003-17-4.
Temporarily sold out of hard copies, but available for e-readers.

JACQUELINE KENNEDY ONASSIS
A Life Beyond Her Wildest Dreams

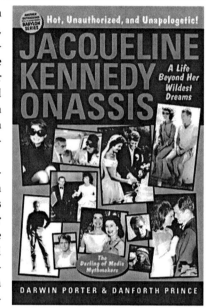

After floods of analysis and commentary in tabloid and mainstream newspapers worldwide, this has emerged as the world's most comprehensive testimonial to the flimsier side of Camelot, the most comprehensive compendium of gossip ever published about America's unofficial, uncrowned queen, **Jacqueline Kennedy Onassis**. Its publication coincided with the 20-year anniversary of the death of one of the most famous, revered, and talked-about women who ever lived.

During her tumultuous life, Mrs. Onassis zealously guarded her privacy and her secrets. But in the wake of her death, more and more revelations have emerged about her frustrations, her rage, her passions, her towering strengths, and her delicate fragility, which she hid from the glare of the world behind oversized sunglasses. Within this posthumous biography, a three-dimensional woman emerges through the compilation of some 1,000 eyewitness testimonials from men and women who knew her over a period of decades.

An overview of the life of Mrs. Onassis is a natural fit for Blood Moon, a publishing enterprise that's increasingly known, worldwide, as one of the most provocative and scandalous in the history of publishing.

"References to this American icon appear with almost rhythmic regularity to anyone researching the cultural landscape of America during the last half of The American Century," said Danforth Prince. "Based on what we'd uncovered about Jackie during the research of many of our earlier titles, we're positioning ourselves as a more or less solitary outpost of irreverence within a landscape that's otherwise flooded with fawning, over-reverential testimonials. Therein lies this book's appeal—albeit with a constant respect and affection for a woman we admired and adored."

Based on decades of research by writers who define themselves as "voraciously attentive Kennedyphiles," it supplements the half-dozen other titles within Blood Moon's Babylon series.

JACQUELINE KENNEDY ONASSIS—
A LIFE BEYOND HER WILDEST DREAMS
Darwin Porter and Danforth Prince
Biography/Entertainment   6" x 9"   700 pages with hundreds of photos
ISBN 978-1-936003-39-6   Also available for E-readers.

J. Edgar Hoover & Clyde Tolson
Investigating the Sexual Secrets
of America's Most Famous Men & Women
Darwin Porter

This epic saga of power and corruption has a revelation on every page—cross dressing, gay parties, sexual indiscretions, hustlers for sale, alliances with the Mafia, and criminal activity by the nation's chief law enforcer.

It's all here, with chilling details about the abuse of power on the dark side of the American saga. But mostly it's the decades-long love story of America's two most powerful men who could tell presidents "how to skip rope." (Hoover's words.)

"Everyone's dredging up J. Edgar Hoover. Leonardo DiCaprio just immortalized him, and now comes Darwin Porter's paperback, *J. Edgar Hoover & Clyde Tolson: Investigating the Sexual Secrets of America's Most Famous Men and Women*. It shovels Hoover's darkest secrets dragged kicking and screaming from the closet. It's filth on every VIP who's safely dead and some who are still above ground."

—Cindy Adams, The New York Post

"This book is important, because it destroys what's left of Hoover's reputation. Did you know he had intel on the bombing of Pearl Harbor, but he sat on it, making him more or less responsible for thousands of deaths? Or that he had almost nothing to do with the arrests or killings of any of the 1930s gangsters that he took credit for catching?

"A lot of people are angry with its author, Darwin Porter. They say that his outing of celebrities is just cheap gossip about dead people who can't defend themselves. I suppose it's because Porter is destroying carefully constructed myths that are comforting to most people. As gay men, we benefit the most from Porter's work, because we know that except for AIDS, the closet was the most terrible thing about the 20th century. If the closet never existed, neither would Hoover. The fact that he got away with such duplicity under eight presidents makes you think that every one of them was a complete fool for tolerating it."

—Paul Bellini, FAB Magazine (Toronto)

Winner of Literary Awards from the Los Angeles & the Hollywood Book Festivals
Temporarily sold out of hard copies, but available for E-Readers. ISBN 978-1-936003-25-9

PINK TRIANGLE: *The Feuds and Private Lives of Tennessee Williams,*

Gore Vidal, Truman Capote, and Famous Members of their Entourages
Darwin Porter & Danforth Prince

This book, the only one of its kind, reveals the backlot intrigues associated with the literary and script-writing *enfants terribles* of America's entertainment community during the mid-20th century.

It exposes their bitchfests, their slugfests, and their relationships with the *glitterati*—Marilyn Monroe, Brando, the Oliviers, the Paleys, U.S. Presidents, a gaggle of other movie stars, millionaires, and international *débauchés.*

This is for anyone who's interested in the formerly concealed scandals of Hollywood and Broadway, and the values and pretentions of both the literary community and the entertainment industry.

"A banquet... If PINK TRIANGLE had not been written for us, we would have had to research and type it all up for ourselves...Pink Triangle is nearly seven hundred pages of the most entertaining histrionics ever sliced, spiced, heated, and serviced up to the reading public. Everything that Blood Moon has done before pales in comparison.
Given the fact that the subjects of the book themselves were nearly delusional on the subject of themselves (to say nothing of each other) it is hard to find fault. Add to this the intertwined jungle that was the relationship among Williams, Capote, and Vidal, of the times they vied for things they loved most—especially attention—and the times they enthralled each other and the world, [Pink Triangle is] the perfect antidote to the Polar Vortex."
—Vinton McCabe in the NY JOURNAL OF BOOKS

"Full disclosure: I have been a friend and follower of Blood Moon Productions' tomes for years, and always marveled at the amount of information in their books—it's staggering. The index alone to Pink Triangle runs to 21 pages—and the scale of names in it runs like a Who's Who of American social, cultural and political life through much of the 20th century."
—Perry Brass in THE HUFFINGTON POST

"We Brits are not spared the Porter/Prince silken lash either. PINK TRIANGLE's research is, quite frankly, breathtaking. PINK TRIANGLE will fascinate you for many weeks to come. Once you have made the initial titillating dip, the day will seem dull without it."
—Jeffery Tayor in THE SUNDAY EXPRESS (UK)

PINK TRIANGLE—The Feuds and Private Lives of Tennessee Williams, Gore Vidal, Truman Capote, and Famous Members of their Entourages
Darwin Porter & Danforth Prince
Softcover, 700 pages, with photos ISBN 978-1-936003-37-2 Also Available for E-Readers

THOSE GLAMOROUS GABORS
Bombshells from Budapest, by Darwin Porter

Zsa Zsa, Eva, and Magda Gabor transferred their glittery dreams and gold-digging ambitions from the twilight of the Austro-Hungarian Empire to Hollywood. There, more effectively than any army, these Bombshells from Budapest broke hearts, amassed fortunes, lovers, and A-list husbands, and amused millions of *voyeurs* through the medium of television, movies, and the social registers. In this astonishing "triple-play" biography, designated "Best Biography of the Year" by the Hollywood Book Festival, Blood Moon lifts the "mink-and-diamond" curtain on this amazing trio of blood-related sisters, whose complicated intrigues have never been fully explored before.

"**You will never be Ga-bored...this book gives new meaning to the term compelling.** Be warned, *Those Glamorous Gabors* is both an epic and a pip. Not since *Gone With the Wind* have so many characters on the printed page been forced to run for their lives for one reason or another. And Scarlett making a dress out of the curtains is nothing compared to what a Gabor will do when she needs to scrap together an outfit for a movie premiere or late-night outing.

"For those not up to speed, Jolie Tilleman came from a family of jewelers and therefore came by her love for the shiny stones honestly, perhaps genetically. She married Vilmos Gabor somewhere around World War 1 (exact dates, especially birth dates, are always somewhat vague in order to establish plausible deniability later on) and they were soon blessed with three daughters: **Magda**, the oldest, whose hair, sadly, was naturally brown, although it would turn quite red in America; **Zsa Zsa** (born 'Sari') a natural blond who at a very young age exhibited the desire for fame with none of the talents usually associated with achievement, excepting beauty and a natural wit; and **Eva**, the youngest and blondest of the girls, who after seeing Grace Moore perform at the National Theater, decided that she wanted to be an actress and that she would one day move to Hollywood to become a star.

"Given that the Gabor family at that time lived in Budapest, Hungary, at the period of time between the World Wars, that Hollywood dream seemed a distant one indeed. The story—the riches to rags to riches to rags to riches again myth of survival against all odds as the four women, because of their Jewish heritage, flee Europe with only the minks on their backs and what jewels they could smuggle along with them in their *decolletage*, only to have to battle afresh for their places in the vicious Hollywood pecking order—gives new meaning to the term 'compelling.' The reader, as if he were witnessing a particularly gore-drenched traffic accident, is incapable of looking away."

—New York Review of Books

Those Glamorous Gabors, Bombshells from Budapest, by Darwin Porter.
Softcover, 730 pages, with hundreds of photos   ISBN 978-1-936003-35-8

PETER O'TOOLE
Hellraiser, Sexual Outlaw, Irish Rebel

At the time of its publication early in 2015, this book was widely publicized in the *Daily Mail,* the *New York Daily News,* the *New York Post,* the *Midwest Book Review, The Express (London), The Globe,* the *National Enquirer,* and in equivalent publications worldwide

One of the world's most admired (and brilliant) actors, Peter O'Toole wined and wenched his way through a labyrinth of sexual and interpersonal betrayals, sometimes with disastrous results. Away from the stage and screen, where such films as *Becket* and *Lawrence of Arabia,* made film history, his life was filled with drunken, debauched nights and edgy sexual experimentations, most of which were never openly examined in the press. A hellraiser, he shared wild times with his "best blokes" Richard Burton and Richard Harris. Peter Finch, also his close friend, once invited him to join him in sharing the pleasures of his mistress, Vivien Leigh.

"My father, a bookie, moved us to the Mick community of Leeds," O'Toole once told a reporter. "We were very poor, but I was born an Irishman, which accounts for my gift of gab, my unruly behavior, my passionate devotion to women and the bottle, and my loathing of any authority figure."

Author Robert Sellers described O'Toole's boyhood neighborhood. "Three of his playmates went on to be hanged for murder; one strangled a girl in a lovers' quarrel; one killed a man during a robbery; another cut up a warden in South Africa with a pair of shears. It was a heavy bunch."

Peter O'Toole's hell-raising life story has never been told, until now. Hot and uncensored, from a writing team which, even prior to O'Toole's death in 2013, had been collecting under-the-radar info about him for years, this book has everything you ever wanted to know about how THE LION navigated his way through the boudoirs of the Entertainment Industry IN WINTER, Spring, Summer, and a dissipated Autumn as well.

Blood Moon has ripped away the imperial robe, scepter, and crown usually associated with this quixotic problem child of the British Midlands. Provocatively uncensored, this illusion-shattering overview of Peter O'Toole's hellraising (or at least very naughty) and demented life is unique in the history of publishing.

PETER O'TOOLE: Hellraiser, Sexual Outlaw, Irish Rebel
Softcover, with photos. ISBN 978-1-936003-45-7.
Also available for e-readers

Less than an hour after the discovery of Marilyn Monroe's corpse in Brentwood, a flood of theories, tainted evidence, and conflicting testimonies began pouring out into the public landscape.

Filled with rage, hysteria, and depression, "and fed up with Jack's lies, Bobby's lies," Marilyn sought revenge and mass vindication. Her revelations at an imminent press conference could have toppled political dynasties and destroyed criminal empires. Marilyn had to be stopped...

Into this steamy cauldron of deceit, Marilyn herself emerges as a most unreliable witness during the weeks leading up to her murder. Her own deceptions, vanities, and self-delusion poured toxic accelerants on an already raging fire.

MARILYN

Rainbow's End

THE FINAL VERDICT

Sex, Lies, Murder, And The Great Cover-Up

Darwin Porter

MARILYN AT RAINBOW'S END
SEX, LIES, MURDER, AND THE GREAT COVER-UP, BY DARWIN PORTER
ISBN 978-1-936003-29-7
Temporarily sold out of hard copies, but available for E-Readers

"Darwin Porter is fearless, honest and a great read. He minces no words. If the truth makes you wince and honesty offends your sensibility, stay away. It's been said that he deals in muck because he can't libel the dead. Well, it's about time someone started telling the truth about the dead and being honest about just what happened to get us in the mess in which we're in. If libel is lying, then Porter is so completely innocent as to deserve an award. In all of his works he speaks only to the truth, and although he is a hard teacher and task master, he's one we ignore at our peril. To quote Gore Vidal, power is not a toy we give to someone for being good. If we all don't begin to investigate where power and money really are in the here and now, we deserve what we get. Yes, Porter names names. The reader will come away from the book knowing just who killed Monroe. Porter rather brilliantly points to a number of motives, but leaves it to the reader to surmise exactly what happened at the rainbow's end, just why Marilyn was killed. And, of course, why we should be careful of getting exactly what we want. It's a very long tumble from the top."

—ALAN PETRUCELLI, Examiner.com, May 13, 2012

Elizabeth Taylor, *There is Nothing Like a Dame*
All the Gossip Unfit to Print from the Glory Days of Hollywood

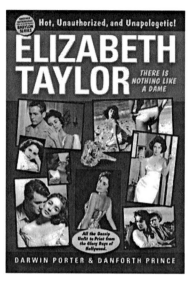

For more than 60 years, Elizabeth Taylor dazzled generations of movie-goers with her glamor and her all-consuming passion for life. She was the last of the great stars of Golden Age Hollywood, coming to a sad end at the age of 79 in 2011.

But before she died, appearing on the Larry King show, she claimed that her biographers had revealed "only half of my story, but I can't tell the other half in a memoir because I'd get sued."

Now, Blood Moon presents for the first time a comprehensive compilation of most of the secrets from the mercurial Dame Elizabeth, whose hedonism helped define the jet set of the tumultuous 60s and beyond.

Throughout the many decades of her life, she consistently generated hysteria among her fans. Here, her story is told with brutal honesty in rich, juicy detail and illustrated, with a new revelation on every page.

It's all here, and a lot more, in an exposé that's both sympathetic and shocking, with a candor and attention to detail that brings the *femme fatale* of the 20th century back to life.

"What has never been denied about Elizabeth Taylor is that the young actress, though small for her age, was mature beyond her years, deeply ambitious, and sexually precocious...Insiders agreed she always had a strong rebellious streak. Could the studio system's vice-like grip on publicity have stopped scandals about their most valuable child star from leaking out?

"A recent biography of Taylor claims that as a teenager, she lost her virginity at 15 to British actor Peter Lawford, had flings with Ronald Reagan and Errol Flynn, was roughly seduced by Orson Welles, and even enjoyed a threesome involving John F. Kennedy.

The authors—Darwin Porter and Danforth Prince—also allege Taylor was just 11 when she was taught by her close friend, the gay British actor, Roddy McDowall, the star of Lassie Come Home, *how to satisfy men without sleeping with them."*
Tom Leonard in THE DAILY MAIL, October 19, 2015

"Before they wither, Elizabeth Taylor's breasts will topple empires."
—Richard Burton

Softcover, 460 pages, with photos ISBN 978-1-936003-31-0.
Temporarily sold out of hard copies, but available as an E-book.

James Dean, *Tomorrow Never Comes*

Honoring the 60th anniversary of his violent and early death

America's most enduring and legendary symbol of young, enraged rebellion, James Dean continues into the 21st Century to capture the imagination of the world.

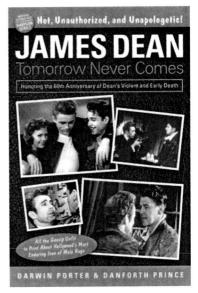

After one of his many flirtations with Death, which caught up with him when he was a celebrity-soaked 24-year-old, he said, "If a man can live after he dies, then maybe he's a great man." Today, bars from Nigeria to Patagonia are named in honor of this international, spectacularly self-destructive movie star icon.

Migrating from the dusty backroads of Indiana to center stage in the most formidable boudoirs of Hollywood, his saga is electrifying.

A strikingly handsome heart-throb, Dean is a study in contrasts: Tough but tender, brutal but remarkably sensitive; he was a reckless hellraiser badass who could revert to a little boy in bed.

A rampant bisexual, he claimed that he didn't want to go through life "with one hand tied behind my back." He demonstrated that during bedroom trysts with Marilyn Monroe, Rock Hudson, Elizabeth Taylor, Paul Newman, Natalie Wood, Shelley Winters, Marlon Brando, Steve McQueen, Ursula Andress, Montgomery Clift, Pier Angeli, Tennessee Williams, Susan Strasberg, Tallulah Bankhead, and FBI director J. Edgar Hoover.

Woolworth heiress Barbara Hutton, one of the richest and most dissipated women of her era, wanted to make him her toy boy.

Tomorrow Never Comes is the most penetrating look at James Dean to have emerged from the wreckage of his Porsche Spyder in 1955.

Before setting out on his last ride, he said, "I feel life too intensely to bear living it."

Tomorrow Never Comes presents a damaged but beautiful soul.

JAMES DEAN—TOMORROW NEVER COMES
DARWIN PORTER & DANFORTH PRINCE
Softcover, with photos. ISBN 978-1-936003-49-5

INSIDE LINDA LOVELACE'S DEEP THROAT

DEGRADATION, PORNO CHIC, AND THE RISE OF FEMINISM

DARWIN PORTER

An insider's view of the unlikely heroine who changed the world's perceptions about pornography, censorship, and sexual behavior patterns

The Most Comprehensive Biography Ever Written of an
Adult Entertainment Star
and Her Relationship with the Underbelly of Hollywood

Darwin Porter, author of some twenty critically acclaimed celebrity exposés of behind-the-scenes intrigue in the entertainment industry, was deeply involved in the Linda Lovelace saga as it unfolded in the 70s, interviewing many of the players, and raising money for the legal defense of the film's co-star, Harry Reems. In this book, emphasizing her role as a celebrity interacting with other celebrities, he brings inside information and a never-before-published revelation to almost every page.

The Beach Book Festival's Grand Prize Winner: "Best Summer Reading of 2013"

Runner-Up to "Best Biography of 2013" *The Los Angeles Book Festival*

Winner of a Sybarite Award from HedoOnline.com

"This book drew me in..How could it not?" Coco Papy, *Bookslut.*

the Award-Winning overview of a story that changed America and the Entertainment Industry forever:

Another hot and insightful commentary about major and sometimes violently controversial conflicts of the American Century by

Darwin Porter

Softcover, 640 pages, 6"x9" with photos.
ISBN 978-1-936003-33-4

Scarlett O'Hara,

Desperately in Love with Heathcliff,

Together on the Road to Hell

Damn You, Scarlett O'Hara
The Private Lives of Vivien Leigh and Laurence Olivier

Here, for the first time, is a biography that raises the curtain on the secret lives of **Lord Laurence Olivier**, often cited as the finest actor in the history of England, and **Vivien Leigh**, who immortalized herself with her Oscar-winning portrayals of Scarlett O'Hara in *Gone With the Wind*, and as Blanche DuBois in Tennessee Williams' *A Streetcar Named Desire*.

Dashing and "impossibly handsome," Laurence Olivier was pursued by the most dazzling luminaries, male and female, of the movie and theater worlds.

Lord Olivier's beautiful and brilliant but emotionally disturbed wife (Viv to her lovers) led a tumultuous off-the-record life whose paramours ranged from the A-list celebrities to men she selected randomly off the street. But none of the brilliant roles depicted by Lord and Lady Olivier, on stage or on screen, ever matched the power and drama of personal dramas which wavered between Wagnerian opera and Greek tragedy. *Damn You, Scarlett O'Hara* is the definitive and most revelatory portrait ever published of the most talented and tormented actor and actress of the 20th century.

Darwin Porter is the principal author of this seminal work.

Roy Moseley, this book's co-author, was an intimate friend of both Lord and Lady Olivier, maintaining a decades-long association with the famous couple, nurturing them through triumphs, emotional breakdowns, and streams of suppressed scandal. A resident of California who spent most of his life in England, Moseley has authored or co-authored biographies of Queen Elizabeth and Prince Philip, Rex Harrison, Cary Grant, Merle Oberon, Roger Moore, and Bette Davis.

"**Damn You, Scarlett O'Hara** *can be a dazzling read, the prose unmannered and instantly digestible. The authors' ability to pile scandal atop scandal, seduction after seduction, can be impossible to resist.*"

—THE WASHINGTON TIMES

DAMN YOU, SCARLETT O'HARA
THE PRIVATE LIFES OF LAURENCE OLIVIER AND VIVIEN LEIGH

Darwin Porter and Roy Moseley

Winner of four distinguished literary awards, this is the best biography of Vivien Leigh and Laurence Olivier ever published.

ISBN 978-1-936003-15-0   Hardcover, 708 pages, with about a hundred photos and hundreds of insights into the London Theatre, the role of the Oliviers in the politics of World War II, and the passion, fury, and frustration of their lives together as actors in the West End, on Broadway, and in Hollywood.
Also available for E-Readers

Paul Newman, The Man Behind the Baby Blues

His Secret Life Exposed

Darwin Porter

Drawn from firsthand interviews with insiders who knew Paul Newman intimately, and compiled over a period of nearly a half-century, this is the world's most honest and most revelatory biography about Hollywood's pre-eminent male sex symbol.

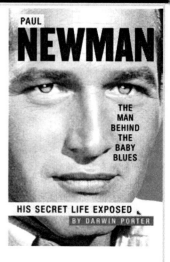

This is a respectful but candid cornucopia of once-concealed information about the sexual and emotional adventures of an affable, impossibly good-looking workaday actor, a former sailor from Shaker Heights, Ohio, who parlayed his ambisexual charm and extraordinary good looks into one of the most successful careers in Hollywood.

Whereas the situations it exposes were widely known within Hollywood's inner circles, they've never before been revealed to the general public.

But now, the full story has been published—the giddy heights and agonizing crashes of a great American star, with revelations and insights never before published in any other biography.

"Paul Newman had just as many on-location affairs as the rest of us, and he was just as bisexual as I was. But whereas I was always getting caught with my pants down, he managed to do it in the dark with not a paparazzo in sight. He might have bedded Marilyn Monroe or Elizabeth Taylor the night before, but he always managed to show up for breakfast with Joanne Woodward, with those baby blues, looking as innocent as a Botticelli angel. He never fooled me. It takes an alleycat to know another one. Did I ever tell you what really happened between Newman and me? If that doesn't grab you, what about what went on between James Dean and Newman? Let me tell you about this co-called model husband if you want to look behind those famous peepers."

—Marlon Brando

Paul Newman, The Man Behind the Baby Blues,
His Secret Life Exposed
Recipient of an Honorable Mention from the New England Book Festival
Hardcover, 520 pages, with dozens of photos.
ISBN 978-0-9786465-1-6   Also available for e-readers

Merv Griffin, A Life in the Closet

by Darwin Porter

HOT, CONTROVERSIAL, AND RIGOROUSLY RESEARCHED,

HERE'S MERV!

Merv Griffin began his career as a Big Band singer, moved on to a failed career as a romantic hero in the movies, and eventually rewrote the rules of everything associated with the broadcasting industry. Along the way, he met and befriended virtually everyone who mattered, including Nancy Reagan, and made billions operating casinos and developing jingles, contests, and word games. All of this while maintaining a male harem and a secret life as America's most famously closeted homosexual.

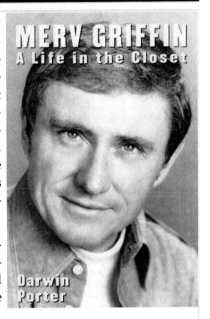

In this comprehensive and richly ironic biography, Darwin Porter reveals the amazing details behind the richest, most successful, and in some ways, the most notorious mogul in the history of America's entertainment industry.

***

"Darwin Porter told me why he tore the door off Merv's closet.......*Heeeere's Merv!* is 560 pages, 100 photos, a truckload of gossip, and a bedful of unauthorized dish."

Cindy Adams, The New York Post

"Darwin Porter tears the door off Merv Griffin's closet with gusto in this sizzling, superlatively researched biography...It brims with insider gossip that's about Hollywood legends, writ large, smart, and with great style."

Richard LaBonté, BOOKMARKS

Merv Griffin, a Life in the Closet, by Darwin Porter.
Hardcover, with photos. ISBN 978-0-9786465-0-9. Also available for E-Readers.

FRANK SINATRA, THE BOUDOIR SINGER

All the Gossip Unfit to Print from the Glory Days of Ol' Blue Eyes

Darwin Porter & Danforth Prince

"Every time I sing a song, I'm actually making love on stage. Call me 'The Boudoir Singer.'" —Frank Sinatra

"When Sinatra dies, they'll donate his zipper to the Smithsonian." —Dean Martin

Hot, Unauthorized, and Unapologetic!

SINATRA
Frank
The Boudoir Singer

ANOTHER OUTRAGEOUS BABYLON SERIES

All the Gossip Unfit to Print from the Glory Days of Ol' Blue Eyes

BY DARWIN PORTER & DANFORTH PRINCE

"F-R-A-N-K-I-E-E-EE! Take my virginity!" screamed a bobby-soxer in midtown Manhattan in 1943

"Our problems were never in bed," said Ava Gardner, his greatest love. "We were always great in bed. Ten pounds of Frank, 110 pounds of cock."

Even If You Thought You'd Heard It All Already, You'll Be Amazed At How Much This Book Contains That Never Got Published Before.

Vendettas and high-octane indiscretions, fast and furious women, deep sensitivities and sporadic psychoses, Presidential pimping, FBI coverups, Mobster mambos, and a pantload of hushed-up scandals about **FABULOUS FRANK AND HIS MIND-BLOWING COHORTS**

"Womanizer Sinatra's Shocking Secret Sins are revealed in a blockbuster new book, including his raunchy romps with Liz Taylor, Marilyn Monroe, Jackie-O, and Nancy Reagan. Every time the leader of the Free World would join him in Palm Springs, the place was a sun-kissed brothel, with Kennedy as the main customer."

— THE GLOBE

Frank Sinatra, The Boudoir Singer
Hardcover, 465 pages with hundreds of photos
ISBN 978-1-936003-19-8 Also available for E-readers

Finally—A COOL biography that was too HOT to be published during the lifetime of its subject.

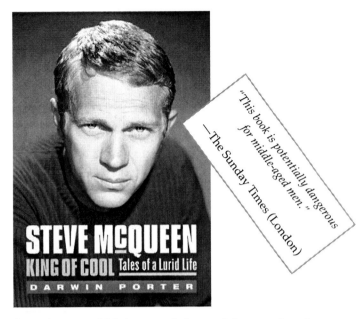

"This book is potentially dangerous for middle-aged men."
—The Sunday Times (London)

The drama of Steve McQueen's personal life far exceeded any role he ever played on screen. Born to a prostitute, he was brutally molested by some of his mother's "johns," and endured gang rape in reform school. His drift into prostitution began when he was hired as a towel boy in the most notorious bordello in the Dominican Republic, where he starred in a string of cheap porno films. Returning to New York before migrating to Hollywood, he hustled men on Times Square and, as a "gentleman escort" in a borrowed tux, rich older women.

And then, sudden stardom as he became the world's top box office attraction. The abused became the abuser. "I live for myself, and I answer to nobody," he proclaimed. "The last thing I want to do is fall in love with a broad."

Thus began a string of seductions that included hundreds of overnight pickups--both male and female. Topping his A-list conquests were James Dean, Paul Newman, Marilyn Monroe, and Barbra Streisand. Finally, this pioneering biography explores the mysterious death of Steve McQueen. Were those salacious rumors really true?

Steve McQueen
King of Cool
Tales of a Lurid Life
Darwin Porter

A carefully researched, 466-page hardcover with dozens of photos
Temporarily sold out of hard copies, but available now for e-readers

ISBN 978-1-936003-05-1

Humphrey Bogart, *The Making of a Legend*

Darwin Porter

A "CRADLE-TO-GRAVE" HARDCOVER ABOUT THE RISE TO FAME OF AN OBSCURE, UNLIKELY, AND FREQUENTLY UNEMPLOYED BROADWAY ACTOR.

Whereas **Humphrey Bogart** is always at the top of any list of the Entertainment Industry's most famous actors, very little is known about how he clawed his way from Broadway to Hollywood during Prohibition and the Jazz Age.

This pioneering biography begins with Bogart's origins as the child of wealthy (morphine-addicted) parents in New York City, then examines the love affairs, scandals, failures, and breakthroughs that launched him as an American icon.

It includes details about behind-the-scenes dramas associated with three mysterious marriages, and films such as *The Petrified Forest, The Maltese Falcon, High Sierra,* and *Casablanca.* Read all about the debut and formative years of the actor who influenced many generations of filmgoers, laying Bogie's life bare in a style you've come to expect from Darwin Porter. Exposed with all their juicy details is what Bogie never told his fourth wife, Lauren Bacall, herself a screen legend.

Drawn from original interviews with friends and foes who knew a lot about what lay beneath his trenchcoat, this exposé covers Bogart's remarkable life as it helped define movie-making, Hollywood's portrayal of macho, and America's evolving concept of Entertainment itself.

This revelatory book is based on dusty unpublished memoirs, letters, diaries, and often personal interviews from the women—and the men—who adored him.

There are also shocking allegations from colleagues, former friends, and jilted lovers who wanted the screen icon to burn in hell.

All this and more, much more, in Darwin Porter's *exposé* of Bogie's startling secret life.

WITH STARTLING NEW INFORMATION YOU'VE NEVER SEEN BEFORE ABOUT BOGART, THE MOVIES, AND GOLDEN AGE HOLLYWOOD

542 PAGES, WITH HUNDREDS OF PHOTOS   ISBN 978-1-936003-14-3
ALSO AVAILABLE FOR E-READERS

Katharine the Great

HEPBURN, A LIFETIME OF SECRETS REVEALED

BY DARWIN PORTER

Katharine Hepburn was the world's greatest screen diva--the most famous actress in American history. But until the appearance of this biography, no one had ever published the intimate details of her complicated and ferociously secretive private life.

Thanks to the "deferential and obsequious whitewashes" which followed in the wake of her death, readers probably know WHAT KATE REMEMBERED. Here, however, is an unvarnished account of what Katharine Hepburn desperately wanted to forget.

"Darwin Porter's biography of Hepburn cannot be lightly dismissed or ignored. Connoisseurs of Hepburn's life would do well to seek it out as a forbidden supplement."
The Sunday Times (London)

"Behind the scenes of her movies, Katharine Hepburn played the temptress to as many women as she did men, ranted and raved with her co-stars and directors, and broke into her neighbors' homes for fun. And somehow, she managed to keep all of it out of the press. As they say, Katharine the Great is hard to put down."
The Dallas Voice

"The door to Hepburn's closet has finally been opened. This is the most honest and least apologetic biography of Hollywood's most ferociously private actress ever written."
Senior Life Magazine, Miami

Katharine
The Great

HEPBURN
A Lifetime of Secrets
Revealed

Darwin Porter

The First Book of Its Kind, A Fiercely Unapologetic Exposé of the Most Obsessively Secretive Actress in Hollywood

Softcover, 569 pages, with photos

ISBN   978-0-9748118-0-2
Also Available for E-Readers

BANDO UNZIPPED

An Uncensored *Exposé* of America's Most Visible
Method Actor and Sexual Outlaw

by Darwin Porter

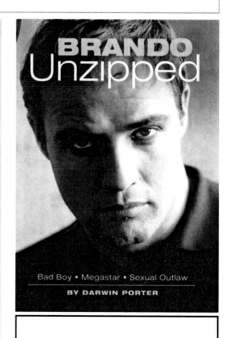

BRANDO EXPOSED!! This "entertainingly outrageous" (*Frontiers Magazine*) biography provides a definitive, blow-by-blow description of the "hot, provocative, and barely under control drama" that was the life of America's most famous Postwar actor.

"Lurid, raunchy, perceptive, and certainly worth reading...One of the ten best show-biz biographies of 2006." *The Sunday Times (London)*

"**Yummy**. An irresistably flamboyant romp of a read."

Books to Watch Out For

"Astonishing. An extraordinarily detailed portrait of Brando that's as blunt, uncompromising, and X-rated as the man himself."

Women's Weekly

"This shocking new book is sparking a major re-assessment of Brando's legacy as one of Holly-wood's most macho lotharios."

Daily Express (London)

"As author Darwin Porter finds, it wasn't just the acting world Marlon Brando conquered. It was the actors, too."

Gay Times (London)

"*Brando Unzipped* is the definitive gossip guide to the late, great actor's life."

The New York Daily News

Extensively serialized in London's *MAIL ON SUNDAY*, this is history's most definitive biography of Marlon Brando,

An artfully lurid hardcover with 625 indexed pages and hundreds of photos, it's the book that redefined the icon who ALWAYS raised headlines, heartrates, and expectations of what HOT ACTORS are supposed to be.

One of the most talked-about Hollywood bios EVER, it's still available for E-readers

ISBN 978-0-9748118-2-6.

Jacko, His Rise and Fall

The Social and Sexual History of Michael Jackson

Darwin Porter

He rewrote the rules of America's entertainment industry, and he led a life of notoriety. Even his death was the occasion for scandals which continue to this day.

This is the world's most comprehensive historical overview of a pop star's rise, fall, and to some extent, rebirth as an American Icon. Read it for the real story of the circumstances and players who created the icon which the world will forever remember as "the gloved one," Michael Jackson.

"This is the story of Peter Pan gone rotten. Don't stop till you get enough. Darwin Porter's biography of Michael Jackson is dangerously addictive."
—*The Sunday Observer* (London)

"In this compelling glimpse of Jackson's life, Porter provides what many journalists have failed to produce in their writings about the pop star: A real person behind the headlines."
— *Foreword Magazine*

"I'd have thought that there wasn't one single gossippy rock yet to be overturned in the microscopically scrutinized life of Michael Jackson, but Darwin Porter has proven me wrong. Definitely a page-turner. But don't turn the pages too quickly. Almost every one holds a fascinating revelation."
—*Books to Watch Out For*

This book, a winner of literary awards from both *Foreword Magazine* and the Hollywood Book Festival, was originally published during the lifetime of Michael Jackson. This, the revised, post-mortem edition, with extra analysis and commentary, was released after his death.

Hardcover 600 indexed pages with about a hundred photos

ISBN 978-0-936003-10-5   Also available for E-readers

Out of the Celluloid Closet, a Half-Century Review of HOMOSEXUALITY IN THE MOVIES
A Book of Record, Reference Source, and Gossip Guide to 50 Years of Queer Cinema

Out, outrageous, provocative, and proud, this comprehensive anthology and library resource reviews 500 of the best of Hollywood's output of gay, bisexual, lesbian, transgendered, and queer questioning films, with a special emphasis on how gays changed the movies we know and love.

Conceived as a working guide to what viewers should stock within their DVD Queues, it reviews everything from blockbusters to indie sleepers, with about a dozen special features discussing the ironies, betrayals, subterfuge, and gossip of who, what, and how it happened when the film world's closet doors slowly creaked open beginning in 1960.

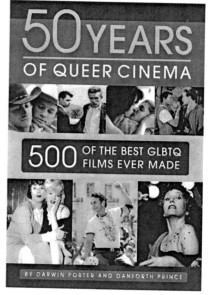

***

"In the Internet age, where every movie, queer or otherwise, is blogged about somewhere, a hefty print compendium of film facts and pointed opinion might seem anachronistic. But flipping through well-reasoned pages of commentary is so satisfying. Add to that physical thrill the charm of analysis that is sometimes sassy and always smart, and this filtered survey of short reviews is a must for queer-film fans.

"Essays on Derek Jarman, Tennessee Williams, Andy Warhol, Jack Wrangler, Joe Gage and others — and on how The Front Runner *never got made — round out this indispensable survey of gay-interest cinema."*

RICHARD LABONTÉ
BOOK MARKS / QSYNDICATE

Winner of the New England Book Festival's
Best GLBT Title of 2010

50 YEARS OF QUEER CINEMA
500 of the Best GLBT Films Ever Made

Softcover, 400 pages, with photos. ISBN 978-1-936003-09-9

HOLLYWOOD BABYLON STRIKES AGAIN!

THE PROFOUNDLY OUTRAGEOUS VOLUME TWO OF BLOOD MOON'S BABYLON SERIES

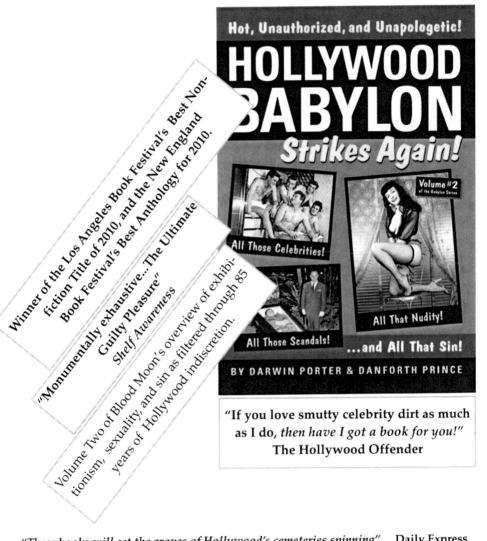

Winner of the Los Angeles Book Festival's Best Non-fiction Title of 2010, and the New England Book Festival's Best Anthology for 2010.

"Monumentally exhaustive...The Ultimate Guilty Pleasure" Shelf Awareness

Volume Two of Blood Moon's overview of exhibitionism, sexuality, and sin as filtered through 85 years of Hollywood indiscretion.

Hot, Unauthorized, and Unapologetic!

HOLLYWOOD BABYLON Strikes Again!

Volume #2 of the Babylon Series

All Those Celebrities!

All That Nudity!

All Those Scandals!

...and All That Sin!

BY DARWIN PORTER & DANFORTH PRINCE

"If you love smutty celebrity dirt as much as I do, *then have I got a book for you!"*
The Hollywood Offender

"These books will set the graves of Hollywood's cemeteries spinning" **Daily Express**

Hollywood Babylon Strikes Again!

Darwin Porter and Danforth Prince
Hardcover, 380 outrageous pages, with hundreds of photos

ISBN 978-1-936003-12-9

This is What Happens When A Demented Billionaire Hits Hollywood

HOWARD HUGHES
HELL'S ANGEL
BY DARWIN PORTER

From his reckless pursuit of love as a rich teenager to his final days as a demented fossil, Howard Hughes tasted the best and worst of the century he occupied. Along the way, he changed the worlds of aviation and entertainment forever.

This biography reveals inside details about his destructive and usually scandalous associations with other Hollywood players.

"The Aviator flew both ways. Porter's biography presents new allegations about Hughes' shady dealings with some of the biggest names of the 20th century"
—**New York Daily News**

"Darwin Porter's access to film industry insiders and other Hughes confidants supplied him with the resources he needed to create a portrait of Hughes that both corroborates what other Hughes biographies have divulged, and go them one better."
—**Foreword Magazine**

"Thanks to this bio of Howard Hughes, we'll never be able to look at the old pinups in quite the same way again."
—**The Times (London)**

Winner of a respected literary award from the Los Angeles Book Festival, this book gives an insider's perspective about what money can buy —and what it can't.

814 pages, with photos. Also available for E-Readers

ISBN 978-1-936003-13-6

**BLOOD
MOON**
Productions, Ltd.

*Entertainment
About How America
Interprets
Its Celebrities*

CPSIA information can be obtained
at www.ICGtesting.com
Printed in the USA
LVOW12s1534131216

517085LV00003B/546/P